T0261227

MULTIMEDIA INFORMATION EXTRACTION

Press Operating Committee

Chair
James W. Cortada
IBM Institute for Business Value

Board Members
Richard E. (Dick) Fairley, *Founder and Principal Associate, Software Engineering Management Associates (SEMA)*
Cecilia Metra, *Associate Professor of Electronics, University of Bologna*
Linda Shafer, *former Director, Software Quality Institute, The University of Texas at Austin*
Evan Butterfield, *Director of Products and Services*
Kate Guillemette, *Product Development Editor, CS Press*

IEEE Computer Society Publications
The world-renowned IEEE Computer Society publishes, promotes, and distributes a wide variety of authoritative computer science and engineering texts. These books are available from most retail outlets. Visit the CS Store at *http://computer. org/store* for a list of products.

IEEE Computer Society / Wiley Partnership

The IEEE Computer Society and Wiley partnership allows the CS Press authored book program to produce a number of exciting new titles in areas of computer science, computing and networking with a special focus on software engineering. IEEE Computer Society members continue to receive a 15% discount on these titles when purchased through Wiley or at wiley.com/ieeecs.

To submit questions about the program or send proposals please e-mail kguillemette@computer.org or write to Books, IEEE Computer Society, 10662 Los Vaqueros Circle, Los Alamitos, CA 90720-1314. Telephone +1-714-816-2169.

Additional information regarding the Computer Society authored book program can also be accessed from our web site at *http://computer.org/cspress*.

MULTIMEDIA INFORMATION EXTRACTION

Advances in Video, Audio, and Imagery
Analysis for Search, Data Mining,
Surveillance, and Authoring

Edited by

MARK T. MAYBURY

A JOHN WILEY & SONS, INC., PUBLICATION

Published by John Wiley & Sons, Inc., Hoboken, New Jersey.
Published simultaneously in Canada.

Library of Congress Cataloging-in-Publication Data:

Maybury, Mark T.
     Multimedia information extraction : advances in video, audio, and imagery analysis for search, data mining, surveillance, and authoring / by Mark T. Maybury.
       p. cm.
Includes bibliographical references and index.
       ISBN 978-1-118-11891-7 (hardback)
     1. Data mining.   2. Metadata harvesting.   3. Computer files.   I. Title.
       QA76.9.D343M396 2012
       006.3'12–dc23

                                                                    2011037229

Printed in the United States of America

10 9 8 7 6 5 4 3 2 1

CONTENTS

FOREWORD

I was delighted when I was asked to write a foreword for this book as, apart from the honor, it gives me the chance to stand back and think a bit more deeply about multimedia information extraction than I would normally do and also to get a sneak preview of the book. One of the first things I did when preparing to write this was to dig out a copy of one of Mark T. Maybury's previous edited books, *Intelligent Multimedia Information Retrieval* from 1997.[1] The bookshelves in my office don't actually have many books anymore—a copy of Keith van Rijsbergen's *Information Retrieval* from 1979 (well, he was my PhD supervisor!); Negroponte's book *Being Digital*; several generations of TREC, SIGIR, and LNCS proceedings from various conferences; and some old database management books from when I taught that topic to undergraduates. *Intelligent Multimedia Information Retrieval* was there, though, and had survived the several culls that I had made to the bookshelves' contents over the years, each time I've had to move office or felt claustrophobic and wanted to dump stuff out of the office. All that the modern professor, researcher, student, or interested reader might need to have these days is accessible from our fingertips anyway; and it says a great deal about Mark T. Maybury and his previous edited collection that it survived these culls; that can only be because it still has value to me. I would expect the same to be true for this book, *Multimedia Information Extraction*.

Finding that previous edited collection on my bookshelf was fortunate for me because it gave me the chance to reread the foreword that Karen Spärck Jones had written. In that foreword, she raised the age-old question of whether a picture was worth a thousand words or not. She concluded that the question doesn't actually need answering anymore, because now you can have both. That conclusion was in the context of discussing the natural hierarchy of information types—multimedia types if you wish—and the challenge of having to look at many different kinds of

---

[1] Maybury, M.T., ed., *Intelligent Multimedia Information Retrieval* (AAAI Press, 1997).

information at once on your screen. Karen's conclusion has grown to be even more true over the years, but I'll bet that not even she could have foreseen exactly how true it would become today. The edited collection of chapters, published in 1997, still has many chapters that are relevant and good reading today, covering the various types of content-based information access we aspired to then, and, in the case of some of those media, the kind of access to which we still aspire. That collection helped to define the field of using intelligent, content-based techniques in multimedia information retrieval, and the collection as a whole has stood the test of time.

Over the years, content-based information access has changed, however; or rather, it has had to shift sideways in order to work around the challenges posed by analyzing and understanding information encoded in some types of media, notably visual media. Even in 1997, we had more or less solved the technical challenges of capturing, storing, transmitting, and rendering multimedia, specifically text, image, audio, and moving video; and seemingly the only major challenges remaining were multimedia analysis so that we could achieve content-based access and navigation, and, of course, scale it all up. Standards for encoding and transmission were in place, network infrastructure and bandwidth was improving, mobile access was becoming easy, and all we needed was a growing market of people to want the content and somebody to produce it. Well, we got both; but we didn't realize that the two needs would be satisfied by the same source—the ordinary user. Users generating their own content introduced a flood of material; and professional content-generators, like broadcasters and musicians, for example, responded by opening the doors to their own content so that within a short time, we have become overwhelmed by the sheer choice of multimedia material available to us.

Unfortunately, those of us who were predicting back in 1997 that content-based multimedia access would be based on the true content are still waiting for this to happen in the case of large-scale, generic, domain-independent applications. Content-based multimedia retrieval does work to some extent on smaller, personal, or domain-dependent collections, but not on the larger scale. Fully understanding media content to the level whereby the content we identify automatically in a video or image can be used directly for indexing has proven to be much more difficult than we anticipated for large-scale applications, like searching the Internet. For achieving multimedia information access, searching, summarizing, and linking, we now leverage more from the multimedia collateral—the metadata, user-assigned tags, user commentary, and reviews—than from the actual encoded content. YouTube videos, Flickr images, and iTunes music, like most large multimedia archives, are navigated more often based on what people say about a video, image, or song than what it actually contains. That means that we need to be clever about using this collateral information, like metadata, user tags, and commentaries. The challenges of intelligent multimedia information *retrieval* in 1997 have now grown into the challenges of multimedia information *mining* in 2012, developing and testing techniques to exploit the information associated with multimedia information to best effect. That is the subject of the present collection of articles—identifying and mining useful information from text, image, graphics, audio, and video, in applications as far apart as surveillance or broadcast TV.

In 1997, when the first of this series of books edited by Mark T. Maybury was published, I did not know him. I first encountered him in the early 2000s, and I remember my first interactions with him were in discussions about inviting a keynote speaker for a major conference I was involved in organizing. Mark suggested somebody named Tim Berners-Lee who was involved in starting some initiative he called the "semantic web," in which he intended to put meaning representations behind the content in web pages. That was in 2000 and, as always, Mark had his finger on the pulse of what is happening and what is important in the broad information field. In the years that followed, we worked together on a number of program committees—SIGIR, RIAO, and others—and we were both involved in the development of LSCOM, the Large Scale Ontology for Broadcast TV news, though his involvement was much greater than mine. In all the interactions we have had, Mark's inputs have always shown an ability to recognize important things at the right time, and his place in the community of multimedia researchers has grown in importance as a result of that.

That brings us to this book. When Karen Spärck Jones wrote her foreword to Mark's edited book in 1997 and alluded to pictures worth a thousand words, she may have foreseen how creating and consuming multimedia, as we do each day, would be easy and ingrained into our society. The availability, the near absence of technical problems, the volume of materials, the ease of access to it, and the ease of creation and upload were perhaps predictable to some extent by visionaries. However, the way in which this media is now enriched as a result of its intertwining with social networks, blogging, tagging, and folksonomies, user-generated content of the wisdom of crowds—that was not predicted. It means that being able to mine information from multimedia, information culled from the raw content as well as the collateral or metadata information, is a big challenge.

This book is a timely addition to the literature on the topic of multimedia information mining, as it is needed at this precise time as we try to wrestle with the problems of leveraging the "collateral" and the metadata associated with multimedia content. The five sections covering extraction from image, from video, from audio/graphics/behavior, the extraction of affect, and finally the annotation and authoring of multimedia content, collectively represent what is the leading edge of the research work in this area. The more than 80 coauthors of the 24 chapters in this volume have come together to produce a volume which, like the previous volumes edited by Mark T. Maybury, will help to define the field.

I won't be so bold, or foolhardy, as to predict what the multimedia field will be like in 10 or 15 years' time, what the problems and challenges will be and what the achievements will have been between now and then. I won't even guess what books might look like or whether we will still have bookshelves. I would expect, though, that like its predecessors, this volume will still be on my bookshelf in whatever form; and, for that, we have Mark T. Maybury to thank.

Thanks, Mark!

ALAN F. SMEATON

PREFACE

This collection is an outgrowth of the Association for the Advancement of Artificial Intelligence's (AAAI) Fall Symposium on Multimedia Information Extraction organized by Mark T. Maybury (The MITRE Corporation) and Sharon Walter (Air Force Research Laboratory) and held at the Westin Arlington Gateway in Arlington, Virginia, November 7–9, 2008. The program committee included Kelcy Allwein, Elisabeth Andre, Thom Blum, Shih-Fu Chang, Bruce Croft, Alex Hauptmann, Andy Merlino, Ram Nevatia, Prem Natarajan, Kirby Plessas, David Palmer, Mubarak Shah, Rohini K. Shrihari, Oliviero Stock, John Smith, and Rick Steinheiser. The symposium brought together scientists from the United States and Europe to report on recent advances to extraction information from growing personal, organizational, and global collections of audio, imagery, and video. Experts from industry, academia, government, and nonprofit organizations joined together with an objective of collaborating across the speech, language, image, and video processing communities to report advances and to chart future directions for multimedia information extraction theories and technologies.

The symposium included three invited speakers from government and academia. Dr. Nancy Chinchor from the Emerging Media Group in the Director of National Intelligence's Open Source Center described open source collection and how exploitation of social, mobile, citizen, and virtual gaming mediums could provide early indicators of global events (e.g., increased sales of medicine can indicate flu outbreak). Professor Ruzena Bajcsy (UC Berkeley) described understanding human gestures and body language using environmental and body sensors, enabling the transfer of body movement to robots or virtual choreography. Finally, John Garofolo (NIST) described multimodal metrology research and discussed challenges such as multimodal meeting diarization and affect/emotion recognition. Papers from the symposium were published as AAAI Press Technical Report FS-08-05 (Maybury and Walter 2008).

In this collection, extended versions of six selected papers from the symposium are augmented with over twice as many new contributions. All submissions were critically peer reviewed and those chosen were revised to ensure coherency with related chapters. The collection is complementary to preceding AAAI and/or MIT Press collections on *Intelligent Multimedia Interfaces* (1993), *Intelligent Multimedia Information Retrieval* (1997), *Advances in Automatic Text Summarization* (1999), *New Directions in Question Answering* (2004), as well as *Readings in Intelligent User Interfaces* (1998).

Multimedia Information Extraction serves multiple purposes. First, it aims to motivate and define the field of multimedia information extraction. Second, by providing a collection of some of the most innovative approaches and methods, it aims to become a standard reference text. Third, it aims to inspire new application areas, as well as to motivate continued research through the articulation of remaining gaps. The book can be used as a reference for students, researchers, and practitioners or as a collection of papers for use in undergraduate and graduate seminars.

To facilitate these multiple uses, *Multimedia Information Extraction* is organized into five sections, representing key areas of research and development:

- *Section 1*: Image Extraction
- *Section 2*: Video Extraction
- *Section 3*: Audio, Graphics, and Behavior Extraction
- *Section 4*: Affect Extraction in Audio and Imagery
- *Section 5*: Multimedia Annotation and Authoring

The book begins with an introduction that defines key terminology, describes an integrated architecture for multimedia information extraction, and provides an overview of the collection. To facilitate research, the introduction includes a content index to augment the back-of-the-book index. To assist instruction, a mapping to core curricula is provided. A second chapter outlines the history, the current state of the art, and a community-created roadmap of future multimedia information extraction research. Each remaining section in the book is framed with an editorial introduction that summarizes and relates each of the chapters, places them in historical context, and identifies remaining challenges for future research in that particular area. References are provided in an integrated listing.

Taken as a whole, this book articulates a collective vision of the future of multimedia. We hope it will help promote the development of further advances in multimedia information extraction making it possible for all of us to more effectively and efficiently benefit from the rapidly growing collections of multimedia materials in our homes, schools, hospitals, and offices.

MARK T. MAYBURY
Cape Cod, Massachusetts

ACKNOWLEDGMENTS

I thank Jackie Hargest for her meticulous proofreading and Paula MacDonald for her indefatigable pursuit of key references. I also thank each of the workshop participants who launched this effort and each of the authors for their interest, energy, and excellence in peer review to create what we hope will become a valued collection.

Most importantly, I dedicate this collection to my inspiration, Michelle, not only for her continual encouragement and selfless support, but even more so for her creation of our most enduring multimedia legacies: Zach, Max, and Julia. May they learn to extract what is most meaningful in life.

MARK T. MAYBURY
Cape Cod, Massachusetts

CONTRIBUTORS

MATUSALA ADDISU, Department of Computer Science, Sapienza University of Rome, Via Salaria 113, Roma, Italy 00198, *matusala.addisu@gmail.com*

GEETU AMBWANI, StreamSage/Comcast, 1110 Vermont Avenue NW, Washington, DC 20005, USA, *Geetu_Ambwani@cable.comcast.com*

DANILO AVOLA, Department of Computer Science, Sapienza University of Rome, Via Salaria 113, Roma, Italy 00198, *danilo.avola@gmail.com, avola@di.uniroma1.it*

AMIT BAGGA, StreamSage/Comcast, 1110 Vermont Avenue NW, Washington, DC 20005, USA, *Amit_Bagga@cable.comcast.com*

ERHAN BAKI ERMIS, Boston University, 8 Saint Mary's Street, Boston, MA 02215, USA, *ermis@bu.edu*

ROBIN BARGAR, Dean, School of Media Arts, Columbia College of Chicago, 33 E. Congress, Chicago, IL 60606, *rbargar@colum.edu*

KOBUS BARNARD, University of Arizona, Tucson, AZ 85721, USA, *kobus@cs.arizona.edu*

PAOLA BIANCHI, Department of Computer Science, Sapienza University of Rome, Via Salaria 113, Roma, Italy 00198, *pb.bianchi@gmail.com*

ANDREW C. BLOSE, Kodak Research Laboratories, Eastman Kodak Company, Rochester, NY 14650, USA, *andrew.blose@kodak.com*

PAOLO BOTTONI, Department of Computer Science, Sapienza University of Rome, Via Salaria 113, Roma, Italy 00198, *bottoni@di.uniroma1.it*

STANLEY M. BOYKIN, The MITRE Corporation, 202 Burlington Road, Bedford, MA 01730, USA, *sboykin@mitre.org*

GASPARD BRETON, Orange Labs, 4 rue du Clos Courtel, 35510 Cesson-Sevigne, France, *gaspard.breton@orange-ftgroup.com*

RICHARD BURNS, University of Delaware, Department of Computer and Information Sciences, Newark, DE 19716, USA, *burns@cis.udel.edu*

ALESSANDRO CAPPELLETTI, FBK-IRST, Via Sommarive, 18, 38123 Trento, Italy, *cappelle@fbk.eu*

SANDRA CARBERRY, University of Delaware, Department of Computer and Information Sciences, Newark, DE 19716, USA, *carberry@cis.udel.edu*

CHING HAU CHAN, MIMOS Berhad, Technology Park Malaysia, 57000 Kuala Lumpur, Malaysia, *cching.hau@mimos.my*

DANIEL CHESTER, University of Delaware, Department of Computer and Information Sciences, Newark, DE 19716, USA, *chester@cis.udel.edu*

LESLIE CHIPMAN, StreamSage/Comcast, 1110 Vermont Avenue NW, Washington, DC 20005, USA, *Leslie_Chipman@cable.comcast.com*

INSOOK CHOI, Emerging Media Program, Department of Entertainment Technology, New York City College of Technology of the City University of New York, 300 Jay Street, Brooklyn, NY 11201, USA, *insook@insookchoi.com*

MADIRAKSHI DAS, Kodak Research Laboratories, Eastman Kodak Company, Rochester, NY 14650, USA, *madirakshi.das@kodak.com*

ANTHONY R. DAVIS, StreamSage/Comcast, 1110 Vermont Avenue NW, Washington, DC 20005, USA, *tonydavis0@gmail.com*

SENIZ DEMIR, University of Delaware, Department of Computer and Information Sciences, Newark, DE 19716, USA, *demir@cis.udel.edu*

STEPHANIE ELZER, Millersville University, Department of Computer Science, Millersville, PA 17551, USA, *elzer@cs.millersville.edu*

FLORIAN EYBEN, Technische Universität München, Theresienstrasse 90, 80333 München, Germany, *eyben@tum.de*

RYAN FARRELL, StreamSage/Comcast, 1110 Vermont Avenue NW, Washington, DC 20005, USA, *farrell@cs.umd.edu*

DIETER W. FELLNER, Fraunhofer Austria Research GmbH, Geschäftsbereich Visual Computing, Inffeldgasse 16c, 8010 Graz, Austria; Fraunhofer IGD and GRIS, TU Darmstadt, Fraunhoferstrasse 5, D-64283 Darmstadt, Germany, *d.fellner@cgv.tugraz.at*

RANDALL K. FISH, The MITRE Corporation, 202 Burlington Road, Bedford, MA 01730, USA, *fishr@mitre.org*

FRED J. GOODMAN, The MITRE Corporation, 202 Burlington Road, Bedford, MA 01730, USA, *fgoodman@mitre.org*

WARREN R. GREIFF, The MITRE Corporation, 202 Burlington Road, Bedford, MA 01730, USA, *greiff@mitre.org*

MARCO GUERINI, FBK-IRST, I-38050, Povo, Trento, Italy, *guerini@fbk.eu*

ALEXANDER G. HAUPTMANN, Carnegie Mellon University, School of Computer Science, 5000 Forbes Ave, Pittsburgh, PA 15213, USA, *alex@cs.cmu.edu*

SVEN HAVEMANN, Fraunhofer Austria Research GmbH, Geschäftsbereich Visual Computing, Inffeldgasse 16c, 8010 Graz, Austria, *s.havemann@cgv.tugraz.at*

DAVID HOUGHTON, StreamSage/Comcast, 1110 Vermont Avenue NW, Washington, DC 20005, USA, *dfhoughton@gmail.com*

QIAN HU, The MITRE Corporation, 202 Burlington Road, Bedford, MA 01730, USA, *qian@mitre.org*

PIERRE-MARC JODOIN, Université de Sherbrooke, 2500 boulevard de l'Université, Sherbrooke, QC J1K2R1, Canada, *pierre-marc.jodoin@usherbrooke.ca*

OLIVER JOJIC, StreamSage/Comcast, 1110 Vermont Avenue NW, Washington, DC 20005, USA, *Oliver_Jojic@cable.comcast.com*

GARETH J. F. JONES, Centre for Digital Video Processing, School of Computing, Dublin City University, Dublin 9, Ireland, *gjones@computing.dcu.ie*

STEPHEN R. JONES, The MITRE Corporation, 202 Burlington Road, Bedford, MA 01730, USA, *srjones@mitre.org*

VAIVA KALNIKAITE, University of Sheffield, Regent Court, 211 Portobello Street, Sheffield S1 4DP, UK, *vaivak@gmail.com*

HIDETOSHI KAWAKUBO, The University of Electro-Communications, Tokyo, 1-5-1 Chofugaoka, Chofu-shi, Tokyo, 182-8585, Japan, *kawaku-h@mm.cs.uec.ac.jp*

MICHAEL KIPP, DFKI, Campus D3.2, Saarbrücken, Germany, *michael.kipp@dfki.de*

ANDREJ KOŠIR, University of Ljubljana, Faculty of Electrical Engineering, Tržaška 25, 1000 Ljubljana, Slovenia, *andrej.kosir@fe.uni-lj.si*

BRUNO LEPRI, FBK-IRST, Via Sommarive, 18, 38123 Trento, Italy, *lepri@fbk.eu*

STEFANO LEVIALDI, Department of Computer Science, Sapienza University of Rome, Via Salaria 113, Roma, Italy 00198, *levialdi@di.uniroma1.it*

WEI-HAO LIN, Carnegie Mellon University, School of Computer Science, 5000 Forbes Ave, Pittsburgh, PA 15213, USA, *whlin@cs.cmu.edu*

ALEXANDER C. LOUI, Kodak Research Laboratories, Eastman Kodak Company, Rochester, NY 14650, USA, *alexander.loui@kodak.com*

EHRY MACROSTIE, Raytheon BBN Technologies, 10 Moulton Street, Cambridge, MA 02138, USA, *emacrost@bbn.com*

NADIA MANA, FBK-IRST, Via Sommarive, 18, 38123 Trento, Italy, *mana@fbk.eu*

MARK T. MAYBURY, The MITRE Corporation, 202 Burlington Road, Bedford, MA 01730, USA, *maybury@mitre.org*

STEPHEN R. MOORE, The MITRE Corporation, 202 Burlington Road, Bedford, MA 01730, USA, *srmoore@mitre.org*

PREM NATARAJAN, Raytheon BBN Technologies, 10 Moulton Street, Cambridge, MA 02138, USA, *prem@bbn.com*

JAN NEUMANN, StreamSage/Comcast, 1110 Vermont Avenue NW, Washington, DC 20005, USA, *Jan_Neumann@cable.comcast.com*

ADRIAN NOVISCHI, Janya Inc., 1408 Sweet Home Road, Amherst, NY 14228, USA, *anovischi@janyainc.com*

DAVID D. PALMER, Autonomy Virage Advanced Technology Group, 1 Memorial Drive, Cambridge, MA 02142, USA, *dpalmer@autonomy.com*

EMANUELE PANIZZI, Department of Computer Science, Sapienza University of Rome, Via Salaria 113, Roma, Italy 00198, *panizzi@di.uniroma1.it*

FABIO PIANESI, FBK-IRST, Via Sommarive, 18, 38123 Trento, Italy, *pianesi@fbk.eu*

ROHIT PRASAD, Raytheon BBN Technologies, 10 Moulton Street, Cambridge, MA 02138, USA, *rprasad@bbn.com*

MARC B. REICHMAN, Autonomy Virage Advanced Technology Group, 1 Memorial Drive, Cambridge, MA 02142, USA, *mreichman@autonomy.com*

GERHARD RIGOLL, Technische Universität München, Theresienstrasse 90, 80333 München, Germany, *rigoll@tum.de*

ROBERT RUBINOFF, StreamSage/Comcast, 1110 Vermont Avenue NW, Washington, DC 20005, USA, *Robert_Rubinoff@cable.comcast.com*

VENKATESH SALIGRAMA, Boston University, 8 Saint Mary's Street, Boston, MA 02215, USA, *srv@bu.edu*

JOSE SAN PEDRO, Telefonica Research, Via Augusta 177, 08021 Barcelona, Spain, *jsanpedro@mac.com*

BJÖRN SCHULLER, Technische Universität München, Theresienstrasse 90, 80333 München, Germany, *schuller@tum.de*

RENAUD SEGUIER, Supelec, La Boulaie, 35510 Cesson-Sevigne, France, *renaud.seguier@supelec.fr*

BAGESHREE SHEVADE, StreamSage/Comcast, 1110 Vermont Avenue NW, Washington, DC 20005, USA, *Bageshree_Shevade@cable.comcast.com*

STEFAN SIERSDORFER, L3S Research Centre, Appelstr. 9a, 30167 Hannover, Germany, *siersdorfer@L3S.de*

ALAN SMEATON, CLARITY: Centre for Sensor Web Technologies, Dublin City University, Glasnevin, Dublin 9, Ireland, *alan.smeaton@dcu.ie*

ROHINI K. SRIHARI, Dept. of Computer Science & Engineering, State University of New York at Buffalo, 338 Davis Hall, Buffalo, NY, USA, *rohini@cedar.buffalo.edu*

OLIVIERO STOCK, FBK-IRST, I-38050, Povo, Trento, Italia, *stock@fbk.eu*

NICOLAS STOIBER, Orange Labs, 4 rue du Clos Courtel, 35510 Cesson-Sevigne, France, *nicolas.stoiber@orange-ftgroup.com*

CARLO STRAPPARAVA, FBK-IRST, I-38050, Povo, Trento, Italy, *strappa@fbk.eu*

JURIJ TASIČ, University of Ljubljana, Faculty of Electrical Engineering, Tržaška 25, 1000 Ljubljana, Slovenia, *jurij.tasic@fe.uni-lj.si*

MARKO TKALČIČ, University of Ljubljana, Faculty of Electrical Engineering, Tržaška 25, 1000 Ljubljana, Slovenia, *marko.tkalcic@fe.uni-lj.si*

EVELYNE TZOUKERMANN, The MITRE Corporation, 7525 Colshire Drive, McLean, VA 22102, USA, *tzoukermann@mitre.org*

TORSTEN ULLRICH, Fraunhofer Austria Research GmbH, Geschäftsbereich Visual Computing, Inffeldgasse 16c, 8010 Graz, Austria, *torsten.ullrich@fraunhofer.at*

JONATHAN WATSON, Raytheon BBN Technologies, 10 Moulton Street, Cambridge, MA 02138, USA, *jwatson@bbn.com*

NOAH WHITE, Autonomy Virage Advanced Technology Group, 1 Memorial Drive, Cambridge, MA 02142, USA, *nwhite@autonomy.com*

STEVE WHITTAKER, University of California Santa Cruz, 1156 High Street, Santa Cruz, CA 95064, USA, *swhittak@ucsc.edu*

MARTIN WÖLLMER, Technische Universität München, Theresienstrasse 90, 80333 München, Germany, *woellmer@tum.de*

PENG WU, University of Delaware, Department of Computer and Information Sciences, Newark, DE 19716, USA, *pwu@cis.udel.edu*

KEIJI YANAI, The University of Electro-Communications, Tokyo, 1-5-1 Chofugaoka, Chofu-shi, Tokyo, 182-8585, Japan, *yanai@cs.uec.ac.jp*

MASSIMO ZANCANARO, FBK-IRST, Via Sommarive, 18, 38123 Trento, Italy, *zancana@fbk.eu*

HONGZHONG ZHOU, StreamSage/Comcast, 1110 Vermont Avenue NW, Washington, DC 20005, USA, *Hongzhong_Zhou@cable.comcast.com*

CHAPTER 1

INTRODUCTION

MARK T. MAYBURY

1.1 MOTIVATION

Our world has become massively multimedia. In addition to rapidly growing personal and industrial collections of music, photography, and video, media sharing sites have exploded in recent years. The growth of social media sites for not only social networking but for information sharing has further fueled the broad and deep availability of media sources. Even special industrial collections once limited to proprietary access (e.g., Time-Life images), or precious books or esoteric scientific materials once restricted to special collection access, or massive scientific collections (e.g., genetics, astronomy, and medical), or sensors (traffic, meteorology, and space imaging) once accessible only to a few privileged users are increasingly becoming widely accessible.

Rapid growth of global and mobile telecommunications and the Web have accelerated both the growth of and access to media. As of 2012, over one-third of the world's population is currently online (2.3 billion users), although some regions of the world (e.g., Africa) have less than 15% of their potential users online. The World Wide Web runs over the Internet and provides easy hyperlinked access to pages of text, images, and video—in fact, to over 800 million websites, a majority of which are commercial (.com). The most visited site in the world, Google (Yahoo! is second) performs hundreds of millions of Internet searches on millions of servers that process many petabytes of user-generated content daily. Google has discovered over one trillion unique URLs. Wikis, blogs, Twitter, and other social media (e.g., MySpace and LinkedIn) have grown exponentially. Professional imagery sharing on Flickr now contains over 6 billion images. Considering social networking, more than 6 billion photos and more than 12 million videos are uploaded each

Multimedia Information Extraction: Advances in Video, Audio, and Imagery Analysis for Search, Data Mining, Surveillance, and Authoring, First Edition. Edited by Mark T. Maybury.
© 2012 IEEE Computer Society. Published 2012 by John Wiley & Sons, Inc.

month on Facebook by over 800 billion users. Considering audio, IP telephony, pod/broadcasting, and digital music has similarly exploded. For example, over 16 billion songs and over 25 billion apps have been downloaded from iTunes alone since its 2003 launch, with as many as 20 million songs being downloaded in one day. In a simple form of extraction, loudness and frequency spectrum analysis are used to generate music visualizations.

Parallel to the Internet, the amount of television consumption in developed countries is impressive. According to the A.C. Nielsen Co., the average American watches more than 4 hours of TV each day. This corresponds to 28 hours each week, or 2 months of nonstop TV watching per year. In an average 65-year lifespan, a person will have spent 9 years watching television. Online video access has rocketed in recent times. In April of 2009, over 150 million U.S. viewers watched an average of 111 videos watching on average about six and a half hours of video. Nearly 17 billion online videos were viewed in June 2009, with 40 percent of these at Youtube (107 million viewers, averaging 3–5 minutes each video), a site at which approximately 20 hours of video are uploaded every minute, twice the rate of the previous year. By March 2012, this had grown to 48 hours of video being uploaded every minute, with over 3 billion views per day. Network traffic involving YouTube accounts for 20% of web traffic and 10% of all Internet traffic. With billions of mobile device subscriptions and with mobiles outnumbering PCs five to one, increasingly access will be mobile. Furthermore, in the United States, four billion hours of surveillance video is recorded every week. Even if one person were able to monitor 10 cameras simultaneously for 40 hours a week, monitoring all the footage would require 10 million surveillance staff, roughly about 3.3% of the U.S. population. As collections of personal media, web media, cultural heritage content, multimedia news, meetings, and others develop from gigabyte to terabyte to petabyte, the need will only increase for accurate, rapid, and cross-media extraction for a variety of user retrieval and reuse needs. This massive volume of media is driving a need for more automated processing to support a range of educational, entertainment, medical, industrial, law enforcement, defense, historical, environmental, economic, political, and social needs.

But how can we all benefit from these treasures? When we have specific interests or purposes, can we leverage this tsunami of multimedia to our own individual aims and for the greater good of all? Are there potential synergies among latent information in media awaiting to be extracted, like hidden treasures in a lost cave? Can we infer what someone was feeling when their image was captured? How can we automate currently manually intensive, inconsistent, and errorful access to media? How close are we to the dream of automated media extraction and what path will take us there?

This collection opens windows into some of the exciting possibilities enabled by extracting information, knowledge, and emotions from text, images, graphics, audio, and video. Already, software can perform content-based indexing of your personal collections of digital images and videos and also provide you with content-based access to audio and graphics collections. And analysis of print and television advertising can help identify in which contexts (locations, objects, and people) a product appears and people's sentiments about it. Radiologists and oncologists are beginning to automatically retrieve cases of patients who exhibit visually similar conditions in internal organs to improve diagnoses and treatment. Someday soon, you will be able to film your vacation and have not only automated identification of the people and places in your movies, but also the creation of a virtual world of reconstructed people, objects, and buildings, including representation of the happy, sad, frustrating, or exhilarating moments of the characters captured therein. Indeed, multimedia information extraction technologies promise new possibilities for personal histories, urban planning, and cultural heritage. They might also help us better understand animal behavior, biological processes, and the environment. These technologies could someday provide new insights in human psychology, sociology, and perhaps even governance.

The remainder of this introductory chapter first defines terminology and the overall process of multimedia information extraction. To facilitate the use of this collection in research, it then describes the collection's structure, which mirrors the key media extraction areas. This is augmented with a hierarchical index at the back of the book to facilitate retrieval of key detailed topics. To facilitate the collection's use in teaching, this chapter concludes by illustrating how each section addresses standard computing curricula.

1.2 DEFINITIONS

Multimedia information extraction is the process of analyzing multiple media (e.g., text, audio, graphics, imagery, and video) to excerpt content (e.g., people, places, things, events, intentions, and emotions) for some particular purpose (e.g., data basing, question answering, summarization, authoring, and visualization). Extraction is the process of pulling out or excising elements from the original media source, whereas abstraction is the generalization or integration across a range of these excised elements (Mani and Maybury 1999). This book is focused on the former, where extracted elements can stand alone (e.g., populating a database) or be linked to or presented in the context of the original source (e.g., highlighted named entities in text or circled faces in images or tracked objects moving in a video).

As illustrated in Figure 1.1, multimedia information extraction requires a cascading set of processing, including the segmentation of heterogeneous media (in terms of time, space, or topic), the analysis of media to identify entities, their properties and relations as well as events, the resolution of references both within and across media, and the recognition of intent and emotion. As is illustrated on the right hand side of the figure, the process is knowledge intensive. It requires models of each of the media, including their elements, such as words, phones, visemes, but also their properties, how these are sequenced and structured, and their meaning. It also requires the context in which the media occurs, such as the time (absolute or relative), location (physical or virtual), medium (e.g., newspaper, radio, television, and Internet), or topic. The task being performed is also important (its objective, steps, constraints, and enabling conditions), as well as the domain in which it occurs (e.g., medicine, manufacturing, and environment) and the application for which it is constructed (e.g., training, design, and entertainment). Of course, if the media extraction occurs in the context of an interaction with a user, it is quite possible that the ongoing dialogue will be important to model (e.g., the user's requests and any reaction they provide to interim results), as well as a model of the user's goals, objectives, skills, preferences, and so on. As the large vertical arrows in the figure show, the processing of each media may require unique algorithms. In cases where multiple

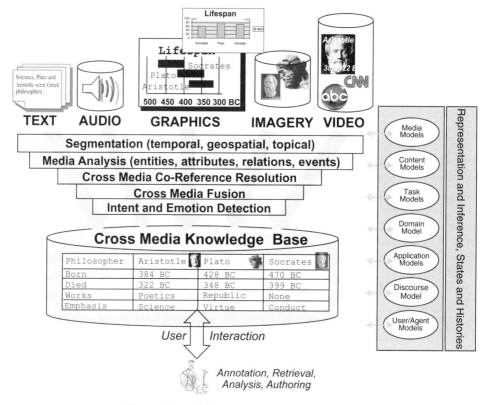

Figure 1.1. Multimedia information extraction.

media contain synchronous channels (e.g., the audio, imagery, and on screen text in video broadcasts), media processing can often take advantage of complementary information in parallel channels. Finally, extraction results can be captured in a cross-media knowledge base. This processing is all in support of some primary user task that can range from annotation, to retrieval, to analysis, to authoring or some combination of these.

Multimedia information extraction is by nature interdisciplinary. It lies at the intersection of and requires collaboration among multiple disciplines, including artificial intelligence, human computer interaction, databases, information retrieval, media, and social media studies. It relies upon many component technologies, including but not limited to natural language processing (including speech and text), image processing, video processing, non-speech audio analysis, information retrieval, information summarization, knowledge representation and reasoning, and social media information processing. Multimedia information extraction promises advances across a spectrum of application areas, including but not limited to web search, photography and movie editing, music understanding and synthesis, education, health care, communications and networking, and medical sensor exploitation (e.g., sonograms and imaging).

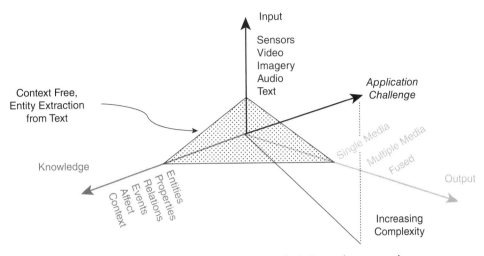

Figure 1.2. Some dimensions of multimedia information extraction.

As Figure 1.2 illustrates, multimedia information extraction can be characterized along several dimensions, including the nature of the input, output, and knowledge processed. In terms of input, the source can be single media, such as text, audio, or imagery; composite media, such as video (which includes text, audio, and moving imagery); wearable sensors, such as data gloves or bodysuits, or remote sensors, such as infrared or multispectral imagers; or combinations of these, which can result in diverse and large-scale collections. The output can range from simple annotations on or extractions from single media and multiple media, or it can be fused or integrated across a range of media. Finally, the knowledge that is represented and reasoned about can include entities (e.g., people, places, and things), their properties (e.g., physical and conceptual), their relationships with one another (geospatial, temporal, and organizational), their activities or events, the emotional affect exhibited or produced by the media and its elements, and the context (time, space, topic, social, and political) in which it appears. It can even extend to knowledge-based models of and processing that is sensitive to the domain, task, application, and user. The next chapter explores the state of the art of extraction of a range of knowledge from a variety of media input for various output purposes.

Figure 1.3 steps back to illustrate the broader processing environment in which multimedia information extraction occurs. While the primary methods reported in this collection address extraction of content from various media, often those media will contain metadata about their author, origin, pedigree, contents, and so on, which can be used to more effectively process them. Similarly, relating one media to another (e.g., a written transcript of speech, an image which is a subimage of another image) can be exploited to improve processing. Also, external semi-structured or structured sources of data, information, or knowledge (e.g., a dictionary of words, an encyclopedia, a graphics library, or ontology) can enhance processing as illustrated in Figure 1.3. Finally, information about the user (their knowledge, interests, or skills) or the context of the task can also enhance the kind of information that is extracted or even the way in which it is extracted (e.g., incrementally or in batch

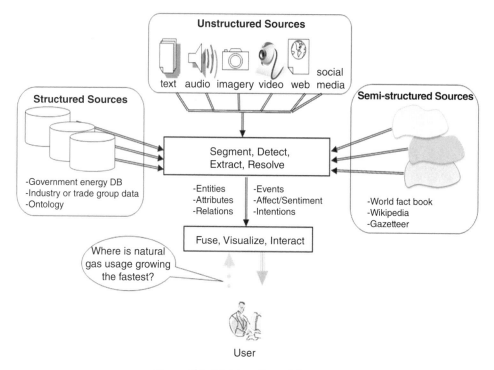

Figure 1.3. Multimedia architecture.

mode). Notably, the user's question itself can be multimedia and may require multimedia information extraction during query processing.

1.3 COLLECTION OVERVIEW

The five sections of *Multimedia Information Extraction* represent key areas of research and development including audio, graphics, imagery, and video extraction, affect and behavior extraction, and multimedia annotation and authoring.

1.3.1 Section 1: Image Extraction

Exponential growth of personal, professional, and public collections of imagery requires improved methods for content-based and collaborative retrieval of whole and parts of images. This first section considers the extraction of a range of elements from imagery, such as objects, logos, visual concepts, shape, and emotional faces. Solutions reported in this section enable improved image collection organization and retrieval, geolocation based on image features, extraction of 3D models from city or historic buildings, and improved facial emotion extraction and synthesis. The chapters identify a number of research gap areas, including image query context, results presentation, and representation, and reasoning about visual content.

1.3.2   Section 2: Video Extraction

The rapid growth of digital video services and massive video repositories such as YouTube provide challenges for extraction of content from a broad range of video domains from broadcast news to sports to surveillance video. Solutions reported in this section include how processing of the text and/or audio streams of video can improve the precision and recall of video extraction or retrieval. Other work automatically identifies bias in TV news video through analysis of written words, spoken words, and visual concepts that reflect both topics and inner attitudes and opinions toward an issue. Tagging video with multiple viewpoints promises to foster better informed decisions. In other applied research, global access to multilingual video news requires integration of a broad set of image processing (e.g., keyframe detection, face identification, scene cut analysis, color frame detection, on screen OCR, and logo detection), as well as audio analysis (e.g., audio classification, speaker identification, automatic speech recognition, named entity detection, closed captioning processing, and machine translation). Performance can be enhanced using cross media extraction, for example, correlating identity information across face identification, speaker identification, and visual OCR. In the context of football game processing, another chapter considers speech and language processing to detect touchdowns, fumbles, and interceptions in video. The authors are able to detect banners and logos in football and baseball with over 95% accuracy. Other solutions provide detection and recognition of text content in video (including overlaid and in-scene text). Notably, a majority of entities in video text did not occur in speech transcripts, especially location and person names and organization names. Other solutions do not look at the content but rather frequency of use of different scenes in a video to detect their importance. Yet a different solution considers anomaly detection from uncalibrated camera networks for tasks such as surveillance of cars or people. Overall, the chapters identify a number of research gap areas, such as the need for inexpensive annotation, cross-modal indicators, scalability, portability, and robustness.

1.3.3   Section 3: Audio, Graphics, and Behavior Extraction

Media extraction is not limited to traditional areas of text, speech, or video, but includes extracting information from non-speech audio (e.g., emotion and music), graphics, and human behavior. Solutions reported in this section include identity, content, and emotional feature audio extraction from massive, multimedia, multilingual audio sources in the audio hot spotting system (AHS). Another chapter reports extraction of information graphics (simple bar charts, grouped bar charts, and simple line graphs) using both visual and linguistic evidence. Leveraging eye tracking experiments to guide perceptual/cognitive modeling, a Bayesian-based message extractor achieves an 80% recognition rate on 110 simple bar charts. The last chapter of the section reveals how "thin slices" of extracted social behavior fusing nonverbal cues, including prosodic features, facial expressions, body postures, and gestures, can yield reliable classification of personality traits and social roles. For example, extracting the personality feature "locus of control" was on average 87% accurate, and detecting "extraversion" was on average 89% accurate. This section reveals important new frontiers of extracting identity and emotions, trends and relationships, and personality and social roles.

1.3.4   Section 4: Affect Extraction from Audio and Imagery

This section focuses on the extraction of emotional indicators from audio and imagery. Solutions described include the detection of emotional state, age, and gender in TV and radio broadcasts. For example, considering hundreds of acoustic features, whereas speaker gender can be classified with more than 90% accuracy, age recognition remains difficult. The correlation coefficient (CC) between the best algorithm and human (where 1 is perfect correlation) was 0.62 for valence (positive vs. negative) and 0.85 for arousal (calm vs. excited) traits. Another chapter explores valenced (positive/negative) expressions, as well as nonlinguistic reactions (e.g., applause, booing, and laughter) to discover their importance to persuasive communication. Valenced expressions are used to distinguish, for example, Democrat from Republican texts with about 80% accuracy. In contrast, considering images annotated with induced emotional state in the context of systems such as Flickr and Facebook, 68% of users are provided better (in terms of precision) recommendations through the use of affective metadata. The last chapter of the section reports the extraction of low-level, affective features from both the acoustic (e.g., pitch, energy) and visual (e.g., motion, shot cut rate, saturation, and brightness) streams of feature films to model valence and arousal. Scenes with particular properties are mapped to emotional categories, for example, a high-pitched human shouting with dark scenes might indicate horror or terror scenes, whereas those with bright colors might indicate funny or happy scenes. Together, these chapters articulate the emergence of a diversity of methods to detect affective features of emotion in many media, such as audio, imagery, and video.

1.3.5   Section 5: Multimedia Annotation and Authoring

This final section turns to methods and systems for media annotation and authoring. Solutions include the more precise annotation of human movement by extending the publicly available ANVIL (http://www.anvil-software.de) to perform 3D motion capture data annotation, query, and analysis. Another chapter employs a display grammar to author and manage interactions with imagery and extracted audio. A related chapter demonstrates how semantic query-based authoring can be used to design interactive narratives, including 2D images, sounds, and virtual camera movements in a 3D environment about historical Brooklyn. Ontology-based authoring supports concept navigation among an (SoundFisher system) audio analysis of non-speech natural sounds. The last chapter of the section describes the MADCOW system for annotation of relations in multimedia web documents. One unique feature of MADCOW is the ability to add annotations not only to single but also multiple portions of a document, potentially revealing new relations. By moving media assembly to the point of delivery, users' preferences, interests, and actions can influence display.

1.4   CONTENT INDEX

This content index is intended for researchers and instructors who intend to use this collection for research and teaching. In order to facilitate access to relevant content, each chapter is classified in Table 1.1 according to the type of media it addresses,

TABLE 1.1. Content Index of Chapters

Section	Chapter	Media Type					Task Application							Architecture Emphasis				Technical Approach			
		Text	Audio	Imagery	Graphics	Video	Web Access/Exploit	Image Processing/Mgmt	Facial Processing/Mgmt	Broadcast News Video	Meetings	Surveillance	Affect Detection	Annotation	Extraction	Retrieval	Authoring	Statistical	Symbolic/Model Based	Recommender	Social
	2	■	■	■	■	■	■	■	■	■	■	■		■	■	■	■	■			
I	3			■			■							■		■		■			
	4			■				■						■		■		■			
	5			■										■	■			■			
	6			■				■			■			■	■			■			
II	7			■				■						■	■			■			■
	8					■			■	■				■	■	■		■			
	9	■				■						■		■	■			■			
	10	■				■						■		■	■			■			
	11	■							■					■	■			■			
	12	■												■	■			■			■
	13			■			■		■					■	■			■	■		
III	14		■						■					■	■			■	■		
	15			■			■							■	■			■			
	16	■					■							■	■			■			
IV	17	■							■				■	■	■			■			
	18	■							■				■	■	■			■			■
	19			■		■			■					■		■			■		
	20			■		■								■	■			■			
V	21	■											■	■	■			■			
	22		■	■	■									■		■		■			
	23													■		■		■			
	24	■		■		■								■	■			■			

the application task addressed, its architectural focus, and the technical approach pursued (each shown in four main columns in the Table). The table first distinguishes the media addressed by each chapter, such as if the chapter addresses extraction of text, audio, imagery (e.g., Flickr), graphics (e.g., charts), or video (e.g., YouTube). Next, we characterize each chapter in terms of the application task it aims to support, such as World Wide Web access, image management, face recognition, access to video (from broadcast news, meetings, or surveillance cameras), and/or detection of emotion or affect. Next, Table 1.1 indicates the primary architectural focus of each chapter, specifying whether the research primarily explores media annotation, extraction, retrieval, or authoring. Finally, Table 1.1 classifies each chapter in terms of the technical approach explored, such as the use of statistical or machine learning methods, symbolic or model-based methods (e.g., using knowledge sources such as electronic dictionaries as exemplified by WordNet, ontologies, and inference machinery such as that found in CYC, and/or semi-structured information sources, such as Wikipedia or the CIA fact book), recommender technology, and, finally, social technology.

1.5 MAPPING TO CORE CURRICULUM

Having seen how the chapters relate to core aspects of multimedia, we conclude by relating the sections of this collection to the required body of knowledge for core curriculum in human computer interaction, computer science, and information technology. This mapping is intended to assist instructors who plan to use this text in their classroom as a basis for or supplement to an undergraduate or graduate course in multimedia. The three columns in Table 1.2 relate each section of the book (in rows) to the ACM SIGCHI HCI Curricula (SIGCHI 1996), the ACM/IEEE computer science curricula (CS 2008), and the ACM/IEEE information technology curricula (IT 2008). In each cell in the matrix, core topics are listed and electives are italicized. For example, the Association for Computing Machinery (ACM) and the IEEE Computer Society have developed a model curricula for computer science that contains core knowledge areas, such as Discrete Structures (DS), Human–Computer Interaction (HC), Programming Fundamentals (PF), Graphics and Visual Computing (GV), Intelligent Systems (IS), and so on. Some of these topics are addressed throughout the collection (e.g., human computer interaction), whereas others are specific to particular sections (e.g., geometric modeling). Finally, the NSF Digital Libraries Curriculum project (DL 2009) is developing core modules that many of the sections and chapters in the collection relate directly to, such as digital objects, collection development, information/knowledge organization (including metadata), user behavior/interactions, indexing and searching, personalization, and evaluation.

Moreover, there are many additional connections to core curricula that the individual instructor can discover based on lesson plans that are not captured in the table. For example, face and iris recognition, addressed in Chapter 2 and Chapter 6, is a key element in the ACM/IEEE core requirement of Information Assurance and Security (IAS). There are also Social and Professional Issues (SP) in the privacy aspects of multimedia information extraction and embedded in the behavior and affect extraction processing addressed in Sections 3 and 4. Finally, there are, of

TABLE 1.2. Book Sections Related to Core Curricula in HCI, CS, and IT (Electives Italicized)

Book Section	ACM SIGCHI Core Content	ACM/IEEE CS Core Curricula	ACM/IEEE IT Core Curricula
All Sections	User Interfaces, Communication and Interaction, Dialogue, Ergonomics, Human–Machine Fit and Adaptation	Human–Computer Interaction (HC), Discrete Structures (DS), Programming Fundamentals (PF), Algorithms and Complexity (AL) Intelligent Systems (IS), Information Management (IM), Net-Centric Computing (NC) Software Engineering (SE), Programming Languages (PL), *Multimedia Technologies, Machine Learning, Data Mining, Privacy and Civil Liberties*	Human Computer Interaction (HCI), Information Management (IM), Integrative Programming and Technologies (IPT), Math and Statistics for IT (MS), Programming Fundamentals (PF), *History of IT, Privacy and Civil Liberties, Digital Media*
Introduction and State of the Art	Evaluation	*Information Storage and Retrieval*	
I. Image Extraction	Image Processing	Graphics and Visual Computing (GV), *Perception, Geometric Modeling*	
II. Video Extraction	Audio/Image/Video Processing	Graphics and Visual Computing (GV), *Computer Vision, Natural Language Processing*	*Social Software*
III. Audio/ Graphics/ Behavior Extraction	Computer Graphics, Audio/Image/Video Processing	Graphics and Visual Computing (GV), *Natural Language Processing*	
IV. Affect Extraction in Audio and Video	Communication and Interaction, Audio/Image/Video Processing	*Signal Processing, Computer Vision, Natural Language Processing*	
V. Multimedia Annotation and Authoring	Input/Output Devices, Dialogue Techniques, Design	*Hypermedia, Multimedia and Multimodal Systems*	Web Systems and Technologies (WS)

course, System Integration & Architecture (SIA) challenges in creating a multimedia information extraction system that integrates text, audio, and motion imagery subsystems.

1.6 SUMMARY

This chapter introduces and defines multimedia information extraction, provides an overview of this collection, and provides both a content index and mapping of content to core curricula to facilitate research and teaching.

ACKNOWLEDGMENTS

Appreciation goes to all the authors for their feedback, especially to Björn Schuller and Gareth Jones for a careful reading of the final text.

CHAPTER 2

MULTIMEDIA INFORMATION EXTRACTION: HISTORY AND STATE OF THE ART

MARK T. MAYBURY

2.1 ORIGINS

Figure 2.1 summarizes two decades of scientific history of information extraction. Notably, the multidisciplinary nature of multimedia information extraction has required the bridging of traditionally independent scientific communities, including but not limited to audio and imagery processing, speech and language processing, music understanding, computer vision, human–computer interaction, databases, information retrieval, machine learning, and multimedia systems.

In the early 1990s, research emphasized text retrieval and fact extraction. This would later expand to audio extraction and indexing, imagery, and, more recently, video information extraction. In the mid-1990s, workshops on content-based retrieval of multimedia began to appear. For example, the International Workshop on Content-Based Multimedia Indexing has been held since 1999 (http://cbmi.eurecom.fr) and the International Society for Music Information Retrieval (http://www.ismir.net) conference has met since 2000. Some workshops developed into international conferences on multimedia information retrieval, such as the ACM SIGMM International Conference on Multimedia Information Retrieval (http://riemann.ist.psu.edu/mir2010) which spun off into its own independent event and will combine with the International Conference on Image and Video Retrieval (http://www.civr2010.org) in 2011 into a dedicated ACM International Conference on Multimedia Retrieval (ICMR, http://www.acmicmr2010.org). Thirteen years after the publication of *Intelligent Multimedia Information Retrieval* (Maybury 1997), this book captures advances in information extraction from various media.

Scientific progress in multimedia information extraction has principally arisen from rigorous application of the scientific method, exploring hypotheses in

Multimedia Information Extraction: Advances in Video, Audio, and Imagery Analysis for Search, Data Mining, Surveillance, and Authoring, First Edition. Edited by Mark T. Maybury.
© 2012 IEEE Computer Society. Published 2012 by John Wiley & Sons, Inc.

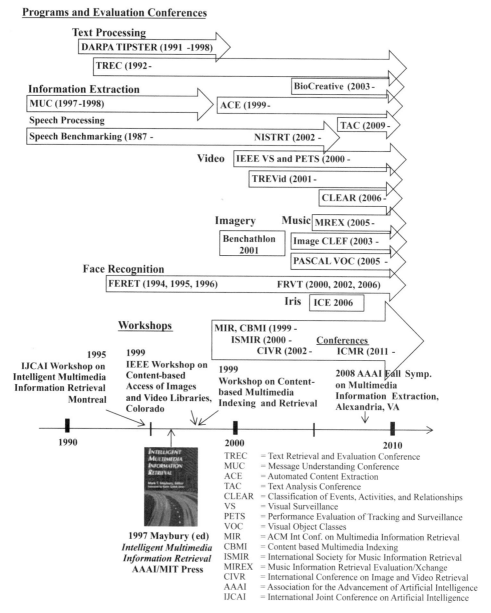

Figure 2.1. Research history.

large-scale multimedia data (e.g., text, audio, imagery, and video). Because of their expense and complexity, multimedia data sets are often collected in the public interest and analyzed and annotated by many human experts to ensure accuracy and consistency of gold standard data sets. Common tasks that are relevant to some user mission are defined. As a community, researchers then develop evaluation methods and metrics, and, frequently, apply machine learning methods to create detectors and extractors. Community evaluations have been used successfully by U.S. government funded research in programs for text processing, speech processing, and video processing to advance new methods for jointly defined user challenges by leveraging collaborative efforts of government, industry, and academia researchers. This chapter next considers each media history in turn, moving from text to audio to images to graphics to video, and, finally, to sensors.

2.2   TEXT EXTRACTION

The most technologically mature area of multimedia information extraction is text extraction. Information extraction from text is the automated identification of specific semantic elements within a text such as the entities (e.g., people, organizations, locations), their properties or attributes, relations (among entities), and events. For example, Figure 2.2 illustrates a document that an analyst has retrieved on a United Nations (UN) resolution on Iran in which text extraction software has annotated and color-coded entities (reproduced here in grayscale), such as people (Ali Kohrram, Mohammad ElBaradei), locations (Iran, Islamic Republic), organizations (IAEA [International Atomic Energy Agency], the UN, Mehr News Agency, UN Human Rights and Disarmament Commission), and dates (Sunday, September).

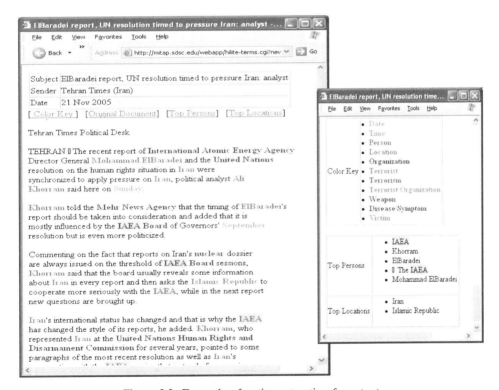

Figure 2.2. Example of entity extraction from text.

While the system has done an excellent job, it is not perfect. For example, it misclassifies IAEA as a person (green).

One of the first major efforts in this area was the multiagency TIPSTER text program led by the Defense Advanced Research Projects Agency (DARPA) from 1991 to 1998. Participants annotated shared data, defined domain tasks (e.g., find relevant documents, extract entities from a document), and performed objective evaluations to enable benchmarking and codiscovery. TIPSTER focused on three underlying technologies: document detection, information extraction, and summarization. Through the Text Retrieval Conferences (TREC), new developments were advanced in query expansion, passage (as opposed to document) retrieval, interactive retrieval, dealing with corrupted data, training for term selection for routing queries, and multilingual document retrieval (Spanish and Chinese). Starting in 1992, by 1998, TREC had grown from 25 to 35 participating systems, and document detection recall had improved from roughly 30% to as high as 75%.

In addition to TREC, TIPSTER made significant advances through the Message Understanding Conferences (MUC), which focused on information extraction from text. Extraction systems were evaluated both in terms of the detection of the phrase that names an entity as well as the classification of the entity correctly—that is, for example, distinguishing a person from an organization from a location, for example, "Hilton" meaning a person, global company, or physical hotel. The two primary evaluation metrics used were precision and recall for each entity class, where:

$$Precision = \text{Number-of-Correct-Returned/Total-Number-Returned}$$

$$Recall = \text{Number-of-Correct-Returned/Number-Possible-Correct}$$

The harmonic mean of precision and recall is used as a "balanced" single measure and is called the *F*-score or *F*-measure.

In its first of three major phases, TIPSTER participants advanced information extraction recall from roughly 49 to 65% and precision from 55 to 59%. In its second phase, from April 1994 to September 1996, a common architecture was created to enable plug and play of participant components. Finally, in phase 3, summarization was added as a new task.

The message understanding conferences ran for over a decade focusing on extracting information about naval operations messages (MUC-1 in 1987, MUC-2 in 1989), terrorism in Latin American countries (MUC-3 in 1991 and MUC-4 in 1992), joint ventures and microelectronics (MUC-5 in 1993), management changes in news articles (MUC-6 in 1995), and satellite launch reports (MUC-7 in 1998). Key tasks included named entity recognition, coreference resolution, terminology extraction, and relation extraction (e.g., PERSON located in LOCATION or PERSON works in ORGANIZATION). A Multilingual Entity Task (MET) was pursued in MUC-6 and MUC-7 in Chinese, Japanese, and Spanish yielding best F-scores of 91% for Chinese, 87% for Japanese and 94% for Spanish. While the domain for all languages for training was airline crashes and the domain for all languages for testing was launch events, the formal test scores were still above the 80% operational threshold set by customers without any changes being made to systems for the domain change.

The Automated Content Exploitation (ACE) Program developed extraction technology for text and automated speech recognition (ASR)- and optical character recognition (OCR)-derived text, including entity detection and tracking (EDT), relation detection and characterization (RDC), and event detection and character-ization (EDC). A fourth annotation task, entity linking (LNK), groups all references to a single entity and all its properties together into a composite entity. Data in English and Arabic included newswire, blogs, and newsgroups, but also transcripts of meetings, telephone conversations, and broadcast news. Systems were evaluated by selecting just over four hundred documents from over ten thousand documents each for English and Arabic text. Assessment included, though was not limited to, entities such as person, organization, location, facility, weapon, vehicle, and geopo-litical entity (GPEs). Relations include but are not limited to physical, social, employment, ownership, affiliation, and discourse relations. ACE became a track in the Text Analysis Conference (TAC) in 2009 with three evaluation tasks: knowledge base population, text entailment, and summarization.

A more focused activity, the NSF-funded BioCreative evaluation (BioCreative II 2008; Krallinger et al. 2008) emphasizes the extraction of biologically significant entities (e.g., gene and protein names) and their association to existing database entries, as well as detecting entity–fact associations (e.g., protein–functional term associations). Twenty-seven groups from 10 countries participated in the first evalu-ation in 2003, and 44 teams from 13 countries participated in the second evaluation in 2006–2007.

Arising from those programs shown in historical context in Figure 2.1, the results displayed in Figure 2.3 summarize the best performing systems across the MUC, ACE, and BioCreative evaluations. Figure 2.3 contrasts human performance with the best performing systems across various tasks, such as text extraction of entities (people, organization, location), relations, events, and genes/proteins. For each of the tasks in Figure 2.3, the first bar in each group displays human performance, and the second bar displays the best information extractors in English. Where available (entities and relations), Mandarin extraction performance is shown in the third bar and Arabic in the final one in the first two groups. The figure illustrates that humans can extract entities with 95–97% agreement, whereas the best English entity extrac-tor has about 95% F-scores, and Mandarin drops to about 85% and Arabic about 80%. Current systems are able to extract named entities in English news with over 90% accuracy and relations among entities with 70–80% accuracy.

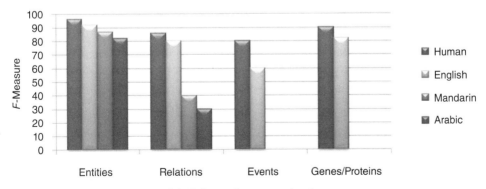

Figure 2.3. Information extraction from text.

In contrast to entities, humans can extract about 90% of relations (e.g., X is-located-at Y, A is-the-father-of B) from free text. However, machines can only extract English relations with about 80% accuracy, and Mandarin and Arabic relation extraction drops to 40 and 30% F-scores. Additionally, whereas humans agree about 80% of the time what events are, current event extraction performance is less than 60%, improving slowly. A range of languages are being evaluated (e.g., English, Japanese, Arabic, Chinese, German, Spanish, and Dutch). Finally, evaluations on bioinformatics texts have shown that current information extraction methods perform better on newswire than on biology texts (90 vs. 80% F-score), but also that newswire is easier for human annotators, too (interannotator agreement results of F=97 from MUC). It is worth noting that information extraction performs less well on biology texts than newswire for several reasons, including less experience (systems improve with practice), less training data, and lower interannotator agreement (in part perhaps because genes are less well defined than, e.g., person names).

These intensive scientific endeavors have advanced the state of the art. Accordingly, today, many commercial or open source information extraction solutions are available, such as Bolt Baranek and Neuman's IdentiFinder™ (Cambridge, MA), IBM's Unstructured Information Management Architecture (UIMA) (New York), Rocket Software's Aerotext™ (Newton, MA), Inxight's ThingFinder (Sunnyvale, CA), MetaCarta GeoTagger (Cambridge, MA), SRA's NetOwl Extractor (Fairfax, VA), and others.

2.3   AUDIO EXTRACTION

Just as information extraction from text remains important, so too there are vast audio sources from radio to broadcast news to audio lectures to meetings that require audio information extraction. There has been extensive exploration into information extraction from audio. Investigations have considered not only speech transcription but also non-speech audio and music detection and classification. Automated speech recognition (ASR) is the recognition of spoken words from an acoustic signal. Figure 2.4 illustrates the best systems each year in competitions administered by NIST to objectively benchmark performance of speech recognition systems over time. The graph reports reduction of word error rate (WER) over time. As can been seen in Figure 2.4, some of automated recognition algorithms (e.g., in read speech or in air travel planning kiosks) approaches the range of human error in transcription.

The systems were assessed on a wide range of increasingly complex and challenging tasks, moving from read speech, to broadcast (e.g., TV and radio) speech, to conversational speech, to foreign language speech (e.g., Chinese Mandarin and Arabic). Over time, tasks have ranged from understanding reading *Wall Street Journal* text, to understanding foreign television broadcasts, to so called "switchboard" (fixed telephone and cell phone) conversations. Recent tasks have included recognition of speech (including emotionally colored speech) in meeting or conference rooms, lecture rooms, and during coffee breaks, as well as attribution of speakers.

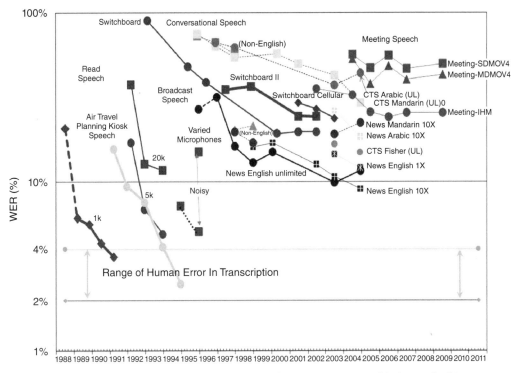

Figure 2.4. NIST benchmark test history (*Source*: http://www.itl.nist.gov/iad).

For example, in the NIST Rich Transcription (RT) evaluation effort (Fiscus et al. 2007) using head-mounted microphones, speech transcription from conference data is about 26% WER, lectures about 30%, and coffee breaks 31% WER, rising to 40–50% WER with multiple distant microphones and about 5% higher with single distant microphones. The "who spoke when" test results (called speaker diarization) revealed typical detection error rates (DERs) of around 25% for conferences and 30% for lectures, although one system achieved an 8.5% DER on conferences for both detecting and clustering speakers. Interestingly, at least one site found negligible performance difference between lecture and coffee break recognition.

2.3.1 Audio Extraction: Music

In addition to human speech, another significant body of audio content is music. The Music Genome Project (Castelluccio 2006) is an effort in which musicians manually classify the content of songs using almost 400 music attributes into an *n*-dimensional vector characterizing a song's roots (e.g., jazz, funk, folk, rock, and hip hop), influences, feel (e.g., swing, waltz, shuffle, and reggae), instruments (e.g., piano, guitar, drums, strings, bass, and sax), lyrics (e.g., romantic, sad, angry, joyful, and religious), vocals (e.g., male and female), and voice quality (e.g., breathy, emotional, gritty, and mumbling). Over 700,000 songs by 80,000 artists have been catalogued using these attributes, and the commercial service Pandora (John 2006), which claims over 35 million users and adds over 15,000 analyzed tracks to the Music Genome each month, enables users to define channels by indicating preferred songs. Unlike collaborative filtering which recommends songs others enjoy that are similar to the ones you like, this content-based song recommender is based on music content, and users set up user-defined channels (e.g., 80s rock, European Jazz, and Indian folk music), in which songs are selected by calculating distances between vectors of other songs and responding to listener feedback.

While useful to audiophiles, manual music classification suffers inconsistency, incompleteness, and inaccuracy. Automated music understanding is important for composition, training, and simply enjoyment. Acoustic feature extraction has proven valuable for detecting dominant rhythm, pitch or, melody (Foote 1999). These capabilities are useful for beat tracking for disc jockeys or for automated pitch tracking for karaoke machines. Humans can predict musical genre (e.g., classical, country, jazz, rock, disco) based on 250 ms samples, and Tzanetakis et al. (2001) report "musical surface" features for representing texture, timbre, instrumentation, and rhythmic structure in 20 ms windows over a second to predict musical genre in samples from an over 6-hour diverse music collection. Blum et al. (1997) SoundFisher system performs both acoustic and perceptual processing of sounds to enable users, such as sound engineers, to retrieve materials either based on acoustic properties (e.g., loudness, pitch, brightness, and harmonicity) or user-annotated perceptual properties (e.g., scratchy, buzzy, laughter, and female speech) or via clusters of acoustic or perceptual features (e.g., bee-like or plane-like sounds). Blum et al. augment this with music analysis (e.g., rhythm, tempo, pitch, duration, and loudness) and instrument identification. The authors demonstrated SoundFisher's utility by retrieving example laughter, female speech, and oboe recordings in the context of a modest 400 sound database of short (1–15 second) samples from animals, machines, musical instruments, speech, and nature. One challenge of this early work was the lack of standardized collection both to develop and evaluate innovations.

Inaugurated in 2005 and supported by the National Science Foundation and the Andrew W. Mellon Foundation, the Music Information Retrieval Evaluation eXchange (MIREX) (http://www.music-ir.org/mirex) is a TREC-like community evaluation with standard collections, tasks, and answers (relevancy assessments or classifications) organized by the International Music Information Retrieval Systems Evaluation Laboratory (IMIRSEL) at the University of Illinois at Urbana-Champaign (UIUC). Because of copyright violation concerns, unlike TREC, data is not distributed to participants, but instead algorithms are submitted to IMIRSEL for evaluation against centralized data, consisting of two terabytes of audio data representing some 30,000 tracks divided among popular, classical, and Americana subcollections. Unfortunately, the same ground truth data has been used for 2005, 2006, and 2007 evaluations, risking overfitting. Evaluations have taken place at the International Conferences on Music Information Retrieval (ISMIR), with multiple audio tasks, such as tempo and melody extraction, artist and genre identification, query by singing/humming/tapping/example/notation, score following, and music similarity and retrieval. One interesting task introduced in 2007 is music mood/ emotion classification, wherein algorithms need to classify music as one of five clusters (e.g., passionate/rousing, cheerful/fun, bittersweet/brooding, silly/whimsical, and fiery/ volatile). Approximately 40 teams per year from over a dozen countries compete, most recently performing an overall 122 runs against multiple tasks (Downie 2008). Sixteen of the 19 primary tasks require audio processing, the other three symbolic processing (e.g., processing MIDI formats). Three hundred algorithms have been evaluated since the beginning of MIREX. For example, the recognition of cover songs (i.e., new performances by a distinct artist of an original hit) improved between 2006 and 2007 from 23.1 to 50.1% average precision. Interestingly, the 2007 submissions moved from spectral-based "timbral similarity" toward more musical features, such as tonality, rhythm, and harmonic progressions, overcoming what were perceived by researchers as a performance ceiling. Another finding was that particular systems appear to have unique abilities that address specific subsets of queries, suggesting that hybrid approaches that combine the best aspects of the individual systems could improve performance. A new consortium called the Networked Environment for Music Analysis (NEMA) aims to overcome the challenges with the distribution of music test collections by creating an open and extensible web service-based resource framework of music data and analytic/evaluative tools to be used globally.

Related, the innovative TagATune evaluation (tagatune.org) compares various algorithms' abilities to associate tags with 29-second audio clips of songs. A TagATune game is used to collect tags of audio clips by giving two players audio clips and having them tag them and then try to figure out if they have the same clip by looking only at the tags of each other. Interestingly, negative tags are also captured (e.g., no piano and no drums). This data annotation method is a promising approach to otherwise expensive and time-consuming creation of ground truth data. Whereas humans can tag music at approximately 93% accuracy, in early 2009, four of five systems performed with 60.9–70.1% accuracy (Law et al. 2009).

2.4 IMAGE EXTRACTION

Image extraction has received increased attention given vast collections of industrial, personal, and web images (e.g., Flickr) inspiring the detection and classification of objects, people, and events from images. Early image processing was motivated by challenges, such as character recognition, face recognition, and robot guidance. Significant interest has focused on imagery retrieval. For example, early applications, such as IBM Research Almaden's Query by Image Content (QBIC), analyzed color, shape, and texture feature similarity and allowed users to query by example or by drawing, selecting, or other graphical means in a graphical query language (Flickner et al. 1995; Flickner 1997). Early feature-based methods found their way into Internet search engines (e.g., Webseek, Webseer) and later into databases (e.g., Informix, IBM DB2, and Oracle). Feature-based methods proved practical for such tasks as searching trademark databases, blocking pornographic content, and medical image retrieval. Researchers sought improved methods that were translation, rotation, and scale invariant, as well as for ways to overcome occlusion and lighting variations. Of course, storage and processing efficiency were desirable.

While feature-based image retrieval provided a great leap beyond text retrieval, very soon, researchers recognized the need to bridge the semantic gap from low-level feature recognition (e.g., color, shape, and texture) to high-level semantic representations (e.g., queries or descriptions about people, locations, and events).

Along the way, a number of researchers explored mathematical properties that reflected visual phenomena (e.g., fractals capture visual roughness, graininess reflects coarseness, and entropy reflects visual disorder). Recently, the Large Scale Concept Ontology for Multimedia (http://www.lscom.org) was created to provide common terms, properties, and taxonomy to use for manual annotation and automated classification of visual material. Common ontologies also enable the possibility of using semantic relations between concepts for search. Originally designed for news videos, LSCOM needs to be extended to new genres, such as home video, surveillance, and movies.

Another issue that arose early was the need (and desire) to process cross media, for example, the use by web image search engines (e.g., Google and Yahoo!) of the text surrounding an image to index searches or the subsequent use by sites, such as YouTube and Flickr, leverage user-generated tags to support search. Researchers have also used the digital camera manufacturer-adopted exchangeable image format (exif.org) standard to help process images that includes metadata such as the camera model and make, key parameters for each photo (e.g., orientation, aperture, shutterspeed, focal length, metering mode, and ISO speed), time and place of the photo, a thumbnail, and any human tags or copyright information. In addition to exploiting related streams of data and metadata, other researchers considered user interactions and relevance feedback as additional sources of information to improve performance.

Scientific research requires access to realistic and accessible data along with ground truth. Researchers (e.g., Muller et al. 2002) found that working with artificial data sets, such as the Corel Photo CD, images could actually do more harm than good by misleading research because they don't represent realistic tasks (they are all in a narrow, unrealistically easy domain leading to overgeneralization) and lack a query set and associated relevancy judgments. The SPIE Benchathlon (www.benchathlon.net) was an early (2001) benchmarking effort associated with the SPIE Electronic Imaging conference. It included specifying common tasks (e.g., query by example, sketch), a publically available annotated data set, and software. More recently, the multimedia image retrieval Flickr collection (Huiskes and Lew 2008) consists of 25,000 images and image tags (with an average of about nine per image) that are realistic, redistributable (under the Creative Commons license), and contain relevance judgments (press.liacs.nl/mirflickr) related to visual concept/topic and subtopic classification (e.g., animal [cat, dog], plant [tree, flower], water [sea, lake, river]), and tag propagation tasks (press.liacs.nl/mirflickr). The 2011 ImageCLEF visual concept detection and annotation task used one million Flickr images which are under the Creative Commons license.

Deselaers et al. (2008) quantitatively compared the performance of a broad range of features on five publically available, mostly thousand image data sets in four distinct domains (stock photos, personal photos, building images, and medical images). They found color histograms, local feature SIFT (Scale Invariant Feature Transform) global search, local feature patches histogram, local feature SIFT histogram, and invariant feature histogram methods performed the best across the five data sets with average error rates less than 30% and mean average precisions of over 50%. Local features capture image patches or small subimages of images and are promising for extraction tasks (e.g., face and objects), although more computationally expensive. Notably, color histograms were by far the most time efficient in terms of feature extraction and retrieval. The processing and space efficient

Motion Pictures Expert Group (MPEG)-7 scalable color also had excellent overall performance. For texture, the authors found that a combination of features usually improved results.

2.4.1 ImageCLEF and ImageCLEFmed

The first broad community evaluation of progress on common, realistic data sets arose out of the Text Retrieval Conference (TREC). As illustrated initially in Figure 2.1, starting from a track in TREC, the Cross Language Evaluation Forum (CLEF) initiated a multilingual image retrieval track in 2003 (ImageCLEF, http:// www.imageclef.org) and then a medical image retrieval track in 2004 (ImageCLE-Fmed). ImageCLEF contains a number of tasks, such as visual concept detection in photos, medical images, photo retrieval, and robot vision. In 2009, a record 85 research groups registered for the seven sub tasks of ImageCLEF. For example, for the photo annotation task, 5000 annotated images from the 25,000 Multimedia Image Retrieval Flickr image collection are used to train image classifiers for 53 "concepts," such abstract category (e.g., landscape and party), season, time of day, person or group, image quality, and so on. These visual concepts are organized into a small ontology, including hierarchy and relations. Systems are then tested on 13,000 images. For the visual concept detection task, 19 groups submitted a total of 73 runs in 2009 and the best equal error rate (EER), in which false rejects equal false positives, was as low as 0.23. The organizers also created a hierarchical measure that considered the relations between concepts and the agreement of annotators on concepts and reporting a best area under curve (AUC) score of 0.84 (where 1 is perfection).

The 2009 photo retrieval task of ImageCLEF, in contrast, uses 50 topics (e.g., Olympic games, Hillary Clinton, beach soccer, stock exchange, Bulgarian churches, Brussels airport, flood, and demonstrations) based on an analysis of 2008 Belga News Agency query logs to reflect more realistic tasks. The job of systems is to provide a rank ordered list of photo IDs most relevant to the query. Evaluation aims to maximize precision and recall. Retrieval is evaluated on almost a half-million images from the Belga News Agency. Diversity of retrieval is important so evaluation includes how many relevant images that are representative of the different subtopics within the results are included in the top 20 hits returned. Eighty-four runs were submitted from 19 different groups. The top system achieved an 81% F-score (harmonic mean of precision and recall), although interestingly, the best image-only system achieved only a 21% F-score.

For the first time in 2009, ImageCLEF hosted the Robot Vision task. Given individual pictures or a sequence of pictures, systems must report the room location of an image from a five-room subsection of an office environment (e.g., kitchen, corridor, printer area, and one- or two-person office) taken under three different illumination settings (night, sunny, cloudy) over a time frame of 6 months. Nineteen groups registered for the Robot Vision task, and seven submitted at least one run for a total of 27 runs. A point is given for each correctly annotated frame and a half-point is deducted for misannotation from about a thousand training and test images over the three lighting conditions. The highest scores had approximately 70% accuracy.

Each year, about 12–15 groups participate in ImageCLEFmed. In 2007, while 31 groups from 25 countries registered, in the end, 13 groups submitted 149 runs (see ir.ohsu.edu/image) using a consolidated test collection consisting of 66,662 images

(5.15 GB) from 47,680 cases and 85 topics in English, French, and German. Images, typically with associated clinical case descriptions as annotations (a total of 55,485 of them), come from a broad range of medical collections in radiology, nuclear medicine, pathology, and endoscopy. Interestingly, topics are visual, textual, or both, for example, referring to an imaging modality (e.g., photograph, computed tomography, magnetic resonance imaging, and x-ray), anatomical location, view, and/or disease or finding. As in TREC, test collections are built on realistic samples of tasks that serve as topics that are submitted to systems as queries to retrieve images. Human-created relevance judgments, which indicate which documents in the collection are relevant to which topics (about 800–1200 per topic), are used to measure recall and precision, although the mean of average precision (MAP) across all topics is the most frequently used aggregate performance measure.

One observation about the current state of the art from ImageCLEFmed is that text processing retrieval methods (based on the image annotations) fare better than image processing methods; however, combined methods do better still. Groups apply a range of text and image processing methods, such as single or multilingual term frequency/inverse document frequency (TF/IDF), bag of words, and query expansion for text and color, shape, and texture processing. Results from the open source GIFT (GNU Image Finding Tool) and FIRE (Flexible Image Retrieval Engine) were made available to participants that did not have their own visual system retrieval engine. The results of methods on textual topics achieved as high as about 40% MAP, whereas the best methods on visual topics fared about 24%, suggesting the value of both better language processing as well as the importance of visual processing. In an unrelated study, when users were asked to browse images organized by visual similarity or text caption similarity, in 40 of 54 searches to find pictures to illustrate a travel website, users preferred the text caption view (Rodden 2001).

A second ImageCLEFmed task focused on automatic annotation of medical images into 120 classes. Systems must identify the body orientation, body region, and biological system captured in a particular image, as well as what type of image it is (e.g., an x-ray of the front of a cranium showing the musculoskeletal system). About 10 groups from 29 who registered participated submitting a total of 68 runs. A broad range of image processing methods were applied. One observation was that methods using local as opposed to global image descriptions performed better, and the more training data available, the more likely images were to be classified correctly. Error rates ranged from a high of 86.8 to a low of 10.3.

Extending the TREC evaluations, the ImagEVAL workshop focuses on user-centered evaluation of CBIR, including measures, such as the quality of user-interface, response time, and adaptability to a new domain. Four tasks included object (e.g., tree, cow, glasses) and attribute (e.g., indoor/outdoor, night/day, natural/urban) detection with mean average precision used for basic performance assessment.

2.4.2 Object Detection

In the past few years, the computer vision and image understanding community have developed a number of standard data sets for evaluating the performance of general object detection and recognition algorithms. For example, the PASCAL VOC (Visual Object Classes) (Everingham et al. 2009, 2010) (http://www.pascal-network.org/challenges/VOC) evaluation challenge has grown from the detection of four object classes (motorcycle, bicycle, people, and car) in a few hundred images and few thousand objects in 2005 to a 2009 competition with over 30 thousand images evaluated against data sets for 20 object classes, including person, animal (bird, cat, cow, dog, horse, and sheep), vehicle (aeroplane, bicycle, boat, bus, car, motorbike, and train), and indoor object (bottle, chair, dining table, potted plant, sofa, and TV/monitor). Three main tasks were classification (predicting presence/absence of an object class), detection (bounding box and label of each object), and segmentation (pixel-wise segmentation of objects and "background"). A single smaller scale "taster" competition looked at person layout, that is predicting the bounding box and label of each part of a person (head, hands, and feet).

In 2005, there were 12 participants and two major test sets, an "easier" challenge from the PASCAL image databases and a second "harder" one from freshly collected Google Images. Performance measures included standard receiver operating characteristic (ROC) measures of equal error rate (EER) and AUC. A variety of methods were applied (e.g., interest points, region features), and the most successful for classification used interest points plus SIFT plus clustering (histogram) plus SVMs. The mean EER of "best" results across all classes (motorcycle, bicycle, people, and car) was more or less uniform across the classes achieving 0.946 on the easy test and 0.741 on the more difficult one. For the detection task, 50% overlap in bounding boxes was considered a success with multiple detections considered as (one true +) false positive with average precision (AP) as defined by TREC (mean precision interpolated at various recall levels). The mean AP of "best" results across classes was 0.408 on the easy test and 0.195 on the hard test, with significant variance across the classes. Detection for people was the poorest, for bicycles was around 0.1, for cars about 0.6 and 0.3 on the easy and difficult data, and 0.9 and just over 0.3 for motorbikes. One entry used a group's own training data and raised AP to 0.4. In summary, there was more encouraging performance on cars and motorbikes than people and bicycles.

By 2009, the competition attracted 12 groups who tested 18 methods representing a variety of approaches (e.g., sliding window, combination with whole-image classifiers, segmentation-based). 17,218 objects were annotated in 7,054 images randomly selected from 500,000 downloaded images from Flickr. Separately, about 15,829 objects in 6,650 images were annotated for a test set. Objects were annotated with bounding boxes, as well as degree of occlusion, truncation, and pose (e.g., facing left). A 50% area of overlap (AO) between the detected and ground truth bounding box was a correct detection. Figure 2.5 shows the average precision results for various object classes. Unlike the 2005 case, use of external training data based on 3D annotations for "person" detection showed only modest improvement (43.2 vs. 41.5% AP) over methods using VOC training data. Also, the increased number of object classes in the 2009 data set not only increased the annotator's cognitive load, making it difficult to maintain quality, but it was also expensive, costing around 700 person-hours.

2.4.3 Face Recognition

In addition to general image retrieval, face recognition is an important specialized task. While early methods searched for whole faces, subsequent approaches

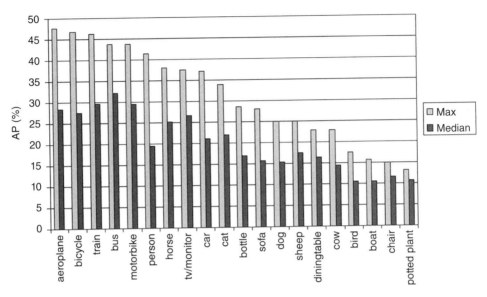

Figure 2.5. Average precision (AP) for visual object classes (VOC). (*Source*: Everingham et al. 2009).

integrated separate detectors and extractors for eyes and noses, as well as new feature similarity measures based on color, texture, and shape. And while early systems performed very highly in detecting frontal face views, nonfrontal views, low quality images, and occluded faces remain challenging. More powerful methods, such as relevance feedback and the use of machine learning methods (e.g., hidden Markov models and support vector machines), improved retrieval performance.

The National Institute of Standards and Technology (NIST)-managed Face Recognition Grand Challenge (FRGC) pursued the development and independent evaluations of face recognition technologies, including high-resolution still image, three-dimensional face scans, and multiple-sample still imagery (http://www.nist.gov/itl/iad/ig/frvt-home.cfm). Face recognition evaluations started with three FERET evaluations (1994, 1995, and 1996), followed by Face Recognition Vendor Tests (FRVT) 2000, 2002, and 2006. By 2004, the FRGC had 42 participants, including 13 universities.

By providing 50,000 recordings and including not only still images but high-resolution (5–6 megapixel) still images, 3D images, and multi-images of a person, the evaluation helped advance metrology and the state of the art in face recognition. For example, the FRGC high-resolution images consist of facial images with 250 pixels between the centers of the eyes on average (in contrast to the 40–60 pixels in current images). Also, three-dimensional recognition ensures robustness to variations of lighting (illumination) and pose. Finally, this was the first time that a computational–experimental environment was used to support a challenge problem in face recognition or biometrics through the use of an XML-based framework for describing and documenting computational experiments, called the Biometric Experimentation Environment (BEE). Experimental data for validation included images from 4003 subject sessions exhibiting two expressions (smiling and neutral) under controlled illumination conditions. An order of magnitude performance was obtained in 2006 over 2002, one of the goals of the FRGC. For example, the false rejection rates at 0.001 (1 in 1000) false acceptance rates dropped from nearly 79% in 1993 to 1% in FVRT 2006.

The related Iris Challenge Evaluation (iris.nist.gov/ICE) in 2006 reported iris recognition performance from left and right iris images. In this independent, large-scale performance evaluation of three algorithms on 59,558 samples from 240 subjects, NIST observed false nonmatch rates (FNMRs) from 0.0122 to 0.038, at a false match rate (FMR) of 0.001. In a comparison of recognition performance from very high-resolution still face images, 3D face images, and single-iris images (Phillips et al. 2007), recognition performance was comparable for all three biometrics. Notably, the best-performing face recognition algorithms were found to be more accurate than humans.

2.4.4 Graphics Extraction

Just as facial recognition and extraction emerged as an important, distinct task from general image processing, so too extraction from data graphics (e.g., tables, charts, maps, and networks) has been identified as a special case. An early effort, SageBook (Chuah et al. 1997) enables search for and customization of stored data graphics (e.g., charts, tables). Nonexpert users can pose graphical queries, browse results, and adapt and reuse previously successful graphics for data analysis. Users formulate queries with a graphical direct manipulation interface (SageBrush) by selecting and arranging spaces (e.g., charts and tables), objects contained within those spaces (e.g., marks and bars), and object properties (e.g., color, size, shape, and position). Sage-Book represents the syntax and semantics of data graphics, including spatial relationships between objects, relationships between data domains (e.g., interval and 2D coordinate), and the various graphic and data attributes. As in document and imagery retrieval, representation and reasoning about both data and graphical properties enables similarity matching as well as clustering to support search and browsing of large collections. Finally, automated adaptation methods support customization of the retrieved graphic (e.g., eliminating graphical elements that do not match the specified query).

An illustration of the practical utility of content-based graphics retrieval, the SlideFinder tool (Niblack 1999) used the IBM QBIC system described above to perform image similarity together with text matching to enable a user to index and browse Microsoft PowerPoint and Lotus Freelance Graphics. However, in spite of the exciting possibilities, no community-based evaluations have been conducted so common tasks, shared data sets, and practical performance benchmarks do not exist. The Chapter 15 contribution by Carberry et al. in this collection explores the automated extraction of information graphics in multimodal documents.

In conclusion, there are important data, algorithmic, and method gaps for a number of challenges, including image query context, results presentation, and representation and reasoning about visual content. While methods such as SIFT (Scale Invariant Feature Transform) features have become widespread, new methods are needed to advance beyond the current state of the art.

2.5 VIDEO EXTRACTION

Video has become an increasingly voluminous and essential media source as exemplified by the desire for content-based access to video mail/teleconferences, large collections such as YouTube, and real-time broadcasts. Early methods of detecting shot boundaries using changes in color histograms over two consecutive video frames (Flickner et al. 1995) were improved by Haas et al. (1997) using motion within video to also classify shots into zoom (in/out), pan, and so on. Others investigated content-based search and browsing of news (e.g., Hauptmann and Witbrock 1997; Maybury et al. 1997) requiring multimodal processing of imagery, speech, and text.

2.5.1 TRECVid

Progress on video extraction has been accelerated through the use of shared data collections, common evaluation tasks, and community workshops that have helped benchmark and promote advancement under the sponsorship of the U.S. government's TRECVid (trecvid.nist.gov) conference series (Smeaton et al. 2006, 2009). Participants leverage common tasks and shared data, allowing them to advance technologies and build systems at significantly less cost and time than if done on their own (Maybury 2009). Starting in 2001 under the text retrieval evaluation conference (TREC), in 2003, TRECVid became its own evaluation. Over the years, TRECVid has grown in data, participation, and scope as illustrated in Figure 2.6. Initial tasks of shot boundary detection and simple search have been augmented with tasks for feature and story extraction, as well as summarization. Publications grew from 10 peer-reviewed publications in 2001 to 56 in 2007 and participation has grown fivefold.

In 2009, this international event included evaluation tasks for surveillance event detection, high-level feature extraction (e.g., indoor/outdoor, people, speech), search (24 topics), and copy detection. Whereas video was originally from English-speaking sources (e.g., BBC, CNN), Chinese and Arabic sources were added in 2005 and 2006. By 2009, data for testing included 100 hours of Gatwick Airport surveillance video

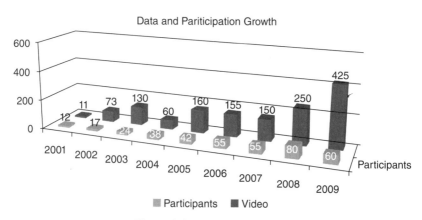

Figure 2.6. TRECVid growth.

Figure 2.7. TRECVid global participation in 2009.

data (courtesy of the U.K. Home Office), 100 hours of video materials from many sources for copy detection (e.g., web video clips, TV archives, movies covering programs including documentaries, movies, sports events, TV shows, cartoons, etc.), and 280 hours of data for search and feature tasks, including MPEG-1 content from the Netherlands Institute for Sound and Vision news magazine, science news, news reports, documentaries, educational programming, and archival video. Evaluations include both fully automatic systems, as well as those that have a human in the loop. Figure 2.7 depicts the geographic distribution of the 63 finishers of the 2009 evaluation who came from universities and industrial labs from across North America, Europe, and Asia.

For search, an example task could be to find video material (including from commercials) that includes a specific person, location, event/activity, or one or more instances of some combination of these. System evaluation varies by task. Precision, recall, and average precision are used for the search and feature tasks plus time and user satisfaction measures for interactive search. Summarization (evaluated in 2007 and 2008 only) was measured in terms of how much of the significant, nonredundant original material was included in the summary. That is, how redundant, pleasant, and so on the summary was. Copy detection and surveillance event detection, new evaluation events in 2009, considered two error types: missed detections (MD) and false alarms (FA). A linear combination of these two error types creates a single error measure called the detection cost rate (DCR) model. In addition to DCR measures, detection error tradeoff (DET) curves are produced to graphically depict the tradeoff of the two error types over a wide range of operational points. Consistent with TREC's tradition of attempting new evaluation tasks to advance knowledge, in the case of copy detection, there remain unanswered issues about the extent to which the constructed test collection resembles a real one. In the case of the surveillance event detection, the amount of data and lack of location-annotated training material presented the community with some very large, new challenges.

The performance of participant systems varies greatly by topic, collection, and user. The easiest task with the most participants is shot boundary detection (e.g., cut and gradual transition). Cut detection is considered "solved," with the best systems achieving 90+% precision and recall, and detecting these essentially in real time, whereas gradual transitions (e.g., fades) demonstrate lower precision (around 70–90%) and recall (around 60–80%).

Feature detection is a broad category of queries with a broad range of difficulty and includes people, such as Madeleine Albright or Bill Clinton, objects, such as trains, places, such as a beach (with water and shore visible) or road (paved or not), and events, such as an airplane taking off, violence between people and/or objects, or people walking or running. Smeaton et al. (2009) provides a summary of features and performance from TRECVid campaigns from 2002 to 2006. Changes in data and tasks over the years makes assessment of trends difficult. In 2003, an abstract category such as physical violence was found to be harder than more concrete ones such as weather news; systems obtained only a mean average precision of only 0.05 for physical violence shots but about eight times that for the weather news (over 0.4 on average with several systems around 0.85 average precision).

In 2004, performance also varied greatly. In general, median scores were very low, around 0.1% or at most 0.2% median average precision, in part because of the difficulty of features and the low density of events in the data. Some systems performed well on particular features, for example, "basketball score" had a median of 0.2 with some systems above 0.5 because of discriminating textual features in a score. Some search tasks had high variability (e.g., shots of Madeleine Albright). Many systems used combinations of low-level features (e.g., color, texture).

While not directly comparable, 2005 scores on 10 new queries on new data showed improvement, with many systems achieving over average precision greater than 0.4 for half the features. Moreover, interactive systems combining human and machine could find nearly 90% of video segments on Tony Blair and nearly 100% of those with tennis players, but only about 10% of those of people entering and leaving buildings. In 2006, 36 features from "LSCOM-lite" were selected, and 20 were evaluated. An unprecedented 159 hours of annotated training data, as well as shot boundaries and keyframes (also provided in the past) were made available to the 30 participants who submitted a total of 125 runs. As in previous years, sports and weather shots were the easiest detected, and abstract concepts such as office or corporate leader proved challenging. Support vector machines were the dominant classifier with robust results. Successful systems combined various features (e.g., color, shape, texture, edges acoustic, face, and text) and operated a multiple levels of granularity. Speech transcription was valuable for finding many topics, but not all, given search topics vary widely in terms of objects, people, locations, and events. Also, speech recognition errors diminished performance. TRECVid interactive searches make use of positive and negative relevance feedback by users. Notably, the top 10 interactive systems outperform manual and fully automatic ones.

In addition to this task progress, many important findings have been discovered in the TRECVid evaluations. For example, in contrast to some of the annotated imagery retrieval tasks described above, some groups (e.g., IBM and MediaMill) found their visual-only search performed better than their text-only search. And in 2005, groups found utility in query typing (CMU), near-duplicate detection (Columbia University), multimodal over text-only search (Helsinki Univ. of Technology), cluster-temporal browsing (Oulu University), and enhanced visualizations (FX Palo

Controlled
Access Door

Waiting
Area

Debarkation
Area

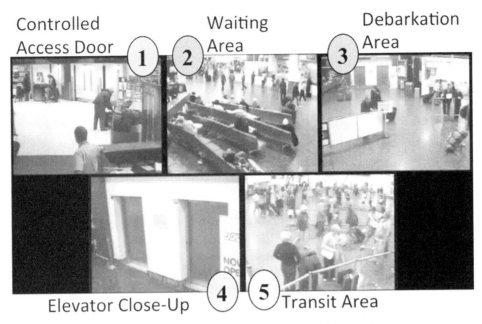

Elevator Close-Up   Transit Area

Figure 2.8. TRECVid multi-camera surveillance task.

Alto). It's worth noting that these findings depend critically on the data used, the query types, and the visual search task. In short, community evaluations are instrumental to global learning and advancement helping to mature technologies more rapidly, readying them for transition.

TRECVid includes a surveillance video challenge data set consisting of 100 hours (10 days × 2 hours/day × 5 cameras) of Gatwick Airport surveillance video data (courtesy of the U.K. Home Office), including ground truth created manually under contract by the Linguistic Data Consortium (see http://www-nlpir.nist.gov/projects/tvpubs/tv8.papers/tv8overview.pdf). There were multiple, synchronized camera views, including elevator close-up and four high traffic areas to capture naturally occurring events (See Figure 2.8). Sixteen sites completed the first evaluation to detect any 3 of 10 required events (PersonRuns, Cell-ToEar, ObjectPut, People-Meet, PeopleSplitUp, Embrace, Pointing, ElevatorNoEntry, OpposingFlow, and TakePicture). Outputs included the temporal extent, as well as a confidence score and detection decision (yes/no) for each event observation. Some events are much rarer (e.g., take pictures and opposing flow) than others (e.g., pointing, objectput, and people meeting) in the data. A 50-hour test set was found insufficient for low frequency events, but 12 hours was sufficient for most events. Annotation was performed using the Video Performance Evaluation Resource (ViPER), located at http://viper-toolkit.sourceforge.net. Annotation rates averaged 10–15 times real time, for example, 50–75 minutes per 5-minute clip, with five events under consideration per clip (Ajot et al. 2008). Human annotators exhibited low recall rates suggesting the difficulty of the task. Not surprisingly, annotation was affected by video quality. Participant performance varied in accuracy across events—detecting an open or closed door or a person running was easier than detecting someone putting a cell to ear or two people embracing (Over 2009).

Related, the Multiple Camera Person Tracking Challenge Evaluation (http://www.itl.nist.gov/iad/mig/tests/avss/2009) measures the ability to track a specified person within a video sensor field. The challenge uses 44 hours of video data from a five-camera airport surveillance field at London Gatwick Airport and consists of 107 five-camera excerpt sets from 12 collection epochs. Evaluation results are available at a special session of the 6th Advanced Video and Signal Based Surveillance (AVSS) IEEE Conference.

2.5.2 VideoCLEF

Building on TRECVid and starting with five participants in 2008, VideoCLEF (www.multimediaeval.org) develops and evaluates video analysis tasks for research on intelligent access to multilingual video collections. Encouraging the combination of speech and visual features, the 2008 pilot included tagging videos from the Netherlands Institute of Sound and Vision with thematic subject labels (e.g., architecture, chemistry, dance, and history), translating metadata to English, and extracting a keyframe as a surrogate for the video. The 2009 exploratory tasks include selecting a set of keyframes that represent the entire video, classifying videos as popular or not, detecting narrative peaks in affect, and finding related resources to enable comprehension of Dutch videos. MediaEval (multimediaeval.org) expands into social video collections, exploring the use of user-generated tags and ratings, as well as relationships between users in social networks to enhance video retrieval.

2.5.3 IEEE VS and PETS

Since 2000, the IEEE Visual Surveillance (VS) and Performance and Evaluation of Tracking and Surveillance (PETS) workshops have evaluated a number of systems to detect and track people and vehicles from single and networked cameras. Motivated by visual surveillance in counter-terrorism and counter crime, public safety, and transport efficiency domains, evaluations have included low-level information about the positions of people and vehicles, as well as high-level descriptions of scene activity over time. Evaluation tasks have included people tracking (e.g., travelers and soccer players), surveillance of public areas (e.g., unattended luggage and loitering people), and smart meetings (e.g., facial expressions, gaze, and gesture). For example, the 2007 data set (pets2007.net), processed by approximately 15 participants, was obtained from the British Airports Authority to test detection of events (loitering, luggage theft, unattended luggage) in crowded public areas, including challenges, such as indoor lights turning on and off, skylighting, people dropping objects, and crowds. Unlike VACE, described below, which also includes text, face, and hand tracking tasks from meetings and broadcast news, PETS focuses primarily on person and vehicle tracking (See Figure 2.9). In a pedestrian counting scenario, several systems could achieve less than 5% error rates, although lighting, crowds, and loitering could lower performance. A person loiters if they stay in one spot for more than a minute. The middle image in Figure 2.9 (Ferryman and Tweed 2007) is a sample from the unattended luggage detection task where if a person crosses a 2-m inner yellow radius and passes a 3-m outer red radius around their luggage (marked by a green cross), an alarm is sounded if the luggage remains unattended

Figure 2.9. PETS: person/vehicle tracking, unattended luggage, crowd tracking.

for 25 seconds. While there were only 10 video clips from four cameras for evaluation, several systems were able to perform easy and difficult examples of luggage abandonment task nearly perfectly, as well as the easier task of loiter detection in near real time. For a 2009 crowd analysis tasks (rightmost image in Figure 2.9), images came from the University of Reading, UK (Ferryman and Shahrokni 2009). The associated task was to count and track people in the three bounded regions annotated in the image (R0, R1, and R2). The best systems achieved about one error per frame on the counting task.

2.5.4 CLEAR

Related is the CLassification of Events, Activities and Relationships (CLEAR) is an international effort initiated in 2006 to evaluate systems to detect people's identities, activities, interactions, and relationships in human–human interaction scenarios (http://www.clear-evaluation.org). CLEAR is a collaboration between the U.S. government-funded Video Analysis and Content Extraction (VACE), the European Commission-funded Computers in the Human Interactive Loop (CHIL) programs, and the Augmented Multiparty Interaction (AMI) program. CLEAR is organized in conjunction with the RT 2007 evaluation, described in the audio extraction section above. Their deadlines were harmonized, and in 2007, the workshops were collocated. While the RT evaluations focus on speech and text recognition, other CLEAR evaluation tasks include person, face, and vehicle tracking, head pose estimation, as well as acoustic scene analysis (Stiefelhagen 2007). Included are tasks performed in the visual, acoustic, and audio-visual domains for meeting room and surveillance data, thus effectively bridging the vision and speech research communities. While consistent annotation proved too difficult, original plans were to include an unmanned aerial vehicle (UAV) person detection and tracking task using data from the DARPA Video Verification of Identity (VIVID) program.

CLEAR data includes 5 hours of 25 lecture seminars based on four fixed cameras, a fisheye ceiling camera, and microphone arrays. VACE data sets included approximately 100 clips each of faces, people, and moving vehicles, split into training and test sets from multisite meetings and surveillance video from the United Kingdom's Home Office. Figure 2.10 illustrates some of the kinds of visual data annotations from a range of VACE tasks from Manohar et al. (2006), including point annotations for hands and bounding boxes for text, people, faces, and vehicles. A common metric of precision and accuracy of multiple object tracking (MOT) was used for person, face, and vehicle tracking, considering imprecision in object location, correct number of objects, and consistency in object labeling over time.

Figure 2.10. VACE detection tasks: face/text, hands, person, and vehicle.

Key CLEAR tasks include tracking (person, face, and vehicle), person identification, head pose estimation, and acoustic event recognition. The best system of seven systems from four sites achieved 73% accuracy (up over 15% from the previous year in spite of increased and more diverse data) for visual tracking using a 3D voxelized foreground map, whereas the most precise system achieved 91 mm of precision by tracking faces in 2D views. For 3D person tracking using audio tracking across microphone pairs or arrays, the best system of eight systems from five sites achieved 140 mm of precision with 54% accuracy in real time or near real time. The best multimodal tracking system achieved a 58% accuracy and 155 mm of precision. A key challenge remains reliable detection in multiple poses and with occlusion. Five systems from three sites participated in the two face tracking from a multisite meeting room video and achieved MOT accuracy of 85% and precision of 70% precision in spite of very small (10×10 pixels), occluded, and blurred/highly compressed faces. The best of six 2D person (including arms and legs) tracking systems in video surveillance achieved 55% accuracy and 63% precision. The best moving vehicle tracker achieved about 70% accuracy and 61% precision. Visual and acoustic far afield person identification in meetings (28 people) were measured on 1-, 5-, 10-, and 20-second test segments on 200 ms annotated visual data. The best visual results achieved 84–96% accuracy on the easiest and hardest tests, an over 10% increase over the previous year. The best acoustic person identification systems from 11 systems from six sites had a near-perfect score of 98% for 20-second test condition and another achieved 100% recognition for a 30-second test. The best multimodal person identification system from four sites was near perfect on 20-second test conditions even on 15-second training. In fact, the advantages of multimodal fusion could only be observed in the 1-second test condition, showing about a 10% improvement over acoustic only recognition.

In the CLEAR head tracking task, ground truth was captured with magnetic sensors. The best system trained and tested on a data set of 1-minute clips of 16 subjects achieved less than 10° mean absolute pan, tilt, and roll errors. In a second data set of 3 minute clips of 15 subjects, even with smaller face sizes, the best system of two achieved remarkable errors rates as low as 6.7° pan, 8.8° tilt, and 4° roll. A final acoustic event recognition task recognized non-speech audio events in seminar video data, such as door knock, steps, chair moving, phone ring, applause, and laugh. The best recognizer from six sites performed relatively poorly, with 36% event detection accuracy and nearly always incorrectly determining the temporal boundaries of the acoustic event. One reason is the data was challenging, with 64% of these events overlapping with speech. For example, low energy "steps" events alone accounted for 40% of events. Tasks, data, annotation, and scoring tools are available through NIST and the Evaluations and Language Distribution Agency (ELDA).

Stiefelhagen et al. (2007) provide a comprehensive overview of CLEAR evaluation tasks, metrics, data sets, and achieved results.

2.6 AFFECT EXTRACTION: EMOTIONS AND SENTIMENTS

Each of the media summarized in this chapter can capture and convey human, or even animal or robot, emotions. For example, sentiments can be expressed in text (e.g., choice of colorful adjectives, adverbs, or nouns), audio (e.g., attitudes expressed vocally via intonation or in non-speech sounds, such as laughing, clapping, or booing), imagery (e.g., facial expressions), and/or video (e.g., facial expressions, as well as gesture, body pose, and motion). Picard (1997) pioneered technologies for sensing, modeling, and communicating people's emotions, exploring practical applications, such as driver safety, motivating exercise, reducing frustration, and enhancing customer experience. The most commonly used classes of emotions are surprise, fear, disgust, anger, happiness, and sadness, specified as faces, for example, in Ekman's Facial Action Coding System (FACS), a collection of movements of characteristic face points in different emotive states (Ekman and Friesen 1978). Another approach models emotions as a state vector of valence, arousal, and dominance (Posner et al. 2005). There is even a proposed W3C XML-based standard markup language for the description of emotive states, EmotionML (Schröder 2009). Sentiment extraction from text of product or movie reviews has been an active area although evaluations have focused on opinion oriented information extraction (Cardie et al. 2004). The Multiperspective Question Answering (MPQA) opinion corpus, OpinionFinder, and subjectivity lexicon have been used to explore extracting answers from text news by extracting sentiment-bearing phrases that express an emotion (positive or negative polarity). For example, using a subjectivity lexicon, the OpinionFinder automatically identifies subjective sentences, as well as agents who are sources of opinion, direct subjective expressions and speech events, and sentiment expressions (http://www.cs.pitt.edu/mpqa).

Extracting affect in media is important for a number of reasons. First, it can help characterize macro level features of a person (e.g., regular cheerful expressions), a group (e.g., positive acoustic cues or non-speech audio such as clapping), or a collection (e.g., the negative bias toward a particular topic by a specific author, editor, or publication). Second, in some cases, the relevant content in a media object may be entirely nonverbally expressed (e.g., an expression or a gesture), which nonetheless serves a communicative function (e.g., to express disagreement) or to signal an emotional state (e.g., anger or embarrassment). Third, emotions may simply be more intuitive for user query. For example, it is easier for a user to search for "exciting scenes" or "happy" videos as opposed to "rapid shot cuts and elevated audio energy." In short, affect extraction and affect-based retrieval is an important future capability and so Section 4 in this collection addresses affect extraction in audio and imagery. Chapter 17 by Schuller et al. considers the detection of the speaker's emotional state from spoken content in TV and radio broadcasts. Chapter 18 by Guerini et al. explores audience emotional reactions to political communications. Chapter 19 by Tkalčič et al. presents a recommender system based on affective features of color images. And Chapter 20 by Jones et al. explores automated extraction of affective labels (e.g., frightening vs. funny vs. happy) from feature films. In addition, Chapter

6 by Stoiber et al. reports a simple and intuitive structure for meaningful information extraction from emotional facial expressions. Finally, Chapter 8 by Lin and Hauptmann explores automated detection of ideological bias in video.

2.7   SOCIAL MEDIA EXTRACTION

Social media has grown rapidly and incorporates many of the media discussed in the sections above. User-generated content has given rise to entire new application areas including wikis (e.g., Wikipedia), blogs, microblogs (e.g., Twitter), image sharing (e.g., Flickr), video sharing (e.g., YouTube), and recommender systems (e.g., GroupLens for movies, Firefly for music, and Amazon for books and products). Social networking (e.g., Facebook, MySpace, and LinkedIn) has exploded, with over 850 million unique visitors to Facebook and 135 million LinkedIn users in 2012, as large as many nations in the world. Social media sites serve both as sources for information to be extracted (e.g., shared text, images, audio, and video), as well as sinks for extracted material. For example, Chapter 12 in this collection describes how interesting passages from YouTube videos can be captured by analyzing commonly edited video subsegments. Social media also capture new kinds of artifacts, such as networks of link diagrams that capture relationships among individuals (e.g., family, friends, and coworkers). This forms a new kind of information that can be extracted: social structure. Threaded newsgroups or blogs also often implicitly capture relationships (e.g., coparticipants in a blog), reputations (e.g., of buyers and sellers on eBay), sentiments, and/or preferences. While there are not yet community evaluations of social media extraction, prototypes are emerging in this area, and it could be the focus of a future evaluation task if not commercialization.

2.8   SENSOR EXTRACTION

While this chapter has focused primarily on media that is perceivable by humans, there are sensors that can provide information beyond human sensory abilities. These include acoustic sensors that capture signals beyond human hearing (e.g., very low or high frequencies as in radio frequencies), highly sensitive motion sensors (e.g., for seismology), or sensors beyond the visible spectrum (e.g., infrared allowing the detection of heat and cold). The latter, for example, can be used to track sea or land surface temperatures or to identify and track animals or people or hot objects, such as cars or heat escaping from buildings. For example, O'Connor et al. (2009) extract and fuse information from both in-situ and remote satellite sensor data to enhance the temporal resolution and spatial coverage of sea surface temperature for more effective water quality monitoring in Galway Bay in Ireland. Related, multispectral sensors can be used to remotely differentiate among vegetation or chemicals. There are a broad range of domains in which sensors exist, such as weather (e.g., temperature, pressure, wind speed, precipitation, and humidity), oceans (e.g., surface and subsurface temperatures, tides, currents, waves, and turgidity), traffic (e.g., along land, sea, air, and space), micro and macro biology (e.g., temperature, pressure), neurology (e.g., awareness), psychology (e.g., emotional state), and even sociology (see the social media discussion). Physiologically, sensors include data gloves and body suits for tracking human motion to extraction information, such as pose, gestures, and choreography. Output from these sensors needs to be temporally, spatially, and semantically integrated with other extracted information. For example, in Chapter 21, in the context of video annotation, Kipp discusses issues of coding agreement, unimodal transition diagrams, and cross-modal association analysis in relation to a 3D motion capture viewer.

2.9 FUSION

Cross-media fusion has been used in a variety of settings. For example, text surrounding imagery in web pages has been used to classify content, tags on imagery or video has similarly enhanced retrieval, and tracking user interactions (e.g., relevancy feedback) has been used to improve retrieval performance. In video understanding, the integration of audio, visual text, and closed captions has been used to enhance the processing of imagery in video (Maybury et al. 1997).

As was evident in the discussion above of extraction from meeting videos, broadcast news, and surveillance videos, multiple media streams (e.g., containing acoustic and visual channels) can provide complementary indicators of objects and events. When there are points of temporal or spatial synchronization, these can be used to link across media (e.g., audio and imagery) or channels within compound media (e.g., the audio and visual channels in video) or across sensors (e.g., multiple microphones or cameras). Once channels are related or fused, this can assist in enhancing detection and extraction precision and robustness by dealing with incomplete, uncertain, and/or ambiguous input. Consider media that is:

- *Incomplete:* If a portion of a media is missing (e.g., unrecorded audio or visual segment), another microphone or camera might be able to be substituted or correlated.
- *Uncertain:* A media or channel or the environment in which it was captured might be noisy resulting in lack of clarity regarding what was said or done. Duplication from a phased array microphone or networked video camera can help increase the certainty of recognition. In addition, a low-quality extractor from one media with high error rates could be augmented with results from another. For example, imperfect speech recognizers have been augmented by lip reading to resolve the meaning of unclear utterances. Also, there might be certainty enhancing information, such as the use of acoustic and linguistic recognition to identify metadata, such as speaker age and gender (see Chapter 17) if those are not readily apparent in the visual channel (e.g., because of occlusion or lighting challenges).
- *Ambiguous:* Sometimes, what is said or done could mean two different things but another media can make it clear. For example, if someone is recorded standing on a riverbank saying "I want to leave this bank," it is clear from the visual image (but not necessarily the audio) that they are refereeing to a place as opposed to a financial institution. Similarly, if a speaker identification module has a high error rate during recognition, it can be augmented by partial face recognition to support person identification. This might be particularly valuable in emotion detection because of ambiguity.

- *Enriched:* New information fused from across media can enrich both media. For example, in Chapter 17 Schuller et al. explore the extraction of paralinguistic information in talk shows and find that arousal (calm vs. excited) can be detected more accurately than valence (positive vs. negative). Similarly, the authors found gender was more automatically detectable that age in the acoustic signal. This metadata could possibly be used to enhance the processing in other channels by taking advantage of affect or gender-tuned detectors.

- *Coreferent across Media:* Sometimes, someone says something in one media that must be resolved by information in another media. For example, when someone points to a visible object such as a vase and says "put that there" and then gestures to another location, the physical context is necessary to understand the intended meaning. Similarly, the visual channel alone will not be unambiguous. Methods to resolve these cross media references are needed.

2.10   A ROADMAP TO THE FUTURE

A number of gaps are required to advance toward the community vision of multimedia information extraction. The foundation for the roadmap illustrated in Figure 2.11 was collaboratively generated by many of the authors in this collection at the 2008 AAAI Fall Symposium. Three major lanes show forecasted progress over the next 5 years along data, resources, and annotation tools, algorithm development and metrology, and components and applications. The line to the left of the roadmap illustrates how sources that are the target of extraction are migrating from the tra-

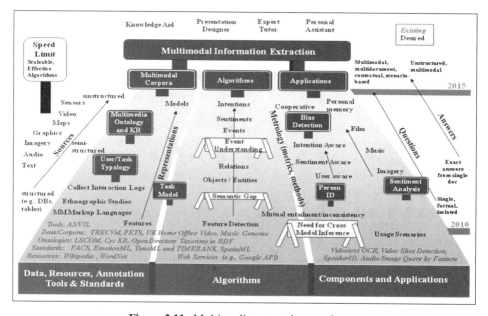

Figure 2.11. Multimedia extraction roadmap.

ditional areas of text, audio, and imagery to newer areas of graphics, maps, and videos, and, over time, to novel sensors. The arrows to the right of the roadmap illustrate how questions posed by users requiring media extraction are moving from single, factual, isolated queries to multimodal, scenario-based questions that require contextualized answers from multiple, multimodal documents.

As captured in italics in the first data lane, there are a number of currently available general resources (e.g., Wikipedia and WordNet), standards (e.g., FACS, EmotionML, TimeML, and its associated corpora TIMEBANK, SpatialML), ontologies (e.g., LSCOM, Open Directory taxonomy in RDF, and CYC common sense knowledge base), and data/corpora (e.g., TREC (trec.nist.gov/data.html), TRECVid, PASCAL VOD, PETS, U.K. Home Office surveillance video, and Music Genome), annotated corpora (e.g., TIMEBANK and Music Genome Project). Current annotation standards could be extended into common multimodal markup languages, ultimately leading to multimodal ontologies, an off-ramp (i.e., an interim milestone capability). Also needed are common typologies of users and tasks. As the arrow indicates, representations will move from low level features (e.g., color, shape, texture) to higher level models (e.g., objects and events). A number of annotation tools, such as ANVIL (described in Chapter 21), are also available. However, annotation of complex media is tedious, error prone, and very expensive, implying a need for better semi-automated annotation tools. Also, ethnographic studies, enriched by interaction logs, could help create deeper and broader user and task models.

In terms of algorithms, many existing general purpose tools can assist in information discovery and extraction (e.g., Google's API). As the algorithm lane illustrates with an arrow, advances are forecasted to progress from feature detection through extraction of objects and/or entities, then relations among them (e.g., geospatial, temporal, and ontological), then simple and complex events, then sentiment extraction, and, finally, intention understanding. Two key gaps along this progression include the so-called semantic gap between features and entities, as well as the challenge with understanding simple and complex events. Cross-media inference will also be required to overcome gaps of understanding caused by inconsistency, uncertainty, and ambiguity within and across media. This higher level understanding should also assist in the detection of bias. Affecting both algorithms and applications, and therefore, annotating the line between these lanes, evaluation metrics and methods will need to be advanced to address more advanced tasks (e.g., affect extraction) and broader measures (e.g., usefulness, usability, adaptability). Also, while imagery detection evaluation efforts have advanced the state-of-the-art on automatic object detection, there are still significant challenges ahead, especially for nonrigid objects or even for many common objects.

Finally, in the components and applications lane, early progress can be made in articulating a range of user scenarios. In the near term, content-based access to imagery will be followed with semantic music retrieval via activities such as the Music Genome Project (Castelluccio 2006; John 2006), followed by semantic film retrieval. Applications will become more user aware, then more sentiment aware, and, lastly, more intention aware as multimodal extractors and sensors increase in sophistication. This promises to enhance personal memory and enable more cooperative applications. Taken as a whole, advances in multimedia corpora, algorithms, and applications should enable new knowledge aids, presentation designers, expert tutors, and/or personal assistants.

2.11 CONCLUSION

This chapter has outlined the history, current state of the art, and near term potential of multimedia. Advances in multimedia information extraction have brought new capabilities previously unimaginable, including automated extraction and tracking of entities and events from written and spoken materials, semantic retrieval of music, and automated tracking of people and vehicles. Users can now perform query by example or content based retrieval of business, medical, or vacation imagery. They can also summarize family, news, or surveillance video. Furthermore, new personal, professional, and social insights and connections are possible via social media or affective media containing or resulting in affect. Finally, content-based access to graphics, maps, and even sensor outputs are rapidly emerging. In conclusion, while many have been overwhelmed by the onslaught of new media, at its bes, multimedia information extraction promises to enhance the way we learn, labor, lead, laugh, and live.

ACKNOWLEDGMENT

I thank all of the authors in the collection for their input but especially Gareth Jones, Alexander Loui, Nicolas Stoiber, Björn Schuller, and Paolo Bottoni for feedback on this chapter. I also thank Alan Smeaton for sharing the most recent TRECVid results.

IMAGE EXTRACTION

This section addresses the extraction of elements from images, including objects, visual concepts, shape, emotional faces, and social media. With the explosion of digital photography and exponential growth of image sharing sites such as Flickr, the need for image extraction to support retrieval, summarization, and analysis is increasing. Challenges include scaling up to large collections, learning and relating linguistic descriptions and visual or semantic features, improving precision and recall, and intuitive interaction.

In the first chapter, Madirakshi Das, Alexander Loui, and Andrew Blose from Eastman Kodak address the challenge of searching large collections of digital photographs. The authors report novel methods for retrieving consumer images with the same object, typically taken at some location. High precision matching between two photos coupled with searches on date, events, and people in images provides a powerful consumer ability to help tag events with location. This approach enables search by location (e.g., "find all pictures taken in my living room") or for objects in a location (e.g., "look for picture of a friend at party in my backyard"). The authors' system uses SIFT (Scale Invariant Feature Transform) features to match unique keypoints in a scene, next it clusters matched points into spatial groups, and then it removes false matches by constraining clusters to those that are correlated, have consistent trajectories, and are compact. The authors evaluated their system by creating a consumer application for retrieving and tagging images from the personal image collections of 18 subjects each having 1–2 thousand images from a 1–2 year time frame. Ninety groups of images with two to five images each containing objects were carefully selected, which could not be matched using standard color histograms or texture cues and which included occlusion, partial visibility, varying viewpoints, and variable objects. The authors' algorithm provides 85% recall and

63% precision. Using an additional step of pruning retrieved images with a match score lower than a threshold, the precision improves to 85%. In contrast, logo detection in consumer images is particularly challenging on deformable three-dimensional objects, such as containers, billboards, or clothing. The authors tested logo detection using 32 images from a stock car race event where corporate sponsorship appears in many forms (e.g., car logos and logo billboards). Images were captured by spectators using consumer digital cameras. False positive rates (FPR) decreased as feature resolution increased. Applications of this research include personal and social media retrieval, as well as content-based targeted advertising.

The second chapter by Keiji Yanai and Hidetoshi Kawakubo at the University of Electro-Communications in Tokyo and Kobus Barnard at the University of Arizona turns to the analysis of annotations or tags on photos in collections such as Flickr or Picasa. The authors use entropy to analyze two types of image tags: those about image visual features and those about image geolocation. Using a 40 thousand-image collection from the World Wide Web using Google Image search on 150 adjectives, the authors assess 150 adjectives with respect to visual features and relations between image features and 230 nouns with respect to geotags. Using entropy to analyze the distribution of features, the authors discovered that concepts with low image feature entropy tend to have high geolocation entropy and vice versa. For example, sky-related concepts such as "sun," "moon," and "rainbow" have low image region entropy and high geolocation entropy, whereas concepts related to places such as "Rome," "Deutschland," and "Egypt" have high image region entropy and low geolocation entropy. The authors developed two methods to compute image region entropy, one using Gaussian mixture models and simple image features, and an alternative method using probabilistic latent semantic analysis (PLSA) and the bag-of-features (BoF) representation that is regarded to have more semantically discriminative power than other representations. The authors represent regions using color, texture, and shape features, and then probabilistically associate regions with concepts. A generic statistical model for image region features is based on about 50 thousand regions randomly picked up from the gathered Web images. Also, the authors create a generic distribution of image features from about 10 thousand randomly picked web images using probabilistic latent semantic analysis (PLSA). Geolocation entropy is computed by dividing the world map into 36×36 grids (or 1296 bins) and making a probability distribution of geolocations of a given concept. The authors plan to explore cultural and regional differences, for example, how concept usage differs based on location, such as how Western-style houses are different from Asian-style ones and African-style ones.

Whereas the first two chapters focus on improving image retrieval, which is essential for consumer photo collections, the third chapter turns toward automated extraction and generation of semantically enriched models from three-dimensional scans. Sven Havemann from Graz Technical University and Torsten Ullrich and Dieter Fellner from Fraunhofer IGD and GRIS depart from three-dimensional scanning, similar to taking a photograph but with added depth dimension. The authors describe the most important techniques for retrieving semantics from such acquired three-dimensional data, including parametric, procedural, and generative 3D modeling. The authors illustrate these concepts with two active and challenging domains: urban reconstruction and cultural heritage. For example, their ambitious CityFIT project aims to automatically reconstruct 80% of the facades in the architecturally diverse city of Graz, Austria by statistically inferring facade templates from LIDAR sensor data. The authors' digital sampling of the world coupled with the augmentation of shapes with semantics is an essential step toward representing reality within a computer in a meaningful, ideally even editable, form. The authors' contribution is twofold: A scalable solution for model-based production of new models, and information extraction from existing models by means of automated fitting procedures.

Just as we need improved models for extracting meaningful shape from human created edifices, so too we want to extract meaning from human faces. In the fourth chapter, Nicolas Stoiber and Gaspard Breton from Orange Labs in France and Renaud Seguier from Supelec, France report reliable and accurate emotional facial feature extraction. Features can be used for identity or pattern recognition (e.g., a frown or smile). To bridge the gap between conceptual models of emotion and actual facial deformations, the authors present a high-level representation of emotional facial expressions based on empirical facial expression data. By identifying the basic emotions (e.g., sadness, joy, surprise, fear, anger, and disgust) on a simple two-dimensional colored disc interface, the facial representation remains true to the real world yet becomes intuitive, interpretable, and manipulatable. Accordingly, it has been successfully applied to facial analysis and synthesis tasks. In the former case of facial analysis, even unseen, mixed facial expressions not included in the original database are recovered. In the latter case, the representation is used for facial expression synthesis on a virtual character. While applied primarily to emotional facial expressions, the representation space could apply the analysis method to other types of expressions, like speech-related facial configurations (visemes).

Taken together, the image extraction chapters illustrate the range of important applications enabled by image extraction, from improved organization and retrieval in consumer collections to extraction of 3D models from city or historic buildings to improved facial emotion extraction and synthesis. While the authors make a number of important data, algorithmic, and method contributions, they also outline a number of remaining challenges including image query context, results presentation, and representation and reasoning about visual content.

CHAPTER 3

VISUAL FEATURE LOCALIZATION FOR DETECTING UNIQUE OBJECTS IN IMAGES

MADIRAKSHI DAS, ALEXANDER C. LOUI, and ANDREW C. BLOSE

3.1 INTRODUCTION

The proliferation of digital cameras and scanners has led to a significant increase in the number of digital images, creating large personal image databases in which it has become increasingly difficult to locate specific images. In the absence of manual annotation specifying the content of the image (in the form of captions or tags), most current image management software only allow search and browsing along the time dimension, which limits the content-based search functionality severely. When the user does not remember the exact date a picture was taken, or if the user wishes to aggregate images over different time periods (e.g., images taken at Niagara Falls during many visits over the years, images of person A, etc.), they would have to browse through a large number of irrelevant images to extract only the desired image(s). Many scenes captured in images contain unique objects that are characteristic of the location, which can be matched with other images captured at the same location. The ability to retrieve photos taken at a particular location can be used for image search by capture location (e.g., "find all pictures taken in my living room"). This feature can be used in conjunction with other search dimensions, such as date and people present in images to narrow the search space for other searches. (e.g., "look for picture of a friend at party in my backyard"). The scene may also contain unique objects of commercial interest, such as logos and special signs. Detection of such objects can be used as input for targeted advertising and social networking applications.

The use of scale-invariant features (Bay et al. 2006) (Lowe 2004) (Mikolajczyk and Schmid 2004) for matching feature-rich scenes has been widely investigated in recent years. These techniques have been applied mainly to registering and

Multimedia Information Extraction: Advances in Video, Audio, and Imagery Analysis for Search, Data Mining, Surveillance, and Authoring, First Edition. Edited by Mark T. Maybury.
© 2012 IEEE Computer Society. Published 2012 by John Wiley & Sons, Inc.

modeling entire scenes. In the Photosynth application (Snavely et al. 2006a,b), keypoints common between multiple images of the same scene are registered, and a 3D representation of the scene is created to aid browsing. Parikh and Chen (2007) have used Lowe's (2004) SIFT (Scale Invariant Feature Transform) features to model objects in the scene, assuming the same objects are present in both candidate images. The problem of ascertaining where an image was captured has also been addressed. Schindler et al. (2007) propose a vocabulary tree that uses the most informative features for matching a given city scene to a very large collection of street side images of the city. Wu and Rehg (2008) determine the scene category and specific instances of a scene. Ma et al. (2008) represent a scene as a set of cluster centers, and use Earth Mover's Distance to measure similarity with other images. The application of these techniques to object recognition in cluttered scenes has proved to be challenging, as objects of interest may occupy a relatively small portion of the image and background pixels can affect the detection and matching of object features. Stein and Hebert (2005) propose a modification to SIFT to incorporate local object boundary information to achieve some degree of background invariance. Suga et al. (2008) propose the combination of Graph Cuts and SIFT as a method for segmenting an object from background clutter. Bouganis and Shanahan (2008) combine the use of local features and their spatial relationship to identify correspondences between an object of interest and a given cluttered scene containing the object.

Some of the work on SIFT has influenced the work on near-duplicate image detection, typically in video keyframes. These include interest point matching (Zhao et al. 2007), nonrigid image matching (Zhu et al. 2008) and spatially aligned pyramids (Xu et al. 2008) for detecting near-duplicates. Chapter 12 of this book discusses content-based techniques used for finding near-duplicates (or copies). Our work in this area focuses on consumer image collections, where near-duplicates occur only in images captured within seconds of each other. Most images captured at the same location have very different appearances due to changes in illumination, viewpoint, and the presence of people in the scene creating occlusions. Content-based matching techniques cannot handle major changes in the image, such as the presence of people in the foreground, changes in the clothing of people, change in the visibility of background objects due to viewpoint changes, and color shifts due to changes in illumination.

In our earlier work (Das et al. 2008; Das and Loui 2008), we address the problem of ascertaining whether two images could have been taken at the same scene—the two candidate images are not assumed to be from the same scene a priori and do not even necessarily contain any of the same objects. The objects of interest that can be used to match the two images are also not known a priori. In consumer image collections, images are typically quite cluttered and contain many common objects (e.g., furniture, cabinetry, windows, and doors) that can easily be falsely matched using current techniques, making images captured at different households appear to match when in fact they should not match.

There has been much work in the area of logo detection, both in documents (Pham 2003; Zhu and Doermann 2007) and from video (Yan et al. 2005). However, existing work mostly focuses on logos appearing on two-dimensional surfaces. Logo detection in consumer images poses a unique challenge, as these logos are embedded on three-dimensional objects (such as beverage containers, cars, billboards, etc.)

that may also be deformable, for example, clothing. Color may be a useful feature in logo detection. Van de Sande et al. (2008) study the performance of color variants of SIFT in object recognition when there are changes in light intensity and light color.

This chapter describes the use of SIFT features to match unique objects in a scene with applications to location matching and logo detection in the consumer image domain. A major contribution of this work is to provide a set of constraints that narrows down potential matched features to produce reliable matching with high precision in cluttered images. Section 2 describes scene matching in consumer images. Section 3 provides details about the logo detection system. Section 4 presents conclusions and discusses future work.

3.2 SCENE MATCHING IN CONSUMER IMAGES

This section describes scene matching in consumer collections. The aim is to be able to group images captured at the same scene, thus enabling retrieval based on location. Some recent digital capture devices provide location information in the form of global positioning system (GPS) data or cell tower location. However, most digital media currently being captured and the billions of earlier digital images taken before the availability of GPS have no location-related data. GPS data also does not have the fine resolution necessary to distinguish between close locations, for example, different rooms in a home. In the absence of this information, the location where the photograph was captured can be described in terms of the stationary background of the image. We exploit the observation that images with similar backgrounds are likely to have been taken at the same location.

3.2.1 Our Approach

In consumers' personal image collections, it is possible to identify unique objects present in the images that can be tied to specific rooms in the house, such as the living room or the children's playroom, or to specific locations, such as the office or grandma's house. Typical examples include pictures hanging on the wall, patterns on curtains, wallpapers or rugs, furniture upholstery, and children's play equipment. These unique objects in the scene can be reliably matched even with significant occlusion and viewpoint changes. The objects that produce the most reliable matches in the consumer image domain happen to be primarily 2D objects, such as the examples listed above, or 3D objects viewed from a distance (such as outdoor buildings and architectural features), because the appearance of these types of objects does not change substantially with viewing angle. Another desirable feature of objects to be matched is having a dense set of localized features so that they can be matched reliably with fewer false matches. Our approach to determine whether two images were captured at the same location is based on automatically matching such reliable objects.

Matching SIFT features between two images using the method described by Lowe (2004) produces a set of matched keypoints between the reference and target images. However, in cluttered scenes, such as consumer images, false positives are quite common. False positives occur when points matched do not correspond to the

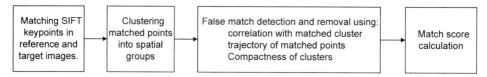

Figure 3.1. Matching reference and target image by adding postprocessing steps to SIFT keypoint matches to eliminate most false positives.

same objects in the two scenes. To overcome this problem, we propose a number of constraints on the matched points, as shown in Figure 3.1, to produce matches with high precision.

The first step in matching two images is to identify regions of interest in the images that have some likelihood of matching. This is achieved by spatially clustering the matched SIFT keypoints (Lowe 2004) independently in each image. This is followed by a filtering process (shown in the third box in Figure 3.1) that aims to apply constraints that will increase the certainty that the match is derived from an underlying common object. The clusters are analyzed to determine whether there are correspondences between pairs of clusters. Because keypoints on the same object are spatially constrained to the region occupied by the object, it is expected that for true matches, clusters in the reference image will correspond to cluster(s) in the target image. The next constraint ensures that the global trajectory of points from the reference to the target is consistent, that is, all clusters in the scene move in the same general direction. This is expected because true objects in the scene are likely to maintain the same spatial configuration relative to each other. The final constraint aims to ensure that the clusters are compact, which is achieved by removing outlier points. The clustering and filtering steps are described in greater detail in the next section.

A match score is computed based on the keypoints that remain after the filtering process. This match score can be used in applications to determine the likelihood that two images could be co-located. Thus, the success of the matching process depends upon the presence of compact, feature-rich objects in the scene. However, such objects are unlikely to occur in every image, for example, portraits of people taken at the scene may not include background details. Also, even in a room with a distinctive object, all capture viewpoints will not include that object. The applicability of our approach can be expanded to a significantly larger set of images when we take temporal information into account. Using the domain knowledge that an entire event (Loui and Savakis 2003) typically takes place at the same location in consumer image collections, when a pair of images (one from each event) matches, we can assign the same location tag to other images in the same events.

3.2.2   Computing Image Matches

This subsection describes our approach in more detail. In particular, we examine the steps in Figure 3.1 and algorithmic components used to determine a match score between two images. Our experimental test bench places the two images side by side with the target image on the left and a reference image on the right. Scene matching begins by extracting scale-invariant features from each image.

3.2.2.1   Extracting and Matching Features   We generate SIFT keypoints using Lowe's (2004) SIFT algorithm. Each feature has a corresponding descriptor, which considers location and localized image gradients at some scale. Multiple orientations may be extracted from the gradient directions with one orientation assigned to each feature. Hence, there may be multiple features described for the same location and indeed for the same location and scale. A variation of Lowe's "Fast Nearest Neighbor" search is used to find corresponding pairs of matched SIFT keypoints between the target and reference images. For each keypoint in the target image, the algorithm finds a reference keypoint that minimizes the Euclidean distance between the corresponding target and reference descriptors. If the minimized reference keypoint has no neighbors (subject to an inlier threshold), then the search returns a match to the given target keypoint.

For spatial clustering of SIFT keypoints, only the subpixel location information of participating matched pairs is used. However, the set of matched keypoints must be filtered for subpixel location redundancy before proceeding to the spatial clustering step. For different target locations that map to the same reference location, the matched keypoint pair with the lowest Euclidean distance is retained. The remaining redundant match pairs are eliminated. Likewise, for redundantly matched target locations (differing only in scale and/or orientation), the keypoint pairs with the lowest Euclidean distance are retained while the others are eliminated. The remaining keypoint pairs represent either probable matching object features between the two images or false positives.

Figure 3.2 shows a typical example of a pair of consumer images taken at different locations, showing SIFT matches without using our clustering step or applying our constraints. Note the dense match that was obtained due to the cluttered nature of these types of scenes. Using our approach described below, no matches are found between these two scenes (the correct conclusion).

3.2.2.2   Clustering Matched Features   Scene matching continues by forming spatial clusters within the set of matched keypoint pairs. Keypoints within the target image are clustered first. Variance-based partitions are formed using 2D subpixel location data while the Euclidean metric is employed for measuring the distance

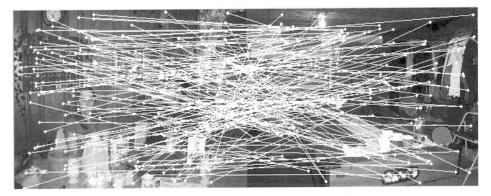

Figure 3.2. Typical image pair (from different locations) showing SIFT matches without using our approach. No matches are found after using our approach.

between keypoints. The clustering algorithm defines a criterion function, which attempts to find the partition for each keypoint that minimizes the mean distance of member keypoints from the partition's center. If the number of scene objects is known, then the k-means algorithm (Duda et al. 2001) may be leveraged to form spatial clusters. Typically, though, the number of feature-rich scene objects within the image is unknown.

Instead of using k-means to form spatial clusters of keypoints within the target image, a different iterative optimization algorithm is employed. Like k-means, ISODATA ("iterative self-organizing data") (Shapiro and Stockman 2001) is a "hard clustering" algorithm that matches each keypoint to a specific partition. ISODATA attempts to find the partition for each keypoint, which minimizes the mean distance of member keypoints from the partition's center. Once ISODATA partitions all keypoints, it examines the variances of the resulting k clusters and makes one of three decisions: discard, split, or merge. Upon convergence (or termination), ISODATA yields a set of partitions that may differ in number from its initial value for k. When examining the resulting clusters, ISODATA will discard any cluster that fails a minimum membership threshold. ISODATA declassifies data members from unviable clusters (if any) and reduces the value of k to $k - 1$. This process continues until a minimum value of k results in all valid clusters. Thereafter, ISODATA examines each of the cluster variances, as well as the distance between neighboring clusters. ISODATA will split a large cluster into two separate groups if the collections of keypoints' attributes are too dissimilar.

Currently, our approach uses only a keypoint's 2D subpixel location attribute so ISODATA splits a large cluster if the partition's dissimilarity metric (membership distance from the partition center) variation exceeds some threshold. If ISODATA indeed splits a cluster, it reclassifies the keypoint members (of the original large cluster) into one of two new partitions and increases the value of k to $k + 1$. If ISODATA does not split any large clusters, it goes on to examine the distance between neighboring clusters. ISODATA will merge two proximate clusters into a single partition if the two groups of keypoints share similar features. So in our case, ISODATA merges two proximate clusters if their partition centers are separated by less than some distance threshold. If ISODATA indeed merges two clusters, it reclassifies the keypoint members (of those two clusters) into a single partition and reduces the value of k to $k - 1$. ISODATA seeks a stable value for k. If after determining a minimum value for k (by discarding invalid clusters), the value of k changes because of a split or merge decision, ISODATA repartitions the keypoints. The algorithm starts again by recalculating the criterion function for each keypoint. The algorithm begins with a new value for k and also with a new guess for the partition centers. If the value of k does not change, then k has stabilized, and no keypoints change membership from one partition to another, so the algorithm terminates.

Keypoints within the reference image are clustered next, using the same ISODATA clustering as the target image. After clustering the target image, though, the number of expected feature-rich objects k is known. However, some of these objects may not be visible in the reference image because of occlusion or change of viewpoint. The scenes may also not be related at all, and thus have a different number of interesting regions. So clustering the matched keypoints in the reference image is done independently of the results of clustering in the target image.

3.2.2.3 *Applied Constraints* Scene matching continues by creating a pseudo-confusion matrix where target clusters form rows and clusters in the reference image form columns. The matrix entries show the number of keypoint matches between the cluster indicated by the row and the one indicated by the column. For clusters in the reference image $i = 1 \ldots N$, and clusters in the target image $j = 1 \ldots M$, matrix entry, c_{ij}: number of point matches between cluster i and cluster j.

Thus, this matrix shows the mapping of keypoints between the clusters of the two images. For each row, membership within the target cluster is correlated to membership within each reference cluster. Our matrix construction is motivated by the use of a confusion matrix (Duda et al. 2001) in determining the precision of matching. In a typical scenario, the confusion matrix shows the correlation between the "ground truth" and the algorithm output. The results are highly correlated when the matrix diagonal approaches identity. In our approach, however, clusters within the reference image may not be enumerated in the same order as those within the target. In addition to inconsistent cluster enumeration, the actual number of clusters may differ. That is, when ISODATA is used to build reference partitions, then the number of resulting partitions in the reference image may not agree with the number of partitions in the target. This could occur when some objects are not visible in both images, or when a single cluster in one image is represented by more than one cluster in the other image. Therefore, the cluster map we construct is not a true confusion matrix and the matrix diagonal alone may not be used to judge the quality of cluster matches. However, the pseudo-confusion matrix may be leveraged to form the basis of a scene match score.

The next step in filtering the matched keypoints is the determination of the best match for each cluster in the target image from among the clusters in the reference image. A correlation score is determined for each cluster in the target image, which is computed as the proportion of points in this cluster that match points in the cluster's strongest match (i.e., largest number of points matched with this cluster). Clusters that have correlation scores below a threshold (empirically determined to be 0.5) are eliminated in the target image. In addition, our approach applies a minimum membership threshold as a filter. That is, scene regions are defined using some minimum number of keypoints. Entire rows and columns of the cluster map may be excluded when their respective sums fail the membership threshold. Using the terminology defined in the previous paragraph, cluster i in the reference image is eliminated if:

$$\frac{\max_j c_{ij}}{\sum_j c_{ij}} \leq 0.5 \quad \text{or} \quad \sum_j c_{ij} < 5.$$

The remaining matrix cells are filtered further using two additional criteria. Further filtering of spurious keypoint matches is obtained by checking the direction of movement of the matched point from the target to the reference. Recall that our experimental test bench places the target and reference images horizontally side by side. Each matching keypoint forms a Cartesian angle with respect to its host image's frame of reference. Using the remaining clusters, an average keypoint angle is determined that represents the general trajectory of regions from one image to

Figure 3.3. Example of filtering false keypoint matches by adding constraints. In matched pairs (top) vs. mismatched pair (bottom), the initial set of keypoint matches is shown first, and the filtered set of keypoint matches (if any) are shown next.

the other. To ensure that the global trajectory of points from the reference to the target is consistent (i.e., all objects in the scene move in the same general direction), keypoints that form a Cartesian angle that is more than a certain standard deviation (empirically determined to be 1.0σ) away from the average keypoint angle are eliminated from the pseudo-confusion matrix row or column.

Target and reference partitions are defined as having both a spatial center and a spatial size. The size of each cluster is determined by the result of the criterion function applied by the particular iterative optimization strategy (i.e., ISODATA). The current criterion leverages only members' subpixel distance from a respective center so the size of each scene region is inversely proportional to the density of features distributed normally about the center. Given in units of Mahalanobis distance, a spatial threshold (empirically set at 2.0σ) eliminates keypoints from a cluster that exceeds a maximum distance from the partition center.

Figure 3.3 shows an example of the effect of these postprocessing steps on false keypoint matches. Note that our test bench scene-matching application draws ellipses around target and reference partition centers, where the width and height of each oval represent the sample standard deviations in x and y pixels, respectively. The denser the partition of feature points, the smaller the ellipse. Our experiments show that the order of applying the constraints during the filtering process is not important to the accuracy of the final match.

3.2.2.4 Match Scores   If there are keypoints that remain after the filtering process, this indicates a match between the reference and target image. The larger the number of keypoints left, the more reliable the match, so the likelihood of a match is proportional to the number of matching keypoints that remain. The scene match score we currently use is simply a count of the remaining features that survive all four threshold tests, that is, $score = \sum_i \sum_j c_{ij}$ after the filtering process has removed clusters and points. However, more sophisticated match scores can be formulated that take into account the confidence level of each of the remaining matches.

Figure 3.4. Examples of image pairs and match results.

3.2.3 Use Scenarios and Results

To test the use of scene matching in the consumer image domain, a software application was created based on our approach. The application allows the detailed viewing of matches to show the keypoints matched between an image pair. It also allows the retrieval of matched images when provided with a query image, and has the capability of tagging retrieved image groups with location. No standardized collections are available for personal image collections. The test images and events used in this work were gathered from personal image collections of 18 subjects. Each collection had one to two thousand images spanning a timeframe of one to two years.

3.2.3.1 Scene Match Examples A significant contribution of this work is to constrain the matching process such that objects that can be reliably matched across images are automatically selected and done so with high precision. Figure 3.4 shows four examples of scene matches obtained using our approach, which illustrates some of the strengths of the approach. In the first example, only a small part of the painting is visible, while the rest of the image (the two guitars) looks very different in terms of color and texture. In the second example, a different part of the room is visible in each image, with the common object visible being a colorful window hanging. In the third example, note that the images are taken many months apart, as can be seen by the fact that the baby has grown considerably. In the last example, note that because of the nature of clusters retained using our method, distinctive objects (the patterned rug), rather than the generic objects (such as the storage units), are matched, even though SIFT features are extracted from these objects as well.

Figure 3.5 shows more examples of typical consumer images where the scenes have been matched by matching specific objects in the scene. Note that the images have been displayed using a contour transformation to protect the privacy of individuals shown in the images. However, the processing steps are all based on the original image pixels.

3.2.3.2 Retrieving Matched Scenes Our application can be used to retrieve co-located images based on an example query image. The retrieved images are ranked by decreasing match scores. In the example shown in Figure 3.6, the query image is on the left, and the retrieved images are shown in the right-hand panel. The bottom panel allows the user to choose an image from their collection as the query. Most of the retrieved images in this example match some part of the picture on the wall, even under large variations in lighting.

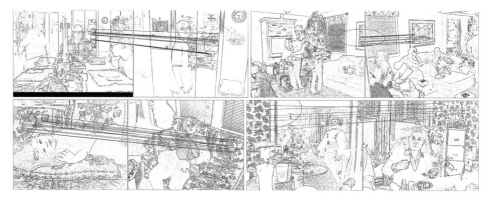

Figure 3.5. Examples of matching image pairs obtained using our algorithm. The objects matched are typical in consumer image collections (from top left: refrigerator, painting, upholstery, wallpaper).

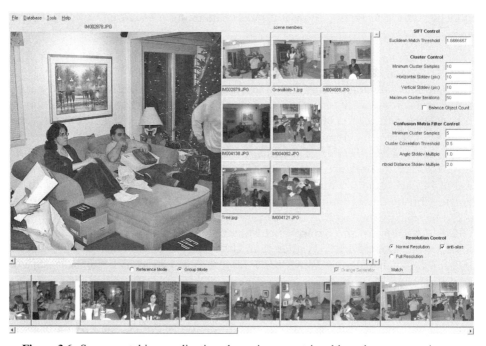

Figure 3.6. Scene-matching application shows image retrieval based on a query image.

For testing the performance of the scene-matching algorithm, 90 image groups (of 2–5 images each) were chosen from the overall image collection, such that they can be judged to be from the same scene by careful human inspection because of the presence of specific objects; however, the images are different enough to be impossible to match using content-based image retrieval strategies, such as color histograms or texture cues. The set is very challenging in a variety of ways. In many images, the rest of the scene, other than the matched region, is very different because

TABLE 3.1. Retrieval Performance of Scene-Matching Application

Scene Match Using	Recall (%)	Precision (%)	Avg. Rank of Best Match
SIFT only	81	21	1.95
SIFT + clustering	85	42	1.3
SIFT + clustering + filters	85	63	1.05

they show the location from a different viewpoint. In most cases, there is considerable occlusion due to the presence of people in images, and only parts of objects are visible. A variety of different objects are included (see Figure 3.5), captured under different lighting conditions and across large time spans.

Table 3.1 shows the quantitative results of raw SIFT-based scene matching, and that of adding the postprocessing steps described in this chapter. The recall is the proportion of correct matches out of all of the correct matches present in the database, and the precision is the proportion of correct matches out of the images retrieved. The recall and precision scores shown are computed by considering the top five images retrieved. The last column shows the average rank of the best (correct) match to the query.

Rather than examining the top five image matches, the match score can be considered in order to eliminate weak matches. Using the additional step of pruning retrieved images with a match score lower than a threshold, the precision using our method improves to 85%, whereas the precision using SIFT alone improves to just 28%. The recall remains the same using this threshold. This operating point is appropriate for our application because the high precision allows the matching of entire events using a small set of single-image matches. Using SIFT alone, there is a very large number of false matches for each query, making the method unusable for our application.

3.3 LOGO DETECTION IN CONSUMER IMAGES

In this section, we present our findings on using SIFT-based visual features similar to those presented in previous sections for detecting logos in images. The automatic detection and identification of company and brand logos in consumer imagery has many applications, including targeted advertising and market research studies. The matching SIFT features must be evaluated to determine a valid match between a target logo and a source image. This processing phase is not part of the SIFT algorithm and was explored and developed during this research. Due to legal issues, the actual logos used in this research do not appear. Public domain images and imagery based on actual logos are included instead.

3.3.1 The Nature of Logos

As research on this topic progressed, it became apparent that certain company logos are more easily detected in images than others. It is important to understand why some logos are more easily identifiable than others so that potential logos or "targets" can be evaluated for suitability as input to automated detection systems.

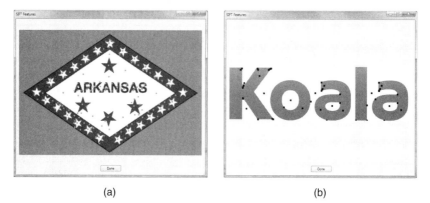

(a)   (b)

Figure 3.7. Examples of logos: (a) a good target for matching; (b) not readily detectable.

It is probable that there will be a significant number of logos that simply cannot be automatically detected with sufficient accuracy to be actionable. A true understanding of the nature of unsuitable targets can be used to suggest modifications to targets or to specify design criteria for new targets that will ensure detection.

Figure 3.7 shows two examples of logos. Figure 3.7a shows a logo with the 280 features (or keys) identified by SIFT. Logos with quantities of features greater than 150 were generally found to be an excellent targets for the SIFT algorithm. There is a sufficient quantity of unique features providing good "feature density," analogous to the compact spatial keypoint clusters of the previous section. The logo shown in Figure 3.7b was not found to be readily detectable in the test images. It has 87 features, but there is some repetition. The inner portions of the "a"s are identical, and the open portions of the "o" tend to match many circular shapes encountered in images. Overall, the features are sparse.

To better understand how shapes and SIFT features are related, some common geometric shapes can be used. Figure 3.8 shows the SIFT features identified for some common shapes and polygons. As evidenced in this figure, large curved surfaces are mostly lacking in features while intersections and near proximities of straight edges are rich in features. The circle in Figure 3.8 has only 1 SIFT feature while the star has over 20 (some are superimposed). While symmetry and curvature are rotationally invariant, they do not scale well, as apparent in the circle. Generally speaking, the greater the number of unique features, the easier a logo will be to detect.

An understanding of logo similarity is also important. As the set of target logos for detection increases, the probability that logos will have similar features increases as well. Increasing logo similarity will inevitably lead to an increase in false positive detections. Color can also play an important role in feature identification, even though no color information is directly used in the generation of feature points, since color provides contrast.

The first step in feature identification for a color image is to convert it to a grayscale image. The conversion from a color RGB image to grayscale is important especially with synthetic images, such as logos, although this is implementation specific. Figure 3.9 shows a logo design that was created from an actual corporate

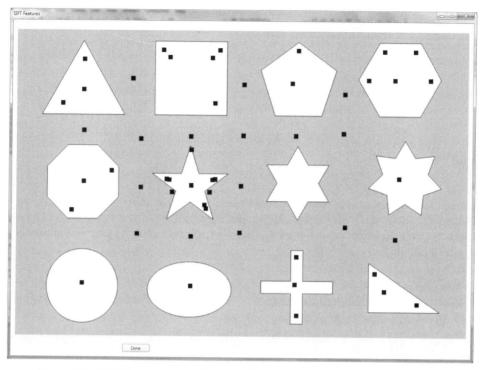

Figure 3.8. SIFT feature points detected for some common geometrical shapes.

Figure 3.9. Effect of color to grayscale conversion on SIFT feature points detected.

logo color scheme. The identified feature points (black squares) of the full-color design are shown on the grayscale image generated as input to feature identification. In the full-color design, considerable contrast exists between the blue background and a red design in the foreground at the top of the logo. During the conversion to grayscale, the contrast between the red foreground and blue background was greatly reduced, and ultimately that portion of the logo was eliminated in the feature identification process as no feature points were identified in that area.

3.3.2 SIFT Feature Matching

A feature descriptor is created from a vector containing the values of orientation histogram entries. Most SIFT implementations (including Lowe's original experiments) use a 128-element feature vector created from a 4×4 array of orientation histograms, each with 8 orientation bins ($4 \times 4 \times 8 = 128$). The size of the feature vector can be thought of as the "feature resolution." Although Lowe's experiments showed the algorithm performed best with a resolution of 128, lower resolutions were used to test the limitations of the algorithm for logo detection. Feature resolutions 64 ($4 \times 4 \times 4$), 72 ($3 \times 3 \times 8$), and 96 ($4 \times 4 \times 6$) were used in testing.

The second part of the SIFT algorithm is feature matching. Details of this phase of the algorithm can be found in Lowe's (2004) paper. The result of this algorithm is a list of zero or more "matches" between target and source features. A match includes, among other things, the 2D image coordinates of the matching features and a relative strength of the match. There are three major steps to SIFT image feature matching:

1. Construction of kd-tree.
2. Best-bin first search of kd-tree.
3. Descriptor distance calculation and comparison.

The first step of the matching process is to construct a multidimensional kd-tree with a depth equal to the number of features in the source image. The number of dimensions is equal to the number of feature descriptors (feature resolution). The tree is then searched using a best-bin first search for the two nearest neighbors of each feature in the target image. There is a configurable upper limit to the number of neighbors searched (default is 200). If two neighbors are found, the Euclidian distance of the feature to the nearest (D0) of the two neighbors is compared against the distance of the feature to the farthest (D1) neighbor. A positive match is scored when $D0 \leq (D1/ratio)$, where the default ratio is 2.

3.3.3 Match Evaluation and Logo Detection

Once features have been extracted from target and source images and matched, the resulting matches must be evaluated to determine if an occurrence of the target is present in the source image. This determination is made based on an evaluation of the data provided by the extraction and matching. Criteria for determining a positive detection can be based on some or all of the following information:

(a) Total number of features in the target.
(b) Total number of features in the source.
(c) Number of matches.
(d) Strengths of the matches.
(e) Locations of the matches.

Note that the object of interest (logo) is known a priori in this case, unlike the scene matching application of the previous section, so different match criteria can be used to provide more accurate match scores. Detecting partially occluded logos is also less important for typical logo detection applications.

3.3.3.1 Match Evaluation Criteria   Two criteria were established to make the logo detection determination. The first, match percentage (MP), is computed as the number of matches between the target and source images divided by the number of features in the target:

$$MP(T, S) = \text{Matches}(T, S)/\text{Total Features}(T),$$

where T is the target logo image and S is the source image.

The second criterion, mean match strength (MMS), is calculated using the relative match strength provided by the Euclidian distance of the feature to the nearest of the two nearest neighbors. The MMS can be easily calculated and used to obtain an overall sense of the strength of the target-to-source similarity as:

$$\text{MMS} = \frac{1}{N} \sum_{i=1}^{N} \text{Match Strength}(T, S_i).$$

The determination of a match between a target logo image and a source image was made using a simple linear threshold classifier. Minimum matching thresholds were learned for both MP and MMS. Source images with MP and MMS values above both thresholds were considered positive matches.

3.3.3.2 Test Image Set   A logo detection test set was compiled from images captured at a stock car race event where corporate sponsorship is evident in many forms. The cars have logos of various sizes painted on different surfaces, and there are logo billboards around the race track itself. The images were captured by spectators using consumer grade digital cameras.

3.3.4 Match Performance

There are two important aspects of feature matching performance that are pertinent to logo detection: the speed in which the feature matching completes and the accuracy of the match.

3.3.4.1 Speed   Performance tests were run on a 1.83 GHz Intel® (Intel Corporation, Santa Clara, CA) Dual Core windows system with 4 GB of memory. The tests were run in single-threaded mode on relatively low resolution test images. The target being matched had 227 features, which was between the median (177) and mean (246) of 32 target images tested. The features were persisted in text files stored on an external hard drive accessed via USB 2.0. Figure 3.10 shows feature matching time by image and feature resolution. Image resolution impacts feature matching time because higher resolution images with greater image detail produce larger numbers of features to be matched. Although not at the same rate, execution time increases with feature resolution.

3.3.4.2 Accuracy   The accuracy of the matching must inform any decision regarding image or feature resolution. As with the matching speed, the accuracy of

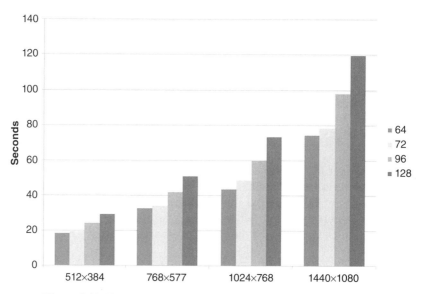

Figure 3.10. Feature match time by feature and image resolution.

TABLE 3.2. False Positive Rates by Logo and Feature Resolution

	Feature Points	64	72	96	128
Company A	227	12.50	0.69	0.00	1.39
Company B	327	0.69	0.69	0.69	0.69
Company C	353	1.39	2.08	0.00	2.08
Company D	396	4.86	0.00	1.39	1.39
Company E	102	17.36	7.64	11.81	3.47
Company F	136	1.39	9.03	2.08	0.69
Company G	71	1.39	2.08	0.69	0.69
Company H	621	43.75	0.00	2.08	0.00
Company I	548	7.64	0.69	0.69	1.39
Company J	84	0.69	0.69	0.69	0.69
Company K	117	30.56	3.47	17.36	7.64
Company L	58	17.36	0.00	1.39	0.69
Company M	104	1.39	4.17	0.00	0.00
Mean	241.85	10.84	2.40	2.99	1.60
Median	136.00	4.86	0.69	0.69	0.69

the matching algorithm is dependent upon the feature resolution. Table 3.2 show the false positive rate for various logos at the four features resolutions examined. In general, the FPR decreased as feature resolution increased. However, for a few of the logos tested, the FPR for feature resolution 96 was significantly greater than the FPR for feature resolution 72. This may indicate that the number of orientation bins is more important than the size of the orientation histogram array. It should be noted that the FPRs shown above were generated using the aforementioned test image set and are not necessarily indicative of future rates for random image sets.

However, tests on random consumer imagery show extremely low FPR for detectable logos.

3.4 CONCLUSIONS

This chapter describes a new approach to reliably matching unique objects embedded in consumer photos. The approach explores filtering steps necessary for producing high precision matches in the consumer image domain, where standard application of scale-invariant feature matching produces numerous false matches because of the clutter that appears in typical scenes. A major contribution of this work is to present a set of constraints that retain feature clusters of distinctive objects while eliminating feature points arising from generic objects and clutter. Experimental results evaluating the performance of this method using real consumer images show very significant improvements when our method is compared against scene matching based on SIFT features alone. This approach can enable consumers to tag entire collections with location labels with very little effort, and can thus enable image search and organization. We also investigate the use of SIFT-based visual features for automatic logo detection in images. Experiments have been conducted to examine logo false-positive rate and feature match time versus feature resolution. Preliminary results have provided good insight into the robustness of this approach.

Future work in the scene-matching area will focus on the efficiency of implementing such a system. For example, we can avoid explicitly matching many potential image pairs by intelligently selecting a few images that can represent groups of images and have a higher likelihood of matching other images. Efficient indexing structures are needed to produce retrieval results within a reasonable time. It is also possible that a set of interesting objects could be created for a specific user's collection, thus focusing the search for matching features in the reference and target images. For unique objects such as logos, the determination of the optimum feature resolution is also needed by experimentation with a larger image set.

ACKNOWLEDGMENTS

The authors would like to thank Jens Farmer for his work on the design and implementation of the scene matching prototype application.

CHAPTER 4

ENTROPY-BASED ANALYSIS OF VISUAL AND GEOLOCATION CONCEPTS IN IMAGES

KEIJI YANAI, HIDETOSHI KAWAKUBO, and KOBUS BARNARD

4.1 INTRODUCTION

Recently, consumer-generated media (CGM) on the Web has become very popular. For example, photo-sharing sites, such as Flickr and Picasa, are representative CGM sites, which store a huge number of consumer-generated photos people uploaded, and make them accessible via the Web for everyone. Photo sharing sites collect not only photos but also metadata on uploaded photos. Regarding metadata for photos, textual information such as keywords and comments is common. Keywords associated with uploaded photos are sometimes called "tags." In addition to textual tags, some photos are associated with "geotags," which represent locations where the photos are taken. A "geotag" is expressed by a pair of values for latitude and longitude.

Such recent growth of photo sharing systems on the Web has made large-scale analysis of visual concepts much easier, since we can obtain a large number of photos associated with various kinds of textual tags and geotags easily. Using a large number of images gathered from the Web, we propose new methods to analyze visual characteristic, geographical distribution, and their relations regarding various concepts in this chapter. To do that, we use entropy to analyze the distribution of image features and geographical locations. We propose two kinds of entropy-based indicators: "image region entropy" and "geolocation entropy." Image region entropy represents to what extent concepts have visual characteristics, while geolocation entropy represents how concepts are distributed over the world. In the experiment, we analyze image region entropy for 150 adjectives and relations between image region entropy and geolocation entropy regarding 230 nouns. From the results, we found that the concepts with low image entropy tend to have high geolocation entropy and vice versa.

Multimedia Information Extraction: Advances in Video, Audio, and Imagery Analysis for Search, Data Mining, Surveillance, and Authoring, First Edition. Edited by Mark T. Maybury.
© 2012 IEEE Computer Society. Published 2012 by John Wiley & Sons, Inc.

Our objective in this article is twofold: examining "visualness" of various concepts, and exploring the relations between word concepts and geographical locations. Both are carried out by entropy-based analysis. In the following two subsections, we explain the details of both objectives.

4.1.1 Visualness of Concepts

"Visualness" as examined in the first part of this chapter is the extent that concepts have visual characteristics. Knowing which concept has visually discriminative power is important for image annotation, especially automatic image annotation by generic image recognition systems, since not all concepts are related to visual contents. Such systems should first recognize the concepts that have visual properties. Not all words are appropriate for image annotation, since some words are not related to visual properties of images. For example, "red" is expected to be tied with visual features strongly, while "interesting" and "artificial" are not expected to link to visual properties represented in images directly.

Recently, there has been much work related to semantic image classification (e.g., Fei-Fei et al. 2004; Li and Wang 2003; Yanai 2003) and automated annotation of images (e.g., Barnard et al. 2003; Barnard and Forsyth 2001; Fan et al. 2004; Jeon et al. 2003; Mori et al. 1999). Our work is mostly related to an approach to learn the labeling of regions from images with associated text, but where the correspondence between words and image regions is not known (Barnard et al. 2003; Duygulu et al. 2002). So far, most of the work related to image annotation or image classification has either ignored the suitability of the vocabulary, or selected the concepts and words by hand. The popularity of sunset images in this domain reflects such choices, often made implicitly. We propose that increasing the scale of the endeavor will be substantively helped with automated methods for selecting a vocabulary that has visual correlates.

To estimate the visualness of a concept, we could consider how well an automated annotation system reliably attaches this concept to an appropriate image region. We could then measure visualness using standard approaches, such as precision and recall, on the task of finding those regions. However, doing so requires significant ground truth, that is, region-labeled regions. While such data is available on a modest scale, mining large data sets for visual vocabulary terms chosen among thousands of words based on this approach is not practical.

To address determining visualness without image region ground truth, we propose a method based on entropy. Our method performs probabilistic region selection for regions that can be linked with concept "X" from images that are labeled as "X" or "non-X," and then we compute a measure of the entropy of the selected regions based on a GMM for generic regions. Intuitively, if such entropy is low, then the concept in question can be linked with region features. Alternatively, if the entropy is more similar to that of random regions, then the concept has some other meaning that is not captured by our features.

To investigate these ideas, we collected 40 thousand images from the World Wide Web using the Google Image search for 150 adjectives. We examined which adjectives are suitable for annotation of image contents. We describe the experimental results in Section 4.1.

4.1.2   Relation between Visual Concepts and Geolocations

In the second part, we propose geolocation entropy that represents how concepts are distributed over the world, and analyze relations between image region entropy and geolocation entropy using a large number of geotagged images on the Web. Some concepts are distributed broadly over the world, while some are concentrated on specific areas. Therefore, analyzing relations between distribution of locations in the world and distribution of image features in the visual feature space for various concepts is a logical first step on analysis of dependency of concepts on locations.

In the experiments, we analyzed relations between image region entropy and geolocation entropy in terms of 230 nouns, and we found that the concepts with low image entropy tend to have high geolocation entropy and vice versa.

The rest of the chapter is as follows. In Section 4.2, we overview related work of this chapter. In Section 4.3, we describe the method to select regions that are likely related to a given concept, to compute "image region entropy" and "geolocation entropy." In Section 4.4, we explain the experimental results in terms of probabilistic region selection and "image region entropy" for 150 adjectives and 230 nouns, and analyze relations between "image region entropy" and "geolocation entropy." In Section 4.5, we conclude this chapter. Note that this chapter is based on two previous papers (Yanai and Barnard 2005; Yanai et al. 2009).

4.2   RELATED WORK

To analyze distribution of visual features regarding given concepts, we proposed "region image entropy" to measure visualness of word concepts with images gathered from the Web (Yanai and Barnard 2005). Word concepts with low entropy are more appropriate for automatic image annotation efforts, such as the ones cited in the previous section. Our initial work on entropy analysis for visual concepts in terms of distribution of visual features has been followed by several others such as Koskela et al. (2007), who used entropy to analysis the large-scale ontology for multimedia (LSCOM) (Naphade et al. 2006). In addition, Wu et al. (2008) proposed the Flickr distance that measures dis-similarity between visual concepts using Jensen–Shannon divergence of the probability distributions of visual features, and Moxley et al. (2009) categorized concepts into places, landmarks, and visual terms with mutual information.

We are not aware of any other analogous work on entropy analysis for relations between words and locations. This kind of study has only recently become relatively easy; a large number of images with location metadata have been very expensive to acquire in the past. Hence, early research on geotagged images focused on location-based photo browsing for a personal geotagged photo collection (Naaman et al. 2004; Toyama et al. 2003), since it was difficult to obtain a large number of geotagged images. However, the situation has changed after Flickr launched an online geotagging interface in 2006. At present, Flickr has become the largest geotagged photo database in the world. Geotagging with GPS devices is expensive and inconvenient, but the Flickr online geotagging system allows users to indicate the place where photos are taken by clicking the online map. In addition, the Flickr database is open to everyone via the FlickrAPI, which allows users' programs to search the whole Flickr photo database for geotagged images.

Therefore, several researchers have recently taken advantage of the huge Flickr geotagged image database to study geotagged image recognition. Cristani et al. (2008) proposed methods on event recognition of geotagged images by integrating visual features and geographical information. In its raw form, a geotag is simply a pair of values for latitude and longitude. To convert this 2D vector into a richer representation, Luo et al. (2008) and Yaegashi and Yanai (2009) converted geotags into visual information from the sky using aerial images, and Joshi and Luo (2008) transformed geotags to words using a reverse geo-coding technique. On the other hand, Yuan et al. (2008) used GPS trace data, which is a series of geotags, instead of a single pinpoint geotag in order to classify images into several predefined events. Yu and Luo (2008) used time and seasons for geotagged image recognition in addition to visual information and geolocation data. While event or scene recognition on geotagged images is common, the "IM2GPS" project (Hays and Efros 2008) proposed a unique idea of estimating a place from just one nongeotagged image based on six million geotagged images gathered from Flickr.

4.3 ENTROPY ANALYSIS

In this section, we describe a new method to analyze relations between location and concepts in terms of image features. We compute both image region entropy and geolocation entropy for many concepts using geotagged images gathered from the Flickr.

4.3.1 Image Region Entropy

Originally, "image region entropy" was proposed in Yanai and Barnard (2005), which is a measure of visualness of concepts, which is the extent that concepts have visual characteristics. In the original method to compute image region entropy, we first perform probabilistic region selection for regions that can be associated with concept "X" from images that are labeled as "X" or "non-X." We then compute a measure of the entropy of the selected regions based on a Gaussian mixture model (GMM) for regions. By introducing a probabilistic region selection method, we can separate foreground regions from background regions, and compute the entropy using only the foreground regions. Intuitively, if this entropy is low, then regions associated with a concept have typical appearances, and the image features of the concept are relatively concentrated. Alternatively, if the entropy is high, then the image features of the concepts are distributed, and the concept has no typical image regions.

In this chapter, we describe two methods to compute image region entropy. One is the original method we proposed in Yanai and Barnard (2005), which employs color and texture features and uses a GMM. The other uses a bag-of-feature representation (BoF) (Csurka et al. 2004) and probabilistic latent semantic analysis (PLSA) (Hofmann 2001) to model their statistics.

We were motivated to develop the second approach, because it is regarded that the BoF representation has more semantically discriminative power than other representations (Csurka et al. 2004), and PLSA is more appropriate for the BoF vectors than GMM. In addition, while the original method uses probabilistic generative methods to select foreground regions, in the second method, we use the multiple instance support vector machine (mi-SVM) (Andrews et al. 2003), which is a multiple instance learning (MIL) approach. Discriminative approaches have distinct advantages for this kind of application provided that sufficient training data is available. However, to capitalize on this, we need to use MIL because the positive training labels (e.g., a word naming a foreground object) are typically correct labels for only a relatively small subset of the image features, making the data too noisy for a naive application of discriminative learning.

In general, since the original method employs color and texture features, it is appropriate to analyze abstract concepts, such as adjectives. On the other hand, since the modified method employs BoF representation, it is appropriate for object and scene concepts which usually correspond to nouns.

4.3.2 Image Region Entropy with Simple Features

The algorithm of the original method (Yanai and Barnard 2005) is as follows:

1. Prepare several hundred "X" images that are associated with "X" and several hundred "non-X" images that are unrelated to "X." ("X" corresponds to a certain concept.)

2. Carry out region segmentation for all the "X" and "non-X" images and extract image features from each region of each image.

3. Select n "X" regions and n "non-X" regions randomly from the regions which come from "X" and "non-X" images, respectively. (In the experiment, we set n as 200.)

4. Applying the EM algorithm to the image features of regions which are selected as both "X" and "non-X," compute the GMM for the distribution of both "X" and "non-X."

5. Find the components of the Gaussian mixture that contributes to "X" regions greatly. They are regarded as "X" components and the rest are "non-X" components. They are the generative models of "X" regions and "non-X" regions, respectively.

6. Based on "X" components and "non-X" components, compute $P(X|r_i)$ for all the regions that come from "X" images, where r_i is the ith region.

7. Compute the entropy of the image features of all the regions weighted by $P(X|r_i)$ with respect to a generic model for image regions obtained by the EM in advance. This "image region entropy" corresponds to the "visualness" of the concept.

8. Select the top n regions regarding $P(X|r_i)$ as "X" regions and the top $n/2$ regions regarding $P(nonX|r_i)$ as "non-X" regions. Add $n/2$ regions randomly selected from "non-X" images to "non-X" regions.

9. Repeat from (4) to (8) for t times. (In the experiments, we set t to 10.)

4.3.2.1 *Segmentation and Feature Extraction*   Images gathered from the Web using keyword search include irrelevant images unrelated to the concept. Further, images with relevant regions typically also have a number of regions that are irrelevant. Thus, we use a probabilistic method to detect regions associated with concepts from a pool of regions assumed to contain some relevant ones.

For a set of images gathered from the Web the concept "X," we begin with region using JSEG (Deng and Manjunath 2001), since the source code is available on the author's Web page. Note that our method does not assume any specific region segmentation method. After segmentation, we extract image features from each region whose size is larger than a certain threshold. We present regions using three kinds of features: color, texture, and shape features, which include the average RGB value and their variance, the average response to the difference of four different combinations of two Gaussian filters, region size, location, the first moment, and the area divided by the square of the outer boundary length.

4.3.2.2 *Detecting Regions Associated with "X"*   To obtain $P(X|r_i)$, which represents the probability that the region is associated with the concept "X," simultaneously with the parameters of the GMM for the statistic of "X" regions, we propose an iterative algorithm. At first, we assign "X" regions and "non-X" regions at random. Using EM, we obtain the GMM for both the image region features of "X" and "non-X," and assign components of the mixture model according to the following formula.

$$p_j^X = \sum_{i=1}^{n_X} P(c_j|r_i^X, X)$$

$$= \sum_{i=1}^{n_X} P(X|r_i^X, c_j)P(c_j),$$

where c_j is the jth component of the mixture model, n_x is the number of "X" regions, and r_i^X is the ith "X" region.

The top m components in terms of p_j^X are regarded as the model of "X," and the rest are the model of "non-X." With these models of "X" and "non-X," we can compute $P(X|r_i)$ for all the regions that come from "X" images. Assume that $p1(X|r_i)$ is the output of the model of "X," and $p2(nonX|r_i)$ is the output of the model of "non-X," given r_i, we can obtain $P(X|r_i)$ as follows:

$$P(X|r_i) = \frac{p1(X|r_i)}{p1(X|r_i) + p2(\text{non}X|r_i)}.$$

For the next iteration, we select the top n regions regarding $P(X|r_i)$ as "X" regions and the top $n/2$ regions regarding $P(\text{non}X|r_i)$ as "non-X" regions. Add $n/2$ regions randomly selected from "non-X" images to "non-X" regions. In this way, we mix newly estimated "non-X" regions and randomly selected regions from "non-X" images after the second iteration. We adopt mixing rather than using only newly estimated "non-X" regions empirically based on the results of the preliminary experiments. After computing the entropy, we repeat estimation of the model of "X" and "non-X," and computation of $P(X|r_i)$.

4.3.2.3 Computing Entropy of Concepts

We compute the entropy of the image region features associated with a concept using a generic statistical model for image region features, again a GMM using the features mentioned above. Intuitively, if the concept region set maps mostly onto a limited set of mixture components in the generic model, then the entropy is low, and the concept is considered visual. Note that the association between region and concept as determined above is soft in that we only have the probability $P(X|x_i)$ that we use to weight the calculations below across all regions associated with the concept word. Note also that we only use the GMMs computed per concept to compute the association $P(X|x_i)$.

To get a generic statistical model for image region features, we used about 50 thousand regions randomly picked up from the images gathered from the Web. Fitting models using EM always includes randomness from the initial assignment, so we prepare k such models and compute the entropy of concepts with respect to each of the k models and average the values to obtain a less biased estimate.

The average probability of image features of "X" weighted by $P(X|x_i)$ with respect to the jth component of the lth generic base represented by the GMM is given by

$$P(c_j^l \mid X) = \frac{w_{j,l} \sum_{i=1}^{N_X} P(f_{X,i}; \theta_{j,l}) P(X|r_i)}{\sum_{i=1}^{N_X} P(X|r_i)}$$

where $f_{x,i}$ is the image feature of the ith region of "X," $P(f_{X,i}|\theta_{j,i})$ is the generative probability of $f_{X,i}$ from the jth component, $w_{j,i}$ is the weight of the jth component of the lth base, and N_X is the number of all the regions which come from "X" images.

The entropy for "X" is given by

$$H(X) = \frac{1}{k} \sum_{l=1}^{k} \sum_{j=1}^{N_{base}} -P(c_j^l \mid X) \log_2 P(c_j^l \mid X).$$

where N_{base} is the number of the components of the base. In the experiment, we set N_{base} and k to 250 and 5, respectively.

4.3.3 Image Region Entropy with BoF

In this subsection, we describe an alternative approach (Yanai et al. 2009) that employs BoF (Csurka et al. 2004) and PLSA (Hofmann 2001) instead of color and texture features and the GMM.

4.3.3.1 Feature Extraction

By using the region-based BoF representation (Csurka et al. 2004), we represent each image region as a collection of independent local patches. To build BoF vectors, we vector-quantize them by voting on the representative patches. We use the Scale Invariant Feature Transform (SIFT) descriptor (Lowe 2004) to represent local patches.

The SIFT descriptor consists of Gaussian derivatives computed at 8 orientation planes over a 4×4 grid of spatial location, giving 128-dimension vector. The SIFT descriptor is invariant to rotation and scale-change. Much research (Csurka et al. 2004; Nowak et al. 2006) suggests that the SIFT descriptor is the best as representation of image patches for object recognition.

Before constructing the bag-of-features (BoF) vector, we apply region segmentation for all the images. To obtain the region-based BoF vector, we extract the BoF vector from each region. For region segmentation, we again use JSEG (Deng and Manjunath 2001) in the first approach.

The main steps to obtain image representation are as follows:

1. Carry out region segmentation with the JSEG algorithm.
2. Sample 3000 patches per image randomly following Nowak et al. (2006).
3. Generate feature vectors for the sampled patches by the SIFT descriptor (Lowe 2004).
4. Construct a codebook with k-means clustering over all the extracted feature vectors. A codebook is constructed for each concept independently. We set k to 300.
5. Assign all SIFT vectors to the nearest code word of the codebook, and convert the set of SIFT vectors for each region into one k-bin histogram vector for the counts of the assigned code words. This applies equally to image regions from additional images used as a source of negative examples in the step for selecting positive regions.

4.3.3.2 Detecting Regions Associated with the Given Concept   To select regions that are highly related to give concepts in this approach, we use the following iterative procedure based on mi-SVM (Andrews et al. 2003) to select foreground regions:

1. Prepare a positive image set gathered from Flickr and a random background image set, and extract a region-based BoF vector from each region in each image.
2. Sample one-third of positive images and negative background images. Train a SVM with them.
3. Classify all the regions of the positive images with the trained SVM.
4. Select one-third of regions in the descending order of the output values of the SVM. The selected regions can be regarded as positive regions.
5. If the number of iteration is more than the predefined value r, finish the selection of positive images. In the experiment, we set r to 5.
6. Otherwise select one-sixth of positive regions in the ascending order of the output values of the SVM as negative samples. Sample one-sixth of negative background images, and add them to negative samples.
7. Train an SVM, and jump back to (3).

4.3.3.3 Representing the Distribution with PLSA Latent Topics   In the next step, we estimate the entropy of the image features of selected regions with respect

to a generic distribution of image features. To represent a generic model, we use the PLSA (Hofmann 2001), which is the probabilistic method to identify latent topics with the given number of topics. PLSA was originally proposed as a probabilistic model to extract latent topics from text documents represented by bag-of-words. Similarly, images can be regarded as document and represented by BoF, and hence PLSA can be applied to images for discovering the object categories in each image. To obtain the generic base, we used about 10 thousand images randomly picked up from the images gathered from the Web similar to the first method which employs GMM to represent the generic base.

The PLSA model represents the joint probability of each word w in a document d by

$$P(w, d) = P(d) \sum_{z \in Z} P(w|z) P(z|d),$$

where $z \in Z = (z_1, \ldots, z_k)$ is a latent topic variable, k is the number of topics, $d \in D = (d_1, \ldots, d_N)$ is an image region expressed by the BoF vector, and $w \in W = (w_1, \ldots, w_M)$ is one element of the BoF vector, which corresponds to a "visual" word. The joint probability of the observed variables, w and d, is the marginalization over the k latent topics Z. The parameters are estimated by the EM algorithm. In the experiments, we set 300 to the number of base topics k. We carry out this estimation of $P(w|z)$ in advance, which is regarded as the training process of the PLSA.

For each positive region i for the concept "X," we estimate $P(z|d_i^X)$ employing "fold-in heuristics" (Hofmann 2001). The entropy for the concept "X" $H_{img}(X)$ is given by

$$H_{img}(X) = -\sum_{z \in Z} P(z|X) \log_2 P(z|X),$$

$$\text{where } P(z|X) = \frac{1}{|I_{selected}|} \sum_{i \in I_{selected}} P(z|d_i^X),$$

and $|I_{selected}|$ is the number of selected positive regions.

4.3.4   Geolocation Entropy

We obtain location information for images downloaded from Flickr in the form of latitude and a longitude with the FlickrAPI. In this work, we calculate entropy regarding geolocation in addition to image region entropy. To estimate geolocation entropy, we build a histogram regarding location distribution on each concept by dividing latitude and longitude by every 10 degrees as shown in Figure 4.1. Because the world map is divided into 36×36 grids, the total number of bins is 1296.

Geolocation entropy $H_{geo}(X)$ is given by:

$$H_{geo}(X) = \sum_i b_i \log_2 b_i,$$

where b_i represents the ith bin of the geolocation histogram, which is normalized in advance so that the sum of the values of all the histogram bins equals one.

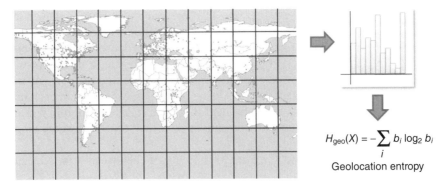

$$H_{geo}(X) = -\sum_i b_i \log_2 b_i$$

Geolocation entropy

Figure 4.1. Overview of computation of "Geolocation entropy." We divide the world map into 36×36 grids, and make a normalized histogram with 1296 bins, which corresponds to the probability distribution of geolocations of a given concept.

Figure 4.2. "Yellow" regions after 1 iteration.

4.4 EXPERIMENTS

4.4.1 Experiments on Visualness of Adjectives

To test the first method, we gathered 250 images per concept from the Web for 150 adjective concepts using the Google Image search. In total, we used about 40 thousand images.

Figure 4.2 and 4.3 show images with high probability "yellow" regions after one and five iterations of the region selection process, respectively. Regions with high probability $P(\text{yellow}|r_i)$ are labeled as "yellow," while the regions with low probability $P(\text{yellow}|r_i)$ are labeled as "nonyellow." At the start, the assignment of yellow regions is essentially random, whereas after only five iterations, most of the high

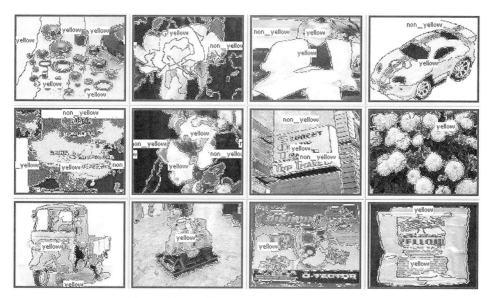

Figure 4.3. "Yellow" regions after 5 iterations.

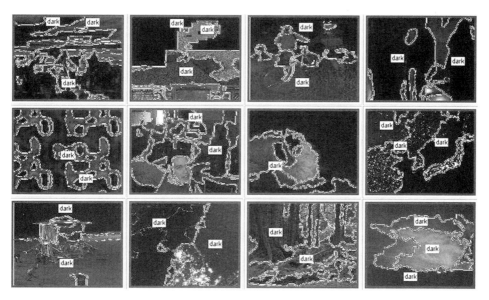

Figure 4.4. "Dark" regions after 5 iterations.

probability yellow regions are appropriate. This indicates the iterative region selection worked well in the case of "yellow."

Table 4.1 shows the 15 most visual adjectives and their image region entropy. Since the entropy of "dark" is the lowest, "dark" can be regarded as being the most visual adjective among the 150 adjectives under the condition of this experiment. Figure 4.4 shows some examples of "dark" images. Most of the regions labeled with "dark" are essentially uniformly black. Images associated with the highly ranked adjectives, "senior" and "beautiful," include many human faces and thus these

TABLE 4.1. Top 15 Adjectives and Color Adjectives in the Entropy Ranking

Rank	Adjective.	Entropy
1	Dark	0.0118
2	Senior	0.0166
3	Beautiful	0.0178
4	Visual	0.0222
5	Rusted	0.0254
6	Musical	0.0321
7	Purple	0.0412
8	Black	0.0443
9	Ancient	0.0593
10	Cute	0.0607
11	Shiny	0.0643
12	Scary	0.0653
13	Professional	0.0785
14	Stationary	0.1201
15	Electric	0.1411
(Color adjectives)		
7	Purple	0.0412
8	Black	0.0443
36	Red	0.9762
39	Blue	1.1289
46	Yellow	1.2827

concepts have lower entropy than one might guess. Interestingly, most images associated with "visual" are not photos but graphical images, such as screenshots of Windows Visual C++.

Table 4.2 shows the 15 least visual adjectives. In the case of "religious" shown in Figure 4.5, which is ranked as 145th, the region selection did not work well and their entropy is also relatively large, since the image features of the regions included in "religious" images have no prominent tendency. Therefore, we can consider that "religious" has no or only a few visual properties.

We show the ranking of color adjectives in the lower part of Table 4.1. They are relatively common in the upper ranking, even though images from the Web included many irrelevant images. This shows the effectiveness of the probabilistic region selection method we propose. Initially, we expected that all of them would be ranked near the top, but some were not. This is because all the images we used are collected from the Web automatically, and the test image sets always include some irrelevant images and others that reflect how culture has adopted color words in many ways (e.g., "Pink Floyd"). We note that we observed some variation in the ranking under different experimental conditions, such as tuning parameters, image features, and the image search engine to gather web images.

4.4.2 Experiments on Relations between Visual Concepts and Geolocations

We experimented with image region entropy and geolocation entropy for 230 nouns, which include abstract nouns, person names, and location names, as well as nouns

TABLE 4.2. Bottom 15 Adjectives in the Entropy Ranking

Rank	Adjective.	Entropy
135	Female	2.4986
136	Medical	2.5246
137	Assorted	2.5279
138	Large	2.5488
139	Playful	2.5541
140	Acoustic	2.5627
141	Elderly	2.5677
142	Angry	2.5942
143	Sexy	2.6015
144	Open	2.6122
145	Religious	2.7242
146	Dry	2.8531
147	Male	2.8835
148	Patriotic	3.0840
149	Vintage	3.1296
150	Mature	3.2265

Figure 4.5. "Religous" regions after 5 iterations.

related to objects and scenes in order to mix words that are likely to be related to location and words unrelated to location.

For these experiments, we gathered 500 images for each concept from Flickr using the FlickrAPI. We show the top 20 and bottom 20 results in terms of region entropy and geolocation entropy in Table 4.3 and in Table 4.4, respectively. Figure 4.6 shows the relations between image region entropy (x-axis) and geolocation entropy (y-axis) regarding 230 nouns in terms of absolute entropy values.

TABLE 4.3. Image Region Entropy $H_{img}(X)$ of Top 20 and Bottom 20 of 230 Nouns

Top 20		Bottom 20	
Concepts	$H_{img}(X)$	Concepts	$H_{img}(X)$
Sun	3.6497	Horse	7.3057
Rainbow	4.5538	Pizza	7.3071
Moon	4.6686	Salad	7.3093
Dragonfly	4.7550	Africa	7.3101
Sky	5.1049	Japan	7.3387
Mantis	5.1897	Oyster	7.3435
Egg	5.2288	Flea	7.3590
Airplane	5.3851	Tiger	7.3874
Bee	5.4210	Rice	7.3906
Light	5.4524	Rome	7.4013
Fly	5.4916	USA	7.4020
Coffee	5.6160	Backpack	7.4086
Bug	5.6407	Italia	7.4111
Mouse	5.6558	Town	7.5177
Butterfly	5.6785	Santa-Claus	7.5431
Lemon	5.7096	House	7.5598
Dream	5.7173	Napoleon	7.5704
Lamp	5.7347	School	7.6173
Insect	5.7560	Lincoln	7.7327
Tulip	5.7700	Mozart	7.8349

TABLE 4.4. Geolocation Entropy $H_{geo}(X)$ on Top 20 and Bottom 20 of 230 Nouns

Top 20		Bottom 20	
Concepts	$H_{geo}(X)$	Concepts	$H_{geo}(X)$
Deutschland	0.2602	Beetle	5.3225
Rome	0.3843	Grasshopper	5.3301
Tokyo	0.6253	Rice	5.3425
Paris	0.6730	Waterfall	5.3449
Eiffel-tower	0.7461	Monkey	5.3600
California	0.8776	Boat	5.3755
New-York	1.0264	Sun	5.1409
Italia	1.3105	Pool	5.4225
France	1.4833	Banana	5.4674
Egypt	1.8476	Parrot	5.4767
Japan	2.2973	Sea	5.4936
Mozart	2.6904	Mother	5.5114
Lincoln	2.7962	Teacher	5.5417
Europe	3.0379	Lizard	5.5448
Canada	3.2612	Fruit	5.5779
Castle	3.3948	Hibiscus	5.5856
Bach	3.4406	Ant	5.6147
Napoleon	3.4686	Coral	5.6565
India	3.4874	Fish	5.7831
Shakespeare	3.5342	Mosquito	5.9759

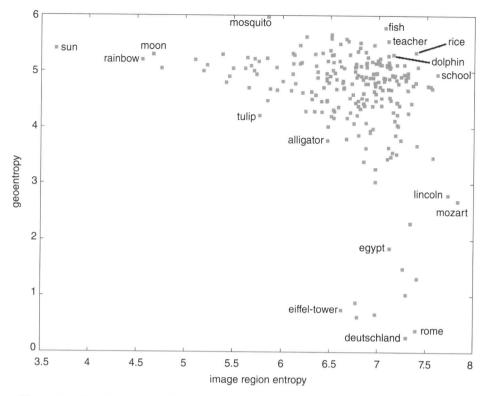

Figure 4.6. Relations of visual entropy and geo-entropy in terms of the entropy values.

4.4.3 Discussion

A prominent tendency shown in Figure 4.6 is that the relatively small geolocation entropy of location concepts, such as "Deutschland," "Rome," and "Egypt," and proper names of historical persons, such as "Mozart" (Figure 4.7) and "Lincoln," is often associated with relatively large image region entropy. In general, the geolocation of person and place names is strongly tied with the concepts themselves, while images related to them have varied appearance since they are relatively abstract concepts.

We found that concepts related to sky such as "sun" (Figure 4.8) and "rainbow" had relatively small image region entropy, while their geolocation entropies were larger. This is because appearances related to such concepts tends to be very similar or almost the same everywhere over the world. Therefore, geolocation entropy was high, and image region entropy was low.

The concept "tulip" (Figure 4.9) exhibited low image entropy and middle geolocation entropy. "Tulip" images were mainly concentrated in the United States and Europe, especially Holland, and most of the tulip photos included tulip flowers and tulip farms.

Both the image region and geolocation entropies for "rice" (Figure 4.10) were large. Although rice is a food concept that is common everywhere over the world, the way it is typically prepared varies greatly depending on the country. Moreover, it is also a well-known person's name. "Dolphin" also was distributed over the world,

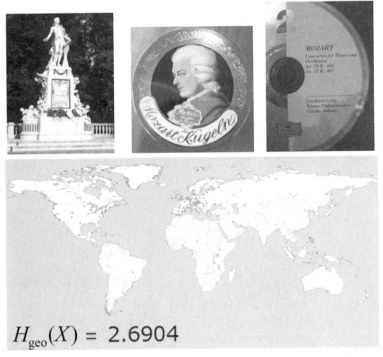

$$H_{\text{geo}}(X) = 2.6904$$

Figure 4.7. "Mozart" images over the world. This concept has high image region entropy and low geolocation entropy.

$$H_{\text{geo}}(X) = 5.4109$$

Figure 4.8. "Sun" images over the world. This concept has low image region entropy and high geolocation entropy.

$$H_{geo}(X) = 4.2091$$

Figure 4.9. "Tulip" images over the world. This concept has relatively low image region entropy and low geolocation entropy.

because dolphins live in the ocean and aquariums over the world. Most dolphin photos are taken in aquariums rather than the ocean, and thus have wider geographical distribution and more diverse appearance than one might guess, leading to higher entropies.

As show in Figure 4.6, the concepts with low image entropy tend to have high geolocation entropy and vice versa. The concepts related to sky, such as "sun," "moon," and "rainbow," have low image region entropy and high geolocation entropy, while the concepts related to places, such as "Rome," "Deutschland," and "Egypt," have high image region entropy and low geolocation entropy. Most of the other concepts have high image entropy and high geo-entropy, while there are no concepts both entropies of which are low in terms of entropy values.

4.5 CONCLUSIONS AND FUTURE WORK

In this chapter, we proposed two entropy-based indicators: "image region entropy" and "geolocation entropy." We developed two methods to compute image region entropy, one using GMMs and simple image features, and an alternative method using PLSA and the BoFrepresentation that is regarded to have more semantically discriminative power than other representations. With them, we analyzed visualness

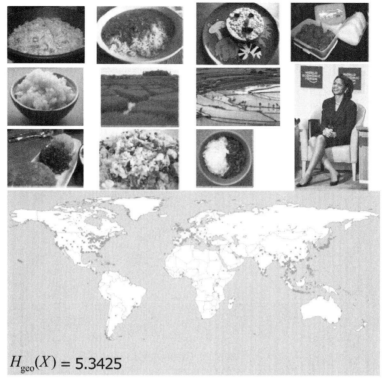

$$H_{geo}(X) = 5.3425$$

Figure 4.10. "Rice" images over the world. This concept has high image region entropy and high geolocation entropy.

of 150 adjective concepts, and relationship between 230 noun concepts and geographical locations using a large number of geotagged images on the Flickr photo sharing websites. In the experiment, we found that the concepts with low image entropy tend to have high geolocation entropy and vice versa.

For future work, we plan to investigate deeper relations between locations and concepts. We would like to investigate methods to discover differences of concepts depending on location such as how Western-style houses are different from Asian-style ones and African-style ones. Finally, we will consider methods to discriminate concepts which have larger cultural differences from concepts with high image entropy and high geolocation entropy.

CHAPTER 5

THE MEANING OF 3D SHAPE AND SOME TECHNIQUES TO EXTRACT IT

SVEN HAVEMANN, TORSTEN ULLRICH, and DIETER W. FELLNER

5.1 INTRODUCTION TO 3D OBJECTS

In the context of information extraction, the question to begin with is: Which semantic information can a 3D model be expected to contain? The truth is that 3D data sets are used for conveying very different sorts of information. A 3D scanning process typically produces a number of textured triangle meshes, or maybe just a large set of colored points. So a single 3D scan is conceptually very much like a photograph; it is a result of an optical measuring process, only with additional depth information. One 3D scan may contain many objects at the same time, or a set of 3D scans may contain different views of the same object. The notion of an *object* is highly problematic in this context, of course, and must be used with care. For the time being, we define a *3D object* pragmatically as a distinguishable unit according to a given *interpretation* or a given *query*. So the notion of what is regarded as an object may change as a function of interpretation and query context.

5.1.1 The 2D/3D Analogy

The strong analogy between 2D images and 3D objects is useful and illustrative, but this analogy also has its limits. As explained, 3D scans are analogous to photographs, with the same issues concerning, for example, resolution and noise. But 3D scenes are usually stitched together from several scans, which is rarely done with photographs, and which complicates the resolution and noise issues. Nevertheless, extracting semantic information can be done in 3D with similar techniques as in computer vision, for example, segmentation, object recognition, object retrieval, shape/image matching, and the like.

Multimedia Information Extraction: Advances in Video, Audio, and Imagery Analysis for Search, Data Mining, Surveillance, and Authoring, First Edition. Edited by Mark T. Maybury.
© 2012 IEEE Computer Society. Published 2012 by John Wiley & Sons, Inc.

5.1.2 Vector Data

The 3D analogy to vector-based 2D drawings are computer-aided design (CAD) data. They are *synthetic data* in the sense that they are the result of a design or construction idea, and not of a measuring process. Such *digitally born* 3D data may use a variety of methods to represent shape beyond the (still predominant) triangle meshes. For example, boundary representations (B-rep) and spline patches, such as nonuniform rational B-splines (NURBS), are used in many CAD systems (Farin 2002) since the 1970s. NURBS are the main industrial shape representation for smooth freeform shapes.

5.1.3 Hierarchical 3D Data

Three-dimensional data can be arranged hierarchically, which is seldom done with images. A *scene graph* typically has a root node representing the origin, inner nodes are transformations, and leaf nodes contain actual 3D objects. This can express coarse-to-fine transformation chains, for example:

$$\text{city} \rightarrow \text{quarter} \rightarrow \text{house} \rightarrow \text{floor} \rightarrow \text{room} \rightarrow \text{table} \rightarrow \text{cup}.$$

In this case, objects are typically moveable things, but can also be semantic units. The roofs and floors of a house may be separated simply because the user wishes to be able to move them in order to show what is inside the house. If the parts are not in separate scene graph nodes, they cannot be moved separately.

5.1.4 Creative 3D

In commonly used approaches object modeling (3D design) is separated from viewing (3D inspection and walk-through). As a result, objects may only be moved but may not be changed dynamically at runtime. This has the implication that the purpose of a 3D object, including the information it conveys and the queries it allows to answer, must often be known in advance at a very early state in the design process. This is illustrated by the 3D analogy to a painter or a comic strip artist, namely the *digital content creation* (DCC) team. It consists typically both of artists and of technicians who collaboratively create the 3D scenery for interactive computer games. The objects need to have a small data footprint (low polygon count) to allow fluent interaction, and cannot be used for documentation purposes, which would require higher resolution and measurement accuracy.

5.1.5 3D Has More Structure than 2D

To summarize, the main difference between 2D images and 3D objects is that images are typically treated as self-contained units. Segmentation is typically applied for recognition purposes (foreground—background separation), but rarely for cutting an image into pieces that are stored separately and recombined to create new images. With 3D data, this is done routinely. The consequence is that in 3D, the spatial interobject relations are more changeable, and more significant: Collision of 3D objects is more significant than 2D collision, which typically means only that one object occludes another from the point of view of the camera. In some sense, of

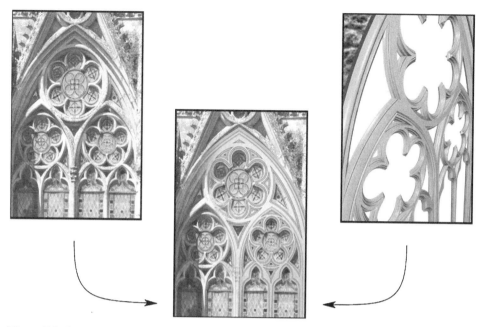

Figure 5.1. Semantic enrichment of 3D shapes. The problem of missing semantics in sampled data goes far beyond detection of object classes; the question is: What is the point? Even complex, detailed, man-made 3D constructions with many internal dependencies can typically be expressed concisely as generative models, exposing only a few high-level parameters. When these are determined, the original input data can be tagged with the ID of the shape part they belong to.

course, 3D subsumes 2D since an arbitrary number of virtual photographs can be shot from a 3D scene.

5.1.6 Semantic Enrichment

The problem of extracting semantic information from 3D data can be formulated simply as *What is the point?* to express that it is a priori not clear whether a given point belongs to a wall, to a door, or to the ground. To answer this question is called *semantic enrichment*, and it is, as pointed out, always an act of interpretation. As suggested in Figure 5.1, one option for providing such an interpretation is to use *generative shape templates* (as defined in Section 5.2).

5.2 GEOMETRY AND SEMANTICS: RECIPE WITH SOME OPEN QUESTIONS

Now that the scene is set, a more rigorous and systematic approach is needed. Which are the steps—the technical requirements—needed, to solve the problem of extracting information from a shape? According to Sven Havemann and Dieter W. Fellner (2001), seven research challenges have to be met:

Classification of Shape Representations: Dozens if not hundreds of digital representations for shape exist, from points and triangles over parametric and implicit (level-set) surfaces to generative and parametric models, and for each there are several subrepresentations with different attribute sets. Conversion is usually not possible without loss of information. So far, no exhaustive classification is available that would allow more uniform approaches and algorithms to be formulated in a generic way to cover a whole class of shape representations sharing similar properties.

A Sustainable Encoding in a 3D File Format: There is a plethora of different incompatible file formats for storing shape representations in different ways. For many important shape representations, there is not even a commonly accepted file format (point clouds, range maps, and compressed meshes), because for a 3D software package to support a given specified file format is difficult and expensive. Most commercial systems therefore have their own formats, which have become proprietary de facto standards. A commonly accepted general file format approach would be highly desirable.

Generic, Stable, and Detailed 3D Markup: The problem is to attach semantic information to a portion of a shape (point, line, surface, and volume) in a sustainable way. The shape markup ("nose of a statue," or even "noise of a statue") should survive simple mesh editing operations ("extracting the head"), so that a minimum of sustainability is guaranteed. Again, the problem is to define this in a generic way compatible to solutions found for the first two problems.

Generic Query Operations: Once a markup is attached, the markup needs to be queried. That means the denoted geometric entities need to be identified, for example, by simply highlighting a portion of a surface on the screen. A generic approach is needed that works for many shape representations and encodings. Purely geometric shape query operations that need to be standardized are ray casting/picking, screen-based selection, distance query (how close is a point to an object's surface), and box containment.

Para Data, Processing History, Provenance: Three-dimensional models are often obtained from combining other 3D models, for example, by stitching together partial scans or by arranging many objects in a scene. For professional applications, it is highly desirable to be able to assess the authenticity of a given set of data by tracing back its *digital provenance* to see which processing steps it underwent. Unfortunately, most 3D software does not store this information, and even if it does, in some rare cases, there is no general standard for it.

Close the Semantic Gap, Determine the Meaning of Shape: The goal is to assign a meaning (car, house, screw) to a given 3D model only by considering its geometry. This entails classical questions, such as measures for shape similarity, shape retrieval, and query-by-example. But also more fine-grained questions, such as determining dimensions, parameters, part-of relationships, as well as symmetries, self-similarity (ornaments, patterns), and speculation about deteriorated parts need to be considered.

Maintain the Relation of Shape and Meaning Consistent: Assuming that the meaning of a shape was determined, how can that information be stored in a sustainable way? Currently, there is no commonly accepted, domain-independent method to store and exchange the meaning of a shape. Note that this not only requires solving the previous problems, but it additionally requires a common approach for knowledge engineering, for example, using standardized *shape ontologies* to express the relations between the different shapes.

To transform the aforementioned recipe at least partly into practice, it is necessary to look at some existing workflows and acquisition technologies.

5.3   WHY ARE SHAPE SEMANTICS SO URGENTLY NEEDED?

Techniques to digitize shape are currently becoming available to a wide audience. Also, shape modeling, that is, the creation of synthetic 3D models, has become more accessible due to proliferation of free, easy-to-use 3D modeling software, for example, Google SketchUp (Gossweiler and Limber 2006). As a consequence, it is highly probable that *masses* of 3D data will be produced very soon. Therefore, the problems from Section 2 are actually very urgent.

Shape acquisition is a measurement process using dedicated devices like a computer tomograph, or a laser scanner, or simply sequences of uncalibrated photographs to which photogrammetry and computer vision techniques are applied (Koch et al. 2000). In any case, the result of the measurement is typically a point cloud, either with color per point, or with texture coordinates per point and a set of texture images. The next (nontrivial) processing step converts the point cloud to a higher-level geometric surface description with less redundancy: Note that also a perfectly planar surface can yield millions of points when it is 3D scanned, although maybe four corner points would be sufficient to represent the shape with high accuracy. This goes without saying that creating a surface from a set of points is in fact already an interpretation; strictly speaking, it is a hypothesis.

5.3.1   What Questions Are 3D Models Supposed to Answer?

The idea of *generalized documents* is to treat multimedia data, in particular 3D data sets, just like ordinary text documents, so that they can be inserted into a *digital library* (DL). For the DL to be able to handle a given media type, it must be integrated with the generic services that a DL provides, namely *markup, indexing,* and *retrieval.* This defines a DL in terms of the function it provides (Fellner 2001; Fellner et al. 2007). Like any library, a DL contains meta-information for all data sets. In the simplest case, the metadata are of the *Dublin Core Metadata Initiative* (1995) type (title, creator/author, and time of creation, etc). This is insufficient for large databases with a huge number of 3D objects, because of their versatility and rich structure. Scanned models are used in raw data collections, for documentation archival, virtual reconstruction, historical data analysis, and for high-quality visualization for dissemination purposes (Settgast et al. 2007). Navigation and browsing through the geometric models must be possible not only in 3D, but also on the semantic level. The need for higher-level semantic information becomes immediately clear when considering typical questions users might want to ask when a large database of 3D objects is available.

- How many different types of chairs are stored in the library?
- Are there any similar objects to the object I have here?
- I want to compare the noses of all these statues, can you extract them?
- Is there an amphora with a wider diameter, or with a smaller height?
- What is the quality of this surface with respect to the original measurement?
- How many rooms does this building have?
- What is the shortest way from one room to another?
- What is visible from this point of view?

These questions cannot be answered if the library simply treats 3D objects as binary large objects (BLOB), as it is done quite often. For a heap of geometric primitives without semantics, it is hard—if not impossible—to realize the mandatory services required by a DL, especially in the context of electronic data exchange, storage, and retrieval (Fellner 2001; Fellner et al. 2007).

5.4 DESCRIPTION OF GEOMETRICAL KNOWLEDGE

While describing a 3D model on the geometric level is a problem that has been researched reasonably well, it is still an open-ended question how to describe the shape and its structure on a higher, more abstract level. We will briefly review a few possible approaches, which also illustrate the complexity of the task.

5.4.1 Description by Definition and by Example

The traditional way of classifying objects, pursued both in mathematics and, in a less formal manner, in dictionaries, is to define a class of objects by listing their distinctive properties:

> **chair** – a seat, esp. for one person, usually having four legs for support and a rest for the back and often having rests for the arms.
>
> http://dictionary.reference.com

This approach is not amenable for computers not only because of the natural language used, but more fundamentally because of the fact that definitions typically depend on other definitions (e.g., seat). This often leads to circular dependencies (hen–egg) that cannot be resolved automatically by strict reasoning, but rely on intuitive understanding at some point. The dictionary example also illustrates the difficulty of making implicit knowledge explicit: Most people will agree on which objects fall into the class "chair," but it is far more difficult to synthesize an explicit definition for this class. So building up a dictionary of definitions is a sophisticated and tedious task.

An alternative, nonrecursive approach for describing shape is to use a picture dictionary. Each entry in the dictionary is illustrated with a photo or a drawing. This description by example approach is widely used, for example, in biology for plant taxonomy. This avoids listing an exhaustive list of required properties for each entry. However, it requires some notion of similarity, simply because the decision whether object x belongs to class A or B requires measuring the closeness of x to the exemplars $a \in A$ and $b \in B$ of both classes.

5.4.2 Statistical Approaches and Machine Learning

A large body of literature on 2D segmentation, detection, recognition, and matching exists in the field of computer vision, based on machine learning techniques. Many of these approaches use a *classifier*. A classifier decides to which class an object x belongs, or, more formally: it is a function f that maps input feature vectors $x \in X$ to output class labels $y \in C = \{1, \ldots, k\}$. The *feature space* X is often $\mathcal{R}^d$. The goal in machine learning is to derive f from a set of labeled training data (x_i, y_i). Probabilistic approaches compute the *posterior probability* $p(y|x)$ that feature vector x belongs to the class y. Then, the classifier can simply choose the class with the highest probability, $p(y = c|x) = \max_{c \in C}$. Modeling the a posteriori probability directly is called a *discriminative model*, since it discriminates between given classes. A *generative model*, however, uses Bayes' rule to compute the posterior probabilities using

$$p(y|x) = \frac{p(x|y)p(y)}{\sum_{y' \in C} p(x|y')p(y')}.$$

The advantage is that $p(x|y')$ and $p(y')$ can be learned separately, which makes the classifier more robust against partly missing data, it can handle combined features, and new classes can be added incrementally. Details can be found in the computer vision literature (Bishop 2007; Ulusoy and Bishop 2005).

5.4.3 Machine Learning and 3D

Many of the machine learning techniques are applicable to 3D problems, for example, for feature-based similarity search; some even use computer vision techniques directly. 2D computer vision is clearly ahead with respect to machine learning, so much progress can be expected in the near future when more of these techniques are lifted to 3D. The new term *visual computing* was coined for the confluence of graphics and vision.

A good survey on content-based 3D object retrieval is provided by Benjamin Bustos et al. (2007). One example is the approach from Ding-Yun Chen et al. (2003), who calculate the similarity between a pair of 3D models (taken from a 3D database) by comparing heuristically chosen sets of 2D projections rendered from the two models. Each projection is then described by image features, for instance, the silhouette. The similarity between two objects is then defined as the minimum of the sum of distances between all corresponding image pairs over all camera rotations.

Statistical approaches clearly have their strength in discriminating object classes. However, it is generally difficult to describe with a "flat" feature vector objects that have a rich hierarchical structure, which is often the case with 3D objects, for example, a hierarchy of joints or a graph of rooms connected by doors. Furthermore, feature-based object detection, for example, of rectangular shapes, does not yield object parameters: width and height of a detected rectangle must typically be computed separately.

5.5   REVERSE ENGINEERING AS INVERSE PROBLEM

Given a shape, the reverse engineering problem is to answer the question: How has this shape been created? This is an inverse problem in the sense that it tries to infer from the result of a construction process the construction process itself. Simple examples would be to infer from points sampled from a sphere the center and radius of the sphere, or, given the shape created by a milling process, to compute the path of the milling tool. This shows that reverse engineering always makes certain assumptions about the underlying design space, that is, the tools that were used for creating a given object. This can also go wrong: Fitting a sphere to an ellipsoid or to a box yields bad results.

5.5.1   The Pipeline Concept

According to the definition by Tamás Vradi et al. (1997), reverse engineering requires identifying the structure of the model and the creation of a consistent and accurate model description. It comprises a number of different problems and techniques, such as fitting, approximation, and numerical optimization, described in more detail in the processing pipeline from Fausto Bernardini et al. (1999). Applying knowledge to reverse engineering problems improves the recovery of object models (Fisher 2002): "*computers are good at data analysis and fitting; humans are good at recognizing and classifying patterns.*" Robert Fisher demonstrated that general shape knowledge enables the recovery of an object even if the given input data is very noisy, sparse, or incomplete.

5.5.2   An Example that Works

One example of a well-established, complete reverse engineering pipeline is the field of urban reconstruction. Raw data, unorganized 3D point clouds, are captured using aerial imagery processed photogrammetrically, optionally complemented by aerial or terrestrial laser scans. Using strong assumptions about the objects to be reconstructed, excellent results can be obtained fully automatically by now (Karner et al. 2001, Fruh and Zakhor 2003, Remondino 2003). This yields a well-defined set of semantic information, that is, ground polygons and building heights, as well as the "roof landscape" (Zebedin et al. 2006). Unfortunately, this semantic information is highly domain dependent and thus, not very generally applicable. It is difficult to extend the information model to represent the number of floors, windows, entries, and walking paths, or by a detailed street model.

5.5.3   Further Generalization Is Needed

The extraction of semantic content from 3D data is an important topic for a wide field of applications, which is quite a burning topic in the context of cultural heritage, as well explained by David Arnold (2006): In the future, many more detailed geo-metrical, logical, and semantic substructures need to be identified in historical 3D data than today. After all, an arch is an arch, and not just a bunch of triangles.

5.5.4 Structural Decomposition

Urban reconstruction is in fact an example for structural decomposition. The idea is to postulate a certain type of semantic structure in the data, typically "part-of" relations, and then to search and extract this structure in unstructured data, such as point clouds or triangle sets. Structural decomposition can be implemented in various ways. Tahir Rabbani and Frank van den Heuvel (2004) for instance, use the constructive solid geometry (CSG) paradigm (Shapiro 2002), where primitive objects (box, sphere, cylinder etc.) can be added to or subtracted from each other. So they decompose a triangulated object into a tree of CSG operations with primi-tive objects in the tree leafs. Cheng et al. (2004) decompose a triangulated free-form surface into a subdivision surface. Similar to splines, subdivision surfaces define a smooth surface with a comparably coarse control mesh.

5.5.5 Psychological Evidence

Structural decomposition is well in line with human perception. In general, shapes are recognized and coded mentally in terms of relevant parts and their spatial con-figuration or structure. While this was only postulated, for example, in the influential *Gestalt theory* (King and Wertheimer 2005) in the late nineteenth century, psycholo-gists like Irvin Biederman (1987) have found also empirical evidence. One idea to operationalize this concept was proposed, among others, by Masaki Hilaga et al. (2001), who introduces an interesting structural descriptor, the *multiresolution Reeb graph*, to represent the skeletal and topological structure of a 3D shape at various levels of resolution. Another school around Bianca Falcidieno and Michela Spag-nuolo is pursuing the idea of *shape ontologies* (AIM@SHAPE 2006). They propose, in the context of shape retrieval, the notion of a *shape prototype* represented as an attributed graph with nodes containing shape descriptors (Biasotti et al. 2006; Marini et al. 2007).

5.5.6 The RANSAC Approach

A simple and elegant conceptual framework to extract primitive shapes is the random sample consensus (RANSAC) paradigm by Martin A. Fischler and Robert C. Bolles (1981). This technique is capable of extracting a variety of different types of primitive shapes out of unstructured, noisy, sparse, and incomplete data. RANSAC-based algorithms proceed by randomly taking (ideally few) samples to calculate the free parameters of a shape (e.g., of a plane). Then all samples of the input data set "vote," whether they agree with the hypothesis, that is, if they are close to the suggested plane. This procedure is repeated a few times, and the hypoth-esis with the highest acceptance rate wins by "consensus." Samples that agree with the hypothesis are removed from the input data set, and the process starts again. This is basically repeated until no samples remain.

Ruwen Schnabel et al. (2007a,b) have presented a RANSAC-based framework that detects planes, spheres, cylinders, cones, and tori in massive point clouds. They use the detected objects as *shape proxies* that are much more efficient to render than the point cloud (Wahl et al. 2005). The approach by Benkő et al. (2002) refines this idea to process a point cloud by using a hierarchy of tests, that is, a tree where in each node a decision is taken which kind of primitive to choose for the fitting process.

Another interesting refinement of the same idea has been done by Ruwen Schnabel et al. (2007a,b). In addition to the detected shape, they also consider the geometrical neighborhood relations between these shapes and store them in a topology graph. A query graph captures the shape configuration to be detected, for instance, a pair of symmetrically slanted planes describing a gabled roof. These query graph templates represent the knowledge about the shape of an entity. The templates have to be provided by the user, again by making implicit knowledge explicit. The matching of a semantic entity to the data then corresponds to a subgraph matching of the topology graph, which can be carried out automatically.

5.5.7 Symmetry Detection and Instancing

One very active branch in the field of geometry processing is the detection of shape regularities. An obvious problem is instance detection: Aurélien Martinet et al. use generalized moments to detect self-similarities of parts and subparts, which can yield impressive compression rates with triangle soups containing masses of similar objects, for example, tubes and pipes. Another idea is the detection of symmetries, as carried out by Mark Pauly et al. (2008). This can be done on multiple levels, for example, for architectural buildings, or even to detect that the deformed body of an animal is symmetric (Mitra et al. 2007). The latter approach can be further extended to undeform and straighten out a deformed symmetric shape so that it becomes symmetric to a plane (Mintra et al. 2006).

To summarize, structural decomposition proceeds by postulating that a certain type of general regularity or structure exists in a class of shapes. This approach clearly comes to its limits when very specific structures are to be detected, that is, complicated constructions with many parameter interdependencies, like in bridges, buildings, bicycles, or steam engines.

5.5.8 Procedural Descriptions and Generative Surface Reconstruction

The term *generative modeling* reflects a paradigm change in representing shape. The key idea is to identify a shape with a sequence of shape-generating operations, and not just with a list of low-level geometric primitives. This is a true generalization, since static objects are equivalent to constant operations that have no input parameters. The benefit of this approach is that parameter dependencies can be expressed, as the output of one operation may serve as input to another. The practical consequence is that every shape needs to be represented by a computer program, that is, encoded in some form of programming language.

This approach was maybe first realized by John Snyder and James T. Kajiya (1992) with his C-like shape language GENMOD, followed by Conal Elliott's TBAG (1994), and Alberto Paoluzzi's et al.'s (1995) PLaSM. A first general theory of generative shape was developed by Michael Leyton (2001). This academic development was paralleled by the advent of parametric design in high-end CAD systems in the mid-1990s, pioneered by Pro/Engineer (PTC), soon followed by all its competitors. Today, almost all CAD systems have an integrated scripting language that is internally used as a procedural shape representation, such as AutoLISP (AutoCAD), MaxScript (3D Studio Max), and MEL (Maya). It is interesting, though, that there is still no common exchange standard for procedural models, so that even high-end programs can still exchange only "dumb" low-level geometry reliably (Pratt 2004)— a very profitable situation for the CAD industry.

5.5.9 Generative Modeling

With ever-increasing computing power becoming available (Moore's law), generative approaches become more important since they trade processing time for data size. At runtime, the compressed procedural description can be "unfolded" on demand to very quickly produce amounts of information that are several classes of complexity larger than the input data. The advantages of the generative approach are:

- Complex models become manageable through a few high-level parameters (Havemann and Fellner 2004)
- Models are easier to store and to transmit, as only the process itself is described, not the processed data, that is, the end result (Berndt et al. 2005)
- Changeability and reusability of existing solutions to modeling problems can be very much improved (Havemann and Fellner 2007)
- Smaller parameter space can lead to much better results in model-based indexing and retrieval (Fellner and Havemann 2005)

These results were obtained using the *generative modeling language* (GML) originally developed by Sven Havemann (2005). GML is a very simple stack-based programming language, syntactically similar to Adobe PostScript, but with many 3D instead of 2D operators. GML realizes the *stream-of-tokens* concept, where tokens can be either data, which are pushed on an operand stack, or processing instructions, which are executed; so data and programs are expressed in the same formalism. This solves the *code generation* problem, traditionally one of the major obstacles of using generative design in practice: Encoding shape as program code clearly has the greatest flexibility, but it requires coding (programming), which is usually done by humans. But a text editor is not necessarily the best user interface for 3D shape design. The GML syntax greatly facilitates automatic code generation, either in background of an interactive 3D application, or to encode the result of a shape reconstruction process. The ambitious goal of GML is to serve as a common exchange format for all kinds of procedural models, as a smallest common denominator, very much like triangles are for surface approximations.

5.5.10 Generative Shape Reconstruction

The first method to create generative 3D models from point clouds was presented by Ravi Ramamoorthi and James Arvo (1999). They use the GENMOD language to construct a hierarchy of generative shape templates. The root of the hierarchy describes the overall object shape only roughly with one primitive object; the templates in child nodes subsequently refine the parent shape. The shape templates in each node are basically just parametric surface patches, that is, functions $\mathcal{R}^2 \to \mathcal{R}^3$. The resulting shape is parametric in the sense that the shape can be regenerated in different ways. The drawback of the approach is that not much of the semantic structure is preserved: a coffee mug, a banana, and a candle holder are all treated basically the same way.

5.5.11   Shape Grammars

Generative design was used much earlier in theoretical architecture than in computer science. Shape grammars were introduced by George Stiny and James Gips as early as 1971 (Stiny and Gips 1972). Recently, new interest in shape grammars was triggered by Pascal Muller et al. (2006), who have introduced *CGAShape*. The basic idea is simple: A replacement rule specifies how a box carrying a specific symbol is split into smaller boxes carrying other symbols. Sizes can also be relative so that a box can be split, for example, along the *x*-axis into four boxes, the inner ones twice as wide as the outer ones. Therefore, such shape grammars are also called *split grammars*. Many variations of this basic scheme exist; for a survey on shape grammars, refer to Ozkar and Kotsopoulos (2008).

This idea has proved very useful especially in the area of urban reconstruction (Watson and Wonka 2008). Based on input data of geographical information systems (GIS), such as building footprints, population density maps, street maps, and so on, complete virtual cities can be generated fully automatically. Müller et al. obtained a "statistically correct" reconstruction of ancient Pompeji by Roman building styles encoded in a shape grammar.

For reverse engineering purposes, the split grammar approach can also be combined with image-based reconstruction techniques (Müller et al. 2007). Using *mutual information*, the reconstruction algorithm detects symmetries and repetitions, and thus can extract horizontal/vertical split lines in rectified facade images. This yields the elementary building blocks of an *irreducible façade*, for each of which an appropriate 3D replacement is identified in a database. Although the resulting facade is 3D, the reconstruction process is performed in 2D.

5.6   EXAMPLES OF 3D INFORMATION EXTRACTION

To illustrate the process of semantic enrichment, we present results from two ongoing research projects, CityFIT and 3D-COFORM.

5.6.1   Template-Based Facade Reconstruction in CityFIT

Currently, the state-of-the-art for automatically generated city models are basically just extruded ground polygons with roofs. Still missing are detailed 3D models of facades, which are indispensable for realistic roadside walkthroughs, for example, in car navigation systems, or for services like Google Earth or Microsoft VirtualEarth. The goal of the CityFIT project is to reconstruct fully automatically 80% of the facades in the city of Graz, Austria. Graz is an especially challenging example since many building styles coexist—for instance, there are highly decorated neoclassical facades (*Gründerzeit* style) in the downtown area. Essentially, the whole development of European architecture has left its traces in the city.

5.6.2   Facade Templates through Inductive Reasoning

The main idea of CityFIT is to turn the general implicit architectural knowledge about facades into explicit knowledge, based on both architectural theory and empirical evidence. To achieve this, it combines inductive reasoning with statistical inference. CityFIT uses the shape grammar concepts from CGA-Shape (Muller et al. 2006), but they are integrated into a procedural formalism, the GML: for each individual façade, one GML procedure is generated.

The goal is not to reconstruct only individual facades, but to identify general patterns in a larger set of reconstructed facades. This is possible only through the extensive amount of input data containing many different facade styles.

A floor of one building might be of the form *aba*, meaning that the center window is different from the left and right windows. Another building might have two equal center windows, resulting in *abba*. When other buildings of forms *abbba* and *abbbba* are found (see Figure 5.2), this can be generalized to the pattern *ab*a*, meaning "any number of center windows." This can be further generalized in a hierarchical way: A complicated facade of the form *cdeffffedc* can still be understood as *ab*a′*, where *a* is replaced by *cde*, and *a′ = edc* is the inversion. By systematically searching for patterns like repetition, symmetry, hierarchical replacement, and so on in facade reconstructions, general *facade templates* can be obtained by statistical inference. The expectation is that these facade templates correspond to characteristic architectural styles. This is inductive reasoning in the sense that a general principle is identified in a set of concrete observations.

5.6.3   Emerging Trend: Combination of Data with Programs

The immediate benefit on the technical level is that the amount of information (i.e., the number of bits) required to encode, store, and transmit the facades of a whole

Figure 5.2. Semantic enrichment of a facade. The CityFIT workflow starts with the massive acquisition of street-side images and laser scans (LIDAR), from which true orthophotos are produced. Facade elements that occur repeatedly are detected, resulting in a set of labeled boxes. Each box is considered a "word" generated by a grammar, in this case a *shape grammar*. With the appropriate grammar rules, the facade and its semantics can be compactly described.

city is drastically reduced: a set of rules like $\{ab^4a'; a \to cdef\}$ can be shorter by whole orders of complexity than the unfolded information *cdefbbbbfedc*. This shows that one important trend in multimedia information extraction, the striving for ever more compact data descriptions (including, e.g., data compression techniques), can in fact be understood as a trend to replace *data* by the combination of *data + processing instructions*.

5.6.4   Shape Reconstructions in Cultural Heritage: 3D-COFORM

Especially in the field of cultural heritage, the interplay of content and metadata, as well as *paradata*, is extremely complex and difficult to model. At the same time, it is of prime importance in order to assess the provenance and authenticity of a digital 3D data set. A useful conceptual basis to meet these requirements in this domain are *The London Charter* (TLC) (Beacham et al. 2006) and the *Conceptual Reference Model* of the International Committee for Documentation of the International Council of Museums (CIDOC-CRM) (Crofts et al. 2003). The TLC introduces the notion of *intellectual transparency*, which reflects the necessity of maintaining the distinction between measurement (wall with measured height) and interpretation (wall inferred from foundation wall, height is only "educated guess"). As a consequence, it prescribes collecting *paradata* describing the provenance and the processing history throughout the work flow.

5.6.5   Sustainable Semantics in Cultural Heritage

The Conceptual Reference Model CIDOC-CRM is an emerging standard for semantic networks in Cultural Heritage. It is an ontology that provides (in version 5.0) 90 entity types (actor, place, time-span, man-made object, etc.) and 148 property types (participated in, performed, has created, etc.) to describe relations between pairs of entities. The semantic network can be represented, for example, as list of resource description framework (RDF)-triplets, each RDF triplet corresponding to one edge of the network. The great value of CIDOC-CRM is that it provides a standard way of storing the results of semantic enrichment algorithms. As mentioned before, sustainability is a great issue there: Where to store the semantics? Often, ad hoc or very domain-dependent methods are used to encode the results of shape detection, structural decomposition, or reverse engineering.

CIDOC-CRM is capable of describing the fact that a photograph exists of Churchill taking part in the Crimea Conference 1945, which resulted in the creation of the Yalta agreement:

E39 Actor:
  Churchill
	P11 participated in	E07 Activity:
		  Crimea Conference

E65 Creation:
  ID-2f2f
	P86 falls within	E07 Activity:
		  Crimea Conference

E65 Creation:
  ID-2f2f
	P94 has created	E31 Document:
		  Yalta Agreement

E07 Activity:
  Crimea Conference
	P67 is referred to by	E38 Image:
		  ID-d034

5.6.6 Semantic Enrichment by Matching of Generative Shape Templates

One possibility to answer questions like "How many of our models are amphorae?" or "Which is the amphora with the largest diameter?" is to use a shape template, that is, a generative model (Section 5.2) of a standard amphora. All models in the database are compared against this standard model. For those that match, the deviation between model and template is minimized by a numeric fitting procedure that adjusts the template parameters. This fact is entered to the semantic network, thus establishing a connection between the (unique) ideal amphora, which is an abstract *E28 conceptual object*, and the concrete 3D model. Thus, all amphorae can be found using a simple database query on the semantic network. Since model parameters can be stored as well (*E54 Dimension*), the amphora with the largest diameter can also be identified. The shape template should therefore be created by a domain expert who knows the essential shape parameters.

5.6.7 Fitting a Generative Model

The goal is not only to identify object types, but also part-of relations and compound objects, including their substructures. In this context, a generative model can simply be regarded as an algorithm that is started via a function call with suitable parameters. These parameters have a semantic meaning and have to be estimated. Our parameter estimation is based on minimizing an error function:

$$f(x) = \sum_{i=1}^{n} \psi(d(\mathrm{M}(x), p_i)) = \min_x.$$

In this equation the input data set is represented by a point cloud $p_1, \ldots, p_n$ (e.g., from a laser scan). The shape template is described by an algorithm M. With this data, the parameter estimation determines some instance parameters x so that as many points as possible are close to the corresponding model instance $\mathrm{M}(x)$; that is, the sum of Euclidean distances d between a point and a model instance is minimal.

In order to eliminate a disproportionate effect of outlying points, an additional weighting function ψ is used. Weighting functions and generalized maximum likelihood estimators (Zhang 1997) are well known in the context of statistics and computer vision. They are of big importance in order to overcome the sensitivity to outliers. A commonly used weighting function is $\psi(x) = x^2$, which results in nonlinear least squares fitting. As the squares of the distances are used, outlying points have a disproportionate effect on the fit. Even worse, if *one* model shall be fitted to a data set, least squares methods implicitly assume that the entire set of data can be interpreted by *one* parameter vector. Multiple instances of a model in one data set cannot be handled this way.

A Gaussian weighting function

$$\psi(x) = 1 - \exp(-x^2 / \sigma^2),$$

is the basis of the so-called *decreasing exponential fitting*, which can handle outlying points and multiple model instances. The resulting minimization process can be

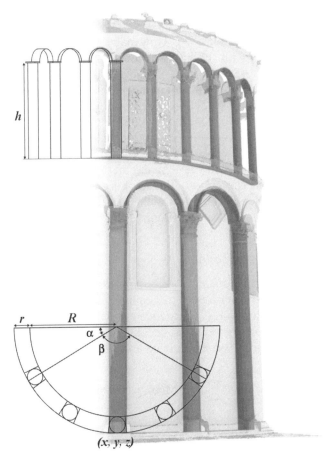

Figure 5.3. This illustration shows a laser scan of the Pisa Cathedral and two fitted, generative models: an upper and a lower arcade. The arcades are rendered with a color coding according to their distance to the laser scan. This fitting result is blended with the shape template's construction plan.

interpreted geometrically. If σ tends to zero, the globally best solution, respectively, the global minimum of the error function is reached, if the maximum number of points have distance zero to the model to fit; for example, the model parameters will be determined so that most of the input data points belong to the model's surface. This characteristic behavior of this parameter estimation technique is comparable to the RANSAC-based hypothesis testing.

Figure 5.3 shows an example data set, a point cloud of the Cathedral in Pisa. It was generated by the Visual Computing Laboratory at the Institute of Information Science and Technologies (ISTI) of the Italian National Research Council (CNR). Just like the whole building, the apse of the Duomo consists of many similar columns in typical Romanesque style. The shape template is a compound shape, an arcade, with nine free parameters. Compared with detecting individual columns and arches, the compound shape has the great advantage that it encodes prior knowledge about regularities: All columns and all arches are fitted simultaneously, which makes the arcade more robust against noise. The whole algorithm does not need any user interaction. It is able to create an initial rough guess, and converges to the global minimum with a precision in the scale of millimeters. Technical details are described in "Semantic Fitting and Reconstruction" (Ullrich and Fellner 2007; Ullrich et al. 2008).

5.7 CONCLUSION

Much remains to be done in order to make 3D models really useful. Adding semantics to shapes is an important, if not the vital, step toward the great vision of *visual computing*: To not only capture reality by sampling the world with 2D and 3D acquisition devices, but also to represent reality within a computer in a meaningful, ideally even in an *editable* form. This will also be the key to interacting with the real world in more meaningful ways: Today computers have left the office and are becoming part of the outside world, in particular of *our view* of the outside world, with mobile phones today and augmented reality tomorrow.

But pervasive and ubiquitous computing, that is, computers everywhere, are useless as long as computers have such a limited understanding of the 3D environment. The information theoretic approach, which is still prevalent in the 3D community, interprets the world as a *signal*. Improving the world model then only means to increase the sampling density or the signal to noise ratio. This view is clearly naive and insufficient, since it leads only to quantitative improvements.

Qualitative leaps can only be expected if the many open problems that were mentioned in this chapter are solved, and the semantic gap is eventually closed in a reliable and sustainable way, using commonly agreed standards and procedures.

CHAPTER 6

A DATA-DRIVEN MEANINGFUL REPRESENTATION OF EMOTIONAL FACIAL EXPRESSIONS

NICOLAS STOIBER, GASPARD BRETON, and RENAUD SEGUIER

6.1 INTRODUCTION

Communication between two or more human beings is a complicated phenomenon we have not yet been able to fully understand. Its richness comes mainly from the multiple communication channels that help transmit the sense, the context, or the tone of a message. While some of these channels explicitly deliver the content of a message, other *nonverbal* communication channels are unconsciously accounted for by the human brain to interpret this message. It seems crucial, when trying to extract meaningful information from human speeches or behaviors, to consider the content of the speech and the nonverbal information jointly (refer to Chapter 16 for more detail on human behavior analysis).

Facial expressions are a well-known example of nonverbal communication. They enrich the speech and are often compared with the reflection of a person's inner emotional state and personality. They are also believed to play an important role in social interactions, as they give clues to a speaker's state of mind and therefore help the communication partner to sense the tone of a speech, or the meaning of a particular behavior (Pelachaud et al. 1996).

Specialists often distinguish between three categories of facial expressions: visemes, conversational displays, and emotional expressions. The visemes are the labial movements corresponding to the production of speech, and do not carry any particular information. Conversational displays are facial movements that augment the message delivered by the speech. They can be used to confirm the

Multimedia Information Extraction: Advances in Video, Audio, and Imagery Analysis for Search, Data Mining, Surveillance, and Authoring, First Edition. Edited by Mark T. Maybury.
© 2012 IEEE Computer Society. Published 2012 by John Wiley & Sons, Inc.

verbal information (nodding while saying "yes") or to emphasize a particular word or sentence (raising the eyebrows usually indicates that this part of the speech is important). Finally, emotional facial expressions are related to the person's emotional state. Under this label, we consider expressions of moods (joy and sadness) as well as spontaneous affects (surprise and disgust).

Chapters 18 and 19 elaborate on the importance of adding affective information to the description of multimedia data. Similarly in the present chapter, we focus exclusively on *emotional* facial expressions. We believe that they represent the most interesting type of nonverbal facial communication. If conversational displays are important to accentuate and reinforce the message delivered by the speech, emotional expressions bring additional information that can considerably affect the interpretation of the message and solve ambiguities. For instance, the sentence "*you have been a big help today*" may be interpreted differently if pronounced with a neutral face (serious message) or a joyful one (sarcasm). Bates also emphasized the role of emotional facial expressions when trying to reproduce realistic human behaviors with virtual characters (Bates 1994). The use of emoticons in emails and instant messaging programs further proves that we are naturally inclined to use facial expressions to transmit or extract information.

While modern speech recognition systems have exhibited impressive performance in commercial applications, the reliable extraction of meaningful information from facial expressions is not yet a reality. An important aspect in that matter is the representation of this information. State-of-the-art computer vision algorithms are doing a good job at detecting and tracking facial features. Some of them are even capable of identifying specific patterns (smile detection in modern digital cameras). Yet we face an issue already identified in Chapter 5 for shape extraction techniques: these algorithms only manipulate low-level information (geometrical data) and do not extract more abstract information related to the semantics of this data. Consequently, several studies have proposed associating facial deformation data with higher-level representations of the emotional content of facial expressions. In practical applications, this tendency is illustrated by the presence of subjective classes or categories in expression classification tasks, or the use of psychological models of human emotion in analysis and synthesis tasks.

The latter association from low-level data and more abstract emotional concepts enables rich and intuitive information extraction from expressive faces. However, until now, the high-level representations have been exclusively subjective, relying on theoretical considerations and psychological studies. They obviously introduce a bias in their association with potentially incompatible real-world facial deformation data. This may ultimately lead to annoying distortions in the concerned extraction and synthesis systems.

The successful extraction of emotional facial expressions—and its reuse—requires an adapted high-level representation for this information. In this chapter, we will see that it is possible to automatically construct an objective representation space for emotional facial expressions. The structure of the representation naturally emerges from the unsupervised analysis of a rich facial expression database. The resulting representation space thus keeps a strong link with the low-level data, and yet presents a simple and intuitive structure ideal for higher-level processing, such as expression recognition and synthesis.

6.2 RELATED WORK AND CONTRIBUTION

6.2.1 Related Work

From a certain point of view, many extraction tasks can be viewed as two-level procedures. The first level is the detection level, or "lower level," where specific features of interests are extracted from the raw data and converted into an application-specific representation. This process might involve removing the noise and redundancies, and removing unwanted context dependencies. The second level is the interpretation level, or "higher-level," where meaningful, valuable information is extracted from the low-level features. Most facial analysis systems can be segmented that way. The lower-level generally consists in tracking and modeling specific facial features that efficiently describe facial configurations. The most intuitive features are the remarkable elements of the face, such as the eyes, the nose, and the mouth. Typical tracking systems detect the positions and shapes of these elements to register the configuration of a face. This raw geometric information can be converted into standardized formats of facial motion description. The Facial Action Coding System (FACS) for instance, developed by Ekman and Friesen (1978), describes facial expressions as a combination of localized unitary movements (Tian et al. 2001). A similar system has later been developed for the MPEG-4 compression standard (Eleftheriadis and Puri 1998). Under one of these formalisms, the captured motion can be easily compared with or retargeted to other faces (Curio et al. 2006, Tsapatsoulis et al. 2002).

Often, linear dimensionality reduction schemes based on principal component analysis (PCA) are used to simplify the parameter set and remove the description redundancy. Moreover, several studies have rightly pointed out that the deformation of the skin caused by expressive motion is a reliable source of information when analyzing moving faces. Schemes like active appearance models (AAM [Cootes et al. 1998]) combine the extraction of geometric and textural information from facial images to improve the robustness of image analysis systems. Facial analysis approaches based on this type of techniques (Chuang et al. 2002; Du and Lin 2002), although more computationally intensive, obtained improved tracking performances. The most recent works have introduced the use of nonlinear dimensionality reduction techniques to further simplify the data description space (Chang et al. 2004; Zhao et al. 2005). These methods generally provide a very compact, low dimensional representation of the training data, but the non-linear reduction generally leads to important distortions when analyzing new, unknown data. For many applications, linear reduction techniques usually present better generalization abilities.

By using any of the techniques mentioned above, we ultimately produce a reduced set of parameters that describes a certain range of facial configurations. This parameter space, however, does not have any semantic meaning. To extract valuable high-level information, the data has to be interpreted. Most of the research that has tackled this question have proposed to associate the low-level data with higher-level models of human emotion.

One of the most successful study on emotional facial expressions was presented by Ekman et al. (2002), and Ekman (1982). Based on cross-cultural psychological research, Ekman identified a set of universal facial expressions (anger, disgust, fear, joy, sadness, and surprise) that can be identified on the face of any human being. As indicated by Pantić and Rothkrantz (2000), this supposedly universal expression set forms an attractive basis for most of the automatic classification systems. In Essa and Pentland (1997), Yacoob and Davis (1996), and Zhao et al. (2005), trained systems are able to classify unknown expressive faces into one of Ekman's categories. Most of early facial animation systems also featured the six universal expression categories for the portrayal of emotional states.

This *categorial* approach has practical advantages, but clearly does not correctly encompass the diversity of emotional facial expressions. In ordinary human interactions, facial expressions seldom display such exaggerated emotions. The majority of feelings are more differentiated, or "blended." The concept of emotional intensity also needs to be considered, as human faces exhibit mostly low- to mid-range facial deformations. Such natural expressions cannot easily be classified into the well-defined classes of categorial emotion models. Thus, other representations of human emotion on faces have been proposed, known as *dimensional* approaches. Emotions are not classified into discrete categories anymore, but are associated to a point in a continuous emotional space. Chang et al. (2006), Chang, Hu, and Turk (2004), Du (2007), and Du and Lin (2002) chose to quantify the closeness of a given facial expression to the stereotypical categories of Ekmanian classification. Facial expressions are then described as a weighted blending of pure emotions. Other dimensional models exhibit the concept of emotion intensity more explicitly. Whissell (1989) and Cowie et al. (2000) organize human emotions around two continuous axes, one (*activation*) representing the degree of arousal of the emotion intensity and the other one (*evaluation* or *valence*) the positive or negative nature of the feeling. Mehrabian (1996) adds a social dimension to his model: the *dominance*, which reflects the subject's dominant or submissive relation with the environment. These representation have been used in several extraction, analysis, and synthesis applications (Albrecht et al. 2005; Du et al. 2007; Zhang et al. 2007). Other psychologists pointed out that the organization of human emotion may not be linear, but cyclic: Schlosberg (1952) and Plutchik (2001) have constructed 2D disk-shaped space of human emotions that have been used successfully in a few studies (Tsapatsoulis et al. 2001).

Using high-level representation of the emotions associated with facial expressions provides an interpretation of facial expressions based on understandable, intuitive emotional concepts. This structure is ideal for the extraction of valuable information from low-level data, and its reuse in end applications like expression recognition, user-behaviour modeling or intuitive facial animation. A drawback of using one of the structures cited above is that they are theoretical. They where constructed based on psychological consideration, without any concern for actual morphological data. It is thus not guaranteed that the topology of the emotion model matches the one of the facial low-level parameters space (whether MPEG-4, FACS, or AAM). In particular, we note that close feelings in the emotional spaces may correspond to completely different parameter values in the facial parameter space. This is illustrated in the emotional space used in Du et al. (2007) in which the representatives of "Anger" and "Fear," as well as "Sadness" and "Disgust," share almost the same emotional coordinates, whereas they correspond to very different facial configuration parameters (the reciprocal problem exists as well). The

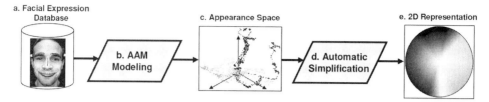

Figure 6.1. Overview of the representation generation system.

construction of a link between incompatible high- and low-level parameter spaces may lead to important distortions in the performances of the final applications.

6.2.2   A Novel Approach

We propose a novel approach that reconciles the simplicity and interpretability of emotion models and the rigor of real-world data. Based on the analysis of a facial expression database we automatically generate a simple and intuitive representation space that can be used to efficiently describe the expressional state of a face. Our system relies on the construction of an *appearance space*. The appearance space is the low-level description of the information contained in our facial expression database (Figure 6.1a). Using a modeling scheme based on AAM (Figure 6.1b), we obtain the appearance space (Figure 6.1c) in which the samples of the database can be efficiently analyzed. The specific structure of the appearance space will allow us to automatically design a simpler, intuitive representation space (Figure 6.1e) that possesses the qualities and interpretability of formerly used emotion models. The remaining of this chapter will describe how the appearance space is constructed (Section 3), how an optimal representation can be derived from the appearance space (Section 4), and finally practical facial analysis and synthesis applications will be presented (Section 5).

6.3   CONSTRUCTION OF AN APPEARANCE SPACE

In this section, we describe the construction of the appearance space using AAM. We then identify interesting properties we will take advantage of to extract valuable information about facial expressions. The starting point is the acquisition of sequences of images of an actor performing facial expressions. The database is meant to contain an important quantity of natural expressions, both extreme and subtle, categorical, and mixed. A crucial aspect of the analysis is that the captured expressions do not carry any emotional label. More generally, all database analysis and generating processes are completely unsupervised. The facial images, associated with additional geometrical data, will allow us to model the deformation of the face according to a scheme used in AAM (Cootes et al. 1998). This procedure delivers a reduced set of N_a parameters ($N_a \approx 30$) which represent the principal variation patterns observed on the face (refer to Section 3.2 for more details). Every facial expression can be projected onto this N_a-dimensional parameter space (Figure 6.1c) that will from now on be referred as the appearance space. Note that this process

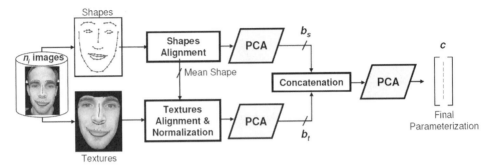

Figure 6.2. The AAM modeling stage.

is invertible: it is always possible to transform any N_a-dimensional point of the appearance space back to a facial configuration, and thus synthesize the corresponding facial expression.

6.3.1 AAMs

Active appearance models have been introduced as a computer vision scheme by Cootes et al. (1998). They include a modeling step that allows parameterizing the observable appearance modifications of a deformable object. The purpose is to facilitate the tracking of a similar object in an image by the use of the obtained parameterization. In this article, we focus on the modeling phase (Figure 6.2).

The modeling procedure starts with a database of *ni* images of the considered object, displaying the appearance modifications the object can be subject to. Several remarkable points are manually or automatically annotated on the object for each image of the database. Together, they form the object's *shape*. The pixel intensities contained in the area spanned by the shape is called the *texture*. In the database, the object is presented with varying shapes and textures. The role of the model is to identify the principal variation eigenmodes of the shape and the texture of the object when deformations occur. These variation modes then serve as an efficient parameter set to describe the object's appearance changes.

To detect the variation modes, the modeling uses PCA for both the shape and the texture. The shape of the *i*th element of the database is a collection of N_s-dimensional points ($N_s = 2$ or 3), and its texture is generally a collection of pixel values, but both can be treated as vectors $\mathbf{s}^i$ and $\mathbf{t}^i$ and feed the PCA routine:

$$\mathbf{s}^i = \overline{\mathbf{s}} + \mathbf{\Phi}_s \times \mathbf{b}_s^i$$
$$\mathbf{t}^i = \overline{\mathbf{t}} + \mathbf{\Phi}_t \times \mathbf{b}_t^i.$$

where $\overline{\mathbf{s}}$ and $\overline{\mathbf{t}}$ are the database mean shape and texture, $\mathbf{\Phi}_s$ and $\mathbf{\Phi}_t$ the matrices formed by the PCA eigenvectors, and $\mathbf{b}_s^i$ and $\mathbf{b}_t^i$ are the decomposition of $\mathbf{s}^i$ and $\mathbf{t}^i$ on the identified eigenmodes. A third PCA is usually performed on the mixed vector $\mathbf{b}^i = \left(\mathbf{b}_s^i \middle| \mathbf{b}_t^i\right)$:

$$\mathbf{b}^i = \mathbf{\Phi} \times \mathbf{c}^i,$$

where $\mathbf{\Phi}$ is the matrix formed by the eigenvectors. Its role is to identify the correlations between shape variation $\mathbf{b}_s^i$ and texture variation $\mathbf{b}_t^i$ and take advantage of them to reduce the size of the final parameter vector $\mathbf{c}^i$. The vector $\mathbf{c}^i$ represents the final parameterization of the ith element of the database. It contains the contribution of the identified eigenmodes of both shape and texture for this element. The variation modes $\mathbf{\Phi}_s$, $\mathbf{\Phi}_t$, and $\mathbf{\Phi}$ are then used to depict any appearance change of the modeled object within the scope of the database.

In this study, we use the previous modeling scheme applied to deforming faces. The AAM $\mathbf{c}$-parameter space is very interesting for facial parameterization because it only models the perceptible variations of the face, and not the underlying mechanisms causing these deformations. Therefore, the appearance space forms a compact and continuous space, with no incoherencies (zones of the parameter space that would correspond to unnatural facial configurations).

6.3.2 Analysis of the Appearance Space

The idea of simplifying the appearance space emerged when observing how the samples from the human database were distributed throughout this space. Obviously, the samples cannot be visualized as N_a-dimensional points, but we can visualize them as 3D points by drawing their three most important principal components. As we can see on Figures 6.3 and 6.4, the point cloud of the database samples in the appearance space has an interesting structure: the neutral facial expressions are located at the center of the cloud while highly expressive faces are located on the edges of the cloud. Intermediate expressions are located in the continuous space between neutral and extreme expressions. This structure is not specific to the appearance model used here, and has been identified in other studies (Hu et al. 2004a, b; Shan et al. 2005). To highlight the peculiarity of the structure on the figure, the database samples have been manually colored according to their resemblance to one of Ekman's expressions (groups E_1–E_6 on Figure 6.3). It is important to note, however,

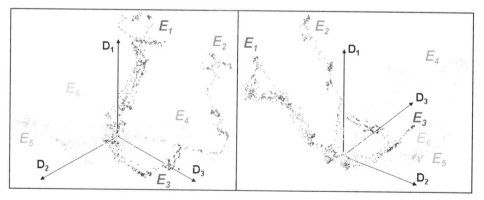

Figure 6.3. Two different views of the database samples distribution in the appearance space ($\approx$5000 samples). Only the first three dimensions D_1, D_2, and D_3 of the appearance space are drawn. The sample coloring is based on an emotional label subjectively assigned to each facial expression (blue = sadness, cyan = joy, green = surprise, yellow = fear, red = anger, and magenta = disgust).

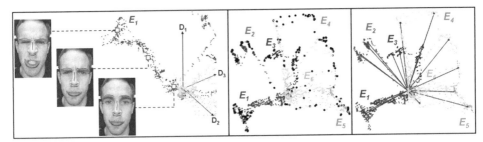

Figure 6.4. Characteristics of the appearance space. *Left:* The central part of the appearance space is occupied by neutral expressions. The other expressions of varying intensities are concentrated on dominant directions in space. Extreme expressions are located on the edge of the point cloud. *Middle:* Extreme expressions are detected as the convex hull points (black dots). *Right:* The dominant directions (black lines) are identified as the segment between the neutral expression and a few selected extreme points.

that this subjective labeling was not used in the modeling process, but only for the convenience of the display.

We observe that the point cloud possesses a few dominant directions, which are identified as the segments separating the neutral expression and the extreme ones. The natural expressions are distributed either along these directions to form a given expression at different intensity levels, or between these directions to form transitional expressions between the dominant ones. This structure naturally associates the low-level data with a semantic meaning. However, the high dimensionality of the appearance space is somewhat unpractical for navigation and interpretation. It is tempting to consider the topology spanned by the dominant directions in the appearance space and try to reorganize it in a more straightforward form in order to allow intuitive manipulation of the data. This process will be depicted in the next section.

6.4 SIMPLIFICATION OF THE APPEARANCE SPACE

The appearance space described in the previous section reveals the presence of dominant directions subject to interesting interpretation properties, but its high dimensionality complicates the intuitive manipulation of the corresponding facial information. We have chosen to organize the space spanned by the dominant directions of the appearance space on a comparable structure in a lower dimensional space: a 2D disk. The relation between these two spaces will be described following three sequential operations:

- *Dominant Directions Detection* (Section 4.1): The first step towars warping a part of the appearance space on a simpler 2D space is to detect the dominant high dimensional directions forming the region of interest in the appearance space. This process is illustrated on Figure 6.4.
- *Expression Space Embedding* (Section 4.2): The purpose of this process is to find a distribution of the identified dominant directions on a 2D space that satisfies an appropriate optimization criterion (see Figure 6.5).

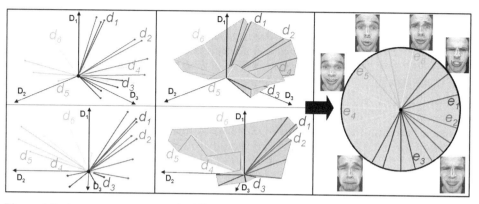

Figure 6.5. Appearance space embedding on a 2D disk. *Left top and bottom:* Two views of the detected dominant directions in the appearance space (only the first three dimensions D_1, D_2, and D_3 are drawn). *Middle top and bottom:* Two views of the path (gray surface) determined by the traveling salesman optimization routine. *Right:* Embedding of the dominant directions on a 2D disk.

- *Mapping Construction* (Section 4.3): The latter embedding determines only a one-to-one discrete link between the dominant directions and their embedded versions. The last operation uses this correspondence as a basis to construct a dense, analytical mapping between the 2D representation and the appearance space.

6.4.1   Dominant Directions Detection

We have defined the dominant directions as the segment between the neutral expression and the extreme expressions in the human database. The database sample representing the neutral expression can be easily designated manually. On the other hand, the extreme expressions have to be objectively and automatically chosen so that the most significant part of the appearance space is encompassed in the 2D space. In that sense, the most appropriate candidates are the samples located on the convex hull of the sample cloud. The hull points detected by a hull detection process at high dimensionalities usually contain important spatial redundancy, as the convex hull intersects the sample cloud at several neighboring points. These neighboring points, however, represent one single dominant direction of the database distribution. They have to be merged into a single representative hull sample. This can be achieved by running a mean-shift algorithm on the set of detected hull points, so that groups of neighboring samples are merged into one mean-shift mode while isolated hull samples remain unchanged (Figure 6.4).

6.4.2   Expression Space Embedding

Figures 6.4 and 6.5 present a symbolic 3D view of the detected dominant directions, but in reality these directions are of higher dimension. Our purpose now is to warp these directions onto a 2D disk. For this operation, we regard the dominant directions as the segments of unit length of a N_a-dimensional hypersphere centered on the neutral expression sample. The goal of the embedding is to distribute a set of directions on a disk (2D hypersphere), so that each dominant direction $\mathbf{d_i}$ in the appearance space correspond to one 2D direction $\mathbf{e_i}$ on the disk, and the distortion between the two directions distributions is minimized. Simply put, when n_d dominant directions $\mathbf{d_i}$, $i \in \{1, \dots, n_d\}$ have been identified in the appearance space, we want to find a set of n_d 2D directions $\mathbf{e_i}$, $i \in \{1, \dots, n_d\}$ distributed on the disk that represent the N_a-dimensional direction as "well" as possible. The distortion measure we use is based on the angular distance between the dominant directions.

A traditional 2D embedding scheme would require that the angular distribution between the 2D embedded directions is similar to the original angular distribution in the appearance space:

$$\Theta^{i,j} = \alpha.\theta^{i,j}, \text{ for all } (i, j) \in \{1, \dots, n_d\}^2$$

$$\text{with } \Theta^{i,j} = \arccos(\mathbf{d_i} \cdot \mathbf{d_j})$$

$$\text{and } \theta^{i,j} = \arccos(\mathbf{e_i} \cdot \mathbf{e_j}).$$

At this point, it is essential to note that the 2D case that we consider is degenerate. The set of directions we want to scatter on the 2D disk is actually 1D (parameterized by the direction angle). The direct consequence of this is that the embedded directions of a 1D embedding are *ordered*. A given direction $\mathbf{e_i}$ only has two direct neighbors, and no direct adjacency with the other directions. The relations between one direction and the ones that are not its direct neighbors are therefore irrelevant and should not be considered. The embedding objective becomes:

$$\Theta^{i,j} = \alpha.\theta^{i,j}, \text{ for all } (i, j) \in \Omega$$

$$\Omega = \{(i, j) | \mathbf{e_i} \text{ and } \mathbf{e_j} \text{ are neighbors}\}.$$

We see that the nature of the present embedding problem differs from the traditional formulation: the challenge here is not to compute the values of the $\theta_{i,j}$, but to determine which directions will actually be neighbors once embedded. Thus, instead of turning to traditional embedding methods (like MDS, Isomap, or LLE), we have to pose the optimization problem in a different way: when running along the 1D circle, we are supposed to pass by each of the embedded directions in a given order, forming a *path* through the directions $\{\mathbf{e^{i_1}}, \mathbf{e^{i_1}}, \dots, \mathbf{e^{i_k}}\}$. The idea is to find such a path $\{\mathbf{d^{i_1}}, \mathbf{d^{i_1}}, \dots, \mathbf{d^{i_k}}\}$ in the high dimensional hypersphere that travels through each dominant directions exactly once, and meanwhile minimizes the angular distance accumulated during the travel (which we identify as the overall distortion of the path):

$$\text{distortion} = \sum_{k=1}^{n_d} \Theta^{i_k, i_{k+1}}$$

$$\text{where } i_{n_d+1} = i_1.$$

Expressed in these terms, we recognize the well-known traveling salesman optimization problem (TSP). The TSP is a NP-complete problem whose purpose is to determine the shortest path running through a set of cities, when the distance between them is known. By replacing the cities by the N_a-dimensional directions and the intercity distance by the interdirection angle, we can solve our specific optimization task by using any generic method solving the traveling salesman problem. Because of the NP nature of the TSP, the optimization task becomes excessively costly when the number of detected directions grows. In this study, we used such a stochastic method based on simulated annealing. Our experiments showed that with a reasonable number of directions, the TSP optimization always reaches a stable possibly optimal solution in a reasonable time (less than 2 minutes for 30 directions). Once solved, the TSP optimization delivers the sequence of directions we have to run through to minimize the overall distortion. The directions are then embedded on the circle following the order of the delivered sequence. The result of the embedding on the 2D circle can be seen on Figure 6.5.

6.4.3 Mapping Construction

The purpose of the mapping is to bind analytically the 2D representation and the appearance space based on the discrete correspondence established between the directions in both spaces (see Section 4.2). Many fitting scheme can be considered for this purpose, like traditional regression methods (linear, polynomial, etc.). Another interesting option is the thin plate spline (TPS) approximation, which can be viewed as an extension of traditional 1D splines (Bookstein 1989). The attractive characteristic of TPS is to present a tradeoff between the accuracy of interpolation of the known samples and the smoothness of the mapping. Here, due to the local coherence of the appearance space, an exact interpolation of the samples is not necessarily relevant. With a TPS mapping, we allow a limited interpolation error in order to accentuate the smoothness of the mapping.

6.4.4 Results

We mentioned in the introduction that contrary to previous approaches, the new facial expressions representation does not rely on a theoretical emotional space like Cowie's activation–evaluation space or Plutchik's emotion wheel (Cowie et al. 2000; Plutchik 2001). It is interesting to observe that if we segment our final disk-shaped space according to the type of emotional expression that each area produces (based on Ekman's six fundamental expressions), we obtain the formulation of a *morphology-based* emotional space (Figure 6.6, left). The difference with previous emotional spaces is that this one is derived from actual facial deformation data, and not from theoretical considerations. The disk-based structure, with the emotion type as the rotational parameter and the emotion intensity as the radial one, reminds us particularly of Plutchik's emotion wheel (Figure 6.6, right). Plutchik formalized the relationships between eight primary emotions according to his psychoevolutionary theory on adaptive biological processes. We observe that the closeness identified by Plutchik between some of the basic emotions still holds from the morphological point of view. The triplet Anger–Disgust–Sadness is common to both representations, as well as the proximity of Surprise and Fear. Obviously, we do not claim to offer a new formal description of human emotions, but our data-driven expression space enriches the purely theoretical models with considerations on the mechanical aspect of facial expressions. Moreover, since it originates from facial

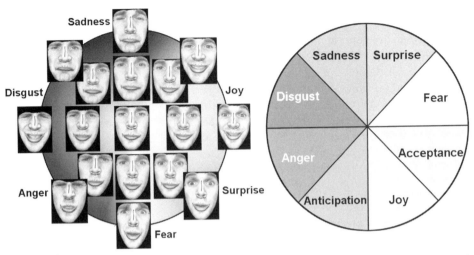

Figure 6.6. Comparison between emotion model and our data-based representation. *Left:* Interpretation of the expressions' semantic of our data-driven representation. *Right:* The relations between eight basic emotions according to Plutchik's (2001) theory.

motion data, it can more efficiently be associated with low-level data and avoid the typical distortions of previous representations (in which close representations would correspond to very different expressions, and vice versa). The next section will illustrate the use of the 2D intuitive representation for facial analysis and synthesis tasks.

6.5   APPLICATIONS

Figure 6.7 displays an example of facial analysis based on our simplified expression space. Any facial configuration can be captured and projected on the 2D representation. The location on that representation provides the system with valuable information, easy to interpret and exploit. Obviously, stereotypical expressions represented in the database are well localized in that space, but it is important to note that even unseen, mixed facial expressions that were not included in the database are recovered as well. This generalization capacity is linked to the AAM modeling's ability to learn from a few examples and successfully extrapolate the appearance changes for unseen configurations. Moreover, the appearance space is based on real visual data, and thus presents no inconsistencies or discontinuities. It is consequently very well adapted to the intuitive parameterization of natural facial expressions.

The new representation we have introduced has been constructed based on a person-specific database. Arguably, only the facial characteristics of a single individual are considered in the appearance space. Nevertheless, a more extensive study on this topic has proved that it is possible to easily construct equivalent appearance faces for other faces using only a few database examples (corresponding to the dominant direction identified in Section 3.2) (Stoiber et al. 2009). Analysis and synthesis of unknown faces could then be performed with our 2D representation, requiring only a few samples of the new face. The proposed representation space is

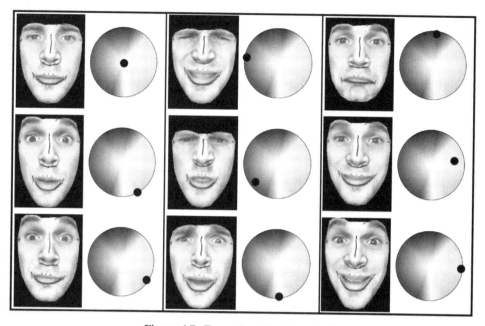

Figure 6.7. Example of facial analysis.

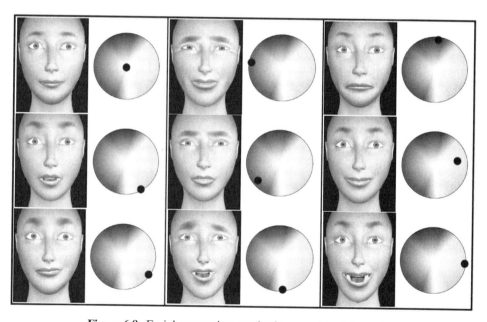

Figure 6.8. Facial expression synthesis on a virtual character.

then perfectly adapted for real-world applications (affective annotation, facial expression recognition and cloning in video games and virtual worlds, etc.).

In Stoiber et al. (2009), facial expression synthesis is intuitively carried out on virtual characters using the 2D disk as a user interface (Figure 6.8). Usual facial animation systems involve complex sets of control parameters that only trained animators can manipulate efficiently. Moreover, due to the conflicting nature of some of these parameters, careless manipulations can lead to the synthesis of unpleasant, and even incoherent facial configurations. Using our representation as a control space ensures that only natural facial expressions can be generated. Besides, the simplicity of the interface makes facial animation accessible and intuitive for experts, as well as nonexpert users.

6.6 CONCLUSION

In this chapter, a novel representation space of human facial expressions has been presented. This representation is generated from the analysis of captured facial movement on a real face. The generation process is able to identify the main variation patterns of the moving face, and reorganize them on a simpler, more intuitive space, ideal for higher-level applications. Despite its purely visual origin, the resulting representation can be linked with emotional concepts, which enables the extraction of meaningful, reliable information from human faces. Moreover, the representation has successfully been used for facial analysis and synthesis task (see Section 5). It can produce profitable affective metadata (Chapters 18 and 19), and help understand the human emotional behavior (Chapter 16).

The representation space is currently limited to emotional facial expressions, which we consider to be the most interesting facial communication channel. It could be interesting to apply the analysis method to other types of expressions, like speech-related facial configurations (visemes). The use of a continuous appearance would constitute an interesting solution to the frequently encountered coarticulation problem (realistic visual interpolation between discrete speech poses).

We have generated the final representation space from a facial expressions database of a single individual. In Section 5, we mentioned the fact that it is easy to adapt the obtained representation to other unknown faces, whether real or synthetic. Nevertheless, the expressions' diversity represented by our 2D space would certainly be improved by the analysis of a multi-individual database. The method we describe reaches its limitation in that case. When analyzing different faces simultaneously, it appears that interpersonal differences are often more important than variations due to the expressions. This is illustrated by the presence of clusters in the resulting appearance space, which make it impossible to extract relevant facial movement patterns. Therefore, judiciously chosen invariant features must be used in the facial description to ensure an accurate alignment of similar visual variations across individuals. This task is still considered an ongoing research problem by the community, and the extension of our approach to a multi-individual facial analysis has to be considered as an important future extension of the system.

SECTION 2

VIDEO EXTRACTION

Understanding video has been a challenge since the dawn of broadcasting. This section reports on novel methods to extract elements from video. One common strategy is the use of additional media, such as processing the text or audio accompanying a video to more accurately identify relevant passages or retrieve more fine grained segments. The integration of cross-modal indicators can increase both the precision and recall of algorithms. Authors in this section explore a range of video exploitation applications to support video indexing, searching, browsing, and summarization in a variety of video domains from broadcast news to sports to surveillance video.

The first chapter by Rohini Srihari at State University of New York at Buffalo and Adrian Novischi at Janya reports on the use of visual semantics from audio and text accompanying video to enhance the precision and granularity of video search (e.g., searching for specific segments within a long clip). This work extends prior research that enhanced image retrieval by using text surrounding a photograph on a web page. With video, frequently accompanying text or audio content (e.g., voiceovers) can be exploited for semantic indexing and search. A key challenge is associating linguistic features with visual properties of accompanying video, as the two can be inconsistent. For example, the authors identify that certain linguistic expressions (e.g., modal verbs like "might," modal expressions like "it's possible," and certain adjectives like "alleged") indicate unreal or uncertain events that will not likely appear in accompanying video. Such linguistic knowledge can help reduce false positives during video search. Performing machine learning on data from a Foreign Broadcast Information Service (FBIS) corpus, the authors use a set of 95 event seeds and 295 nonevent seeds to automatically tag instances as positive and negative examples, building a probabilistic model consisting of vectors of features

Multimedia Information Extraction: Advances in Video, Audio, and Imagery Analysis for Search, Data Mining, Surveillance, and Authoring, First Edition. Edited by Mark T. Maybury.
© 2012 IEEE Computer Society. Published 2012 by John Wiley & Sons, Inc.

for each word. They achieve average expression detection accuracy results of 79% on FBIS data and 71% on video transcripts. To evaluate the effect on video search, the authors assembled and labeled a 176 video clips corpus, (including the TREC 2002 Video Track) and generated 50 queries from the content. Giving more importance (term frequency) to the nouns referring to actual events in the video clip increases the ranking performance mean average precision (MAP) scores by 12–15% and improves average reciprocal rank (ARR) by 9% to 11 %. The authors hypothesize a more dramatic effect will be seen applying more useful linguistic triggers and training in larger collections.

The second chapter by Wei-Hao Lin and Alex Hauptmann from CMU explores methods for automated detection of highly biased imagery in news video. For example, Yasser Arafat's death in 2004 was portrayed by American broadcaster (NBC) using stock footage of Arafat, whereas Arabic broadcaster (LBC) showed footage of interviews with the general public and scenes of the funeral. The authors argue that tagging and providing users with multiple viewpoints can foster better informed decisions. They report a system that automatically classifies television news video using both text (linking news stories on the same topic based on automatic speech recognition transcriptions) as well as visual indicators. The authors introduce a statistical model of ideological discourse called the joint topic and perspective model (jTP), which is based on emphatic patterns and simultaneously captures the topical and ideological factors in a unified statistical model. Working with the 2005 TREC Video Evaluation broadcast news video archive (which includes Arabic, Chinese, and English news), the authors automatically segment these into 4436 news stories. After removing anchor and advertisement shots, 10 international news events were chosen (e.g., Iraq war, Arafat's health, and AIDS). Visual content was annotated using the 449-item Large-Scale Concept Ontology for Multimedia (LSCOM), averaging 10 visual concepts per shot. LSCOM consists of tags describing, e.g., the scene, people, objects, events. A same/different news event detector was trained using multinomial distributions to achieve 70% classification accuracy. They then learned a joint topic and ideological set of weights associated with each word in the video corpus. This is used to predict ideological perspective of new videos. Using simulated perfect LSCOM annotations, their jTP algorithm achieved F-scores of 70% for American news, and about 65% for Chinese and Arabic. Using empirically trained LSCOM visual concept classification drops jTP F-scores about ten percentage points. In summary, the authors demonstrate that perspectives on controversial issues can be successfully identified by statistically modeling of the written words, spoken words, and visual concepts used in news video, which reflect not only topics, but also reflect inner attitudes and opinions toward an issue. Notably, their classifiers, based *only* on emphatic patterns of visual concepts, can clearly identify bias in TV news. The authors conclude by articulating a number of benefits of their system such as custom retrieval and filters of extreme views to protect children.

The third chapter by David Palmer, Marc Reichman, and Noah White from Autonomy Virage addresses the challenge of global access to multilingual video news. They describe the Enhanced Video Text and Audio Processing (EVITAP) to access to news in over 20 languages, including Arabic, Mandarin Chinese, Persian, Russian, Spanish, and English. EVITAP performs audio and video content analysis and machine translation to support archiving, indexing, searching, and browsing large-scale, multilingual video news collections. Video and image analysis includes keyframe detection, face identification, scene cut analysis, color frame detection, on screen OCR, and logo detection. Audio analysis includes audio classification, speaker identification, automatic speech recognition, named entity detection, closed captioning processing, and machine translation. The authors discuss the challenges and benefits of cross-media extraction, for example, correlating information across face identification, speaker identification, and visual OCR for training and recognition algorithms. A fully operational system in use in several locations by hundreds of simultaneous users, EVITAP must provide real time processing requirements put severe constraints on speech (requiring 300 times real-time processing) and machine translation. The authors emphasize the importance of an effective user interface, for example, a cross-lingual search can result in transcribed and translated broadcast information with search terms shown in context along with the most frequently named entities.

The fourth chapter by Evelyne Tzoukermann et al. from StreamSage Comcast similarly uses fully automatic speech, text, and video content analysis to support video segment retrieval. The authors report two methods: one that uses audio and language processing to find relevant passages and another that uses speech, text, and video processing to extract segments. Using mutual information, they compute "relevance intervals" of single and multiple terms, pronominal references, and term expansions, to create "virtual documents" corresponding to topics of interest. The authors focus initially on American football, aiming to capture meaningful segments of a game to enable viewers to browse salient moments of a football game, for example, touchdowns, fumbles, and interceptions. They also process video, including detection and extraction of commercials, static and dynamic logo and sport replay detection, and static overlay detection and text extraction via OCR. They report the detection of banners and logos in football and baseball with precision and recall over 95%. The authors describe an intuitive interface for searching and browsing the results and claim that techniques similar to sports are applicable to a wide range of other domains, such as cooking and home improvement shows.

The fifth chapter by Prem Natarajan, Ehry MacRostie, Rohit Prasad, and Jonathan Watson from BBN focuses on the analysis of visual natural language content in broadcast video. The chapter reports methods for detecting and recognizing text content in video (including overlaid text and in-scene text or scene text). The authors describe their statistically based trainable system, which incorporates BBN's Byblos automatic speech recognition engine and an optical character recognition (OCR) system, both founded on the BBN (Raytheon BBN Technologies, Cambridge, MA) Byblos™ hidden Markov model (HMM) based toolkit. Output from ASR and OCR are fed into BBN Identifinder™ named entity (NE) extraction engine. The authors present the results of an analysis of the correction of the appearance of named entities in audio and video text, demonstrating the complementary nature of video text to the audio track. They used 13.5 hours of video from the NIST TDT-2 corpus, which contains approximately even amounts of video from ABCNews and CNN from 1998. In the video text, the authors manually annotated a total of 8421 entities, as defined by the automatic content extraction (ACE) named entity detection task. Surprisingly, when the authors looked within a 1-minute window of an entity's occurrence in the video text stream, 79% do not occur in the ASR results. Even when the time window is expanded to equal the entire duration of the video clip (30 minutes), 62% of entities in video text did not occur in the ASR results.

These results were consistent with a previous 2002 study. Upon closer inspection, entities contained in video text not appearing in audio ranged from over 50% novel location and person names to over 85% novel organization names. Also, video text can help audio analysis identify out of vocabulary words, which are frequently named entities. In particular, the authors found that 16% of the unique named entities in video text had at least one out-of-vocabulary (OOV) word in the ASR dictionary. The results demonstrate the importance of video text even when ASR is possible. Furthermore, as the authors point out, even redundant audio and video content can be valuable to automatic identification of key ideas or concepts in a video.

The sixth chapter by Jose San Pedro, Vaiva Kalnikaite, and Steve Whittaker at the University of Sheffield and Stefan Siersdorfer at the University of Hannover departs from the primarily video content-based approaches discussed so far. In contrast, the authors' approach exploits social media technology to improve search and browsing from social media sites, such as YouTube. In particular, the frequency with which different scenes in a target video have been uploaded is used to determine the importance of those scenes. The authors first use redundancy (independent selection and uploading of the same video) to detect regions of interest within the timeline of a video and then use redundancy to propagate tags across sparsely tagged collections. Robust hash fingerprint techniques are used to find similar video sequences, augmented by a color histogram difference-based shot detection algorithm to select region boundaries. Studies have shown over 25% near-duplicate videos detected in search results. The authors evaluated the efficacy of automatically extracted highlights by having 45 expert film critics assess the selected highlights from seven popular films, generating a total of 86 sessions and 945 clip judgments. The more knowledgeable an expert was with a particular film, the higher the correlation of their ratings of clips with those generated by the authors' algorithm based on frequency of content redundancy. Film experts also spent less time replaying the clips before judging them. Also, action films had better correlated ratings than slower pace films perhaps because there are fewer visually salient regions. One limitation of the social summarization technique is it can only be applied to popular media streams where there is sufficient content overlap. Moreover, these often lack consistency. Accordingly, the authors explore a variety of algorithms for propagating tags across similar clips. They created a test collection using 579 queries extracted from Google's Zeitgeist archive from 2001 to 2007 to help create a 38,283 YouTube video file test collection (a total of over 2900 hours of video). Augmenting feature vectors from the original manual video tags with those from videos with overlap redundancy improved the accuracy of classifying videos into YouTube categories (e.g., comedy, sports, news & politics, and music) by as much as 5–6%.

The final chapter of the section by Erhan Ermis and Venkatesh Saligrama at Boston University and Pierre-Marc Jodoin and Université de Sherbrooke, Canada addresses the challenge of remote scene sensing from a network of uncalibrated video cameras. Low-level pixel correspondence across cameras is utilized together with high-level activity clustering, segmentation of scenes into behavior regions, and cross-camera behavior region association to address challenges of unknown camera topology, epipolar geometry, and zoom levels. The authors demonstrate anomaly detection from uncalibrated camera networks with different zoom levels and orientations. In an indoor evaluation with two cameras over a plane measuring a remote-controlled car in the scene, the authors capture a 5000-frame video, and when comparing the automated matching algorithm to manually annotated ground truth, their error rate is less than 10 pixels after about 250 frames, which is within 1/6th of the length of the car. After about 1000 frames, the maximum likelihood has the smallest error. In examples such as surveillance of cars or people, the authors demonstrate automated behavior clustering, that is, classification of pixels that exhibit similar behavior, such as distinguishing busy from idle space across cameras. They demonstrate information fusion and anomaly detection by transmitting the behavior model trained on one camera to another camera that observes that same location, promising freedom from calibration. The method enables sharing of information in a dynamic camera network for wide-area surveillance applications.

A number of video understanding challenges remain. Large-scale, heterogeneous collections of annotated "gold standard" data remain expensive but essential to automatically trained video extractors. Also important is the development of cross-modal indicators for identifying and tracking topics or events of interest. Robust methods that will operate across a wide range of genre and phenomena from news to meetings to surveillance video remain elusive. Finally, effective interfaces to support natural video exploitation and analysis are needed. Advances addressing these gaps promise effective detection, extraction, and exploitation of the increasing volumes, variety, and velocity of video.

CHAPTER 7

VISUAL SEMANTICS FOR REDUCING FALSE POSITIVES IN VIDEO SEARCH

ROHINI K. SRIHARI and ADRIAN NOVISCHI

7.1 INTRODUCTION

This chapter investigates the interaction of textual and photographic information in a video and image search system. With the rising popularity of websites such as YouTube, the need for a semantic and granular search of video content is apparent. Currently, such material is being indexed purely by metadata and keywords provided by the users contributing the content. While this is often sufficient for ranking video clips, it is not sufficient if a more granular search of video content is necessary, that is, searching for specific segments within a long clip corresponding to a specific event. Even in such cases, there is often text/audio content accompanying the video (e.g., voiceovers) that can be exploited for more semantic indexing and search. Applications, such as question–answering, have focused on granular text search, whereby the unit of retrieval is a phrase or a text snippet; video search is beginning to require similar levels of granularity, especially when mobile, small-form devices such as the iPhone are being used.

There has been considerable research in the area of multimedia indexing and retrieval. Much of the early focus was on content-based indexing and retrieval of images (Smeulders et al. 2000). This body of work was concerned with using image features such as color, texture, shape, and so on in indexing images. Evaluation was typically on a large collection of images, such as the Corel data set; queries were typically similarity based, where an image was used as a query. It is felt that most of the achievable gains in image-based retrieval have already been realized. The new frontier focuses on exploiting the temporal dimension in content-based video indexing and retrieval (CBVIR) in order to detect entities and events; several DARPA and NIST programs have focused on this task (Smeaton et al. 2006). This

Multimedia Information Extraction: Advances in Video, Audio, and Imagery Analysis for Search, Data Mining, Surveillance, and Authoring, First Edition. Edited by Mark T. Maybury.
© 2012 IEEE Computer Society. Published 2012 by John Wiley & Sons, Inc.

is an extremely challenging task since, in most cases, no collateral audio/text is available. PICTION (Srihari and Burhans 1994) was a system that identified human faces in newspaper photographs based on information contained in the associated caption. It was noteworthy since it was (1) one of the first systems to combine both text and image data in semantic image search, and (2) provided a computational framework for text-guided image interpretation in situations where pictures are accompanied by descriptive text. More recent work (Feng and Lapata 2008) focuses on the use of machine learning techniques that combine both text features (such as bag-of-words) along with video/image features in joint indexing of video/images. The assumption is that this will: (1) allow for both text-based and similarity-based search, and (2) eliminate the need for manual video/image annotation. While the initial results have been impressive, they have not focused on the problem of granular, semantic video search. Text features have typically been restricted to variants of bag-of-words features and have not exploited advances in information extraction technology. Thus, a search for video clips of Clinton giving a speech will also result in video clips of an empty hall; the latter would have been retrieved due to the accompanying audio saying *volunteers are getting the museum building ready in preparation for Clinton's speech tonight.*

The focus of this chapter is on exploiting advances in text-based information extraction for more granular and accurate searching of video. In particular, we focus on reducing false positives such as the above by finding key linguistic triggers in the form of nominal events. We first discuss some initial results in detecting events in video. The techniques are based on a traditional text-based IE system. We revisit the theory of visual semantics (Srihari and Burhans 1994), a framework used in situations where visual and textual/audio materials are jointly presented to a user: visual semantics is concerned with correlating linguistic structures with the semantics of a scene. Semantics of a scene include the objects present, the events taking place, and background context (e.g., scenic background vs. city setting). The focus of this chapter is on how they contribute to accurate searching of video/images by filtering out noise. Such a text-based technique can be eventually combined with the advances made in CBIVR to enable the most accurate video search possible.

7.2 EVENT DETECTION IN VIDEO

This section describes how a text-based information extraction system was customized to find events of interest in video. The text transcripts of audio accompanying the video were indexed by the Semantex™ (Srihari et al. 2008) engine. Semantex is a hybrid engine for information extraction, incorporating both machine-learning and grammatical paradigms. It is capable of extracting entities, events, and relationships and attributes, as well as other nontraditional IE output, such as sentiment analysis. Events of interest included marriage, divorce, and stealing, and were extracted from a corpus of about 300 documents containing about 872 kB of text. In this corpus, Semantex automatically found 191 instances of marriage events, 59 instances of divorce events, and 94 instances of stealing events. The accuracy of event detection for each type is presented in Table 7.1.

We found that some of the detected events that are mentioned in the audio transcripts do not correlate with events presented in the video. A simple indexing

TABLE 7.1. Accuracy of Semantex System in Finding Three Types of Events: Marriage, Divorce, and Stealing

Event Type	Correct	Attempted	Accuracy (%)
Marriage	178	191	93.2
Divorce	56	59	94.9
Stealing	77	94	81.9

based on keywords would lead to retrieval of false positives. For example, in the following paragraph:

> "I, unfortunately, in the last couple years, did not have any conversations with her because she was withdrawn so much," said Jane Doe,[1] who was maid of honor at the couple's 1990 wedding. The couple had met through a dating service a few years before their marriage, she said.

The system found the phrase *at the couple's 1990 wedding* as being an instance of a marriage event. Although this is counted as a correct detection of a wedding event in text, it unfortunately does not correspond to a wedding event in an accompanying video clip. Later sections discuss this discrepancy and how it can be avoided.

7.3 VISUAL SEMANTICS

Visual information in collateral text answers the questions who or what is present in the accompanying scene and provides valuable information on how to locate and identify these objects or people. When combined with a priori knowledge about the appearance of objects and the composition of typical scenes, visual information conveys the semantics of the associated scene. The resulting semantics provides the basis for semantic searching of video and images. We refer to the theory of extracting visual information (and the associated semantics) from text as visual semantics.

7.3.1 Entity Classification

A primary task is to correctly detect and determine the semantic category of key entities in the accompanying video. Examples of such classes include person, place, organization, and so on. Considerable progress has been made on accurate tagging of named entities; considerable work remains in tagging and categorizing nominal entities, such as the protestors, the herd, and so on. As an example of how difficult this problem can get, consider the caption *"Winning Colors with her trainer Tom Smith prior to the start of the Kentucky Derby,"* which accompanied a clip of a horse and her trainer. Determining that "Winning Colors" is not a human and is actually

---

[1] Name changed to protect identity.

a horse involves understanding the meaning of the word "trainer," as well as contextual knowledge about the Kentucky Derby.

7.3.2   Linguistic Triggers Useful in Predicting Video Content

The description of a video clip may contain the mentions of several events. Most of the time only one event in this description is presented in the video clip. For example, in the video clip where *Tom Smith and his wife Mary Jane are preparing for the visit of President Clinton on Tuesday*, the visit of President Clinton is not expected to be in the video clip. Most of the concern is finding the main events and their entities and rejecting those events and entities that are not expected to appear; not all entities mentioned in the accompanying description are in the video. Using linguistic triggers to detect relations between events can help one in predicting the event(s) described in the video together with their relevant entities. We identified three situations:

1. *One Event Is the Argument of the Other*: This situation is possible if, by the use of reification of one event, the event is expressed as a verb nominalization and becomes an argument of the other event. This is why it is important to address the detection of nominal events. For example in the following video description from the CNN website *CNN political analyst Mark Preston talks about John McCain's accusations of Barack Obama's "financing flip-flop,"* the "flip-flop" event is an argument of the accusation event which in turn is an argument of the discussion event. In these cases, prepositions like "about," "of," "for" represent very good linguistic triggers for indicating that one event is an argument of another.

2. *Linguistic Modality*: Some events described in the text are real and others are unreal or uncertain. These events that are unreal or uncertain are introduced by modal verbs like "may," "might," "can," and "could," or modal expressions like "it is possible" and "it is probable," or intentional adjectives for nominal events like "alleged," "fake," "possible," or "probable" (Palmer 2001). All these are important linguistic clues to detect events and entities that are not likely to appear in the video content. As an example, in the following description from CNN website: *Possible floods force earthquake refugees in China to put what little they have onto bikes and evacuate their tents*. The "floods" event is not real, and it will not be shown in the video because it is modified by the adjective "possible" (Peters and Peters 2000).

3. *Temporal Relations between Events*: In some cases, there is a temporal relation between events where the time frame of the main event in the description is given using some temporal relationship to other event. For example, in the following video description from the CNN website *Italian soccer fans set fireworks off after a victory against France in Zurich in the Euro 2008 games*, the "victory" event prefixed by the preposition "after" is in a temporal relationship with the main event, "setting fireworks off." Temporal relationships between events are expressed by prepositions like "before" and "after," which are important linguistic triggers to select the most important event and entities.

7.4 EXPERIMENTATION WITH NOMINAL EVENT DETECTION

Nominal event detection plays an important role in avoiding false positives in video search. This section presents our approach for detecting nominal events, inspired by Creswell et al. (2006). This approach is based on a probabilistic model called the multinomial model. This model uses vectors of features computed for each word in a certain class: event or nonevent. In two different instances, a word can be classified both as an event and nonevent, but for a given classification of a word, we are interested in those features that are correlated with that classification. For a given word in a set corresponding to a certain classification, the frequencies of all the features in its vector are computed from a corpus. The multinomial model has two requirements:

1. Future instances of words with features similar to the words within a certain class should receive the same class label (words with similar features to words that are events should be labeled as events).
2. All the words in the set of words corresponding to a certain classification should have a contribution proportional to their frequency in the training corpus.

These requirements are incorporated naturally into a mixture model formalism where there are as many components as the number of words with a given label. Let Λ be the set of all the words that were assigned label L in the training corpus. The ith component s^i build around word i from the set Λ is a multinomial probability of its vector of features v:

$$p(v|s^i) = \prod_{f=1}^{F} (\hat{s}_f^i)^{vf},$$

where $\hat{s}_f^i$ is the proportion of times the word i was seen with feature f in the training corpus compared with the number of times the word i was seen with any feature. $\hat{s}_f^i$ is simply the (i,f) entry in row–sum normalized matrix:

$$\hat{s}_f^i = \frac{s_f^i}{\sum_{f'=1}^{F} s_{f'}^i},$$

vf represents the number of times the word i is seen with the feature f in the test corpus.

The second requirement is realized by forming a weighted mixture of the above multinomial distribution for all the words i from the set Λ. The weighting of the ith component $p(s^i)$ is the ration between the number of times the word i occurred in the training corpus with label L and the total number of all occurrences of words with label L:

$$p(s^i) = \frac{|s^i|}{\sum_{i' \in \Lambda} |s^{i'}|}.$$

The generative probability for the vector v of features for the words in set Λ with label L is the following:

$$p(v|L) = \sum_{i \in \Lambda} p(v|s^i)p(s^i).$$

The new instance in the test corpus, the probability for $L = $ EVENT is computed together with the probability for $L = $ NONEVENT. Then the difference between the logarithm of the two probabilities (log odds ratio) is computed:

$$d(v) = \log p(v|\text{EVENT}) - \log p(v|\text{NONEVENT}).$$

The sign of $d(v)$ gives the label of the new instance. The training corpus was taken to be the Foreign Broadcast Information Service. A set of 95 event seeds and 295 nonevent seeds was used to automatically tag instances in this corpus as positive and negative examples. The multinomial model used features the set of strings created from the relations output by the Semantex system by concatenating the relation string with the lemma of the relation word. In addition, we used a set of 50 topic labels computed offline from the same corpus using Gibbs sampler HMM-LDA model (Griffiths et al. 2005) (with the following parameters: number of syntactic states NS = 12, number of iterations $N = 200$, ALPHA = 1, BETA = 0.01, and GAMMA = 0.1). For comparison with the previous work, we used the same test corpus described in Creswell et al. (2006) consisting of 77 documents with 1276 positive instances and 8105 negative instances for a total of 9381 labeled instances. For each instance in the test corpus, we considered three ways to compute the feature values: (1) word—the feature values are computed from the vector of features from the training corpus; (2) context—the feature values are computed from the current context of the word in the test set, and (3) word + context—for each instance, we multiply the probability of word vector with the probability from the context vector. Table 7.2 presents the results for each type of test: word, context and word + context. Table 7.3 presents the original results reported in Creswell et al. (2006) for comparison.

The multinomial model was also tested on the corpus of video transcripts. The 300 files in the corpus were split randomly into 250 files used for training and 50 files used for testing. All the 9348 nouns in these 50 files were manually labeled with an EVENT or NONEVENT label. This annotation effort resulted in 1035 instances labeled as EVENT and 8313 instances labeled as NONEVENT. Table 7.4 presents the evaluation of the Multinomial Model of the corpus of video transcripts. The

TABLE 7.2. Results of the Experiments with Multinomial Model Using Three Ways to Compute the Feature Vector: (1) Word, (2) Context, and (3) Word + Context

Feature Vector	Event			Nonevent			Total			Average (%)
	Correct	Total	%	Correct	Total	%	Correct	Total	%	
Word	1127	1276	88.3	5892	8105	72.7	7019	9381	74.8	78.6
Context	608	1276	47.7	2897	8105	35.7	3505	9381	37.4	41.9
Word + context	1147	1276	89.9	5903	8105	72.8	7040	9381	75.0	79.2

TABLE 7.3. Results of the Original Experiments Reported in (Creswell et al. 2006)

Feature Vector	Event			Nonevent			Total			Average %
	Correct	Total	%	Correct	Total	%	Correct	Total	%	
Word	1236	1408	87.7	4217	6973	60.5	5453	8381	74.8	74.1%
Context	627	1408	44.5	2735	6973	39.2	3362	8381	37.4	41.9
Word + context	1251	1408	88.8	4226	6973	60.6	5477	8381	75.0	74.7

TABLE 7.4. Results of the Experiments with Multinomial Model on the Corpus of Video Transcripts

Feature Vector	Event			Nonevent			Total			Average %
	Correct	Total	%	Correct	Total	%	Correct	Total	%	
Word	570	1035	55.1	5916	8313	71.2	6486	9381	69.4	65.2
Context	737	1035	71.2	5075	8313	61.0	5812	9381	62.2	64.8
Word + context	622	1035	62.2	6387	8313	76.8	7009	9381	75.0	71.3

overall accuracy of nominal event detection is above 70% in the best case. These results are promising and will allow future use of lexical triggers in identifying the main events occurring in a video and thereby avoid false positives.

7.5 IMPACT OF NOMINAL EVENTS IN KEYWORD-BASED SEARCH OF VIDEO CLIPS

To test the impact of detecting nominal events on the performance of an information retrieval system for searching video clips using keywords, we created a corpus of video clips and their accompanying text files using the test collection of TREC 2002 Video Track[2]. About 174 video clips were downloaded from the Internet Archive website[3] and two clips from The Open Video Project[4] for a total of 176 video clips. For each video clip, we created an accompanying text file using the following information gathered from the clip web page: title, description, reviews, and shot list. In the end, this effort resulted in a collection of 176 video clips and their corresponding text files. For each text file in the corpus, we created a list with all the nouns that describe events presented in the video clip and that have instances of events in the text file. There are two reasons for these annotations:

- They serve as labels for events that appear in the video in order to automatically detect linguistic triggers.
- They provide an upper bound for the improvement of the performance in retrieving video clips using keyword search.

---

[2] http://www-nlpir.nist.gov/projects/t2002v/t2002v.html.
[3] http://www.archive.org/index.php.
[4] http://www.open-video.org.

TABLE 7.5. Single-Word Queries Used for Information Retrieval System Experiments

Interview	Harvest	Ad
Parade	Extraction	Selling
Aluminum	Processing	Feeding
Living	Assembly	Auction
Defense	Effect	Cutting
Appliance	Production	Barbecue
Innovation	Light	Herding
Iteration	History	Tribute
Explosion	Physics	Preservation
Maintenance	Property	Communication
War	Giving	Breakfast
Blast	Invention	Presentation
Testing	Therapy	Fight
Computer	Measuring	Development
Technology	Discovery	Comfort
Manufacturing	Importance	Beauty
Functionality	Visit	

Here we address the second reason, and we performed experiments in order to see the improvement in the retrieval and ranking of video clips using their corresponding text files. We used the Lucene[5] information retrieval system with default settings to perform the experiments. The previous annotations were used to boost term frequency scores of the nouns that relate to events in the video clip with a weight w. We experimented with three values: $w = 3$, $w = 5$, and $w = 10$.

We created 50 queries based on words found in the text files corresponding to video clips. We noticed that queries based on two or more keywords (linked with the AND operator) would retrieve only a single document most of the time, and cannot be used to show improvement in retrieval performance or ranking. This happens because the size of the corpus is small. Therefore, we used single-word queries based on nouns that appear in text files corresponding to video clips. The queries are presented in Table 7.5. About 34 (68%) of the nouns used in the queries can refer to a nominal event. For each query, we annotated the set of relevant documents.

We used two types of performance measures: mean average precision (MAP) and average reciprocal rank (ARR). The MAP measure is defined as:

$$MAP(Q) = \frac{1}{|Q|} \sum_{j=1}^{|Q|} \frac{1}{m_j} \left(\sum_{k=1}^{m_j} \text{Precision}(R_{jk}) \right).$$

where $Q = \{q_1, q_2, \ldots, q_j, \ldots q_{|Q|}\}$ is the set of queries, $|Q|$ is the number of elements of the set Q, m_j is the number of relevant documents for query j, and R_{jk} is the set of ranked retrieval results of the first k documents for query j ($j = 1 \ldots |Q|$). The ARR measure is defined as:

[5] http://lucene.apache.org.

$$\mathrm{ARR}(Q) = \frac{1}{|Q|} \sum_{j=1}^{|Q|} \frac{\sum_{k=1}^{m_j} \frac{1}{\mathrm{rank}(d_{jk})}}{\sum_{k=1}^{m_j} \frac{1}{k}},$$

where $Q = \{q_1, q_2, \ldots q_j, \ldots q_{|Q|}\}$ is the set of queries, $|Q|$ is the number of elements of the set Q, m_j is the number of relevant documents for query j, and $\{d_{j1}, d_{j2}, \ldots, d_{jk}, \ldots d_{jmj}\}$ is the set of relevant documents for query j and $\mathrm{rank}(d_{jk})$ is the rank of the document d_{jk} in the set of retrieval results.

We performed four experiments: one experiment using an unmodified information retrieval system with default settings, and three experiments where we increased the term frequency of the relevant nouns with the weight w: $w = 3$, $w = 5$, and $w = 10$. Table 7.6 presents the results of these experiments. We can see from the table that giving more importance to the nouns referring to actual events in the video clip does increase the ranking performance. The MAP scores increase by 12–15% and the ARR scores increase by 9–11% when we increase the term frequency of the relevant nouns.

We found some specific examples where increasing the importance of the nominal events appearing in the video provides better ranking. We found eight relevant documents for the query "parade." The document retrieval system using normal indexing retrieves two relevant documents in the first two positions; however, in the third position, we found a document related to the video clip "*Aluminum on the march (Part II)*," which does not have any parade event because one of the reviewers metaphorically compares the events in the video clip with a military parade: "*an aluminum man and his metallic minions lurching across the screen in military parade fashion.*" The document related to the first part of this clip "*Aluminum on the march (Part I)*" is returned in the fifth position. The retrieval system that uses the term frequency of nominal events increased by $w = 3$ returns these "aluminum" documents in positions six and eight and the systems with $w = 5$ and $w = 10$ returns them in the seventh and ninth positions. Table 7.7 presents the ranking of nonrelevant "aluminum" documents and the MAP and ARR scores for each retrieval system for this specific query.

While the improvement in ranking using nominal events over simple keyword search may be relatively modest in these experiments, a more dramatic effect will be seen in much larger collections. Due to the ground truth experiments, we are limited in the size of data sets we can experiment with.

TABLE 7.6. The Results of the Information Retrieval Experiments

System	MAP Score (%)	ARR Score (%)
Unmodified term freq. (tf)	77.08	83.67
tf increased with $w = 3$	89.55	92.67
tf increased with $w = 5$	90.57	93.45
tf increased with $w = 10$	91.95	94.18

TABLE 7.7. The Position of Nonrelevant "Aluminum" Documents for the Query "Parade" and the MAP and ARR for Each Retrieval System

System	Position of "Aluminum" Nonrelevant Documents	MAP Score (%)	ARR Score (%)
Unmodified term freq. (tf)	3 and 5	76.84	84.46
tf increased with $w = 3$	6 and 8	93.00	97.03
tf increased with $w = 5$	7 and 9	96.65	98.42
tf increased with $w = 10$	7 and 9	96.65	98.42

7.6 SUMMARY

We have focused on the problem of granular and semantic searching of video, for example, searching for specific events involving specific entities. We are interested in situations where collateral audio or text is available, thereby permitting recent advances in text-based information extraction to be exploited. The problem of detecting nominal events and their significance in accurate event search has been explored in depth. Initial results are promising. Although the problem is challenging, the impact on video search is expected to be significant. Our next step will be to derive more useful linguistic triggers and test on larger data collection.

CHAPTER 8

AUTOMATED ANALYSIS OF IDEOLOGICAL BIAS IN VIDEO

WEI-HAO LIN and ALEXANDER G. HAUPTMANN

8.1 INTRODUCTION

Our goal is to develop a system that can automatically identify highly biased television news video based on imagery. The difference in framing news events becomes clear when we compare news broadcasters across national boundaries, languages, and media. Video has been a popular medium for expressing different opinions and value judgments. For example, Figure 8.1 shows how an American broadcaster (NBC) and an Arabic broadcaster (LBC) portray Yasser Arafat's death in 2004. The two broadcasters' footages are very different: NBC shows stock footage of Arafat, while LBC shows footage of interviews with the general public and scenes of the funeral.

Our approach is to discover emphatic visual patterns in biased presentations. Although bias or ideology is difficult to define well, the unique emphatic pattern that results from the presentation can be objectively defined. These emphatic patterns are pervasive and exhibit themselves through words or visual concepts. The emphatic patterns in ideological discourse are the result of two factors that influence word frequency in text or visual concept frequency in video: a topical factor commonly shared by different viewpoints and an ideological factor emphasized by individual viewpoints.

We define a statistical model for ideological discourse, called the joint topic and perspective model (jTP). The model is based on emphatic patterns, and simultaneously captures the topical and ideological factors in a unified statistical model. Given a training corpus, the model can simultaneously uncover both the topical and the ideological factors. After a training step, the model can predict the ideological viewpoint of a new document using the learned topical and ideological weights. jTP provides an understandable explanation on the difference between two viewpoints

Multimedia Information Extraction: Advances in Video, Audio, and Imagery Analysis for Search, Data Mining, Surveillance, and Authoring, First Edition. Edited by Mark T. Maybury.
© 2012 IEEE Computer Society. Published 2012 by John Wiley & Sons, Inc.

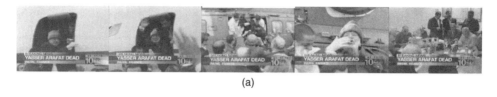

(a)

(b)

Figure 8.1. Television footage on Yasser Arafat's death from two broadcasters. (a) Keyframes of a television news story from the American news broadcaster NBC. (b) Keyframes of a television news story from an Arabic news broadcaster, LBC.

(categories) by exposing the learned topical and ideological weights. This is very different from many classifiers that focus solely on improving accuracy and provide little explanation on why a model returns particular results on some set of data.

We start with a brief summary of related work in video analysis. Section 8.2 describes the data we use, a collection of video news broadcasts, a set of contrasting stories by different broadcasters and an ontology of visual concepts used to label the imagery in the news broadcasts. Section 8.3 discusses our basic idea of using visual concept labels to characterize imagery in video documents. Section 8.4 details the technical approach and model for automatically recognizing both events (topics) and biased perspectives within a topic. Section 8.5 presents a series of results obtained by applying the model to our data, and Section 8.6 gives brief concluding remarks.

8.1.1   Related Work in Video Analysis

Very few researchers in multimedia have studied the problem of identifying different perspectives or bias in video. The most relevant prior work has been in the form of a video generation system and some multimedia art installations that promote mutual understanding between people holding different ideological viewpoints. *Vox Populi* (Bocconi and Nack 2004) is a video synthesis system that can make a documentary from a pool of interview clips based on the viewer's position on an issue, for example, "Iraq War." *Minions* (Ireson 2004) is an interactive art installation that confronts visitors with videos from two religious perspectives, Christianity and Islam. Arango (2005) displays a multimedia art work, *Vanishing Point*, that shows us how mainstream news media in industrialized countries give uneven coverage of countries around the world. *"Terminal Time"* (Mateas et al. 2000) is a video generation system that automatically generates ideologically biased documentaries based on Carbonell's ideology goal trees (Carbonell 1978). However, all assume that a video's biased perspectives are known or manually labeled, which makes it almost impossible to analyze large numbers of videos. There has been research on linking stories on the same topic across news sources, also known as "topic detection" (Allan 2002), using cues in keyframe images (Zhai and Shah 2005), or near-duplicates (Wu et al. 2007, 2008) to cluster news on the same event across different news channels. In our work, we also link news stories on the same topic based on automatic speech recognition transcriptions, which worked well enough for our purposes.

Much of our work is derived from statistical modeling and inference techniques in research on topic modeling (Blei et al. 2003; Griffiths and Steyvers 2004; Hofmann 1999). These focus mostly on modeling text collections that contain many *different* (latent) topics (e.g., academic conference papers and news articles). In contrast, we are interested in modeling ideology manifestations that are mostly on the *same* topic but mainly differ in their ideological perspectives. There have been studies going beyond topics, such as modeling authors (Rosen-Zvi et al. 2004). In our work, we are interested in modeling lexical and concept variation collectively from multiple authors/editors sharing similar beliefs, not variations due to individual authors' styles and topic preference.

8.2 VIDEO CORPUS

To study methods that identify differing ideological perspectives in video, we used the 2005 TREC Video Evaluation (TRECVID) collection (Over et al. 2005). The TRECVID'05 video collection is comprised of almost 160 hours of broadcast news programs recorded in late 2004 in three languages: Arabic, Chinese, and English. We ran a story segmentation program to detect news story boundaries (Hauptmann et al. 2005), resulting in 4436 news stories. The story segmentation program detected a news story's boundary using cues such as an anchor's presence, commercials, color coherence, and average story length. We removed anchor and commercial shots because they contained mostly talking heads and conveyed little ideological perspective. We identified 10 international news events from late 2004 and found news videos of these events that had been covered by broadcasters in more than one language (Lin 2008).

We also used the visual concepts annotations from the Large-Scale Concept Ontology for Multimedia (LSCOM) v1.0 (Kennedy and Hauptmann 2006). The LSCOM annotations labeled the presence of 449 LSCOM visual concepts in every video shot of the TRECVID 2005 videos. A (manually) LSCOM labeled keyframe is shown in Figure 8.2.

8.3 VISUAL SEMANTIC CONCEPTS FOR DESCRIBING VIDEO

Recent work on using a concept ontology for video retrieval (Hauptmann et al. 2007a,b) showed that visual semantic concepts, such as those in LSCOM, can provide highly accurate descriptions of video for the purposes of retrieval. We treat visual semantic concepts as words describing a video and consider a specific kind of visual grammar for analysis, expressed through the *composition of concepts that comprise the video*. News video footage, like paintings, advertisements, and illustrations, is not randomly designed, and has its own visual "grammar" (Efron 1972). Some visual concepts are shown more frequently because they are highly related to a specific

Figure 8.2. Keyframe from TRECVID'05 with LSCOM labels: Vehicle, Armed Person, Sky, Outdoor, Desert, Armored Vehicles, Daytime Outdoor, Machine Guns, Tanks, Weapons, and Ground Vehicles.

(a)   (b)

Figure 8.3. The text clouds show the frequencies of the visual concepts used by two broadcasters (CNN and LBC) for Iraq War stories. The larger a visual concept, the more frequently it was shown in news footage. (a) Frequent visual semantic concepts found in CNN news stories on Iraq. (b) Frequent visual semantic concepts found in news stories on Iraq from Lebanese channel LBC.

news topic regardless of broadcasters, and we call these concepts *topical* (e.g., Military Personnel and Daytime Outdoor for the Iraq War news). Some visual concepts are shown more frequently because broadcasters with a particular ideological perspective choose so in portraying a particular news event (e.g., Weapons in American news media vs. Civilian Person in Arabic news media for the Iraq War news), and we call these concepts *ideological*. Therefore, if we can automatically identify the visual concepts in that news footage, we may be able to learn the difference between broadcasters' differing ideological perspectives. We illustrate the idea in Figure 8.3. We count the visual concepts in the television news footage about the Iraq War from two different broadcasters (an American broadcaster CNN vs. an Arabic broadcaster LBC), and display them in text clouds.

Due to the nature of broadcast news, it is not surprising to see many people-related visual concepts (e.g., *Adult, Face*, and *Person*). Because the news stories are about the Iraq War, it is also not surprising to see many war-related concepts (e.g., *Weapons, Military Personnel*, and *Daytime Outdoor*). The surprising differences, however, lie in the subtle emphasis on some concepts. *Weapons* and *Machine Guns* are shown more often in CNN (relative to other visual concepts in CNN) than in LBC. In contrast, *Civilian Person* and *Crowd* are shown more often in LBC than in CNN. Thus, we find broadcasters holding different ideological beliefs choose to emphasize certain visual concepts when they portray a news event.

8.4   JOINT TOPIC AND PERSPECTIVE MODEL

To identify the perspective of videos, we have developed a statistical model for ideological discourse. The model associates *topical* and *ideological* weights to each word in the vocabulary. Topical weights represent how frequently a word is chosen because of a document's topic regardless of an author or speaker's ideological perspective. Ideological weights, dependent on an author or speaker's ideological perspective on an issue, modulate topical weights to increase or decrease a word's frequency.

We illustrate the interaction between topical and ideological weights in a three-word simplex in Figure 8.4. Any point in the three visual-concept simplex represents the proportion of three visual concepts (i.e., *Outdoor, Weapon*, and *Civilian*) chosen to be shown in news footage (also known as a multinomial distribution's parameter). Let T denote the proportion of the three concepts for a particular news topic (e.g., the Iraq War). T represents how likely an audience would see Outdoor, Weapon, or Civilian in the news footage about the Iraq War. Now suppose a group of news broadcasters holding a particular ideological perspective choose to show more *Civilians* and fewer *Weapons*. The *ideological* weights associated with this group of news broadcasters in effect move the proportion from T to V_1. When we sample visual concepts from a multinomial distribution of a parameter at V_1, we would see more Civilians and fewer Weapons. Now suppose a group of news broadcasters holding

Figure 8.4. A three-visual concept simplex illustrates the core idea of the joint topic and perspective model. T denotes the proportion of the three concepts (i.e., topical weights) for a particular topic. V_1 denotes the proportion of the three concepts after the topical weights are modulated by broadcasters holding one particular ideological perspective; V_2 denotes the proportion of the weights modulated by broadcasters holding another set of beliefs.

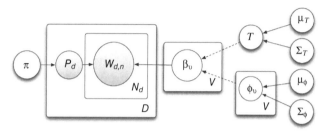

Figure 8.5. The joint topic and perspective model in a graphical model representation. A dashed line denotes a deterministic relation between parent and children nodes.

a contrasting ideological perspective choose to show more *Weapon* and fewer *Civilian*. The ideological weights associated with this second group of news broadcasters move the proportion from T to V_2. When we sample visual concepts from a multinomial distribution of a parameter at V_2, we would see more *Weapon* and fewer *Civilian* onscreen. The topical weights determine the position of T in a simplex, and each ideological perspective moves T to a biased position according to its ideological weights.

We can apply the jTP to simultaneously uncover topical and ideological concept weights and then use the model to predict the bias of a new video.

8.4.1 Model Specification

The graphical representation of the jTP is shown in Figure 8.5. Formally, the jTP assumes the following generative process for ideological discourse:

$$P_d \sim \text{Bernoulli}(\pi), d = 1, \dots, D$$
$$W_{d,n} | P_d = v \sim \text{Multinomial}(\beta_v), n = 1, \dots, N_d$$
$$\beta_v^w = \frac{\exp(\tau^w \times \phi_v^w)}{\sum_{w'} \exp(\tau^{w'} \times \phi_v^{w'})}, v = 1, \dots, V$$
$$\tau \sim N(\mu_\tau, \Sigma_\tau)$$
$$\phi_v \sim N(\mu_\phi, \Sigma_\phi).$$

The ideological perspective P_d from which the dth video in a collection was produced (i.e., its author's or editor's ideological perspective) is assumed to be a Bernoulli variable with a parameter π. In this chapter, we focus on bipolar ideological perspectives, that is, those political or ideological issues with only two perspectives of interest ($V = 2$). There are a total of D videos in the collection. The nth tag in the dth video $W_{d:n}$ is dependent on its author's ideological perspective P_d and assumed to be sampled from the multinomial distribution of a parameter β. There are a total of N_d visual concepts associated with the dth video.

The multinomial parameter, β_v^w, subscripted by an ideological perspective v and superscripted by the wth word in the vocabulary, consists of two parts: a topical weight τ_w and ideological weights $\{\phi_v^w\}$. Every word is associated with one topical weight τ_w and two ideological weights ϕ_1^w and ϕ_2^w. β is an auxiliary variable and is deterministically determined by (unobserved) topical and ideological weights.

τ represents the *topical* weights and is assumed to be sampled from a multivariate normal distribution of a mean vector μ_τ and a variance matrix Σ_τ. ϕ_v represents the *ideological* weights and is assumed to be sampled from a multivariate normal distribution of a mean vector μ_ϕ and a variance matrix Σ_τ. Every concept is associated with one topical weight τ_w and two ideological weights ϕ_1^w and ϕ_2^w. Topical weights are modulated by ideological weights through a multiplicative relationship, and all the weights are normalized through a logistic transformation.

Given a set of D documents on a particular topic from differing ideological perspectives $\{P_d\}$, the joint posterior probability distribution of the topical and ideological weights under the jTP is

$$P(\tau, \{\phi_v\}|\{W_{d,n}\}, \{P_d\}; \Theta)$$

$$\propto P(\tau|\mu_\tau, \Sigma_\tau)\prod_v P(\phi_v|\mu_\phi, \Sigma_\phi)\prod_{d=1}^{D} P(P_d|\pi)$$

$$\prod_{n=1}^{N_d} P(W_{d,n}|P_d, \tau, \{\phi_v\})$$

$$= N(\tau|\mu_\tau, \Sigma_\tau)\prod_v N(\phi_v|\mu_\phi, \Sigma_\phi)\prod_d \text{Bernoulli}(P_d|\pi)$$

$$\prod_n \text{Multinomial}(W_{d,n}|P_d, \beta),$$

where $N(\ )$, Bernoulli($\ $), and multinomial($\ $) are the probability density functions of multivariate normal, Bernoulli, and multinomial distributions, respectively. We call this model the jTP.

8.4.2 Classifying Ideological Perspective

We can apply the jTP to predict the ideological perspective from which a video is produced. We first fit the jTP on a training corpus where each of video story is labeled with its ideological bias. Given a video of an unknown ideological perspective, we use the model with the learned parameters to predict its ideological bias. The joint posterior probability distributions of topics and perspectives, however, are computationally intractable because of the nonconjugacy of the logistic-normal prior. We have developed an approximate inference algorithm (Lin et al. 2008) based on variational methods, and parameters are estimated using variational expectation maximization (Attias 2000).

8.5 EXPERIMENTS ON DIFFERENTIATING IDEOLOGICAL VIDEO

We used the TRECVID'05 video archive because the ideological perspectives from which the news videos were produced (i.e., its broadcaster) were clearly labeled. We first conducted the experiments using the LSCOM annotations, and later replaced manual annotations with predictions from empirically trained concept classifiers.

Given that the state-of-the-art classifiers for most visual concepts are far from perfect, we start from manual annotations that simulate perfect concept classifiers, because manual annotations allow us to test the idea of measuring similarity in visual concepts without being confounded by the poor accuracy of current empirical concept classifiers. If we started from poor concept classifiers and found that our idea did not work, we could not know whether (1) our idea indeed cannot identify a news video's ideological perspective or (2) the idea could work but the classifier accuracy was too low.

Manual annotations also establish the performance upper bound of our method. We can relax the "perfect" assumption by injecting noise into manual annotations to decrease classifier accuracy until the accuracy reaches the state of the art in automatic concept detection, with MAP around 0.1–0.2. We thus have both realistic and optimistic pictures of what our method can achieve.

8.5.1 Identifying News Videos of Differing Ideological Perspectives

Given two news videos are on the same news event, we can then use our method to test if they portray the news from differing ideological perspectives. We implicitly equate American news broadcasters with "American" ideological beliefs, and similarly Arabic news broadcaster with "Arabic" ideological beliefs. We evaluated the idea of using emphatic patterns of visual concepts to identify a news video's ideological perspective in a classification task. For each ideological perspective, we trained a one-against-all binary classifier (e.g., the American perspective vs. non-American perspectives) using the jTP. We then evaluated the performance of the ideological perspective classifier on held-out news videos. We compared the perspective classifiers based on the jTP with a random baseline (i.e., predicting one of the two perspectives with equal probabilities). We conducted a total of 22 binary perspective classification experiments, and calculated the average $F1$ for each ideological perspective. The positive data of a perspective classification experiment consist of videos on the same news topic from a particular ideological perspective (e.g., news stories about "Arafat's death" from Arabic news broadcasters). The negative data consist of news videos on the same news topic but from contrasting ideological perspectives (e.g., news stories about "Arafat's death" from non-Arabic news broadcasters, that is, American plus Chinese news broadcasters). We conducted 10-fold cross-validation in each binary classification task. We also varied the amount of training data from 10% to 90%. We adopted the commonly used evaluation metrics for binary classification tasks: precision, recall, and F1 (Manning et al. 2008). Precision is the fraction of the predicted positive news stories that are indeed positive. Recall is the fraction of all positive news stories that are predicted positive. F1 is the geometric average of precision and recall. The random baseline's F1 may not be 0:5 because the proportion of positive and negative data is not the same in our data.

We plot the classification results in Figure 8.6. The ideological perspective classifiers based on the jTP significantly outperformed the random baselines in three ideological perspectives. American perspective classifiers achieved the best performance of average F1 around 0:7. There were, however, more American news stories available for training than Arabic and Chinese perspectives. The significantly better-than-random classification performance can be attributed to:

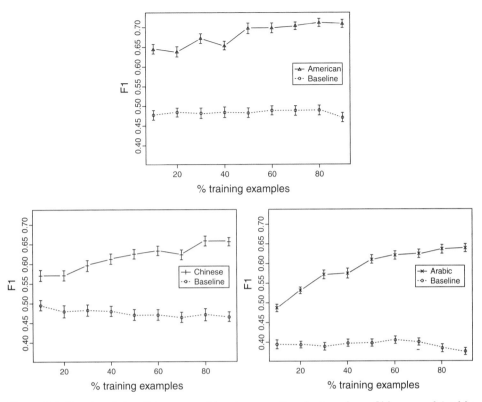

Figure 8.6. Results of classifying news videos' perspectives in American, Chinese, and Arabic news. x-axis is the amount of training data, and y-axis is the average $F1$.

- *Emphatic Patterns of Visual Concepts*: News broadcasters holding different ideological beliefs seem to exhibit strongly and consistently emphatic patterns of visual concepts when they cover international news events. Therefore, by modeling the emphatic patterns of visual concepts, our classifiers can identify the ideological perspective from which a news video was produced.
- *The jTP*: The model seems to closely capture the emphatic patterns of visual concepts. The model assumptions (e.g., the multiplicative relation between topical and ideological weights and normal priors) do not seem to contradict real data much.
- *Sufficient Coverage of LSCOM*: The visual concepts in the LSCOM ontology seem very extensive, at least in terms of covering news events in the TRECVID 2005 archive. Although LSCOM was initially developed to support video retrieval (Naphade et al. 2006), LSCOM seems to cover a wide variety of visual concepts so that the choices made by news broadcasters holding different ideological perspectives can be closely captured.

Although our method achieved significant improvement over the random baseline, there is considerable room for improvement. We focused on the visual concepts chosen differently by individual news broadcasters, but this did not exclude possibilities for improving the classification by incorporating signals other than visual concepts. For example, broadcast news videos contain spoken words from anchors, reporters, or interviewees, and the word choices have been shown to exhibit a broadcaster's ideological perspectives (Lin and Hauptmann 2006).

It could be argued that because we already knew a video's broadcaster when the video was recorded, the task of determining whether two news videos portray the news event from differing ideological perspectives should be as trivial as checking if they came from different broadcasters. Although we can accomplish the same task using metadata, such as a news video's broadcaster, this method is unlikely to be applicable to videos that contain little metadata (e.g., web videos). We opted for a method of broader generalization and developed our method solely based on visual content and generic visual concepts. In the following section, we will refute the argument that the difference in video presentations is merely due to individual broadcaster idiosyncrasies.

8.5.2   Effect of Broadcasters' Idiosyncratic Production Styles

The experimental results above seem to suggest that broadcasters with differing ideological beliefs choose different imagery to portray the same news event. However, there is an alternative theory for the high classification accuracy. Each broadcaster usually has idiosyncratic production styles (e.g., adding station logo in the corner and unique studio scenes) and a fixed number of anchors and reporters. Although we have removed nonnews segments and news studio scenes, individual news broadcasters may still have idiosyncratic ways of editing and composing news footage. These news channel-specific product styles may be reflected in the visual concepts, and the high accuracy classification results in Section 5.1 (Figure 8.6) may be mostly due to production styles and have little to do with ideological perspectives. Is it possible that the classifiers in Section 5.1 learned only broadcasters' idiosyncratic production styles to determine if they portray a news event differently? We developed the following classification task to test this theory. Similar to the last experiments, we conducted classification experiments with a key difference: we did not contrast news stories on the same news event.

If the jTP captured only individual news broadcasters' production styles, we would expect the classifiers to perform well in this new setting, no matter whether we contrasted news stories on the same news topic or not. Production styles should exist independent of news events. We conducted three ideological classification experiments. For each ideology, we randomly sampled positive data from all possible labeled news events, and randomly sampled negative data from the news stories from the other two ideologies. For example, in classifying Chinese ideology, we collected positive data by randomly sampling Chinese news stories (about any news events), and negative data by randomly sampling from Arabic and American news stories (also without regard to their news topics). We trained the perspective classifiers based on the jTP, and performed 10-fold cross-validation. We also varied the amount of training data from 10% to 90%. We compared the perspective classifiers with random baselines (i.e., randomly guessing one of two perspectives with equivalent probabilities). The experimental results in Figure 8.7 show that it is very unlikely that the high classification accuracy in the previous section is due to broadcasters' idiosyncratic production styles. The classification accuracy is slightly better than a

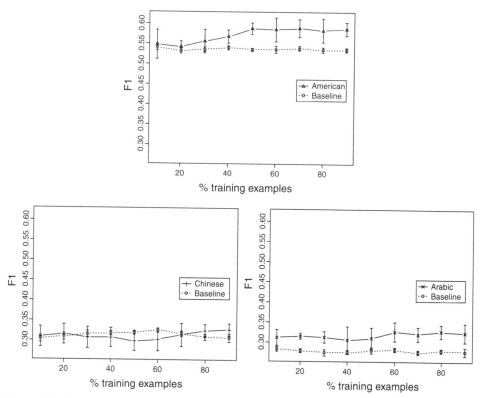

Figure 8.7. The results of testing if the joint topic and perspective model captures only individual news broadcasters' production styles but not emphatic patterns of visual concepts. *x*-axis is the amount of training data, and *y*-axis is the average F1.

random baseline (*t*-test, $p < 0.02$) but very close to random. The production styles seem to contribute to classifying whether or not news video pairs come from the same broadcasters, but the magnitude was minimal and cannot account for the high accuracy achieved earlier.

Except for Chinese ideology, Figure 8.7 shows statistically significant differences when training data are large ($p < 0.01$). Therefore, the classifiers seemed to recognize some production styles, at least in American and Arabic news stories, that allow classifiers to outperform random baselines. However, the difference is minor and much smaller than the difference we observed in Figure 8.6 when news stories were contrasted on the *same* news event. Therefore, individual broadcasters' production styles contribute to but cannot account for the high accuracy of the perspective classification results in Figure 8.6. In addition to a minor effect from production styles, broadcasters holding different ideological perspectives seemed to exhibit strongly emphatic patterns of visual concepts when they covered international news events. By exploiting these emphatic patterns, we can successfully identify the ideological perspective from which a news video was made.

8.5.3 Topical and Ideological Weights

We illustrate the emphatic patterns of visual concepts by visualizing the topical and ideological weights recovered from the news videos in the TRECVID 2005 archive. JTP explicitly models the emphatic patterns of visual concepts as a product between a concept's *topical* weight (i.e., how frequently a visual concept is shown for a specific news event) and *ideological* weights (i.e., how much emphasis a broadcaster holding a particular ideological perspective puts on it). These topical and ideological weights succinctly summarize the emphatic patterns of visual concepts. We visualized the topical and ideological weights of visual concepts in a color text cloud. Text clouds, or tag clouds, have been a very popular way of displaying a set of short strings and their frequency information (e.g., bookmark tags on Del.icio.us (http://del.icio.us) and photo tags on Flickr (http://www.flickr.com). Text clouds represent a word's frequency in size, that is, the value of topical weights τ in the model. The larger a word's size, the more frequently the word appears in a collection. To show a visual concept's ideological weight, we painted a visual concept in color shades. We assigned each ideological perspective a color, and a concept's color was determined by which perspective uses a concept more frequently than the other. Color shades gradually change from pure colors (strong emphasis) to light gray (almost no emphasis). The degree of emphasis is measured by how far away a concept's ideological weight ϕ is from 1. Recall that when a concept's ideological weight ϕ is 1, it places no emphasis. We fitted the jTP on the news videos about a specific news event from two contrasting ideologies, (e.g., American vs. non-American, i.e., Chinese plus Arabic). For example, Figure 8.8 shows the topical weights (in word sizes) and ideological weights (in color shades) of the news stories about the Iraq War. The visual concepts of low topical and ideological weights are omitted due to space limits.

In reporting the Iraq War news, Figure 8.8 shows how American and non-American (i.e., Chinese and Arabic) news media presented stories differently. Concepts such as *Outdoor*, *Adult*, and *Face* were frequently shown (see Figure 8.3), but they were not shown more or less frequently by different ideologies. Compared with

Figure 8.8. The color text cloud summarizes the topical and ideological weights uncovered in videos about the Iraq War. The larger a word's size, the larger its topical weight. The darker a word's color shade, the more extreme its ideological weight. Red represents the American ideology, and blue represents non-American ideologies (i.e., Arabic and Chinese).

Computers Protesters Sunny Corporate_Leader Attached_Body_Parts Sidewalks Host People_Crying Police_Private_- Security_Personnel Dresses_Of_Women Guard Smoke Parade Reporters Microphones Security_Checkpoint Windy Funeral Police Explosion_Fire Apartment_Complex Residential_Buildings Walking Office Road Guest Adobehouses Conference_Room Scene_Text Female_Reporter Muslims Car Demonstration_Or_Protest Exiting_Car Trees Vegetation Rocky_Ground Building Dirt_Gravel_Road Armed_Person Military_Personnel Flags Athlete Grandstands_Bleachers Sky Truck Urban_Scenes Computer_Or_Television_Screens People_Marching Streets Beards Exploding_Ordinance Nighttime Airport Congressman Celebration_Or_Party Suburban Highway Single_Family_Homes Handshaking Sports Politics Cityscape Clouds Landscape Text_Labeling_People Election_Campaign Waterways Text_On_Artificial_Background Greeting Overlaid_Text Maps Waterscape_Waterfront George_Bush Us_Flags Caucasians Motorcycle Head_Of_State Asian_People Non-uniformed_Fighters Non-us_National_Flags

Figure 8.9. The text cloud summarizes the topical and ideological weights uncovered from the news videos about the Arafat's death. The larger a word's size, the larger its topical weight. The darker a word's color shade, the more extreme its ideological weight. Red represents Arabic ideology, and blue represents non-Arabic ideologies (i.e., American and Chinese).

non-American news broadcasters, American news media showed more battles (*Fighter Combat*, and *Street Battle*), war zones (*Exploding Ordnance*, *Explosion Fire*, *Smoke*, and *Shooting*), soldiers (*Military Personnel*, *Armed Person*, and *Police Private Security Personnel*), and weapons (*Machine Guns*, *Weapons*, and *Rifles*). In contrast, non-American news media showed more non-American people (*Muslims* and *Asian People*) and symbols (*Non-U.S. National Flags*), and civilian activities (*Parade* and *Riot*). Although some visual concepts were emphasized in a manner that defied our intuition, the military versus nonmilitary contrast clearly distinguishes how Western and Eastern media covered the Iraq War. We show how Arabic news media and non-Arabic (i.e., Chinese and American) news media covered Arafat's death in Figure 8.9.

We can see that Arabic news media reported more reactions from Palestinian people (*People Crying*, *Parade*, and *Demonstration—or Protest* and *People March-ing*), which is what we might expect. In contrast, non-Arabic news media showed more still images (*Still Image*) of Yasser Arafat (*Yasser Arafat*) and reactions from political leaders (*Head of State* and *George Bush*). Again, we observe how news broadcasters holding contrasting ideological perspectives choose to emphasize different visual concepts. An alternative way of estimating the frequency visual concepts is to obtain maximum likelihood estimates of a language model.

There are also alternative ways of estimating what visual concepts are emphasized by each ideology (e.g., chi-square test, mutual information, etc.). The jTP differs from these techniques in the following aspects:

- Our model provides a probability model that unifies topical and ideological weights in the same model. Most of the previous techniques answer only one aspect of the question. The statistical model allows us to learn parameters and infer a news video's ideological perspective in a very principled manner.

- Our model explicitly models the emphatic patterns of visual concepts as a multiplicative relationship. The assumption may be arguably naive, but the concrete relationship allows future work for refinement. In stark contrast, most previous techniques are not able to explicitly model how visual concepts are emphasized.

8.5.4 Effects of Visual Semantic Concept Classification Accuracy

So far our experiments were based on manual annotations of visual concepts. Using manual annotation is equivalent to assuming that perfect concept classifiers are available. The state-of-the-art classifiers are far from perfect for most visual concepts (Naphade and Smith 2004). So how well can our approach determine if two news videos convey a differently ideological perspective on an event using empirically trained visual concept classifiers?

We empirically trained all LSCOM visual concept classifiers using support vector machines. For each concept, we first trained unimodal concept classifiers using many low-level features (e.g., color histograms in various grid sizes and color spaces, texture, text, and audio), and then built multimodal classifiers that fused the outputs from top unimodal classifiers (Hauptmann et al. 2005). We obtained a visual concept classifier's empirical accuracy by training on 90% of the TRECVID 2005 development set and testing on the held-out 10%. We evaluated the performance of the best multimodal classifiers on the held-out set in terms of average precision. We varied visual concept classifiers' accuracy by injecting noise into manual annotations. We randomly flipped the positive and negative LSCOM annotations of a visual concept until we reached the desired break-even points of recall and precision, which approximates a rank-based evaluation metric like average precision.

Recall-precision break-even points are shown to be highly correlated with average precision (Manning et al. 2008). We varied the classifiers' break-even points ranging from average precision obtained from empirically trained classifiers to 1.0 (i.e., the original LSCOM annotations), and repeated the perspective classification experiments in Section 5.1. The noise injection allows us to easily manipulate a classifier's accuracy, but the real classification errors may not be completely random. The experimental results in Figure 8.10 show that using the empirically trained visual concept classifiers (the leftmost data points) still outperformed random baselines in identifying Arabic, Chinese, and American ideological perspectives (t-test, $p < 0.01$). The improvement, however, is smaller than that found by using manual LSCOM annotations (the rightmost data points). The median average precision of the empirically trained classifiers for all LSCOM concepts was 0.0113 (i.e., the x-axis of the leftmost data point in Figure 8.10). Not surprisingly, perspective identification improved as the concept classifiers' performance increased. With recent advances in computational power and statistical learning algorithms, it is likely that visual concept classifier accuracy will steadily improve. Moreover, we may be able to compensate for concept classifiers' poor accuracy by increasing the number of visual concepts, as suggested in a recent simulation study of video retrieval performance using thousands of visual concepts (Hauptmann et al. 2007a,b).

8.6 SUMMARY

We investigated how ideological perspectives are reflected in news video imagery. When people discuss controversial issues, their choices of written words, spoken words, and visual concepts are not only about the topic (i.e., topical), but also reflect inner attitudes and opinions toward an issue (i.e., ideological). Although automatically understanding perspectives from written or spoken text documents and video is a scientifically challenging problem, it will enable many applications that can

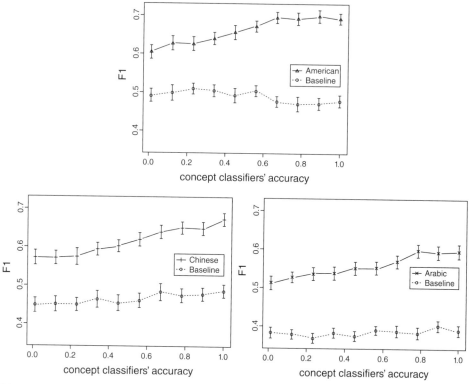

Figure 8.10. The results of varying visual concept classifier accuracy. The *x*-axis is concept classifier accuracy in terms of recall-precision break-even point. The leftmost data point is using empirically trained visual concept classifiers. The rightmost point is using perfect concept classifiers, that is, LSCOM annotations.

survey public opinion on social issues and political viewpoints on a much larger scale. Machine understanding of subjective beliefs, however, has been deemed "a vain hope" (Abelson and Carroll 1965). In this work, we took up the challenge and approached the problem in a statistical learning framework. The experimental results show that perspectives could be successfully identified by statistically modeling documents and their relationship.

We studied the problem of automatically identifying the ideological perspective from which a news video was produced. We presented a method based on specific, computable emphatic patterns of visual concepts: given a news event, contrasting ideologies emphasize different subsets of visual concepts. We explicitly modeled the emphatic patterns as a multiplicative relationship between a visual concept's topical and ideological weights, and developed an approximate inference algorithm to cope with the nonconjugacy of the logistic-normal priors. The experimental results suggest that the ideological perspective classifiers based on emphatic patterns are effective, and the high classification accuracy cannot be simply attributed to individual news broadcasters' production styles. What is perhaps the most interesting is not the perspective classification task per se, but that classifiers based *only* on emphatic patterns of visual concepts can clearly identify bias in TV news.

CHAPTER 9

MULTIMEDIA INFORMATION EXTRACTION IN A LIVE MULTILINGUAL NEWS MONITORING SYSTEM

DAVID D. PALMER, MARC B. REICHMAN, and NOAH WHITE

9.1 INTRODUCTION

The explosion in the availability of global news broadcasts, via satellite, cable television, and Internet sources, has made it possible for a person in one location to view news video from around the world, broadcast in dozens of languages. This access to an overwhelming quantity of multilingual video has created an urgent need for tools that enable archiving, indexing, searching, and browsing large quantities of multilingual news video. A key component of this technology is multimedia information extraction, which distills the raw video broadcast into a rich textual metadata profile of the information content of the source.

In this paper, we describe the multimedia information extraction capabilities of the Enhanced Video Text and Audio Processing (EVITAP) system, a news navigation system that continuously captures live news broadcasts in over 20 languages, including Arabic, Mandarin Chinese, Persian, Russian, Spanish, and English. The EVITAP system uses a broad set of multimedia information extraction tools to analyze the raw video and audio contained in the broadcast. EVITAP transcribes each broadcast in the source language using automatic speech recognition (ASR) and translates each source into a single target language (usually English) using machine translation (MT); additional information extraction components analyze the raw images, audio, and language content of the broadcast to create a metadata profile of the information contained in the broadcast. The system enables cross-lingual searching of the archive in the target language, as well as monolingual searching in the source language for any set of broadcasts. EVITAP provides a single system that achieves continuous 24/7 processing of multilingual video sources

Multimedia Information Extraction: Advances in Video, Audio, and Imagery Analysis for Search, Data Mining, Surveillance, and Authoring, First Edition. Edited by Mark T. Maybury.

and provides users with a single interface for searching, browsing, viewing, editing, and exporting multilingual news.

EVITAP contains a combination of commercial software products and research components, and it is currently a fully operational system with multiple independent installations in use in several locations by hundreds of simultaneous users. In this paper, we provide a general overview of all the components contributing to the multimedia information extraction in EVITAP. Due to its operational nature and the continuous processing of several simultaneous broadcast feeds, EVITAP has a strict real-time processing requirement: all components analyzing the input video must maintain real-time performance at all times on all sources in order to keep up with the flow of incoming data. Speech recognition transcripts must be produced as the live audio is received, for all languages; image analysis must be completed as frames arrive. And the resulting metadata from all multimedia processing components must be indexed and searchable by a user immediately. The real-time constraint results in essential speed versus accuracy tradeoffs in practice. Optimal accuracy for any speech system in the research lab is attained via multiple adaptation and decode passes, and in formal evaluations, the best accuracy (lowest word error rate, or WER) is produced at upwards of 300 times real-time processing. Similar processing times are common for MT evaluations, and information retrieval (IR) evaluations rarely place any time or processing constraints on the actual indexing step. This is obviously unacceptable for continuous live data, and a great deal of engineering effort in EVITAP has focused on balancing this real-time requirement with the need for high quality output.

In Section 9.2, we describe the EVITAP system and its multimedia information extraction components. In Section 9.3, we describe how the wide range of information extracted in EVITAP can be used to create a complete model of the content of the video source. In Section 9.4, we discuss joint training techniques that help to improve the overall performance of the multimedia information extraction.

9.2   EVITAP SYSTEM OVERVIEW

The EVITAP system continuously ingests live video news broadcasts from around the world, analyzes the broadcast content in real time, and makes the broadcasts searchable by users and available for immediate and archived playback. In Section 9.2.1, we describe the core video ingest components of EVITAP, and in Section 9.2.2, we describe the multimedia information extraction components that distill the raw broadcast into its core content. In Section 9.2.3, we describe the information fusion enabled by the range of information sources, and in Section 9.2.4, we discuss methods for improving the overall performance of information extraction components by training them jointly. In Section 9.2.5, we briefly summarize previous work in the area of broadcast monitoring systems.

9.2.1   Video Ingestion and Archiving Components

The *video ingestion and archiving* components in EVITAP schedule the processing of all broadcasts, route the video to the appropriate language-specific processing

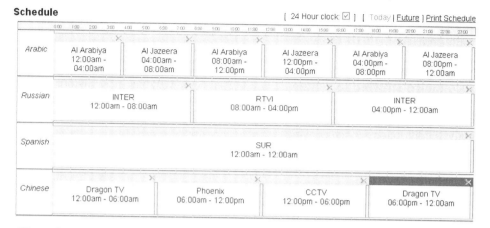

Figure 9.1. Example of the schedule of channels to be processed in an EVITAP system.

module, encode the raw video signals into a common format, and store the video files for live or archived user playback. The primary source of video data in the EVITAP system is a series of live video feeds from consumer and free-to-air satellite dishes and receivers, which provide access to a constant supply of live news broadcasts from around the world. The processing of satellite feeds proceeds according to a predefined schedule, which allows the source feed for any given language to switch frequently between available channels in that language, as shown in Figure 9.1.

All incoming video feeds are simultaneously streamed from a server for live playback within the EVITAP interface and encoded to video files for archived playback. As each source is ingested by the EVITAP system, it is also prepared for analysis by the information extraction components. The video signal is split into image and audio components by the commercial Virage VideoLogger, which communicates with the components described in Section 9.2.2 via a plug-in architecture. For each piece of metadata produced by the analysis components, VideoLogger stores a time stamp that contains the information label start and end times. The time stamps allow the EVITAP system to access and play back the exact point in any broadcast containing a particular item, such as a face detection, speaker segment, or spoken word.

9.2.2 Multimedia Information Extraction Components

As each video news broadcast is captured, it is processed by a set of *multimedia information extraction* tools, which produce time-stamped textual metadata describing the content of the video. The *video and image analysis tools* process the video frames of the source signal; these tools include keyframe detection, scene analysis, and face identification, and are described in Section 9.2.2.1 The *audio and language analysis tools* process the audio component of the source signal and the resulting spoken language; these tools include audio classification, speaker identification,

ASR, named entity detection, and machine translation, and are described in Section 9.2.2.2.

9.2.2.1 Video and Image Analysis The composition of individual frames of the video can be analyzed to determine whether specific persons or items are shown, and the sequence of image frames can be analyzed to determine a pattern of image movement. The EVITAP system contains several different types of video and image analysis components, each of which produces a time-stamped textual metadata tag describing one or more frames of the video.

Keyframes are defined roughly as video frames that are "significantly different" from previous frames; a sequence of keyframes can thus represent a condensed view of the full video. EVITAP keyframes are detected based on the comparison of edge and luminance histograms derived from adjacent frames. A sensitivity threshold allows for adjustments to the difference required in order for a frame to be judged different from its neighbor.

Face identification detects human faces within individual video frames and compares the face to a library of known faces. Detected faces are labeled with the name from the library or as unknown faces, if no known face is recognized.

Scene cut analysis analyzes sequences of video frames to detect four classes of video sequence changes of variable length. The sequence changes are detected and classified based on analysis of 16-bin histograms populated with features derived from the raw amounts of RGB color in the frames. A *scene cut* is classified as a sudden, hard change within a small number of frames. A *transition* is a short progression from one scene into another, while a *transient* is a long transition between scenes. A *fade* is a frame progression to or from a frame that is completely black.

Color frame detection analyzes the pixels of each image frame and detects frames that primarily consist of a single color. This detection of single-color frames can be useful for commercial detection and story segmentation.

On-screen text recognition (OCR) analyzes each video frame (or keyframe), detects the presence of text within the frame, and recognizes the text strings. An optional *language model* (LM) and vocabulary can be used to correct some OCR errors.

Logo detection, like face identification, detects logos within individual video frames and compares the logo to a library of known logos.

9.2.2.2 Audio and Language Analysis A great deal of the information in a news broadcast is contained in the raw acoustic portion of the signal. Much of the information is contained in spoken audio, both in the characteristics of the human speech signal and in the sequence of words spoken. This information can also take the form of nonspoken audio events, such as music, background noise, or even periods of silence. The EVITAP system contains many audio and language analysis components, each of which produces a time-stamped textual metadata tag describing a region of the source audio.

Audio classification segments and labels the audio signal based on a set of acoustic class models, including speech, non-speech noise, music, and silence.

Speaker identification models the speech-specific acoustic characteristics of the audio and labels the gender of the speaker. It also identifies speakers that match trained examples in a library of known speakers.

Automatic speech recognition (ASR), or *speech-to-text* (STT), provides an automatic transcript of the spoken words, with a (real-time) WER of approximately 15–30% for each of the 20+ languages supported.

Named entity detection identifies names of people, locations, and organizations within the ASR and MT output transcripts.

Closed captioning is a human-generated transcript of the spoken transcript that can be embedded in a broadcast video signal. In addition to transcribed words, the closed captioning often contains speaker names and story and speaker delimiters (usually ">>>" or ">>"). Closed captioning is rarely available for non-U.S. broadcasts.

Machine translation (MT) provides an automatic translation from a source language into a target language. In the EVITAP system, an MT system translates all ASR transcripts into a common target language (usually English).

9.2.3 Indexing and Retrieval

Text-based IR techniques have been successful at indexing large corpora, such as the Internet, for retrieval by users of search engines. The same IR techniques can be used to index the textual metadata produced by the analysis components in EVITAP. In our system, the indexing of all data in all languages must happen continuously and seamlessly in order to allow for searching of live broadcasts as soon as information is extracted. The textual metadata generated by the multimedia information extraction components in EVITAP, represented as a single UTF-8 XML file, is indexed in one-minute batches by the Autonomy IDOL engine, a commercial text-based IR engine that uses Bayesian techniques to index large document collections. Since the metadata for a given broadcast is usually in multiple languages, each transcript and translation is treated as a separate document for indexing and retrieval. In this way, the ASR transcript can be indexed and searchable at the same time that it is being translated by the MT engine; the translation is subsequently indexed as soon as it is complete. Since all transcripts are translated into a common target language, and since most users of the system search exclusively in that language (usually English), we optimize the indexing and retrieval for the target language while still enabling searching in the source languages.

9.2.4 User Interface

The user interface is an important factor in the success of any news navigation system. Transcribing and indexing the data are useless if the user does not have the tools to navigate and interpret complex search results. This is especially important due to the inherent uncertainty in the automatically generated data. An intuitive interface must be available for a user to view and navigate search results, to interpret the key broadcast information, and to play back segments of interest. The

Figure 9.2. Simultaneous live broadcasts viewed within the EVITAP interface.

browser-based user interface in EVITAP provides several tools for helping a user navigate the news archive.

Live View of All News Broadcasts: All news broadcasts can be viewed live. Figure 9.2 shows 12 simultaneous live broadcasts displayed within EVITAP.

Cross-Lingual Search and Alerting: Users can search all broadcasts cross-lingually in a single target translation language, such as English, and they can also search in the broadcast source language. Users can set up saved searches and be alerted in the interface or via email when a new broadcast matches their search criteria. Searches can be restricted to particular languages and broadcasters, as well as date and time ranges. All textual metadata created by the analysis components described in Section 9.2.2 are indexed using the textual IR system described in Section 9.2.3. The user can search the entire archive using this same textual IR system, utilizing the entire range of standard and advanced search functionality provided by the commercial Autonomy IDOL engine, including Boolean queries, natural language queries, phrase queries, wildcards, stemming, result clustering, and related document search. Within the search interface, the user can enter the query text and parameters, as well as restrict the search to specific broadcasters, languages, and date range.

For each search, the list of matching broadcasts contains the broadcast information, including source and date/time, search terms in context, and a list of the most-frequently named entities in the transcript/translation, as shown in Figure 9.3. Note that the search term was "Barack Obama" in English, and the cross-lingual search results can be in any broadcast language in the archive (Arabic Al-Jazeera in this case).

Audio/Video Playback with Full Transcript: Users can play the audio/video for any broadcast, and they can view the ASR transcript and the translation with

52273 - Al Jazeera (Qatar)   2009-03-18 07:00:00

while, the face of fifteen parliamentarians us
from Democrats and Republicans a letter to
President **Barack Obama** asked him to
reconsider the new strategy in Afghanistan and
sent more troops there and say that the motive
dead GEO as

- People: Arab, Li, Arabs
- Locations: Iraq, World, Gaza
- Organizations: Means of, Government,
  Ministry of Foreign Affairs

Figure 9.3. EVITAP search result showing broadcast information, search terms in context, and most frequently named entities.

Figure 9.4. Video Playback interface, with synchronized speaker-segmented transcript and keyframe storyboard.

search terms and named entities highlighted and segmented by speakers, as shown in Figure 9.4.

The words in the transcript are highlighted as they are spoken in the audio; search terms ("Ahmadinejad," in this case) are also highlighted in the transcript. Users can search for the output of on-screen text recognition, Face ID, and all other multimedia information extraction systems, and the full list of words and phrases detected by these systems can be viewed. A closer view of the transcript display is shown in Figure 9.5.

Words in any transcript can be located using the find box. The transcript displays are synchronized with the video playback, such that as the video plays, the corresponding words in the transcript are highlighted. The user can click on any word or speaker label in the transcript, and the video will immediately jump to the point in the video where that word is spoken. Users can edit any transcript, and all edits are reindexed and searchable immediately. Users can also export any portion of a transcript, with its corresponding audio/video clip, to a separate file outside the interface. They can also add custom annotations within the transcripts to indicate visual or audio events that are present in the video.

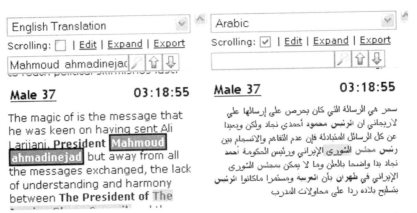

Figure 9.5. ASR and MT transcripts with search terms and named entities highlighted, segmented by speaker.

9.2.5 Related Work

Research groups first started focusing on large-scale news video processing in the mid-1990s, and there has been significant progress in video news archiving over the past two decades. Much of the impetus for early work came from the DARPA-sponsored Hub-4 news transcription evaluations, which focused on improving the ASR performance on news data, initially in English and later in Mandarin and Spanish; see Kubala (1999) for a summary of the results of these programs. The TRECVID evaluations have similarly focused on improving performance of video retrieval systems, with an emphasis on cross-lingual retrieval of news broadcasts; see Smeaton et al. (2009) for a summary of the recent TRECVID evaluations.

Early video news processing systems, led by MITRE's Broadcast News Editor and Broadcast News Navigator (BNE/BNN) system (Merlino et al. 1997), processed English-language broadcasts and relied primarily on human-generated closed captioning embedded in the video signal. BNE/BNN was one of the first systems to index and archive large quantities (several broadcasts per day) of news video and to make the archive available to users via a web-based interface. The BNE/BNN interface displayed story "summaries" as a single keyframe with broadcast source and time and a list of frequent names occurring in the closed caption data; we include several of these elements in the user interface of the eViTAP system.

The next generation of systems, such as Speechbot (Van Thong et al. 2000) and BBN's Rough "N" Ready (Kubala et al. 1999), used speech recognition to generate transcripts automatically. Due to the lack of real-time speech processing, the number of daily broadcasts that could be processed was limited, and broadcasts were rarely processed live. The Rough "N" Ready system used several audio and language analysis systems in addition to speech recognition, including speaker identification and named entity extraction, which have become standard audio indexing components for news processing systems, including our system.

The Informedia project at Carnegie-Mellon University (Hauptmann and Witbrock 1997; Wactlar et al. 1999) has continuously contributed novel audio and video analysis research since its inception in 1994. The stated goal of the Informedia project is "to achieve machine understanding of video and film media, including all aspects of search, retrieval, visualization and summarization in both contemporane-ous and archival content collections" using speech, language, and image analysis techniques, and an active prototyping interface has served as a testbed for new analysis results.

In our work, we have built on the previous work to develop a single system that can continuously process multilingual news video, transcribe and translate each broadcast, and provide real-world users access to an intuitive browser-based inter-face that allows them to search the news archive, play news video, view and edit transcripts, and export video and transcripts to external reporting tools. In doing so, we have brought together many existing real-time audio and video analysis compo-nents, and we have developed additional novel capabilities.

9.3 TRANSMEDIA INFORMATION FUSION

The range of video, audio, and natural language information extraction components in EVITAP open the door to information fusion across media types. At any point in any video in any language, EVITAP can provide a user details from the audio about who is speaking and what they are saying, as well as details from the video frames about whose face is displayed in the video and what text is displayed on the screen. Users can search for all broadcast segments containing a certain person speaking in the audio component at the same time a specific word or a specific face appeared in the video frame.

By combining all information sources available in a news broadcast, users can get a full model of everything happening in a video segment, across modalities. For example, Figure 9.6 shows a graphical representation of the multimedia information extraction for a short segment of video in EVITAP. Each row is a metadata track, such as Face ID or STT transcript, and the x-axis represents the change in the metadata over time. The graph in Figure 9.6 shows that the Face ID system recog-nizes the face "Lynne Russell" (a news anchor) in a keyframe at time stamp 8:26:12 in the broadcast, at the same time that the Speaker ID system recognizes Lynne Russell's voice, and the On-Screen Text system recognizes the words "Special Report" on the screen; these sources combined clearly show that a news anchor is introducing a special report. The Closed Caption and STT transcripts of the audio ("Clinton spoke with reporters") indicate that the special report is about Hillary Clinton giving an interview. At 8:34:29, the Face ID system detects Hillary Clinton, and the On-Screen Text system recognizes the words "Medicare Issues," indicating that Clinton is speaking with reporters about Medicare. At 8:40:00 the Speaker ID system recognizes Hillary Clinton's voice: the broadcast has switched from the anchor to video footage of Clinton speaking. While any one of the information extraction components can provide information about one aspect of the broadcast, fusing the information from all the multimedia extraction components enables a higher level analysis of the broadcast content.

9.4 JOINT TRAINING OF INFORMATION EXTRACTION COMPONENTS

The information fusion across video and audio modalities described in Section 9.3 is a powerful combination. However, success depends on having meaningful results

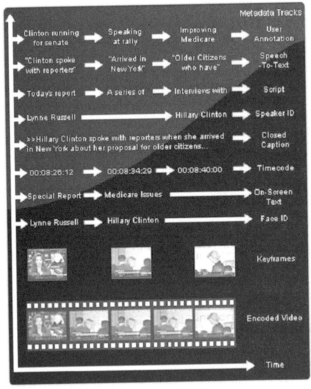

Figure 9.6. A graphical representation of multimedia information extraction from a news broadcast.

from all the components, such that identified faces and speaker voices can be connected to the same person. This is a significant challenge since the information extraction components have a range of training and recognition algorithms, which makes it difficult to coordinate the libraries and vocabularies of all systems to optimize cross-component recognition. Dynamic updating of all components is essential, as new information is constantly entering the news in the form of new words, new speakers, and new faces. For example, successful retrieval of a word or phrase from the output of a cascade of automatic audio and language processing components (ASR, NE, MT) depends on the performance of each of the components, as well as the successful indexing of the output transcripts in the IR engine. Similarly, correlating information across Face ID, Speaker ID, and OCR systems trained from libraries depends on overlap between the libraries: identifying a face in a video frame is much more significant if that person's voice can also be identified in the audio and the person's name can also be recognized in an on-screen caption. In this section, we discuss joint training of multimedia components in the EVITAP system.

9.4.1   Joint Vocabulary Updating for Language Components

To locate a desired name phrase in the English translation of a non-English audio segment, the name must first be correctly transcribed by the ASR engine, and then correctly tagged as a name by the named entity system. Finally, the phrase must be correctly translated into English by the MT engine. Each system can be tuned for optimal overall accuracy; however, independent of accuracy, the desired word must be present in the vocabulary and accurately represented in the language model (LM) of each of the three systems.

New words, usually proper names, are constantly entering the news. In addition, the frequency of different words and names can change dramatically in a short period of time, especially from one country to the next. The vocabularies and language models of the various components in a global news monitoring system must be dynamically updated to reflect this reality. While this is a sensible goal in principle, in reality the coordinated updating of models in different components is nearly impossible, given the computational resources required for retraining and the fact that the processing of live data cannot be disabled during the retraining of component models. In our work, we use commercial MT and IR engines that cannot be easily tuned, so we focus on the coordinated updating of vocabularies and models in the ASR and NE systems in order to optimize speech retrieval performance.

The first step in updating the vocabulary is updating the pool of training data to contain examples of new words and to better reflect the relative importance of existing words. We maintain a list of Internet news sites for each of the languages we update; this list includes the websites for broadcasters being ingested, since online content often parallels broadcast stories. We download data regularly from these sites and convert it to a format consistent with existing training data by extracting news content from web pages, then cleaning up and normalizing content. Retraining the ASR language model involves first adding all new words to the vocabulary by applying language-specific automatic pronunciation generation. The new training data is then either appended to the existing training set for retraining of the full LM, or a separate LM is trained for the new data and is interpolated with the existing LM.

Since existing Named Entity training data is only available for a small set of the languages processed by the EVITAP system, and since regular automatic NE retraining on new data does not allow for manual annotation, we train the Named Entity models using an unsupervised algorithm. The unsupervised training first labels names in the training files based on a set of name lists; these name lists are compiled from existing NE training data where available, manually created by native speakers, harvested from Internet sites, or created by running MT on existing lists in other languages. The labeling in new data follows a simple greedy longest-match algorithm. Since NE training requires much less training data than ASR LM training, we prune the resulting data set based on a tag density measure, selecting those training files containing the most NE tags. Automated retraining can occur as frequently as every few hours, if required.

9.4.2 Joint Library Updating for Face and Speaker ID

Unlike language models in ASR, NE, and MT systems, which can be trained automatically from text sources harvested from the Internet, Face and Speaker ID libraries require significant manual preparation of training data from very different sources. Face library training requires manual filtering and labeling of a collection of image files in order to identify images containing faces suitable for training.

Speaker library training requires manual chopping and labeling of a collection of audio files of suitable acoustic quality, in order to identify audio files suitable for training. In order to identify news segments containing both the face and the voice of a given person, the Face and Speaker ID libraries must both contain the necessary training examples.

There are two directions from which the joint Face and Speaker ID training problem can be approached. A list of high-value people can be used to target the training, or a large collection of unlabeled data can be manually culled to create a training library. In the first approach, training works from a known set of people that need to be identified. Examples of images and audio clips of appropriate quality need to be located and labeled in order for both the Face and Speaker libraries to contain the same people. In the second training approach, the process builds from an existing collection of images and speaker segments. Images and audio clips containing known people are extracted, usually manually, from the data set to create a targeted library. The second approach has the advantage of starting from an existing data set; however, this approach requires more manual effort and is not guaranteed to result in Face and Speaker libraries that overlap significantly.

9.5 CONCLUSION

In this paper, we described the EVITAP system, a news broadcast navigation system that captures and analyzes live news broadcasts in over 20 languages. We described briefly the variety of multimedia information extraction components in EVITAP and the function of each component. We have not focused on detailed descriptions of the information extraction components or the algorithms contained therein, but rather we have focused on how information from video, audio, and language sources are combined to create a full model of information content within the multimedia source. We also provided a brief discussion, in Section 9.4, of how the performance of individual information extraction components can be improved by leveraging other IE components running on the same data.

The EVITAP system described in this paper builds on the previous research and development in a wide range of areas, including image analysis, audio processing, natural language processing, and systems engineering. While many of the components and ideas described in this paper are not novel in the academic sense, the EVITAP system and its components make several important contributions to the scientific community. First, the range of multimedia information extraction components running on all broadcasts in EVITAP enables new possibilities for information fusion and data mining. Face ID, logo ID, and on-screen text recognition systems extract information from the individual video frames. Speaker ID, audio classification, and ASR systems extract information from the raw audio in the video transmission. Named entity detection and MT systems extract information from the natural language in the audio. And all information extracted is stored, indexed, and searchable, via a single IR system. Faces and speakers can thus be identified as they appear in news broadcasts and correlated with additional information extracted from the spoken language. Patterns of appearance of names and phrases can be analyzed over a period of time. In addition, information can be compared and contrasted across broadcasters and languages, such that the many facets of international coverage of an important news event can be accessible and searchable. See, for example, Chapter 7 on Automated Analysis of Ideological Bias in Video in this collection for a detailed discussion of this problem.

A second contribution of the EVITAP system is the demonstration of the feasibility of large-scale continuous real-time analysis of live broadcasts. By focusing on strict real-time processing and long-term software stability requirements for all multimedia analysis components, from both commercial and research sources, this work advances the state of the art in these component information extraction systems. EVITAP also provides an opportunity for research components to be used outside the lab in a fully operational environment by real users, thus providing valuable feedback to researchers on practical matters of system usability and stability.

A third major contribution of the EVITAP system is the variety of languages and sources supported. The full list of languages currently supported by EVITAP for automatic transcription and translation (into English) is: English (U.K., U.S., Australian, and Canadian), Spanish (Spain, North American, Latin American), Portuguese, Japanese, Mandarin Chinese, Korean, French (French, Canadian), German, Italian, Dutch, Arabic (Modern Standard), Farsi/Persian, Russian, Romanian, Polish, Danish, Swedish, Greek, Catalan, and Slovakian. This set of languages enables real-time analysis, by an English speaker, of broadcasts from all countries in North and South America, and most major countries in Europe, the Middle East, and East Asia. Notable gaps in the current coverage are the major languages of Africa and other regions of Asia (South, Southeast, and Central), as well as minority languages and dialects.

EVITAP is an active applied R&D project. Moving forward, we anticipate adding additional multimedia information extraction components to the existing capabilities, in addition to improving the performance of current IE components. We also plan to add new languages as they become available in the speech and MT communities in order to expand the range of broadcast sources that can be indexed and analyzed.

ACKNOWLEDGMENTS

The authors would like to thank Greg Smith, Andrew Sprouse, Shahin Hosseini, Mahesh Krishnamoorthy, Alvin Garcia, Ronald Adams, and Igor Helman, who have made significant technical contributions to the EVITAP project and its many components.

CHAPTER 10

SEMANTIC MULTIMEDIA EXTRACTION USING AUDIO AND VIDEO

EVELYNE TZOUKERMANN, GEETU AMBWANI, AMIT BAGGA,
LESLIE CHIPMAN, ANTHONY R. DAVIS, RYAN FARRELL,
DAVID HOUGHTON, OLIVER JOJIC, JAN NEUMANN, ROBERT RUBINOFF,
BAGESHREE SHEVADE, and HONGZHONG ZHOU

10.1 INTRODUCTION AND MOTIVATION

Improving search capabilities in video has implications ranging from the Internet to television. Browsing a movie while looking at the gist of a related document, watching a sports broadcast while simultaneously browsing statistics about athletes, directly accessing important plays of a particular game or highlights of the football season, obtaining a recipe seen on a cooking show—all these applications require a better understanding of the multimedia content so that searching, browsing, and retrieving are made easier and more accurate.

The last 5 years have seen a tremendous growth in the number of videos available via the Internet. YouTube alone, which is the third most visited website, has 100,000 videos uploaded every day and had about 5 billion videos viewed just during the month of July 2008 ("YouTube draws 5 Billion U.S. Online Video Views in July 2008". comScore. http://www.comscore.com/press/release.asp?press=2444. Retrieved on November 29, 2008). It is estimated that 13 hours of new videos are uploaded to the site every minute.[1] The Internet traffic generated by multimedia content dwarfs that of text and image-based content.

Likewise, the amount of television consumption in developed countries is impressive. According to the A.C. Nielsen Co., the average American watches more than 4 hours of TV each day. This corresponds to 28 hours each week, or 2 months of

---

[1] Stelter, Brian. "Some Media Companies Choose to Profit From Pirated YouTube Clips." *The New York Times*. http://www.nytimes.com/2008/08/16/technology/16tube.html?_r=1&8dp. Retrieved on November 29, 2008.

Multimedia Information Extraction: Advances in Video, Audio, and Imagery Analysis for Search, Data Mining, Surveillance, and Authoring, First Edition. Edited by Mark T. Maybury.
© 2012 IEEE Computer Society. Published 2012 by John Wiley & Sons, Inc.

nonstop TV-watching per year. In an average 65-year lifespan, a person will have spent 9 years watching television[2].

Nonetheless, research is still at the beginning in the area of video processing and understanding of multimedia content. This chapter addresses some of the challenges that need to be solved in order to search, extract, and retrieve multimedia documents. The approach taken in these different projects clearly reflects our belief that fusing information sources, such as automatic speech recognition, natural language processing, and image and video processing techniques yield better results that any one of these methods in isolation.

The following section describes some of the related research in multimedia processing. Section 10.3 shows the work that has been done on the semantic extraction using speech recognition and text. By applying natural language and statistical techniques, we have been able to accurately retrieve segments that are highly relevant to the user's query. Section 10.4 presents our work on multimedia semantic extraction using video, text, and speech. While most of the examples here are based on American football, similar techniques as the ones described in Section 10.4 can be applied to other types of multimedia content, incorporating domain-specific knowledge where applicable. For sports in particular, we want to capture meaningful segments of a game, so that a viewer can browse salient moments of a football game, for example, events such as touchdowns, fumbles, interceptions, and other plays.

The diagram in Figure 10.1 presents the overall architecture of the system. The input can be either a collection of written documents or a collection of media documents. The system processes the text, audio, and video fully automatically.

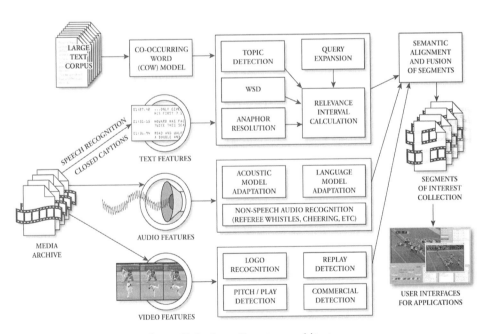

Figure 10.1. Overall system architecture.

---

[2] Compiled by TV-Free America; 1322 18th Street, NW; Washington, DC 20036 (202) 887-4036.

The algorithm makes use of (1) video analysis that aligns the audio, video, and text data of the document; (2) external sources that assist in establishing guidelines to determine information about the document such as the beginning and ending; (3) technology such as optical character recognition (OCR), acoustics, video analysis, speech recognition, and natural language analysis of closed caption information to identify the structural components of the document; and (4) a taxonomy based on known structures of specific content to categorize document types. These diverse information sources collectively provide attributes for describing each segment. Using these attributes or metadata, the identified segments are then tagged, indexed, and classified for retrieval and viewing by the user. While this work focuses on the domain of sports video, for other content genres, the relative abundance of these data sources determines how well the described techniques will generalize. Section 10.5 presents some concluding remarks, as well as some perspectives on future research directions.

10.2 RELATED RESEARCH

On the audio side, the work done at Carnegie Mellon University on the Informedia project (Hauptmann and Witbrock 1997) is the closest to our work. Hauptmann and Witbrock (1997) discuss how speech recognition is used to create transcripts from video, to time-align closed captions, and to segment paragraphs for multimedia information retrieval. Within the vision community (Efros et al. 2003) is an approach similar to ours for scene recognition, focusing on recognizing human action in a range of sports using motion descriptors based on optical flow combined with similarity measures. Wang et al. (2006) describe recognition of action classes using an unsupervised learning approach. Classes are discovered in a large collection of training images, and clusters are organized by group of people in a similar pose. Then distance is computed between image pairs to assign an action class.

The original contribution of this research is in the combined use of sources of evidence for video indexing. By sources of evidence, we mean the actual use of text and speech to guide video processing, associated with content-based features, for example, texture, shape, and color, as discussed in del Bimbo (1999). Other research that uses combined evidence can be found in Palmer, Reichman, and White (Chapter 9, this volume) as well as in Lin and Hauptmann (Chapter 8, this volume).

Gibbon and Liu (2008) provide an overview of video search engines and present a discussion of media processing that is relevant for the work presented in this paper. Media segmentation consists of dividing audio or video into semantically coherent units, combining shot boundary detection, different models for computing feature-based models, to guide other metadata with the segmentation. Gibbon and Liu (2008) also discuss the level of granularity that is variable and thus needs to be clearly defined to perform scene analysis (p. 100). The article by Lew et al. (2006) gives a thorough review of the state of the art in the field of multimedia information retrieval, focusing more on image analysis than video.

There is wealth of research in the area of video analysis applied to American football or soccer (Babaguchi et al. 2004; Gong et al. 1995; Reede and Jose 2005; Yu and Zhang 2001). For example, Babaguchi et al. analyzed football videos for the purpose of automatic highlight selection. The goal is to generate personalized abstracts of American football broadcasts by detecting significant events. They detect salient events that may be included in the video summary, whereas we collect all football segments and cluster them based on their saliency and their similarity. Other approaches (Reede and Jose 2005) base segmentation on frames that establish some of the game structure, such as for example, play, focus, replay, and break. They use a statistical model to parse the video structures. Zhu et al. (2007) focus on soccer broadcast videos, capturing trajectory pattern and interaction pattern in which they develop a model to identify tactic strategies of goal attacks. Similar to our work, authors in Xu et al. (2006) present an event detection model using the broadcast source text, as well as the video to create a personalized summary of the game.

10.3   SEMANTIC MULTIMEDIA EXTRACTION USING AUDIO OR CLOSED-CAPTIONS

In addition to the video signal, multimedia files contain audio information that can guide search and retrieval. In particular, the speech signal contains a lot of important information. Closed captions are available for many commercial-quality videos; however, in their absence, we can fall back on speech-to-text systems. In either case, we use the resulting text output to construct what we refer to as relevance intervals (RIs). An RI is a continuous segment of an audio or video document that is relevant to a particular search term. We construct RIs for every term in the document, providing a complete index of the document covering everything that is mentioned in the audio track. We can also construct RIs from transcripts instead of speech recognition output, but reliable transcripts are not available for most documents.

10.3.1   Construction of RIs

An RI for a given term (which can be any word or phrase that occurs in a document) is constructed starting with the sentence containing the term (see Davis et al. 2004; Tzoukermann et al. 2005). The RI is then expanded forward and backward to take in relevant material, as described below, and a magnitude is assigned based on its assessed importance to the user's query. These magnitudes provide a ranking of how important and germane the interval is to the query term. For each term, all of the RIs generated for that term in a single document are combined into a virtual document (henceforth VD) for that term. For multiterm queries (unless the terms occur as a phrase in the document), we combine the RIs for each term if they are near one another and calculate magnitudes of these conjoined intervals. Only the single-term RIs and VDs are constructed at indexing time. The RIs and VDs for multiterm queries are computed at query time, because the number of possible multiterm queries is exponentially larger than the number of single-term queries. The resulting set of RIs for a media file then constitutes the corresponding VD for the query; there will in general be a large number of VDs produced for each media file, one for each term in the file.

10.3.1.1   *Topical and Structural Expansion of RIs*   RIs are expanded based on both topical and structural factors. Topical expansion of an RI relies on a mutual

information model built up from a text corpus of over 300 million words. This model measures the mutual information associated with two content words co-occurring within a window of approximately three sentences. Using this model, we expand RIs to include nearby sentences whose words have a high mutual information score with the query term, indicating a strong topical connection. The farther away a sentence is from the original occurrence, the stronger this connection needs to be. Topical expansion continues until either several consecutive sentences are judged not strongly related or a structural boundary is reached. The topical expansion process allows the system to build up RIs whose extent is specific to the particular query term. This allows the system to tailor the span of the returned material to the particular query term, rather than having to use the same segment boundaries for all terms. In effect, the system produces a different set of segment boundaries for each query term.

Structural factors both promote and limit expansion of RIs. Syntactic cues can indicate the need to expand intervals; for example, a pronoun whose antecedent is in the previous sentence may induce expansion. Similarly, discourse cues can indicate connections that will trigger expansion (e.g., a sentence that starts with "in that case"). Intervals may also be expanded to include a complete discourse unit when the structure of that discourse unit is important to the meaning of the already included piece. For example, an interval that starts with "The first problem is . . ." would be expanded if the previous sentence contained "There are several problems with . . ." Conversely, structural factors can block further expansion if they indicate a topical boundary. Phrases such as "Turning now to . . ." or "On another subject" indicate such a boundary, and any apparent topical connections across such a boundary are likely to be spurious and are ignored. If the edge of a fully expanded interval is close to such a boundary (i.e., within a sentence or two), we expand it up to the edge of the boundary, paying the price of a small amount of less relevant material for the advantage of including a complete, explicitly marked discourse segment. RIs are limited and expanded in a similar fashion at boundaries located by our topic segmentation module.

We use a three-part algorithm to determine topic boundaries in a document. The first part is based on work by Choi (2000); the measurement of topical continuity involves calculating the overlap and the mutual information value of content words in adjacent sentences. At points where the topic shifts, these values tend to decrease. The second links sentences in the document containing the same low or medium frequency noun, or two different such words with high mutual information, and places boundaries to minimize the breaking of these links. The third induces topic boundary markers by detecting n-grams preferentially found near the boundaries determined by the other two (for instance, markers like "For NPR news, this is . . ." commonly found in broadcast news). In addition to identifying topic boundaries, we extract the words or phrases with the strongest within-segment links as topics of the segment. Note that these topic terms are not used directly in topical expansion or other phases of constructing the RIs, although they can be used in other ways once the RIs have been built, as described in Section 10.3.3 below.

10.3.1.2 *Building RIs for Pronominal References* Additional RIs for an index term are created for pronominal references to the term in nearby sentences. Anaphors are typically found in subsequent sentences, but not always. Because

speech recognition output is not of the quality that permits accurate parsing, we use an anaphora resolution method based on that of Kennedy and Boguraev (1996), which assigns points to potential antecedents based on the position of the anaphora and the potential antecedent in their respective sentences and on guesses about their syntactic functions. In general, the separate RIs created at this step are merged with the RI containing the index term itself, if they are reasonably close, and all the intervening sentences become part of an expanded RI.

10.3.1.3 Term Expansion and RIs   A limited amount of term expansion is currently implemented in RI calculation as well. When we can be confident that two terms are very nearly synonymous, we treat the terms as indistinguishable in creating RIs. We use several symbolic and statistical methods to generate lists of equivalent terms. One is to inspect WordNet for monosemous terms in the same synset. Another is to treat as equivalent certain rearrangements of phrases, and to use lists of equivalent nouns and adjectives. Thus "garbage collection in the city," "city garbage collection," and "municipal garbage collection" are treated as one. Finally, the mutual information model is exploited to determine how similar the contexts of two terms are. If they are highly similar, the terms are safely regarded as equivalent, even if they have some nonoverlapping senses. "Film," for example, has several senses, but in our corpus, its distribution with other words is so similar to that of "movie" that we can see this sense is overwhelmingly prevalent. We also treat more specific terms as instances of a more general term. For example, if we are building RIs for "mammal," we will treat a sentence containing "dog" or "cat" as if it had an occurrence of "mammal," since dogs and cats are kinds of mammals. We only do this in one direction; we don't treat the word "mammal" as an occurrence of "dog," since the discussion may be focused on other kinds of mammals. A sentence containing "dog" is still likely to be included in an interval for the term "mammal" if it is near an occurrence of "mammal." But the system will not create an RI for "mammal" based on an "occurrence" of dog.

10.3.2 Creation of VDs

Once the RIs for a media file have been constructed, each interval is assigned a relevance magnitude, combining local and global factors. Local scoring assigns a measure to each sentence in the interval based on the count of occurrences of the query term, pronouns (or other phrases) that are co-referential with an occurrence in another sentence, and words that have a high mutual information score with the query term. The precise score depends in part on what kind of occurrence it is. The index term itself (or an exact synonym) gets the highest score. "Partial" synonyms get a lower score, because they are less directly connected to the index term. Finally, related words get a score based on their mutual information score with the index term, reflecting the strength of the relation. These scores give us a measure of how relevant each individual sentence in the RI is to the index term. We then factor in how long the interval is and how many of the sentences have nonzero relevance. Note that sentences included for structural reasons may not be directly relevant to the index term at all, and so may get a local score of 0.

After the relevance magnitudes are assigned, the RIs from a single document for a particular term are combined to create a VD containing all and only the relevant material in the original document. In effect, this VD is (an approximation of) the version of the original document that would have been produced if the author(s) had intended to focus solely on the topic of the query term. The VD is assigned the magnitude of the highest-rated RI it contains, with a bonus added if there are other RIs whose relevance is nearly as high. The VDs for each term in the document are then added to a database tailored to allow rapid search by query term, along with all the necessary information to allow smooth playback of the contents of a VD and to construct merged VDs for multiterm searches.

10.3.3 Further Uses of Topic Extraction

The topic word extraction process described above allows us to do more than simply construct RIs and VDs and present them to the user. We use the representative topic words derived from topic segmentation to correct speech recognizer errors. The SR system uses purely local criteria (trigrams) to make decisions about which words have been spoken, but using our knowledge of the local topic, we up weight SR alternatives that have high mutual information with the topic words, and where applicable overrule the SR's decision. The topic terms can also be presented to the user to give a brief description of what the VD is about. While the original multimedia document may have metadata providing a brief description, this will often include topics that have been omitted in the VD and/or leave out topics that are minor in the original document but prominent in the portions extracted for the VD. Finally, the topic terms can be used to guide clustering of multiple VDs for the same search terms into topically coherent groups.

10.4 SEMANTIC MULTIMEDIA EXTRACTION USING VIDEO

In addition to text-based metadata (either manually annotated, or automatically generated by speech recognition software), video data contains a lot of useful information that can make multimedia search more powerful. In this section, we describe how we have exploited the presence of visual entities that are strongly correlated with the program content to segment the video stream into semantically meaningful parts. Examples are static visual overlays (banners) that provide the viewer with information about the current game status, or network- or station-specific dynamic logos that indicate transitions between different semantic segments, such as live broadcasts, replays, and commercials. In the following section, we will summarize the functionality of the modules that constitute our system for semantic media segmentation, including a short description of the display interface that allows the user to browse and search the segmented video parts.

A number of steps are necessary to segment multimedia into meaningful units:

1. *Preprocessing*: Ingesting text-based metadata or capturing the time of the play and the text associated with it.
2. *Semantic Video Analysis*:
    (a) detection and extraction of commercials
    (b) static and dynamic logo and sport replay detection
    (c) static overlay detection and text extraction via OCR

3. *Data Management*: Searching and browsing segmented entities in the database.
4. *User Interface*: Interacting with the segmented video on a semantic level.

We will describe each of these steps in detail in the following sections.

10.4.1 Preprocessing Data

This process converts the input data into entity objects, and stores them in a database, a process called ingestion. We have data available to us in the form of four partially aligned streams: audio, video, closed caption texts, and, particularly for sports, metadata provided in near real-time by other organizations, such as Stats, Inc. and MLB.com (Major League Baseball). All this data describes real-world entities, individuals, and events, with their own ontological structure. The ingestion step extracts the evidence in these different data streams to produce virtual representations of the real-world entities; these virtual entities are then serialized into a database.

At this point, these four streams of data have been merged into a semi-structured collection of XML documents. The only steps remaining are to extract events from event descriptions and to collect all the known facts about particular entities. Here's an example of such a description from baseball, from one of the metadata sources noted above:

> Andre Ethier grounds out softly. Second baseman Chase Utley to first baseman Ryan Howard. Rafael Furcal to 2nd.

Among the events detected for this segment are Andre Ethier "grounding out" and Chase Utley fielding the ball and throwing it to Ryan Howard. Events may be represented as a tuple consisting of a label, a super-segment, a tuple of participants, and a mapping between participant order and event roles. In fact, the language of the description is sufficiently formulaic that we can identify the label and extract the player tuple with a simple regular expression. In practice, we generate the regular expression for a particular event type from a template together with entities, such as players and teams, known to be participating in the super segment. For example, for a baseball event such as this, we know the pitch containing the event, the at-bat containing the pitch, the inning containing the at-bat, and so on. This tells us which individuals are named in the event description, along with some constraints on their roles. The class that generates the regular expression also participates in the generation of a master regular expression matching a super set of all event descriptions particular to any event type. The generated regular expressions are nonbacktracking, so matching is deterministic and fast, scaling well to large numbers of event types, though the process of hand-discovering formulas does not scale very well. A statistical approach would be less brittle and laborious, but would require tagged data, which we did not have available at the time the research was performed. The manual approach resulted in various pieces of code to facilitate the discovery of formulas, and the process shows great promise for the domains we have explored.

The entities constructed from the data should correspond in relations and properties to the ontology inherent in the domain being searched. For baseball, this includes team entities, person entities, game entities, and so forth. We use Hibernate (http://www.hibernate.org) to facilitate the translation back and forth between the database and the Java code. Java's object model allows us to abstract the common properties of related ontologies into an inheritance hierarchy, so most of the code for the baseball and football ontologies is shared. In each ontology designed so far, there has been a base level entity on which we can search: a play or down in football and a pitch in baseball.

10.4.2   Semantic Video Analysis: Commercial Segmentation and Extraction

Broadcast videos usually contain a large number of commercials, which, in general, are semantically unrelated to the program content and thus should be filtered out. Several techniques have been used to detect commercials from regular programming, most of them based on visual features. Since each television channel has its own peculiarities, the display of commercial entities varies from one channel to another. Thus, a battery of techniques was developed to take advantage of the peculiarities of the various channels:

10.4.2.1   Black Frame Detection   Black frames often occur at the beginning and at the end of a commercial, particularly at a commercial break boundary, and this technique has been successfully applied to sports broadcasts.

10.4.2.2   Video Frame Entropy   Video frame entropy captures the entropy using the red, green, and blue features in a frame. High entropy indicates content-rich frames, while low entropy usually indicates a black frame, pure color frame, or a frame that contains sharp contrast text. Such features can be used for commercial detection.

10.4.2.3   Pairwise Joint Entropy for the Red, Green, Blue, Hue, Saturation, and Value Feature   We computed the pairwise joint entropy and the matrix of joint entropy; we then tried to analyze the matrix for visual patterns that suggest commercial and program boundaries (Černeková et al. 2002).

10.4.2.4   Pairwise Kullback–Leibler (KL) Divergence   We computed KL divergence for the red, green, blue, hue, saturation, and value feature, as well as the matrix of KL divergence; we then tried to analyze the matrix for visual patterns that suggest commercial and program boundaries (Kullback and Leibler 1951).

10.4.2.5   Cut Rate Analysis   Uses a 15-bin HSV feature vector in conjunction with the Mahalanobis distance. The intuition being there are more cuts in commercials than programs (Lienhart 2001).

10.4.2.6   Audio Duplicate Detection   Commercials tend to occur several times during a relatively short period. Our audio duplicate detection algorithm divides the audio into 5-second segments and compares the average difference and the KL divergence. Segments with high duplicate rates can be used to detect commercials. The same algorithm can also be used to detect video duplicates.

Figure 10.2. Examples of logos and banners being extracted in a baseball game (top), CW channel, Disney, ZEETV, and football game.

Each of these modules was separately evaluated and results ranged between 94 and 98% in precision. Using statistical fusion techniques, we combined the different cues described above to optimize the performance of the commercial detection module.

10.4.3   Semantic Video Analysis: Logo Detection

We have observed that many TV broadcasters use channel or program logos to indicate the beginning or end of a specific program segment, or during a program, to inform the viewer about the network affiliation of the current program. These logos tend to exhibit consistency in both position and visual appearance, making it possible to build statistical appearance models for detecting their presence in a video segment. In our system, we distinguish between the two cases of static and dynamic logo detection.

10.4.3.1   Static Logo Detection   Our video logo detection is able to detect static logos contained in a video. Frames containing logos have a high probability of being a show, while frames that do not contain any logo are more likely to be commercials. While different TV channels may have different behaviors, we believe that detecting such logos will provide a useful feature for future video analysis. Logo detection has been especially useful in the video analysis of football and baseball, allowing the detection of banners and logos with high precision and recall over 95%, helping us to separate game content from commercials, commentators, news, and so on, and providing support for more advanced video analysis, such as replay detection. Figure 10.2 clearly shows the banner of a baseball game that is being extracted by the system along with logos from different channels.

10.4.3.2   Dynamic Logo Detection   By dynamic logo, we refer to the flashy logos that consist of short, animated video clips used as network advertisements to promote brands in videos or to indicate the beginning of a new program segment (see Figure 10.3). The problem of detecting dynamic logos is important as a part of our larger objective to detect replays in football and baseball sports games. After analyzing the content structure of a few videos of football and baseball games, it became apparent that replay segments are marked by the presence of dynamic logos at the start and at the end of the segment.

Figure 10.3. Sequential frames depicting an example of a dynamic logo in baseball.

The detection performance was further increased by fusing the output of this module with the output of the module that detects the visual overlay containing the scores and/or game clock (see Sections 10.4.4 and 10.4.3.1). We have observed that this banner is consistently present during normal play but disappears during replays. Thus, these two cues used in combination work very well to detect the beginning and the end of replays.

Using dynamic logo detection, we are able to identify the audio-visual segments that correspond to signatures or templates that are consistently shown by the providers at the end of a TV show. For a 5-hour ZEETV recording, we successfully identified 7 out of 8 end-of-show boundaries.

10.4.4 Semantic Video Analysis: Textual Overlay Detection Using OCR Technology

While logo detection can be applied more generally in video analysis, we have developed algorithms based on logo detection specifically for reading the game clock in football broadcasts. We used external metadata sources noted earlier, such as Stats, Inc. that are available for sports domains called "game stats." Game stats typically describe the significant events of the game and are a rich source of information about the game's progression. If we can align the descriptors from the game stats data with the actual video stream, we can achieve rich information and event detection for the sports video broadcast. We make use of the textual overlay in the sports video to do this time alignment and thus generate a rich visual description of the video streams.

There are several kinds of textual overlays in sports TV programs. In American football, we have a game clock; in baseball games, we have a banner containing score, inning, count, and so on. Throughout a broadcast of a given game or match, the location where the overlay appears and the layout of textual data are typically unchanged.

As an example, game stats for an NFL American football broadcast consists of a linear progression of plays, with each play associated with a specific time on the game clock. This game clock time, however, does not correspond to the video time but simply to the game time. However, the textual overlay of football games always contains a game clock. If we can read the time in the clock correctly, then we can align the video frames with the play events described in the game stats data. In the case of baseball, the alignment involved extracting information from the banner, such as the count (balls, strikes) and pitch speed. Thus, we can see that reading the banner or overlay text in video frames gives us reliable anchor points to align external metadata with the information from the broadcast. The general procedure we follow is described below:

1. We first determine the location of the textual overlay for a given broadcast, either manually or by use of automatic logo detection.
2. Once we have the location of the overlay, we extract a specific region of it as a subimage to which we then apply a preprocessing filter (resizing, filtering, and binarization), depending on the underlying video broadcast quality.
3. This preprocessed image is now fed to an open source OCR package. We used the Google Tesseract-OCR engine (http://code.google.com/p/tesseract-ocr/downloads).
4. The text descriptor for each video frame is aligned with the corresponding game stats data.

10.4.5 Searching and Browsing Video Segments

Search involves the localization of entities that are typically both similar to a reference entity and are inherently interesting. The reference entity is some subevent in a larger event: a play in football, the last pitch in an at-bat in baseball, or some step or expository aside in a cooking show. For this search process to be beneficial to the user, a great many segments must be searchable. The number of searchable events in turn produces an engineering challenge: sufficient events to make an interesting search mean more events than can reasonably be held in memory. The natural solution is to store events in a database, but the problem then is that generic DBMs are unlikely to be tuned to the needs of this particular join-intensive problem, and that database query languages are relatively poor formalisms for representing the complex logic of the search. Our search algorithm, therefore, involves an initial database query to obtain an unranked superset of the events to be culled, ranked, and returned as search results. The culling and ranking are done by a Java program outside the database.

10.4.5.1 Connecting Video Segments by Saliency and Relatedness The results are ranked by a combination of both similarity and intrinsic level of interest, hereafter called saliency. The database results are initially ranked by similarity. The most similar segments are chosen for reranking by both similarity and salience. This reranked, most similar subset is returned as the search result. Similarity is calculated as a weighted combination of various domain-specific similarity functions. Examples of identity or similarity function include the same batter in baseball, or batters on the same team with the same fielding position, or the identity or similarity of subevents, both the reference and comparison segment contain a fielding error. The

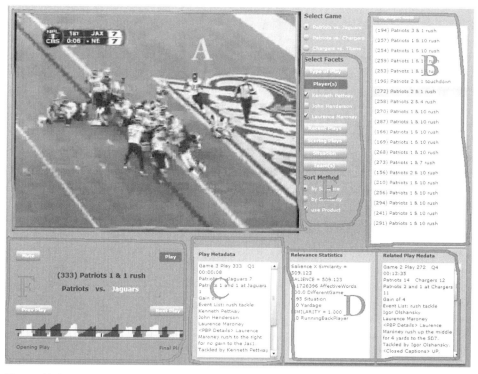

Figure 10.4. Interface for exploring American football videos and the corresponding aligned metadata.

composite similarity function maps a pair of segments, a reference and comparison segment, to a non-negative floating point value. A similar salience function, mapping individual segments to non-negative floating point values, is then applied to the most similar subset. Lastly, we apply a ranking function that maps the similarity of the comparison and reference functions with the salience of these two functions to a final ranking value.

10.4.6 User Interface

Our ability to align metadata with video segments enables us to create powerful interfaces for viewing and searching video. In Figure 10.4 is a demo interface created to explore metadata on American football games that is aligned to the corresponding plays within the games, created using the processes described in this chapter. When a game is selected, it is streamed to the video display (Figure 10.4, part A). A list of related plays is presented nearby (Figure 10.4, part B). This list is updated each time the video progresses to a new play. The metadata associated with the current play is also displayed (Figure 10.4, part C). Selecting a related play from the list (B) also displays metadata for that play (Figure 10.4, part D) and information about its relevance to the current play in the video. The related play list (B) can be filtered based on selected aspects, or facets (Figure 10.4, part E) of the current play metadata. This includes facets specific to each given play, such as the names of

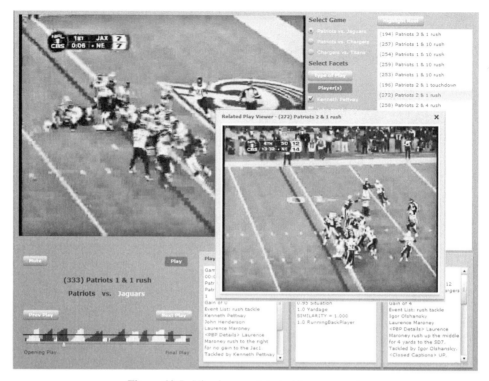

Figure 10.5. Viewing a related video segment.

players involved in the play. This makes it simple for users to search for, filter, and sort other segments of the same video, or other videos, that are similar to the current segment, and also to view the related segments (Figure 10.5).

In addition, metadata for all segments in a video can be used to create much more sophisticated navigation controls than the standard timeline found in video viewers. Videos can be navigated by segment (Figure 10.4, part F, and Figure 10.6), enabling users to automatically cue up on the beginning of interesting segments (in this case, the snap in a football play). Representation by segment is more powerful than a timeline because it contains a higher level of semantic knowledge, which is better fitted to a user's understanding of the content. This can be used to either replace or supplement video timelines. In addition, visualizations of the segment metadata can make such a navigation tool more powerful. In the interface shown (Figure 10.6), a bar graph is used to indicate the field position, and color is used to represent which team possesses the football. This enables a user to jump specifically to portions of the game corresponding to a given team's offensive drive. Equally important, with a glance, a user gains an understanding of the duration and depth of each offensive drive. Sudden changes in possession give the user a clue to turnovers, while dips in field position give indications of setbacks, such as sacks or penalties. Such visualizations enable powerful exploratory search processes, an important counterpart to the directed search enabled by a facet filtered list.

Note that the UI tool was designed for experts; specifically, it was created to be a tool for examining system output. It was also used as a sandbox for experimenting

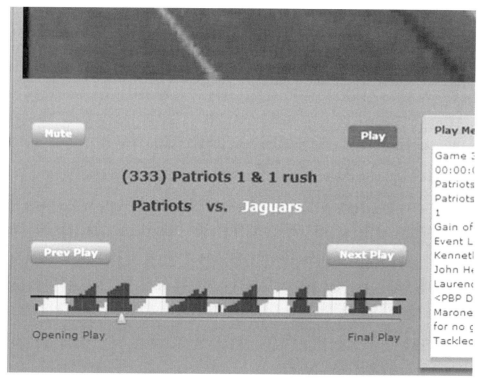

Figure 10.6. Zoomed in on the lower left of Figure 10.2 showing navigation controls based on segmented video and metadata.

with interesting UI widgets based on segment metadata. Part F of the UI is an example of one experiment. But even as an experiment, it was not based on a detailed profile of the sports fan. It does not reflect either the needed features or the usability of any end-user application.

The authors are currently in the process of designing an application for end users. This design is based on users' needs and desires and will be tested by the target audience (sports fans and casual watchers). Details of the design and results of testing are not yet available.

10.5 CONCLUSION AND FUTURE WORK

The automatic segmentation and annotation of multimedia content is challenging, because most of the information that is of interest is not directly accessible, but has to be inferred using additional contextual information. Nevertheless, it is worth pursuing this challenge because it will allow users to interact in a much more intuitive manner with multimedia content, for example, as described in this chapter, by browsing a TV sports broadcast based on game events rather than in the traditional linear fashion.

We presented two different approaches to semantic multimedia extraction from broadcast television programs, one approach is based on extracting semantic information from metadata and audio using speech recognition, while the other approach integrated metadata with information extracted from a video signal using video content analysis. In both projects, we utilize natural language processing to relate the extracted information to preexisting knowledge representations. The results are very promising, and while each multimedia content requires the particular knowledge of a given domain, techniques similar to the ones described in Section 10.5 are applicable and extendable to a wide range of other domains, such as cooking and home improvement shows.

We also described how the semantic information can be mapped to a user interface, because the extraction of semantic information needs to be complemented by appropriate and intuitive ways to present this information to the user. Therefore, in addition to testing each module individually, we are currently also conducting usability evaluations to make sure that interfaces will be build with the user's needs in mind.

CHAPTER 11

ANALYSIS OF MULTIMODAL NATURAL LANGUAGE CONTENT IN BROADCAST VIDEO

PREM NATARAJAN, EHRY MacROSTIE, ROHIT PRASAD, and JONATHAN WATSON

11.1 INTRODUCTION

Language content is pervasive in many multimedia sources and typically conveys specific information about objects and events within the media itself (e.g., the name of a person whose face is displayed on screen) and within the larger outside world (e.g., an anchor speakers commentary on a developing news story). While it is easy for humans to extract and synthesize content from multiple modalities simultaneously, such multimodal synthesis is still beyond the reach of automated systems. A small but important step toward multimodal systems is the successful application of automatic speech recognition technology to language-rich video domains, such as real-time broadcast news monitoring, resulting in valuable analytic tools, such as real-time alerting and keyword search.

While speech is a rich source of language content, it is only one part of such content in broadcast video. Often, a significant amount of language information is conveyed through on-screen video text. Video–text comes in two flavors—*overlaid* text and *in-scene* text (also referred to as *scene* text). Overlaid text is the result of the studio production process and is used to reinforce the story being discussed by the news anchors, or to identify the current speaker, and so on. Scene text is text from sources such as road signs, posters, and placards that are part of the scene being captured by the camera. In this case, rather than serving an editorial purpose, it often provides natural clues that may help in understanding the scene.

There has been considerable research in the area of semantic representation in video in the past decade (Naphade and Huang 2002; Snoek et al. 2006; Yang and Hauptmann 2004). While much of this work has focused on representation of non-linguistic content, some researchers have investigated the semantic relationship between linguistic and nonlinguistic content (Fleischman et al. 2007).

Multimedia Information Extraction: Advances in Video, Audio, and Imagery Analysis for Search, Data Mining, Surveillance, and Authoring, First Edition. Edited by Mark T. Maybury.
© 2012 IEEE Computer Society. Published 2012 by John Wiley & Sons, Inc.

It is obvious that when present, language content is a powerful source of semantic information in video. In particular, the relationship between video text and audio content plays an important role in how the semantic information is synthesized and interpreted by viewers. To date, there has been relatively little systematic study of the relationship between these two language sources. Empirical evidence suggests that the human mind is wired to process auditory and visual information simultaneously using visual information to reinforce what is heard (Sugihara et al. 2006). Therefore, understanding the relationship between spoken language and video text is one step toward developing systems that can exploit redundancy between the modalities to improve content extraction performance or to identify and synthesize differences in the two modalities to generate a more robust semantic representation of the content contained in the video source.

In this chapter, we present new results from an investigation of the relationship between natural language content in audio and video text. First, we describe an integrated system for automatically extracting language content from video—from speech in the acoustic signal and video text in the visual signal. Next, we describe our experimental analysis methodology for comparing language content in audio and video text modalities. We conclude with experimental results and detailed analysis of the results.

11.2 OVERVIEW OF SYSTEM FOR CONTENT EXTRACTION FROM AUDIO AND VIDEO TEXT

Figure 11.1 shows a block diagram of our integrated system that extracts content from audio and video text tracks. As shown in the figure, BBN's (Raytheon BBN Technologies, Cambridge, MA) Byblos™ automatic speech recognition engine converts the audio track into electronic text, while an optical character recognition (OCR) system converts the video text into electronic text. Next, a named entity (NE) extraction engine processes the text from both audio and video text track for detecting entities. Note that all three components in our end-to-end system, namely automatic speech recognition (ASR), OCR, and NE extractor are statistically based trainable systems. In fact, both our ASR (Nguyen et al. 1995) and OCR (Natarajan et al. 2001a) systems are hidden Markov model (HMM)-based engines and use the BBN Byblos HMM toolkit. For NE extraction, we use the BBN Identifinder™ (Bikel et al. 1999), which uses a Perceptron (Gallant 1990) classifier to detect entities in text. In the following section, we describe each of the components in detail.

11.2.1 Broadcast News Speech Recognition Using BBN Byblos

The BBN Byblos recognition system uses phonetic HMMs with one or more of the following parameter tying forms depending on the amount of training data and computing resources: phonetic-tied mixture (PTM), state-tied mixture (STM), and state-clustered-tied mixture (SCTM) models. The states of each phonetic model are clustered based on the triphone or quinphone context into different "codebooks" (groups of Gaussian mixture components). The mixture weights are clustered using linguistically guided decision trees.

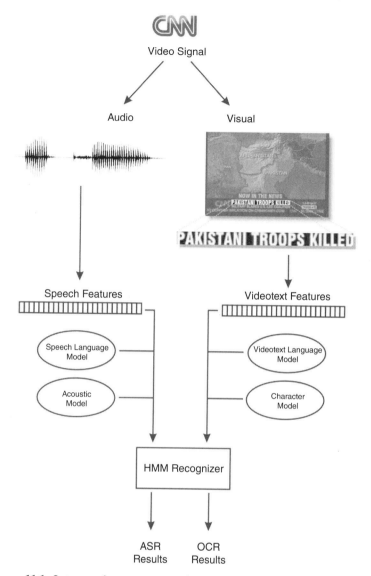

Figure 11.1. Integrated content extraction from audio and video text tracks.

Decoding in the BBN Byblos system is performed in two passes (Schwartz et al. 1996). The forward pass uses PTM or STM acoustic models and a composite set bigram language model (LM). The output of the forward decoding pass consists of the most likely word ends per frame, along with their partial forward likelihood scores. The backward decoding pass then operates on the output of the forward pass using SCTM within-word acoustic models and an approximate trigram LM to either generate an N-best list or a word lattice. The word lattice or the N-best is typically rescored with a more detailed between-word SCTM models.

For the experiments described here, the BBN Byblos ASR engine was trained on 200 hours of broadcast news (BN) audio. The phonetic HMMs were estimated

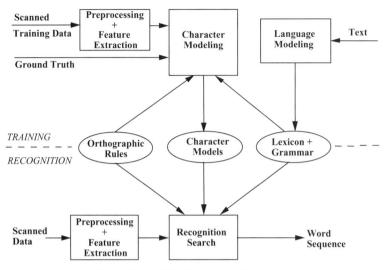

Figure 11.2. BBN Byblos OCR system.

via maximum likelihood followed by discriminative training using minimum phone error (MPE) criterion (Povey and Woodland 2002).

11.2.2 Overlaid Video Text Recognition Using BBN Byblos

The video text OCR system is an extended version of the HMM-based BBN Byblos OCR system that was originally developed for recognizing text in printed documents. A pictorial representation of the BBN Byblos OCR system (Natarajan et al. 2001a) is given in Figure 11.2. Knowledge sources are depicted by ellipses and are dependent on the particular language or script. The OCR system components themselves are identified by rectangular boxes and are independent of the particular language or script. Thus, the same OCR system can be configured to perform recognition on any language.

As shown in Figure 11.2, the BBN Byblos OCR system can be subdivided into two basic functional components: training and recognition. Both training and recognition share a common preprocessing and feature extraction stage. Preprocessing and feature extraction start off by first deskewing the scanned image and then locating the positions of the text lines on the deskewed image. Next, the feature extraction program computes a feature vector, which is a function of the horizontal position within the line. Each line of text is horizontally segmented into a sequence of thin, overlapping frames. For each frame, we compute a script-independent, feature vector that is a numerical representation of the frame.

The character models comprise of multistate, left-to-right HMMs. Each state has an associated output probability distribution over the features. The character HMMs are trained on transcribed text lines using the expectation maximization (EM) algorithm. The model topology including the number of states and the allowable transitions between them is typically optimized for each script.

The LM used in the BBN Byblos OCR engine is a character or word n-gram LM estimated from the character HMM training data and other available sources of text. The default configuration uses character n-grams in order to support the recognition of new words that were not seen during training. The recognition algorithm is fundamentally the same as the one used in the ASR engine described above.

The video text OCR problem can be broken down into these three broad steps (Natarajan et al. 2001b):

1. *Text Detection and Location*: Detecting the presence and location of text within each frame in the video stream.
2. *Preprocessing*: Enhancing (removing nontext artifacts, background noise, upsampling, etc.) and binarizing the text image.
3. *Recognition*: Recognizing the detected and preprocessed video text.

Preprocessing of video text involves two key steps that are different from the processing of document images. The first step is to upsample the video text region by a fixed factor (typically a factor of 4). Upsampling is performed to mitigate the effect of low resolution of video text by trading off resolution in the color-space for spatial resolution in a binarized image. The second step is to binarize the color text images into black text on white background or vice-versa, depending on the text and background characteristics. For binarization, we use several different approaches, including a simple intensity-based procedure in which all pixels with intensity greater than some threshold are set to black in the output image. For images with low-intensity text, pixels with intensity less than the threshold are set to black. The thresholds on the intensity are determined empirically on a development set as a percentile of intensity for each frame.

Following binarization, we extract the same set of features from video text as for machine-printed OCR (Natarajan et al. 2001a). In the OCR model training stage, we estimate character HMMs from the available training data. Next, the two-pass recognition strategy described earlier is used to recognize all text regions in a development set of video I-frames. Then, we empirically determine the I-frame that results in the lowest character error rate (CER) or word error rate (WER). On a validation set as well as for the runtime system, the recognition result from the empirically determined lowest CER/WER I-frame is used for evaluating performance.

11.2.3 Named Entity Detection Using BBN Identifinder

Our name-finding engine detects NEs in input text by classifying each word in a sentence as one of the three classes: start of an NE ("NE-Start"), continuation of an NE ("NE-Continue"), or not part of an NE ("None"). A separate perceptron classifier is trained for each class (NE-Start/NE-Continue/None). The features for the perceptron are computed for each word using the identity of the word, the word cluster to which the word belongs, the neighboring words, and the prefix and suffix of the word.

The data-driven nature of our system allows us to optimize system performance for a target language or domain without requiring language or domain-specific rules. Optimizing the system for new dialects, fonts, or unique image degradations only requires representative training data from that dialect, font, or image source.

The trainable aspect of the HMM methodology is of particular value since input signals from video can be highly degraded or noisy after conversion from color to bi-level or after encoding and compression *and* because such degradations are a statistical function of the specific sources of input signals. Apart from binarization artifacts, video text data exhibits a variety of challenges, including low resolution, a wide variety of variations due to illumination, movement, complex backgrounds, distortion introduced by the camera, and the perspective of the text in relation to the camera. As a result of these challenges, even for languages such as English, commercial OCR and ASR systems are unable to reliably process video text and speech data.

11.3 METHODOLOGY FOR COMPARING CONTENT IN AUDIO AND VIDEO TEXT

In this chapter, our primary goal was to characterize the value of the visual text content in video. We used the video text ground truth transcriptions and ground truth named entity annotations as a reference point and asked the question: How often do entities in video text not show up in aligned ASR results?

Our definition of an entity in this context is the same as the automatic content extraction (ACE) named entity detection task. An entity is an object or set of objects in the world. Entity mentions are references to entities within the text (ACE 2005). We compared named entity mentions (referred to as named entities) that are entity mentions that are referred to by name or common noun. We did not consider entities mentioned by pronoun reference.

We chose to compare named entities because of their critical importance to information retrieval (IR). Also, named entities are a well-defined concept for which significant investments have been made in developing annotation guidelines and metrics for measuring performance. Finally, named entities are of acknowledged importance in analytical processes.

Our corpus consisted of 13.5 hours of video from the NIST TDT-2 corpus. This data contained approximately even amounts of video from ABC News and CNN recorded in 1998. While the video duration was approximately even, the text content was weighted in favor of CNN since it was more text-dense than ABC. There were a total of 8421 entities in the video text.

We manually transcribed each line of video text. The location, size, and angle of rotation for each text line were marked, and the ground truth textual content was transcribed. Since our video text annotation was performed on a line-by-line basis, we did not have information about the semantic relationship of groups of lines. Video text lines within the same frame can be completely unrelated semantically so we could not use time alignment to draw semantic associations among video text regions.

Named entities were manually marked in the video text ground truth. We marked entities only within the bounds of individual lines of text. The manually marked

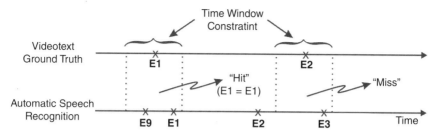

Figure 11.3. Entity comparison within a time window.

entities were extracted into a unique list of entities, which formed the world of known entities for this study.

We generated text content for the speech track by running ASR with models trained on English broadcast news. Named entity comparison was defined as a simple case-insensitive string match. All punctuation characters were ignored in the comparison, and only alphanumeric characters were compared.

We constrained our named entity annotation guidelines for this task to exclude certain name references that we felt were "unspeakable" or otherwise unlikely to be seen in the speech track. These included abbreviations, stock symbols, channel names (such as ABC and CNN), and all text from the scrolling news ticker. It is understood that if these types of information are of interest, then the only way to access them is through recognition of the video text content.

The entity comparison iterated through each entity mention in the video text ground truth and asked the question: *Is this entity present in the corresponding ASR result?* In order to answer the question in a meaningful manner, we imposed a time constraint window centered at the start time of the video text segment containing the current entity. We then searched the ASR results within that time window for the target entity. If the entity was found, it was counted as a hit. Otherwise, it was counted as a miss. Figure 11.3 illustrates our alignment method.

11.4 EXPERIMENTAL RESULTS AND ANALYSIS

We compared every named entity in the ground truth against the entities present the corresponding ASR output within the defined time window constraint. We performed multiple runs for a range of time window widths. For each run, we used as a metric the percent of misses. The overall results for all of the video clips in our corpus are shown in Figure 11.4.

These results show that when we look within a 1-minute window of an entity's occurrence in the video text stream, 79% do not occur in the ASR results. The magnitude of the increase in named-entity content when video text is included well exceeded our most optimistic expectations. Even when the time window is expanded to equal the entire duration of the video clip (30 minutes), 62% of entities in video text did not occur in the ASR results. These results are consistent with another study conducted in 2002, which measured IR results on video data using both ASR and OCR results (Hauptmann et al. 2002). The conclusion of that study was that when

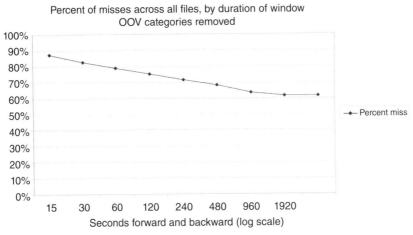

Percent of misses across all files, by duration of window
OOV categories removed

Figure 11.4. Named entity miss rates for different time window widths.

IR was performed using the union of OCR and ASR results, the performance was far better than either modality alone. The earlier study focused on IR performance, and did not attempt to measure the richness of named entities in either stream (speech and video text), nor did it attempt to methodically characterize the overlap between streams.

There are several reasons that video text entities might not have a match in ASR. One possibility is that there was no mention of the entity in the spoken track accompanying the video. Another possibility is that the ASR contained a mention but in a different form than in video text. For example, in some cases, people are referred to only by their last name in speech dialog, whereas in video text, their full name is used. Finally, differences in spelling or ASR errors could contribute to the overall miss rate. We found that 16% of the unique named entities in video text had at least one out-of-vocabulary (OOV) word in the ASR dictionary. This means that we would never be able to find a match for these entities in ASR output simply because the ASR system would never be able to recognize them correctly.

It is also important to consider that when a match is found between an entity mention in video text and an entity mention in ASR, the two may refer to different actual entities in the real world. Without semantic level annotation, we do not have the ability to detect these cases in our current experimental setup. We must rely on proximity in time as a crude approximation of dialog context. In other words, we assume that entity mentions that occur close in time are more likely to refer to the same actual entity because they are likely to be from the same dialog context. We believe this assumption is more appropriate for the broadcast news domain than in general conversational dialog. News broadcasts often follow a tightly scripted format in which short unrelated stories follow each other in quick succession. The semantic context from one news story to the next is often completely different.

Using this definition of relatedness, we show in Figure 11.5 a breakdown of entity miss rates on a per-category basis. The numbers in this figure are based upon a 1-minute time window centered at the start of the video text entity.

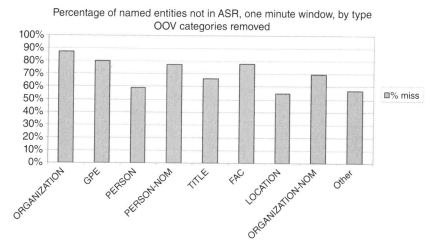

Figure 11.5. Per-category miss rates for a 1-minute time window.

11.5   CONCLUSIONS AND FUTURE WORK

The results from our study demonstrate that video text contains a significant amount of additional information, specifically named entity mentions, beyond that which is available in the speech content in broadcast news videos. These findings make a strong case that exploitation of video text is an important part of an overall video content extraction system. Continued investment in video text technology to improve the quality of text recognition technologies is, therefore, important for enabling the next generation of video information exploitation tools. It is important to underscore the fact that we have established a case for continued investment in videotext OCR technology even when accompanying spoken language information is available. In the case of many types of videos where there is no accompanying spoken language track, the case for videotext is even more compelling!

In addition to content that is present only in video text, there is also a significant amount of overlap in entities that appear in both video text and ASR. We believe that this redundant information has an important role to play in automatically identifying key ideas or concepts in a story. Understanding how this redundant information can be used by automatic reasoning and understanding systems will likely be a fruitful research area.

Unlike state-of-the-art speech recognition systems, our OCR system is not constrained to only recognize words that are contained within a predefined lexicon. Given that named entities are often the most important class of out-of-vocabulary words in a speech recognition system, there is another possible synergy that can be gained through the use of a videotext OCR system—that of augmenting the speech recognition lexicon with new words, especially named entity words, that are recognized by the OCR system. How to best leverage this potential synergy is clearly a promising area of research. For example, should only new words recognized with high confidence by the OCR system be incorporated into the speech lexicon?

In the future, we would like to compare the entity results in two directions; both from the point of view of the video text as we did in this study and from the point of view of the spoken language track. In addition, we would like to do an entity comparison using manual speech transcriptions in place of ASR results. This would eliminate the effect of OOV words and errors present in ASR output. We would also like to perform the entity alignment using true semantic annotations rather than a string match criteria. Finally, we would like to expand the study to include nonlinguistic modalities, such as speaker ID and face recognition, modalities that are under active research at BBN and other sites.

CHAPTER 12

WEB-BASED MULTIMEDIA INFORMATION EXTRACTION BASED ON SOCIAL REDUNDANCY

JOSE SAN PEDRO, STEFAN SIERSDORFER, VAIVA KALNIKAITE, and STEVE WHITTAKER

12.1 INTRODUCTION

Social networking sites are among the most frequently visited on the Web (Cha et al. 2007), and their use has expanded into professional contexts for expertise sharing and knowledge discovery (Millen et al. 2006). These virtual communities can be enormous, with millions of users and shared resources. Social multimedia websites, such as YouTube, are particularly popular. Network traffic involving YouTube accounts for 20% of web traffic and 10% of all Internet traffic (Cheng et al. 2007). This chapter focuses on new techniques for information extraction from such social multimedia sites to support improved search and browsing.

Social multimedia sites are organic and user-centric, with few centralized control policies or systematic ways to organize content. They rely on user annotations, feedback, and access behaviors to manage and present content. The drawbacks of this user-centric focus are:

- *Sparsity and Limits of Tags*: Although user annotations have been shown to support various applications such as topic detection and tracking (Allan et al. 1998), information filtering (Zhang et al. 2002), and document ranking (Zhang et al. 2005), they nevertheless have limitations. Manually annotating content is a time consuming process. And not all content receives equal attention from taggers (Sun and Datta 2009). As a consequence, metadata and annotations are often very sparse for large parts of the collection. Furthermore, keywords and community-provided tags may lack consistency and present

Multimedia Information Extraction: Advances in Video, Audio, and Imagery Analysis for Search, Data Mining, Surveillance, and Authoring, First Edition. Edited by Mark T. Maybury.
© 2012 IEEE Computer Society. Published 2012 by John Wiley & Sons, Inc.

numerous irregularities (e.g., abbreviations and typos). In addition, only a minority of users generate tags so that metadata may represent the interests of a small minority (Paolillo and Penumarthy 2007). Overall, this makes it hard to rely on tag-based techniques for automatic data organization, retrieval, and knowledge extraction.

- *Lack of Granular Access*: The reliance on user tags and related metadata mean that the majority of the tools used to access multimedia data are not directly content based. Instead, they apply to the entire file. For example, tags or popularity scores are applied to an entire video, music track, or movie. Yet for extended content, users may want to identify specific elements within that content, for example, highlights or favorite moments, and neither tags nor popularity applies at this level of granularity.

- *Duplicated Content*: Despite the use of tools for its removal, recent studies (Cha et al. 2007; Wu et al. 2007) report significant amounts of redundant footage in video-sharing websites, with over 25% near-duplicate videos detected in search results. Such redundant content can affect retrieval performance, by increasing browsing time to skip repeated entries, or require additional processing to eliminate highly overlapping content. For this reason, the literature has considered redundancy a problem for social multimedia, and various studies have proposed techniques for its elimination (Wu et al. 2007; Zhang et al. 2005).

In this chapter, we focus on the analysis of the leading social multimedia platform, YouTube, addressing the above problems using a novel hybrid approach which combines content analysis and user-centric metadata. Rather than viewing redundancy as a problem to be excised from the system, we exploit it. We use state-of-the-art content-based copy retrieval (CBCR) techniques to identify visually overlapping data—which provide us with two types of information. First, we use redundancy to detect multimedia highlights, and, second, we use it to propagate tags across sparsely tagged collections. More specifically, we use content techniques to compute the network of connections between elements of a video collection in an unsupervised way. We call this the Visual Affinity Graph. It conveys information about the data set provided manually by the community, but extracted automatically by the content analysis technique. This implicit user behavior can be used to generate high level semantic cues for multimedia content in an unsupervised way, helping to bridge the so called "semantic gap," that is, the problem of inferring the high-level concepts by which humans perceive the world, from the set of low-level features that can be automatically extracted from multimedia data (Enser and Sandom 2003). In this chapter, we show how to harness this content-derived social knowledge to solve two video-related problems:

- *Summarization of Video Content*: Summarizing multimedia is known to be an extremely difficult problem (Yang and Hauptmann 2008). Automatic methods rely on low-level features that do not tend to map well to aspects of content that users find interesting or useful (Christel et al. 1998). The analysis of redundancy in YouTube enables us to study uploaders' behavior. When several users have independently selected and uploaded the same video, a consensus about its importance can be inferred. We use this idea to derive an importance metric for uploaded video sequences. Such a metric enables us to derive highlights: regions of socially agreed interest within the timeline of the video.

- *Improvement of Annotations*: We also take advantage of the Visual Affinity Graph to propagate annotations (i.e., tags) between related videos, utilizing the graph edges to spread community knowledge into the network. Uploaders of overlapping sequences of the same video provide their personal perspective on its content in the form of different annotations. This propagation addresses the tag sparsity problem: by combining tags for a related resource to achieve a more comprehensive description.

In both cases, we describe our algorithms and present an evaluation showing the utility of our new approach.

The approach differs from other chapters in this book that address video analysis. Several chapters point to the need to use contextually available metadata (Chapter 7). Others analyze the speech contained in the video using NLP methods (Chapters 10 and 11), or combine metadata and linguistic content. Our approach is perhaps closest to that of Chapter 8, which combines visual content analysis with speech analysis. However, one important contrast is that in our approach we use content analysis to analyze people's social behaviors to determine important regions, as well as to propagate end user tags across videos. Although various later chapters address human social behavior (Chapters 16 and 18), in our approach, we are not interested in social behavior per se, but rather in how we can apply this to solve summarization or tagging problems.

This chapter is organized as follows. In Section 12.2, we first describe the CBCR techniques that allow us to detect redundancy in video collections and to generate the network of content-based connections. Section 12.3 describes the related work, algorithm, and evaluation for a social summarization tool for video. Section 12.4 describes a method to improve annotations of elements in community websites, again presenting related work, algorithm, and evaluation. We conclude in Section 12.5, with a discussion of future work.

12.2 REDUNDANCY DETECTION AND GENERATION OF THE VISUAL AFFINITY GRAPH

Here we introduce the tools used for the automatic detection of redundant content in video-based Web 2.0 sites, commonly referred to as content-based copy retrieval (CBCR) tools. These techniques achieve very high accuracy in the detection of exact and near duplicates, providing reliable insights into the properties of the video collection. CBCR analysis provides a set of connected video pairs that we represent, for convenience, as a graph.

12.2.1 CBCR Methods

There is a plethora of literature about near-duplicate detection of video content. CBCR can be considered a particular case of query-by-example content-based information retrieval (Joly et al. 2007), where the result set only includes duplicates of the target sample. Two main problems need to be tackled by CBCR systems. On the one hand, the computational complexity associated to the comparison process requires sophisticated representation (Liu et al. 2006) and indexing (Joly et al. 2007) techniques. On the other, the concept of "identity" has to be carefully dealt with, as videos may experience transformations of visual content during different stages of their life cycle. The detection of near-duplicate text documents presents analogous problems (Huffman et al. 2007). Many of the principles used by text-based duplicate detection techniques can be adapted to the video domain. Fingerprints are the most commonly used detection tool; they are generated using specific features of visual content, such as temporal video structure (San Pedro et al. 2005) or time-sampled frame invariants (Joly et al. 2007).

CBCR's main application is to digital rights management (DRM), where it is used to detect unauthorized usage of video footage. The proliferation of multimedia content broadcasting channels, from current standards of TV (DVB-T/S) to the latest trends in mobile and wireless communications (UMTS), produce a massive amount of broadcast multimedia content that requires advanced content-based analysis algorithms to guarantee copyright agreements. CBCR is also used in many other applications. The ability to obtain airtime statistics for specific clips can be exploited in many different ways, for instance to monitor advertisement campaigns, an application of fundamental importance in the advertising industry.

12.2.2 System Description

We use a copy detection system based on robust hash fingerprint techniques. Robust hash functions generate similar hash values for similar input messages, in contrast to standard hash functions, which try to reduce collisions and specifically create very different values for similar messages (useful in cryptographic applications). All videos used by the system are preanalyzed and transformed into strings of hash values, that is, fingerprints, which represent the evolution of their visual features in time.

Robust hash fingerprints achieve very high comparison effectiveness, and allow us to handle significant changes in visual quality, including frame size reduction, bitrate reduction, and other artifacts generated in reencoding processes (Oostveen et al. 2001). On the other hand, the string-based nature of the comparison makes these systems very sensitive to changes in the temporal features. Hash signatures are sequentially created from video frames; this may create problems as frame rate may differ between videos being compared: larger frame sequences will create larger hash strings.

To handle these difficulties, we base our system on (San Pedro and Dominguez 2007a). The chosen robust hash function works in the luminance color space and uses a 2×2 spatio-temporal Haar filter to compute values using pairs of video frames, as illustrated by Figure 12.1. Frame pairs are selected using an entropy-based subsampling approach. Shannon's entropy is computed for the luminance distribution of each frame. The time series generated by computing this value for every time t of the video is analyzed using a sliding window. For each window W_k, a pair of frames is selected using points of maximum, t_M, and minimum, t_m, entropy in this local scope.

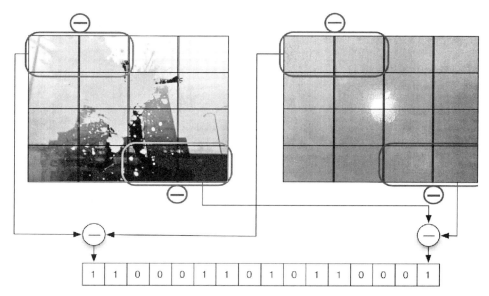

Figure 12.1. Hash value computation using a 2×2 spatio-temporal Haar filter. A 16-bit hash code is produced for every pair of selected frames.

This content-based subsampling approach aims to repeatedly select the same time points for different variations of the input video. The resulting subsampled set of frames can therefore be used to generate a temporal resolution independent fingerprint for video v, that we denote $h(v)$. Video comparison is then performed in the hash space, using standard string matching algorithms. Such algorithms allow the duplicate detection both at the string level (near-duplicate videos) and at the substring level (overlapping videos) (San Pedro and Dominguez 2007b).

At the application level, our CBCR system maintains a collection of searchable content:

$$C = \{v_i : 1 \le i \le |C|\},$$

where $|C|$ denotes the cardinality of the collection.

This video collection, C, can be queried using input video streams, which we denote as Q_j. The system is able to identify if a given incoming stream, Q_j, is a near-duplicate or overlaps with one or more elements in collection C. This process is depicted in Figure 12.2.

12.2.3 Building the Visual Affinity Graph

In our social website application, we want to analyze the whole collection of resources, C, for redundancy. Note that every video $v_i \subset C$ may potentially include sequences from every other v_j. To perform a comprehensive identification, we need to consider the set $C' = C - \{v_i\}$ and the input query $Q_i = v_i$ for every element $i \in [1, |C|]$.

We transform this set of connected video pairs into a weighted undirected graph, the visual affinity graph, $G = (V, E)$. In this graph, nodes (V) represent individual

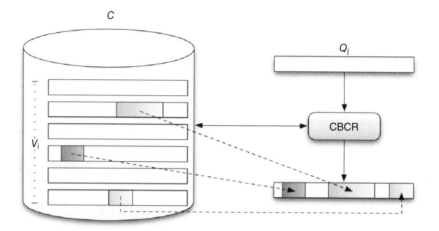

Figure 12.2. Video identification scenario. A video collection, C, is queried via the CBCR system using Q_j as input query.

videos of collection C. On the other hand, edges (E) link together nodes when the corresponding videos overlap. Formally, these two sets are defined as:

$$V = \{v_i \in C : \exists v_j \rightarrow v_i \cap v_j \neq \varnothing\}$$
$$E = \{\{v_i, v_j\} : v_i \cap v_j \neq \varnothing\}, \quad v_i, v_j \in V.$$

Every edge is then weighted as a function of the duration of the overlap between the pair of videos it connects

$$w(v_i, v_j) = |v_i \cap v_j|.$$

A graph representation enables us to take advantage of the numerous mathematical tools available for these structures, and provides an intuitive and organized view of the derived relationships. This graph formalizes all the visual connections in the video set.

12.3 SOCIAL SUMMARIZATION

12.3.1 Description

Summarization of content is crucial, as it provides a compact, rapidly analyzable, representation of a larger resource. However, it is hard for the following two reasons:

Summarization requires a high level of content understanding to enable selection of the scenes that best represent the entire content. For video, this understanding is limited by the Semantic Gap; audio-visual content summarization techniques are currently restricted to the use of low-level features to infer the semantic high-level features that users demand. The inference process achieves poor precision, and results are often far from being semantically meaningful (Yang and Hauptmann 2008).

Summarization is known to be a highly subjective task (Jones 1993). The set of summary scenes selected by different users are often very different. But standard machine learning/test collection methods that depend on having multiple human judges to rate video content are known to be time-consuming and costly.

In this section, we present a summarization technique that circumvents these limitations by obtaining implicit ratings inferred from user behavior on Web 2.0 sites. This community-based approach is important because it provides an alternative way to bridge the Semantic Gap, exploiting social consensus to reveal video highlights.

Our algorithm harnesses users' redundant uploading patterns from the Visual Affinity Graph, to obtain human-generated semantic cues about content in an unsupervised fashion. We exploit the idea that the intentional uploading by multiple users of the same clip from within a given video indicates the importance of that particular video clip. This intentional clip selection is analogous to users' active website linking behavior: popularity information that is exploited by major search engines in algorithms, such as PageRank (Page et al. 1999). If such a clip is a part of a larger original video (normally the case given the duration limits imposed on uploading content to Web 2.0 sites), such duplication provides information about regions of importance within the larger event. We exploit this information about important regions to build a summary of the entire video.

12.3.2 Methodology

The first stage in our social video summarization technique involves locating all relevant video resources from a social sharing site, such as YouTube. In our scenario, we work externally to the social website, so we need to recreate the topology of the relevant subnetwork in our local context, enabling us to restrict our study to this subset. We are looking to extract highlights, that is, clips of the highest interest, of a specific video, v, for which we already know some meta-information (e.g., title, director, publisher, etc.). We use these metadata to construct a query to identify relevant content using the social website search engine. The returned results constitute our subset of relevant items. Optionally, we can supplement the results set by using "related content" recommended lists, provided by many of these portals.

We construct the Visual Affinity Graph using all collected results, along with the original video footage we are trying to summarize, v. Following the notation introduced in Section 12.2, we consider our collection C to contain just our target video v. Each of the results obtained from the social website will constitute our input queries, Q_j. The CBCR system will then detect all the time points where results collected overlap with v. Discovering these overlaps between content enables us to define an importance metric. This metric is based on the frequency with which different scenes of the target video v have been uploaded into the social sharing engine. We choose frequency as a simple and intuitive metric, although of course other metrics are possible. We can express this importance value for any given time, t, of the target video as

$$v_t = \frac{\left|\{Q_j : Q_j \cap v^{(t)} \neq \varnothing\}\right|}{\left|\{Q_j : Q_j \cap v \neq \varnothing\}\right|},$$

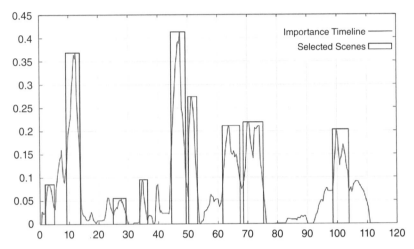

Figure 12.3. Importance timeline. The time series depicts the values of υ_t found for each time point of a given video. Bounding boxes delimit highlights selected.

where $v(t)$ denotes the frames at time t of video v, and the set intersection represents the visual overlap, which we find automatically using our CBCR algorithm. The time series obtained by the computation of υ_t for all possible values of t we call the "importance timeline" (see Figure 12.3). The importance timeline conveys information about the video scenes that are most frequently uploaded, and, therefore, most important according to our definition. Peaks indicate potential highlights of V.

12.3.3   Highlights Selection

The importance timeline is a continuous function, but for our analysis, we need to identify discrete regions to present to users. In this last stage of the analysis, we identify specific highlighted regions, by analyzing the neighborhood around maximal points υ_k in the series to find the appropriate boundaries of each region. To select the region boundaries, we compute a threshold $\theta(\upsilon_k, D)$ dynamically as a function of two variables: the importance value at the current maximal point being considered, υ_k, and an optional maximum duration for the selected region, D:

$$\theta(\upsilon_k, D) = \omega \cdot \upsilon_k \cdot \varphi(l, D).$$

In the previous expression, ω is a fixed weight factor, l denotes the current length of the region selected so far, and $\varphi(l, D)$ is an increasing weighting function so that

$$\lim_{l \to D} \varphi(l, D) = \frac{1}{\omega}, \quad \text{i.e.,} \quad \varphi(l, D) = \frac{l}{\omega \cdot D}.$$

To enhance the boundaries for our detected regions, we proceed to analyze the video to identify its shot structure. A shot is a continuous set of frames captured in a single camera operation. It is the lowest level meaningful unit into which videos can be divided. We use a color histogram difference-based algorithm (San Pedro et al. 2005) to detect abrupt transitions between consecutive shots and take advantage of these partitions to constrain the time points which will be later used as region boundaries. Figure 12.3 shows an example of the result obtained with this procedure.

12.3.4 Evaluation

We evaluated the quality of automatically extracted highlights by comparing them to subjective judgments by film experts. For the experiment, we selected seven popular films: *The Godfather* (1972), *Star Wars* (1977), *Forrest Gump* (1994), *The Matrix* (1999), *Lord of the Rings* (2001), *Pirates of the Caribbean* (2003), and *300* (2006). First, we crawled YouTube to retrieve all the uploaded videos related to these films, and applied our algorithm to derive highlights. We then presented film experts with a series of these highlights and asked them to rate their significance compared with other clips selected from the film. We wanted to see whether film experts' judgments replicated our automatic analysis of region significance.

We built a web-based application to collect experts' importance ratings. For each film, participants were asked to rate a set of 18 clips presented 3 clips at a time: one clip our algorithm rated as of high importance, another of intermediate, and a final one of low importance. Each triplet was selected from a random pool of clips (containing 6 top, 6 medium, and 6 low importance clips), and the order of presentation was randomized with respect to algorithm importance. Detected highlights, that is, peaks in Figure 12.3, were classed as high importance. Clips below this but with more than 0 uploads were categorized as medium, and clips with no uploads were classed as low. Each clip represented a full scene, ranging from 1 to 3 minutes. Clip cuttings were adjusted using shot boundaries to preserve the integrity of self-contained individual regions.

We recruited 45 participants by posting to special interest film sites and social networking sites. They generated a total of 86 sessions, and 945 clip judgments, with 15 users rating multiple films. We asked our participants to select a film and provide their knowledge level about it (passing knowledge, knowledgeable, expert, and world expert). Users were only allowed to rate the same film once, although they could rate multiple films. Users could choose different knowledge levels for each film, although we asked them to focus on films they were familiar with. Users were asked to decide on their "favorite," "not so favorite," and "least favorite" clip in each triplet. We also recorded how long users played each clip and collected qualitative comments about their ratings. They had no prior knowledge of this project.

12.3.4.1 *Experimental Results* For each clip we analyzed the relation between (a) the ratings provided by participants and (b) the importance coefficient generated by the algorithm. Both metrics ranged in value between 1 (for important regions), 2 (for intermediate regions) and 3 (for unimportant regions). We first correlated all user and algorithm importance metrics. This was significant (Spearman's rho = 0.351, $p < 0.01$, 944 df) showing a clear relation between automatic methods and user judgements.

Effects of Knowledge Level Despite our instructions, some users rated films that they were less familiar with. Such nonexpert ratings are likely to correlate less well with our algorithm. If we consider just those judgments where participants rated

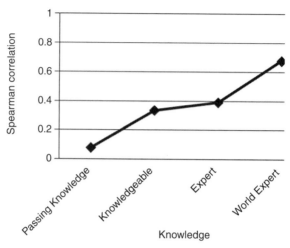

Figure 12.4. Correlation as a function of the knowledge of participants.

TABLE 12.1. Contingency Table for Participants of Two Top Knowledge Levels: (a) Expert and (b) World Expert

Count		Algorithm Importance Rating			Total
		1	2	3	
User	1	72	21	14	107
importance	2	18	55	34	107
rating	3	17	31	59	107
Total		107	107	107	321

themselves as "expert" or "world expert," The correlation increases to 0.467 ($p < 0.01$, 320 df). As Figure 12.4 shows, higher correlations are obtained for higher user knowledge levels. The contingency table is shown in Table 12.1. The main diagonal represents the frequency of agreement, while the values off the diagonal represent disagreements between automatic and user provided judgements. The table shows high agreement, with the main diagonal being more highly populated than off-diagonal scores.

Film experts also spent less time re-playing the clips before judging them. A one-way analysis of variance with play time as the dependent variable and knowledge level as the independent variable showed a significant effect ($F(3, 944) = 7.53$, $p < 0.0001$). These findings validate our method, offering behavioral support for participants' self-evaluations of expertise, as experts should have less need to access films to make their judgments.

There were also differences between films. Figure 12.5 suggests that action films led to better correlated ratings. For slower-pace films, it is somewhat more difficult to agree on key moments, as there may be fewer visually salient regions, and subjective rating factors become more significant.

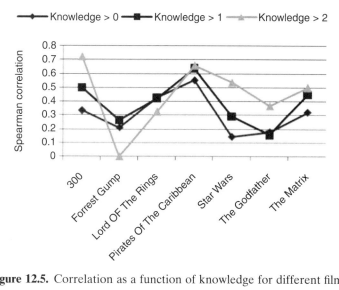

Figure 12.5. Correlation as a function of knowledge for different films.

Number of Uploads and Relation between User Judgments and Algorithm Scores
We then applied a linear regression test to determine the extent to which our algorithm's accuracy was affected by the number of overlapping uploads. We found that the number of uploads was unrelated to correlations between algorithm and user judgements ($R^2 = 0.0001, p > 0.10$). This suggests we had collected enough overlapping videos to generate sufficient data to obtain accurate algorithm scores.

12.3.5   Discussion

We proposed a social video summarization method based on the frequency of content redundancy detected and formalized on the Visual Affinity Graph. An extensive user evaluation revealed that our algorithm is able to derive highlights judged by experts to be important. Further tests confirmed that the correlation between algorithmic and user judgments tend to increase when experts are more knowledgeable. Last, we found no relation between the number of redundant videos found and the user-algorithm correlation, indicating that YouTube contains enough overlaps to systematically produce dense Visual Affinity Graphs, and therefore accurate highlight detection. However, this social summarization technique can only be applied to popular media streams where there is enough content overlap.

12.4   IMPROVING ANNOTATIONS

12.4.1   Description

Metadata allow us to attach structured information to data objects, videos in our case, with the purpose of providing easily parseable meta-information about them. These annotations can be automatic or manual in origin. Automatic annotations are normally restricted to technical and low-level aspects of the content. For example,

DV video capturing devices encode in the stream meta-information about time/date, zoom, and white balance, among other things. On the other hand, manual annotations such as tags, titles, and descriptions are provided by users and normally describe the data object at a much higher, semantic level. For this reason, manual annotations are commonly exploited for the effective retrieval of complex kinds of information contained in multimedia data. However, content annotation in social multimedia sites requires active intellectual effort and is very time consuming. In consequence, community-provided annotations can lack consistency and present numerous irregularities (e.g., abbreviations and typos) that degrade the performance of applications, such as automatic data organization and retrieval. Furthermore, users tend to tag content of interest so that tags can be unevenly distributed in a collection, again potentially compromising retrieval.

In this section, we analyze content to achieve more comprehensive and accurate annotations of video content. We use the Visual Affinity Graph to locate groups of videos with duplicated content. Each uploader provides annotations in the form of different tags expressing their personal perspective on a given clip, including characters, dates, and other more general concepts. We use the new content-based links provided by the Visual Affinity Graph to propagate tags between related videos, utilizing visual affinity to extend community knowledge in the network. With this approach, we exploit visual redundancy to combine information about related clips extending the (currently limited) set of metadata currently available for that content. We propose and evaluate different tag propagation techniques, and show systematic improvements in quality and applicability of the resulting annotations.

12.4.2 Methodology

Our algorithm uses edges of the Visual Affinity Graph to propagate tags between neighbors. Neighbors of this graph are known to share the same visual content, indicating joint semantic content that is often reflected by corresponding annotations. For each connected video in the Visual Affinity Graph, we compute a set of autotags, that is, tags imported from visually overlapping videos. Every element of autotags is assigned a weight that determines the importance of the new tag for the video. These weights are determined by the amount of overlaps occurring between the source and the target videos. Different propagation strategies can be defined, affecting the set of autotags and their associated weights.

For neighbor-based tagging, we transform the undirected overlap graph into a directed and weighted graph $G'(V, E')$, with (v_i, v_j) and $(v_i, v_j) \in E'$ iff $\{v_i, v_j\} \in E$. The weight $\omega(v_i, v_j)$ assigned to an edge (v_i, v_j) reflects the influence of video v_i on video v_j for tag assignment. In this chapter, we use the heuristic weighting function

$$ w(v_i, v_j) = \frac{|v_i \cap v_j|}{v_j}, $$

where $|v_j|$ is the (temporal) length of video v_j, and $|v_i \cap v_j|$ denotes the length of the intersection between v_i and v_j. This weighting function describes to what degree video v_j overlaps with video v_i. Note that when v_i and v_j overlap, if v_i is a parent of v_j (meaning that v_i is the more general video, and v_j can be considered as a specific

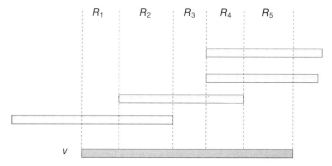

R_1 R_2 R_3 R_4 R_5

v

Figure 12.6. Overlap regions $R_1, \ldots, R_5$ for a video v covered by four other videos.

region from this video), then the weighting function ω assigns the maximum value 1 to (v_i, v_j).

Let $T = \{t_1, \ldots, t_n\}$ be the set of tags originally (manually) assigned to the videos in V, and let $I(t, v_i)$ be an indicator function for original tags $t \in T$, with $I(t, v_i) = 1$ iff v_i was manually tagged by a user with tag t, $I(t, v_i) = 0$ otherwise. We compute the relevance $\mathrm{rel}(t, v_i)$ of a tag t from adjacent videos as follows:

$$\mathrm{rel}(t, v_i) = \sum_{(v_j, v_i) \in E'_O} I(t, v_j) w(v_j, v_i),$$

that is, we compute a weighted sum of influences of the overlapping videos containing tag t. For a set of overlapping videos, that is, neighbors in the graph, situations with multiple redundant overlaps as shown in Figure 12.6 can occur. In order to avoid a too high increase of the relevance values for automatically generated tags in comparison with original tags, we propose a relaxation method for regions with redundant overlap, reducing the contribution of each additional video in each region by a factor α ($0 < \alpha \le 1$). We call this variant *overlap redundancy aware tagging*.

We use the obtained relevance values for all tags from the overlapping videos to generate sets of autotags (v_i) of automatically assigned new tags for each video $v_i \in V$ applying a threshold δ for tag relevancy:

$$\mathrm{autotags}(v_i) = \{t \in T \mid I(t, v_i) = 0 \wedge \mathrm{rel}(v_i, t) > \delta\}.$$

In order to compute feature vectors (e.g., for clustering or classification) for videos v_i, we use the relevance values $\mathrm{rel}(t, v_i)$ of tags t as features weights. Enhanced feature vectors can be constructed as a combination of the original tag weights ($I(t, v_i)$ normalized by the number of tags) and the relevance weights for new, automatically added tags (normalized by the number of tags).

12.4.3 Evaluation

We have presented different methods for automatically generating tags, resulting in richer feature representations of videos. Machine learning algorithms can make use of this feature information to generate models, and to automatically organize the data. We hypothesize that these extended feature representations of videos lead to the generation of better models, improving the quality of automatic data organization. We test this by performing a quantitative evaluation of the new set of tags by examining the influence of enhanced tag annotations on automatic video classification.

12.4.3.1 Test Collection We created our test collection from YouTube by formulating queries and subsequent searches for "related videos," analogous to the typical user interaction with Web 2.0 sites. Note that, in our scenario, we require access not just to metadata, but to the actual video content. Therefore, crawling and storage requirements are much higher, imposing a limit on the subset size we could gather. Given that an archive of the most common queries does not exist for YouTube, we selected our set of queries from Google's Zeitgeist archive from 2001 to 2007. These are generic queries, used to search for web pages and not videos. Therefore, some of them might not be suitable for video search (e.g., "windows update"). We set a threshold on the number of search results returned by queries. Those for which YouTube returned less than 100 results were considered not suitable for video search, and ignored. In total, 579 queries were accepted, for which the top 50 results were retrieved. Altogether, we collected 28,216 videos using those queries (some of the results were not accessible during the crawling because they were removed by the system or by the owner). A random sample of these videos was used to extend the test collection by gathering related videos, as offered by the YouTube API. In total, 267 queries for related videos were performed, generating 10,067 additional elements. The complete test collection included 38,283 video files for a total of over 2900 hours.

12.4.3.2 Classification Classifying data into thematic categories usually follows a supervised learning paradigm and is based on training items that need to be provided for each topic. Linear support vector machines (SVMs) construct a hyperplane $\vec{w} \cdot \vec{x} + b = 0$ that separates the set of positive training examples from a set of negative examples with maximum margin. We used the SVMlight (Joachims 1999) implementation of SVMs with linear kernel and standard parameterization in our experiments; SVMs have been shown to perform very well for text-based classification tasks (Dumais et al. 2006).

As classes for our classification experiments, we chose YouTube categories containing at least 900 videos in our collection. These were: "Comedy," "Entertainment," "Film & Animation," "News & Politics," "Sports," "People & Blogs," and "Music." We performed binary classification experiments for all 21 possible combinations of these class pairs using balanced training and test sets. Settings with more than two classes can be reduced to multiple binary classification problems that can be solved separately. For each category, we randomly selected 400 videos for training the classification model and a disjoint set of 500 videos for testing. We trained different models based on $T = 10, 25, 50, 100, 200$, and all 400 training videos per class. We compared the following methods for constructing feature vectors from video tags:

> *BaseOrig*: Vectors based on the original tags of the videos (i.e., tags manually assigned by the owner of the video in YouTube). This serves as the baseline for the comparison with our vector representations based on automatic tagging.

TABLE 12.2. Classification Accuracy with T = 10, 25, 50, 100, 400 Training Videos Using Different Tag Representations for Videos

	BaseOrig	NTag	RedNTag
$T = 10$	0.5794	0.6341	0.6345
$T = 25$	0.6357	0.7203	0.7247
$T = 50$	0.7045	0.7615	0.7646
$T = 100$	0.7507	0.7896	0.7907
$T = 200$	0.7906	0.8162	0.8176
$T = 400$	0.8286	0.8398	0.8417

NTag: Vectors constructed based on the tags and relevance values produced by simple neighbor-based tagging (Section 12.4.2) in addition to the original tags.

RedNTag: Vectors using tags generated by overlap redundancy aware neighbor-based tagging plus the original tags as described in Section 12.4.2. We did not pursue any extensive parameter tuning and chose $\alpha = 0.5$ for the relaxation parameter.

Our quality measure is the fraction of correctly classified videos (accuracy). Finally, we computed micro-averaged results for all topic pairs. The results of the comparison are shown in Table 12.2. We observe that classification taking automatically generated tagging into account clearly outperforms classification using just the original tags. This holds for both tag propagation methods. For classification using 50 training documents per class, for example, we increased the accuracy from approximately 70 to 76%, quite a significant gain. Overlap redundancy aware neighbor-based tagging provides slightly, but consistently more accurate results than the simple neighbor-based tagging variant.

12.4.4 Discussion

In this section, we have proposed a methodology to improve annotations of shared video resources in Web 2.0 sites. We take advantage of the existing annotations in the network, and use the edges of the Visual Affinity Graph to spread this social knowledge to other resources. Different propagation strategies are discussed and evaluated, resulting in significant improvements on the amount and quality of video annotations. Our experiments show that with the enriched set of tags, better classification models can be generated, allowing for improved automatic structuring and organization of content.

12.5 CONCLUSIONS

In this chapter, we have presented a novel approach for information extraction in multimedia-enabled Web 2.0 systems. We take advantage of what is usually viewed as an undesirable feature of these websites, content redundancy, to establish connections between resources, and exploit them to increase the knowledge about the collection. Such connections are formalized into the so-called Visual Affinity Graph. We have presented two applications of such a graph.

First, we present an approach to the unsupervised selection of highlights from video footage. Our method successfully circumvents the limitations of current content analysis methods, exploiting knowledge implicitly available in video-sharing social websites. The Visual Affinity Graph is computed and used to identify redundant region uploads from different users. We use this information to build time series of important sequences within the videos that we then analyze to locate highlights. The results were shown to be reliable in a subsequent user evaluation when expert users' judgments agreed with our algorithm.

The ability to detect semantically meaningful regions from video clips in an unsupervised fashion has many applications. For example, techniques that analyze users' repeated access and annotation behaviors have been used to detect important regions of both recorded lectures and meetings (Kalnikaite and Whittaker 2008). A similar social summarization approach might also be used for finding favorites in collection of other kinds of shared media, such as Flickr's photo collections. However, there are interesting future empirical questions about the influence of content: Would there be user consensus about highlights for data such as political debates or news, where content is less well structured and evaluations of it more esoteric?

Second, we have also shown that content redundancy in social sharing systems can be used to obtain richer annotations for shared objects. More specifically, we have used content overlap in the video sharing Web 2.0 environments to establish new connections between videos forming a basis for our automatic tagging methods. Classification experiments show that the additional information obtained by automatic tagging can largely improve automatic structuring and organization of content. We think that the proposed technique has direct application to search improvement, where augmented tag sets can reveal previously concealed resources.

This work reports another important direction for future Web 2.0 and social information processing research. So far, previous work has focused on using social information (such as tags) to organize and retrieve textual data. Techniques for accessing text are relatively well understood, however. But with the massive recent increases of multimedia data, such as pictures and video, we desperately need new methods for managing multimedia information. Hybrid social and content analysis methods such as those we report here represent a promising future direction for accessing such data.

CHAPTER 13

INFORMATION FUSION AND ANOMALY DETECTION WITH UNCALIBRATED CAMERAS IN VIDEO SURVEILLANCE

ERHAN BAKI ERMIS, VENKATESH SALIGRAMA,
and PIERRE-MARC JODOIN

13.1 INTRODUCTION

In the United States, 4 billion hours of surveillance video is recorded every week (Vlahos 2008). Even if one person were able to monitor 10 cameras simultaneously for 40 hours a week, monitoring all the footage would require 10 million surveillance staff, roughly about 3.3% of the U.S. population. This is evidently impractical, and automated systems are necessary to aid the monitoring and reviewing the contents of the footage.

A common setup in the surveillance systems is to have a network of cameras collaboratively collect information from a region of interest. Therefore, automated systems need to fuse the collected information and perform a number of tasks based on the fused information. However, information fusion in multi-camera systems requires data association, and this poses a significant challenge that does not exist in single camera systems. Observe, for example, Figure 13.1, which depicts the standard approach taken in automated video analytics systems. While the single camera systems follow the dashed arrows, the multi-camera systems have to follow the solid arrows, which requires a data association step in order to be able to fuse information.

However, data association, without precise calibration, proves to be a major challenge due to the significant variability of geometry from one camera to another. More precisely, due to the variability in the observation geometry, we do not know where a feature vector in one camera maps to in the second camera, as depicted in Figure 13.2.

One approach to overcome the difficulties with data association is to perform calibration after deploying the system such that each camera has access to the

Multimedia Information Extraction: Advances in Video, Audio, and Imagery Analysis for Search, Data Mining, Surveillance, and Authoring, First Edition. Edited by Mark T. Maybury.
© 2012 IEEE Computer Society. Published 2012 by John Wiley & Sons, Inc.

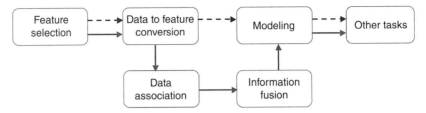

Figure 13.1. Information processing in single and multi-camera systems.

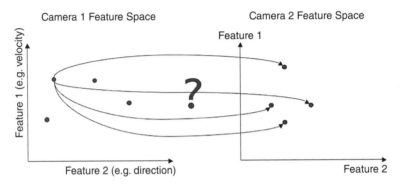

Figure 13.2. Feature space of two uncalibrated cameras.

parameters of all the other cameras along with their exact locations, orientations, and zoom levels. While calibration makes information fusion an easier task to accomplish, as the size and scope of these networks increase, calibration itself becomes a significant challenge, which also hinders the scalability and flexibility of the systems. Furthermore, in the case of dynamic camera networks that include pan-tilt-zoom cameras, calibration requirements make scalability even harder to achieve, requiring frequent updates. In order to overcome these difficulties, information fusion techniques for uncalibrated cameras are required.

In this chapter, we consider a network of video cameras that observe a scene from various orientations with different zoom levels, and use video dynamics to develop a new approach to several important problems in uncalibrated camera networks. We propose a simple yet powerful method to characterize behavior in videos, which lends itself to a wide variety of applications involving multi-camera fusion. The novelty of our work stems from the fact that the camera orientations and zoom levels are not constrained, yet the proposed method requires the knowledge of neither camera topology, nor epipolar geometry, nor zoom levels.

13.1.1 Multi-Camera Fusion Problems

The multi-camera fusion problem can manifest itself in several forms, including dense matching, behavior modeling, multi-camera anomaly detection, occlusion mapping, and multi-camera tracking. Consider, for example, the dense matching problem. In the classical stereo matching setup, the cameras are implicitly assumed

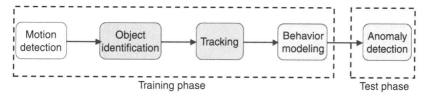

Figure 13.3. Block diagram of object-based anomaly detection methods.

to have similar orientations and zoom levels. Scharstein and Szeliski (2002) presented an evaluation of dense two-frame stereo correspondence algorithms. One of the main points made there is that most algorithms use strong assumptions about the camera calibration and epipolar geometry (see Black and Rangarajan 2005; Bobick and Intille 1999; Boykov et al. 1998; Scharstein and Szeliski 1998; Ogale and Aloimonos 2005; Veksler 2002, and references therein for prominent methods on dense matching). Furthermore, a majority of dense matching methods have stringent requirements on camera placement and zoom levels, which are limitations for their applicability to large and dynamic systems.

13.1.2 Location Based Anomaly Detection

The ultimate objective in a camera-surveillance system is the identification of activities of interest in the field of view, possibly adapted to prior information available from other sources. Such activities in many cases can be thought of as abnormalities, namely, activities that are outside the range of normal behavior. As discussed in a review paper by Hu et al. (2004), many surveillance methods are *object based* (Bouthemy and Lalande 1993; Elgammal et al. 2002; Paragios and Deriche 2000; Stauffer and Grimson 2000; Toyama et al. 1999), and follow a general pipeline-based framework as depicted in Figure 13.3; moving objects are first detected, then they are classified and tracked over a certain number of frames, and, finally, the resulting paths are used to distinguish "normal" objects from "abnormal" ones. In general, these methods contain a training phase, during which a probabilistic model is built using paths followed by "normal" objects. We call these methods *object based*, as the features of interest are generally related to specific objects.

Although object-based method is simple in principle, it is sensitive to detection and tracking errors, and suffers from computational complexity. Consider, for example, the urban scene in Figure 13.4. The object based method would have to identify and track all the objects in the scene, which is impractical for many scenarios that contain objects as well as clutter.

This issue motivates an alternative approach that is *location based*. More specifically, instead of collecting features that pertain to specific objects and follow the process described above, we investigate the data that describes the behavior patterns observed at a particular location. We first generate behavior models for each location and detect anomalies in the behavior patterns exhibited in different locations. We then identify and track objects that generate the anomalous patterns, and this approach immediately reduces the amount of objects that need to be identified and tracked, and eliminates false alarms due to clutter. Figure 13.5 depicts how our

Figure 13.4. A common urban scene encountered in surveillance applications.

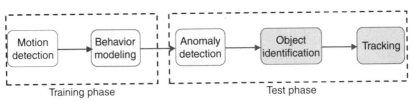

Figure 13.5. Block diagram of the proposed location-based anomaly detection method.

Figure 13.6. Location-based method eliminates clutter, reduces complexity (Jodoin et al. 2008).

method differs from the aforementioned object-based methods, and Figure 13.6 gives an example of how location-based methods can reduce the amount of objects that need to be identified and tracked.

In this work, we propose simple motion-based features to address the problem of information fusion in multi-camera systems. These features also lend themselves to the development of a location-based approach for anomaly detection. The strength of the proposed features is that they are geometry independent in the following sense: no matter what the camera orientations and zoom levels are, a location carries the same features in each camera up to a scaling factor. This scaling factor can be accounted for with little difficulty since the observations belong to a family of signals parameterized by a single parameter.

13.2 GEOMETRY INDEPENDENCE OF ACTIVITY

In a video sequence, once the background is subtracted, a pixel p_1 has a time series of ones and zeros, as depicted in Figure 13.7 (right). We use these time series to characterize behavior and as activity features for a given location. These features have the geometry independence property, as discussed in the next section. These time series or features derived from them can also be used for information fusion and anomaly detection in multi-camera surveillance systems, as discussed in Section 13.4.

13.2.1 Geometry Independence

Consider a cuboid object that moves over a point x_0 on a surface. We describe the idea over a cuboid object, since a cuboid bounding box around any object can be drawn, and a majority of the objects can be approximated by this bounding box. Assume that the object moves with velocity v, and its length in the direction of motion is l. Assume that two infinite resolution cameras observe the object from different views with different zoom levels. Let α be the ratio of the object's height h to its length l, for example, 1/4 for a car, 1/10 for a truck, and about 6 for people. Let θ_i and ϕ_i be the observation angles defined as in Figure 13.8 for Camera $i, i = 1,2$. In each camera's frame (projection plane), there is a point that corresponds to x_0. Call these points p_1 in Camera 1, and q_1 in Camera 2.

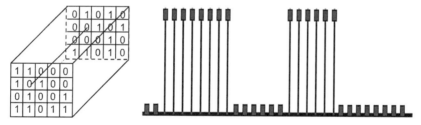

Figure 13.7. Binary time series of a pixel after background subtraction.

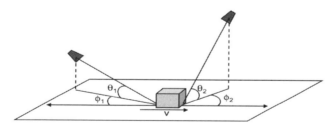

Figure 13.8. Multi-camera observation angles.

Let $t = l/v$ be the actual occupancy duration of x_0 by the object. Define t_{p_1} and t_{q_1} as the occupancy duration of pixels p_1 and q_1 by the projection of the object in each camera. First consider the case where $\phi_1 = 0$, that is, Camera 1 is placed at some height along the direction of motion. Assume for simplicity that the camera is placed in front of the object. In this case, the back-projection of the object's image onto the surface will have length $l_{C_1} = l + h/\tan(\theta_1)$, where h is the height of the object. Rewriting this in terms of the aspect ratio, we have $l_{C_1} = l + \alpha l/\tan(\theta_1) = l(1 + \alpha/\tan(\theta_1))$. Observe that the occupancy duration of p_1 will be the same as the amount of time it takes for the back-projection to cross over x_0. Then, we have $t_{p_1} = l_{C_1}/v = (l/v)(1 + \alpha/\tan(\theta_1)) = t(1 + \alpha/\tan(\theta_1))$. As we increase the angle ϕ_1 from 0 to 180°, the extension term $\alpha/\tan(\theta_1)$ in l_{C_1} begins to shrink. At 90°, it becomes precisely zero, and at 180°, it again becomes $\alpha/\tan(\theta_1)$. Therefore, to model this effect, we multiply the extension term with a function $\chi(\phi_i)$, which is bounded to $[0,1]$, and takes a value of 0 at $\phi_i = 90$ and 1 at $\phi_i = 0$ and $\phi_i = 180$. This leads to the following approximations for t_{p_1} and t_{q_1}:

$$t_{p_1} = t(1 + \alpha\chi(\phi_1)/\tan(\theta_1)), \quad t_{q_1} = t(1 + \alpha\chi(\phi_2)/\tan(\theta_2)).$$

Here, we are only interested in accounting for the scaling effect for a given α. Therefore, we can define $\gamma_i = \chi(\phi_i)/\tan(\theta_i)$, and treat the scaling factor as a single parameter. With this setup, the observations belong to a family of signals parameterized by a single parameter and can be accounted for without the knowledge of θ_i and ϕ_i through statistical methods. Furthermore, the uniqueness property presented below guarantees reliable disambiguation among different pixels, and this information can be used for multi-camera fusion.

Remark: For many real-world objects, the expressions $t[1 + \alpha/\tan(\theta_i)\chi(\phi_i)]$ turn out to be upper bounds on the occupancy durations. Below, we present a simulation study that examines $1 + \alpha/\tan(\theta_i)\chi(\phi_i)$ as a function of camera placement for $\alpha = 1/4$ and $\alpha = 6$, representing the cases for a car and a human, respectively. We also demonstrate real-world examples where the scaling factor turns out to be nearly zero for very plausible scenarios.

Remark: While γ_i characterizes the discrepancy between the observed and actual occupancy rates, we need only care about how t_{p_1}/t_{q_1} behaves for multi-camera fusion. This ratio is always smaller than t_{p_1}/t, which means that the discrepancy between the cameras is smaller than the discrepancy between the cameras and actual occupancy rates.

13.2.2 Uniqueness Property

Geometry independence property states that given two pixels observe the same location, they have the same time series up to a scaling factor. However, it does not establish that two pixels that observe different regions do not have the same time series. When the events are independent, the probability that two pixels have the same time series goes to zero. We state this result as a lemma below.

Lemma: Let p_i be a pixel in Camera 1, and q_j be a pixel in Camera 2. If p_i and q_j do not observe the same location, and if the events occur randomly in the observed region, then the Hamming distance between the time series of p_i and q_j is positive with high probability for sufficiently long video sequences.

Nowhere in our development of geometry independence did we use any assumptions about the zoom levels of cameras. This leads us to the lemma below.

Lemma: The time series of a particular location is invariant to different zoom levels with which it is observed.

13.2.3 Examples

In order to characterize the discrepancy between the observed and actual occupancy rates, we set up an experiment using 3ds Max, where we placed cameras for all combinations of $\theta = \{15, 30, \ldots, 90\}$ degrees and $\phi = \{0, 15, \ldots, 90\}$ degrees. In total, we had 36 cameras covering the first octant, all observing the same point in the middle of their field of view. Note that once $\theta = 90$, there is no need to vary ϕ, hence 36 cameras and not 42.

Next, we made two cuboids to simulate the bounding box of a car and the bounding box of a human, both with appropriate dimensions. These objects moved through the point, and we recorded the videos with each of the cameras. Then we looked at the occupancy duration of the point of interest in each camera, and finally calculated the ratio of observed occupancy duration to that of actual, that is, $\tau = t_{p_i}/t$. The results are presented in Figure 13.9 for both cuboids. Once the singular observation angles are ignored, τ has a narrow range, which also narrows the parameter search space.

We next present an example of geometry independence of traffic information in real-life scenarios, where two cameras overlook a street from the top of a nine-floor building. We recorded the videos simultaneously from both cameras, and performed background subtraction on both sequences with the same method. We then looked at the time series data of one pixel from each camera, each corresponding to the same point on the road. The results are presented in Figure 13.10.

In Figure 13.11, we demonstrate the claim that the time series are invariant to different zoom levels. Time series generated by cars passing by are the same for both videos, irrespective of the zoom levels.

In the view of our discussion related to Figure 13.2, the geometry independence allows us to eliminate the data association problem, because the features we select are independent of the cameras' positions, orientations, and zoom levels. Consequently, we know exactly where a feature in the space of one camera falls in the space of another, depicted in Figure 13.12.

		Phi					
		0	15	30	45	60	75	90
Theta	15	2.05	1.87	1.44	1.26	1.15	1.05	1
	30	1.49	1.49	1.38	1.23	1.13	1.05	1
	45	1.28	1.28	1.26	1.21	1.13	1.05	1
	60	1.15	1.15	1.13	1.10	1.08	1.05	1
	75	1.08	1.08	1.05	1.05	1.03	1.03	1
	90	-	-	-	-	-	-	1

		Phi					
		0	15	30	45	60	75	90
Theta	15	20.8	3	2.2	1.4	1.6	1.2	1
	30	10.4	2.8	2.2	1.6	1.4	1.2	1
	45	6.4	2.8	1.8	1.6	1.4	1.2	1
	60	4.2	2.8	1.8	1.6	1.4	1.2	1
	75	2.6	2.4	1.8	1.6	1.4	1.2	1
	90	-	-	-	-	-	-	1

Figure 13.9. Table of discrepancy ratios (τ) for various angles of observation.

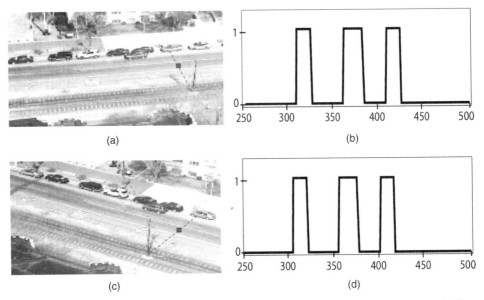

Figure 13.10. Camera 1 view and time series (a,b); Camera 2 view and time series (c,d).

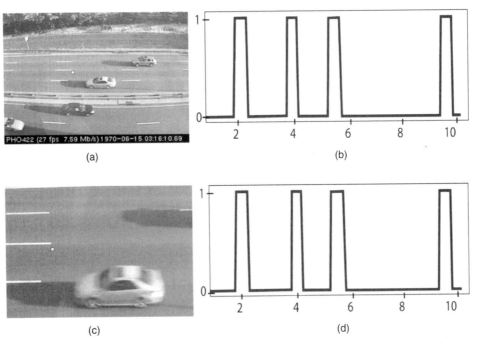

Figure 13.11. No-zoom view and time series (a,b); zoom-vie and time series (c,d).

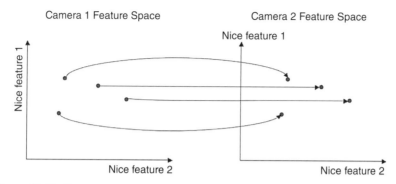

Figure 13.12. Feature space of two cameras with geometry-independent features.

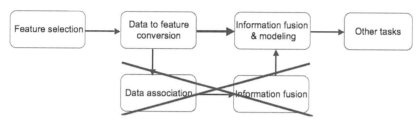

Figure 13.13. Information processing in multi-camera systems with geometry independence.

As consequence of the geometry independence, we can now eliminate the data association block and go directly to information fusion and modeling block as depicted in Figure 13.13.

13.3 DENSE MULTI-CAMERA MATCHING

In order to perform the dense stereo matching, we first subtract the background from the video. Researchers have investigated a number of methods to perform motion detection and background subtraction (Elgammal et al. 2002; Konrad 2005; Neri et al. 1998; Zhang and Lu 2001). Once the background is subtracted, we obtain a binary motion video $V(.,.)$, where $V(i,\tau)$ denotes the binary value of a pixel, indexed with i, in frame number τ. Throughout the chapter, V_1 will denote the binary video obtained from Camera 1, V_2 will denote the binary video obtained from Camera 2. Similarly, p will denote a pixel in Camera 1, and q will denote a pixel in Camera 2. For simplicity, we assume that both V_1 and V_2 are composed of m-pixel frames.

13.3.1 Mapping Activity Regions

Let p_i be a pixel in Camera 1, and $V_1(i,.)$ be its binary time series. For each pixel q_j in Camera 2, we compute a variation of Euclidean distance, that is,

$$d(p_i, q_j) = \frac{1}{\eta} \sqrt{\sum_{\tau=1:T} (V_1(i, \tau) - V_2(j, \tau))^2},$$

where

$$\eta = \max \left\{ \sum_{\tau=1:T} V_1(i, \tau), \sum_{\tau=1:T} V_2(j, \tau), 1 \right\},$$

is a normalization factor, and T is the length of the video sequences. The normalizing constant η diminishes the effect of small discrepancies in sequences where there is a large amount of activity, yet retains the importance of errors when there is little activity. Let $d_i^{\max} = \max_{q_j} d(p_i, q_j)$ and $d_i^{\min} = \min_{q_j} d(p_i, q_j)$. We then find a similarity measure between the time series of p_i and q_j as $s(p_i, q_j) = [d_i^{\max} - d(p_i, q_j)]/[d_i^{\max} - d_i^{\min}]$, $s(p_i, q_j) \in [0,1]$.

When there is very little activity in the region of observation, as in the cases where a very short video is available, pixels in different regions may exhibit high similarities. In order to be able to handle these situations, we assign the corresponding pixel in Camera 2 to be q_{j*}, where we obtain the index $j*$ by using the least median of squares (LMS) algorithm, which is robust to as much as 50% outliers in the data (Rousseeuw and Leroy 1987).

13.3.1.1 Activity Matching Initialize with $Q^0 = \{q_j : s(p_i, q_j) \geq 0.9\}$, set convergence threshold γ.

1. Find the center of mass $C^t = (C_x^t, C_y^t)$ of Q^t using the least-squares (LS) method.
2. $\forall q_j \in Q^t$, find its Euclidean distance to $C^t = (C_x^t, C_y^t)$, that is, $d_E(C^t, q_j) = \sqrt{(C_x^t - q_{jx})^2 + (C_y^t - q_{jy})^2}$ where q_{jx} denotes the x-coordinate of pixel q_j and q_{jy} denotes the y-coordinate of pixel q_j.
3. Let $d_Q^t = d_E(C^t, q_j)$ and $med_q^t = \text{median}\{d_q^t\}$.
4. Set $Q^{t+1} = \{q_j : q_j \in Q^t, d_E(C^t, q_j) \leq med_Q^t\}$.
5. Calculate the new C^{t+1}. If $d_E(C^t, C^{t+1}) > \gamma$, go to step 2, else set $q_{j*} = C^t$.

We compared the performance of this method to the maximum likelihood estimate and least squares estimate. We present the comparison results below.

13.3.2 Results

13.3.2.1 Performance Evaluation In order to quantify the performance of our dense matching algorithm, we devised an indoor example where we placed two cameras with opposite orientations to a plane of observation. A schematic of the setup is presented in Figure 13.14. We obtained a 5000-frame video, where we generated activity on the plane by driving a remote-controlled car in the scene. We also took a snapshot of a grid on the scene. Then, we used the snapshot of the grid to calculate a ground truth dense map. To get the ground truth, we first hand-selected pixels in one camera and manually found their matches in the second camera. Using these matching pixels, we estimated the homographic transformation matrix, and

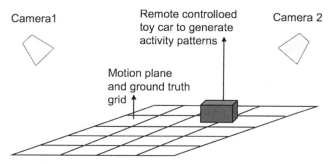

Figure 13.14. Setup of the indoor experiment.

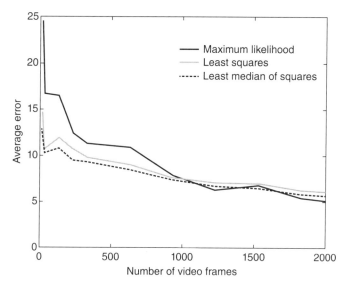

Figure 13.15. Average Euclidean distance between the ground truth matches and the matches found using the proposed method.

using this matrix, we calculated the mapping for each pixel from one camera to another.

In order to quantify the performance of our method, we randomly selected a number of pixels in Camera 1 and found their matches in Camera 2 using the method described previously, where we used a simple median filter to subtract the background from the videos. We then calculated the Euclidean distance between our match and the ground truth match, and defined average error as the average Euclidean distance between our estimate and ground truth across selected pixels.

In order to understand the effect of the number of frames on the error, we performed this experiment with videos of different lengths, and plotted the average error as a function of the number of frames used. The results, demonstrated in Figure 13.15, indicate that with sufficiently long videos, we can estimate the dense mapping accurately. The error was obtained using a toy car that was approximately 60 pixels long in the camera with which the matching error was measured. Noting that the error is less than 10 pixels with the proposed method after about 250 frames, this translates to about $\frac{1}{6}$th the length of the toy car. Back projecting this rate onto real-life scenarios, it corresponds to about 80 cm of error. For a video sequence of 2000 frames, we can reduce this error to about 40 cm.

The least median of squares method is more robust than the maximum likelihood and least squares methods when the video sequence is short. However, after about 1000 frames, the maximum likelihood has the smallest error.

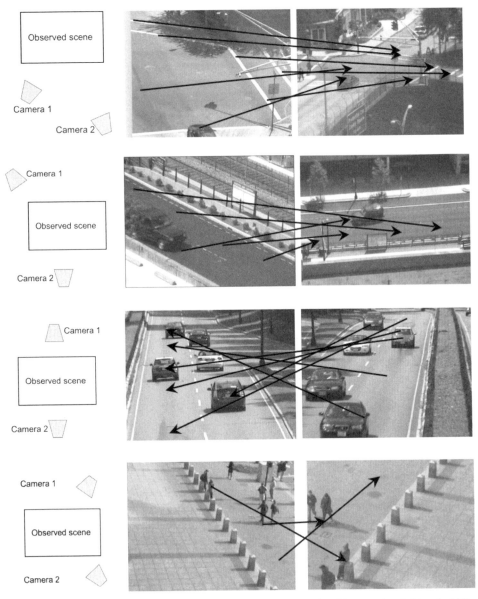

Figure 13.16. Camera setup (left column), matching results using 90 seconds of video (middle and right columns).

13.3.2.2 *Dense Mapping in Outdoor Scenarios* Here, the cameras have different orientations with respect to the observed scene, as well as different zoom levels. Unlike the standard stereo-matching problems, presenting a visual disparity map here can hardly provide the reader with an intuitive understanding of the mapping function. Hence, we picked several pixels in one camera and drew arrows to their corresponding pixels in the other camera. The results are presented in Figure 13.16.

13.4 MULTI-CAMERA INFORMATION FUSION AND ANOMALY DETECTION

Consider the binary time series data for pixel p_i: $V_1^i = (V_1(i, 1), V_1(i, 2), \ldots, V_1(i, \tau))$. Let B_n^i (busy rate) denote the length of nth set of consecutive ones in V^i and I_n^i (idle rate) denote the length of the nth set of consecutive zeros in V^i. For each pixel p_i, (B_n^i, I_n^i) tuples are samples of a two-dimensional distribution, where the unknown distribution is the behavior context and characterizes the behavior at p_i. The set of pixels that carry the same type of behavior can be collected in a cluster, and this can be done for the whole image frame, yielding to a number of behavior clusters.

Remark: While a number of powerful methods can be employed to extract complex structures in the data for this purpose (see Jain et al. 1999; von Luxborg 2006, and references therein), in this chapter, we present a basic approach for simplicity.

Behavior Clustering: Let $\{B_n^i, I_n^i\}_{n=1}^{s_i}$ be the set of busy-idle samples for pixel p_i. Define

$$\hat{B}^i \doteq \frac{1}{s_i} \sum_{n=1}^{s_i} B_n^i, \quad \hat{I}^i \doteq \frac{1}{s_i} \sum_{n=1}^{s_i} I_n^i,$$

the mean busy and idle rates for pixel p_i. We treat $(\hat{B}^i, \hat{I}^i)$ as the coordinates of pixel p_i in the busy-idle space, and use k-means to obtain the clusters.

Behavior Modeling: Without loss of generality, assume $C = \{p_1, p_2, \ldots, p_l\}$ is the set of pixels that belong to the first behavior cluster. Let

$$\mathcal{BI} = \{\{(B_i^1, I_i^1)\}_{i=1}^{s_1}, \{(B_i^2, I_i^2)\}_{i=1}^{s_2}, \ldots, \{(B_i^l, I_i^l)\}_{i=1}^{s_l}\},$$

be the collective set of busy-idle rate samples of all the elements of C. Let F_C be the probability distribution learned from $\mathcal{BI}$ using a given method, and f_C be the corresponding density function. We call F_C the behavior model of cluster C. For generality, we do not specify a learning method here; however, in our experiments, we used smoothed histograms.

Remark: Behavior clustering requires very little data, whereas obtaining a reliable behavior model requires a much longer video sequence. This is because behavior clustering is a classification problem, whereas obtaining the behavior models is an estimation problem.

Remark: Behavior models of corresponding clusters in different cameras can be used interchangeably, which leads to flexibility and scalability of the camera network. For example, in situations where a new camera is added to a network, it can learn the relevant behavior clusters and obtain the behavior models, which allow the new camera to benefit from the *experience* of the network. We present results of this nature below.

Anomaly Detection: Once the behavior models are obtained using the training video, it is possible to test for anomalous behavior in a test video of the same scene. Consider the time series for pixel p_i in the test sequence, a sequence of ones and zeros:

$$\hat{V}_1^i = (\hat{V}_1(i,1), \hat{V}_1(i,2), ..., \hat{V}_1(i,\tau')).$$

Now define the observed busy-idle rates for p_i, $\hat{B}_n^i$, and $\hat{I}_n^i$, similar to B_n^i and I_n^i. In order to detect the abnormal behavior at the nth tuple, we use the following algorithm, which keeps the false alarm probability below a desired threshold γ.

Abnormal Behavior Detection:

1. Find the likelihood of the tuple under the model F_C: $L = f_C(\hat{B}_n^i, \hat{I}_n^i)$.
2. Find the set $A = \{(B, I) : f_C(B, I) \leq L\}$.
3. Calculate the probability of set A under the measure associated with F_C:

$$P(A) = \int_A f_C(x)dx.$$

4. If $P(A) < \gamma$ label pixel p_i as carrying abnormal behavior over frames $\hat{B}_n^i$ and $\hat{I}_n^i$.

13.4.1 Results

13.4.1.1 Behavior Clustering
We now demonstrate that the pixels that exhibit similar behavior can be placed in the same cluster. For this demonstration, we filmed a road from two cameras, subtracted the background, and applied the clustering algorithm described above. The results are demonstrated in Figure 13.17 for one behavior cluster in two distinct cameras. Observe that in the busy–idle space, the clusters fall into the same region in both cameras.

13.4.1.2 Information Fusion and Anomaly Detection
Next, we demonstrate that the behavior model obtained from one camera can be transmitted to another camera that observes that same location, and that the anomaly detection can be performed based on the received model. For this demonstration, we used two cameras and obtained two videos of the same location by adjusting the cameras for different zoom levels and placing them with different orientations (Camera 1 is located to the south of the scene, while Camera 2 is located to the northwest of the scene). Then, we obtained the behavior clusters and corresponding behavior models in Camera 1, whereas on Camera 2, we only obtained the behavior clusters and matched them to those of the Camera 1.

Figure 13.17. Clusters of mean busy–idle rates for train tracks (left column), and the corresponding pixels in views of Camera 1 and Camera 2 (right column).

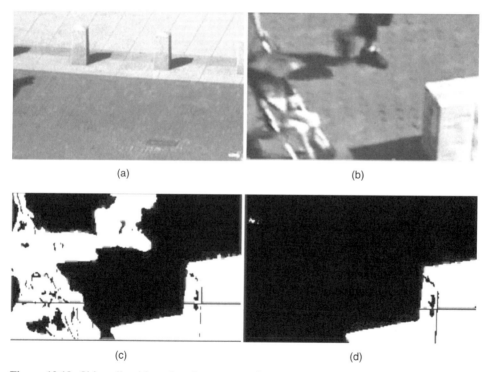

Figure 13.18. Sidewalk with pedestrians as seen from two cameras. The system is trained on the first camera (a) and tested on camera (b). Image (c) shows a binary motion mask in the test camera and (d) shows a detected anomaly in the test camera.

We next transferred the behavior models from Camera 1 to Camera 2, and in Camera 2 we used the "imported" behavior models to perform anomaly detection.

In the training videos, we recorded a sidewalk where pedestrians walk around, and for the test videos, we recorded the same sidewalk with an abandoned object. The abandoned object created a different busy rate, and we were able to correctly detect it in Camera 2, even though the behavior models were obtained from Camera 1. Note that the cameras have very different orientations and zoom levels; however, our method is indifferent to such parameters. Figure 13.18 demonstrates these results.

13.5 SUMMARY AND CONCLUSIONS

In this chapter, we considered the problem of information fusion in uncalibrated video networks. Motivated by wide-area surveillance applications, we deviated from the common setup of stereo matching problems and allowed cameras to have different orientations and zoom levels. Here, a major challenge was the significant variability of geometry from one view to another. In order to eliminate the stringent requirement of camera calibration, we used features that are geometry independent in the sense that no matter what the camera orientations and zoom levels are, an object generates the same feature in each camera. The presented approach makes it possible to share information in a dynamic camera network.

SECTION 3

AUDIO, GRAPHICS, AND BEHAVIOR EXTRACTION

Whereas the first two sections focus on extracting imagery and video, this section turns attention to the extraction of content from some unique sources, including audio, graphics, and human behavior. Each of these chapters provides a novel perspective and, taken together, illustrates how often overlooked channels or information sources can provide unique and valuable insights into artifacts or users.

The first chapter by Qian Hu et al. from the MITRE Corporation describes how their Audio Hot Spotting (AHS) system indexes and retrieves content from crosslingual audio or video by detecting multiple audio attributes. AHS provides audio content search and retrieval using a patented, integrated phonemic and word model-based approach. The system performs spoken language identification, and, where possible, speaker identification. Additional features, such as speech rate and vocal effort (e.g., shouting and whispering), are exploited to capture the speaker's emotional state. For example, even using errorful phone recognition, the authors find that speech rate estimation can both indicate emotion (e.g., stress, excitement, anger, or urgency) and also aid the speech recognizer itself, as recognizer error rate correlates with speech rate. Using linear predictive coding to analyze vocal effort, the authors report greater than 95% separation between soft and loud articulation using the Speech Under Simulated and Actual Stress Database (SUSAD) and Emotional Prosody Corpora. Finally, AHS automatically identifies non-speech audio, such as background noise (e.g., group laughter and applause), which can be very valuable for identifying significant audio (and associated video) passages. For example, their algorithm identified all instances of applause in the 2003 State of the Union address with only a 2.6% false alarm rate. In addition, preliminary results to retrieve meaningful information from meeting room data using combined word- and phoneme-based recognition suggests that for single-word queries, word models work well up

Multimedia Information Extraction: Advances in Video, Audio, and Imagery Analysis for Search, Data Mining, Surveillance, and Authoring, First Edition. Edited by Mark T. Maybury.
© 2012 IEEE Computer Society. Published 2012 by John Wiley & Sons, Inc.

to a 75% word error rate, beyond which point phoneme-based retrieval is superior. For multiple-word phrasal queries, however, the phoneme-based retrieval exhibited superior performance. In experiments on 679 keywords used to search 500 hours of broadcast news from the TREC SDR corpus (cross corpus error rate of 30%+), the authors found that passage retrieval rate was 71.7% when the passage was limited to only the query keyword, but increased to 76.2% when the passage length was increased to 10 seconds and rose to 83.8% if the returned document was allowed to be as long as 120 seconds. In summary, AHS illustrates that rich identity, content and emotional features available in the audio channel can be exploited to retrieve relevant material within massive, multimedia, multilingual content.

The second chapter by Sandra Carberry et al. from the Universities of Delaware and Millersville turns attention to the relatively unaddressed area of information graphics. Figures, such as bar charts, pie charts, and line graphs, are found in a broad range of media and convey valuable information. The authors argue that the message of information graphics (e.g., a trend or relation) cannot be ignored either in summarizing a document or extracting from it as it often is not repeated in the surrounding text. Further, it can be exploited to enhance the robustness of multimodal document extraction. The authors focus on three kinds of information graphics: simple bar charts, grouped bar charts, and simple line graphs. The authors collected and analyzed a corpus of 110 simple bar charts, 150 grouped bar charts, and 234 line graphs. They identified 14 categories of possible messages conveyed by the graphics, such as same trend (increasing, decreasing, and stable), contrast trend, rank of an entity in a class with respect to some variable, the trend of a gap, contrast relation, and so on. They used WordNet and a thesaurus to identify a set of potentially helpful verbs and divided them into categories according to semantic similarity. Following part of speech tagging and stemming, this verb categorization is then used as input to a Bayesian network to identify the intended message. Other inputs include identifying nouns in captions that match labels in the graphics, which assists in detecting which bars are salient in a graphic. The system also considers visual evidence of the intended message, such as contrasting colors of bar, positioning, or annotations. Also, using eye-tracking experiments and perceptual/cognitive modeling, the authors measure the relative difficulty of different perceptual tasks as an additional source of evidence and report on a method to estimate relative task effort on grouped bar charts. For example, preliminary experiments observed fewer bar fixations and shorter processing time when patterns, such as straight lines and quadratic curves, were present and relevant to the particular message extraction task. The experiments support the intuition that the intended message of a graphic should not require significant effort to recognize. Interestingly, the authors also found that subjects were using peripheral vision to process multiple trends in parallel and to attend to several successive bars in a trend with a single fixation. They describe a graph segmentation algorithm trained on 234 line graphs collected from newspapers and popular magazines that transforms graphs into visually distinguishable trends. These trend segments are used to reason about messages. Finally, the authors describe a message recognition system that includes a visual extraction module, caption extraction module, and feature extraction module that serve as input to a Bayesian model for message extraction. When tested on 110 simple bar charts, their system had an almost 80% recognition rate. The authors are in the process of implementing it for line graphs and grouped bar charts and investigating storage and retrieval of information graphics based on their recognized messages.

The third chapter by Fabio Pianesi, Bruno Lepri, Nadia Mana, Alessandro Cappelletti, and Massimo Zancanaro from FBK-IRST addresses extracting information from human behavior. The authors' premise is that many systems can only succeed if they have a much deeper understanding of human attitudes, preference, personality, and past and current activities. They argue that "thin slices" of social behavior are enough for a reliable classification of personality traits, and that personality shows up in a clear form in the course of social interaction and has a direct influence on human computer interaction (e.g., acceptability, control). This can be used, for example, to coach individuals, facilitate group interaction, or provide more effective access to knowledge elicited during the meeting. The authors aim to create "socially aware machines" and focus on social behavior and aim to understand static (e.g., personality) and dynamic (e.g., social roles) aspects of people interaction from audio-visual cues. The authors focus on multiple nonverbal cues, including prosodic features, facial expressions, body postures and gestures, whose understanding is a prerequisite of social intelligence. The authors extract audio and visual features from two mission survival corpora and then describe two studies targeting the automatic classification of functional roles and personality traits. For example, subsets of 22 acoustic features were used to measure excitement, emphasis, mimicry (often used to signal empathy), and influence (measured by overlapping speech). Similarly, visual features were used to measure energy (fidgeting) of both hands and head. They report automated extraction of both social roles (e.g., attacker, protagonist, supporter) and personality traits (extraversion and locus of control) using a thin slicing approach considering visual (e.g., movement) and acoustic (e.g., tone, energy) features. Detection of locus of control was on average 87% accurate, and extraversion was on average 89% accurate, well above the performance of a trivial classifier. The authors provide evidence that knowledge of the social context can improve personality assessment, lending support to the well-known thesis that the behavioral expression of one's personality is modulated by the interaction partners' behavior.

Collectively, these chapters explore much less frequently addressed aspects of information extraction, notably audio, graphics, and behavior extraction. Each chapter provides unique insights: the first about identity and emotions, the second about trends and relationships, and the final one about social roles and personality. Taken together, these chapters reveal that much remains to be discovered from innovative processing of multiple media.

CHAPTER 14

AUTOMATIC DETECTION, INDEXING, AND RETRIEVAL OF MULTIPLE ATTRIBUTES FROM CROSS-LINGUAL MULTIMEDIA DATA

QIAN HU, FRED J. GOODMAN, STANLEY M. BOYKIN, RANDALL K. FISH, WARREN R. GREIFF, STEPHEN R. JONES, and STEPHEN R. MOORE

14.1 INTRODUCTION

The large volume of available multimedia data presents many challenges to content retrieval. Sophisticated modern systems must efficiently process, index, and retrieve terabytes of multimedia data, determining what is relevant based on the user's query criteria and the system's domain specific knowledge. Research systems for spoken document retrieval (SDR) have been developed and evaluated against radio and broadcast news data through TREC SDR 6, 8, 10. These systems primarily rely on the automatic speech recognition (ASR) transcribed text for retrieval purposes and return whole documents or stories (Garofolo et al. 2000; Johnson et al. 2000; Rendals and Abberley 2000). Our system's objective is to return passages within documents rather than entire documents, based upon an extension of attributes beyond the ASR transcript (Hu et al. 2002a,b). In addition to the machine-generated speech transcripts, our system also includes phoneme-based recognition, speaker and language identification, and less obvious nonlexical audio cues, such as speech rate, shouting and whispering, laughter, and applause (Hu et al. 2003, 2004a,b, 2009a) Our intent is to begin to explore the rich nonlexical information available in the audio track. In high transcription error rate domains, reading the ASR output is problematic. When users wish to listen to the original audio, we believe that optimum productivity depends upon the system's ability to retrieve the desired portion of the audio file at its precise location rather than just identifying the entire document or story segment in which the event occurred (Hirschberg et al. 1999). As described later, we locate and return short passages of text and original media conducive to rapid review and evaluation. Finally, we have experimented with task conditions

Multimedia Information Extraction: Advances in Video, Audio, and Imagery Analysis for Search, Data Mining, Surveillance, and Authoring, First Edition. Edited by Mark T. Maybury.
© 2012 IEEE Computer Society. Published 2012 by John Wiley & Sons, Inc.

more challenging than the broadcast news quality of the TREC evaluations, including:

- Different language models and genres: lectures, spontaneous speech, meetings, teleconference recordings, and so on
- Multimedia sources
- Multimedia in different languages
- Uncontrolled acoustic environment with ambient background noise and multiple speakers

Early audio information retrieval systems applied straightforward text-based queries to transcripts produced by ASR (Allan 2002; Colthurst et al. 2000; Garofolo et al. 2000; Johnson et al. 2000; Rendals and Abberley 2000). However, audio contains more information than is conveyed by the text transcript produced by an automatic speech recognizer. Information such as: (1) who is speaking, (2) the vocal effort used by each speaker, and (3) the presence of certain non-speech background sounds, are lost in a simple speech transcript. Current research systems make use of speaker identification and prosodic cues for topic segmentation and sentence or discourse boundary detection (Johnson et al. 2000; NIST 1997; Rendals and Abberley 2000; Stevens and Hanson 1995; Stolcke et al. 1998, 1999). Some also include these non-lexical cues in their search; the most common being the combination of keyword and speaker ID. While there has been no formal evaluation of retrieval performance using nonlexical cues, we hypothesize that expanding the list of nonlexical cues will assist multimedia content access and retrieval.

Relying on the text alone for retrieval is also problematic when the variability of noise conditions, speaker variance, and other limitations of current automatic speech recognizers results in errorful speech transcripts. Deletion errors can prevent the users from finding what they are looking for from audio or video data, while insertion and substitution errors can be misleading and/or confusing. In order to discover more and better information from multimedia data in the presence of imperfect speech transcripts, we have incorporated multiple speech technologies and natural language processing techniques to develop our research Audio Hot Spotting (AHS) prototype. By utilizing the multiple attributes detected from the audio, AHS technology allows a user to automatically locate regions of interest in an audio/video file that meet his/her specified criteria. These regions of interest or "hot spots" can be found through keywords or phrases, speakers, keywords in combination with speaker ID, nonverbal speech characteristics, or non-speech signals of interest.

In Section 14.2, we describe how multiple attributes are detected and used to discover information and refine query results.

In Section 14.3, we describe keyword retrieval combining word-based and phoneme-based speech recognition engines, as well as our indexing algorithms to automatically identify potential search keywords that are information rich and also provide a quick clue to the document content. Since speech-to-text ASR engines are limited by the language model and lexicon, they will not find words missing from the speech recognizer's lexicon. Furthermore, sensitivity to audio quality results in speech-to-text transcripts with wide variations in accuracy. To mitigate the effects of these deficiencies on retrieval rate, the AHS system combines a phoneme-based audio retrieval engine with a speech-to-text engine. In this section, we explain our fusing algorithms to merge and rank order two speech processing engines' results to aid AHS performance.

In Section 14.4, we discuss our query expansion mechanism to improve retrieval rate. We also present different approaches to cross-lingual multimedia AHS based on the characteristics of the source and target languages, and use of the speech recognition engine for a particular language based on its accuracy.

In Section 14.5, we describe the AHS system architecture and work flow that allow both interactive and batch processing of multimedia data and query requests. We also discuss some current and future work in automatic multimedia monitoring and alert generation when an attribute of interest is detected by the system.

14.2   DETECTING AND USING MULTIPLE ATTRIBUTES FROM THE AUDIO

Automatic speech recognition has been used extensively in audio and multimedia information retrieval systems. However, high speech word error rate (WER) (NIST 1997) in the speech transcript, especially in less-trained domains, such as spontaneous and nonbroadcast quality audio, greatly reduces the effectiveness of navigation and retrieval using the speech transcript alone. Even in applications where WER is low, our approach recognizes that there is more information in the audio file than just the words, and that other attributes, such as speaker identification and the type of background noise, may be helpful in the retrieval of information that words alone fail to provide. One of the challenges facing researchers is the need to identify "which" nonlexical cues are helpful. Since the retrieval of these nonlexical audio cues has not been available to users in the past, we have chosen to implement a variety of nonlexical cues in the AHS system to stimulate feedback from our user community.

14.2.1   Spoken Language ID

Current ASR relies on the manual determination of the language spoken in the multimedia. In order to speed up the automation of audio processing, we integrated a commercial spoken language ID engine with our custom-built language model aiming to identify the set of specific languages required by the user. There are multiple benefits when the language being spoken is automatically detected. The productivity of a human analyst is improved when media is sorted by language. The accuracy of downstream processes that are language-dependent, such as ASR, is improved when the tool is matched with the intended language. Finally, it allows the expansion of audio query criteria to include spoken language ID.

14.2.2   Speaker ID and Its Application

Another valuable audio attribute is speaker ID. By extending a research speaker identification algorithm (Reynolds 1995), we integrated speaker identification into the AHS prototype to allow a user to retrieve three kinds of information. First, if the user cannot find what he/she is looking for using keyword search but knows who spoke in the audio, the user can retrieve content defined by the beginning and ending time of the chosen speaker, assuming enough speech exists to build a model for that speaker. Second, we provide summary speaker statistics indicating how many turns each speaker spoke and the total duration of each speaker in the audio. Finally, we use speaker identification to refine the query result by allowing the user to query keywords and speaker together. For example, the user can find when President Bush spoke the word "anthrax".

14.2.3   Detection of Group Laughter and Applause

In addition to language and speaker identification, we wanted to illustrate the power of other nonlexical sounds in the audio track. As a proof-of-concept, we created detectors for crowd applause and laughter. The algorithms used both spectral information, as well as the estimated probability density function (PDF) of the raw audio samples to determine when one of these situations was present. Laughter has a spectral envelope that is similar to a vowel, but since many people are voicing at the same time, the audio has no coherence. Applause, on the other hand, is spectrally speaking, much like noisy speech phones such as "sh" or "th." However, we determined that the pdf of applause differed from those individual sounds in the number of high amplitude outlier samples present. Applying this algorithm to the 2003 State of the Union address, we identified all instances of applause with only a 2.6% false alarm rate. One can imagine a situation where a user would choose this nonlexical cue to identify statements that generated a positive response.

14.2.4   Speech Rate Estimation

The rate at which a person speaks is often indicative of the person's mental state. Fast speech is often associated with elevated emotions, including stress, excitement, anger, or urgency. We have begun to look at speech rate as a separate attribute. Speech rate estimation is important, both as an indicator of emotion and stress, as well as an aid to the speech recognizer itself (see e.g., Mirghafori et al. 1996; Morgan and Fosler-Lussier 1998; Zheng et al. 2000). Currently, ASR error rates are highly correlated to speech rate. For the user, marking that a returned passage is from an abnormal speech rate segment and therefore more likely to contain errors allows him/her to save time and ignore these passages if desired. However, if passages of high stress are desired, these are just the passages to be reviewed. For the recognizer, awareness of speech rate allows the modification of HMM state probabilities, and even permits different sequences of phones.

One approach to determining speech rate accurately is to examine the phone-level output of the speech recognizer. Even though the phone-level error rate is quite high, the timing information is still valuable for rate estimation. By comparing the phone lengths of the recognizer output to phone lengths tabulated over many speakers, we have found that a rough estimate of speech rate is possible (Mirghafori et al. 1996). Initial experiments have shown a rough correspondence between human perception of speed and the algorithm output. One outstanding issue is how to treat audio that includes both fast rate speech and significant silences between utterances. Is this truly fast speech?

14.2.5 Vocal Effort Estimation

Vocal effort is the continuum between whispering and shouting. Detecting this attribute is valuable in a variety of situations. For example, current speech recognition performance is negatively impacted by either extreme; thus, through detection we can avoid getting worthless transcriptions. In this case, we give the user the opportunity to listen to, for example, all shouted segments, because such segments may indicate situations of high importance. To determine the vocal effort of a speaker, LPC (linear predictive coding) analysis is performed using several different orders (14–20). The best fit to the incoming spectrum is then determined and used for inverse filtering. Inverse filtering removes (most of) the effects of the vocal tract shape, leaving a train of glottal pulses during voiced speech. We examine the shape of these pulses to determine the vocal effort. Higher vocal effort pulses have different time and frequency characteristics than lower effort (softer) speech. Softer glottal pulses are less peaky in the time domain and have a lower spectral bandwidth. Using the SUSAS (Hansen and Bou-Ghazale 1997) and Emotional Prosody (Liberman et al. 2002) Corpora, we were able to get good separation (>95%) between the soft and loud cases. More subtle effort distinctions could not be reliably made because of interspeaker variations.

The issue of truly whispered speech (no voicing) has not been studied extensively, and is heavily dependent on signal quality. If the noise level is low, whispering can be detected by spectral shape, because the formants of the vowels still appear (though with low energy).

14.3 KEYWORD RETRIEVAL USING WORD-BASED AND PHONEME-BASED RECOGNITION ENGINES

Even with the option to use nontextual audio cues for the query, the primary criterion in a hot spotting search is still likely to be a key word or phrase. There are two methods for keyword retrieval from multimedia. The most common one is using an automatic speech recognizer to turn speech into words followed by standard text search. Another approach is to turn speech into phonemes without making a hard decision on the word. Thus, a sequence of phonemes like [k-eh-r-i-a] can represent words like "career" and "Korea". There are advantages and disadvantages of both approaches. The word-based approach is dependent on the engine's lexicon and language model. Given a reasonable audio quality that matches the acoustic and language model of the recognition engine, the word-based approach will transcribe the speech accurately enough for keyword retrieval when the spoken words fall within the lexicon of the speech recognition engine. If those conditions are not met, the speech transcripts will degrade significantly, leading to lower keyword retrieval accuracy. In other words, the word-based approach yields high precision but limited recall due to its dependence on lexicon and language model. On the other hand, the phoneme-based approach is lexicon and language model independent. It can retrieve words that are not in the lexicon as long as the phonemes match. This is helpful especially for proper names and domain-specific words that fall outside of a general lexicon. For example, during our testing, since the proper name *Nesbit* was not in the speech recognizer vocabulary, it was transcribed as *Nesbitt* (with two "t"s) and thus not identified during word-based search. With the phoneme-based engine, *Nesbit* was retrieved.

However, the same sequences of phonemes, particularly short sequence of phonemes, may have multiple or partial matches to the query words. Because of this, a phoneme only-based search may yield false positives, trading poor accuracy for improved recall. While the word-based approach provides a transcript beneficial to downstream processes, such as keyword indexing and translation, the phoneme-based approach produces no transcript. The word-based speech recognition requires significantly more processing time than phoneme-based indexing. Speech-to-text speech recognition is typically real time—1 hour of speech takes 1 hour of processing time, while a phoneme engine only takes a few minutes to process an hour of audio.

The AHS research prototype takes advantage of both word-based and phoneme-based indexing engines by fusing outputs from both engines and rank ordering the results to improve both precision and recall of keyword retrieval.

In Section 14.3.3, we discuss our fusing approach using both word-based and phoneme-based recognition engines However, we begin our discussion of keyword retrieval in Section 14.3.1 with a discussion of our keyword indexing algorithm to take advantage of word-based transcripts and also explore other speech processing and NLP techniques. In Section 14.3.2, we report the preliminary findings of keyword retrieval and compare the retrieval results from a word-based approach with those using a phoneme-based engine.

14.3.1 Keyword Indexing

Knowing that not every machine-transcribed word is correct and that not every word has equal information value, we developed a keyword indexing algorithm to assist the user in the selection of keywords for search. The algorithm finds words that are information rich (i.e., content words) with high likelihood of being correctly recognized by the recognition engine. The AHS prototype examines speech recognizer output and creates an index list of content words. Our approach is based on the principle that short duration and weakly stressed words are much more likely to be misrecognized, and are less likely to be important (Hu et al. 2002a,b). To eliminate words that are information poor and prone to misrecognition, our index-generation algorithm takes the following factors into consideration: (1) absolute word length, (2) the number of syllables, (3) the speech recognizer's own confidence score, and (4) the part of speech (i.e., verb, noun) using a POS tagger. Experiments we have conducted using broadcast data, with Gaussian white noise added to achieve the desired signal-to-noise ratio (SNR), indicate that the index list produced typically covers about 10% of the total words in the ASR output, while more than 90% of the indexed words are actually spoken and correctly recognized given a WER of 30%. The following table illustrates the performance of the automatic indexer as a function of SNR during a short pilot study.

Table 14.1 shows the keyword indexer performance with audio files having a range of SNR to explore the correlation among audio quality, ASR accuracy measured by WER, and the keyword indexing word error rate (IWER). In the table, Index Coverage is the fraction of the words in the speech transcript chosen as index words, and IWER is the Index WER.

TABLE 14.1. Key Word Indexer Performance

SNR (dB)	ASR WER (%)	Index Coverage (%)	IWER (%)
Inf	26.8	13.6	4.3
24	32.0	12.3	3.3
18	39.4	10.8	5.9
12	54.7	8.0	12.2
6	75.9	3.4	20.6
3	87.9	1.4	41.7

As expected and shown in Table 14.1, increases in WER result in fewer words meeting the criteria for the index list (Index Coverage). However, the indexer algorithm manages to find reliable words even in the presence of very noisy data. At 12dB SNR, while the recognizer WER has jumped up to 54.7%, the index WER has risen modestly, to only 12.2%. Note that an index word error indicates that an index word chosen from the ASR output transcript did not in fact occur in the original reference transcription.

Whether this index list is valuable will depend on the application. If a user wants to get a feel for a 1-hour conversation in just a few seconds, automatically generated topic terms, such as those described in Kubala et al. (2000), or an index list such as this could be quite valuable.

14.3.2 Keyword Retrieval from Meeting Room Data Using Word-Based and Phoneme-Based Recognition Engines

This section describes preliminary results of our attempts to retrieve meaningful information from meeting room data (Hu et al. 2004a). This search for information included the use of both a word- and a phoneme-based ASR system. For a limited test set, our results suggest that the word-based recognizer is better than the phoneme-based system at retrieving information based on single keyword queries for WER up to about 75%. As the WER degrades, the phoneme-based system performance surpasses the word-based system. When the information search is based upon multiword phrases, the phoneme based recognizer is superior at all three examined WERs.

Excerpts of the selected audio files were processed by a commercial word-based speech recognition engine with no tuning of the language or acoustic models for the meeting room domain. NIST's SCLITE alignment tool was used to align the output of the recognizer with the NIST-provided transcripts and to determine the WER for each file. The same files were also processed by a commercial phoneme-based recognition engine, also without any tuning (Cardillo et al. 2002). The reference transcripts were used to select information-bearing keywords as query terms. The keywords were manually selected by two researchers working independently; the agreed-upon list of single keywords is shown in Table 14.2, and the list of selected query phrases is shown in Table 14.3.

Our system response to a keyword query is a temporal pointer into the multimedia file. We consider this audio hot spot to be *correct* if the queried keyword actually exists in the audio at a time within half of the audio segment duration from the

TABLE 14.2. Keywords Selected from the Reference Transcripts

File: 20020627	File: 20020214	File: 20020304
Agonizing	Computer	Castle
Backslashes	Disk	Detail
Computer	Door	Evil
Debugging	Help	Healed
Decorations	Knobs	Idea
Emily	Move	King
Function	Office	Kingdom
Graffiti	Officemate	Love
InstallShield	Paper	Mother
Joe	Problem	People
Keyboard	Room	Prince
Linux	Shelf	Princess
Meeting	Space	Queen
Messages	Survived	Road
Module	Table	Stepmother
Onscreen	Temperature	Story
Operate	Vent	Village
Package	Window	
Palm		
PWS		
Remote		
Unpack		
VIP		
Web		
Wednesday		
Windows		

TABLE 14.3. Key Phrases Selected from the Reference Transcripts

File: 20020214	File: 20020627	File:20020304
Air conditioner	Having trouble	Evil spell
Real problem	High priority	Wonderful deeds
Leg room	July seventeenth	
Plant division	Onscreen keyboard	
Prime location	Scrolling frame	
Control the temperature	Successfully packaged	
Storage problem		

returned pointer. For our evaluation, the desired duration of a returned audio segment is 6 seconds; therefore, the keyword must exist in the audio within +/–3 seconds of the returned temporal pointer (Hirschberg et al. 1999). A response is flagged as a *missed detection* if the keyword exists in the audio, but no temporal pointer within half the audio segment duration is returned. Finally, a response is flagged as a *false alarm* if the temporal pointer is too far away from an actual occur-

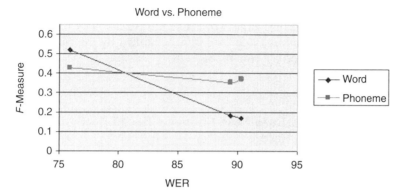

Figure 14.1. Single-word retrieval performance (*F*-measure) for word-based versus phoneme-based recognizers.

TABLE 14.4. Single-Word Retrieval Performance: Word- versus Phoneme-Based Recognition

WER	Precision Word Based	Precision Phoneme Based	Recall Word Based	Recall Phoneme Based	*F*-M Word	*F*-M Phone
90.3	1.00	0.438	0.091	0.318	0.167	0.368
89.4	0.83	0.381	0.102	0.327	0.182	0.352
75.9	0.85	0.500	0.370	0.369	0.516	0.425

rence of the queried keyword in the audio or the queried keyword does not exist in the audio.

For the keyword query performance, we report precision and recall. Precision indicates the percentage of returned audio pointers that actually identify audio segments containing the query term. Recall indicates the percentage of the total number of audio segments containing the query term that are actually identified by the returned audio pointers. We also report *F*-measure, which is the harmonic mean of precision and recall. *F*-measure performance as a function of WER for our three excerpts is shown in Figure 14.1.

Since the word based recognizer makes a hard decision about each word in the transcript, searching for a particular keyword is very straightforward; the word is either there or it is not. When using the phoneme-based recognizer, the return for each query is a list of possible matches sorted by a confidence measure. Without some stopping criterion, the recognizer will return an endless list of possible matches, resulting in excessive false alarms. We have investigated using both fixed and relative confidence thresholds, as well as a fixed number of false alarms for each keyword. We have found that the fixed false alarm threshold gives the best performance. In the work reported here, phoneme-based returns were ignored after a single false alarm for each keyword.

Table 14.4 shows a precision/recall/*F*-measure comparison between word-based and phoneme-based systems on the single-word retrieval task.

Phrases presented a problem for the word-based recognizer. In this high WER domain, having all of the contiguous words in a phrase correctly recognized is rare. None of the phrases listed in Table 14.2 were identified by the word-based recognizer. The phoneme-based system recovered an average of 75% of the phrases across the three tested WERs.

14.3.3 Fusing of Word-Based and Phoneme-Based Recognition to Improve Precision and Recall

To take advantage of the high precision of a word-based recognition engine and high recall of phoneme-based recognition engine shown in the above evaluations, we experimented with merging the results from both recognition engines and rank ordering the results. As stated earlier, our research suggests that word-based recognition results generally are more likely to represent true hits than phoneme-based results if the query word falls within the ASR engine's lexicon. The sorting used in our fused search results reflects this hypothesis. In our approach, segments that are retrieved by the word-based engine alone are assigned a constant weight. Words returned by only the phoneme-based system are assigned a weight equal to the confidence score for that return. Results retrieved by both engines combine the arbitrary word-based score with the phonetic confidence score. Using these scores to rank order returns results in words identified by both engines being given the highest rank followed by those identified by only the word-based system and finally those identified only by the phoneme-based recognizer.

When Fuse Search type is selected by the user, the AHS prototype aligns results from the other two search types with a fused rank order of a single set of results. Therefore, the Fused Search not only retrieves a single set of rank ordered exact segments of the audio containing the query keyword with combined system scores, but also the accompanying transcript. To make the system flexible and user-need selectable, the AHS system also provides two other search types: Transcript Search based on the ASR output only, and Phonetic Search based on the phonetic engine only.

14.4 QUERY EXPANSION

TREC SDR found both a linear correlation between Speech WER and retrieval rate, and that retrieval was fairly robust to WER. However, the robustness was attributed to the fact that misrecognized words are likely to also be properly recognized in the same document if the document is long enough. Since we limit our returned passages to roughly 10 seconds, we do not benefit from this long document phenomenon. The relationship between passage retrieval rate and passage length was studied by searching 500 hours of broadcast news from the TREC SDR corpus. Using 679 keywords, each with an error rate across the corpus of at least 30%, we found that passage retrieval rate was 71.7% when the passage was limited to only the query keyword. It increased to 76.2% when the passage length was increased to 10 seconds, and rose to 83.8% if the returned document was allowed to be as long as 120 seconds.

In our AHS prototype, we experimented with query expansion to achieve two purposes, (1) to improve the retrieval rate of related passages when exact word match fails, and (2) to allow cross lingual query and retrieval.

14.4.1 Keyword Query Expansion

The AHS prototype made use of the Oracle 10 g Text engine to expand the query semantically, morphologically, and phonetically. For morphological expansion, we activated the stemming function. For semantic expansion, we utilized expansion to include hyponyms, hypernyms, synonyms, and semantically related terms. For example, when the user queried for "oppose," the exact match yielded no returns, but when semantic and morphological expansion options are selected, the query was expanded to include *anti*, *anti-government*, *against*, *opposed*, and *opposition*, and returned several passages containing those expanded terms.

Obviously, more is not always better. Some of the expanded queries are not exactly what the users are looking for, and the number of passages returned increases. In our AHS implementation, we made query expansion an option, allowing the user to choose to expand semantically or morphologically.

14.4.2 Cross-Lingual Query Expansion

In some applications, it is helpful for a user to be able to query the multimedia source in a single language and retrieve passages of interest from multimedia in another language. For some language pairs, the AHS system treated translingual search as another form of query expansion. For these language pairs, we created a bilingual thesaurus by augmenting Oracle's default English thesaurus with target language dictionary terms. With this type of query expansion enabled, the system retrieves passages that contain the keyword in either English or other target languages. A straightforward extension of this approach will allow other languages to be supported using other relational databases as well.

This multilanguage thesaurus approach must be modified when using phonetic search. The phonetic search engine uses the written form of a word to determine its phonetic composition. For some languages, the written form of a word does not capture all of the phonemes present in its spoken form. This mismatch between expected and actual phonetic content results in a degradation in search performance. In these cases, we utilized and integrated other commercial translation, transliteration, and phoneme supplementation engines to turn English query terms into the target language in forms of written words and phonetic representations, which included the normally omitted phonemes. The written word translated to the target language is used for cross-lingual Transcript Search, while the transliteration with augmented phonetic representation is used for cross-lingual Phonetic Search of the multimedia. Both forms of translation are used for cross-lingual Fused Search.

14.5 AHS RESEARCH PROTOTYPE

The AHS research prototype consists of two primary components: the AHS media processor and the AHS query processor.

The AHS media processor allows users to prepare media files for search and retrieval. It automatically detects information from the media file for the downstream processes. This includes the media format, acoustic channel (telephone, microphone), and primary language spoken in the media. With this information, the media processor will determine which media processing engines are available for the current media type. For example, given a multimedia file in microphone speech for English, the media processors available will be speech-to-text transcription, phoneme indexing, keyword indexing, background noise detection, and vocal effort detection. Once the media file is media processed, the file is available for the user to search and retrieve segments of interest by different types and combinations of searches using the AHS Query engine.

The AHS Query Processor allows users to search for and retrieve information from the media processed media files. It supports single media and cross media search as long as the media contains speech, cross-lingual search, and multiple attributes search, such as searching for a key word by a particular speaker. The supported cross-lingual search in the current AHS prototype supports English, Spanish, Modern Standard Arabic, Iraqi Arabic, and Gulf States Arabic. The query processor supports a variety of search criteria. It allows the user to search the processed media by language, by speaker, by word-based search, by phoneme-based search, by fused search, by background noise, such as applause and laughter, by speech rate, and by vocal effort, such as shouting and whispering. The system already supports cross-attribute search, such as keyword and speaker. With a relational database as the backend of the AHS system, we plan to link other attributes for the user to search information, such as shouting by a particular speaker and the other combinations of the multiple attributes.

Both processors work in a web-based environment to support current users for processing and query. The system provides the interface for both interactive query and media processing, as well as batch query and media processing so that the user can submit multiple queries and media process multiple files without having to set the query and processing criteria every time.

Although the AHS research prototype offers query and retrieval capability for multiple attributes from multimedia, each module can function alone with the exceptions of keyword indexing and speech rate estimation, which depend on the output of ASR.

14.6 CONCLUSION

By detecting multiple audio attributes from multimedia, our AHS prototype (Hu et al. 2003, 2004b, 2009a) allows a user to apply the range of lexical and nonlexical audio cues available in audio to the task of information retrieval. Areas of interest can be specified using keywords, phrases, language, and speaker ID, information-bearing background sounds, such as applause and laughter, and prosodic information, such as vocal effort (i.e., shouting and whispering). When matches are found, the system displays the recognized text and allows the user to play the audio or video in the vicinity of the identified "hot spot." See Figure 14.2 for a screenshot of the AHS prototype.

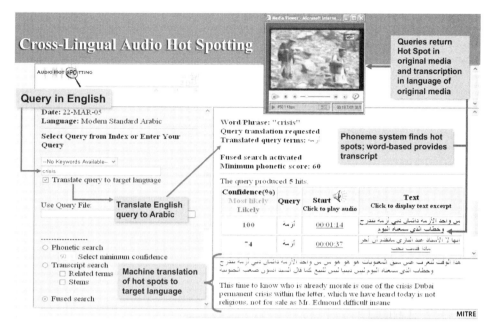

Figure 14.2. Audio Hot Spotting prototype.

With the advance of component technologies, such as ASR, language and speaker identification, and audio feature extraction, there will be a wider array of audio attributes for the multimedia information extraction and for the systems to query and retrieve segments of interest, allowing the user to access the exact information desired both in postprocessing and live monitoring modes. The multimedia information extraction using multiple audio attributes can be applied for other downstream processing, such as machine translation, speech-to-speech translation, and live monitor and alert systems in different application domains.

CHAPTER 15

INFORMATION GRAPHICS
IN MULTIMODAL DOCUMENTS

SANDRA CARBERRY, STEPHANIE ELZER, RICHARD BURNS, PENG WU,
DANIEL CHESTER, and SENIZ DEMIR

15.1   INTRODUCTION

Information graphics are nonpictorial graphics, such as bar charts, grouped bar charts, and line graphs, that depict attributes of entities and relations among entities. Although some information graphics are only intended to display data, the majority of information graphics in popular media, such as magazines and newspapers, are intended to convey a message. For example, the information graphic shown in Figure 15.1 ostensibly conveys the message that there was a substantial increase in 6-month growth in consumer revolving credit in contrast with the preceding decreasing trend from July 1997 to July 1998; the graphic in Figure 15.2 ostensibly conveys the message that CBS ranked second from last in average price of advertisements among the networks listed.

This chapter addresses the importance of information graphics in extracting information from multimodal documents. It argues that information graphics in multimodal documents cannot be ignored, either in summarizing the document or in extracting information from it, and then provides a brief overview of our methodology that uses communicative signals as evidence in a Bayesian network in order to identify what we view as the primary content of the graphic—namely, its intended message. The chapter focuses on three commonly occurring types of information graphics: simple bar charts, simple line graphs, and grouped bar charts. We describe the categories of messages that are conveyed by each, and the kinds of communicative signals that help to convey these messages. The signals themselves are multimodal in that some are extracted from the graphic and some from the textual

Multimedia Information Extraction: Advances in Video, Audio, and Imagery Analysis for Search, Data Mining, Surveillance, and Authoring, First Edition. Edited by Mark T. Maybury.

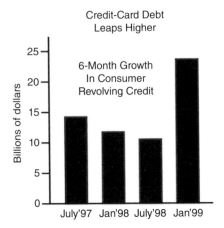

Figure 15.1. Graphic from popular media, conveying that there was a substantial increase in 6-month growth in consumer revolving credit in contrast with the preceding decreasing trend from July 1997 to July 1998.

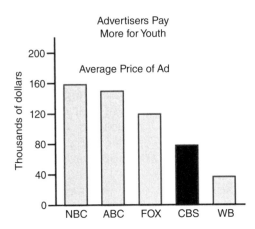

Figure 15.2. Graphic from popular media, portraying that CBS ranked second from last in average price of advertisements among the networks listed.

caption or the article's accompanying text. We then discuss two important modules that we have had to develop for use in our Bayesian recognition system: a model of relative task effort for simple and grouped bar charts and a model of graph segmentation for line graphs. Our Bayesian methodology has been successfully implemented and tested for simple bar charts (Elzer et al. 2005b); we are in the process of implementing it for line graphs and grouped bar charts. We contend that a graphic's recognized message captures the high-level content of the graphic and thus can be used as the basis for taking information graphics into account in extracting information from multimodal documents.

15.2 ROLE OF INFORMATION GRAPHICS IN MULTIMODAL DOCUMENTS

15.2.1 The Importance of Information Graphics in Popular Media

Information graphics in popular media, such as magazines and newspapers, generally have a message that they are intended to convey. This message is often not
duplicated in the surrounding text (Carberry et al. 2006). For example, Figure 15.3
shows a graphic from a *Newsweek* article entitled "Microsoft's Cultural Revolution."
The primary message conveyed by the graphic is ostensibly that the percentage of
pirated software in China is much higher than in the world as a whole. Our analysis
of a corpus of grouped bar charts suggests that they can also have a secondary
message that is strongly conveyed, although it does not appear to be the primary
communicative goal of the graphic designer. For example, the graphic in Figure 15.3
has a strong secondary message that the decrease in pirated software in 2002 compared with 1994 was smaller in China than in the world. The article containing these
graphics is about Microsoft's commitment to China and the issues of pirated software. The closest the article comes to mentioning either the graphic's primary or
secondary message is: "Ninety percent of Microsoft products used in China are
pirated." No comparison is ever made between piracy in China and in the world,
nor the decline in piracy between 1994 and 2002. Figure 15.4 shows a grouped bar
chart from a *BusinessWeek* article entitled "A Small Town Reveals America's Digital
Divide." The article itself interviews individuals who are separated from technology
either because of geography or limited income. This graphic[1] supplements the article's text with two high-level messages: that a smaller percentage of households have
Internet access in rural areas than urban areas at every income level, and second-
arily, that the percentage of households with Internet access increases with income
level.

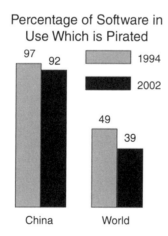

Figure 15.3. Graphic from *NewsWeek*.

---

[1] Figure 15.4 was part of a set of graphics, the first of which showed that they were all depicting households with Internet access. We have added this to the caption of Figure 15.4 for clarity of this article.

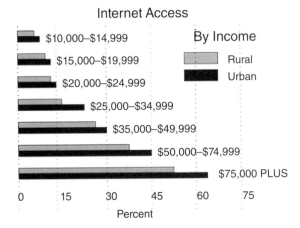

Figure 15.4. Graphic from *BusinessWeek*.

These two examples illustrate the important role of information graphics in multimodal documents. In terms of the discourse theory espoused by Grosz and Sidner (Grosz and Sidner 1986), the message conveyed by an information graphic constitutes the discourse goal of the graphic, and, together with the discourse goals of the textual discourse segments, contributes to achieving the discourse purpose of the overall article. Thus, it is impossible to fully comprehend a multimodal document without understanding its information graphics.

15.2.2 Extracting Information from Graphics in Popular Media

We contend that a graphic's intended message captures the high-level content of the graphic and should be used along with the article's text when extracting information from a multimodal document. For example, consider again the graphic in Figure 15.4, which is about Internet access in rural and urban households. Both the primary message (pertaining to the contrast between rural and urban households with respect to Internet access) and the secondary message (pertaining to the relationship between income level and Internet access) capture the high-level knowledge that the graphic is intended to convey. Thus, they can be used as the basis for taking the graphic into account when extracting information from the document. Furthermore, using the intended message to index a graphic allows it to be efficiently retrieved to extract more detailed information in a question-answering system.

For example, the primary message of the graphic in Figure 15.4 can be logically represented as:

- Same-relation ({Rural, Urban}, less-than, Internet-access, percent, income-levels)

The message category Same-relation captures message types in which the entities being compared are in the same relationship (less than, equal, and greater than), as is the case for the Rural and Urban bars in the groups in Figure 15.4. Based on the message category of Same-relation, as well as the instantiated parameters in the logical representation of the message, a system could answer questions, such as "What is the difference between rural and urban Internet access for low-income families?" or "Does the difference between rural and urban Internet access change as income changes?"

Similarly, the secondary message of the graphic in Figure 15.4 can be logically represented as:

• Same-trend({Rural, Urban}, increasing, Internet-access, percent, income-levels)

The Same-trend message category captures messages in which the same trend (rising, stable, and falling) holds for the values of a set of entities in the graph. These entities might be displayed across different groups (as the rural and urban households are in the graphic in Figure 15.4) or within their own group. Based on this logical representation, a system could answer a question such as, "What is the impact of income level on rural Internet access?"

However, the logical representations of the high-level messages conveyed by an information graphic may not directly contain the answer to the detailed questions being asked. Nonetheless, the message category and the instantiated parameters can be used to draw inferences regarding the detailed information that might be obtained from the graphic and a decision made about whether the graphic should be retrieved and analyzed further to answer the question. For example, consider a question such as "What are the percentages of low income rural and urban households with Internet access?" Even though the logical representation of the secondary message of the graphic in Figure 15.4 does not contain specific data points, such as the percentages of low income rural and urban households with Internet access (and the system may not even have a clear definition of the user's definition of "low income"), the fact that the graphic conveys trends for Internet access for rural and urban households based on income level suggests that this graphic will contain the desired information.

In summary, we contend that information graphics in multimodal documents play an important role in achieving the discourse purpose of the document and cannot be ignored. Furthermore, the intended message of the graphic captures its high-level content, represents a graphic's core summary, and can be used for taking information graphics into account in extracting information from a multimodal document.

15.3 METHODOLOGY FOR PROCESSING INFORMATION GRAPHICS

Our methodology for identifying the primary intended message of an information graphic contains several components. A visual extraction module (VEM) first processes an electronic information graphic image and produces an XML representation of the graphic that captures all features of the graphic, such as the height and value of each bar, the color of bars, any annotations, the caption, and so on (Chester and Elzer 2005). Analogous to the detection of specific identifiable features from audio tracks in Hu et al. (Chapter 14, this volume), the goal of our VEM is the ability to extract visual features from information graphics. Although VEM must process a raw image, the task is much more constrained, and thus much easier, than most image recognition problems. Currently, the VEM can handle electronic images of simple bar charts that are clearly drawn in a fixed set of fonts and with standard placement of labels and captions. Current work is extending the VEM to grouped bar charts and line graphs.

A caption processing module then performs a shallow processing of the graphic's caption to identify helpful verbs and nouns in the caption (discussed later), and enters them into an augmented XML representation of the graphic. A feature extraction module analyzes the augmented XML representation to identify communicative signals present in the graphic and enters them as evidence in a Bayesian network. The Bayesian network then hypothesizes the message that the graphic is intended to convey and outputs its logical representation.

This chapter focuses on three types of information graphics: simple bar charts, grouped bar charts, and simple line graphs. A simple bar chart is a bar chart that displays the value of a single independent attribute and the corresponding values for a single dependent attribute. Figure 15.1 is an example of a simple bar chart. On the other hand, a grouped bar chart is a bar chart that consists of two or more visually distinguishable groups of bars. Groups must share the same ontology, and bars must share the same ontology. For example, the grouped bar chart in Figure 15.4 has seven groups and two bars per group; income range and demographic area are the ontologies, respectively, for the groups and the bars. A simple line graph is a line graph that displays the value of a single dependent attribute over a continuous independent attribute. The next subsections discuss the categories of messages conveyed by such information graphics and the communicative signals that help to convey them.

15.3.1 Categories of Messages

We have collected a large corpus of information graphics including 110 simple bar charts, 150 grouped bar charts, and 234 line graphs. Our analysis of these and other graphics has led us to categorize the kinds of messages that are conveyed by each of the three types of graphics. Simple bar charts can convey a trend (increasing, decreasing, or stable), a change in trend, or a contrast between the value of an entity and a trend; the graphic in Figure 15.1 falls into the latter category. In addition, they can convey that the value of an entity is a minimum or a maximum among the listed entities, the rank of an entity's value, or the relative rank of all the entities; the intended message of Figure 15.2 falls into the rank-of-entity category. They can also convey a comparison of two entities with respect to their value and the degree of difference of these values.

Simple line graphs can convey the same kind of trend messages as simple bar charts, but they do not provide rank or comparison messages. However, simple line graphs can convey other kinds of messages, such as a big fall in the value of an entity (which may be sustained or not sustained over the subsequent values of the independent attribute), a trend that changed and is now returning to the original trend (which we refer to as a change–trend–recover category), and a contrast of a segment at the end of the graph with a previous trend (suggesting the potential for a change in trend, as opposed to a change-trend message where the segment is long enough to be viewed as a new trend).

Grouped bar charts convey more complex relationships among entities; they are in some sense three-dimensional in that the bar labels and the bar values constitute two dimensions and the groups constitute the third dimension. Thus, not surprisingly, they have a richer set of intended messages that they can convey. We have identified 14 categories of possible messages. Below is a sampling:

- *Same-Trend*: Entities have the same trend (increasing, decreasing, or stable) in their values.
- *Contrast-Trend*: Trend for one entity's values differs from the trends for the other entities.
- *Rank*: Rank of an entity, with respect to its values for the members of a class.
- *Gap-Trend*: Gap between two or more entities' values has a trend (increasing, decreasing, or stable).
- *Gap-Comparison*: A comparison of the gap between entities' values for all members of a class.
- *Same-Relation*: Relation among the values of entities is the same for all members of a class.
- *Contrast-Relation*: Relation of entities in one member of a class is different from the relation of entities in all other members of the class.

Consider, for example, the graphic in Figure 15.3. The graphic's primary message (that the percentage of pirated software in China is much higher than in the world as a whole) falls into the Rank category, where the entities are China and World, and the members of the class are the years 1994 and 2002. The secondary message (that the decrease in pirated software in 2002 compared with 1994 was smaller in China than in the world) falls into the Gap-comparison category; in this case, the entities whose values are being compared are 2002 and 1994, and the comparison is for members of the class consisting of China and World. The primary message of the graphic in Figure 15.4 (that a smaller percentage of rural households have Internet access than urban households at all income levels) falls into the Same-relation category, and the secondary message (that the percentage of households with Internet access increases with income level for both rural and urban households) falls into the Same-trend-increasing category.

Although the message categories are useful for classifying the kinds of messages that can be conveyed by a type of information graphic and form the predicate for a logical representation of the conveyed message, our system must identify the full message conveyed by the graphic, not just the message category. For instance, a message involving a Gap-comparison category must include which specific entities have their respective values forming the gaps, over which members of a class the gaps are being compared, and the relationship between the gaps.

15.3.2 Communicative Signals

When designing an information graphic, a designer will incorporate communicative signals to help convey an intended message. Thus, a system that automatically

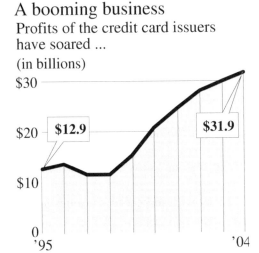

A booming business
Profits of the credit card issuers
have soared ...
(in billions)

Figure 15.5. Graphic from *USA Today*.

recognizes the message conveyed by an information graphic must extract and reason about the communicative signals that appear in the graphic. This is similar to natural language discourse, where signals such as discourse markers and intonation help the listener identify the intended meaning of an utterance.

A graphic's caption is one source of communicative signals. Unfortunately, captions in graphics are often very general and fail to convey the graphic's intended message. For example, the caption on the graphic in Figure 15.2 is very general and does little to convey the intended messages of the graphic. Moreover, even when a caption might be helpful, it is often ill-formed or requires significant domain knowledge to process and understand.

Thus, given the difficulty of automating the full understanding of a graphic's caption, we have focused on the shallow processing of the caption to extract communicative signals about the graphic's message. Verbs in a caption can suggest the general category of message conveyed by the graphic. For example, the verb *boom* (as in the caption for the line graph in Figure 15.5) suggests a message category such as *increasing-trend* or *change-trend* for simple bar charts and line graphs or a *same-trend-increasing* message category for grouped bar charts. Using WordNet and a Thesaurus, we identified a set of potentially helpful verbs and divided them into categories according to semantic similarity. Our Caption Processing Module uses a part-of-speech tagger and a stemmer to identify the presence of one of our identified helpful verbs in a caption (Elzer et al. 2005a). The presence of this verb category is then used as evidence in our Bayesian network for identifying a graphic's intended message.

Communicative signals in an information graphic can make certain entities in the graphic salient, and thereby suggest that they play a prominent role in the message that the graphic is intended to convey. For example, nouns in captions can assist in making a set of bars salient. Consider the graphic in Figure 15.6, which was part of a set of graphics whose overall caption was "Boys Don't Cry: Men and Depression."

Illicit drug use people older than 12

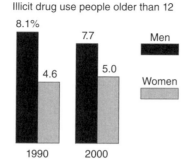

Figure 15.6. Graphic from *NewsWeek*.

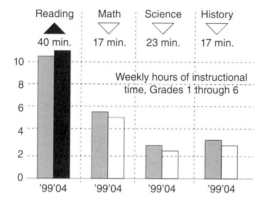

Figure 15.7. Graphic from *Time*.

The noun men matches a reference in the graphic's legend, thereby making the bar referring to men salient in both groups; this suggests that the intended message might be emphasizing men, perhaps in a comparison. In addition to extracting potentially helpful verbs, our Caption Processing Module is also responsible for identifying nouns in a caption that match a label in the graphic.

Entities in a graphic can also become salient via design choices made by the graphic designer. The designer might color some bars differently from other bars in a bar chart. For example, the bar for CBS is colored differently from the other bars in Figure 15.2, thereby suggesting that the intended message of the bar chart is about CBS; similarly, the 2004 bar in the first group in Figure 15.7 is colored differently from the 2004 bars in the other groups, thereby drawing attention to the increased instruction on reading in contrast with the decreased instruction time for the other subjects. Entities also become salient if the entity is positioned first in a bar chart, if the entity is annotated (most often occurring in a line graph when one or more points on the line are annotated with their value or with an event), or if the value of an entity is much larger than the values of the other entities. The presence of these and other communicative signals can be determined by analyzing the XML representation of the graphic that was constructed by the Visual Extraction Module.

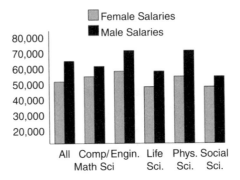

Figure 15.8. Graphic from an NSF publication.

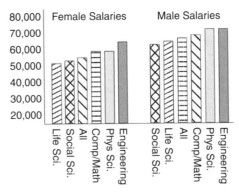

Figure 15.9. A graphic constructed from the same data as the graphic in Figure 15.8.

But for simple bar charts and grouped bar charts, perhaps the most important communicative signal is the relative effort of different perceptual tasks. Consider, for example, the graphic in Figure 15.8. Its intended message is that female salaries lag behind male salaries in each of the science and engineering disciplines.[2] Note that the design of the graphic in Figure 15.8 makes it easy to compare female and male salaries in each discipline. The graphic in Figure 15.9 was constructed from exactly the same data as the graphic in Figure 15.8. However, it is much more difficult to compare female and male salaries in Figure 15.9, and thus the graphic conveys a different message—perhaps that salaries for both men and women are highest in engineering.

The AutoBrief project (Green et al. 2004) was concerned with generating integrated text and graphics; they hypothesized that graphic designers attempt to facilitate as much as possible the perceptual tasks that a viewer is intended to perform. Thus, we hypothesize that the relative difficulty of different perceptual tasks serves as a communicative signal about what tasks the viewer is intended to perform in recognizing the graphic's intended message. The next section describes our work on estimating relative task effort on grouped bar charts; our earlier work on modeling task effort for simple bar charts can be found in Elzer et al. (2006).

---

[2] We know the intended message of this graphic since a colleague was on the committee that constructed the document.

15.3.2.1 *Modeling Perceptual Task Effort in Grouped Bar Charts* Our goal
is a model that, given a graphic, produces an estimate of the relative effort involved
in extracting different messages. We conducted a set of preliminary eye-tracking
experiments with human subjects to gain insight into the factors that affect the effort
required to extract messages from grouped bar charts. Our observations from these
experiments, along with previous research by cognitive psychologists, suggested that
we must take into account both the human visual architecture and human cognitive
limitations. Thus, we chose to implement our model of relative task effort in the
ACT-R programmable framework (Anderson et al. 1997), augmented with EMMA
(Salvucci 2001), an ACT-R add-on that was designed to model peripheral vision.
EMMA adjusts the constant visual encoding time cost of an object into a variable
cost, affected by the proximity of the previous attention location. Thus, it can capture
the ability to *attend to* an object without actually *fixating* on it.

The presence of high-level visual patterns that can be easily perceived by humans
appears to reduce the effort needed to extract messages from grouped bar charts.
Pinker (1990) identified several such patterns, such as straight lines and quadratic
curves. Our preliminary eye-tracking experiments confirmed this phenomenon; we
observed fewer bar fixations and shorter processing time when such patterns were
present and relevant to the particular message extraction task.

Our model takes the presence of common visual patterns into account. For
example, when estimating effort for *Same-relation* and *Contrast-relation* tasks, our
ACT-R model first determines whether the tops of the bars in a group represent a
common visual pattern; if so, this relation is encoded in ACT-R's imaginal buffer
and the task of extracting a *Same-relation* or a *Contrast-relation* message is modeled
as a comparison of the pattern with each group's pattern. For example, a *Same-
relation* message can be extracted from the grouped bar chart in Figure 15.8 (the
relation between female and male salaries for each discipline) and Figure 15.10
(the relation between 2002, 2003, 2004, and 2005 Chinese exports to each of the
three trading partners[3]); in both cases, the tops of the bars in each group form a

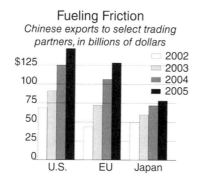

Figure 15.10. Graphic from the *Wall Street Journal*.

---

[3] A *Same-relation* message can be extracted from the graphic in Figure 15.10, but the primary message
of the graphic is that there is an increasing trend in Chinese exports to all three of the trading
partners.

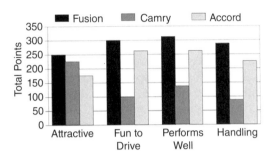

Figure 15.11. Advertisement by Ford in the *Sporting News*.

relatively straight line, which is a common visual pattern. A *Contrast-relation* message can be extracted from the grouped bar chart in Figure 15.11 (contrasting the relation between Fusion, Camry, and Accord for attractiveness with their relation for fun, performance, and handling)[4]; in this case, three of the groups share a "U" pattern (another common visual pattern), while the contrasting group has a straight line pattern. If the tops of the bars in a group do not form a common visual pattern, then our model captures bar-by-bar comparisons to determine the presence of a same or contrasting relation.

Note that the goal of our model is to estimate the relative effort for extracting different messages, even when that message is not the intended message of the graphic. These effort estimates will be used as evidence in our Bayesian network that recognizes the intended message of a graphic—thus, when effort is much higher for perceiving one message than for perceiving a different message, the effort evidence should cause the system to lean toward the less effortful message (subject to other competing evidence that is present in the graphic). Consider again the graphic in Figure 15.9. It is possible to extract the message that female and male salaries have the same relation to one another in all the disciplines, but it is much more difficult than for the graphic in Figure 15.8. In the case of Figure 15.9, our ACT-R model cannot compare adjacent bars in each group. Instead, it is necessary to repeatedly fixate on the female and male salaries for a discipline (which appear as bars in different groups), compare them, and compare their relationship with the relationship between female and male salaries in the disciplines that have already been attended to. This processing reflects the greater difficulty of extracting the *Same-relation* message for this graphic, thereby producing a much greater effort estimate—which is exactly what we would want as evidence in our Bayesian network.

Our eye-tracking experiments also suggested that the use of peripheral vision was affecting the relative effort of different message extraction tasks. For example, when extracting a *Same-trend* message where each trend is across all the groups (such as in Figure 15.4, where Internet access has an increasing trend across income

---

[4] A *Contrast-relation* message can be extracted from the graphic in Figure 15.11. However, the remainder of the advertisement makes it clear that the ad is about the Ford Fusion; thus Fusion becomes salient in the graphic, and the intended message is that the Ford Fusion has the highest points among the three cars for all four categories.

levels for both rural and urban households), subjects did not always fixate on every bar in the series of bars comprising the trends nor did they fixate on bars in every trend. The pattern of fixations led us to hypothesize that the subjects were using peripheral vision to process multiple trends in parallel and to attend to several successive bars in a trend with a single fixation. This is supported by research in several domains that has shown the ability to attend to an object without fixating on it (Salvucci 2001).

Our ACT-R model takes the use of peripheral vision into account. For example, when modeling extraction of trend messages where the trends are across groups (as in Figure 15.4), if the tops of the bars in one series are near the tops of the bars in another series (but the two series do not cross), our ACT-R model marks one series as a "free" attention; attending to the nonfree series is treated as also attending to the bars in the "free" series. In addition, our model does not fixate on every bar in a series, but instead invokes EMMA's ability to capture attending to several adjacent bars (that are located close to one another) with a single fixation.

Our model also takes into account several other factors, but space precludes discussing them in this chapter. The model has been implemented for estimating the relative effort involved in extracting five categories of messages: *Same-relation*, *Contrast-relation*, *Same-trend*, *Contrast-trend*, and *Gap-trend*. We performed a subsequent validation experiment in which 20 human subjects performed message extraction tasks on 52 graphics in these five categories. A Spearman rank order correlation produced a correlation coefficient of 0.809 ($P < 0.001$) between the rank order of the effort estimates produced by our ACT-R model and the rank order of the average completion time for the tasks by the human subjects. This is a very strong correlation, and suggests that our model produces very good estimates of relative effort that can be used in our Bayesian network.

15.3.2.2 Graph Segmentation for Line Graphs Rather than treat a line graph as a large set of data points connected by small line segments, we want to transform it into a sequence of visually distinguishable trends and reason about its intended message in terms of these trend segments. For example, although the graphic in Figure 15.12 consists of a number of short straight line segments, a viewer

Figure 15.12. Graphic from *BusinessWeek*.

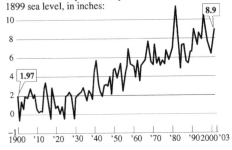

Ocean levels rising
Sea levels fluctuate around the globe, but oceanographers believe
they are rising about 0.04–0.09 of an inch each year.
In the seattle area, for example, the Pacific Ocean has risen nearly
9 inches over the past century. Annual difference from Seattle's
1899 sea level, in inches:

Figure 15.13. Graphic from *USA Today*.

summarizing it would be likely to regard the graphic as consisting of a falling trend
from 2000 to 2002 followed by a rising trend to 2006. Similarly, although the graphic
in Figure 15.13 consists of many short rises and falls, a viewer would likely regard
it as consisting of a short overall stable trend from 1900 to 1930 followed by a long
rising trend (both with high variance). While these trend segments are not
communicative signals in exactly the same way as relative task effort or highlighting
an entity to make it salient, they do have some similarity in that graphic designers
rely on their viewers to perceive these smoothed segments in recognizing the
message that a graphic designer intended to convey via a line graph. Thus, our
Bayesian network relies on a graph segmentation module to hypothesize how a line
graph should be broken into a set of visually distinguishable trends; this segmentation is then used to suggest potential messages that are considered by the Bayesian
network.

Our graph segmentation module takes a top-down approach to identifying
sequences of rising, falling, and stable segments in a graph. It starts with the original
graphic as a single segment and decides whether it should be split into two subsegments; if the decision is to split the segment, then the split is made at the point that
is the greatest distance from a straight line between the two end points of the
segment. This process is repeated on each subsegment until no further splits are
identified. The graph segmentation module returns a sequence of straight lines
representing a linear regression of the points in each subsegment, where each
straight line is presumed to capture a visually distinguishable trend in the original
graphic. For example, Figures 15.14 and 15.15 show the sampled data points and the
regression lines for each segment as produced by our graph segmentation module
for the line graphs in Figures 15.12 and 15.13, respectively.

We used SMO (sequential minimal optimization) for training a support vector
machine that makes a decision about whether a segment should be split (Platt 1999).
The values of 18 attributes are considered in building our model. Some of the attributes are based on statistical tests computed from a sampling of the data points in
the segment, and other attributes capture explicit features of the segment and
graphic. The following are a few of the attributes:

Figure 15.14. Segmentation of the graphic in Figures 15.12.

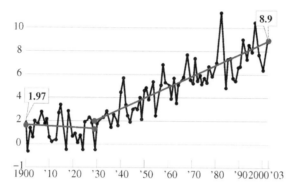

Figure 15.15. Segmentation of the graphic in Figure 15.13.

Correlation Coefficient: The Pearson product-moment correlation (Rodgers and Nicewander 1988) coefficient measures the tendency of the dependent variable to have a linearly rising or falling relationship with the independent variable. If the absolute value of the correlation coefficient is close to 1, then the tendency is strong. We hypothesized that the correlation coefficient might be helpful in determining whether a long set of short jagged segments, such as those between '30 and the end of the graph in Figure 15.13, should be captured as a single rising trend and thus not be split further.

F-Test: The *F*-test measures whether a two-segment regression is significantly different from a one-segment regression (Beckman and Cook 1979). It does this by comparing the differences in their respective standard deviations. Our system bases two binary attributes on the *F*-test, using significance levels of 0.95 and 0.90, respectively; the attribute is set to 1 if, for some sampled point in the segment under consideration, the *F*-test says that a regression on the subsegments to the left and right of the point differs significantly from the regression across the whole unbroken segment. We hypothesize that the *F*-test may be useful when a segment consists of a relatively flat subsegment that is overshadowed by a longer rising segment, thus resulting in a high correlation coefficient even though the segment should be split into two subsegments.

Runs Test: The runs test estimates whether a regression is a good fit for the data points (Bradley et al. 1995). Each sampled point is categorized as $+1$ or -1 based on whether it lies above or below the regression line. A *run* is defined as a sequence of consecutive points that fall into the same category. The number of runs is then compared with an estimate of the expected number of runs R_{mean} and its standard deviation R_{sd}; if the actual number of runs exceeds $(R_{mean} - R_{sd})$, then the runs test suggests that the regression is a good fit and the segment should not be split. We hypothesize that the runs test might be helpful when a segment consists of more than two trends. We use a binary attribute that captures the result of the runs test on a segment, along with four numeric attributes giving the actual number of runs, the expected number of runs, the standard deviation of the expected number of runs, and the difference between actual and expected number of runs as a fraction of the expected number of runs.

Segment Fraction: This attribute measures the proportion of the total graph that comprises this segment. We hypothesize that segments that comprise more of the total graph may be stronger candidates for splitting than segments that comprise only a small portion of the graph.

We trained our model on 234 line graphs collected from newspapers and popular magazines. For each line graph, a split/no-split decision for the segment comprising the whole line graph was recorded; if the decision was to split the line graph, then the process was repeated for each of the two resulting subsegments. This produced a data set consisting of 649 segments and their associated split/no-split decisions. To test our learned model, we used leave-one-out cross validation, in which each of the 649 instances in the data set is used once as the test set and the other 648 instances are used as the training set; the success rate of the resulting 649 models are then averaged to produce the overall success rate, which was 88.29%. A baseline success rate of 67% would occur if we always made a no-split decision, which is the most common correct decision for the data set of segments. Thus, our model produces a relative improvement of 31.78% over the baseline model.

Figures 15.14 and 15.15 display the results of our model of graph segmentation on the line graphs in Figures 15.12 and 15.13. In both cases, the segmentation produced by our system matches what was deemed to be the appropriate segmentation of the line graphs into visually distinguishable trends.

15.4 IMPLEMENTATION OF OUR MESSAGE RECOGNITION SYSTEM

Our methodology for recognizing the intended message of an information graphic uses the communicative signals present in the graphic to hypothesize the graphic's intended message. The entire Bayesian system has been implemented for simple bar charts, using the Netica software (Netica 2005) for constructing and reasoning with Bayesian networks. Figures 15.1 and 15.2 are examples of two simple bar charts that have been processed by our message recognition system. The system hypothesizes that the intended message of Figure 15.1 is to contrast the 6-month growth in consumer revolving credit in January 1999 with the previous decreasing trend from July 1997 to July 1998. For Figure 15.2, the system hypothesizes that the intended message is to convey that CBS ranks second from last in average price of ad among the five networks listed in the bar chart.

Our system was tested on 110 simple bar charts whose intended message had previously been annotated by two human coders. If the system's top-rated hypothesis matched the intended message identified by the human coders (both with respect to the message category and the instantiation of the parameters) and the system assigned the hypothesis a probability above 50%, then the system was judged to have correctly identified the bar chart's intended message. Using leave-one-out cross-validation, the system achieved a success rate of 79.1%. However, it should be noted that even when the system was mistaken about the graphic's intended message, such as if it had hypothesized that the graphic in Figure 15.1 was intended to convey that 6-month growth in consumer revolving credit had a decreasing trend from July 1997 to July 1998, that information was not incorrect—it just was not the intended message of the graphic.

We are now in the midst of extending our Bayesian network to grouped bar charts and line graphs. As discussed earlier in the chapter, we have successfully implemented and tested our model for estimating the relative effort of five different kinds of message recognition tasks on grouped bar charts. We are now implementing the Bayesian network to recognize these kinds of messages. Given a grouped bar chart, the system will construct a Bayesian network capturing all of the possible instantiated messages that might be conveyed by that graphic. Evidence will be extracted from the XML representation of the graphic, the results of our caption processing module, and the relative estimates of effort produced by our model of task effort; these will be entered into the network to hypothesize the graphic's message.

We have also successfully developed a graph segmentation model for line graphs. Given a line graph, the segmentation produced by our graph segmentation module is the basis for constructing possible messages that will be considered by the Bayesian network. For example, the segmentation shown in Figure 15.15 would produce several possible suggestions, including (1) a relatively stable trend from 1900 to 1930, (2) a rising trend from 1930 to 2003, (3) a change trend (relatively stable from 1900 to 1930 and then rising to 2003), and (4) a big jump at 1930 that is sustained. As with grouped bar charts, evidence will be extracted from the graphic and entered into the Bayesian network, which will hypothesize the intended message of the line graph.

The next phase of our project is to investigate the storage and retrieval of information graphics based on their recognized messages and to identify other aspects that would assist the retrieval of the most appropriate graphic for a particular information extraction task.

15.5 RELATED WORK

Bradshaw (2000) notes that work on image retrieval has progressed from systems that retrieve images based on low-level features, such as color and texture, to systems that reason about the semantics of the images being processed. Futrelle and Nikolakis (1995) developed a constraint grammar for parsing vector-based visual displays and producing structured representations of the elements comprising the display. The goal of Futrelle's (1999) more recent work is to produce a graphic that is a summary of one or several more complex graphics. Note that the end result is again a graphic, whereas our goal is to recognize a graphic's intended message so that it can be used in multimodal document summarization and information extraction.

The goal of Zancanaro et al. (this volume) is the realization and understanding of human intention from behavior in audio and video media. While our system focuses on the intention of graphic designers in the domain of information graphics, the works are similar in that both aim to provide a higher-level analysis of multimedia data.

Yu et al. (2002, 2007) use pattern recognition techniques to summarize interesting features of time series data from a gas turbine engine. However, their graphs were automatically generated displays of the physical data from the gas turbines, and not graphs designed by a graphic designer whose intention was to convey a message to the viewer.

A number of researchers have studied the problem of segmenting time series data. For example, Lin et al. (2002) and Toshniwal and Joshi (2005) discuss different ways of finding similar time series segments; Dasgupta and Forrest (1996) present an algorithm for detecting anomalies using ideas from immunology. These and other research efforts have been primarily concerned with detecting similar patterns or anomalies, whereas the goal of our graph segmentation model is the identification of visually apparent trends.

15.6 CONCLUSION

This chapter has argued that information graphics are an important component of a multimodal document and cannot be ignored. We contend that the message conveyed by an information graphic can serve as a brief summary of the graphic's high-level content and thus contribute to effective information extraction from a multimodal document. The chapter has focused on three kinds of information graphics: simple bar charts, grouped bar charts, and simple line graphs. It has presented a brief overview of our methodology for recognizing the primary message of an information graphic. This methodology relies on extracting communicative signals from a graphic. The signals may result from the graphic's design (perceptual task effort), or be part of the text of a graphic's caption or part of the graphic's design (such as coloring, positioning, etc.); thus, the signals are themselves multimodal. The extracted communicative signals are used as evidence in a Bayesian network that hypothesizes the message that the graphic is intended to convey. Our methodology has been successfully implemented for simple bar charts and is now being extended to grouped bar charts and line graphs. To our knowledge, our research is the first to address the problem of recognizing the message conveyed by an information graphic in popular media, and thus serves to advance robust summarization of, and information extraction from, multimodal documents.

ACKNOWLEDGMENT

This material is based upon work supported by the National Science Foundation under Grant No. IIS-0534948.

CHAPTER 16

EXTRACTING INFORMATION FROM HUMAN BEHAVIOR

FABIO PIANESI, BRUNO LEPRI, NADIA MANA,
ALESSANDRO CAPPELLETTI, and MASSIMO ZANCANARO

16.1 INTRODUCTION

The automatic analysis of human behavior is more and more attracting the attention of researchers for its important applicative aspects and its intrinsic scientific interest. Indeed, in many technological fields (pervasive and ubiquitous computing, multimodal interaction, ambient assisted living and assisted cognition, etc.), the awareness is emerging that the system can provide better and more appropriate services to people only if they can understand much more of what they presently do about users' attitudes, preference, personality, and so on, as well as about what people are doing, the activities they have been engaged in the past, and so on. At the same time, progress on sensors, sensor networking, and multimodal analysis are making the building the blocks for the automatic analysis of behavior available. Multimodal analysis—the joint consideration of several perceptual channels—is a powerful tool to extract large and varied amounts of information from the acoustical and visual scene. It has found major applications as applied to multimodal interaction, providing flexible, efficient, and powerfully means for human–computer interaction (see e.g., Oviatt 2008). Apart from the consideration of language, however, multimodal analysis has so far targeted low-level behaviors, only recently attempting to put its power to the service of the reconstruction and understanding of high-level aspects of human behavior. Within this moving picture, an important subfield is emerging that attempts to understand social behavior and socially related aspects by exploiting so-called social signals (Pentland 2008; Vinciarelli et al. 2009), a multiplicity of nonverbal cues, including prosodic features, facial expressions, body postures, and gestures, whose correct manipulation is a prerequisite of social intelligence, hence of one of the most important aspects for human life (Goleman 2006). Arguably, the

Multimedia Information Extraction: Advances in Video, Audio, and Imagery Analysis for Search, Data Mining, Surveillance, and Authoring, First Edition. Edited by Mark T. Maybury.
© 2012 IEEE Computer Society. Published 2012 by John Wiley & Sons, Inc.

possibility of building computer applications able to understand, simulate or manipulate social signals can open new scenarios in human–computer and human–human interaction, by producing a new generation of socially aware machines.

An important feature of the social signal approach is the possibility that it provides direct access to high-level cognitive and social properties of humans, be they dynamic (e.g., social roles) or static (e.g., personality), without the necessity of going through intermediate concepts, such as those commonly employed in a coarse-grained description of social behavior. This minimalist path to high-level properties finds empirical justification in psychological studies that demonstrate how humans can form judgments about complex aspects of social life—for example, other people's personality and preferences (Pianesi et al. 2008a)—or the outcomes of social processes—for example, negotiation (Curhan and Pentland 2007)—just by considering short behavioral sequences—or "thin slices"(Ambady and Rosenthal 1992)—of low-level signals. In these respects, subsets of social signals have been isolated that are both particularly useful for a host of practical tasks and reliable given that they are too hard and/or too costly to fake (Pentland's honest signals).

Systems exhibiting similar capabilities of getting to the core of human attitudes, states, and traits, can exploit this knowledge to predict the future course of social events through minimal amounts of information (André et al. 1999; Castelfranchi and de Rosis, 1999); to provide for more flexible and personalized services in, for example, meeting situations, such as personalized information access and delivery, interaction management (Pianesi et al. 2008a,b); to improve over current user modeling components by providing information about users' personality (Zhou and Conati 2003), preferences, and so on.

A survey of research and applications in the area of social signal processing is beyond the scope of this chapter; but see Vinciarelli et al. (2009) for a thorough introduction to the topic, and Gatica-Perez (2009) for a comprehensive survey of nonverbal signal analysis for small group interactions. Chapter 17 of this volume discusses a related topic: the nonverbal behavior of a large audience in the analysis of political communication. In this chapter, we limit ourselves to showing how social signals can be used to reconstruct both dynamic (the functional roles played by the participants in the course of the interaction) and static (personality traits) characteristics of individual participants in meetings.

The rest of the chapter is organized as follows: we first introduce two corpora, Mission Survival I and Mission Survival II (MSC-I and MSC-II, respectively), that were used for our experiments, and describe the audio and visual features that were extracted from them. We then turn to presenting two studies targeting the automatic classification of functional roles and personality traits, respectively.

16.2   THE MISSION SURVIVAL CORPORA

In order to provide for as much a uniform context as possible, two corpora (MSC-I and MSC-II) of groups engaged in the solution of the Mission Survival Task were collected. The Mission Survival (Hall and Watson 1970) is an often used task in experimental and social psychology to elicit decision-making processes in small groups. The exercise consists in promoting group discussion by asking participants to reach a consensus on how to survive in a disaster scenario, like moon landing or a plane crashing in Canadian mountains. The group has to rank a number (15) of items according to their importance for crew members to survive. A consensus decision-making scenario was chosen and enforced, because of the intensive engagement it requests to groups in order to reach agreement, this way triggering a large set of social dynamics and attitudes. The Mission Survival task was originally designed by the National Aeronautics and Space Administration to train astronauts before the first Moon landing, and it proved to be a good indicator of group decision-making processes. In these cases, each participant is asked to express her/his opinion, and the group is encouraged to discuss each individual contribution by weighing and evaluating their quality. In our case, consensus was enforced by establishing that any participant's proposal would become part of the common sorted list only if she managed to convince the others of its validity. We also added an element of competition by awarding a prize to the individual who proposed the greatest number of correct and consensually accepted items.

MSC-I (Pianesi et al. 2007) consists of the audio-visual recordings of 11 groups of four people involved in the mission survival task. The participants (40% males and 60% females) were clerks from the administrative services of our research centre. In all cases, they knew each other and had often been involved in common group activities. The average age was 35 years. All the groups were mixed gender.

Twelve groups of four members each (male: 51.9%; females: 48.1%; average age: 35 years) participated in the data collection for MSC-II. They were recruited outside our research center and their participation took place on a voluntary basis. Besides involving them in the mission survival task, we also asked participants to fill two standard questionnaire for measuring personality traits: the Italian version of Craig's Locus of Control (LoC) of Behavior Scale (Farma and Cortivonis 2000), and the part of the Big Five Marker Scales (BFMS) that measures the Extraversion dimension (Perugini and Di Blas, 2002).

Both for MSC-I and for MSC-II, the sessions were recorded in a specially equipped room by means of four firewire cameras placed in the corners of the room, and four actively driven web cameras (PTZ IP cam) installed on the walls surrounding the table. Four wireless close-talk microphones (one for each participant) and one omni-directional microphone placed on the tabletop around which the group sat were used to record speech activity.

16.2.1 Acoustic Features

The only acoustic feature we considered for MS-I was the speech activity of each participant. Speech activity refers to the presence/absence of human speech. The audio channels from the microphones were automatically segmented at a 500-ms frame rate and labeled by means of a VAD—voice activity detector (Carli and Gretter 1992). For each session, the VAD detected the participant's speech activity and produced an output of the form "<emporal frame; label-S1; label-S2; label-S3; label-S4>," where <temporal frame> corresponds to a 500 ms interval and <label-*> takes on the values "0" and "1," in correspondence to "non-speech" and "speech," respectively, for each participant (speakers S1, S2, S3, and S4).

For MS-II, a speech analysis of the recorded audio was conducted to extract 22 acoustic features (see Table 16.1) using the extraction toolbox developed by the Human Dynamics group at Media Lab (Pentland 2006, 2008). The 22 acoustic

TABLE 16.1. Acoustic Features

Labels	Acoustic Features
F1	Mean of formant frequency (Hz)
F2	Mean of confidence in formant frequency
F3	Mean of spectral entropy
F4	Mean of largest autocorrelation peak
F5	Mean of location of largest autocorrelation peak
F6	Mean of number of autocorrelation peaks
F7	Mean of energy in frame
F8	Mean of time derivative of energy in frame
F9	SD of formant frequency (Hz)
F10	SD of confidence in formant frequency
F11	SD of spectral entropy
F12	SD of value of largest autocorrelation peak
F13	SD of location of largest autocorrelation peak
F14	SD of number of autocorrelation peaks
F15	SD of energy in frame
F16	SD of time derivative of energy in frame
F17	Average length of voiced segment (seconds)
F18	Average length of speaking segment (seconds)
F19	Fraction of time speaking
F20	Voicing rate
F21	Fraction speaking over
F22	Average number of short speaking segments

features can be grouped in four classes: *Activity*, *Emphasis*, *Mimicry*, and *Influence* (Pentland 2008): *Activity* is meant as a measure of the conversational activity level, and it is an indicator of interest and excitement. In particular, this class is measured by the z-scored percentage of speaking time, voicing time, and by the mean and standard deviation values of the energy (F7, F17, F18, F19, and F20). For computing these values, the speech stream of each participant is first segmented into voiced and nonvoiced segments, and then the voiced ones are split into speaking and non-speaking. The second class, *Emphasis*, consists of two groups of features: (F1, F2, F3, F4, F5, F6, and F8) and (F9, F10, F11, F12, F13, F14, and F16). For each voiced segment, the first group measures mean values of the frequency of the fundamental formant and of the spectral entropy. The second group consists of the estimated standard deviations of those values. Emphasis provides an indication of how strong the speaker's motivation is; moreover, a low degree of variation in Emphasis signals mental focus, while higher variability signals an openness to influence from other people (Pentland 2008). *Mimicry*, meant as the unreflected copying of one person by another during a conversation (i.e., gestures and prosody of one participant are "mirrored" by another one), is expressed through short interjections (e.g., "uh-huh," "yup") or back-and-forth exchanges consisting of short words (e.g., "OK?", "done!"). Usually, more empathetic people are more likely to mimic their conversational partners: for this reason, mimicry is often used as an unconscious signal of empathy. Mimicry is a complex behavior and therefore difficult to measure computationally. A proxy of this dimension is given by the z-scored frequency of short utterances

(<1 second; features F22); *Influence* is the amount of influence, hence dominance, each person has on another one in a social interaction, and is measured by calculating the number of overlapping speech segments (feature F21).

Activity, Emphasis, Mimicry, and Influence signals are all honest ones (Pentland 2008), in that they refer to "behaviors that are sufficiently expensive to fake that they can form the basis for a reliable channel of communication"; hence, they can be reliably used to predict and explain human behavior in social interactions.

16.2.2 Visual Features

Both for MSC-I and MSC-II, the only visual features considered were the amount of energy in participants' bodies (fidgeting). Fidgeting refers to localized repetitive motions such as when the hand remains stationary while the fingers are tapping on the table, or playing with glasses, and so on. Fidgeting was automatically annotated by means of MHI (Motion History Images) (Chippendale 2006), a technique that uses skin region features and temporal motions to detect repetitive motions in the images; an energy value is then associated to such a motion in such a way that the higher the value, the more pronounced the motion. In the corpora, the annotation for fidgeting consists of an absolute timestamp, followed by the values of the fidgeting energy for the head, the hands, and the body, all normalized to the fidgeting activity of the person during the entire meeting.

16.3 AUTOMATIC DETECTION OF GROUP FUNCTIONAL ROLES

Meetings are more and more important in structuring daily work in organizations. For example, according to a survey in (Doyle and Straus 1993) executives spend on average 40–50% of their working hours in meetings; 50% of that time is unproductive, and up to 25% of it is spent discussing irrelevant issues. This situation is determined not only by task-related factors (e.g., a difficult of choosing the right items for the agenda, and/or of focusing the attention on relevant issues), but often by the complexity of group dynamics in small groups, which hinders the performance of teams. Different means can be put at work to support dysfunctional teams, ranging from facilitation to training sessions conducted by experts; moreover, disfunctionalities can be addressed at the individuals and/or at the group levels. The social signal approach together with the availability of rich multimodal information make it attractive exploring the possibility of providing some of these functionalities automatically, by means of systems that first capture and understand group dynamics, and then use this knowledge to either coach individuals, facilitate group interaction, or give better and more structured access to knowledge elicited during the meeting.

For example, DiMicco et al. (2007) and Sturm et al. (2007) proposed two similar systems that provide visual feedback on the group activity during a meeting in order to balance the contribution of the participants. Another system aimed to improve social dynamics is discussed in Pianesi et al. (2008b); here, group behavior is analyzed and relational roles are extracted that the system exploits to generate individual reports; the latter are presented offline to individual participants, with the system acting similarly to a human coach. Curhan and Pentland (2007) proposed a system able to exploit social signals to predict the outcome of a negotiation by observing the first 5 minutes of interaction. Rienks and Heylen (2006) discussed a meeting browsing functionality in which users have access, among other things, to knowledge about the way participants influence each other.

In Zancanaro et al. (2006) we exploited the MSC-I to investigate the possibility of automatically capturing aspects of group behavior by analyzing thin slices of behavior. We modeled group behavior in terms of the roles each member plays inside the group, where this notion is given a functional characterization (Salazar 1996) that differs from that of approaches defining them in terms of the social expectations associated with a given position or status. Once functionally defined, social roles are directly linked to actual interaction, as abstractions over the behavior enacted by individuals in a particular context; this way, the dependence is reduced on knowledge about the group' structure, history, position in the organization, and so on. Our definition of functional social roles is based on that of Benne and Sheats (Benne and Sheat 1948), and on Bale's two dimensional approach (Bales 1970). Both were adjusted according to observations we performed on a number of face-to-face meetings (Pianesi et al. 2007). The result was the Functional Role Coding Scheme (FRCS), which provides five labels for each of two areas: the Task area and the Socioemotional area. The Task area includes functional roles related to the facilitation and coordination of the tasks the group is involved in, as well as to the technical skills of the members as they are deployed in the course of the meeting. The Socioemotional area involves roles oriented toward the functioning of the team as a group. In more detail, the task area functional roles are the following: the *Orienteer* (o) orients the group by introducing the agenda, defining goals and procedures, keeping the group focused and on track and summarizing the most important arguments and group's decisions. The *Giver* (g) provides factual information and answers to questions; she states her beliefs and attitudes about an idea, expresses personal values and factual information. The *Seeker* (s) requests suggestions and information, as well as clarifications, to promote effective group decisions. The *Recorder* (r) uses the resources available to the group, managing them for the sake of the group. The *Follower* (f) only listens, without actively participating in the interaction.

The Socioemotional area includes: the *Attacker* (a), who deflates the status of others, expresses disapproval, attacks the group or the problem; the *Gatekeeper* (gk), the group moderator, who mediates the relations and communications by encouraging and facilitating participation and by regulating the flow of communication; the *Protagonist* (p), the one who takes the floor, driving the conversation, assuming a personal perspective and asserting her authority; the *Supporter* (s), who shows a cooperative attitude demonstrating understanding, attention, and acceptance, as well as providing technical and relational support; the *Neutral* (n), who passively accepts the idea of others, serving as an audience in group discussion.

In order to assess the reliability of the coding scheme, we applied it to a corpus consisting of the video and audio recordings of nine group meetings not included in the MSC-I corpus. Five people were coded on the Socioemotional area and five in the Task area by two trained annotators. In the Task area, Cohen's statistics was $\kappa = 0.70$ ($N = 758$, SE $= 0.02$; $P < 0.001$; confidence interval for $\alpha = 0.05$: 0.67–0.75). According to Landis and Koch's (1977) criteria, the agreement on the task area is good ($0.6 < \kappa < 0.8$). For the Socioemotional area, the interannotator agreement was $\kappa = 0.60$ ($N = 783$, SE $= 0.02$, $P < 0.001$; confidence interval for $\alpha = 0.05$: 0.56–0.65).

TABLE 16.2. Distribution of the Categories in the Reduced Corpus by Considering Speech Events Only (330 ms Time Stamp)

Task Area Roles (Reduced)			Socioemotional Area Roles (Reduced)		
Neutral	10,462	9.72%	Neutral	14,747	13.70%
Orienteer	3,567	3.31%	Gatekeeper	0	0.00%
Giver	17,659	16.41%	Supporter	5,579	5.18%
Seeker	1,275	1.18%	Protagonist	12,460	11.58%
Recorder	0	0.00%	Attacker	177	0.16%
Total	32,963		Total	32,963	

According to Landis and Koch's (1977) criteria, the agreement on the Socioemotional roles is at the borderline between good ($0.6 < \kappa < 0.8$) and moderate ($0.4 < \kappa < 0.6$). For more information about the statistical properties of the FRCS, see (Pianesi et al. 2007). A new set of guidelines for annotators were compiled, resulting in a uniform improvement of the κ statistics.[1]

The FRCS was used to manually annotate the MSC-I: for each participant, units spanning 5 seconds were considered and then resampled every 330 ms to align them with acoustical features. The corpus was quite unbalanced: *Follower* and *Neutral*—unsurprisingly—were the most frequent roles, while *Attacker* was quite rare (the participants knew they were observed and perhaps they tended to avoid aggressive or uncooperative behavior). The *Recorder* and the *Gatekeeper* roles were never observed. The corpus was reduced by considering only the cases corresponding to time intervals where the participant for whom the roles was to be classified was speaking. This lowered the impact of the Follower and Neutral roles even if the data sets remained quite unbalanced (see Table 16.2).

The average duration of the meetings was 25 minutes, the range being 13′.08″–30′.06″. The total time length of the corpus was 3.44.55" hours.

16.3.1 Automatic Classification

In order to take into account the time dimension in the classification task, sliding windows were used: the classifier considers all the data in the time window to assign a Task area role and a Socioemotional area role only at the end of the window. We considered windows of varying size, from 0 to 14 seconds. For each window size, a dataset was built by adding to each row all the features of the previous rows included in the window width. Therefore, for a given time and a given participant, the information that the classifiers had available to classify his/her roles was the information about his/her speech and fidgeting activity, as well as information about all the speaking participants in the window length. Each data set was then split in two equal parts for training and testing.

We modeled role assignment as a multiclass-classification problem on a relative large and very unbalanced dataset, and used Support Vector Machines (SVMs) as

---

[1] See Chapter 21, this volume, for a thorough discussion of issues relating to the hand-annotation of multimodal corpora.

classifier using the bound-constrained SV classification algorithm with a RBF kernel. The cost parameter C and the kernel parameter γ were estimated with the grid technique by cross-fold validation using a factor of 5. In order to account for the unbalanced classes, the cost parameter C was weighted for each class with a factor inversely proportional to the class size. SVMs were originally designed for binary classification, but several methods have been proposed to construct multiclass classifier. We used the "one-against-one" method (Kressel 1999), whereby each training vector undergoes a number of binary comparisons, corresponding to the number of class pairs available (12 for each area in our case), each time minimizing the error between the separating hyperplane margins. Classification is then accomplished through a voting strategy in such a way that the class that most frequently won is selected. By way of comparison, we used two baselines: the *trivial classifier*—that assigns all instances to the most frequent class—and the *equidistributed classifier*—that assigns classes equal prior probabilities. Both accuracy and *F*-score were used as figures of merit, where the latter is computed as the harmonic means of the macro-

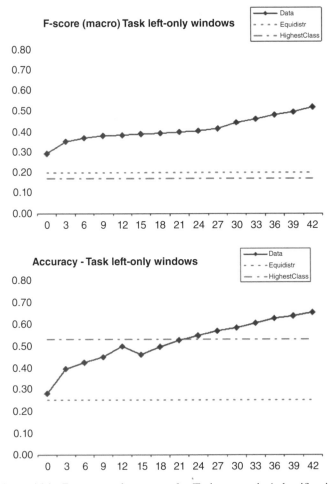

Figure 16.1. *F*-scores and accuracy for Task area roles' classification.

averaged one-class precisions and recalls (macro *F*-score). We also considered average *F*-score computed as the arithmetic average of the one-class *F*-scores.

Fifteen datasets were built considering windows from 0 to 14 seconds to the left of the time point to classify. The number of features varied accordingly, from 4 for the 0 second window to 173 for the 14 seconds window. Figure 16.1 plots accuracy and macro *F*-scores comparing them with the baselines.[2]

The window width with the best accuracy and *F*-score is the 14 seconds one. On both measures, it yielded higher values than the *equidistributed* and the *trivial* classifiers. Accuracy reached 0.65, while the macro *F*-score reaches the value of 0.52 (averaged *F*-score = 0.51).

Similarly, for the Socioemotional task roles (see Figure 16.2), 15 datasets were built considering windows from 0 to 14 seconds to the left of the time point to

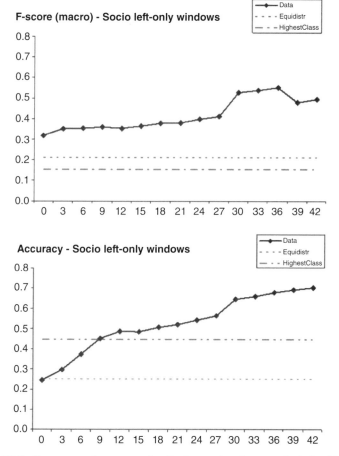

Figure 16.2. *F*-scores and accuracy for Socioemotional area roles' classification.

[2] Notice that the abscissas indicate the window length in terms of the number of database rows they consist of. Since frame rate was 0.333 seconds, the transformation to window length is obtained by dividing the abscissas figure by 3 so that, for example, the 14 seconds window is indicated by abscissa 42.

classify. Because of the small number of examples of the *Attacker* role, accuracy reached its maximum—0.70—at the greater window width, at the expenses, however, of missing all the instances of the *Attacker* role. A better performance was obtained at width 12 seconds, where the highest macro *F*-score is reached (0.55; macro precision = 0.75, macro recall = 0.43) yet, the classifier still under-classified the Attacker role.

16.4 AUTOMATIC PREDICTION OF PERSONALITY TRAIT

In every-day intuition, the personality of a person is assessed along several dimensions: we are used to talk about an individual as being (non-)open-minded, (dis-) organized, too much/little focused on herself, and so on. Several existing theories have formalized those intuitions in the form of multifactorial models, whereby an individual's personality is described in terms of a number of more fundamental dimensions known as traits, derived through factorial studies. A well-known example of a multifactorial model is the Big Five (John and Srivastava 1999), which owes its name to the five traits it takes as being constitutive of people's personality: Extraversion versus Introversion (sociable, assertive, playful vs. aloof, reserved, shy); Emotional stability versus Neuroticism (calm, unemotional vs. insecure, anxious); Agreeableness versus Disagreeable (friendly, cooperative vs. antagonistic, faultfinding); Conscientiousness versus Unconscientiousness (self-disciplined, organized vs. inefficient, careless); Openness to Experience (intellectual, insightful vs. shallow, unimaginative). Besides models that, as the Big Five, attempt to provide a comprehensive assessment of people personality, others have privileged specific dimensions, possibly useful to characterize people attitudes and behavior in specific domains. An interesting example is the so-called LoC (Rotter 1966), which measures whether causal attribution for one's behavior or beliefs is made to oneself or to external events or circumstances. Hence, it consists of a stable set of belief about whether the outcomes of one's actions are dependent upon what the subject does (internal orientation) or on events outside of her control (external orientation) (Rotter 1965). LoC has been used as an empirical tool in several domains; for instance, it was shown that people who feel they are the source or cause of their own attitudes and behaviors (internal LoC), tend to see the computer as a tool that they can control and use to extend their capabilities. On the other hand, those who attribute their own behavior or attitudes to external factors (external LoC) are much more prone to regard computers as an autonomous, social entity with which they are forced to interact (Falaleeva and Johnson 2002).

Several fields in computer science have shown recurring interest in the notion of personality. For instance, it has found a stable place in the repertoire of features a lifelike character should possess in order to improve its believability; the underlying assumption is that a virtual agent would appear more realistic, understandable, and, ultimately, human-like, if, as a human, it exhibited a personality through consistent behaviors that the interacting humans could use to understand its goals, form expectations about future behaviors, and so on. (André et al. 1999; Castelfranchi and Rosis 1999). In the user modeling literature, information about people's personality has been exploited to help inferring their goals from their behavior, as in the work of Zhou and Conati (2003) in the context of a tutoring system. Finally, Goren-Bar et al. (2006) have shown that personality plays a role in the way people use and experience adaptive technology: strong external orientation (LoC) correlates with a preference for nonadaptive systems over adaptive ones. That is, people who are highly sensitive to the social facets of technology because of their external LoC are not comfortable with adaptivity, or other forms of control delegation, in technology.

So far, very few works have attempted to automatically extract personality traits from behavioral outcomes, in most cases using the Big Five model (or parts thereof) as the reference model. As to the kind of behavioral observations exploited, two groups of works can be easily distinguished: those considering mainly verbal material (Mairesse et al. 2007; Oberlander and Nowson 2006), such as that found in weblogs, blogs, and so on, and works exploiting nonverbal audio-visual cues (Pianesi et al. 2008a,b). Given the focus of this paper, we briefly report on the latter. Before doing so, however, it is worth mentioning a recent work that, with different purposes and using still different types of observables, have attempted to connect the latter with Big Five traits. Olguin et al. (2009) collected various behavioral measures of the daily activities of 67 professional nurses in a hospital. The data were collected by means of the *sociometer badge* (Choudhury and Pentland 2003), a wearable device integrating a number of sensors (accelerometer, microphone, and an infrared sensor) measuring aspects, such as physical and speech activity, number of face-to-face interactions with other people, level of proximity to relevant objects (people, but also beds, etc.), and social networks parameters. Although the authors' goal was not that of predicting personality traits from those signals, by exploiting simple correlation analysis, they were able to prove that the signals they targeted can provide quite a lot of information about people's personality.

In our own work (Pianesi et al. 2008a,b), we exploited the MS-II corpus to automatically predict two personality traits, Extraversion and LoC, from low-level features automatically extracted from the acoustical and visual scene. The choice of the two traits was due to the fact that of the Big Five traits, Extraversion is the one that shows up more clearly in, and has the greater impact on, social behavior. For instance, it has been associated with higher pitch and higher variation of the fundamental frequency (Scherer 1979), with fewer and shorter silent and filled pauses, and with a higher voice quality and intensity (Mallory and Miller 1958). LoC, in turn, has a proven effect on attitudes and beliefs towards various kinds of information technologies (Falaleeva and Johnson 2002; Goren-Bar et al. 2006). We could not find studies demonstrating a connection between LoC and social behavior as strong as for Extraversion; however, the often observed relationship (correlation) between LoC and Extraversion (e.g., Goren-Bar et al. 2006) suggest that the pursuance of this hypothesis is not based on arbitrary assumptions.

Extraversion was meas ured by means of the Extraversion subscale of the Italian version of the BFMS (Perugini and Di Blas 2002), while LoC through the Italian version of Craig's LoC scale (Farma and Cortivonis 2000). The scales were administered to participants before they engaged in the interaction task.

The task was given the form of a classification one: on the basis of 1-minute-long behavioral sequences, the system had to assign the subjects to the right class on Extraversion and LoC. To this end, the continuous distributions of Extraversions and LoC were turned into discrete ones (Low, Medium, and High) by assigning to the Medium class the scores comprised between ±1 SD from the average; the Low and the High classes colleted scores below −1 SD and above +1 SD, respectively. The 1-minute-long sequences are our thin slices. In relevant respects, the task is similar to the one we, as humans, are routinely involved in when judging about strangers' personality from very short behavioral sequences. Those *intuitions* about others' personality are based on *thin slices* of behavior, and the process they come by has been the subject of extensive investigation by social psychologists in the last years (Ambady and Rosenthal 1992; Kenny 1994). In our study, we maintained pretty much the same assumptions, attempting to extend them to machines.

SVMs were used again for classification; the multiclass nature of the problem was dealt with through the "one-against-one" method plus voting strategy. The bound-constrained SVM classification algorithm with a RBF kernel was used. The cost parameter C and the kernel parameter γ were estimated through the grid technique by cross-fold validation using a factor of 10. Furthermore, the cost parameter C was weighted for each class with a factor inversely proportional to the class size. The data set was MSC-II. Its acoustic features (see Sections 16.2.1 and 16.2.2) were subjected to a feature selection based on an assessment of their means through analysis of variance (ANOVA): each feature was treated as a dependent variable in two between-subject ANOVA, with the factors Extraversion (three levels: L, M, and H) and LoC (three levels: L, M, and H); significance level was set at $P < 0.05$. No adjustment for multiple comparisons was performed in order to have a more liberal test. Only the features for which the ANOVA gave significant results were retained, for the given factor: F1, F2, F6, F14, a subset of the Emphasis class, and F21, the Influence feature, for Extraversion; F1, F6, F14, again a subset of Emphasis, and F22, the Mimicry feature, for LoC.

16.4.1 Automatic Classification

That classification task can be pursued in (at least) two different manners, each corresponding to a different hypothesis about the way personality, as manifested in social interaction, can be assessed. According to the first, the sole consideration of the target subject's behavior (her thin slices) is enough: the way she moves, the tone and energy of her voice, and so on, are informative enough to get at her personality. The second view maintains that the appreciation of personality requires information not only about the target's behavior, but also about the social context: the same behavior might have a different import for personality assessment if produced in a given social environment than in another. To put things differently, and assuming (as it seems natural) that manifest behavior is causally affected by personality, the first hypothesis has it that such a causal relation is enough to obtain accurate personality estimates. The second hypothesis, in turn, acknowledges that the way personality manifests in behavior is modulated by the social context—that is, by the behavior of the other group members. Hence, thin slices of the other group members are needed as well.

A second aspect to test is the effectiveness of the feature selection procedure. To test these two dimensions, and focusing on the acoustic features, we designed a between-subject study with factors "target" and "others," each relating to different arrangements of the target subject's (target) and of the other group members' (others) features: (1) Target has two levels: all acoustic features + visual features (ALL) versus selected acoustic features (see above) + visual features (SEL); (2) Others has three levels: no acoustic features + visual features (No-Feat); all acoustic features + visual features (ALL); selected acoustic features (see above) + visual features (SEL). A given combination—for example, (ALL, No-Feat)—corresponds to a specific arrangement of the feature vectors used to train and test the classifiers—in the example, all the acoustic plus the visual features of the target subject, and only the visual features for each of the other group members—and to a specific combination of the hypothesis dimensions discussed above—the example corresponds to a condition maintaining that it is enough to consider the thin slices of the sole target subject, and that the whole set of acoustic features are needed. The result is a 2×3 design. For each condition, the training instances included the relevant acoustic and visual feature, computed over a 1-minute window. The analysis was conducted by means of 15-fold stratified cross-validation, with the same 15 training/test sets pairs being used in all the design's six conditions. Stratification was conducted in order to closely reproduce in the training and test sets the distribution of Extraversion and LoC in the whole corpus.

16.4.2 Results

In this chapter, we will limit our discussion to accuracy—see Tables 16.3 and 16.4—and compare our results with those of the trivial classifier that always assigns the most frequent class to each instance (Accuracy = 0.6667).

TABLE 16.3. Means and SDs of Accuracy for Extraversion

		Others			
		No-Feat	ALL	SEL	
Target	ALL	0.8889	0.9021	**0.9438**	0.9116
		(0.029)	(0.028)	(0.021)	(0.035)
	SEL	0.8493	0.8611	0.9035	0.8713
		(0.024)	(0.036)	(0.026)	(0.037)
	Total	0.8691	0.8816	0.9237	0.8914
		(0.033)	(0.038)	(0.031)	(0.041)

Note: Boldface indicates the best results.

TABLE 16.4. Means and SDs of Accuracy for LoC

		Others			
		No-Feat	ALL	SEL	
Target	ALL	0.9014	0.9090	**0.9486**	0.9197
		(0.026)	(0.021)	(0.016)	(0.030)
	SEL	0.7487	0.8278	0.8472	0.8199
		(0.040)	(0.061)	(0.039)	(0.054)
	Total	0.8431	0.8684	0.8979	0.8698
		(0.068)	(0.061)	(0.059)	(0.066)

Note: Boldface indicates the best results.

Both for Extraversion and for LoC, the global average values of accuracy are well above the performance of the trivial classifier (0.8914 and 0.8698, respectively).

Two ANOVA, one for Extraversion and one for LoC, showed that all the main effects are significant ($P < 0.0001$), whereas interaction effects were not. With reference to the marginal means, both for Extraversion and LoC, the usage of all the features for the target subjects yielded much better results in terms of accuracy, the advantage being even more marked for LoC (0.9116 vs. 0.8713 for Extraversion and 0.9197 vs. 0.8199, for LoC).

Concerning the effect of the context, as captured through the factor "Others," contrast analysis shows that the usage of acoustic features yields better results for both Extraversion (contrast value = 0.067, $P < 0.0001$) and LoC (contrast value = 0.080, $P < 0.0001$). Moreover, the best results are obtained when the social context is captured by means of the selected features (condition SEL), both for Extraversion (contrast value = 0.097, $P < 0.0001$) and LoC (contrast value = 0.084, $P < 0.0001$).

Contrary to our expectations, the features selected according to the procedure described above are not effective, as far as the target subject is concerned: when applied to it, they constantly yield results that are worse than those obtained by means of all the acoustic features, as the summary curves in Figure 16.3 shows.

Concerning the other hypothesis, it is confirmed that the encoding of the social context (what the other members of the group do) improves personality classification. It is important to emphasize, however, that even in the absence of any attempt

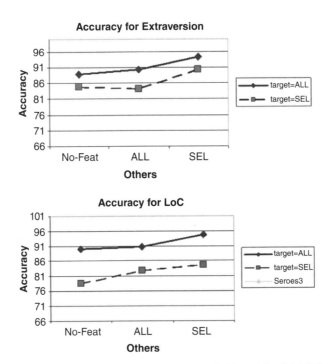

Figure 16.3. Accuracy for Extraversion (left) and LoC (right).

to (acoustically) capture the social context, the performance obtained are all much higher than the baseline provided by the trivial classifier: 0.8691 for Extraversion and 0.8431 for LoC. Considering that the baseline is 0.6667, the relative improvement is 0.607 and 0.529, respectively. Hence, thin slices of the sole target subject's behavior are enough to obtain quite a good automatic classification of the two personality traits considered here.

Moreover, our results show that the way the social context is encoded matters: the best performances are obtained when the selected features are used. A more detailed analysis shows that when all the acoustic features are used for the target subject, the usage of the same features for the social context does not improve the accuracy over the No-Feat condition (comparison between [ALL, No-Feat] and [ALL, ALL]), both for Extraversion and LoC. The improvement is only due to the usage of the selected features for Others (comparisons between (ALL, SEL), and (ALL, No-Feat) and (ALL, ALL) both significant at $P < 0.0001$), again for both personality traits. The role of the selected features for capturing the context is striking and unexpected, given that the choice procedure considered only the relationship between each features and the target subject personality. However, as further studies have shown (Lepri et al. 2009), this datum is quite robust, hence it seems to point to some deep aspect of the way the context (the behavior of other subjects) affects personality expression, which deserves more specific investigation.

16.5   CONCLUSION

In this chapter, we discussed the possibility of exploiting simple audio-visual features from social interaction to automatically extract knowledge about the participants' behavior. The usage of simple nonverbal features and the focus on short behavioral sequences (thin slices) makes the minimalist approach to human behavior understanding discussed here particularly suited to automatic systems. Our results suggest that both dynamic and transitory properties, such as the functional role an individual plays in a meeting, and persistent properties, such as personality factors, can be extracted with a reasonably high accuracy, showing that machines can be made capable to exploit thin slices of behavior in a fashion that closely resembles their usage by humans (Ambady and Rosenthal 1992).

Of course, our results are still based on lab data, and more evidence is needed from real case studies in more ecological setting. Yet, if definitely proven feasible, the automatic extraction of information about human behavior and about human characteristics from thin slices of behavior opens important scenarios both for the field of human–computer interaction and for the field of human–human, computer mediated interaction.

AFFECT EXTRACTION FROM AUDIO AND IMAGERY

Emotional intelligence has long been valued as a key natural human intelligence. This section considers how machines can extract emotional indicators from audio and imagery. The chapters demonstrate how recognition of emotion can enhance information retrieval, human computer interaction, and image recommendation. As such, these chapters explore the representation of emotional ontologies and automated measurement of such indicators as positive or negative valence and degree of arousal caused by (written, spoken, or visual) expressions.

In the first chapter by Björn Schuller, Martin Wöllmer, Florian Eyben, and Gerhard Rigoll from Technische Universität München, the authors explore the recognition of the speaker's emotional state, age, and gender from spoken content in TV and radio broadcasts. The authors experiment with the German TV talk show Vera am Mittag (VAM) corpus, which contains 947 spontaneous and emotionally colored German utterances from 47 talk show guests. The corpus is annotated along three emotional dimensions: *valence* (positive vs. negative), *arousal* (calm vs. excited), and *dominance* (weak vs. strong). Given 90% correlation between arousal and dominance, only valence and arousal (also called *activation*) are used to represent emotional state. The best results for emotion recognition were obtained with a bag of *n*-grams approach (based on closed captions), which could outperform a bag of words technique. Furthermore, roughly 100 (for arousal) and 200 (for valence) relevant audio features were selected out of a set of 760 systematically generated features. These were primarily Mel-frequency cepstral coefficients (MFCC), which performed better than other methods, such as straight pitch detection. For prediction of *valence*, the best result was attained using linguistic only bag of *n*-grams features. However, for *arousal*, a combination of acoustic features and linguistic bag of *n*-grams features gave the best performance. Speaker gender could be classified with accuracy above 90% and could be used for the recognition of affect, although this only led to minimal improvement. Whereas gender was recognized with high accuracy, the recognition of speaker's age was shown to be a more difficult task. Since even humans cannot recognize the exact age from speech, the task of detecting *young people* (<21 years, 217 instances) and *adults* (>20 years, 730 instances) was considered. The best performance on this database (ages 16–69 years, average 30.8 years) was achieved by a combination of 84 acoustic and 32 linguistic features. In concluding, the authors discuss how results could be improved by part of speech tagging, sociolect inclusion, topic analysis, visual information, and fusion of knowledge sources.

In the second chapter by Marco Guerini, Carlo Strapparava, and Oliviero Stock from FBK-IRST, Italy, the authors investigate audience reactions to persuasive language in political communications, focusing on valenced (positive/negative) expressions. The authors point out the limitations of traditional approaches based on word usage (e.g., counting how many times a word such as "*war*" is used in a speech), which fail to highlight important rhetorical phenomena and turn instead to measure the persuasive impact of words. For example, they explore audience reactions to the use of an expected theme, a name, or an expression. The authors describe their freely available (see http://hlt.fbk.eu/corps) 900 speech, 2.2 million word, English CORPS (*COR*pus of tagged *P*olitical *S*peeches) of monologues. The corpus includes nonlinguistic audience reactions, such as positive (e.g., applause, cheer, and standing ovation), negative (e.g., booing), or ironic (e.g., laughter). The authors lemmatize, part-of-speech tag, and named-entity tag the corpus using TextPro and apply Senti-WordNet (which represents the objective, positive, and negative valence of the synset) to compute the valence of words. The authors then apply machine learning to automatically extract positive, negative, ironical, and persuasive expressions based on frequency and proximity measures. The authors find that persuasive expression in four sentences is sufficient to distinguish Democrat from Republican texts with about 80% accuracy. The authors found that the mean polysemy of the "great communicator" Reagan's persuasive words (as opposed to all of his words) is almost double as compared with the whole corpus, consistent with his objective to convey a "simple and conversational" style. The authors also report how political speeches change after key events. The authors found that the negative valence mean of Bush's speech post 9/11 increased 15%. Furthermore, the word "justice" was not persuasive at all prior to 9/11, but became the ninth most persuasive word and was mentioned 10 times more frequently after the attack. Finally, a test on Obama and McCain speeches found their persuasive content was high. In summary, the authors demonstrate the importance of nonlexical audio cues to persuasive communication analysis.

The third chapter by Marko Tkalčič, Jurij Tasič and Andrej Košir from the University of Ljubljana, Slovenia, similarly considers affective signals. However, in this case, they focus on image recommender systems. The authors note that conventional content-based recommender (CBR) systems attempt to overcome information overload by analyzing metadata, such as genre, title, or actors to predict items of interest to individual users. The most used metadata attribute in CBR systems is *genre*. User profiles typically contain a vector of numbers representing the degree of agreeableness of the user with different genre types so that they can better retrieve content from, for instance, 3 billion Flickr photos or 10 billion Facebook photos. Unfortunately, prior research has largely ignored affective metadata. The authors explored the hypothesis that a content-based image recommender system would perform better when images are annotated with the induced emotional state of the end user to include valence, arousal, and dominance. In an evaluation experiment, 52 users (21 male, 31 female) from 17 to 20 years old were asked to choose a wallpaper image for the computer's desktop from a collection of 70 images carefully selected from the approximately 1000 images in the International Affective Picture System (IAPS) database. The IAPS database contains images annotated with metadata about their induced emotive responses to represent the spectrum of affective vector space. The system with affective metadata gave 68% of users better recommendations in terms of precision than the system with standard metadata, and a t-test showed the difference was significant. Finally, the mean value of precision among all users was higher when using affective metadata than standard metadata.

Finally, the fourth chapter by Gareth J. F. Jones and Ching Hau Chan from Dublin City University, Ireland, focuses on the automated extraction of affective labels from multimedia data streams. The authors focus their attention on retrieval of feature films, 4500 of which are released annually. The authors describe a novel system that extracts affective features from visual and acoustic streams of feature films and maps these onto a set of keywords with predetermined emotional interpretations. The prototype first extracts low-level audio and visual features from video (e.g., pitch and energy; motion, shot cut rate, saturation, and brightness), and then combines these to model valence and arousal. Subsequently, verbal emotional labels are assigned to the videos. Scenes with particular properties are mapped to emotional categories, for example, high-pitched human shouting with dark scenes might indicate a horror or terror scenes, whereas those with bright colors might indicate funny or happy scenes. Because of subject interpretations of words used to describe emotion, an open lexical database (i.e., WordNet) was used. The task of video annotation is harder when more abstract descriptions, such as affective labels, are needed, and likely to be more inconsistent because of subjectivity. Thirty-nine movies (approximately 80 hours) were segmented into 5-minute segments, to create a total of 939 segments and were used to create a benchmark data set covering a wide range of genres from action films to comedy and horror films. Eight English-speaking volunteers (average 29 years old) were tested on two tasks. The first task rated the quality of the valence and arousal curves that had been automatically extracted from the films. The second task assessed the three lists of emotional verbal labels automatically detected by the system for each of the randomly assigned movie clips. The results were promising. The authors are exploring the utility of their annotation system for movie retrieval, focusing first on exploring retrieval of and similarity between movie content based on affective annotation.

Collectively these chapters illustrate the rich source of emotion available in media, such as audio, imagery, and video. Affective features come from a variety of different sources, such as human body language, facial expression, and speech intonation. The authors explore a diversity of methods to learn from labeled multimedia corpora ranging from simple frequency analysis, to support vector classification, to CBR methods. These approaches promise new information services, such as affect-based analysis, retrieval, and summarization. Remaining research gaps include the needs for better databases and annotated audio and imagery corpora of emotional content (e.g., drama/films or sports broadcast), improved speech transcription and tagging of prosody and other speech features, improved visual emotion extraction from imagery, and automated detection of user/audience reactions.

CHAPTER 17

RETRIEVAL OF PARALINGUISTIC INFORMATION IN BROADCASTS

BJÖRN SCHULLER, MARTIN WÖLLMER, FLORIAN EYBEN, and GERHARD RIGOLL

17.1 INTRODUCTION

The automatic recognition of emotion, affective states, and paralinguistic phenomena has become more and more important in recent years and is enjoying increasing popularity in the fields of human–machine interaction and multimedia retrieval. As a result of continuous increase of computation power and improvements in the domain of pattern recognition, some applications become feasible, even with today's state of knowledge and technology.

A large field of application where first end-consumer products can already be observed is entertainment electronics. Examples are interactive video games or robot toys that react to the user's emotional state or edutainment systems that are able to adapt the learning scheme if the user loses attention. Closely related to consumer point entertainment electronics are television and radio broadcast systems, where a vast number of content exists. Automatically labeling affective states, spoken content, age, and gender of speakers, for example, at the broadcast site of a radio or television show can be a helpful aid for automatically building statistics for this show without additional personnel costs. Further, implementing such technology on the receiver's side enhances the viewer's experience by giving additional information about the shows. It might not be obvious at first why this kind of information is beneficial. It indeed makes no sense to have a TV display the emotional state of a person in a live TV show, since the person viewing the show will recognize the state intuitively. However, using meta information for retrieval or automatic filtering tasks (parental control, for example) brings a great benefit, for example, searching for shows with participants of a certain age or gender or certain emotional content (e.g., sad, happy, or aggressive films). Further, such information is of crucial

Multimedia Information Extraction: Advances in Video, Audio, and Imagery Analysis for Search, Data Mining, Surveillance, and Authoring, First Edition. Edited by Mark T. Maybury.
© 2012 IEEE Computer Society. Published 2012 by John Wiley & Sons, Inc.

importance in automatic movie or audio play dubbing, for the enhancement of automatically generated subtitles, or for automatic translation with subsequent emotional speech resynthesis.

Apart from information retrieval tasks, the recognition of emotion and emotion-related states also has the potential to become an essential part of future human–machine communication (Cowie et al. 2001; Picard 1997; Shriberg 2005; Zeng et al. 2009). This is because affective states are fundamental to human experience concerning cognition, perception, communication, and even rational decision making. The integration of affective states and social competence as an additional factor of interaction is thus an indispensable component of next-generation human–machine interfaces (Schuller 2006) and next-generation multimedia systems (Nakatsu 1998).

In contrast with audio-visual approaches (such as in Jones and Chan [Chapter 20, this volume] or Hanjalić and Xu 2005), this chapter focuses on recognizing emotion from the *speech* signal and from the spoken content, since occlusions, changing lighting conditions, and diverse angles of the face still are heavy challenges for video-based analyses when confronted with nonprototypical and natural data. The speech signal is often also overlaid by overtalk or music. However, multichannel recordings ease this problem, and the spoken content as secondary stream can often be accessed without error from close captions or subtitles, in contrast to more error-prone automatic speech recognition, which would be used if no captions are available. Likewise, we focus on the human speech signal, which also allows for a reasonable phrase- or sentence-wise segmentation. Still, oncoming highly robust video processing will certainly add more reliability to the estimates (Schuller et al. 2007b; Wimmer et al. 2008).

Following the tradition in the field, a data-driven approach with extensive use of acoustic features will be observed herein. However, in addition, the main focus of this chapter lies in improving recognition robustness using appropriate linguistic features, as spoken or written text also carries information about the underlying affective state (Arunachalam et al. 2001; Chuang and Wu 2004; Dupuis and Pichora-Fuller 2007). This is usually reflected by the use of certain words or grammatical alterations—which means, in turn, by the use of specific higher semantic and pragmatic entities. A number of approaches exist for this analysis: keyword spotting (Cowie et al. 1999; de Rosis et al. 2007; Elliott 1992), rule-based modeling (Litman and Forbes 2003), semantic trees (Zhe and Boucouvalas 2002), latent semantic analysis (Goertzel et al. 2000), transformation-based learning (Wu et al. 2005), world-knowledge-modeling (Liu et al. 2003), key-phrase-spotting (Schuller et al. 2004), and Bayesian networks (Breese and Ball 1998; Rigoll et al. 2005). Context/pragmatic information has been modeled as well, for example, the type of system prompt (Steidl et al. 2004), dialogue acts (Batliner et al. 2003; Litman and Forbes 2003), or system and user performance (Ai et al. 2006). Two methods seem to be predominant, presumably because they are shallow representations of linguistic knowledge and have already been frequently employed in automatic speech processing: *(class-based) n-grams* (Ang et al. 2002; Devillers et al. 2003; Lee et al. 2002; Polzin and Waibel 2002) and *vector space modeling* (Batliner et al. 2006; Schuller et al. 2005, 2006a); these will be dealt with in this chapter. Due to the typical data sparseness in emotion recognition, mostly unigrams have been applied so far (Devillers et al. 2003; Lee et al. 2002), besides bigrams and trigrams (Ang et al. 2002). The actual emotion is calculated by the posterior probability of the emotion given the actual word(s). Vector space modeling based on bag of words (BOW) is a well-known numerical representation form of text in automatic document categorization introduced by Joachims (1998). It has been successfully ported to recognize sentiments by Pang et al. (2002) or emotion and interest by Schuller et al. (2005, 2006b). The possibility of early fusion with acoustic features helped to make this technique very popular, as shown in Batliner et al. (2006).

In the ongoing, we will combine the ideas of n-grams and vector space modeling to profit from word sequence modeling and easy integration at the same time. Likewise, new linguistic approaches in the field of affect recognition, like the bag of n-grams (BONG), are described and compared in terms of benefits for the recognition of affect in spontaneous speech, in particular in the dimensional emotion space. Since the scope of this book is multimedia information retrieval, this chapter will focus on the application field of TV and radio broadcasts. For the illustration of obtainable performances, a database called *VAM corpus* is used in experiments, which is described in detail in Section 17.2. The database was chosen over others (e.g., Douglas-Cowie et al. 2007) because of its close relatedness to media and broadcast applications. The methods and algorithms used to classify speaker emotion, age, and gender from two modalities, namely the audio signal and the transcribed spoken content (e.g., from an automatic speech recognizer or closed captions of broadcast shows), are outlined in Section 17.3 and 17.4. In order to show how suitable such a detection system is for a real application scenario, typical performances are discussed in Section 17.5. At the end of this chapter, in Section 17.6, a summary of the most important aspects is provided along with an outlook, which outlines future trends in paralinguistic information retrieval and affective computing in consumer devices.

17.2   EMOTIONS IN TV BROADCASTS: THE VAM CORPUS

In recent years, great effort has been spent to collect emotional speech data. Douglas-Cowie et al. (2003), Ververidis and Kotropoulos (2003) and Douglas-Cowie et al. (2007) give a comprehensive overview over these efforts. Nevertheless, inferring from these works, there are only few databases dealing with natural, spontaneous speech while offering a considerable amount of data at the same time. Even fewer corpora exist for the TV and radio show broadcast domain. A widely known and fully annotated corpus that is available to the research community is the *"Vera am Mittag" (VAM) corpus*. Other corpora, using material from drama/films or sports broadcast, would be desirable; however, no annotated data exists yet, thus the VAM corpus will be used herein.

The "Vera am Mittag" corpus was first used in Grimm and Kroschel (2005) and was made accessible to the research community with Grimm et al. (2008). It consists of audio-visual recordings taken from the German TV talk show "Vera am Mittag,"[1] whereas only audio and linguistic data is used for emotion recognition herein.

The corpus contains 947 German spontaneous and emotionally colored utterances from 47 talk show guests. The utterances were recorded from unscripted,

---

[1] English: *Vera at Noon*; Vera is the name of the talk show host.

authentic discussions. There were several reasons to build the database on material from a TV talk show (Grimm et al. 2008): a reasonable amount of speech from each speaker is available in each session, and the spontaneous discussions between the guests are often rather affective (cf. Section 17.2.2) and lead to a variety of emotional states, depending on the discussed topics. These topics were mainly personal issues, such as friendship crises, fatherhood questions, or romantic affairs. To obtain nonacted data, a talk show in which the guests were not being paid to perform as actors was chosen. The subjects did not know that the recordings will be analyzed in a study of affective expression. The dialogues contain a large amount of colloquial expressions, nonlinguistic vocalizations, and different German dialects. This emphasizes the natural, spontaneous character of the corpus.

17.2.1 Emotion Representation and Annotation

Within the VAM corpus, emotion is described in terms of three basic primitives as proposed by (Russell and Mehrabian 1977):

- *Valence*: Positive versus negative.
- *Arousal*: Calm versus excited (sometimes: *activation*, e.g., in cognitive studies).
- *Dominance*: Weak versus strong.

Valence describes the intrinsic pleasantness or unpleasantness of a situation. *Arousal* expresses whether a stimulus puts a person into a state of increased or reduced activity. *Dominance* defines the apparent strength of the person. This involves whether the person considers himself as being able to deal with a particular situation.

An emotion can be independently described by each of these primitives on a continuous scale from $(-1, +1)$. Therefore, emotions can be described as a point in a three-dimensional space if the three primitives *valence, arousal (activation)*, and *dominance* are interpreted as orthogonal emotion dimensions (see Figure 17.1). The concept of estimating emotions on a continuous scale is an important alternative to emotion categories for describing human's affective states, because it is able to describe the intensity of emotions. Furthermore, the concept can be used for recognizing dynamics and allows for an adaptation to individual moods and personalities (Grimm et al. 2007; Wollmer et al. 2008).

For the annotation of the speech data, the audio recordings were manually segmented to the utterance level, whereas each utterance contained at least one phrase. A large number of human labelers was used for annotation (17 labelers for one-half of the data, six for the other). As evaluation tool, a text-free method using Self-Assessment Manikins (SAMs) was used (Grimm and Kroschel 2005). The instrument of SAMs is an icon-based method and consists of an array of five images for each emotion dimension. Each human listener had to listen to each utterance in the database in order to choose three icons, one for each emotion dimension. Afterwards, the choice of the icons was mapped on a discrete five-point scale for each dimension in the range from -1 to $+1$. This way of evaluation using SAMs is known to be very fast and intuitive.

The individual listener annotations were averaged using the evaluator weighted estimator (EWE) as described in Grimm et al. (2007). The average results for the

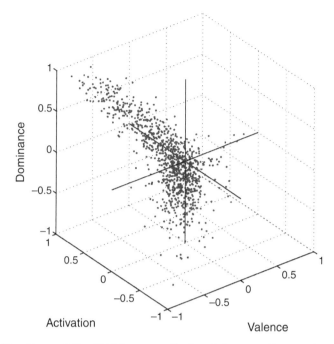

Figure 17.1. Emotions of the VAM corpus displayed in a continuous three-dimensional emotion space.

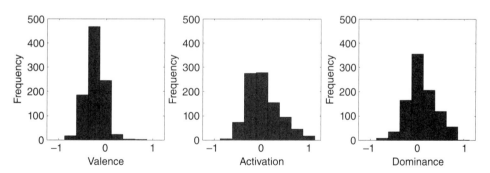

Figure 17.2. Histograms of the emotion distribution in the VAM corpus.

standard deviation between the annotators are 0.29, 0.34, and 0.31 for valence, arousal, and dominance, indicating good evaluation results. The averages for the correlation between the evaluators are 0.49, 0.72, and 0.61, respectively (Grimm et al. 2007). The correlation coefficients for arousal and dominance show suitable values, whereas the moderate value for valence indicates that this emotion primitive was more difficult to evaluate, but may partly also be a result of the smaller variance of valence (see Figure 17.2).

17.2.2 Database Properties

The distributions for the three emotion dimensions, obtained from the evaluation described above, are outlined in Figure 17.2. Due to the topics discussed in the talk show, a large percentage of utterances shows neutral or negative valence with high arousal and dominance. Note that for the performance evaluation in Section 17.5, only valence and arousal were used as emotional dimensions, since arousal and dominance are highly correlated (the correlation coefficient resembles 0.903, the mean linear error 0.10; see Figure 17.1). Thus, the gain of including dominance in the emotional analysis would be marginal. The corpus comes along with a transcription of the spoken content, which can be used for linguistic analysis. This is well in line with exploitation of close captions. However, with close captions stemming from diverse broadcasts, new problems will be inherited: different spellings, potential misspellings, and varieties. This will demand for additional string matching as edit distances.

17.3 CLASSIFICATION AND FEATURE SELECTION METHODS

Automatic recognition of speaker characteristics and emotional states from real-world signals is a classical pattern recognition problem. In the first step, suitable features must be extracted from the input data (audio, text, etc.). The choice of optimal features is important, since the features should in theory only contain information about emotional states. The selection of relevant features is not trivial, thus generally a large feature set is generated and then automatic feature selection methods are applied to reduce the set. Here, correlation-based feature selection (CFS) as a broadly used, fast, and efficient tool is applied.

Two substantially different recognition problems are addressed in this chapter, namely recognition of emotion in a continuous two-dimensional space spanned by the dimensions valence and arousal (see Section 17.2), and classification of gender and age into discrete classes. For the first problem, support vector regression (SVR) is used, for the second problem support vector machines (SVM) are applied. The following sections briefly describe the main characteristics of the selected fundamental methods for feature selection and classification/regression.

17.3.1 Correlation-Based Feature Selection

Correlation-based feature selection was introduced by Hall (1999). The main idea of CFS is that useful feature subsets should contain features that are highly correlated with the class while being uncorrelated with each other. To avoid an exhaustive search of the feature space, a greedy hill climbing forward search is used (Witten and Frank 2005, p. 292).

17.3.2 Support Vector Machines

Support vector machines for classification tasks were introduced by Cortes and Vapnik (1995). The main concept is the discriminative separation of two classes by a linear hyper plane that provides the maximum distance between the vectors of both classes. This margin assures that new, unseen patterns can be classified reliably. To separate very complex problems, an implicit nonlinear extension, the so-called *kernel trick*, is applied, which makes SVM a highly efficient classifier.

17.3.3 Support Vector Regression

Support vector regression makes use of methods derived from SVM theory to solve a regression problem. The goal of SVR is to find a regression function $f(\underline{x})$ that has at the most a deviation of ε from the actually obtained targets, and, at the same time, is as flat as possible. In an analogous manner to SVM theory, the algorithm for SVR is described by dot products between training vectors $\underline{x}_i$, and the new, unseen pattern vector $\underline{x}$. As for SVM, the model is extended nonlinearly to solve complex regression tasks.

   For more details, please refer to Smola and Schoelkopf (1998). Note that in this chapter, a radial basis function kernel and a polynomial kernel are used for SVR and SVM.

17.4 METHODS FOR ACOUSTIC AND LINGUISTIC ANALYSIS

This section describes established methods for acoustic and linguistic analysis tailored for emotion recognition, that is, the extraction of suitable features from the audio signal and the transcriptions (closed captions) of media broadcasts. Extraction of a single static acoustic feature vector for an utterance of variable length and selection of relevant acoustic features is described in Section 17.4.1. Linguistic analysis methods, such as BOW and BONG, that analogously allow the mapping of text of variable length to a static feature vector of a fixed dimensionality are detailed in Section 17.4.2.

17.4.1 Acoustic Analysis

In order to recognize affect from acoustic features, a data-driven approach is commonly used. This means an extensive generation of acoustic features from the speech signal and choosing the most relevant ones through feature selection, for example, (Schuller et al. 2007a). The following section gives a short overview over the extracted acoustic features that form a basis for the feature selection, detailed in Section 17.4.1.2.

17.4.1.1 Audio Feature Extraction   The recognition of affect is based on sentences. Thus, every sentence is windowed in equidistant short-time segments. For every window, a set of low-level descriptors (LLD) is calculated. These LLD can be temporal characteristics, spectral characteristics like formants (i.e., spectral maxima), and other characteristics of the speech signal, like harmonics-to-noise ratio (HNR), Mel-frequency cepstral coefficients (MFCC), or energy. The input is segmented into turns. For every turn, functionals derived from these LLD time series are calculated, for example, mean values, standard deviations, quartiles, extremes, and so on. Additionally, these functionals are calculated from delta coefficients of the time series. Table 17.1 gives an overview over LLD and functionals used for acoustic analysis.

TABLE 17.1. Low-Level Descriptors (LLDs) and Functionals Used Throughout Systematic Construction of a Large Acoustic Feature Space

Low-Level Descriptors	Functionals
Pitch (F0)	Mean, standard deviation
Energy	Zero-crossing-rate
Envelope	Quartile 1/2/3
MFCC coefficient 1–16	Quartile 1—minimum
Harmonics-to-noise-ratio (HNR)	Quartile 2—Quartile 1
Delta pitch	Quartile 3—Quartile 2
Delta energy	Maximum—Quartile 3
Delta envelope	Centroid, skewness, kurtosis
Delta MFCC coefficient 1–16	Maximum/minimum value/range
Delta HNR	Relative maximum/minimum position
	Position of 95% roll-off-point

TABLE 17.2. Feature Reduction through CFS for the VAM Corpus

Number of Features	Valence	Arousal
Total original	760	760
Total after CFS	238	109
Pitch	6	2
Energy	1	1
Envelope	12	1
MFCC	218	101
HNR	1	4

Number of features for whole data set and for different LLD (delta LLD included).

In total, 760 features are considered that proved reliable and well suited in related work (Schuller et al. 2007a; Batliner et al. 2008; Vlasenko et al. 2008).

17.4.1.2 Selection of Audio Features   As described, CFS is used to select relevant features out of the full set of 760 systematically generated features. The CFS has to be executed for the emotion primitives *valence* and *arousal* independently. Table 17.2 shows the number of features before and after CFS and gives the frequencies of occurrence for the different LLD. The total number of selected features differs for the two emotion dimensions; however, the allocation to the different LLD is similar. Mainly MFCC coefficients are chosen to be relevant features. This stems from their high robustness over, for example, pitch, with respect to the naturalness of the data and noisy conditions.

17.4.2 Linguistic Analysis

As Section 17.5 will show, analysis based only on acoustic features cannot solve the task of multimedia affect recognition to complete satisfaction. Therefore, this section shows approaches exploiting a higher level of information. Two different linguistic analysis methods will be introduced: *BOW* is an approach for generating numeric representations of the spoken content. This approach is well known from document retrieval tasks and has shown good results for the recognition of emotion as well. *BONG* is an extension of the BOW well suited for the task (Schuller et al. 2009a,b). While BOW only consider single words, BONG build numeric features from more consecutive words. The linguistic analysis is based on the correct transcription of the spoken content, which in practice is provided for most broadcasts by the transmitted closed captions.

17.4.2.1 *Bag of Words*

17.4.2.1 Bag of Words The BOW approach was originally developed for document retrieval tasks, but also showed good results for emotion recognition (Batliner et al. 2006). The basic idea behind this approach is the representation of text in a numeric feature space. Each feature represents the occurrence of a specific word in a sentence. The recognition of affect herein is based on the sentence level. This means every spoken sentence S has to be assigned to a state of affect. A sentence can be described by the set of words w_i it contains, that is, $S = \{w_1, \ldots, w_S\}$. The BOW method considers these words w_i as semantic units of interest. For a given database, the amount of all different words build the vocabulary $V = \{w_1, \ldots, w_v\}$. For the VAM corpus, the vocabulary size is 1932. However, only a fraction of these words conveys relevant information about the underlying emotional states of a person. In order to reduce the information in a meaningful way, two methods can be applied: stopping and stemming.

Stopping uses simple rules to exclude single words from the vocabulary. A stop list that includes words known to be irrelevant for affect recognition can be applied. Nevertheless, creating a stop list is not trivial because it is not always obvious which terms are emotionally important for a specific database. Therefore, another simple method for reducing the vocabulary is often exploited in addition to data-driven selection as introduced: a minimum database word frequency f_{min} determines the necessary minimum number of occurrences of a word in the database, for being part of the vocabulary. Very rare words are thus discarded.

Stemming is a method for reducing different morphological forms of a word to its base form. As the name implies, the reduction is achieved by using only word stems in the vocabulary, so-called lexemes. For example, the words "*buy*," "*buying*," and "*bought*" can be reduced to the lexeme "*buy*" (Lovins 1968; Porter 2008).

The main idea of the BOW approach is the representation of words (or lexemes if stemming is applied) as numeric features. For each word w_i in the vocabulary, a corresponding feature x_i exists, resulting in a high dimensional feature vector space. Each spoken utterance S_j can therefore be mapped to a vector $\underline{x}_j$ in this feature space. There are different ways to determine the value of each feature x_i. A simple way is to count the number of appearances of a word w_i in the sentence S_j, resulting in the word frequency f_{ij}. This frequency can be transformed in various ways (Witten and Frank 2005, p. 311). A common method is the application of the logarithm to compensate linearities, called the term frequency transformation (TF); see for example, Singhal et al. (1996):

$$\mathrm{TF}_{ij} = \log\left(1 + f_{ij}\right).$$

The offset in the logarithm prevents definition problems in case of $f_{ij} = 0$. Other measures that are widely used for document retrieval are the inverse document frequency transformation (IDF) and TFIDF as a combination of TF and IDF.

17.4.2.2 Bag of n-Grams   Similar to BOW, the BONG approach also represents text in a numeric feature space. The main difference is the observation of a series of consecutive words as semantic units of interest. Whereas BOW observes only single words for the mapping to a numeric feature space, the idea behind BONG makes a simple extension by observing n-grams of words. For $n = 1$, only single words are observed, which corresponds to BOW. For $n = 2$, word bigrams are observed, for $n = 3$ trigrams, and so on. The approach allows to observe several n-gram sizes together, determined by a minimum n-gram length g_{min} and a maximum n-gram length g_{max}. For the exemplary setting $g_{min} = 1$, $g_{max} = 3$, and the exemplary sentence: "*Recognizing affect from speech*," the following linguistic units are built from the sentence:

- *1-Gram (Single Words)*: "*Recognizing*," "*affect*," "*from*," and "*speech*."
- *2-Grams (Bigrams)*: "*Recognizing affect*," "*affect from*," and "*from speech*."
- *3-Grams (Trigrams)*: "*Recognizing affect from*," and "*affect from speech*."

For each of these text units, the generation of a numeric feature is done exactly as described for the BOW. Thus, stopping and stemming are applied (prior to n-gram construction), the n-gram frequency in the sentences are counted, transformed, and normalized. As a basis for investigations, the parameters for stopping, stemming, transformations, and normalization are chosen to be the best setting derived from BOW analysis. Parameters of interest for experiments with BONG are the minimum and maximum n-gram length g_{min} and g_{max}.

17.4.3 Fusion of Acoustic and Linguistic Information

So far, acoustic and linguistic analyses can be used to extract features from spontaneous speech on the sentence level. To make use of both kinds of information, the different features can be combined using early fusion. This means a simple union of acoustic and linguistic features to one super-vector. Since the dimensionality of this resulting vector can be quite high, a feature selection such as the one described is used to discard unimportant features. This feature selection can be applied on the whole acoustic–linguistic vector or on the acoustic and linguistic part separately. However, usually, an additional gain is obtained by the combined optimization.

17.5 PERFORMANCE ON MEDIA BROADCASTS

This section describes obtainable performance results for three recognition tasks, namely recognition of emotional states, speaker age, and speaker gender in a real-world TV show scenario. Automatic labeling of these three tasks is useful in various applications, for example, automated generation of statistics, or automatic generation of meta-information for viewers of a show. For illustration, classification and regression models are trained on data from the *VAM corpus* (cf. Section 17.2). The models are evaluated on *VAM* data sets disjunctive from the training sets to ensure realistic conditions. The VAM set is thereby split into 10 disjunctive folds. The performance is discussed for recognition of all three tasks using (1) only acoustic features, (2) only linguistic features, and (3) acoustic and linguistic features combined on the feature level by early fusion.

17.5.1   Emotion Recognition

In the following, the results of acoustic–linguistic emotion recognition on the *VAM corpus* using SVR are introduced. To evaluate the regression performance, the emotion estimation is compared with the reference given by the human evaluators. Two values are observed: the mean linear error (MLE) for the continuous emotion dimensions in the range of $(-1,+1)$, and the correlation coefficient (CC) between the SVR estimates and the averaged ratings of the human evaluators. The correlation coefficient therefore shows the accuracy in terms of the tendency in the estimates. It can take values from $(-1,+1)$, where 1 indicates perfect correlation and 0 no correlation. Values below 0 indicate a negative correlation, that is, a positive correlation can be achieved by inverting one of the signals.

For the BOW experiment, stopping with $f_{min} = 2$ together with iterated Lovins stemming, term frequency transformation and normalization was applied. After stopping, stemming, and test-disjunctive feature selection (i.e., feature selection carried out only on the training data), 136 linguistic features remained for valence and 130 for arousal. The minimum and maximum n-gram lengths for the BONG experiment was $g_{min} = 1$ and $g_{max} = 2$, respectively. The results are obtained through 10-fold cross-validation for the whole *VAM corpus*. Table 17.3 shows the correlation coefficient, as well as the mean linear error for both, valence and arousal using acoustic, linguistic, and merged acoustic–linguistic features. For linguistic analysis, BOW and BONG was applied, whereas BONG outperforms the simpler BOW approach. For prediction of *valence*, the best result was attained using linguistic BONG features. The combination of acoustic features and linguistic BONG features gave the best performance for *arousal*.

When comparing the results with Grimm et al. (2007), we see that the results obtained with acoustic features only are well in line, with those reported there (CC

TABLE 17.3. Final Results of Acoustic-Linguistic Analysis for the VAM Corpus: Correlation Coefficient (CC) and Mean Linear Error (MLE)

Feature Set	CC (MLE) Valence	CC (MLE) Arousal
Acoustic only	0.451 (0.13)	0.810 (0.16)
Linguistic only (BOW)	0.476 (0.13)	0.533 (0.23)
Linguistic only (BONG)	**0.617 (0.12)**	0.645 (0.22)
Acoustic and linguistic (BOW)	0.565 (0.12)	0.832 (0.15)
Acoustic and linguistic (BONG)	0.575 (0.12)	**0.851 (0.14)**

Observed features: acoustic, bag of words (BOW), bag of n-grams (BONG) with correlation-based feature selection.
Note: Numbers in boldface indicate the best result.

TABLE 17.4. Gender Recognition with Acoustic and Linguistic (BONG) Features: Unweighted and Weighted Average Recall

Feature Set	Recall (Weighted Average)	Recall (Unweighted Average)
Acoustic	91.1	91.1
Linguistic (BONG)	62.8	62.8
Acoustic + BONG	**91.6**	**91.5**

Displayed are best results obtained without feature selection. All results are subject independent. Note: Numbers in boldface indicate the best result.

for valence/arousal with RBF kernel SVR: 0.42/0.82). Combining acoustic and linguistic features, however, significantly outperforms (Grimm et al. 2007) both for valence and arousal. The observed gain for valence is greater than the gain for arousal.

The evaluations in this section show that it does make sense to observe more information than only the acoustic features. The BONG approach can be recommended as an advanced method of linguistic analysis. In the next section, additional paralinguistic high-level information is considered for analysis. Also, the benefit of the knowledge for improved emotion recognition is discussed.

17.5.2 Gender Recognition

In order to recognize the gender of a speaker, acoustic features as introduced in Section 17.4.1 are used for a classification with SVM (see Section 17.3). All evaluations are subject independent, that is, the testing data does not contain data from the speakers the classifier was trained on.

Due to the imbalance of male/female subjects in the *VAM corpus*, the training data used for this experiment was resampled to uniform class distribution. The linguistic features for the *VAM* database are created by a BONG analysis ($f_{min} = 2$, iterated Lovins stemming, $g_{min} = 1$, $g_{max} = 2$). Table 17.4 shows the performance of gender recognition. For gender recognition, a better performance was achieved without feature selection, thus only results computed without feature selection are discussed.

As can be seen from the table, the gender of a speaker can be classified with high accuracy above 90% for the *VAM corpus*. The contextual information of speaker gender can be used for the recognition of affect. This can, for example, be realized by early fusion of the already introduced linguistic–acoustic features with a binary feature, which contains the recognized gender information. However, this method only leads to minimal improvement in recognition performance. But the knowledge of speaker gender can also be used in other ways: for example, different classification/regression models can be built for females and males. Depending on the recognized gender, a specific model is subsequently used for affect recognition. This method is shown to be exemplary for *valence* on the *VAM corpus*. The regression is based on 238 acoustic features selected by CFS. Table 17.5 shows the results obtained by 10-fold cross-validation.

The first entry shows the reference performance using only acoustic features as before (cf. Table 5.2), the second entry the one with an additional binary feature

TABLE 17.5. Estimation of Valence with Use of
Recognized **Speaker Gender: Correlation Coefficient (CC)**
and Mean Linear Error (MLE)

Analysis Method	CC (MLE)
Acoustic	0.451 (0.13)
Acoustic and gender	0.457 (0.13)
Acoustic (only female)	0.447 (0.13)
Acoustic (only male)	**0.576 (0.11)**

Used features: acoustic features and binary gender feature with combined or separate models.
Note: Numbers in boldface indicate the best result.

TABLE 17.6. Age Recognition with Different Feature Types: Unweighted and Weighted Average Recall

Feature Set	Recall (Weighted Average)	Recall (Unweighted Average)
Acoustic	72.6	70.9
Linguistic (BONG)	77.4	50.0
Acoustic + BONG	74.1	74.2

Acoustic and linguistic bag of *n*-grams (BONG) features. All results after correlation-based feature selection. All results are subject independent.

containing the gender information. As said, the benefit of this approach is only marginal. The last two entries in the table show the performance if only females or males are used for both training and testing according to the recognized gender. The affect of female subjects is recognized without relevant change in CC, whereas the estimation shows a clear improvement for the male speakers.

17.5.3 Speaker Age Recognition

The *VAM corpus* is further suited for a basic observation of the speaker age determination in real-life media data. The subjects in this database cover ages from 16 to 69 years, with an average age of 30.8 years. Treating age recognition as a regression problem is not recommended, since it is not possible, even for a human listener, to detect a speaker's age alone from acoustic and linguistic clues with a precision of a fraction of a year or less. Therefore, the labels *young people* (<21 years, 217 instances) and *adults* (>20 years, 730 instances) are introduced considering available data, obtaining a basic two-class problem, which is still of practical relevance.

For classification, SVM with radial basis function kernel are used. The evaluation method is a subject-independent cross-validation as before, where again the training data (not the test data) was resampled to uniform class distribution. Feature reduction was applied by CFS. Table 17.6 shows the performance concerning different feature types. In all cases, feature selection was applied prior to classification. The linguistic features for the *VAM* database are created by a BONG analysis ($f_{min} = 2$, iterated Lovins stemming, $g_{min} = 1$, $g_{max} = 2$).

The best performance is achieved by combined acoustic (84) and linguistic (32) features. It is probably easier to classify young people versus adults instead of

TABLE 17.7. Estimation of Valence Knowing the Speaker Age: Correlation Coefficient (CC) and Mean Linear Error (MLE)

Analysis Method	CC (MLE)
Acoustic	0.451 (0.13)
Acoustic and age group	0.450 (0.13)
Acoustic and exact age	0.452 (0.13)
Acoustic (only young people)	**0.538 (0.13)**
Acoustic (only adults)	0.418 (0.13)

Acoustic features, binary feature young people/adults (age group) and feature with knowledge about exact age (exact age). Training and test with the whole data set or separated for young people and adults. Note: Numbers in boldface indicate the best result.

separating different groups of adults. Thus, altogether, the results show that the classification of age groups is not an easy task.

Similar to the knowledge of gender, the speaker age is considered for bringing improvements in affect recognition (valence as an example, here). Results of the experiments shown in Table 17.7 are based on the knowledge of the correct age. The first entry is the reference using only acoustic features after CFS. The second and third entries denote the results using additional speaker age information by early fusion. One additional binary feature contains the age group (*young people/adults*), a second one the exact age of a speaker in years. Carrying out the measurements with both features does not change the classification results significantly. The last two entries in the table show the results for building separate classifier models for the age groups *young people* and *adults*. For *young people*, the result can be improved and are at the same time better than for the combined analysis method. The results show similar characteristics compared with the experiments with gender meta information. Thus, age as contextual knowledge apparently does not improve performance when integrated by early fusion, but may be used when training different models for classification to use them later for a certain age group. This approach leads to good results only if the different age groups can be classified with high accuracy.

17.6 CONCLUSION AND OUTLOOK

In this chapter, the potential, the technical details, and the performance of a recognition system classifying the paralinguistic information of emotion, gender, and age of speakers in a TV show were outlined. The described approach can be seen as a novel multimedia information retrieval system that exploits acoustic information together with linguistic information obtained from the closed captions. The main ambition was to improve the recognition of affect in spontaneous TV and radio broadcast speech using semantic and contextual analysis. Exemplary basis for all examinations was the *VAM* database, containing nonacted emotions and a sufficient amount of data to obtain significant experimental results.

As main techniques for machine learning, SVM for classification and SVR for regression tasks were used. Next to common acoustic features, different linguistic analysis methods were applied in order to exploit higher level information from the spoken content of a speech signal. The best results for emotion recognition were obtained with the BONG approach that could outperform the BOW technique. Especially for the difficult task of estimating the emotional dimension *valence*, the benefit of using not only acoustic but also linguistic features became obvious. Besides these linguistic observations, contextual information was exploited to determine possibilities to improve affect recognition. Here, the background knowledge of the speaker's gender and age was estimated observing the speech signal. Whereas gender can be recognized with high accuracy, the recognition of speaker's age was shown to be a more difficult task. The knowledge of gender and age allows building separate classification models to improve the recognition performance.

For future work, several suggestions to determine more semantic information out of the spoken content can be made by investigating further linguistic analysis methods. Part-of-speech tagging can be used as basis of further linguistic investigations. This would allow the creation of new features, for example, adjective and adverb frequencies (Schuller et al. 2009a,b). In addition, the examination of grammatical structures, for example, simple versus complex or correct versus incorrect, and the detection of incomplete sentences could also provide important linguistic information for the recognition of affect. The determination of sociolect as a simple separation of different speaking styles, for example, colloquial versus elaborate, can provide additional cues. A sociolect analysis could be based on part-of-speech tagging, observation of the vocabulary size, and use of acoustic criteria, for example, the existence of emphasis at the end of a sentence. Further, topic retrieval based on linguistic analysis could be used to determine discussed topics and therefore receive a coarse semantic knowledge of a specific situation. An additional use of visual information can be beneficial in order to exploit information not contained in the speech signal or when no speech is present. When it comes to the integration of data from different levels of information, other ways of fusion should be explored. Although early fusion works well for linguistic and acoustic information, a union with contextual information seems to be more problematic. Therefore, approaches in the field of meta-classification should be considered.

The recognition of affect in TV shows and radio broadcasts by the use of acoustic, linguistic, and contextual information is still a new area of research with great potential for improvements. Yet, it was shown that advanced machine learning strategies can successfully be applied for reasonably reliable affect recognition from broadcast speech data, which is a challenging multimedia information retrieval task.

ACKNOWLEDGMENT

The research leading to these results has received funding from the European Community's Seventh Framework Programme (FP7/2007-2013) under Grant Agreement No. 211486 (SEMAINE).

CHAPTER 18

AUDIENCE REACTIONS FOR INFORMATION EXTRACTION ABOUT PERSUASIVE LANGUAGE IN POLITICAL COMMUNICATION

MARCO GUERINI, CARLO STRAPPARAVA, and OLIVIERO STOCK

18.1 INTRODUCTION

Persuasive natural language processing focuses on the use of language for inducing desired beliefs and behaviors in the receivers. In order to automatically deal with persuasive communication, we built a resource called CORPS (*COR*pus of tagged *Political Speeches*) that contains transcripts of political speeches tagged with non-lexical audio features about audience reactions. First, we describe the construction of this resource and present some experiments for acquiring a lexicon (i.e., diction-ary) of persuasive expression from it, using a specific measure of the persuasive impact of words. In particular, we focus on the analysis of expressions that provoke audience reactions, such as applause, which we consider audience validation of a speaker's rhetorics. We further argue for the advantages of this measurement in the automatic analysis of political communication, showing that traditional approaches, based on word usage (e.g., counting how many times the word *war* is used in a speech) fail to highlight important rhetorical phenomena. Then we illustrate the usefulness of CORPS for training machine learning algorithms that predict the persuasive impact of novel speeches.

In this chapter, we focus mainly on lexical (i.e., word level) aspects of persuasive communication, and illustrate how our approach can help addressing a number of political analysis questions. For example: how do political speeches change after key historical events? What can be said about the lexical choices of well-known persua-sive speakers? How does the perception of the enemy change in different historical moments? Still, the corpus is potentially useful for many other natural language processing (NLP) and political analysis tasks that involve, for example, reasoning about syntactic and rhetorical aspects of the speeches. Here we emphasize the role

Multimedia Information Extraction: Advances in Video, Audio, and Imagery Analysis for Search, Data Mining, Surveillance, and Authoring, First Edition. Edited by Mark T. Maybury.
© 2012 IEEE Computer Society. Published 2012 by John Wiley & Sons, Inc.

of the audience's intervention, which we think provides valuable information, leaving aside other sources of information in the speech—like prosody—that are not reported in a normal transcription. Their possible integration will be briefly discussed at the end of the chapter.

The chapter is structured as follows. We first give an overview of relevant literature background. We then describe CORPS and some issues related to the annotation of this specific resource. The following sections introduce some NLP techniques tailored to CORPS structure for persuasive expression mining and some examples that show the advantages of using CORPS for political communication analysis. Finally, we present some machine learning experiments for predicting audience reaction on speeches still to be uttered or in the case audio sources are not available.

18.2 PERSUASION AND NLP

Past works on persuasion and NLP focused mainly on natural language generation (NLG). NLG deals with the automatic production of texts in human languages, often starting from nonlinguistic input (Reiter and Dale 2000). Persuasive text generation deals with the production of texts that are meant to affect the behavior of the receiver. The area of health communication is one of the first ones where the potentials of persuasive features for NLG were investigated. For a detailed overview on persuasion and NLG, see Guerini et al. (2011). Since reasoning about emotion can modify/increase the impact of the message, affective NLP is often connected to persuasive NLP. An annotated bibliography on affective NLG can be found in Piwek (2002).

18.2.1 Opinion Mining

This is a topic at the crossroads of information retrieval and computational linguistics, concerned with the identification of opinions (either positive or negative) expressed in a document, for example, "The tax proposal was simple and well received." While opinion mining deals with texts that are meant to persuade, its focus is on polarity (valence) recognition, as seen, for example, in Carenini et al. (2005), Wilson et al. (2004), and Breck et al. (2007). In Carenini et al. (2005), a method for feature extraction that draws on an existing unsupervised method is introduced. The work in Wilson et al. (2004) presents methodologies that use a wide range of features for opinion recognition, including new syntactic features.

18.2.2 Automatic Analysis of Political Communication

While there is a huge amount of theoretical and empirical research on politicians' rhetorics, only in recent years has there been a growing interest in bridging the gap between qualitative analysis of political communication and computational linguistics in order to automatize tasks that were usually carried out manually (mainly on text categorization). A well-articulated discussion on the broader problem of integrating information technologies with social science research can be found in Cousins and Mcintosh (2005).

18.2.3 Text Categorization

This deals with the task of assigning a document to a predefined set of categories, such as determining party position in a text (e.g., Republican or Democratic) or coding legislative activities into subject areas; see for example, Purpura and Hillard (2006).

Franzosi, in many of his writings, for example, Franzosi (2004), focused more closely on persuasive issues of political communication, in particular on narrative and semantic aspects. He created a large-scale corpus of annotated political news from newspapers expressing contrasting positions. His aim was to understand the characteristics of social events during the fascist period, so the interest on persuasive aspects was quite incidental.

Finally, an automatic analysis of the lexical aspects of political communication, similar to the work presented in this chapter (but not considering words' persuasive impact), can be found in Laver et al. (2003) and in Bligh et al. (2004).

18.2.4 Persuasion and Information Extraction

Recently, significant advances have been made in language processing for information extraction from unstructured texts and extraction of objects from imagery, video, and audio. However, up to now, nonlinguistic audio cues have received little attention and often have been treated as "background noise" to be discarded. Some approaches have tried to model extralinguistic phenomena (such as silence, breathing, lip smacks, etc.) mainly for optimizing speech recognition (see e.g., Bertoldi et al. 2002). Other approaches went further, hypothesizing that the recognition and classification of such phenomena (e.g., applause, laughter, and speaker vocal effort) can be used to enrich retrieval. On this point, see Chapter 14.

18.3 CORPS

In this chapter, we adopt persuasive lexical expression mining techniques as a component for persuasive NLP systems in an unrestricted domain. As for emotion, we focus on valenced expressions (i.e., those that have a positive or negative connotation). CORPS is a specific resource aimed at persuasion that includes long and elaborated persuasive texts.

In collecting this corpus, we relied on the hypothesis that tags about public reaction, such as APPLAUSE, are indicators of hot spots where persuasion attempts succeeded, or, at least, a persuasive attempt had been recognized by the audience; on this point, see Bull and Noordhuizen (2000) on mistimed applause in political speeches. We can then perform specific analyses—and extractions—of persuasive linguistic material that caused the audience reaction.

Given that the corpus is composed of transcriptions of speeches mostly given at public mass gatherings, in general, the audience is favorable to the speakers and the context is one of support. Of course, by giving value to the audience reactions, we do not mean that the audience is actually effectively persuaded of some ideas or induced to do something that it did not believe in beforehand, even if the audience can be reassured, inspired, or helped in making sense of events. To the contrary, the audience tends just to react to signals, including an expected theme, a name, an expression, or the tone of the voice. Often the signals are creative, in the sense that the speaker may have produced new forms through creative rhetorical elaboration, but eventually they are recognized. Therefore, the audience, so to say, resonates to a fragment of speech, which is meant to be of a persuasive genre and mostly concerned with a concept or a conceptual framework of which the audience is already persuaded. To be successful, the speaker's expression that immediately leads to the audience reaction must have been coherently composed. So we believe that there is a wealth of material that by virtue of the validation provided by the audience reaction, can be used by a machine to automatically learn and use in different situations, where it may have the goal of effectively persuading someone, or simply to reproduce politicians' speech or be used for analyzing the pragmatic characteristics of novel political speech. Given the textual nature of the corpus, rhetorical artifices based on prosody cannot be addressed. These artifices are used to highlight key passages of a speech, with the help of high-impact words or concepts.

At present, there are approximately 900 speeches in the corpus and about 2.2 million words. The speeches are all in native English language, and all represent monological situations (i.e., there is only one speaker addressing an audience). We took this decision since dialogical situations, like the ones found in political debates, are not in our current focus of research and pose further problems in labeling and analysis.

These speeches have been collected from the Internet, and an automatic conversion of audience reactions tags has been performed to make them homogeneous in formalism and labeling. For example, some discourses contain the tag (BIG-APPLAUSE), while others have (LOUD-APPLAUSE), (SUSTAINED APPLAUSE), and so on. All these tags were converted to (SUSTAINED APPLAUSE). Metadata regarding the speech has also been added: title, event, speaker, date, and description. A special tag COMMENT is used for particular cases, for example: (COMMENT = "An audience member claps"), (COMMENT = "Recording interrupted"). With regard to the problem of interannotator and intersource agreement, it should be noted that:

- The automatic conversion of audience reactions tags drastically reduces the problem of the heterogeneity in tag vocabularies; in fact, various sources were considered in collecting this corpus.
- Given the heterogeneity of the sources, there could be still disagreements in what can be judged to be "loud applause" versus just "applause." To face this problem, and to preserve the richness of the original annotation, we further clustered tags into coherent groups of audience reactions, but only at the analysis stage (see following sections: *Positive-Focus*, *Negative-Focus*, and *Ironical* tags groups).
- Since tags represent audience reactions, in principle, there is an evident high interannotator agreement. In some sense, it is the audience itself that annotates the corpus.

As for the problem of label informativeness, especially if focusing on the problem of mistimed applause, it should be noted that there are no explicit annotations on applause duration, delay, or similar in this corpus (see e.g., Atkinson 1984), so it is difficult to state if and when there has been a mismatching. Still, we believe that for our purposes, this is not a problem, because persuasive dynamics are still present. An *interruptive applause* indicates that there has been an impact on the audience even if not intended by the speaker. A *delayed applause* indicates that there has been a persuasive attempt that has not been promptly recognized by the audience.

For further details and discussions about the corpus, please see (Guerini et al. 2008a).

18.4 EXPLOITING THE CORPUS

In analyzing CORPS, the focus has been posed on the lexical level, both from a persuasive and affective point of view, and just in part on the syntactic level. Exploitation for NLG is briefly mentioned in the conclusions.

To reduce data sparseness, we used a lemmatizer and a part-of-speech tagger on the whole corpus, which gave for each token in the text the corresponding lemma and pos. So, at the lexical level, we considered lemmata (e.g., the verb to *win*) rather than *tokens* (i.e., the form of the word, as it appears in the text: *win, wins, won*). In the following sections, if not differently stated, the term *word* indicates a *lemma#pos*—where pos can be *v* for verbs, *a* for adjectives, *r* for adverbs and *n* for nouns. So the word *to win* is represented as *win#v*. In the lexical analysis, we further considered the following:

- Windows of different width *wn* (where *wn* is the number of tokens considered) preceding audience reactions tags
- Typology of persuasive communication (audience reaction).

As for what concerns the last point in this list, we individuate three main groups of tags:

- *Positive-Focus*: This group indicates a persuasive attempt that sets a positive focus in the audience. Tags considered (about 16,000): (APPLAUSE), (SPONTANEOUS-DEMONSTRATION), (STANDING-OVATION), (CHEERING), and so on.
- *Negative-Focus*: It indicates a persuasive attempt that sets a negative focus in the audience. Note that the negative focus is set toward the object of the speech and not on the speaker themselves (e.g., "Do we want more taxes?") Tags considered (about 100): (BOOING), (AUDIENCE) No! (/AUDIENCE).
- *Ironical*: Indicate the use of ironical devices in persuasion. Tags considered (about 4000): (LAUGHTER).[1]

It should be noted that, rhetorically, positive-focus reactions can be obtained also by means of (sub) fragments of speech that set a temporary negative focus in the audience, or even by means of a complete focusing on negative aspects (usually political opponents' behavior). In fact, about 30% of the time, the rhetorical device

---

[1] If LAUGHTER appears in a multiple tag (e.g., together with APPLAUSE), by default, this tag is associated to the ironical group. This is not the case for BOOING that occurs always alone.

used in political speeches to evoke applauses is *contrast*; see Atkinson (1984) and Heritage and Greatbatch (1986). Let us consider the speech that John F. Kennedy gave in Berlin on the June 26, 1963, and in particular, the following fragment that led to a (APPLAUSE ; CHEERS) reaction:

> Freedom has many difficulties and democracy is not perfect. But we have never had to put a wall up to keep our people in—to prevent them from leaving us.

This fragment sets a double negative focus. First, by means of a *concession*, Kennedy sets a negative focus on the limits of the American social model: "*Freedom has many difficulties and democracy is not perfect,*" then by means of a *contrast* he sets a stronger negative focus on the Soviet social model: "*But we have never had to put a wall up to keep our people in—to prevent them from leaving us.*" Still, the overall effect of the fragment, based on an implicit *concession* and an explicit *contrast*, is to set people to a positive point of view on the American social model.

18.5   CORPS AND PERSUASIVE EXPRESSION MINING

Though there have been various works focusing on the lexical level of political speeches, for example, Laver et al. (2003), and subsequent works, such as Martin and Vanberg (2007), those works were focused only on political position recognition, a task similar to text categorization, and they treated all the words as potentially equivalent, leaving aside aspects such as emotional content or, more generally, persuasive impact. For the analyses presented hereafter, we used the following resources and tools:

(a) The TextPro package to perform lemmatization, POS analysis, named-entity recognition, and sentence splitting; see Pianta and Zanoli (2007).
(b) SentiWordNet[2] scores (Esuli and Sebastiani 2006) to compute the valence of speeches lexical entries (words).

An example of SentiWordNet items is given in Table 18.1. We conducted a preliminary analysis of the corpus focusing on the relation between valence and persuasion:

TABLE 18.1. Examples of SentiWordNet Entries

POS	Offset	PosScore	NegScore	SynsetTerms
a	602,378	0.0	0.875	wrong#a#1 incorrect#a#1
r	60,640	0.75	0.0	better#r#1
n	7,017,251	0.0	0.0	victory#n#1 triumph#n#1

---

[2] *WordNet* is a large lexical database of English. Nouns, verbs, adjectives, and adverbs are grouped into sets of cognitive synonyms (synsets), each expressing a distinct concept and indexed by an offset. Synsets are interlinked by means of conceptual semantic and lexical relations. *SentiWordNet* is a lexical resource in which each WordNet synset is associated to three numerical scores: Obj(s), Pos(s), and Neg(s). These scores represent the objective, positive, and negative valence of the synset. Each entry takes the form *lemma#pos#sense-number*.

The phase that leads to audience reaction (e.g., APPLAUSE), if it presents valence dynamics, is characterized by a valence crescendo. That is to say, persuasion is not necessarily achieved via modification of valence intensity, but, when this is the case, it is by means of an increase in the valence of the fragment of speech.

To come to this result, we computed, for every window, its mean valence ($\bar{w}$), calculated by summing up all the valences of the lemmata (SentiWordNet scores) corresponding to the tokens in the fragment and divided by wn, and subtracted the mean valence of the corresponding speech ($\bar{s}$). In this way, we obtained two classes of windows:

- Windows with mean-valence above the mean-valence of the speech ($\bar{w} > \bar{s}$).
- Windows with mean-valence below the mean-valence of the speech ($\bar{s} > \bar{w}$).

We then summed up all the values for the two classes and normalized the results by dividing it by the total number of cases in the class (nc). We repeated the procedure for various window widths ($5 < wn < 40$); see Equation 18.1. The results show that cases above the speech mean are fewer but far stronger. We are planning to have a finer-grained analysis by means of cluster-based approaches and variable window width.

$$y = \frac{\sum \text{abs} |\bar{w} - \bar{s}|}{n_c} \quad x = wn. \tag{18.1}$$

We then focused on the impact of the lexicon used in the speeches, assuming that for persuasive purposes (both in analysis and generation), not all the words have the same importance. Generally speaking, the idea is that a word is more persuasive if at the same time it appears close to audience reactions tags and it does not occur far from them. We extracted persuasive words by using a coefficient of persuasive impact (pi) based on a weighted tf-idf (term frequency-inverse document frequency) (see Eq. 18.2, $pi = \text{tf} \cdot \text{idf}$). With a similar approach, we also extracted persuasive bigrams, trigrams, and collocations, but for the sake of exposition, we limit our discussion to single words, since the reasoning can be generalized to these groups.

$$\text{tf}_i = \frac{n_i \cdot \sum_{n_i} s_i}{\sum_k n_k} \quad \text{idf}_i = \log \frac{|D|}{|\{d : d \ni t_i\}|}. \tag{18.2}$$

The tf-idf weight is a statistical measure used to evaluate how important a word is to a document in a corpus. To calculate the tf-idf weight, we created a virtual document by unifying all the tokens inside all the windows (of dimension $wn = 15$) preceding audience reactions tags, and considering the number of documents in the corpus as coincident to the number of speeches plus one (the virtual document). Obviously, from the speeches, we subtracted those pieces of text that were used to form the virtual document. Given this premise, we can now define the terms in Equation 18.2:

- n_i = number of times the term (word) t_i appears in the virtual document
- $\sum n_i s_i$ = sum of the scores of the word (the closer to the tag, the higher the score)

TABLE 18.2. List of the Most Persuasive Words

Positive-Focus Words	Negative-Focus Words
bless#v deserve#v victory#n justice#n fine#a relief#n November#n win#v help#n thanks#n glad#a stop#v better#r congressman#n lady#n regime#n fabulous#a uniform#n military#a wrong#a soul#n lawsuit#n welcome#v appreciate#v Bush#n behind#r grateful#a 21st#a defend#v responsible#a safe#a terror#n cause#n bridge#n prevail#v choose#v hand#n love#v frivolous#a sir#n honor#n defeat#v end#v fight#n no#r Joe#n ready#a wear#v future#a direction#n foreign#a death#n single#a democratic#a	household#n Neill#n equivalent#n running#a mate#n horrible#a live#a tip#n criticize#v waste#n page#n front#a opponent#n timidity#n shuttle#n erode#v torpor#n Soviets#n invasion#n scout#n violation#n Castro#n troop#n authority#n Guevara#n Kaufman#n Sachs#n Goldman#n ferociously#r solvent#n international#a direction#n monstrosity#n Cambodia#n unbearable#a drilling#n Soviet#a increase#v intelligence-gathering#a Carolina#n Gerald#n trusted#a drift#n operation#n WTO#n entry#n mcgovern#v coward#n

- $\sum_{\kappa} n_k$ = the number of occurrences of all words = $wn \cdot |\text{tags number}|$
- $|D|$ = total number of speeches in the corpus (included the virtual document)
- $|(d : d \ni t_i)|$ = number of documents where the term t_i appears (we made a hypothesis of equidistribution).

Four lists of words were created according to the group of audience reactions tags they refer to: positive-focus words, negative-focus words, ironical words, and a persuasive words list—computed by considering all tags together. Analyzing the 100 top words of these lists, ordered according to their *pi* score, we found that the negative valence mean of positive-focus and negative-focus groups is the same, while for the negative-focus group the positive valence mean is about 1/4 with regard to the positive-focus group (*t*-test; $\alpha < 0.01$).

These results could be explained by a high use of the CONTRAST relation (that brings negatively valenced words when talking about opponents) in the positive-focus group, while this is not the case for the negative-focus group. In Table 18.2, a comparison between the positive-focus and negative-focus top 50 most persuasive words is given (note that named entities have not been discarded). It is arguable whether these words are "universally" persuasive (i.e., they could be biased by speaker style, audience typology, context of use, and so on). To partially overcome the problem, the corpus was balanced by choosing speakers that are equally distributed within the two major parties in the United States (Democratic and Republican). At present, we do not address negation, hypothetical clauses, and similar topics, but we believe that they do not invalidate the *pi* of a word. Let us hypothesize that the word *bad#a* has a high *pi* in the positive-focus list, and the word is mainly used in contexts like *not bad*. The word *bad#a* should not be discarded from the positive-focus list, rather its co-occurrence score in the bigram with *no#r* should be considered.

18.6   CORPS AND QUALITATIVE ANALYSIS OF PERSUASIVE COMMUNICATION

Often, the user is interested in *interpreting* the information once it has been retrieved. Let us consider the example of a user who wants to find "when President Bush uttered the word *war*." The retrieved information alone does not tell much about the context and the dynamic use of this word. Our goal is to support information extraction with data that helps the user in making sense of the content retrieved (e.g., the role of the words in the social context). Analysis of public reaction can substantiate intuitions about the speaker's use of such words. In general, there are several possibilities, like synchronous and asynchronous comparisons, both inter- and intra-speaker.

Given the formal annotation of the corpus together with the *pi* measure we presented, this analysis can be made automatically on a large scale, allowing the user to gain interesting insights. In fact, there are rhetorical phenomena that do not come into light with traditional approaches—based on the words' *usage* (counting their occurrences). Considering also the words' *impact* (their persuasiveness coefficient *pi*), a much finer analysis is possible. Examples are listed below.

18.6.1   How Do Political Speeches Change After Key Historical Events?

Some works, such as Bligh et al. (2004), investigated the lexicon of Bush's speeches before and after September 11, 2001 (9/11), with tools for automatic analysis of political discourses (DICTION 5.0) focusing on charisma traits. Using CORPS, and analyzing some of the speeches of George W. Bush before and after 9/11 (70 speeches before and 70 after, from 12 months before to 16 months after) at the lexical level, we found that while the positive valence mean remains totally unvaried, the negative mean increased by 15 percent (*t*-test; $\alpha < 0.001$). Then we ran a quantitative/qualitative analysis on Bush's persuasive words before and after 9/11 to understand how his rhetoric changed, making two lists of persuasive words, one for the speeches before 9/11 and another for the speeches after 9/11. We focused on some paradigmatic words and found interesting results.

The words are presented in Table 18.3. In the first column, there is the *lemma#pos* (word), in the second and third columns, its position (persuasiveness)[3] in the lists before and after 9/11, and in the fourth and fifth columns, the number of occurrences in the speeches. An *x* indicates that the word is not persuasive (i.e., when it appears in the corpus but never in proximity of an audience reaction, the persuasiveness ceases around position 2500 in the lists). A hyphen indicates the word is not present in the corpus at all. Bligh et al. (2004) followed a simple approach based on word usage. Here, instead, we adopted also the words' impact, and created for every word a matrix that records an increase or decrease of use compared with an increase or decrease of persuasiveness. Some interesting phenomena emerged. Let us consider the words *military#n* or *treat#v*. Both words are used almost the same number of times before and after 9/11 (respectively 23 vs. 29 times and 25 vs. 20 times). So their informativeness, based on number of occurrences, is null. But considering the persuasiveness score, we see that their impact varies quite a bit (respectively from

---

[3] We use the rank in the list, instead of the *pi*, for readability purposes.

TABLE 18.3. Bush's Words Before and After September

Lemma	Ranking Before	Ranking After	Occur Before	Occur After
win#v	112	7	27	52
justice#n	x	9	15	111
prevail#v	x	15	2	20
defeat#v	x	16	1	44
right#r	x	25	94	55
taliban#n	x	27	1	44
mighty#a	615	30	4	26
military#n	197	36	23	29
victory#n	826	65	9	26
evil#a	–	129	0	44
death#n	4	450	65	32
war#n	36	X	80	258
soldier#n	70	296	20	47
tax#n	x	93	702	81
refund#n	15	–	10	0
wage#n	121	–	4	0
drug-free#a	87	X	9	3
commander-in-chief#n	76	850	25	14
leadership#n	81	261	40	75
future#n	83	394	54	51
dream#n	99	321	77	30
soul#n	23	126	47	32
generation#n	122	442	27	56

position 197 to 36 and from 54 to 473). Let us also consider the word *tax#n*. If we examine only the number of its occurrences, we could infer that before 9/11 this topic was much more important than after (702 occurrences vs. 81). However, if we focus on persuasiveness, we see that before 9/11 the word *tax#n* never got audiences' reactions, while after 9/11 it became very popular (position 93).

Surprisingly, the same, but in an opposite direction, holds for *war#n*: mentioned three times more after 9/11 (80 vs. 254), but never got applause (while before 9/11 it was one of the topmost persuasive words, after 9/11, its *pi* decreased to 0).

The results were divided in four blocks, according to thematic areas. In the first block, there are words that became very popular after 9/11. They usually (indirectly) refer to war, usually from a positive point of view. These words were not considered before 9/11 (i.e., *justice#n* was not persuasive at all before 9/11, but jumped to the ninth position after; at the same time, its frequency increased 10 times after the attack).

The second block represents words that were popular before the attack but became unutterable after 9/11 (e.g., *death#n* fell from position 4 to 450, with the frequency cut in half). These words generally refer to the negative aspects of war or to war itself. The third block contains some words that represent the shift in the political agenda before and after 9/11: taxation, contrasting drugs use, and leadership. The fourth block shows some abstract and moving words that became less used and popular after 9/11, partially in contrast to the findings of Bligh et al. (2004).

18.6.2 What Can Be Said of the Lexical Choices of a Specific Speaker Who Obtains a Certain Characteristic Pattern of Public Reaction?

Ronald Reagan was known as "the great communicator." His rhetorics has been the focus of many qualitative research studies, for example, Collier (2006); such research has also focused on particular aspects of his style, for example, irony; see Weintraub (1986) and Stevenson (2004). We tried to test whether these findings were consistent with our corpus. By considering 32 of Ronald Reagan's speeches, we first found that the mean tag density of this collection is one-half of the mean tag density of the whole corpus (t-test; $\alpha < 0.001$). At first sight, this result is somewhat strange, because his being a "great communicator" is not bound to his "firing up" rate (far below the average rate of others speakers). But interestingly, focusing only on the subgroup of ironical tags, we found that the density in Reagan's speeches is almost double than the one of the whole corpus (t-test; $\alpha < 0.001$). The results are even more striking if they are compared with the mean ironical tags ratio mtr_i (the mean of the ratio of ironical tags to positive-focus and negative-focus tags per speech; see Eq. 18.3) of the two groups.

$$mtr_i \sum \frac{|\text{ironical} - \text{tags}|}{|\text{positive} - \text{focus}| + |\text{negative} - \text{focus}|}. \tag{18.3}$$

In Reagan's speeches, the mtr_i is about 7.5 times greater than the mtr_i of the whole corpus (about 3.5 vs. about 0.5; t-test; $\alpha < 0.001$). That is to say, while normally there is one tag of LAUGHTER for every two other tags, such as APPLAUSE, in Reagan's speeches, there is one tag, such as APPLAUSE, for every three or four tags of LAUGHTER.

With regard to Reagan's overall style, his criterion was, "Would you talk that way to your barber?" as reported in Collier (2006). He wanted his style to appear "simple and conversational." To verify this statement, we made a hypothesis that a simple and conversational style is more polysemic than a "cultured" style (richer in technical and unambiguous terms). We first calculated the mean polysemy of Reagan's speeches and compared it with the mean polysemy of the whole corpus, finding no statistical difference between the two; also, in this case, word usage analysis was not informative. Then we focused on the persuasive lexicon: We made a list of Reagan's persuasive words and compared it with the persuasive words list of the rest of the corpus (we considered all the words whose pi was not 0). We found that the mean polysemy of Reagan's persuasive words is almost double as compared with the whole corpus (t-test; $\alpha < 0.001$).

18.6.3 How Does the Perception of the Enemy Change in Different Historical Moments?

A specific analysis on the valence of the lexical context surrounding named entities that elicit negative-focus audience reactions in different periods of time can provide interesting insights. Looking at Table 18.2, it is clear that there are various named entities in the list of negative-focus words at the topmost positions, while this is not the case for positive-focus words. Given the small amount of negative-focus tags, our approach will include a second, inductive analysis step: After singling out named entities that elicit negative-focus reactions (i.e., the "enemies"), those same entities will be searched in the corpus (in the surroundings of positive-focus tags) by assuming that they are inserted in a CONTRAST relation, which sets a temporary negative focus on enemies' behavior, as described earlier in this chapter.

For the moment, we drove a small analysis on the use of negative-focus tags to single out "enemies." First, we used EntityPro to individuate named entities. Then we selected the two most "persuasive persons" found in positive and negative-focus persuasive words lists: Bush and Castro. Using the NLTK package, we extracted the 100 most similar words to these entities, and scored them using SentiWordNet.

The results shows that while for Castro the positive and negative affective score means—of similar words—are quite balanced (0.025 and 0.026 respectively), for Bush, there is a huge discrepancy (0.036 vs. 0.017). The positive mean for Bush is 70% more, and the negative is 65% less, with respect to Castro.

While these findings could have been intuitively expected (Castro has been one of the most despised enemies of the United States, and so of the majority of speakers considered), the use of negative-focus tag can help finding relations between adverse positions in unknown domains.

18.7   PREDICTING AUDIENCE REACTION

In this section, we explore the use of machine learning techniques for predicting the persuasive impact of novel speeches in terms of audience reactions. In particular, we conducted a series of experiments on the corpus and explored the feasibility of:

(a) Predicting the passages in the discourses that trigger positive audience reactions

(b) Distinguishing in the corpus Democrats from Republicans

(c) Checking audience reaction prediction if training is made on adverse party speeches (e.g., training on Republican speeches and testing on Democratic ones)

(d) Experimenting the classifiers on plain and typical nonpersuasive texts taken from the British National Corpus (BNC) and on speeches from the Obama–McCain political campaign.

For all the experiments, we used the support vector machines (SVM) framework, in particular SVM-light, under its default settings (Joachims 1998). As for data set preprocessing, also in this case, to reduce the sparseness, we considered *lemma#pos* instead of tokens. In these experiments, we included all the tokens, that is, we did not make any frequency cutoff or feature selection. Then we divided all the speeches into fragments of about four sentences (if a tag is present in the fragment the chunk ends at that point). The obtained chunks are then labeled as Neutral (i.e., no tag), and Positive-ironical (i.e., all *positive-focus* and *ironical* audience reactions). In the experiments, we did not consider the *negative-focus* tags, since they are only a few.

Finally, we got a total of 37,480 four-sentence chunks, roughly equally partitioned into the two considered labels. This accounts for a baseline of 0.5 in distinguishing between Neutral and Positive-ironical chunks. In all the experiments, we randomly split the corpus in 80% training and 20% test.

TABLE 18.4. Republicans versus Democrats (4-Sentence Chunks)

	Precision	Recall	$F1$
Democrats	0.842	0.756	0.797
Republicans	0.773	0.854	0.811
Micro average	0.804	0.804	0.804

TABLE 18.5. Positive-Ironical versus Neutral (4-Sentence Chunks: Republican/Democrat Corpus)

	Precision	Recall	$F1$
Positive-ironical	0.646	0.683	0.664
Neutral	0.676	0.641	0.658
Micro average	0.660	0.660	0.660

TABLE 18.6. Positive-Ironical versus Neutral (4-Sentence Chunks: Republicans Only)

	Precision	Recall	$F1$
Positive-ironical	0.660	0.766	0.709
Neutral	0.663	0.549	0.601
Micro average	0.661	0.661	0.661

18.7.1 Experiments on CORPS

18.7.1.1 Democrats versus Republicans First, we simply tested the separation between Democratic and Republican speeches. This experiment was mainly conducted to see if the SVM setting, used for the following experiments, suitably distinguishes between the two parties, given that the topics dealt with by the speakers are often quite similar. The corpus contains a total of 18,384 chunks coming from Republican speeches and 19,096 Democratic ones. From Table 18.4, we see that four-sentences chunks are enough to distinguish between Republicans and Democrats, with a performance of 0.804 ($F1$ measure).

18.7.1.2 Positive Audience Reaction Then we tested the capability to predict a positive audience reaction. As explained above in this case, the tags to be classified are Neutral and Positive-ironical. First, we experimented on the entire corpus (Table 18.5), then we split the corpus in two: Democrats and Republicans. So we verified the classification on the two different parts separately (Tables 18.6 and 18.7) and in addition on the case of cross-classification (i.e., training on Democrats and testing on Republicans and vice versa—Tables 18.8 and 18.9). In all cases, we randomly split in 80/20 training–test partition. We see that the persuasive impact of speeches is quite general, and, as shown in the cross-classification results, to a certain degree independent from the party of the speakers.

TABLE 18.7. Positive-Ironical versus Neutral (4-Sentence Chunks: Democrats Only)

	Precision	Recall	$F1$
Positive-ironical	0.666	0.674	0.670
Neutral	0.686	0.680	0.683
Micro average	0.676	0.676	0.676

TABLE 18.8. Positive-Ironical versus Neutral (4-Sentence Chunks: Training on Democrats, Test on Republicans)

	Precision	Recall	$F1$
Positive-ironical	0.642	0.632	0.637
Neutral	0.579	0.599	0.589
Micro average	0.612	0.612	0.612

TABLE 18.9. Positive-Ironical versus Neutral (4-Sentence Chunks: Training on Republicans, Test on Democrats)

	Precision	Recall	$F1$
Positive-ironical	0.625	0.660	0.642
Neutral	0.658	0.626	0.641
Micro average	0.641	0.641	0.641

TABLE 18.10. Classification on BNC

Total chunks	7,243
Positive-ironical	784
Neutral	6,459
Prec/Rec/$F1$	0.892

18.7.2 Exploiting the Classifier

18.7.2.1 Testing on Nonpersuasive Texts
In order to test the capabilities of distinguishing persuasive from nonpersuasive texts, we conducted some experiments, running the classifier, trained on CORPS, on about 7300 four-sentence chunks extracted from typical nonpersuasive texts of the BNC,[4] so labeled as Neutral. Table 18.10 summarizes the results.

18.7.2.2 Obama/McCain Presidential Campaign
As a last experiment, we could not refrain from testing the classifier trained on CORPS for Obama's and McCain's speeches taken from the latest presidential campaign. These speeches

---

[4] We extract the chunks from A00 to A0H texts of BNC sources.

TABLE 18.11. Classification on Obama/McCain Campaign Speeches

	Obama	McCain
Positive-ironical	2372	2360
Neutral	68	80
Total chunks	2,440	2,440

were not labeled (i.e., it was not possible to train the classifier on that specific political campaign), so the experiment should be regarded as a generic test. The speeches were divided into four sentence chunks similarly to other data sets. The results show that the persuasive content of the speeches was quite high, with slightly better results for Obama.

18.8 CONCLUSIONS AND FUTURE WORK

We have presented the CORPS corpus, which contains political speeches tagged with audience reactions. CORPS is freely available for research purposes (for further details, see http://hlt.fbk.eu/corps), and we want to promote its scaling up. Along with the corpus, we have described techniques for statistical acquisition of persuasive lexical expressions (such as a measure of persuasive impact of words) and for predicting audience reactions when the audio source is not available. Our aim is to contribute to various persuasive NLP tasks. Effective expressions are of paramount importance in this context; still, there are many challenges to face in future research.

18.8.1 Bottleneck of Manual Transcription

Manually transcribed and annotated speeches are present on the Web, but they are limited, given the cost of their creation. Automatic tools are necessary. There are two possible ways:

- If only the audio source is available, tools for automatic transcription and automatic detection of audience reactions can be used. Projects facing the problem have delivered good results. See Chapter 14.
- If only the text is available, either a new text as prepared for delivery, or, in case audio sources are not available, approaches for predicting audience reaction can be used (as described in the previous section).

18.8.2 Enriching the Corpus with Other Nonlexical Information

The proposed techniques focus on the information coming from audience reaction and of course can be integrated with other nonlexical information about the speaker output. Rhetorical artifices expressed with prosody and other speech features are used to highlight key passages of a speech. Tagging the corpus with these pieces of information could foster analysis in a way that complements what tags about audience reaction do. The integration of these features is an open issue. For example, multidimensional vectors for words can be used (using a "rhetorical stressing" measure in addition to occurrences counting and persuasive impact). Interesting approaches for recognizing such features about speaker rhetorics can be found in Chapter 14.

In the present work, we have limited ourselves to lexical analysis, and of course if the corpus is not big enough, this may lead to errors. In the long run, we will add more complex elements. We will possibly include syntactic constraints and negation and, most important, rhetorical analysis of the text. Of course, a larger wealth of information is available if we start from speech analysis and not just from more limited text transcriptions as mentioned above. Anyway, all these more complex techniques will further help identify persuasive lexemes and more in general model persuasive expression understanding and production.

As for exploitation of this work, we focus on tasks related to NLG. For the problem of lexical choice, techniques that use corpus and domain information for choosing appropriate lemmata inside synsets has been proposed, among others, by Jing (1998). In our approach, lexical choice is performed on the basis of lemma impact rather than lemma use (the lemma with the highest pi is extracted). If the typology of persuasive communicative goal is specified (positive-focus, negative-focus, and ironical), the choice can be further refined by selecting the lemma according to the specific pi (i.e., accessing the proper list of persuasive words). These strategies are implemented in the Valentino prototype (Guerini et al. 2008b), and are going to be added to the realization component of the existing Promoter prototype (Guerini et al. 2007). It is also worth reporting that with a methodology similar to the one used for persuasive words, we also extracted chunks of persuasive sentences. We plan to use these chunks for extracting high impact sequences of words and rhetorical patterns. In particular, we want to (1) understand if the results presented by Atkinson (1984) and by Heritage and Greatbatch (1986) about rhetorical devices used to provoke audience reactions can be replicated/verified on a larger scale corpus, and (2) refine the analysis by focusing on complex patterns of rhetorical relations.

Another kind of application scenario is based on this work as a key component of a summarization system that relies on audience reaction tags for extracting automatically key material from political speeches.

A similar concept can be used where the material, instead of being just bound to linguistic communication, includes also a visual component. For instance, the camera may zoom in on the speaker when applause underlines the effectiveness of his speech. Or, working on material produced at different times, rhetorical contradictions in one speaker may be made apparent, by reasoning on extracted material, as said above, and assembling those key passages of the speeches that emphasize discrepancy over time.

CHAPTER 19

THE NEED FOR AFFECTIVE METADATA IN CONTENT-BASED RECOMMENDER SYSTEMS FOR IMAGES

MARKO TKALČIČ, JURIJ TASIČ, and ANDREJ KOŠIR

19.1 INTRODUCTION

Services that provide digital images like Flickr or Facebook are attracting more and more users that generate content. For example, Flickr provides more than 3 billion of photos while Facebook provides more than 10 billion of photos (Flickr 2008). End users are obviously lost in these huge image databases. In order to help end users find the images that are relevant for them, a recommender system could be applied (Leavitt 2006).

State-of-the-art content-based recommender (CBR) systems rely on image meta-data that are available along with the images. These data are stored in item profiles. Based on the users' past choices, user profiles are generated. These profiles contain the users' preferences toward various metadata values. One user might prefer images with calming content, like mountain landscapes, while another user might prefer photos depicting people. The most used metadata attribute in CBR systems is the *genre*. User profiles typically contain a vector of numbers representing the degree of agreeableness of the user with different genre types (Adomavicius and Tuzhilin 2005; Lew et al. 2006; Pogačnik and Tasič 2005; Pogačnik et al. 2005).

Recommender systems that exploit the genre attribute of images have reached a certain level of performance that appears to be the upper limit according to Lew et al. (2006). In order to improve the quality of predictions of CBR systems, a better set of image attributes should be used (Lew et al. 2006). There have been attempts to model the users with affective metadata (González et al. 2004). Limited research has been done on the automatic extraction of induced emotive states from multi-media content (Hanjalić 2006), while there is increasing effort being put in the research of emotion detection of users from multiple modalities (Picard and Daily

Multimedia Information Extraction: Advances in Video, Audio, and Imagery Analysis for Search, Data Mining, Surveillance, and Authoring, First Edition. Edited by Mark T. Maybury.
© 2012 IEEE Computer Society. Published 2012 by John Wiley & Sons, Inc.

2005; Zeng et al. 2009). Despite all the knowledge on the affective representation of users and content, it has not been used widely in the context of recommender systems. The web radio application *Musicovery* makes use of affective metadata of songs for the visualization of music (Musicovery 2010).

We propose to make use of affective metadata to describe multimedia items and users. The underlying assumption is that human decision making (in our case the selection of a multimedia item to consume) is influenced by emotions (Bechara et al. 2000; Naqvi et al. 2006). We present the results of the CBR system experiment for images that uses attributes that describe the induced emotive responses in end users for each image in the database. Experimental results show that the performance of such a recommender system is significantly better than the standard genre-based CBR. Based on the presented results, we argue that there is a strong need for methods for the extraction of affective features from multimedia content. Recommender systems can exploit these features by giving a boost to services that provide digital images.

19.1.1   Related Work

Recommender systems are a well-developed area of research although there still are barriers that do not allow them to find their way on the market. There is considerable literature available on the subject (Adomavicius and Tuzhilin 2005; Burke 2002; Herlocker et al. 2004; Lew et al. 2006; Pazzani and Billsus 2007). Recommender systems are roughly divided into content-based recommender systems and collaborative filtering (CF) systems. CBR systems analyze the content's metadata to identify items that may be interesting to a user (Adomavicius and Tuzhilin 2005; Pazzani and Billsus 2007). CF systems recommend items that users with similar tastes have liked in the past (Adomavicius and Tuzhilin 2005). A taxonomy of recommender systems based on the task they perform, for example, *find all good items* or *recommend sequence*, has been proposed (Herlocker et al. 2004). The recommendation problem is described as the problem of estimating ratings for items that have not been consumed by a user (Adomavicius and Tuzhilin 2005). The main drawback of recommender systems is their relatively low performance (in terms of the most frequently used scalar measures *precision*, *recall* and *F-measure*), especially in generic applications. Several reasons for the recommenders' low performance have been identified by Adomavicius and Tuzhilin (2005): (1) the limited content analysis (noninformative metadata attributes), (2) overspecialization (the system recommends items that are not diverse enough), (3) cold start problem (when a new user or item is added to the system there is not enough knowledge in the system to perform well), and (4) data sparsity (when the system has lots of items, lots of users, but very few ratings to rely on). Several approaches to work around the mentioned reasons for low performance have been suggested by (Lew et al. 2006). They suggest improving along two lines: (1) by improving the algorithms and (2) by creating new features that describe the items. They suggest using color features, texture histograms, shape features, and audio features. They also point out the importance of the semantic meaning of the features (Lew et al. 2006). The main motivation for the inclusion of affective metadata in recommender system is the fact that human decision making is strongly influenced by emotions (Bechara et al. 2000; Naqvi et al. 2006). One of the first attempts to use affective attributes in recommender systems was done by González et al. (2004). They introduced the *smart user model* (SUM) as a collection of key–value pairs describing degrees of inclination toward specific emotional components. In order to apply affective user models in CBR systems, content items need to be annotated with affective metadata. The item's affective attributes describe the induced emotive state in end users. Researchers have taken two approaches: (1) the automatic extraction of the induced emotive state from the content itself or (2) the detection of the end user emotive response while consuming an item through various sensors. In 2005, Hanjalić et al. (Hanjalić and Xu 2005) ascertained that there was little knowledge about the relation between low-level features and induced affect. Since then, they developed a method for the automatic extraction of salient moments (moments with strong arousal) from football video clips. Much more research has been done in trying to detect the emotive response of a user from various modalities, like body sensors, voice, or video (Castellano et al. 2008; Mcintyre and Gocke 2008; Picard and Daily 2005; Vogt et al. 2008). The turning point was when Picard coined the term *affective computing* and paved the way for research in the field of affective human computer interaction (Picard 1997). Since then, many methods have been developed, and a good overview is given in Zeng et al. (2009). Despite all the efforts done in trying to automatically detect emotive states of users from various sources the output format of these detectors appears to be rather vaguely defined. There is still a dispute on the taxonomy of emotions. One popular line of describing emotions is the basic-emotions approach. Started already by Charles Darwin (Darwin 1872), it was further developed and consolidated by Paul Ekman (Ekman 1999). While within the basic emotion field scientist cannot agree on the number of relevant and distinct emotions (Schröder et al. 2008), the most commonly used are *surprise, fear, disgust, anger, happiness,* and *sadness* (Ekman and Friesen 2003). The basic emotions theory is largely based on facial expressions, which was Darwin's starting point. An important milestone was done by Ekman when he specified the *Facial Action Coding System* (FACS), a collection of movements of characteristic face points in different emotive states (Ekman et al. 2002). Another approach is to model an emotive state as a vector in a three-dimensional space with the base vectors being *valence, arousal,* and *dominance* (thus the name VAD space), well described by Posner et al. (2005). They argue that the VAD space is supported by physiological evidence that there are three distinct brain circuits that manage the emotive state of humans. They further propose the circumplex model of emotions which maps the basic emotions into the valence-arousal plane of the VAD space which can be seen in Figure 19.3. An XML based standard for the description of emotive states, the *EmotionML*, is being proposed within the W3C (Schröder et al. 2008). It allows recording the emotive states in a variety of ways including the VAD and basic emotions.

19.1.2 Improving the CBR Performance with Affective Metadata

In this chapter, we will take a closer look at how a CBR system's performance can be improved by introducing affective metadata. In fact, features that are currently used in CBR systems to describe the content, like title, release date, and genre used in the most widely used data set for recommender systems (MovieLens 2009), do not allow recommender algorithms to effectively distinguish relevant items from nonrelevant ones for a specific user. As pointed out by Lew et al. (2006), new features should be sought to improve the performance of CBR systems.

The presented solution uses *affective features* to describe the content items in order to improve the performance of a CBR system. Our hypothesis testing was based on a data set of real users consuming images and giving explicit ratings. We compared the quality of the recommended set of items given by a CBR using two distinct feature sets: (1) a genre-based feature set and (2) an affective plus genre-based feature set. According to the nature of user modeling-related data, there was a need for statistical testing in order to prove the difference between the two feature sets, that is, without and with affective parameters. We validated the proposed procedures on the computed confusion matrices. We first computed the scalar measures *precision* (P), *recall* (R), and F-*measure* (F), and then applied the Pearson χ^2 significance test on the confusion matrices. The results of statistical testing proved that the proposed CBR performs significantly better when affective features are applied in the content description compared with the standard features based on the genre.

19.2   AFFECTIVE-BASED CBR SYSTEMS

19.2.1   Usage Scenario of an Image CBR System

When a user is faced with a large database of images, she/he has a tough task of selecting items that are relevant for her/him. A CBR system performs a significant part of choosing relevant items by narrowing the set of images to a manageable amount. The usage scenario is depicted in Figure 19.1. The choice of the set of recommended items is done by an algorithm that classifies all unseen images by the user into relevant or nonrelevant. The relevant images compose the list of recommended items. The algorithm is based on the knowledge the system has about the

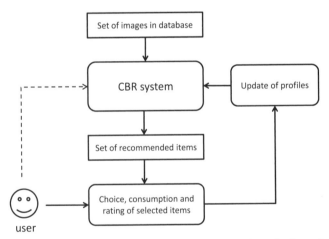

Figure 19.1. Usage scenario of a CBR system for image. Based on the knowledge about the items and users that is stored in the item and user profiles the CBR's algorithm extracts a set of recommended items for the selected user. After the user consumes the items the feedback (rating, emotive response) is used to update the item and user profiles.

TABLE 19.1. Example of an Item Profile

Metadata Field	Metadata Value
Image id	6910
Image tag	Bomber
Genre	Weapon
Watching time t_w	2614 ms
Watching time mean $\overline{t_w}$	5307 ms
Valence mean $\overline{v}$	5.31
Valence st. dev. σ_v	2.28
Arousal mean $\overline{a}$	5.62
Arousal st. dev. σ_a	2.46
Dominance mean $\overline{d}$	5.10
Dominance st. dev. σ_d	2.46

Several metadata key–value pairs are used to describe the knowledge the CBR has on a specific item.

images and the end users. This knowledge is stored in data structures called *item profiles* and *user profiles*.

19.2.2 CBR System

Let us have a set of J images in our database $H = \{h_1, h_2, \ldots h_J\}$. The item profile (metadata) of the image $h \in H$ is a data structure $md(h)$ that contains features (attributes) that describe the item $md(h) = \{a_1, a_2, \ldots a_N\}$. The attributes can be numerical, ordinal, or nominal. An example of an item profile (which has been used in the experiment described later on in Section 19.3) is shown in Table 19.1.

Based on where and how the attributes originate, we give the following taxonomy:

- *Production-Time Attributes*: Are generated at the production of the item (e.g., title, genre, author, date, or resolution).
- *Consumption-Time Attributes*: Are collected during and after the consumption of an image by the users (e.g., explicit ratings or watching times). In MPEG7, these attributes are implicitly included in the usage history.
- *Low-Level Attributes*: Are features extracted from the images using some automatic method (e.g., color, texture, or shape features).

The knowledge about the user u is stored in the user profile $up(u)$. User profiles do not have such a formal structure as item profiles do. They greatly depend on the implementation of the algorithm that predicts the relevancy of images. In the case of a tree classifier, the user profile has the form of a tree (see Figure 19.2), while in the case of the Naive Bayes classifier, it is a table with probabilities.

When calculating a list of recommended items for a specific user u, the CBR takes the set of items H and calculates the similarity measures between the user profile $up(u)$ and the item profiles $md(h)$ of the images in the set H, yielding a set of similarity values

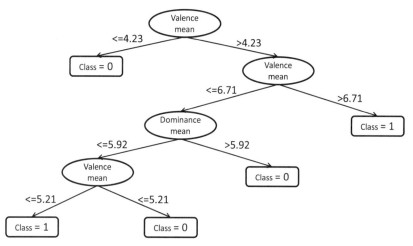

Figure 19.2. User model in the form of a decision tree: based on the metadata values of the item (valence mean, dominance mean), the tree classifier (like the C4.5) that contains the user-specific knowledge classifies the observed item into the class 1 (relevant) or 0 (nonrelevant).

$$\{s(md(h_i), up(u)) : h_i \in H\}.$$

Then, a mapping γ of the set of similarity values is applied. The target space of the mapping γ is the space of two classes $\Omega = \{c_0, c_1\}$, where c_0 represent the class of *nonrelevant items*, and c_1 represents the class of *relevant items*. The mapping yields us two sets of images: H_r and H_{nr}, relevant and nonrelevant, respectively

$$H_r = \{h_i \in H : \gamma(s(md(h_i), up(u))) = c_1\}$$
$$H_{nr} = \{h_i \in H : \gamma(s(md(h_i), up(u))) = c_0\}.$$

The set of relevant items H_r is offered to the user who then consumes some of the recommended items and provides the system with feedback information in an explicit (e.g., rating) or implicit (e.g., emotive response) form. This information is used to update the user and item profiles for better future performance.

19.2.3   Affective Attributes in Item Profiles

The usage of recommender systems that rely on the affective component of multimedia items and the user's response has been suggested already by Picard (1997) and Hanjalić and Xu (2005). It seems intuitively that an item's description with information about the end user's emotive response should resemble more closely the user's preferences than the item's description, with some technical metadata like genre, title, and the like.

Thus, our goal was to annotate the content items, images in our case, with information on how end users respond emotionally when they consume the items. The phenomenon is called *emotion induction* or *emotion elicitation*. The statistical moments of the emotive responses of many users consuming the same item are stored in the item's profile as affective features (see example in Table 19.1).

Despite the noncoherency of various definition of what emotion is (Posner et al. 2005), two distinct notations seem to be suitable for recording the emotive response in the context of user modeling for recommender systems. The first is the *basic emotions* approach, where an emotive response of a user u while watching the item h is the degree of affiliations with the basic emotions (usually surprise, fear, disgust, anger, happiness, and sadness). The second approach of recording an emotive state is a vector in the *VAD space*. The coordinates of the space, namely valence, arousal, and dominance, each describe a quality of the emotion and are believed to be connected with distinct circuitries in the brain (Posner et al. 2005). The value of the valence parameter tells us the position of the emotion on the pleasant–neutral–unpleasant axis. Arousal describes the strength (or activation) of the emotive state, while dominance tells us how much a person is in control of her/his emotions (whether she/he can dominate the emotions). It was showed how the two approaches can be merged into a unified circumplex model of emotions by mapping the basic emotions into the valence–arousal plane of the VAD space (see Figure 19.3) (Posner et al. 2005). For instance, fear, as a basic emotion, has low valence (unpleasant), high arousal (very aroused), and low dominance (the emotion dominates the person more than the person can dominate the emotion).

Another issue in the recording of the affective state of users while consuming an item is the time dimension. In the case of longer consumption times, that is, when consuming movies, the emotive response is a sequence of emotive values that are induced in end users at various time points of the video sequence. In case of short consumption times, like for images, the emotive response is a single value in the selected emotive space.

In the experiment that supports this chapter, we chose to use the VAD space for the notation of emotive values. The main reason for this choice is that the

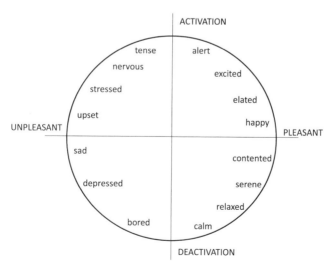

Figure 19.3. The circumplex model of emotions maps the basic emotions into the valence–arousal plane. Figure adapted from Posner et al. (2005).

space of basic emotions has few rough classes, while the VAD space can be segmented in smaller classes. This gives us the possibility of a more detailed analysis of the influence of the emotions on recommender systems that can be done in the future.

The structure of the set of metadata items MD can be either compliant with a metadata standard (TV anytime, MPEG-7, etc. [Martínez and Pereira 2002]) or custom designed. Since we proposed a new approach of modeling the item,s we also proposed a new metadata structure. We annotate each content item $h \in H$ with the genre, average watching time, and with features describing the user emotive response $= \mathcal{R}^6$. The set of metadata descriptions can be decomposed as $MD = A \times S$.

We denote the set of genres and watching times as $A = A_1 \times A_2$, where A_1 is a set of genres and $A_2 = \mathcal{R}_+$ represents the average watching time of all users who consumed the item. Each item has a genre attribute whose value is chosen from the set A_1.

In the absence of any knowledge about the suitability of different forms of affective parameters in recommender systems, we believe that the first two statistical moments of the VAD values carry the information needed for producing good recommendations. These parameters are also attractive to use because they can be easily calculated from the VAD values of the emotive responses of users (assuming that we have an automatic method for the detection of emotion in the VAD space). A further argument for the selection of the first two statistical moments is that they describe the common emotive response of users to an item. The concept is similar to the collaborative tagging known from the Web2.0 world (which should, intuitively, contribute more to the overall variance), as opposed to the tagging done by a single authority (whose contribution to the overall variance might be negligible).

We take all users $U_h \subset U$ who have consumed the item h, and we build the set of their emotive responses $V = \{(v, a, d)\}$ for the observed item h. For every item $h \in H$, we calculate the first two statistical moments of the emotive responses V, which yields us the vector of affective metadata for each item $s_h = \left(\bar{v}, \sigma_v, \bar{a}, \sigma_a, \bar{d}, \sigma_d\right)$, which is a 6-tuple in the space $S = \mathcal{R}^6$.

In the experiment part, we evaluated the performance of the CBR with two metadata sets: $MD_A = A$ and $MD_{AS} = A \times S$. The corresponding item profiles are the vectors $md_A(h) = (g, t_w)$ and $md_{AS}(h) = (g, t_w, \bar{v}, \sigma_v, \bar{a}, \sigma_a, \bar{d}, \sigma_d)$. Table 19.1 shows an example of the item profile.

19.2.4   Acquisition of Affective Features

The goal of the acquisition of affective features is to have an automatic method that yields information about affective responses of users similar to those in the International Affective Picture System (IAPS) database without the need for large experiments like the one performed by Lang et al. (2005). The IAPS database provides the first two statistical moments of the emotive responses of users in the VAD space (the mean and standard deviation for valence, arousal, and dominance) recorded using the Self-Assessment Manikin technique, where each user fills in a questionnaire after viewing an image from the database. Examples of values of these affective features that were used in our experiment can be seen in Tables 19.1 and 19.2.

TABLE 19.2. Excerpt from the Data Set

User id	Genre	t_w	$\bar{t}_w$	Rating	Image id	$\bar{v}$	δ_v	$\bar{a}$	δ_a	$\bar{d}$	δ_d
47	action	2848	2557.8	1	8370	7.77	1.29	6.73	2.24	5.37	2.02
47	action	1207	1946.8	1	5621	7.57	1.42	6.99	1.95	5.81	2.38
47	animal	2190	2698.4	0	1300	3.55	1.78	6.79	1.84	3.49	2.10
47	weapon	1426	2441.6	0	6230	2.37	1.57	7.35	2.01	2.15	2.09
48	weapon	2456	5307.2	0	6910	5.31	2.28	5.62	2.46	5.10	2.46
48	still	1874	2665.4	0	7052	4.93	0.81	2.75	1.80	5.82	1.93
48	animal	1599	3093.4	0	1280	3.66	1.75	4.93	2.01	5.05	2.20
48	action	2055	2857.1	0	3280	3.72	1.89	5.39	2.38	4.06	1.99

The five leftmost columns are the data acquired in our experiment while the seven rightmost columns are imported from the IAPS Data Set (refer to Table 19.1 for notations).

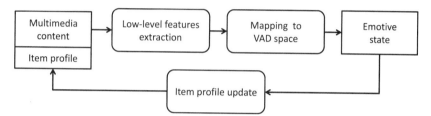

Figure 19.4. Extraction of affective metadata from multimedia content.

We propose two approaches for the extraction of affective features from images and other multimedia content: (1) extraction from content (direct extraction) and (2) extraction through users (indirect extraction).

The first approach (direct extraction) consists of the extraction of certain low-level features from the image items being consumed by users and then mapping them to the value of the induced emotive state in the VAD (or some other affective) space (see Figure 19.4).

So far no generic method for the successful extraction of affective data from multimedia content exists. For audio items, Picard reports that speech bears lots of affective information (Picard 1997; Picard and Daily 2005). Hanjalić tried to extract affective information from video clips, and showed that variations in shot lengths in soccer matches are a good indicator of the arousal component of the emotion experienced by viewers (Hanjalić 2006; Hanjalić and Xu 2005).

The second approach (indirect extraction) for the extraction of affective meta-data from multimedia content consists in measuring the emotive response of real users during the consumption of multimedia items. The value of the induced emotion is then transferred in the multimedia database and the item profile is updated (see Figure 19.5).

The IAPS database, which consists of nearly 1000 images annotated with meta-data about their induced emotive responses, was built using the Self-Assessment-Manikin (SAM), a simple form for filling in the emotion state in the VAD space (Lang et al. 2005). This approach yields very accurate data, but is very intrusive and

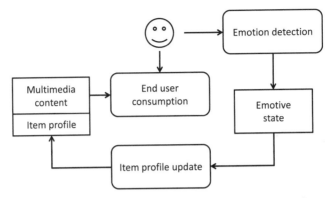

Figure 19.5. Extraction of affective metadata through users' emotive responses.

not suitable for multimedia consumption applications. Significant research has been done on emotion detection of users through a variety of modalities like speech, gesture, posture, face, body sensors, and so on. This collection contains several chapters that deal with indirect emotion detection. Stoiber et al. (2009) present an algorithm for the detection of emotive states from video sequences of the user's face. Acoustic and linguistic signals are being used to detect the emotive state of speakers in the VAD space by Schuller et al. (2009, 2012). In Chapter 16 of this book, Pianesi et al. present a methodology for detecting personality traits (which are sometimes treated as long lasting emotive states) using multimodal analysis. Jones and Chan (Chapter 20, this volume) present a novel system for the extraction of affective features from visual and audio streams.

19.3 EXPERIMENT

19.3.1 Experimental Setup

A two-stage experiment was performed to accept or reject the hypothesis that the inclusion of affective features improves the performance of the CBR. First, we built the data set, and then we simulated the CBR system with two item profiles: the first with standard attributes only and the second with affective attributes.

19.3.2 Data Set Acquisition

A selection of 70 images from the IAPS database was made. The IAPS database provides images annotated with average and standard deviation values of the induced emotive response in end users (Lang et al. 2005). The choice was carefully done to cover as equally as possible the whole valence–arousal plane. There were 52 users aged between 17 and 20 (21 males) taking part in the data set acquisition phase.

The users were further instructed to imagine they were collecting images for the desktop wallpaper on their computer. Each user watched each of the 70 images and then gave a rating to each image (*relevant* or *nonrelevant*, which was the equivalent of *I want it as a wallpaper* and *I don't want it as a wallpaper*). A data set with explicit ratings by all users, recorded watching times, average and standard deviation values of the induced emotion in the VAD space, and the image genre was compiled. The set of available genres used was $A_1 = ($ "*action*," "*animal*," "*erotic*," "*people*," "*plants*," "*portrait*," "*still*," "*violence*," "*weapon*," and "*weather*"$)$. An excerpt from the data set can be seen in Table 19.2.

19.3.3 CBR System Simulation

We performed two CBR simulations, the first with the metadata set $md_A(h) = (g, t_w)$ and the second with the metadata set $md_{AS}(h) = (g, t_w, \bar{v}, \sigma_v, \bar{a}, \sigma_a, \bar{d}, \sigma_d)$. The simulation was done by classifying the metadata items into the space of item relevancy $\Omega = \{c_0, c_1\}$. This was done using the mapping (classifier) γ, which maps an item's profile into a class from the set Ω. The whole procedure of predicting the relevancy of an item h for the user u is a compositum of feature extraction and features classification $\delta = \gamma \circ md$. The corresponding decision maps for the two metadata sets under observations are denoted with $\delta^A = \gamma^A \circ md_A$ and $\delta^{AS} = \gamma^{AS} \circ md_{AS}$. Beside comparing the metadata sets, we also compared two classifiers that form the set $\Gamma = \{$Naïve Bayes, C4.5$\}$.

Each classifier was first trained with the training set $T_r = \{(h, c) : h \in H_{T_r} \subseteq H, c \in \Omega\}$ and then tested with the testing set $T_s = \{(h, c) : h \in H_{T_s} \subseteq H, c \in \Omega\}$. The respective confusion matrices $M(\delta)$ were computed and then compared using the Pearson χ^2 statistical significance test (Lehman and Romano 2005) on each classification class. The confusion matrices are 2 by 2 matrices that contain the amount of correctly (true positives TP and true negatives TN) and incorrectly classified (false positives FP and false negatives FN) instances (see Table 19.3).

19.3.4 The Validation Procedure

We chose the 10-fold cross validation testing scheme (Kohavi 1995). The performance validation was done for each classifier $\in \Gamma$, for each feature set (A and $A \times S$), and for each user $u \in U_s$ separately, where $U_S = \cap U_h, h \in H$. We used two classifiers, the Naive Bayes and the C4.5 tree algorithm, and each of them was applied in the realization of two decision maps δ^A and δ^{AS}. For each user $u \in U_s$, a training set T^u was constructed from experimental data and supplied as the input to the training and testing phase of the validation procedure. For the ith fold of the evaluation, the resulting confusion matrices are denoted by $M(\delta_i^{A,u})$ and $M(\delta_i^{AS,u})$. In the user data acquisition process, every user $u \in U_s$ rated (classified) every item from $h \in H_s$ as $e(u,h) \in \Omega$. Therefore, for each $u \in U_s$, there was a separate data set $T^u = \{(h, e(u, h)) : h \in H_s\}$, and the input data set can be written as $T = \{T^u : u \in U_s\}$. This set was available as the input to the 10-fold cross-validation scheme. Since the

TABLE 19.3. Confusion Matrix of a Classifier that Show the Number of Correctly and Incorrectly Classified Instances

	Relevant	Nonrelevant
Predicted as relevant	TP	FP
Predicted as nonrelevant	FN	TN

validation procedure was ran separately for classifiers on feature sets A and $A \times S$, two sequences of confusion matrices are computed, $\{M(\delta_i^{A,u}) : \gamma \in \Gamma, u \in U_s, 1 \leq i \leq k\}$ and $\{M(\delta_i^{AS,u}) : \gamma \in \Gamma, u \in U_s, 1 \leq i \leq k\}$. These sequences were further analyzed to validate the proposed schemes; details are given in the next section.

19.3.5   Evaluation Measures and Statistical Testing

In order to determine whether the obtained differences in performance are casual or real, we need to perform a statistical test (Lehman and Romano 2005). We used three scalar measures to assess the performance of the CBR simulations: precision P, recall R, and F-measure F (Hastie et al. 2001; Herlocker et al. 2004). These are scalar measures computed from confusion matrices. Precision is the percent of truly relevant items among all recommended items and is calculated using the equation:

$$P = \frac{TP}{TP + FP},$$

while recall is the percent of truly relevant items that were caught by the recommender and is calculated using the equation:

$$R = \frac{TP}{TP + FN}.$$

Both precision and recall can be aggregated into a single scalar measure, the F-measure, using the equation:

$$F = \frac{2PR}{P + R}.$$

As we wanted to have high-quality recommendations, we were mostly concerned that the recommended items were truly relevant. This is why the precision measure was more important than recall or F-measure.

As it is well known from multivariate statistics, there is more information in vector-type data (confusion matrices in our case) than in the derived scalar statistics. Therefore, we analyzed the classifiers' performances using the confusion matrices assigned to the decision maps.

The statistical testing of confusion matrices was transferred to the testing for the equivalence of two estimated discrete probability distributions. The zero hypothesis to be tested was $H_0 = \{M(\delta^A) \cong M(\delta^{AS})\}$, where $\cong$ stands for the equivalence of the underlying discrete distributions. The natural choice here was the Pearson χ^2 test (Lehman and Romano 2005). It tests if a sample $(n_1, \ldots, n_N)$ is drawn from a multinomial distribution $B(n,p)$ with parameters $n = n_1 + \cdots + n_N$ and $p = (p_1, \ldots, p_N)$. Assuming $p_i > 0$ for all $1 \leq i \leq N$, the test statistics is $Q = \sum_{i=1}^{N}(n_i - np_i)^2 / np_i$, distributed as $\chi^2(N-1)$ if $np_i \gg 1$ for all $1 \leq i \leq N$ and n large enough (Lehman and Romano 2005). Experimental studies showed that $np_i \gg 1$ in practice means $np_i \geq 5$. In our case, with only two classes $N = 2(\Omega = \{c_0, c_1\})$, the distribution was binomial.

TABLE 19.4. The Confusion Matrices (TP, FP, FN, and TN), Precision P, Recall R, and F-Measure for Both Feature Sets (A and $A \times S$) and Classifiers (C4.5 and Naive Bayes)

Feature Set	Classifier	TP	FP	FN	TN	P	R	F	Correctly Classified (%)
A	C4.5	656	433	781	1700	0.60	0.46	0.52	66
A	Naive Bayes	829	603	608	1530	0.58	0.58	0.58	66
$A \times S$	C4.5	823	469	614	1664	0.64	0.57	0.60	70
$A \times S$	Naive Bayes	923	691	514	1442	0.57	0.64	0.61	66

19.3.6 Results

The summary confusion matrices and the corresponding numerical P, R, and F measures are shown in Table 19.4. As described in the previous section, the validation procedure we ran on experimental data provided twice of $10|U_s| = 530$ confusion matrices $\{M(\delta_i^{A,u}) : \gamma \in \Gamma, u \in U_s, 1 \le i \le k\}$ and $\{M(\delta_i^{AS,u}) : \gamma \in \Gamma, u \in U_s, 1 \le i \le k\}$ for each of the two classifiers from $\Gamma = \{\text{Navie Bayes, C4.5}\}$.

We applied the statistical significance test Pearson χ^2 (see Lehman and Romano (2005) and section 19.3.5) to compare the confusion matrices $M(\delta^A)$ and $M(\delta^{AS})$. The distribution of the test statistics Q was $\chi^2(1)$, and the critical value at the chosen risk level $\alpha = 0.05$ was 3.84. Since all the listed values were larger than the critical value, all p-values were way below the risk level ($p < 0.001$), and we concluded that the performances of both classifiers were significantly different when the feature set used was A or $A \times S$. In order to find out which of the statistically different results was better, we observed the differences in the scalar measures, which showed that the confusion matrices significance difference is in favor of the affective feature set.

In terms of the assessment of the quality of recommendations, the most important aspect of the system is to minimize the amount of nonrelevant items among the recommended ones. For the satisfaction of the end user, which is choosing a wallpaper image for the computer's desktop, it is a better tradeoff to leave out certain relevant items and include less nonrelevant items than the other way around. Getting recommended lots of nonrelevant items surely annoys the user, while not getting all of the relevant items is not a problem since the user is not aware of how many relevant items are there in the database. Thus, to keep low the amount of FP is crucial even at the expense of having moderately high FN. This makes precision P the most important scalar measure.

Besides the aggregated results, we also analyzed the distribution of the success rate (in terms of precision P) among single users. Figure 19.6 shows the distribution of precision separately for both combinations of feature sets for the C4.5 classifier. The t-test within the multiple comparison procedure showed that the difference of precision means between feature sets A and $A \times S$ (with $A \times S$ outperforming A) was significant at 0.05. The percentage of users for which the system has given better recommendations (in terms of precision P) was 68%.

Furthermore, a visual inspection of the distribution of the images users have rated as relevant or nonrelevant within the VAD space for two different users depicted in Figure 19.7 shows that users have different tastes on what they like in the VAD space.

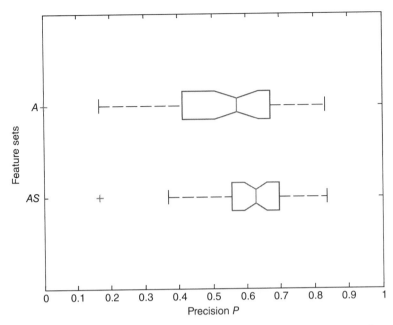

Figure 19.6. Boxplots of the distribution of precision *p*-values across users using different feature sets (A and AS). The lines of the boxes are at the lower quartile, median, and upper quartile values. Whiskers' extreme values are at 1.5 times the interquartile range from the ends of the box.

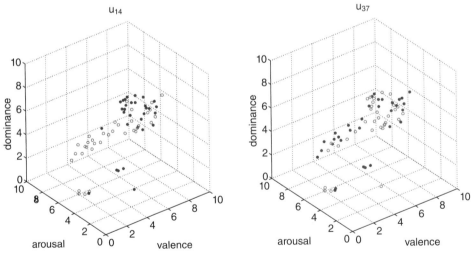

Figure 19.7. Two users with clearly different tastes regarding which items are relevant (full circles) or nonrelevant (empty circles) in the valence–arousal–dominance space.

19.4 CONCLUSION AND OUTLOOK

We showed that affective image attributes significantly improve the performance of a CBR system (see Figure 19.6). This clearly sets the need for the development and wider usage of methods for the extraction of affective information from images and multimedia content in general.

According to the nature of user data, which is stochastic, and the general experience from statistical data analysis, more accurate results can be expected from monitoring the classifier's performance in terms of its confusion matrix $M(\delta)$ than from the scalar measures precision, recall, and F-measure. We applied a statistical significance test to show that the VAD affective parameters significantly improve the performance of a CBR system.

We believe that there is considerable potential in the employment of affective parameters in the development of CBR systems, as well as for general user modeling techniques. The first reason is that there are methods for the extraction of affective features from multimedia content (either direct or indirect extraction) under development that provide promising results (Jones and Chan [Chapter 20, this volume], Schuller et al. [2009, 2012], Stoiber et al. [Chapter 6, this volume], and Pianesi et al. [Chapter 16, this volume]). The second reason is that effective user modeling proved to be a difficult task, and as such depends on data fusion from many sources.

Our work plan for the future will concentrate on the development of methods for the automatic extraction of affective VAD features using several modalities. Statistical evaluation and verification techniques are an unavoidable part of the experimental design required by such development. In particular, our present experience shows a need for further landscape analysis of user modeling-related data, and among others, also the multivariate statistics analysis of factors.

ACKNOWLEDGMENTS

The authors would like to thank all the colleagues of the LDOS group (http://www.ldos.si) at the Faculty of Electrical Engineering in Ljubljana for their assistance in the acquirement of the data set. A special thank goes to Matevž Kunaver and Tomaž Požrl for their ample help.

CHAPTER 20

AFFECT-BASED INDEXING FOR MULTIMEDIA DATA

GARETH J. F. JONES and CHING HAU CHAN

20.1 INTRODUCTION

The amount of professional and user-generated multimedia data is currently increasing dramatically. With such large volumes of data becoming available, manually searching for a piece of video from within a collection, which is already a time-consuming and tedious task, is set to become entirely impractical. Due to its temporal nature, even skimming through a single piece of video to look for a specific scene or event can be very inefficient. The solution to this problem is to provide effective automated and semi-automated video retrieval and browsing applications. Such tools require that the content be suitably annotated with meaningful features to support users in their searching tasks. Unfortunately, it is unrealistic to expect most video to be richly annotated manually in this way; indeed, in many cases, it will not be manually annotated at all. This situation requires that the content be indexed using automated content analysis tools to support subsequent retrieval and browsing.

Additionally, the richness of semantic information contained in multimedia content means that it is difficult to fully describe all aspects of such items. The need to support users in accessing such semantically rich content has led to a significant growth in recent years in research into content-based video retrieval (CBVR) systems aimed at helping users to locate and retrieve relevant video from potentially very large databases. Annotation labels for video content can be made at three levels (Eakins 1996). The lowest level (feature level) extracts details such as colors and textures, which can be used directly for search, but also to identify basic features, such as location of shot cuts, face detection, and camera motion. The next level

Multimedia Information Extraction: Advances in Video, Audio, and Imagery Analysis for Search, Data Mining, Surveillance, and Authoring, First Edition. Edited by Mark T. Maybury.
© 2012 IEEE Computer Society. Published 2012 by John Wiley & Sons, Inc.

describes logical features (cognitive level) that are higher-level features and involve some degree of logical inference about the identity of the content, such as it being a news report, a red car, or an indoor scene. The highest level (affective level) contains abstract features that involve some degree of subjectivity, where the emotional aspects of the content can be described, for example, happy scenes, a girl in fear, or a funny person.

Describing video content at multiple levels in this way relates to the concept of the semantic gap. This refers to the difference between the information that can be extracted from the data and the interpretation of the same data by the user in a given situation (Smeulders et al. 2000). Thus, a viewer's interpretation of a scene in a movie might be determined as police chasing a gang of criminals through a very scared crowd. The lowest level of extraction would describe this in terms of colors and textures. A higher level of interpretation could find men, it might then be able to identify them as policemen if they are wearing uniforms. Extracting a chase among a crowd of randomly moving people would be very difficult, and determining the mood of the participants would be harder still. In practice, current CBVR system must rely on the low-level features including colors and textures, which can be extracted reliably, and do their best to support searchers as they seek to find content relevant to them from a much higher level perspective. This clearly represents a significant gap to interpretation between the CBVR system and that of a human viewer for this scene.

Hauptmann (2005) notes that one step toward bridging the semantic gap between user needs and detected features is to combine these detected features to infer some sort of high-level ontology that nonexpert users can relate to. He favors this method because it splits the semantic gap problem into two stages: mapping low-level features to immediate semantic concepts, and mapping these semantic concepts to user needs. Existing work on video content analysis for CBVR systems has concentrated largely on recognition of objective features (Hauptmann and Christel 2004). Such work includes scene segmentation (Zhang and Jay Kuo 2001; Zhai et al. 2004), object detection (Browne and Smeaton 2004), and highlight detection (Sadlier and O'Connor 2005). These features allow users to make queries for clearly defined features, such as named objects or people (Smeaton et al. 2006). While work in this area is beginning to close the semantic gap by linking low-level extracted features with higher-level descriptions, at best, this provides only a partial solution to the problem of the semantic gap.

Hauptmann also believes that a further contribution to closing the semantic gap can be provided by affective interpretation of the content. Affective features in video contain information about its emotive elements, which are aimed at invoking certain emotional states in viewers with which they can naturally identify. The emotional content in a video can potentially be inferred using extraction of features associated with its affective dimension. Little existing work has reported exploration on the automatic annotation of the emotional or affective dimension of audio-visual content. However, a manual approach to affective labeling of video content is provided by the FEELTRACE system described in Cowie et al. (2000). Automatic extraction and interpretation of affective features of video content lies within the field of affective computing. Work in this area in recent years has significantly improved understanding of the relationship between human–computer interaction and human emotional states to which intelligent machines can react accordingly to provide better results to our information needs (Picard and Cosier 1997). Detecting affective features in a video is not about detecting the viewer's emotional state, but the emotional content of the video itself. This can generally be expected to correspond to the emotional interpretation that the director of a movie is seeking to convey to the viewers, whether this is actually true of course depends on the success of the director in realizing his or her vision. The affective dimension is an important natural component of human interpretation of information and potentially offers users a new modality of interaction with video data (Picard and Cosier 1997), and provides a contribution to closing the semantic gap.

The annotation of video with abstract or subjective labels, such as affective labels, is potentially much harder than labeling objective descriptive features. Affective features require that video be labeled with a mood such as "blue" or "sad." The subjective nature of such labels means that even manual annotation is generally more difficult than labeling objective features. The nature of affective interpretation means that manually assigned affective labels are likely to be the inconsistent between videos and especially between annotators. Even an individual annotator may find it hard to behave consistently for different videos. This is obviously undesirable if annotations are to be used for content management applications, such as browsing and retrieval. As with many areas of feature extraction or labeling, a suitably enabled computer is likely to behave more consistently than a human, leading to more reliable and predictable responses in searching applications.

We are interested in developing a system that can automatically detect and extract features in a multimedia data stream indicative of affective information that the creator of the content wishes to convey. In doing this, we need to identify a range of features that can be extracted reliably and used in combination to describe the affective state that it is intended to communicate. Extracting the sort of subtle signals used by human observers, such as minor variations in facial expression, is extremely difficult; thus, we need to use in combination such low-level features that can be reliably extracted. In doing this, we build on existing work in affect extraction and interpretation.

In existing work, Lew et al. (2006) highlighted affective computing as one of the approaches that holds promise for human-centered systems. For example, using an affect-based video retrieval system to satisfy their information needs, users might find formulating queries of the form "exciting scenes" to be much easier and more helpful than trying to define them in terms such as "rapid shot cuts and elevated audio energy." This higher level of abstraction would potentially allow users more options in searching for relevant content and reviewing the returned results. Thus, a mechanism for distinguishing between "happy" and other video segments may have potential in various video management applications. This chapter describes the development and analysis of a prototype system for affect-based indexing of video content.

This chapter is structured as follows: Section 20.2 reviews the models of affect used in our work, Section 20.3 overviews affect relevant features in multimedia production, Section 20.4 describes our system for cross-modal affect annotation for video and Section 20.5 a subjective experimental investigation of its accuracy, and finally Section 20.6 concludes and outlines directions for further work.

20.2   AFFECT REPRESENTATION AND COMPUTING

Recent years have seen a significant increase in research into affect from both a human psychological or cognitive perspective and from a computational one. Much of this work has been stimulated by Picard's seminal work on affective computing, defined to be computing that "relates to, arises from, or deliberately influences emotions" (Picard 1997). In our work, we are primarily interested in affective computing, but draw on more fundamental work in human affective interpretation of language. Although there are variations in how affect can be expressed (such as the way a joke is being told that might make it funny or not), research in affective computing shows that these problems can be overcome. The affective features in a data stream can be described as the pieces of encoded information that elicit an emotional response. However, affective communication can come from a variety of different sources, such as body language, facial expression, or speech intonation. On its own, each component might not be sufficient to determine the underlying emotional intention, but in combination, these features can often be used to interpret a person's underlying emotional state.

Drawing on neurological studies in her development of affective computing, Picard (1997) inferred that emotion greatly influences human perception. While research into human perception of emotions and its underlying processes is an extremely complex and wide field, for the purposes of our current study, we leave aside details of the explanation of the concepts of human emotions, and focus on useable knowledge about them that can be used to implement a real system for extracting and exploiting affect-related information.

In this section, we review the popular three-dimensional representative model of emotion space which describes how this can be used to form an Affect Curve for temporal representation of affect change over time. This is followed by a review of existing work in affect extraction for context-based video indexing.

20.2.1   Valence–Arousal–Dominance Emotion Space

Research into human physical and cognitive aspects of emotion can help us to model affective features. One such model that is extremely useful in this context is the Valence–Arousal–Dominance (VAD) emotion representation, which breaks emotions into three independent components. Russell and Mehrabian (1977) describe how three independent and bipolar dimensions can represent all emotions experienced by humans. The three components are defined as follows:

- *Valence*: Measures the level of pleasure–displeasure being experienced. This ranges from a "positive" response associated with extreme happiness or ecstasy through to a "negative" response resulting from extreme pain or unhappiness.
- *Arousal*: This is a continuous measure of alertness ranging from one extreme of sleep through to intermediate states of drowsiness and alertness and finally frenzied excitement at the other end of the scale.
- *Dominance*: Dominance (or control) is a measure of a person's perceived control in a situation. It can range from feelings of a total lack of control or submissiveness to the other extreme of complete control or influence over their

situation or environment. It has been observed that this dimension plays a limited role in affective analysis of video, and we follow previous work in concentrating only on valence and arousal (Hanjalić and Xu 2005). The less discriminative power of this dimension to separate emotions compared with the other two is also cited as a contributing factor to its omission by Dietz and Lang (1999).

A person can be said to always be in an emotional state dependent on the level of each of these three dimensions. To visualize this, the three dimensions can be plotted on a three-dimensional coordinate system graph with linear axes ranging from −1 to +1 referred to as the VAD emotion space. Emotional states, such as "happy" or "sad," can be said to exist as areas within a certain boundary of coordinates. Therefore, when the three-dimensional coordinates fall within a boundary region, the person is inferred to be in that particular emotional state. This gives an intuitive representation of emotions that can easily be interpreted. For example, the difference between the emotions "happy" and "sad" is that "happy" falls in the positive regions of arousal and valence, and "sad" falls in the negative regions. Russell and Mehrabian (1977) conducted a study involving a large number of human subjects being given a list of 151 words, each describing a distinct emotional state and asked to rate each of them on a scale based on how they feel toward the emotion terms according to the three dimensions. The subjects' scores were then averaged to give valence, arousal, and dominance values for each of the 151 words.

In affective computing, due to the omission of the dominance dimension, this can be plotted as a two-dimensional graph with the linear axes ranging from −1 to +1, called the valence-arousal (VA) emotion space. The emotional state "happy" falls in the positive and slightly excited region of the VA space, while "excitement" occupies a higher arousal region. The difference between "fear" and "angry" is slightly higher arousal but more negative feelings. The results of Russell and Mehrabian's (1977) study provided relative values that can be used to populate the VA space with 151 emotion labels, which are sufficient to describe a wide range of emotions. Figure 20.1 shows a VA space with the location of some emotion label examples.

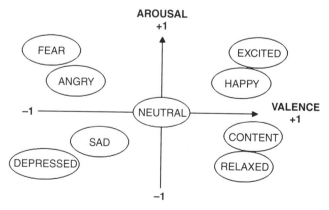

Figure 20.1. Example VA emotion space showing location of emotions in two dimensions.

20.2.2 Affect Curve

For a temporal data source, such as a video, or indeed a person, affective state will change over time. State change will be accompanied by corresponding changes in valence or arousal. A VA plot can be made at any point of the temporal affect measurement. A series of VA samples can be plotted on an affect curve (Hanjalić and Xu 2005). Observing an affect curve enables the affective development and dominant features of a data source to be seen in a single graph. If an affective verbal label is assigned at each sampling point, an affective description of the data can be produced. Annotation of a video in this way requires that the affective dimension of valence and arousal can be extracted with sufficient reliability. This is the subject of the next section.

20.3 AFFECT ANALYSIS FOR CONTENT-BASED VIDEO INDEXING

Clearly, features extracted from complex sources, such as a video, will be subject to some imprecision in terms of feature values. Additionally, there will, of course, also be subjective variations in human interpretations of the emotional content. For these reasons, it is not realistic to expect precision and unambiguous affective labels to be assigned to individual points in a video, but rather we are seeking to develop a method that can identify the appropriate region of the VA space, and assign labels that observers would generally agree are related to the content, although they might quite reasonably be expected to disagree on the extent to which the labels are precise in their description of the content.

As explained previously, reliably extracting complex features, such as slight changes in body language, is very difficult. Recent work in affective computing has focused on the problem of extracting low-level semantic features. For example, Stoiber et al. (2012) use analysis of low-level features as the source for data-driven high-level representation of emotional facial expressions. While the complex nature of emotions means that they cannot be defined simply, affective features that contribute and influence emotions can be. This is why the VA emotion space is such an important foundation for affective computing. As explained in existing work (Picard 1997; Hanjalić and Xu 2005), valence and arousal can be measured based on features in multimedia data. This provides a framework for modeling valence and arousal based on low-level features. Our work extends this existing work on low-level feature extraction to derive affective features to explore a solution to the problem of expressing high-level affective concepts, thus providing a part of the solution to closing the semantic gap. Before looking at low-level feature extraction, this section briefly reviews methods used in movies to generate affective reactions in viewers.

20.3.1 Low-Level Affective Feature Extraction for Movie Content

A central aspect of movie production is that associated with the planned emotional reaction of viewers. To this end, a range of production tools and filmmaking techniques are used to elicit an emotional response from viewers, for example, the art of storytelling, editorial devices, speed effects, and so on. Filmmaking is one of the more mature and popular forms of human entertainment and leverages decades of filmmaking knowledge designed to capture the heart and imagination of its viewers. Film is one of the most affect-laden media and is a great source of data for affective features. Research in affective computing is just beginning to mine information from this domain (Rasheed et al. 2005).

A large body of knowledge and rules have been accumulated in film theory, film language, and cinematography. These guide filmmakers in making not only movies, but also documentaries, sitcoms and other entertainment shows. This makes the results of analysis performed on movies applicable to other domains of entertainment videos as well. These rules are often referred to as "the grammar of film"; while not necessarily implemented as set rules that filmmakers must follow, since it is up to their creativity to portray and tell a story, understanding them can provide guidance in the design of automatic extractors to detect affective features in the content. Some filmmakers intentionally break these "rules" to come up with new perspectives in storytelling. Nevertheless, common techniques designed to elicit an emotional response from viewers are frequently used. Some of the most commonly used devices are the following:

- *Editing*: Scene editing refers to how editors or directors cut up and mix recorded scenes to tell a story. For example, horror movie directors sometimes use long periods of silence and slow scenes to build up tension before following them with a loud bang to surprise the audience. A jump cut (or a shot cut), which is an abrupt switch from one scene to another, can be used to make a dramatic point, or indicate a change of scene. An increase in the rate of these cuts usually indicates an increase in activity or excitement.

- *Camera Movement*: Camera movement refers to how the camera is manipulated to frame the event that is happening in the movie. There are many types of camera movements, including panning left or right, zooming in and out, tilting up and down, or tracking the movement of an object or person. An increase in camera motion can also indicate an increase in activity.

- *Color and Lighting*: Color and lighting can be used to manipulate the viewer's emotions and attention. For example, a flash of bright light can often be used to indicate a near-death scene or a religious experience. In movies such as *The Matrix*, a green tinge or filter is often applied to specific scenes to suggest artificiality (the green color as found on early monochrome computer monitors) and link them together, so that viewers are able to perceive them as being a different but coherent artificial world when they see the green tinge.

- *Sound*: Sound plays an important role in determining the emotional impact of a scene, and is frequently used to great effect by moviemakers to elicit an emotional response. For example, horror movie directors typically use long periods of silence to build up tension before scaring the audience with a loud and high-pitched sound. There are also more subtle uses of different types of music to convey a different mood or feeling, such as using orchestral music to signify grandness or a violin solo to indicate sadness.

The key to exploiting these techniques in affective feature extraction is to identify suitable low-level features that can be associated with them and extracted automatically with reasonable reliability, and to then combine them to infer affective state via the VA representation.

20.3.2 Existing Work in Affective Extraction from Video Content

The features discussed in the previous section have been used to detect valence and arousal levels in various existing studies. Hanjalić and Xu (2005) report pioneering work using the VA emotion space to model low-level video features onto the valence and arousal dimensions. Their work showed that valence and arousal can be effectively modeled by combining low-level video features, such as visual motion, shot cut rates, audio energy, and audio pitch by utilizing basic knowledge of cinematographic techniques. For example, shorter shot lengths are typically perceived as being more action oriented, with a high tempo of action or stressed accented movements, while longer shot lengths are typically used to deaccentuate an action. Also, based on the results of work by Murray and Arnott (1993) and Slaney and McRoberts (2003), and the conclusions of Picard (1997), it can be seen that various vocal effects present in the soundtrack of a video may bear broad relations to its affective content. In terms of affect dimensions, loudness is often related to arousal, while pitch-related features are commonly related to valence. However, as acknowledged by Picard (1997), detecting valence can be more difficult than arousal since valence information is more subtly conveyed. In other work, de Kok (2006) proposed the use of color saturation and scene brightness as visual features for the modeling of the valence component of affect curves, while Schuller et al. (2009) report on the speaker's emotional state in terms of valence and activation (arousal) in a database of TV broadcasts.

Rasheed et al.'s (2005) work on classifying movies into four categories (comedies, action, drama, and horror movies) examined the use of low-level video features that take into account some knowledge of ubiquitous cinematic practices. In the course of their work, they identified shot cuts, color, motion, and lighting as useful and relevant visual features grounded in cinematic practices that can be used for the classification of movies into different genres.

Hang's (2003) work on affective content detection relied on the VA emotion space to model low-level features associated with four emotion categories: fear, anger, joy, and sadness. Using video data, he used an HMM-based classifier to discriminate between the four emotion categories using low-level features, including color, motion, and shot cut rates.

Salway and Graham (2003) presented a method to extract information about a character's emotional state in a movie based on textual descriptions of the content. Their approach used "audio descriptions" provided for the visually impaired that are contained in DVD movie releases. These descriptions were analyzed for possible descriptions of emotions in order to classify them into 22 types of emotion. Using the online dictionary WordNet,[1] each type of emotion, such as "joy," was expanded into keywords, such as "euphoria," "jolly," "happy," and "pleased." Positions in the audio descriptions where these keywords occur were classified into one of the 22 emotion types.

---

[1] http://wordnet.princeton.edu/wordnet/.

Having introduced the VA affect-space for classifying emotion labels and existing work on the extraction of arousal and valence levels based on low-level feature extraction, the following section describes our system for affective annotation of movies, which combines extracted low-level features, VA representation, and textual annotation.

20.4 DESIGN OF A NOVEL AFFECT-BASED VIDEO INDEXING AND RETRIEVAL SYSTEM

This section presents the design of our affect-based video indexing system for application in CBVR-related applications. For users of a system using emotional content for indexing, it is important that they are able to express their annotations in a natural, simple, and descriptive way; for example, by using a text query in a search application. An obvious starting point then is to label the data using words with a known affective interpretation such as the 151 words from Russell and Mehrabian's (1977) study. In our work, we explore the use of three predefined lists of this type. The system is divided into three stages: feature extraction, valence and arousal modeling, and verbal labeling. The system first processes the videos to extract low-level visual and audio features. These are then combined to model valence and arousal, and finally verbal emotional labels are assigned to the videos.

20.4.1 Feature Extraction

Natural and realistic movement requires a minimum frame rate of around 25 frames per second which is adopted in the video used in this study. For visual features, each frame of the visual video stream is decompressed. Following the norms of audio analysis, the audio values are read and processed in frames of 20 ms in duration with 2/3 overlap between adjacent frames. This ensures that rapid changes between frames are captured within the overlapping frames. Once these visual and audio values are obtained, they can be processed to generate low-level features.

While the selection of these low-level features is made in line with previous work and intuition, the subjective nature of evaluating the performance of valence and arousal modeling makes it difficult to determine the significance of the respective features during development. Therefore, a prototype system first needed to be built before the features could be tested for their suitability.

Figure 20.2 shows a summary of the feature extraction components. A total of six low-level features are extracted from the visual and audio streams. Four features are extracted from the visual stream: motion, shot cuts, saturation, and brightness. For audio, as introduced in Section 20.3.2, only the audio energy and pitch are extracted. In Hanjalić and Xu (2005), the modeling of arousal was based on three features (motion, shot cut rate, and energy), with only one audio feature (pitch) for modeling valence. It seems intuitive to assume that visual cues in video would also influence a viewer's feelings of valence toward it. Therefore, we incorporate the findings of de Kok (2006), and use color saturation and brightness as additional visual features to model valence. This aims to improve the quality of the valence modeling, as it was found during the development of the indexing system that valence-based only on pitch is susceptible to large fluctuations, which might not correspond with affect related active-ties in the video. For example, in scenes with high-pitched human

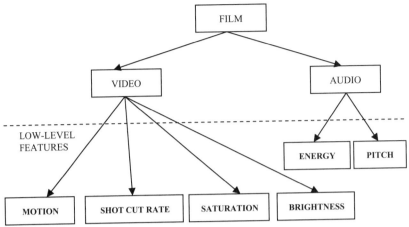

Figure 20.2. Low-level feature extraction from video and audio of a movie.

shouting or sound effects, the dark colors of the scene could indicate a horror or terror scene, while bright colors could indicate a funny and happy scene.

20.4.1.1 Extracted Features This section summarizes the methods used to implement the low-level feature extraction components.

- *Brightness*: To obtain a function $b(k)$ for brightness, each frame of the video is converted into HSV color space. The values of $b(k)$ are then summed, and the average value in the color space is taken and scaled between 0% and 100% to derive the scaled average brightness function $b'(k)$:

$$b'(k) = 100 \times \frac{b(k)}{(b_{max} - b_{min})}\%.$$

- *Saturation*: In order to calculate saturation $s(k)$ for each frame, the video is converted into HSV color space. The saturation values for each frame are summed, and the average value calculated and scaled between 0% and 100% similarly to brightness, to derive the scaled average saturation function $s'(k)$:

$$s'(k) = 100 \times \frac{s(k)}{(s_{max} - s_{min})}\%.$$

- *Pitch*: Pitch tracking is a difficult task that can be approached using a wide range of techniques. In their work, Hanjalić and Xu (2005) used pitch only for voiced segments of video. Since we wish to generate affect annotations for all data, in our work, we calculate the pitch for all audio segments. We extend the original assumption made by Hanjalić and Xu (2005) that higher pitch in voiced segments equals higher valence, and assume that it still holds true when applied to all audio segments. Pitch detection, approximate fundamental frequency estimation, is one of the most important problems in both speech signal and music content analysis. Although equivalent, pitch detection is a rather more perceptual term, while fundamental frequency is a physical measurement. The pitch tracking method used in their work is not explained in detail, and used an off-the-shelf pitch tracker. Our pitch tracker adopts the approach taken in Zhang and Jay Kuo (2001), which, according to the authors, is "to build a method which is efficient, robust, but not necessarily perfectly precise" that works satisfactorily for a wide range of audio signals. The pitch or fundamental frequency is calculated based on peak detection from the spectrum of the sound. The power spectrum is generated with autoregressive (AR) model coefficients estimated from the autocorrelation of audio signals $R_n(k)$. The autocorrelation of the audio signal is computed as,

$$R_n(k) = \frac{1}{N} \times \sum_{m=1}^{N} (x(m) \times w(m+k)) \quad \text{where } 0 < k < P,$$

where P is the order of the AR model. The AR model parameters are estimated from the values of $R_n(k)$ through the Levinson–Durbin algorithm (Haykin 1991). The power spectrum S_{AR} is then estimated as,

$$S_{AR}\left(e^{j(2\pi/N)l}\right) = \frac{E_p}{\left|\sum_{k=0}^{N-1} a_k \times e^{j(2\pi/N)l}\right|^2} \quad 0 \le l \le N-1,$$

where E_P is the mean-square prediction error, and a_k the prediction coefficients. The denominator of S_{AR} can be computed with an N-point FFT. For our work, N was set to 512 to ensure reasonable frequency resolution. The AR model-generated spectrum is a smoothed version of the frequency representation. The AR model is an all-pole expression, making the peaks prominent in the spectrum. The order (P) of the AR model was chosen to be 40, as suggested in Zhang and Jay Kuo (2001), to obtain good precision of the fundamental frequency. The highest peak in the spectrum is chosen as the fundamental frequency for each frame to obtain a pitch $p(k)$, which is again scaled into the range 0–100% to derive the scaled fundamental frequency function $p'(k)$,

$$p'(k) = 100 \times \frac{p(k)}{(p_{max} - p_{min})}\%.$$

- *Motion*: This captures overall motion activity $m(k)$ for each frame k. Motion vectors are calculated using a standard block-matching motion estimation method between consecutive frames k and $k + 1$. The calculated displacement values then form the motion vectors. For this system, only the magnitude of the motion is significant, so motion direction is not used. The motion activity value $m(k)$ is calculated as the average magnitude of all motion vectors $\vec{v}_i(k)$, where there are a total of B motion vectors scaled in the range 0–100%, and then normalized by a maximum possible length motion vector $|\vec{v}_{max}|$ to derive the final scaled average motion function $m'(k)$.

$$m'(k) = \frac{100}{B \times |\vec{v}_{max}|} \times \sum_{i=1}^{B} |\vec{v}_i(k)|\%.$$

- *Shot Cut Rate*: Shot cuts are detected using a color histogram approach shown to perform reliably in Browne et al. (2000). Similar to motion, adjacent frames are compared and a shot cut is detected when the difference between the colors in the two frames exceeds a predetermined threshold. More sophisticated shot boundary detection methods exist, but here, a simple and fairly robust method is used. A large amount of data needs to be processed, and small numbers of errors can be tolerated since only a measure of shot cut rate is required for the affect related feature. After the shot cuts have been detected, the shot cut rate is modeled by defining the scaled shot cut rate function $c'(k)$,

$$c'(k) = 100 \times e^{[1-(n(k)-p(k))]}\%,$$

where $p(k)$ and $n(k)$ are the positions (frame indexes) of the two closest shot cuts to the left and right of the frame k respectively with $c'(k)$ values distributed on a scale between 0% and 100%. The result is a step curve, with each step corresponding to a video segment between two shot cuts and the height of each step being inversely related to the interval between the boundaries; therefore, the shorter the interval, the higher the value $c'(k)$.

- *Energy*: For audio features, one energy value is computed for each audio frame. The short-time energy function $e(k)$ is defined as,

$$e(k) = \frac{1}{N} \times \sum_{i=1}^{N} (x(m) \times w(n-m))^2,$$

where $x(m)$ is the discrete time audio signal, n is the time index of the short-time energy, and $w(m)$ is a rectangular window. This is then scaled between 0% and 100%, again similarly to brightness using maximum and minimum energy values, to derive the scaled short time energy function $e'(k)$. However, because of the size and overlapping of frames, audio features have more than double feature rates of the visual features. In order to ensure that the features are synchronized, the audio values are resampled into the same total number of values as the visual features.

20.4.1.2 *Arousal and Valence Modeling*   Before the low-level features can be combined to measure valence and arousal, they need to fulfill three criteria established in Hanjalić and Xu (2005). The criteria are:

- *Comparability*: The criterion "comparability" ensures that the values of the valence and arousal obtained in different videos are comparable. This means that all values have to be normalized and scaled appropriately so they are directly comparable. This criterion is fulfilled in our system since features are normalized and scaled into the range 0–100%.
- *Compatibility*: The criterion "compatibility" ensures that the curves cover an area in the affect curve that corresponds to the VA emotion space. While Hanjalić and Xu (2005) illustrates that the shape and distribution of emotional labels on the VA emotion space have a parabolic-like contour, in our system, the emotional labels that were used and their distribution (between 0 and 1)

were distributed across the entire on the VA emotion space. Therefore, the valence and arousal values that are calculated here can be linearly mapped to the emotion space between 0 and 1 and still fulfill the criterion.

- *Smoothness*: The criterion "smoothness" accounts for the degree of memory retention of preceding frames and shots. This means that the perception of the content does not change abruptly from one video frame to another, but is a function of a number of consecutive frames. For example, although low-level features can fluctuate significantly between frames, human emotion perception does not follow such rapid changes, since there is a certain "inertia" to the change in affective state. Therefore, a smoothing function has to be applied to the features to fulfill this criterion. To achieve this, the low-level features are convolved with a suitably long Kaiser window. By subjective evaluation, it was found that setting a window of approximately 30 seconds' duration yielded the best result, which is comparable with the details reported in Hanjalić and Xu (2005).

Figure 20.3 shows an example motion feature before and after it has been convolved with a Kaiser window. The large rapid fluctuations are smoothed to produce a stable line that shows the underlying trend of the motion feature.

Once the low-level features have been normalized, they are combined into functions to represent valence and arousal as follows:

- *Valence Modeling*: Valence is defined as the weighted sum of $B(k)$, $S(k)$, and $P(k)$,

$$V(k) = \frac{(\alpha \times B(k)) + (\beta \times S(k)) + (\gamma \times P(k))}{(\alpha + \beta + \gamma)},$$

where $B(k)$, $S(k)$, and $P(k)$ are the smoothed forms of $b(k)$, $s(k)$, and $p(k)$, respectively, and α, β, and γ are scalar the weighting factors. The weights here were set as: $\alpha = 0.69$, $\beta = 0.22$, and $\gamma = 1$, respectively. The different weights for saturation and brightness follow the findings of de Kok (2006), where the values were derived from Valdez and Mehrabian's (1994) work on how saturation and brightness are related to the VA emotion space. Through subjective evaluations, it was determined that these weights worked well for a wide range of movies.

- *Arousal Modeling*: Arousal $A(k)$ is similarly defined as the weighted linear sum of $M(k)$, $E(k)$, and $C(k)$,

$$A(k) = \frac{(\alpha \times M(k)) + (\beta \times E(k)) + (\gamma \times C(k))}{(\alpha + \beta + \gamma)},$$

where $M(k)$, $E(k)$, and $C(k)$ are the smoothed forms of $m(k)$, $e(k)$, and $c(k)$, respectively, and α, β, and γ are again scalar weighting factors. Through subjective evaluations involving random video clips from several movies, it was found that setting all weights to 1 yielded the best practical result. This is a reasonable finding since for the wide variety of movies being analyzed here, at various points different low-level features will be significant in representing the dominant state of arousal.

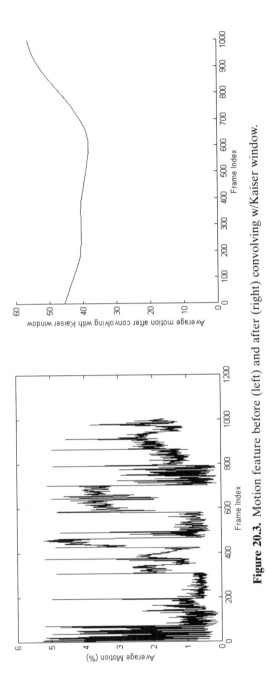

Figure 20.3. Motion feature before (left) and after (right) convolving w/Kaiser window.

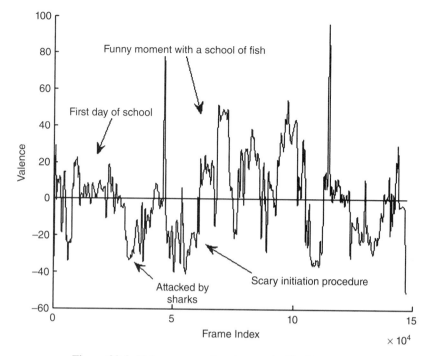

Figure 20.4. Valence curve for the movie *Finding Nemo*.

Figure 20.4 shows the valence curve for the movie *Finding Nemo*. *Finding Nemo* is a comedy movie featuring fishes as the main characters. The horizontal line is the "neutral" value. In the valence curve, it can be observed that during the beginning of the movie, the main characters were in an uplifting mood as they prepare for the first day of school; therefore the curve is in the positive feeling region. When the main character is attacked and chased by sharks in the dark murky waters, the curve drops below neutral and into the negative feeling regions. When the main character undergoes a scary initiation procedure, the curve drops into the negative feeling region again. However, the curve rises up to the positive feeling region again when the main character encounters some fish and experiences a funny moment.

Figure 20.5 shows the corresponding arousal curve for *Finding Nemo*. The horizontal line again shows the "neutral" value. This means that the closer the curve is to this line, the more neutral the scene is in terms of arousal, and the higher the curve, the more positive the arousal. While it seems that there are a lot of peaks and fluctuations, the curve is actually quite compressed as it plots the entire movie. When zoomed in, the lines are smooth (as a result of the convolution with the Kaiser window) and appear to correlate well with the movie. For example, during the scene where the character is chased by sharks, there is high and sustained activity in the arousal curve. When the characters are talking among themselves with little activity, the curve drops to the negative region, suggesting a more relaxed atmosphere. When the main character is suddenly frightened by a scary monster fish, a sudden high peak is observed after a period of low activity.

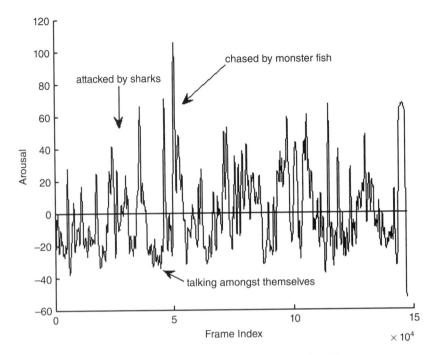

Figure 20.5. Arousal curve of the movie *Finding Nemo*.

While of course such an illustrative example does not constitute formal evaluation of the modeling of valence and arousal, we are encouraged that there are in many instances clear correlations between our expectation of the valence and arousal conditions associated with sampled points in the movie and the values indicated by the modeling functions.

As introduced in Section 20.2.2, the valence and arousal curves can be combined to form an affect curve and mapped onto the VA emotion space as shown in Figure 20.6. Using the *x*-axis for valence and *y*-axis for arousal, the curve starts off at a point and then travels through the VA emotion space "snaking" between different regions until it comes to a halt at the end of the movie. Therefore, each point of the affect curve occupies a position in the VA emotion space that can be associated with an emotional label nearest to this point.

20.4.2   Verbal Labeling of Video Data

In order to automatically annotate video with labels describing its affective dimensions, the VA emotion space has to be populated with emotional verbal labels. In previous work, Hang (2003) labeled the VA emotion space with a small number of very broad terms for classification of multimedia data, such as "happy," "sad," and "fear." While these very broad categories are useful in some applications, we wish to see if a finer level of labeling granularity can be achieved reliably. This could then be used to support more fine-grained affect-based search or classification of multi-

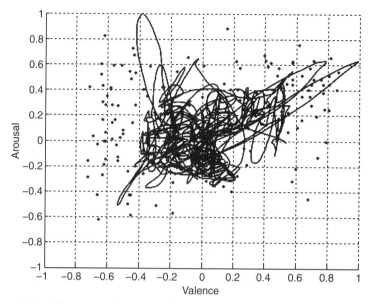

Figure 20.6. Affect curve for the movie *Finding Nemo* on the VA emotion space.

media content. To this end, we adopt a novel use of the findings of Russell and Mehrabian's (1977) study. As introduced in Section 20.2.1, averaged arousal, valence, and dominance values were assigned to 151 words by a group of human assessors. These values were then normalized in the range −1 and +1. Using the values from their findings, the VA emotion space can be populated with the 151 words or verbal labels. For example, "bold" has an arousal value of 0.61 and a valence value of 0.44, and "nonchalant" has an arousal value of −0.25 and a valence of 0.07. Figure 20.7 shows the location of these two labels on the VA emotion space. As can be seen, the affect related labels are quite evenly distributed over the VA space. This list of labels is referred to here as the "Russell list."

Each point on an affect curve extracted from a video can be associated with the closest word or verbal label from the Russell list. This mapping thus produces a verbal label assignment for each frame of the video. While labeling with a vocabulary of this size with very high accuracy is not going to be possible, to some extent because it may sometimes not be possible for assessors to agree on the labels, we are seeking to explore whether the general affective region is correct. We are seeking to allow users to select from as wide a range of words as possible, and to use as accurate an affective interpretation of each point as possible. A similar approach to labeling affective regions to this was used in Cowie et al. (2000), based on manual placement of a limited set of 40 affect labels, for the FEELTRACE system. It was reported that experiments with the FEELTRACE system could distinguish around 20 nonoverlapping affective labels.

We also investigated two other lists of affective labels with coarser levels of granularity. The second list is made up of the 22 emotion types suggested in Salway and Graham (2003), we refer to this as the "Surrey list" (based on the authors'

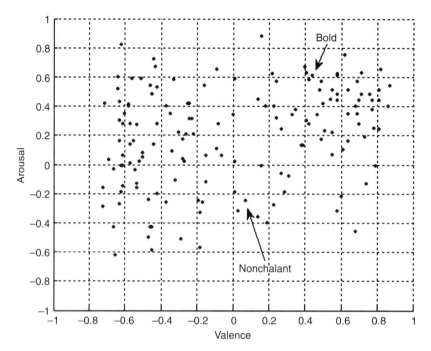

Figure 20.7. The 151 emotional verbal labels plotted as dots in the VA emotion space.

affiliation). The third list is broader still, expressing only six emotion types and is based on emotion recognition from facial gestures (Ekman and Friesen 1978), referred to here as the "Ekman list."

The Surrey list was taken from the work of Ortony et al. (1988). Salway and Graham (2003) expanded the 22 emotion types to a set of 627 emotion keywords using the WordNet ontology. For example, the emotion type "fear" has a number of keywords, such as "alarmed," associated with it. In order to utilize the Surrey list in our work, the 151 Russell keywords were mapped onto the list of 22 emotion types. Fifty of the 627 expanded Surrey keywords appeared in the Russell list, and so were easily mapped to the appropriate one of the 22 emotion types. The remaining 101 Russell words were then manually mapped onto the Surrey emotion list using a standard English dictionary to identify the nearest list entry for each word.

The Ekman list was generated using the positions of the VA emotion space. The 151 labels were mapped onto six broad emotion types used in Ekman's research that was derived from an analysis of facial expression: happy, sad, surprise, anger, fear, and calm, by manually classifying their position into clusters, as shown in Figure 20.8.

The next section describes our experimental investigation of human assessment of the quality of the extracted features and the verbal labels assigned using these features.

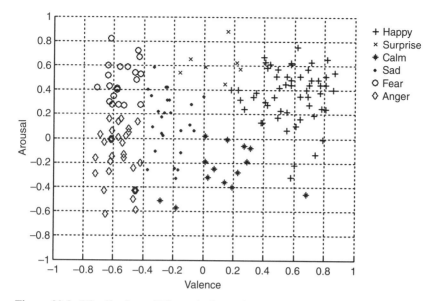

Figure 20.8. Distribution of Ekman's 6 emotion types in the VA emotion space.

20.5 EXPERIMENTAL INVESTIGATION OF AFFECT LABELING

The experimental investigation presented here explores the behavior and potential of our affect-based video indexing system for a variety of commercial Hollywood movies. Movies of this type represent a compelling source of video data especially for an affect-based system due to the richness of their emotional content. In addition, emotional content is much more pronounced in movies than other video material, making it easier to determine what emotions a movie is trying to project. This has the added advantage of making it easier for human viewers to rate how well the system is performing in the evaluation. The evaluation task here requested a group of test subjects to rate the accuracy of the system by examining the video content and assessing the corresponding detected affective features.

In order to explore the system's effectiveness in assigning relevant labels, a suitably large corpus of video data had to be developed. A total of 39 movies were processed, covering a wide range of genres from action movies to comedy and horror movies. This amounted to approximately 80 hours of data comparable with video evaluation campaigns, such as TRECVid (Smeaton et al. 2006). To explore annotation of multiple sections, each movie was broken up into 5-minute segments, giving a total of 939 segments. The 5-minute length was chosen based on the reasoning that it would be sufficiently long to have a clear dominant emotional theme, long enough to allow users to be able to observe and rate the dominant emotional content of each clip, but not require an excessive time commitment to complete the interactive experimental evaluation of each segment.

Eight subjects participated in this investigation; all spoke English, were computer literate, and held higher education qualifications in computer science. The subjects recorded their name, age, and gender, how often they went to the cinema, what genre of movies they liked, and how familiar they were with the individual test movies. One of the subjects was female, and the subjects had an average age of 29. Each subject was assigned a number from 1 to 8. The subjects frequented the cinema on average between once a month and 1–2 times a year. However, this did not include watching movies on television at home or other media. This reveals that most of the subjects enjoy movies and the experience of the cinema.

20.5.1 Experimental Procedure

The experimental session took about 1 hour for each subject to complete. The subjects worked at a prepared computer, and were guided through the process each step of the way by the experimenter. They completed a consent form and were briefed on the general details of valence and arousal curves, as it was vital they understood them before the experiments started. A very important point to maintain data consistency was to explain to each subject clearly that the system is detecting affective features (the emotion that the scene is trying to project to the viewer) as opposed to what the viewer emotions actually are or the movie character's emotions. They were also informed that they were allowed to withdraw from the experiment at any time or take breaks. The session began with the subject indicating the five movies with which they most familiar from among the 39 movies available. The subjects also indicated how familiar they were with each movie.

20.5.1.1 Task 1 The first task was to rate the quality of the valence and arousal curves that had been automatically extracted from the movies. A movie player enabled playback of the first of the five selected movies. Below the movie player in the bottom half of the monitor, a plot of the valence curve was displayed. The timeline on the movie player was lined up with the valence curve, so that the subject could drag the movie player timeline to any part of the movie according to what they see on the valence curve. The subject was then able to quickly browse through the movie to see if the happenings in the movie corresponded to the valence curve. In general, they were told to see if the trend of the valence curve matched the movie scenes. The subjects were told not to spend more than 5 minutes on this task, although they were free to exceed this time if they needed to scrutinize the valence curve further. When they were done, they recorded a score from 0 to 10 to indicate how well the valence curve corresponded to the valence components of emotions conveyed by the movie, as interpreted by the subject. Following this, the movie player was used again to review the corresponding arousal curve, and the subject was asked to score the arousal curve in a similar way. This process was repeated for each of the five movies selected.

20.5.1.2 Task 2 Subjects were assigned a random set of five of the 5-minute movie clips. They were then shown the first clip, which they were allowed to repeat or browse through as many times as they wished. To ensure that they were engaged with the emotional content of the clip, they were asked to write down words that describe the dominant emotions contained in the clip.

Three short lists of the emotional verbal labels automatically assigned to each movie clip using the affect annotation system based on the Russell, Surrey, and

TABLE 20.1. Users Familiarity with Their Chosen Five Movies

	Remember Most Scenes	Remember Some Scenes	Remember Only Plot of Movie	Not Familiar with Movie
Total score	22	14	4	0

Ekman lists were then shown to the subjects. In each case, the labels consisted of labels that occurred most often in the clip. The first list had the top 10 labels in the Russell list, the second list had the top 5 labels from the Surrey list, and the third list had the top 3 labels from the Ekman list. Therefore, each list represented a description of the emotional content of the movie clip at a varying degree of granularity. Subjects were then asked to give a score from 0 to 10 indicating how much they agreed that each list of detected emotional verbal labels described the movie clip. This process was repeated for each of the five movie clips assigned to the subject.

20.5.2 Results and Discussion of the User Evaluation

20.5.2.1 *Task 1* With eight subjects, the total number of movies evaluated was 40, but there were repetitions of the movies selected, since only 20 of the 39 movies were chosen by the subjects, representing slightly more than half of the movies processed. The two movies receiving the highest number of evaluations were *Shrek* and *Titanic* with 5 in each case. While these two movies received more evaluations than others, the range of movies evaluated was still reasonable.

In addition to choosing the five movies, subjects were also required to score how well they remembered each of them. The categories that they could choose were: remember most scenes, remember some scenes, remember only plot of movie, or not familiar with the movie. This was to gauge their degree of familiarity with the movies that they chose. This is important as the task of rating the accuracy of the valence and arousal curves requires some understanding and knowledge of the movie's general structure and plot.

Table 20.1 shows a summary of the subjects' familiarity with their selected movies. The results show that subjects had seen and at least remembered the plot of all the movies they chose. On average, the users had a vivid understanding and memory of each movie they had chosen, therefore hopefully giving the results of their assessment of the valence and arousal curves a high degree of reliability.

After this information had been collected, the subjects were required to rate each movie according to how accurate the valence and arousal curves were across the entire movie. The subjects gave a score for the two curves for each movie, giving a total of 10 scores that ranged from 0 to 10 (0–3 = disagree, 4–6 = agree, 7–10 = strongly agree).

Tables 20.2 and 20.3 show the average valence and arousal accuracy scores assigned by the subjects for their selected movies. For valence, the lowest score was 3 and the highest was 10. The lowest score for the arousal curves was 5 and the highest was 10. It can be observed from these tables that for each subject, the

TABLE 20.2. Valence Accuracy for Each Subject

Subject no.	1	2	3	4	5	6	7	8
Average score	6.8	6.2	3.8	3.6	7	5.4	9	7

TABLE 20.3. Arousal Accuracy for Each Subject

Subject no,	1	2	3	4	5	6	7	8
Average score	7.8	6.6	6.2	6.8	8.2	7.6	9.6	8.4

TABLE 20.4. Comparison of Valence and Arousal (V/A) Scores for Movies Selected 3 or More Times

Subject No.	Shrek (V/A)	Titanic (V/A)	Finding Nemo (V/A)	Pulp Fiction (V/A)	The Godfather Part 1 (V/A)
1	8/9			6/8	
2		6/5			
3	5/5	3/7	4/7		
4				3/6	3/6
5	4/7				8/9
6		6/9		7/5	5/8
7	9/9	8/9	9/10		
8	8/8	8/9	8/9		

difference in the average scores between valence and arousal was small. This small variation can be observed across all subjects except for subjects 3 and 4, where both scored valence poorly. Overall, based on the opinions of the subjects, arousal appears to be captured more accurately than valence. This is consistent with the existing view that capture of valence is more difficult than arousal (de Kok 2006). However, the general similarity of the results here indicates that this system is extracting valence with reasonable accuracy. Although the average valence scores are lower for all movies, compared with those for arousal, it only falls significantly behind for movie 17, *Pirates of the Caribbean*, where the difference was the largest with 7 for arousal against 3 for valence. Only in the case of the movie *Leon* was the average valence score higher than the arousal score. However, each of the movies *Titanic*, *Harry Potter and the Philosophers Stone*, and *Pulp Fiction* also had one instance where the valence score was higher than the arousal score. Overall, only 4 out of the 40 valence scores given by subjects were higher than the arousal scores.

Table 20.4 shows the valence and arousal scores for five movies that were picked by three or more subjects. As can be seen, there was some consistency of scores between the different subjects. The valence and arousal scores can be grouped into high, medium, and low scoring pairs. It can be observed that the movie *Shrek* had three pairs of high valence and arousal scores that were either 8 or 9. The remaining two pairs had medium scores that ranged from 4 to 7. The movie *Titanic* had two pairs of high scores that were either 8 or 9. This is followed by the remaining three pairs of medium scores that ranged from 3 to 9. The movie *Finding Nemo* had two pairs of high scores that ranged from 8 to 10 and a lower pair of scores that were either 4 or 7. The movie *Pulp Fiction* had two pairs of medium scores that ranged from 5 to 8, and a lower pair of scores that were either 3 or 6. The movie *The God-father Part 1* had one pair of high scores that were either 8 or 9, one pair of medium scores that were either 5 or 8, and one pair of low scores that were either 3 or 6.

The variations between the evaluators are not unexpected. Individuals will vary in their affective response or interpretation of any multimedia material or indeed any experience in general. In analysis of the FEELTRACE affect labeling tool, there were significant differences between raters manually tracing their affective interpretation of affective multimedia data. It is thus not surprising that their opinions of automatically labeled content should vary considerably.

The results presented here are the first attempt at quantifying the performance of the valence and arousal features automatically extracted from movies. Previous justifications for valence and arousal modeling relied on presenting the plot of the curves and describing the scenes in detail, which could be subjected to bias or subjective interpretation (Hanjalić and Xu 2005) (de Kok 2006). Due to such an evaluation method, it is difficult to tell if any improvement, such as the selection of weighting or low-level features, constitute an improvement in the valence and arousal detection. This was one of the major problems facing the development of our affect-based indexing system, since there were no baseline results and experimental guidelines to follow that could indicate an improvement over previous work.

20.5.2.2 Task 2 Subjects were asked to assess the three lists of emotional verbal labels automatically detected by the system for each of the randomly assigned movie clips. For each list, subjects were asked to assign a score from 0 to 10 to indicate how well they felt the list of labels describes the affective features of each assigned clip. The results of this experiment for each subject are shown in Table 20.5. The scores for all three lists were spread across the whole scale of 0–10. Subject 5 assigned noticeably higher scores across the three lists. The Russell list exhibited scores that were more evenly distributed across the scale from 2 to 9. In the Surrey list scores, except for two instances where the scores were zero, the results were concentrated around the 4–8 range of the scale. However, in contrast to this, the Ekman list scores exhibited a greater variation with the scores concentrated around the 1–5 range of the scale.

These observations can also be seen when the values are averaged as shown in Table 20.5. Looking at the averaged scores for each list, it can be seen that the

TABLE 20.5. User-Assigned Average Scores of Detected Emotional Labels for Each List

Subject No.	Russell List	Surrey List	Ekman List
1	4.6	2.6	3.2
2	6.0	5.6	5.0
3	5.6	5.8	6.2
4	3.4	4.8	3.6
5	6.8	7.8	9.6
6	3.4	2.2	3.0
7	6.8	7.4	3.4
8	5.6	5.2	4.8
Average score	5.28	5.18	4.85

Russell list's score of 5.28 slightly outperforms the Surrey list's score of 5.18, which is slightly better than the Ekman list's score of 4.85. In addition, looking at the average scores given by each subject, except for subjects 3 and 5, the scores are lower as the labels become more general.

The Russell list labels received the highest scores since the words were more detailed and were able to describe the clips more accurately. When the labels were then summarized to the Surrey list of 22 general labels, subjects still give high precision scores, but on the occasions the labels were wrong, the penalty was quite severe. There is a further drop in precision when the labels were summarized into Ekman's list of six labels; subjects for the most part found the most general set of labels to be less accurate than the more detailed descriptions. However, when the users found the labels to be correct, they marked these labels as accurate.

20.6   CONCLUSIONS AND NEXT STEPS

This chapter has described a system for cross-modal affective annotation of audio-visual content. The system has been shown in an experimental evaluation to give meaningful affective labels to a wide range of commercial movies. Three annotation vocabularies of varying levels of granularity were analyzed. Comparative results suggest that users prefer the use of larger vocabularies that can be more expressive of the emotional content of the movies.

A more objective evaluation of the accuracy of the annotation could probably be performed by comparing the output of our system with a manually extracted affect curve of these movies extracted using a tool, such as FEELTRACE (Cowie et al. 2000). However, as noted earlier, there is considerable variation in the labeling behavior of individuals, and it is not clear that a meaningful gold standard could be developed manually unless a large number of subjects assigned responses, and these were then combined to give an averaged baseline, in the manner of Russell and Mehrabian's (1977) assignment of VAD values for affective words.

The addition of affective annotations to audio-visual content has a range of potential applications in areas including content retrieval and browsing and classification. The subjective nature of affective interpretation and lack of objective specificity means that we envisage the affective dimension of annotation to generally augment rather than replace existing more objective labeling schemes. The integration of affective features with standard genre features is shown to be affective for an image recommendation task in Tkalčič et al. (Chapter 19, this volume). This could also be combined with affective labeling of specific objects, for example, facial expressions as examined in Stoiber et al. (2009).

The annotation method as described here is based on a fixed keyword vocabulary; this may cause problems for untrained users of affect-enriched applications unfamiliar with a fixed keyword vocabulary and more used to free text search applications. Analysis of feedback from the human subjects watching movies in our CDVPlex project at DCU (Rothwell et al. 2006) found that users typically use a wide range of words to describe the emotional content found in movies. While there are a lot of recurring simple words such as "happy," "sad," and "fear," these are usually augmented with more descriptive words, such as "dynamic," "angst," and "triumphant." One way to expand the vocabulary to ameliorate this problem of mismatch between annotation and user labels would be to repeat a study in the style of Russell and Mehrabian (1977) to cover a much greater number of potential affective label words. However, since this would require the participation of a large number of human judges, it would involve considerable expense and the vocabulary would still be restricted. A more low-cost and flexible alternative means of matching words selected by a user would be to utilize a resource such as WordNet to map user-selected words to the nearest entries in one of our existing lists. We are exploring the utility of our annotation system for a movie retrieval application, focusing in the first instance on investigating retrieval of and similarity between movie content based on affective annotation, before considering how it might used to enhance existing objective CBVR applications.

SECTION 5

MULTIMEDIA ANNOTATION AND AUTHORING

This fifth and final section addresses methods and systems that support the annotation and authoring of multimedia content. Reliably annotated multimedia corpora (e.g., that has reliable interannotator agreement) is an essential ingredient to machine learning systems to discover algorithms for automated annotation. These chapters include reports of methods for cross media annotation, as well as authoring by exploiting semantic representations.

The first chapter by Michael Kipp from the German Center for Artificial Intelligence Research motivates the essential role of multimedia for discovering and baselining phenomena, standardizing conceptual classes, terminology, and properties to facilitate scientific sensemaking, creating gold standards for evaluation, and creating corpora to serve as the basis for machine learning and further discovery. Kipp describes ANVIL, a widely used, free and publicly available annotation tool, and introduces novel extensions for 3D viewing of motion capture data to enable human movement annotation. Automatic computation of agreement scores facilitates the validation of annotated corpora, an essential step toward valid scientific discovery. An integrated query facility and cross-modal association analysis facilitate discovery.

The second chapter by Robin Bargar of New York City College of Technology in Brooklyn turns to the challenge of authoring multimedia presentations, describing the use of a display grammar to author and manage interactive multimedia. Display grammars have other media value, having been used in music theory to organize tonality (melody and harmony) and also in architectural design to explore shapes and geometries. The authors focus on digital signal processing to assist in audio extraction or manipulation, which can be exploited during authoring, which

Multimedia Information Extraction: Advances in Video, Audio, and Imagery Analysis for Search, Data Mining, Surveillance, and Authoring, First Edition. Edited by Mark T. Maybury.
© 2012 IEEE Computer Society. Published 2012 by John Wiley & Sons, Inc.

is supported by a display grammar. The authors exemplify the extraction of audio using audio signal processing and its employment together with interactive images. These could include still images, video, computer graphics, and animations. The authors link signal processing to semantic structure, for example, using reverberation for audio presented in a semantic entity, such as a "cathedral," "phone booth," or "concert hall." A more complex semantic concept, such as a Doppler shift, which refers to the simulation of a sound accelerating toward and then away from the listener, could be represented by a display grammar syntax that combines audio signal processing of stereo panning, pitch shift, an amplitude envelope, and reverberation, to create the impression of a moving audio sound source. The authors present a prototype of a manifold representation of a high dimensional control space for managing interactive media.

The third chapter by Insook Choi of New York City College of Technology in Brooklyn explores the automated creation of new media. Extending beyond the "mashing up" of diverse media types from pre-selected resources, such as RSS feeds, Twitter, or YouTube, the author explores media authoring supported by classifying, storing, locating, and retrieving media resources using ontological representations. Ontology-based authoring supports concept navigation as opposed to searching by resource type. The author presents a demonstration system of non-speech natural sounds where interactive authoring is path-planning in ontological space (represented in the ontology web language [OWL]) in which paths consist of concept nodes that generate queries and return media resources coupled to real-time displays. Interactive authoring is enhanced by audio analysis (the SoundFisher system) together with semantic matching to return similarity ranked candidates for each 3-second segment in the current path. When no candidates match the audio, semantic search can find similar sounds, filtered by matches with sounds in adjacent segments in the path. Specialized thesauri (e.g., use Art and Architectural Thesaurus) can provide a controlled vocabulary to support both hierarchical and associative relationships among concepts. The author demonstrates how semantic query-based authoring is used to design interactive narratives, including 2D images, sounds, and virtual camera movements in a 3D environment about historical Brooklyn. By moving media assembly to the point of delivery, users' preferences, interests, and actions can influence the display.

The final chapter of this section and of the collection is by Matusala Addisu, Danilo Avola, Paola Bianchi, Paolo Bottoni, Stefano Levialdi, and Emanuele Panizzi of Sapienza University of Rome, Italy. The authors turn to the annotation of relations in multimedia web documents. The authors note that the current limitation of automated annotation suggests the need for support for manual human annotators. The authors introduce their Multimedia Annotation of Digital Content Over the Web (MADCOW) system, which integrates browsers with tools to produce text, image, or video "web notes." Two case studies illustrate MADCOW as a tool for information extraction and a tool to structure distributed knowledge. The authors highlight a unique feature of MADCOW, namely the ability to add annotations not only to single but also multiple portions of a document, organizing them in a hierarchical structure, which may reveal new relations about them.

While the chapters in this section represent an exciting set of capabilities for multimedia annotation and authoring, many research gaps remain. First, there are many limitations in processing free text, audio, and video to provide robust annotation of semantics, emotions, and intent. Second, some phenomena cut across time or space or media (e.g., human social behavior) and thus are not easily annotated or authored. Third, robust and intuitive methods for machine learning of ontologies, thesauri, and markup are needed. Fourth, we need intuitive and intelligent user interfaces for annotating and authoring complex media, especially recognizing that the annotations themselves might become multimedia. Finally, natural, collaborative authoring/annotation is needed.

CHAPTER 21

MULTIMEDIA ANNOTATION, QUERYING, AND ANALYSIS IN ANVIL

MICHAEL KIPP

21.1 INTRODUCTION

The goal of finding meaning in data has two extreme manifestations. In the computing sciences, researchers search for automatic methods to extract meaning from low-level data. Most of the contributions in this volume pursue this goal. In the empirical sciences, researchers attempt to interpret surface behaviors of humans or animals according to precise guidelines. While the methods of the two fields are different, they share the underlying data (video and audio files, motion capture data, etc.), as well as the general aim. Both approaches can benefit from each other and are in fact often combined. The computer scientist needs to explore his/her data in a qualitative fashion to determine promising predictors and to build training and test corpora. The empirical scientist can use automatic, quantitative methods to bootstrap the manual annotation process and to increase the objectivity of the approach. Both kinds of research need appropriate tools to support this process. For the qualitative annotation, browsing, and analysis of videos, several tools have been developed (Bigbee et al. 2001; Rohlfing et al. 2006). All tools were developed in a specific research context but are generalizable to a certain extent. This chapter presents the ANVIL[1] tool (Kipp 2001, 2008; Martin and Kipp 2002) as one incarnation of multimedia annotation tools. More specifically, recent extensions to ANVIL are presented that make a first step toward an integrated multimedia annotation, browsing, and analysis platform. The extensions comprise of 3D motion capture viewing, database integration, and a number of analysis features. The driving force behind these extensions was the need to go beyond single modality, single media analysis to cross-modal, multimedia analysis.

[1] http://www.anvil-software.de.

Multimedia Information Extraction: Advances in Video, Audio, and Imagery Analysis for Search, Data Mining, Surveillance, and Authoring, First Edition. Edited by Mark T. Maybury.
© 2012 IEEE Computer Society. Published 2012 by John Wiley & Sons, Inc.

A common target of analysis is human behavior. For something as complex as human behavior, research has moved from performing unimodal analysis to multi-modal analysis. Likewise, with an increased availability of capture and storage devices, researchers are moving from few media sources (e.g., a single video) to multiple media sources. For human motion, the most precise media is *motion capture data*, which can be acquired using various techniques, from complex marker-based optical systems to inexpensive inertia-based systems (Roetenberg et al. 2008). A complex data situation for human behavior analysis would consist of multiple video, audio, and motion capture files (Fikkert et al. 2008). Existing annotation tools cannot display motion capture data as a 3D-animated skeleton, which is the most appropriate visualization. This is surprising since the automatic segmentation and classification of motion capture data is a common problem in computer graphics (Barbic et al. 2004). To be useful for, for example, animation, motion capture data must be annotated with semantic information (Arikan et al. 2003). A viewing and annotation tool is a natural starting point for developing automatic annotation techniques.

Apart from viewing the media, complex search and filter operations on existing annotations are necessary, especially in large corpora. An SQL compliant database was integrated into ANVIL to utilize the full power of the SQL query language. One form of cross-modal analysis, association analysis, uses such queries to collect potential association tuples. In association analysis, the annotation categories of co-occurring annotations from different tracks are quantitatively analyzed. Unimodal analysis features focus on a single track, and, for instance, the transition of categories (essentially a Markov model), which can be visualized by a transition diagram. However, before significant analysis can take place, the consistency of the annotations has to be validated. For this, ANVIL offers automatic agreement computation using kappa statistics.

This chapter is organized as follows. First, the main concepts of the ANVIL tool, as a representative for multimedia annotation tools, are briefly introduced, and related work is surveyed. Then, the database and multiple media integration, especially the 3D motion capture viewer, are presented. Furthermore, three analysis features, coding agreement computation, unimodal transition diagrams, and cross-modal association analysis are discussed. The chapter concludes with a brief discussion of tool interoperability and scheme standardization.

21.2   ANVIL: A MULTIMEDIA ANNOTATION TOOL

In the last 10 years, a number of video annotation tools have emerged. In most of them, annotations are placed on parallel time-aligned *tracks* or *tiers*, so that annotations appear like notes on a musical score (Figure 21.1). Another important aspect of these tools is the possibility to define a coding scheme that describes the structure of annotations and imposes certain constraints on how annotations from different tracks relate to each other.

This chapter presents ANVIL, a widely used video annotation tool in multimodality research (Kipp 2001). In ANVIL, the user transcribes events that occur in the video on parallel *tracks* running along the time axis (Figure 21.1). The transcription of a single event is called *annotation element*, which is displayed as a rectangle in

Figure 21.1. ANVIL graphical user interface. The bottom window, the so-called *annotation board*, is the main instrument of the coder who adds *elements* that appear as time-aligned rectangles on screen.

one of the tracks, in time alignment with all other elements. In Figure 21.1, the *annotation board* is the bottom window, containing color-coded elements. The track layout can be fully specified by the user in a separate file, the so-called *coding scheme*, making the tool independent of a specific research field or underlying theory (cf. Allwood et al. 2005 and Kipp et al. 2007, for sample gesture coding schemes).

A single annotation element is the basic carrier for the human coder's information and can usually be considered a time interval defined by two timestamps for begin and end time. Additionally, ANVIL offers the *time point* annotations, which also refer to a single point in time and are displayed as vertical lines in the track. In ANVIL, the information that a single element carries is not a simple label. Instead, each elements is a complex object with attributes and values. For instance, a gesture annotation can contain gesture type, handedness, hand shape, and so on encoded in dedicated attributes. Attributes are *typed*, which allows the user to restrict the scope of an attribute to a predefined set of labels (sometimes called a *controlled vocabulary*), a range of numbers or a Boolean value. Using complex elements with typed attributes allows the compact encoding of complex events, like gestures in a single screen object.

The underlying assumption for tracks is that all encodings in one track have similar properties, more concretely: each track has its own set of typed attributes that have to be defined by the user in the *coding scheme*. For example, for a track, "gesture" could have two attributes, "type'" and "handedness." Tracks come in various flavors to model the fact that a certain relationship holds between a track *A* and a reference track *B*. For instance, an element in *A* may always have a corresponding element in *B* with the exact same begin/end times. In this case, track *A* would be declared a *singleton* type track with reference track *B*. Another type, *span*, models the condition that each element of track *A* consists of a sequence of elements in reference track *B*. The spanning element in track *A* inherits the begin time of the first element in this sequence and the end time of the last one. The inheritance of timestamps is the main advantage of track types: The begin/end times of *singleton* and *span* type tracks are always propagated from the reference track, making manual alignment unnecessary and the coding process more robust.

Relationships between tracks reflect systematic relationships between their contained elements; in the above cases, these are temporal correspondence or containment. However, one may need to encode arbitrary relationships between encoded elements, which is especially important in cross-modal analysis. ANVIL allows this in the form of *logical links*. A link is a special type of attribute that contains a list of links to other elements that can be used, for instance, for coreference coding.

Elements in tracks have a start and end time as inherent properties. However, sometimes, an element in a video exists for the whole duration of the video (e.g., an object on a table) or is not even concrete (a person). In ANVIL, one can encode such nontemporal entities in a data container called a *annotation set*, which is the equivalent of a track, but without time information (Martin and Kipp 2002). A set is visualized using a simple table. In conjunction with logical links, these elements allow the encoding of complex relations.

While ANVIL and related tools are inherently time based, for a number of applications, it is not enough to encode *when* something happened, but also *where on the screen*. In such cases, ANVIL allows to perform *spatial coding* by drawing directly on the video screen (Kipp 2008). In Figure 21.1, the coder marked up point locations on the video screen, which are displayed as connected dots. The screen locations are encoded as timestamped screen coordinates in a special type of attribute. This is an essential feature for video-based information extraction and is also being used for coding facial expression based on FACS (facial action coding system, cf. Ekman and Friesen 1978).

Finally, since a corpus usually consist of numerous media files and corresponding annotation files, a *project tool* facilitates corpus management by grouping multiple annotation files together that are based on the same coding scheme. The project tool allows to perform all search, export, and analysis operations over the whole corpus.

ANVIL is implemented in Java, thus platform independent, and uses XML for data exchange. It is available free of charge for educational and research purposes.

21.3   RELATED ANNOTATION TOOLS

This section gives a concise overview of tools with a functionality similar to that of ANVIL. This survey is not exhaustive—for more thorough tool surveys, consult

Bigbee et al. (2001) and Rohlfing et al. (2006). Note that the whole area of ontological annotation is not mentioned here (see Chapter 24, this volume).

ELAN,[2] developed at the MPI for Psycholinguistics (Wittenburg et al. 2006), is written in Java and is XML-based. Tracks are called *tiers* in ELAN, and on every tier, the annotations consist of single strings, that is, ELAN lacks the ability to encode multiple attributes on each tier. This implies that a single ANVIL track must be expanded to a set of tiers in ELAN. ELAN does, however, offer to predefine so-called controlled vocabularies to restrict the user input to a set of labels. In ANVIL, this can be achieved using that *ValueSet* attribute type. ELAN also knows about track relationships. The *time subdivision* relationship between tiers A and B implies that every element of A is decomposed into a contiguous sequence of elements in tier B. This is the inverse relation to ANVIL's *span* relationship. The major difference is that ELAN's relation forces the coder to first code the whole and then subdivide it, whereas ANVIL forces the coder to first code the parts and then join them (the subtle difference is that ANVIL's relation allow gaps between subelements and ELAN does not). Another important relation in ELAN is *symbolic association*, which is equivalent to ANVIL's *singleton* relation. ELAN also offers multiple video viewing but does not support motion capture viewing. One major difference between ELAN and ANVIL lies in the fact that ANVIL keeps the structure of the annotation (i.e., declaration of tracks and attributes) in a separate file, the so-called *coding scheme*, whereas ELAN stores this information together with the annotated data. This can cause consistency problems when dealing with large collections of annotation files that should conform to the same scheme. ELAN is well known in gesture research and sign language communities. *EXMARaLDA*[3] is a video annotation tool mainly targeted at the research field of conversation analysis (Schmidt 2004). To some degree, it is theory dependent (for instance, each tier has a speaker assigned to it) and based on the general annotation graph framework (Bird and Liberman 2001). It is also Java and XML based, but neither supports track relationships nor complex elements. However, like ANVIL, it has the notion of projects and has a dedicated corpus management tool. *MacVisSTA*[4] is a video annotation tool targeted at human communication and interaction analysis (Rose et al. 2004). The system is restricted to Mac OS and features the integration of multiple data sources, including motion capture data. However, the latter is not displayed in the form of a 3D skeleton but only as curve plots. MacVisSTA features database integration in two ways: first, to an external database for collaborative coding, and second, to an embedded database for querying. The hybrid architecture may be extended through plugins. *PRAAT*[5] is an audio analysis and annotation tool, mainly targeted at phonetics research, developed at the Institute of Phonetic Sciences, University of Amsterdam (Boersma and Weenink 2005). It runs on multiple platforms and is certainly the most widely used tool in phonetics. For annotation, PRAAT also offers multiple tracks, which come in two flavors: one records elements with a duration, one only elements with a single time point. This corresponds to ANVIL's interval and point tracks. The actual information stored in elements are

---

[2] http://www.lat-mpi.eu/tools/elan.
[3] http://www.exmaralda.org.
[4] http://sourceforge.net/projects/macvissta.
[5] http://www.praat.org.

simple strings. Since PRAAT allows very precise playback control on audio files, it is very suitable for speech transcription. ANVIL can import PRAAT encoded data and it is actually recommendable to use PRAAT as a supplementary tool for ANVIL to do both speech transcription and intonation analysis, which can also be imported and displayed in ANVIL. *Advene*[6] is developed at LIRIS Laboratory, University Claude Bernard Lyon 1. It aims at providing a system for sharing annotations on digital videos (movies, courses, etc.) and providing tools for editing and visualization of so-called *hypervideos*, which are generated from annotations and videos. Users can then exchange analyzed and commented multimedia data. Advene can import ANVIL data. Advene can be considered a meta-tool, as it provides services on top of other tools, thus enabling to profit from the strengths of various tools in an integrated workflow.

To sum up, while there are several similar tools for multi-level multimedia annotation, ANVIL has a number of unique characteristics. Most importantly, ANVIL is the only tool that treats annotations as *objects* with typed attributes, making annotations much more compact if the user chooses to exploit this feature. It is also the only tool that keeps the coding scheme strictly separated from the annotated data, which has proven to be a major advantage in the iterative development of coding schemes. Another unique feature are symbolic links, an essential tool when investigating cross-modal relationships. ANVIL is also the only tool that allows the encoding of spatial information on the video frame, important for preparing information extraction training material, and the only tool to offer a fully 3D motion capture viewer. ANVIL shares with MacVisSTA an embedded database for complex queries, with ELAN the use of track relationships to make coding more robust, and with EXMARaLDA a dedicated corpus management tool. There are tools that can be used for importing to ANVIL, namely PRAAT, and tools that consume ANVIL files, namely Advene. For the future, it would be desirable to increase interoperability between tools so that end users can exploit the individuals strengths of various tools on the same data.

21.4 DATABASE INTEGRATION

Multilayer annotations of multiple media can quickly become cluttered, so that the user needs query functionality to efficiently find relevant information. Since ANVIL allows packaging multiple bits of information into a single element, queries are even more important.

The SQL query language is not only very powerful but also an industry standard. Therefore, ANVIL internally maps the user's annotations to a temporary SQL database that is kept in sync at all times. Each track corresponds to a table: each annotation element is a row, each attribute a column (Figure 21.2). The user can use the full expressive power of SQL to post queries. Since formulating such queries requires expert knowledge, we drafted a simplified syntax for the most basic queries: (1) finding elements in a single track using attribute constraints and (2) finding elements of two tracks that have a certain temporal relationship (e.g., overlap). For

---

[6] http://liris.cnrs.fr/advene.

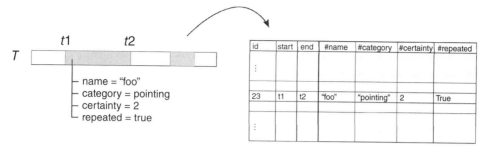

Figure 21.2. Each ANVIL track is mapped to one DB table: elements are rows, attributes are columns; three special columns contain primary key, start, and end time.

TABLE 21.1. Mapping between ANVIL and SQL Data Types

ANVIL Type	SQL Type
String	VARCHAR
Number	INTEGER
Float	FLOAT
Boolean	BOOLEAN
ValueSet	VARCHAR

implementation, we use the Java-based HSQL database engine.[7] Two important restrictions are that the database integration does not handle logical pointers nor explicitly model track relationships.

21.4.1 Mapping Annotations to Database Tables

An annotation track has much in common with a table. A track represents a certain type of information with various properties encoded in attributes. A database table encodes properties in columns, while rows represent instances. In ANVIL, for each track, a specific table is created with columns for each attribute (Figure 21.2). Since tracks elements have begin/end timestamps, they are stored in special columns. We avoid name clashes by prefixing all user-defined attributes with a hash sign. The *id* column is our primary key to annotation elements and is unique across tracks. Query results can easily be mapped back to ANVIL's internal representation of the corresponding annotation elements. Note that the database tables must be kept in sync throughout the annotation session (deletions, additions, and modifications). When ANVIL shuts down, the database is simply closed, to be recreated from scratch on the next launch.

In the mapping depicted in Figure 21.2, we have to convert ANVIL value types to SQL data types. For most types there is a corresponding type (e.g., SQL type *integer* for ANVIL type *number*), for all others, we simply chose the SQL *varchar* type, which is an arbitrary string of alphanumeric characters (Table 21.1).

---

[7] http://hsqldb.org.

21.4.2 Single-Track Queries

A query is a request for a subset of all annotation elements, given some constraints. The single-track query restricts this to a single track. Constraints can be formulated in SQL syntax depending on the SQL data type (Table 21.1): Strings can be queried using regular expressions, numbers can be queried with numeric comparison operators ($<$, $>$, etc.). Since SQL syntax must be learned and can quickly become tedious to write, we offer a simplified scripting language that allows to specify track plus a, possibly nested, combination of attribute constraints, for instance:

```
[mytrack, (att1 = 2H OR att1 = LH) AND anotherAtt <> null].
```

This is translated to the somewhat unwieldy SQL expression:

```
SELECT "mytrack"."id", "mytrack"."#att1", "mytrack"."#anotherAtt"
    FROM "mytrack"
        WHERE ("mytrack"."#att1" = '2H' OR "mytrack"."#att1" = 'LH')
            AND "mytrack"."#anotherAtt" <> 'null'
```

The expression returns all elements in track *mytrack*, which have value 2H or LH in *att1* and have a nonempty attribute called *anotherAtt*. In ANVIL, the returned IDs are used to collect the corresponding ANVIL elements.

21.4.3 Temporal Relationship Queries

To explore cross-modal interactions, researchers have to scrutinize the relationship between elements of *different* tracks, comparing those that temporally coincide or have some other systematic temporal relationship. However, in order to analyze, for example, pairwise relationships between elements of different tracks, one has to define under which conditions element E_1 of track T_1 and element E_2 of track T_2 are compared. One way to do this is to let the user define the *temporal relation* that must hold so that two elements are comparable. We use seven of the Allen relations for this: equals, before, meets, overlaps, starts, finishes, and during. In addition, we let the user specify a *tolerance* limit in seconds (a float value). For example, the relation (*equals, 0.4*) holds if the start time of element E_1 and the start time of element E_2 differ by maximally 0.4 seconds (and if the same holds for the end time).

Again, to spare the user from using long and complex SQL expressions, we have a special syntax to ask for elements from two tracks that are characterized by a certain temporal relationship. An example is:

```
R[overlaps, .8] [firstTrack, hand = 2H] [otherTrack, hand <> null]
```

As one can see, this is an extension of the previously introduced example. It uses two single-track queries and defines a temporal relationship constraint on top of the resulting track elements sets.

Temporal relationship queries are the first step for analysis, for example, in the form of association analysis in ANVIL (Section 21.6.3). For the future, our scripting language will be extended in the direction of other end user oriented query languages, like *Pig Latin* (Olston et al. 2008), which is based on successive filter, grouping, and aggregation operations over data sets.

21.5 INTEGRATING MOTION CAPTURE

ANVIL presupposes that a certain event was documented using multiple types and instances of media. For instance, psychotherapists interested in changes of facial expression, posture, and interpersonal distance and orientation during a therapy session, must record the session with multiple video cameras and microphones. Other media like biometric measurements, eye tracking, and motion capture can complement the setup. In ANVIL, the challenge is to allow for synchronized playback of multiple media streams. In particular, the integration of 3D motion capture playback is desirable because it allows a fine-grained 3D reconstruction of human motion. While nowadays motion capture is mainly used in computer animation, it has the potential of becoming the next generation tool for human behavior research.

21.5.1 Multiple Videos

Video playback in ANVIL is handled by the Java Media Framework (JMF), complemented by the JFFMPEG[8] package, which adds a number of codecs. When playing multiple videos, the internal framework has to synchronize the different media using a single clock. Since in JMF each video is itself modeled as a clock, one video is declared the *master* video, while all others are so-called *slaves*, and are basically controlled by the master video's progression in time. The integration of other media like motion capture also rely on the master video's clock function.

21.5.2 Motion Capture Data

As motion capture (mocap) is becoming more affordable (e.g., through the use of inertial sensors [Roetenberg et al. 2008]), such technology is becoming more likely to be employed in human behavior analysis (Fikkert et al. 2008). Similar technologies like cybergloves have already been used in sign language research (Crasborn et al. 2006). In psycholinguistics, such data could bring long-awaited refinement of theories of human gesture behavior (Kita et al. 1998). In a more general context, the large existing open libraries[9] of motion capture data need the advancement of intuitive retrieval technology to be fully usable (see e.g., Müller et al. 2005). For all these research issues, an annotation tool with an integrated 3D viewer is an important asset to perform qualitative analysis or to create training material.

21.5.2.1 *Visualization*   The primary visualization of mocap data is a 3D reconstruction of the skeleton in the style of a 3D stick figure, as shown in Figures 21.3 and 21.4. The stick figure moves in synchrony to the human shown in the video (if properly synchronized, see below). Additionally, the user can change the camera

---

[8] http://jffmpeg.sourceforge.net.
[9] For instance, the CMU Graphics Lab motion capture database; see http://mocap.cs.cmu.edu.

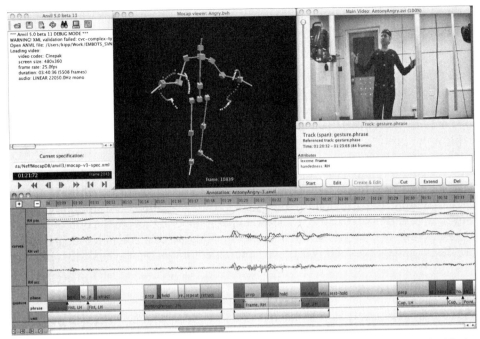

Figure 21.3. ANVIL integrates a 3D viewer for motion capture data, synchronized with the 2D video recording(s) of the capture session.

angle and zoom factor. To visualize movement, ANVIL displays the traces of the hands as a trail of small dots in the same 3D space. We call this *motion trails* (Heloir et al. 2010), which effectively grants a four-dimensional view on the movement, the trail representing time. To unify this visualization with the traditional annotation board (bottom window), ANVIL transfers the color coding of the annotation board elements to the motion (in Figure 21.3, notice the three elements around the play-line on the board, bottom window; their colors are used for the small dots in the top-middle mocap window). This allows researchers to immediately see which part of the trails belongs to, for example, the gesture preparation, and which belongs to the stroke. A third visualization renders 3D movement to curves on the annotation board, so-called *motion curves*. Figure 21.3 shows motion curves of the right hand's wrist joint in three tracks (bottom window). The topmost track represents position in space (decomposed in x, y, and z components), the next is velocity, the next acceleration. These curves can be used to develop motion analysis features or to objectively define certain phenomena, like temporal synchrony or rhythm. Offering arbitrary motion curves in various frames of reference and offering digital filter and aggregation operations is subject of future work to complement the current array of analysis features (Section 21.6).

21.5.2.2 Recording   Motion capture recording requires a specialized studio with several high-speed cameras. The human performer is equipped with either passive or active markers. These markers are then used in postprocessing to reconstruct the relative angles of bones with respect to joints. Fortunately, while there are multiple

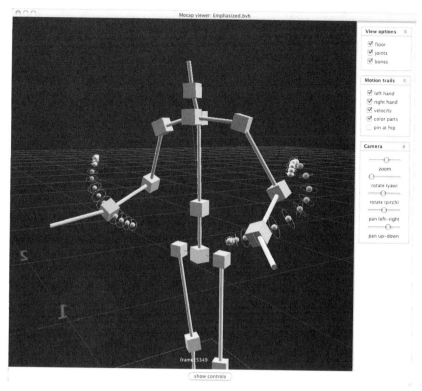

Figure 21.4. Motion trails grant a four-dimensional view on the motion. Velocity is visualized with circles: the radius reflects speed, the circle plane is orthogonal to the motion vector.

ways and technologies to perform motion capture, for the final representation of motion capture data, there are standardized file formats. The most popular ones are Acclaim's ASF/AMC, Biovision's BVH, and the relatively new COLLADA format. The latter is XML-based and currently becoming the new industry standard. All formats store two principal components: (1) the skeleton, that is, the names of joints and their relative position/orientation toward each other, and (2) the motion data, usually represented frame by frame, specifying all angles of all joints for each frame. In ASF/AMC format, the skeleton is defined in the ASF file, and the motion data in the AMC file. In BVH and COLLADA, both are contained in a single file.

21.5.2.3 Synchronization Synchronization between the motion capture data and the video must be done manually. The user first identifies an easy-to-recognize point in the motion capture viewer at time point t_m, then decouples motion capture from video playback. Then, the video is brought to the equivalent point of the motion in the video, at time point t_v in the video. The two time points are then synchronized, which internally means to compute their distance $d = t_v - t_m$ and to use d as an offset when controlling the motion capture viewer.

21.5.2.4 Implementation The ANVIL motion capture viewer is implemented in Java3D and can currently only read BVH files. The skeleton is read from the

BVH file and transformed to a scene graph, where each joint is modeled with a chain of scene graph nodes that have geometry attached to it (the visual representation of a bone). Thanks to the scene graph, the skeleton can be manipulated using local transforms on each joint. The motion file is stored in a separate object and the frame rate, usually around 50–100 fps, is sampled down to the frame rate of the corresponding video, usually 25–30 fps. The mocap viewer does not have its own clock for playback but instead listens to the signal that the master video issues each time a new video frame is displayed.

21.6   ANALYSIS

Analysis procedures must be tailored exactly to the hypotheses at hand. However, having an array of ready-to-use analysis methods in an integrated tool allows for a quick exploration of possible avenues. The first step in any annotation project is to validate the performed annotations by measuring the agreement between different coders. For exploration, data visualization is an important tool. Transition diagrams visualize the sequential behavior of categories in an intuitive fashion. For cross-level analysis, ANVIL offers a custom process for examining the association of two attributes on different tracks that enables the user to single out the specific categories that seem to be correlated.

21.6.1   Validating Coding

Manual annotation relies on the human coder's competence in segmenting and classifying the data. Since there is usually some degree of interpretation involved, it is essential to establish how objective the annotations are and to clarify whether the categories are well-defined and consistently applied across the corpus. Such a validation can be done by measuring intercoder or intracoder agreement: multiple coders annotate the same media (intercoder) or the same coder annotates the same media after some time has passed (intracoder). In both cases, the degree of correspondence between two annotation files has to be measured. ANVIL offers to compute Cohen's *kappa* (κ) as one such measure. This statistic is appropriate for testing whether agreement exceeds chance levels for binary and nominal ratings (Cohen 1960). The input consists of two annotation files (or two sets of files) to compare. The user must decide which track and which attribute to analyze. In the computation of kappa, the elements of two tracks are compared where each element has one out of n behavior categories $C_1, \ldots, C_n$. The $n \times n$ confusion matrix records the occurrences of paired elements in terms of categories. The diagonal in the matrix is the number of occurrences of agreement between the two coders for each behavior. This matrix is also informative for understanding possible sources of disagreement. However, the challenge is to decide which elements to compare in cases where the segmentation is different. In ANVIL, this problem is solved by considering *time slices* instead of elements. For videos with a frame rate of 25 frames per second, ANVIL cuts the annotation file into slices of 0.04 seconds and compares categories on each time slice, adding one additional category VOID for the case that no annotation resides on the slice. These counts are put into a confusion matrix used to

	V-O-I-D	hold	indep-hold	partial-retract	prep	retract	stroke
V-O-I-D	1.875	109	0	0	20	12	49
hold	83	484	7	12	7	10	17
indep-hold	0	14	2	0	3	4	5
partial-retract	0	0	0	32	0	0	0
prep	37	15	9	0	274	1	78
retract	32	2	0	0	0	201	16
stroke	7	38	3	10	120	17	529

Save..

Figure 21.5. Confusion matrix, including the VOID marker for not-annotated areas.

compute kappa (Figure 21.5). ANVIL has the option to neglect all parts of the annotation files where both coders have VOID. Note, however, that the kappa value remains the same because it factors out prior probabilities.

While the kappa value, computed in this way, reflects both the degree of agreement in segmentation and classification, one can use the same method to focus on segmentation only. For this, ANVIL uses only two categories, VOID and ANNOTATED, and then performs the same computation as described above, resulting in a *segmentation kappa*.

For every performed agreement analysis, ANVIL displays the confusion matrix, the computed kappa, and the segmentation kappa. The resulting kappa value can be used to get an impression of how consistent the annotation is. Fleiss (1981) considers a kappa between 0.40 and 0.60 as fair, between 0.60 and 0.75 as good, and over 0.75 as excellent. Bakeman and Gottman (1987) take a kappa of less than 0.70 with some concern. Kappa statistics should not be viewed as the unequivocal standard for computing agreement. However, they are almost always preferable to simple proportion (percentage) of agreement, which does not factor out chance agreement.

21.6.2   Transition Diagrams

A *transition diagram* consists of states and transitions (Figure 21.6). Each transition has a probability attached to it (in Figure 21.5, the probability is given in percent), and all outgoing transitions from a single state add up to 100%—it is therefore a *Markov model* (Press et al. 2007). A transition with 21% between state A and state B means that in 21% of all times that the system was in state A, the immediately following state happened to be B. Transition diagrams visualize the temporal neighborhood of discrete events in a quantitative fashion. For example, if looking at a stream of gestures, we may be interested in how often the speaker changes from left hand (LH) to right hand (RH) to two hands (2H), in all possible combinations (Figure 21.5).

Mathematically, this is modeled with relative frequencies, an approximation for the conditional probability of state B, for example, LH, given that state A, for example, RH, occurred beforehand. Formally, if we have a set of states $s_1, \ldots, s_n$, then the conditional probability $P(s_i|s_j)$ is approximated by the counts: $P(s_i|s_j) =$

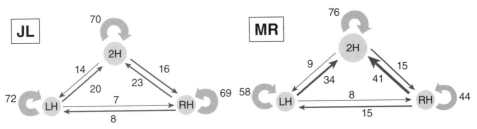

Figure 21.6. Handedness transition diagrams for speakers JL and MR show preferences which hand(s) are used for gesturing and how often the mode is switched. Circle area indicates unigram probability, size of the arrows and number indicate transition probability between gestures. The diagrams show that MR uses 2H more often than JL. Moreover, JL stays in one mode more often than MR, as the high probabilities on the 2H → 2H, LH → LH, and RH → RH arcs show.

$C(s_i, s_j)/C(s_i)$, where $C(s_i, s_j)$ counts the number of occurrences of the states (s_i, s_j), having occurred in this order, and $C(s_i)$ counts the total number of s_i occurrences.

In speech processing (cf. Jurafsky and Martin 2003) this is also called a *bigram*, as opposed to the *unigram* which simply is the probability of a single state s_i, approximated by $P(s_i) = C(s_i)/\sum_k C(s_k)$. The transition diagram as displayed in Figure 21.6 is a visualization of unigrams and bigrams, where the unigram probability is indicated by the size of the circles of $s_1, \ldots, s_n$ and the bigram probabilities are indicated by the size of the arrows between the events.

Transition diagrams give an immediate visualization of the bigram distribution and may guide the detection of regularities. The above example of gesture handedness was used, for example, by Kipp et al. (2007) and Neff et al. (2008) to detect and model idiosyncrasies in gesture behavior for two distinct speakers. The way a human speaker uses the left hand, the right hand, or two hands is quite specific to the individual performer, a hypothesis validated in a recent semiotic study (Calbris 2008).

21.6.3 Association Analysis

While transition diagrams illustrate the sequential behavior of events within a single track, association analysis can discover meaningful co-occurrences of events on different tracks. In a recent study, we were interested in the relation between gesture and emotion (Kipp and Martin 2009). In our study, one track recorded the gesture behavior of a person and another track encoded the person's emotional state. Do certain gesture types coincide with a certain emotional state? Let us assume that the interesting categories are encoded in two attributes A and B located on tracks T_1 and T_2, respectively (where $T_1 \neq T_2$). In our example, A was gesture handedness (LH, RH, 2H) and B emotional state (happy, angry, and so on). Since the attributes are located on different tracks, we first have to decide in which cases elements are paired up, usually based on some notion of temporal co-occurrence. For each pair, we can then compare the values of A and B. "Co-occurrence" can mean, for instance, only those elements in T_1 that are fully contained in an element on T_2, but it could

TABLE 21.2. Exemplary Contingency Table, Including Row and Column Marginals and Total Sum

	LH	RH	2H	N_j
Happy	12	4	1	17
Angry	5	2	20	27
$N_{i\cdot}$	17	6	21	44

TABLE 21.3. Expected Values Matrix, Including the Differences to Actual Observation

	LH	RH	2H
Happy	6.57 (+5.43)	2.32 (+1.68)	8.11 (−7.11)
Angry	10.43 (−5.43)	3.68 (−1.68)	12.89 (+7.11)

TABLE 21.4. Mutual Information Matrix

	LH	RH	2H
Happy	0.14	0.03	0.25
Angry	0.14	0.03	0.25

also be every pair of elements that temporally overlap. The user can formally define such a relation using the Allen relations introduced in Section 21.4.3. This done, we are able to view coinciding events in a *contingency table*.

The next step is to find out whether the two attributes are statistically associated. This is usually measured with a χ^2 test or *Cramer's V* (a normalization of χ^2 to the interval [0,1]). However, this only tells us whether the *attributes* as a whole are related, but not whether two specific *values* are associated. In order to find out the latter, we use an explorative method and a conclusive validation method. For the explorative part, we look at the contingency table (Table 21.2). This table can be used to compute the expected value n_{ij} for each cell, defined by $n_{ij} = N_{i\cdot}N_{\cdot j} / N$, where $N_{i\cdot}$ denotes the row marginals, $N_{\cdot j}$ the column marginals, and N the total number of observations (Press et al. 2007).

The difference between expected value and actual value reveals whether there is a potential association and the direction of this association (Table 21.3). Note that this value is neither normalized nor necessarily statistically significant. To check the hypothesis that value a out of A and value b out of B are associated, we could then run a χ^2 analysis where we treat all non-a values in A as a single value $\bar{a}$, likewise for b. However, in order to arrive at a more precise and comparable measure of association strength, we employ the entropy-based measure of *mutual information* (MI) as suggested by Press et al. (2007), which is defined by $I(x, y) = \sum p_{ij} \ln(p_{ij} / p_{i\cdot}p_{\cdot j})$ where $p_{ij} = N_{ij}/N$. The measure is symmetrical, $I(x,y) = I(y,x)$, and can be used to compare the strengths of various value combinations. ANVIL displays this in an MI matrix (Table 21.4), which one can use to compare strengths of associations.

Using the techniques described in this section, we were able to show, for a limited corpus of theater material, that gesture handedness was closely correlated with emotion in the analyzed speakers (Kipp and Martin 2009). More specifically, the two analyzed speakers consistently used the left hand in a relaxed mood and used the right hand in a hostile mood. This shows that the described steps can lead to significant results in cross-modal analysis. Thanks to the automation of this procedure, new hypotheses about attribute association can quickly be explored and validated.

21.7 CONCLUSIONS

This chapter introduced ANVIL as an example for a multimedia annotation tool, and pointed out the differences to related tools. The most striking difference lies in ANVIL's concept of complex annotation elements with typed attributes and its strict separation of coding scheme and annotation data. The chapter focused on recent extensions to ANVIL, which are aiming at making ANVIL an integrated platform for the annotation, browsing, and analysis of multimedia data. The extensions are a 3D motion capture viewer, an SQL database, and various analysis features (coding agreement computation, transition diagrams and cross-modal association analysis). The association analysis uses contingency tables for identifying possible associations between attribute values and then gives *mutual information* measures to estimate the strength of these associations. Future work has to move toward the inclusion of automated extraction using the techniques described in the first chapters of this volume. Concrete candidates for future extensions are automatic motion detection, using motion capture data or by applying computer vision algorithms on the video files to perform semi-automatic annotation, ideally in an interactive human-in-the-loop process. Such directions have the potential to build new alliances between empirical researchers and information extraction communities.

On a higher level, there are two important issues for future exploration: tool interoperability and scheme standardization. Since many annotation tools exist, each with their own strengths and discipline-specific features, it is highly desirable to establish mechanisms that allow the joint use of several tools in a smooth workflow. This implies data transformation, which can be done with a tool like *Transformer*, or a direct import/export feature—for example, ANVIL users usually do their speech transcription in PRAAT and then import this data into an ANVIL track. However, given N tools, one needs $N \times N$ specific transformation procedures. Instead, if a single exchange format X existed, this could be reduced to $N + N$ transformation procedures (export to X, import from X). This avenue has been explored at a 2007 workshop on multimodal annotation tools (Schmidt et al. 2009), and resulted in a preliminary exchange format based on annotation graphs (Bird and Liberman 2001). However, a number of important features, for example, track relationships, are nontrivial to map, so that for now, such transformations are not lossless. The second issue is that of scheme standardization and has been explored by Bunt et al. (2005). The main idea is to have standard coding schemes in the form of coding scheme files. Along these lines, a decomposable coding scheme in the form of a meta-scheme needs to be developed. For standardization to have an effect, such meta-scheme must be interoperable across many tools. This avenue seems possible, since even now many coders (re-)use similar schemes (e.g., Kita et al. 1998, for movement phases), or are connected in networks with a standardized coding procedure (e.g., the MUMIN network [Allwood et al. 2005]).

ACKNOWLEDGMENTS

Special thanks to my students Quan Nguyen (DFKI) and Gabriel Manolache for their work on export functions and database integration. Thanks to Nele Dael, Marcello Mortillaro, and Klaus Scherer (U Geneva, CISA) for their input on agreement computation. This research has been carried out within the framework of the Cluster of Excellence *Multimodal Computing and Interaction*, sponsored by the German Research Foundation (DFG).

CHAPTER 22

TOWARD FORMALIZATION OF DISPLAY GRAMMAR FOR INTERACTIVE MEDIA PRODUCTION WITH MULTIMEDIA INFORMATION EXTRACTION

ROBIN BARGAR

22.1 INTRODUCTION

Applications of multimedia information extraction (MMIE) for interactive media production depend upon dynamic relationships between prerecorded media resources and on-demand media signal processing. Systems of production and distribution for interactive media are different in fundamental ways from production systems for noninteractive media, and these differences impact applications of MMIE. While interactive media programs utilize preproduced media resources, these are combined with metadata and paradata for additional signal processing on devices where the programs are delivered and displayed. These data may include *descriptions* of resources, the observer or the context where media resources were captured; *instructions* for computation, including scripts and code; *variable data* representing user input or other dynamic conditions; and *network addresses* of media resources located online. The premise of producing a single, final version of an interactive program is antiquated by user-driven on-the-fly content assembly. MMIE must be adaptive to dynamic properties of interactive media content.

An interactive media program will present new content each time the work is observed. The extent of its media content is not bounded by images and sounds transmitted from a source. Variability of users' actions, use contexts, and signal processing algorithms embedded in display devices, all contribute to the media content. Together, these represent the full scope of the interactive media signal that must be taken into consideration when performing information extraction. In an ideal system, each of these factors are represented in data available to MMIE to aid the analysis of dynamic image and sound content. In present systems, these

Multimedia Information Extraction: Advances in Video, Audio, and Imagery Analysis for Search, Data Mining, Surveillance, and Authoring, First Edition. Edited by Mark T. Maybury.
© 2012 IEEE Computer Society. Published 2012 by John Wiley & Sons, Inc.

factors may not be differentiable or exposed in a media signal, or they may be available, but the MMIE application may not be configured to analyze them.

The present research describes a method for differentiation of interactive media signals into (a) media source components and (b) data or instruction set components. Transformations may be applied to (a) or (b), and MMIE should be able to utilize (b) to enhance accuracy of analyses of (a). We examine two distinctions to aid MMIE for interactive media signals: (1) Distinction of media source materials from the *display processing* applied to generate transformations of the source materials: MMIE may be more efficient if media sources can be isolated from signal processing transformations applied during interactive presentation. (2) Distinction of media source materials from the *authoring instructions* that govern the display processing engines: MMIE interpretations of interactive media will be simplified if the MMIE algorithms can access and parse the authoring instructions for display processing embedded in the media signal.

These distinctions are encompassed in the concept of a *display grammar*, which provides symbolic representations of signal processing states associated to interactive media production rules. Display grammar symbols and their associated signal processing states are quantifiable, transformable, and reproducible. A display grammar implementation discussed here will focus on audio examples and audio signal processing related to the application of audio with interactive images. Audio is highly malleable and is often combined with multiple types of visual material—still images, video, computer graphics, and animations. Digital audio brings a long history of computational modeling both of sound sources and acoustics. The principles of Display Grammar applied here may be directly extended to procedural and interactive signal processing of visual media using the demonstrated approach.

22.1.1   Interactive Media Production and MMIE

Interactive media situate elements of program content assembly in the hands of an observer. Interactive media are the primary candidate domain for display grammars due to their use of real-time systems to dynamically and procedurally generate media streams, incorporating continuous control data from system users. For the present discussion, two areas of functionality are relevant: the *program signal* that encodes an interactive program, and *point-of-delivery assembly* of media programs.

An interactive media "program" is a signal that carries both executable and observable information. The MPEG-4 standard is representative of this paradigm (Rao et al. 2006): an end-to-end model from compression to synchronization to delivery of media resources is transmitted as multiplexed streams of media objects encompassing both data and content, decoded under users' actions for point-of-delivery assembly within a digital multimedia integration framework (DMIF). Whereas MMIE is traditionally situated prior to the Compression phase, we will examine its potential in the Delivery phase.

Point-of-delivery assembly is powered by an ecosystem of embedded computation and digital signal processing (DSP) hosted by media display devices: (1) Display of media files requires rudimentary DSP, such as compression–decompression. (2) More advanced signal processing provides transformations of attributes of media content, such as frequency-domain filtering. (3) DSP is required for real-time signal generators, such as computer graphics or sound synthesis software and hardware. (4) Data from users' actions processed with low latency DSP provides pattern recognition to enhance a user's experience of responsive feedback at the point of delivery. Given intensive application of DSP, a point of delivery media synthesis architecture is a locus for MMIE data. Encoded in an interactive program signal, MMIE analysis data may be effectively applied to extend the media synthesis capability of DMIF applications.

22.1.2   MMIE and Display Grammar

The present work applies to production cycles, where media signals are ingested and transformed to generate new media signals. The ingest-transform cycle has consequences for applications of MMIE as methodology, not only for media analysis, but for media production. Patterns and their semantic functions are targeted for extensive and iterative signal processing in media production. When MMIE is applied to a task of media document analysis, the MMIE process must decipher the consequences of layers of signal processing that were applied by media-makers to achieve semantic goals. If data representing semantically oriented DSP were encoded computationally during media production, and if this data was retrievable in the form of signal processing data from media authoring files, it would be of great benefit to the process of decoding the semantic properties of the media and applying these to further production.

Semantically driven data is proliferate during media production, but is rarely preserved or transmitted through media distributors to consumers. Semantic production data is predominantly proprietary and nonstandard, often recorded as informal annotations in formats that reflect individual studio production methodology. From a pragmatic perspective, this potentially valuable data is not reusable. A display grammar encoding semantically driven signal processing data can provide a formalization of the signal-to-symbol decisions made in media production, and preserve this data for future use in MMIE. The direct utilization of MMIE in the production process of new media, based upon the automated acquisition and analysis of existing media resources, is one anticipated consequence of transmitting grammatical representations embedded in media signals.

22.2   DISPLAY GRAMMAR BACKGROUND

Prior to modern applications of computation Wittgenstein in Philosophical Grammar identified the potential of grammar to "show the actual transactions of language, everything that is not a matter of accompanying sensations" (Wittgenstein 1974, p. 87). The function of grammatical rules to "set up a connection between language and reality" (op. cit. p. 89) provides ontological grounding in the designation of signal-to-symbol constructs. While today's digital media are based primarily upon simulation of physical devices and quantization of physical signals, grammatical constructs provide a basis for semantic representations of computational media. Advances in media management and production depend upon robust semantic composition and manipulation of computational representations of media content.

At the root of this inquiry is the ontological relationship of a semantic expression to a corresponding physical phenomenon. In computation, this relationship is embodied in the designation of symbols for signals. This includes the process of sample generation where continuous signals are discretized and quantified, and symbolic operations applied to groups of samples at various time scales to achieve microscopic and macroscopic transformations. The prevalent use of transformations in a media synthesis environment indicates the value of computational grammars for representing and managing transformations.

22.2.1 Generative Grammars

Generative grammars introduced by Chomsky are both descriptive and productive, reflecting the ontological duality of signal analysis and signal generation necessary for computational transformations. A Generative Grammar is "a system of rules that can iterate to generate an indefinitely large number of structures" (Chomsky 1965, pp. 15–16). His identification of competence and performance carries implications for representations of computational processes used in interactive media. The concept of performance indicates a person enacting an utterance based upon structural principles encoded in symbols. Interactive media embodies the process of utterance as an individual's control of a media signal generator in real time. Chomsky's subdivision of generative grammar into syntactic, phonological, and semantic is relevant for interactive media applications, where the control of a media device is analogous to speech acts or to expressive acts, such as musical performance.

Interactive media authoring and production enable a distinction between two use cases of grammars. Generative grammars are one case, primarily used by practitioners to render handcrafted optimized signals, such as the use of fractals to generate computer graphics for simulated natural scenes or special effects. Display grammars are a distinct case, applied to real-time procedural display of multiple media synthesized from previously produced media resources.

22.2.2 Design Computing, Computer Music, and Interactive Narrative

Applications of generative grammars in digital media have a history in the fields of computer graphics, design computing, and computer music research, and, more recently, in interactive game environments. L-systems or Lindenmayer systems were developed to simulate algae growth and have been applied to automatic generation of computer graphic plant images having intricate detail (Prusinkiewicz 2000), as well as other patterned natural and man-made phenomena. Shape grammars were introduced in the architectural design research by Stiny and Gips (1978). Gero and Kumar (1993) combined generative grammars for shapes and the use of genetic algorithms to create alternative designs in 2D and 3D geometries that can be related to components in architecture and construction. Design Computing has emerged as a field of practice that includes the application of generative grammars to create geometric patterns, which are applied to visual designs and 3D forms (Gero 2006). Design Computing practices are highly suggestive for the application of display grammars to interactive media. The primary differences are the cross-media structures required for multimedia communications and the heightened interactivity and real-time procedural display of results.

In the music theory research, community generative grammars have been demonstrated relevant to analysis and production of tonality, the system of organizing musical melody and harmony in temporal hierarchies related to the common practice period of European classical period (Lerdahl and Jackendoff 1983). Limited applications for composing computer-generated music have emerged in contemporary practice (Laske 1993). Efforts at generative music for interactive media, such as video games, are limited to combinatorial segment selection using high-level scripts and preproduced musical segments (Boer 2003), techniques that do not require generative grammars. Additional creative work in generative music composition (Cope 2006) and interactive storytelling (Bocconi 2006; Davenport et al. 2000; Mateas and Stern 2005) primarily utilize techniques of pattern matching and NLP.

22.2.3 Proposed Scope of Display Grammars for Media of Multiple Types

The term display grammar was proposed by Choi to formalize the relationship of display processing with respect to interactive systems for content management and media synthesis (Choi 2008a,b). The intent from a media production standpoint is to develop formal representation of display processing across media of multiple types. Contemporary cross-media representations are notably limited in software interfaces for industrial media production. Interfaces for professional media production software tend to embrace illustrations of controls applied to individual parameters of complex signal processing. Interface semantics tend to be imitations of analog media devices, such as arrays of frames from a physical segment of motion picture celluloid, or audio signals on a magnetic tape. Extreme examples include representations of antiquated analog hardware, such as tape decks, patch panels and mixing consoles. The common limited extent of cross-media representation is a visual timeline depicting motion picture frames aligned with time-domain graphs of audio signals, such as the ProTools™ (Avid Inc., Burlington, MA) or Final Cut Pro™ (Apple Inc., Cupertino, CA) interfaces. Literal renderings of audio sample values and are known to be poor representations of recognizable audible properties, not helpful for synthesis with visual media semantics.

Display grammars are proposed to organize coherent and extensible representations of media signal processing methods, and to apply those methods through semantically expressive control of relationships across media of different types. The term "expressive" refers to the capacity to computationally draw distinctions among multiple properties of media signals, providing a representation of distinct signal processing layers that generate or modify these properties. Distinct representations can be applied to organize DSP layers across media of multiple types, with respect to semantics in the conventional sense of media content.

22.3 DISPLAY GRAMMAR DEFINITION AND CHARACTERISTICS

1. A display grammar is a set of symbols and formation rules. Each symbol represents a unique signal processing state in an n-dimensional state space designated for that grammar.

2. While the symbols are discrete, each symbol represents a point in a continuous space of values of control parameters for display signal processing. This is the control parameter state space.

3. An n-dimensional signal processing algorithm will be represented by an n-dimensional control parameter state space. Each dimension of the state space defines a range of values for one control parameter of the DSP algorithm.

4. A transformation applied to a symbol will produce another symbol representing a point in the state space.

5. Symbols may be grouped in sets or in sequences in terms of their application to media signal processing. Criteria for group formation are particular to the syntax of individual grammars and their media applications, consistent with the underlying general model of display grammars.

A display grammar is intended for optimization of DSP representations for authoring real-time interactive media. A signal processing configuration represented by a display grammar is effectively a set of presentation rules for multimedia authoring. Display grammar production rules consist of a DSP algorithm and an associated n-dimensional control space that designates the phase space of DSP states. As in other grammars, these are production rules. The grammatical symbol provides a pivot between a continuous signal processing state space and a discrete semantic representation. This pivot function is discussed in Section 22.5.3.

22.3.1 Display Grammar for Media of Multiple Types

Media of multiple types may be brought into a common signal processing representation in a display grammar. The DSP state space may be extended over signal processing algorithms for multiple media resources, such that a symbol in the grammar represents a state that applies to multiple media. In some cases, a common DSP process may apply to media of more than one type, such as "fade out" or "cross dissolve" applied in tandem to a visual and an auditory signal. In other cases, the state space may link dissimilar DSP processes that are designated as a single grammatical unit for purposes of a particular syntax. For example, to reproduce a theatrical and cinematic tradition, the end of a scene accompanied by a "fade to black" may be accompanied by an inverse function, a fade up of a musical signal. The "event rate" and "event onset" parameter values of these complementary functions—fade out image while fading in sound—are not necessarily the same rate or time point; selecting these values creates semantic alternatives. The music may emerge from silence and darkness, or the music may onset before the end of a scene to draw attention away from the visual transition. These combinations present alternate semantic consequence, a unique symbol encoded for each set of parameter values. Grammatical transformation of either symbol can produce the other, representing traversal of control parameter space from one state to another. Articulation of scene boundaries is an example of the semantic function of media signal processing encoded in a display grammar, and is particularly relevant for applications of MMIE, which could use grammar data to disambiguate cross-modal features.

22.3.2 Temporal Properties of Display Grammar

Each symbol in a display grammar represents concurrent transformations applied in parallel to all media resources assigned to that grammatical operation. Other than ubiquitous concurrent transformation, temporal range in a display grammar is defined by properties of the signal processing algorithm associated with the grammar. Symbols in a display grammar do not include a temporal designation; the inherent temporality of a given transformation is a property of the associated DSP state space. Each display grammar symbol represents a DSP state that may be applied for a duration that is fixed or variable. For example, applications of "fade out" or "cross dissolve" include specific event duration. Other transformations may be of variable duration, such as a color filter applied to a video signal or a frequency filter applied to an audio signal. Temporality on a larger scale is applied according to syntax, the organization of series of grammatical transformations for interactive performance of media signal processing.

22.3.3 Display Grammar Characteristics

Formalization of display grammar requires a representation of a grammatical unit as an axis or pivot between signal processing data and semantic data. These data are inherently dissimilar in terms of type and implementation. Signal processing data is continuous, quantitative, and ordered. Semantic data is discrete, organized by set membership and unordered. A grammatical pivot requires a robust computational space and reproducible, extensible methods for relating dissimilar constituents in this space. The present work applies a geometric representation of a continuous signal processing control space with embedded discrete symbolic links to semantic data, which are query terms in the form of a controlled vocabulary. Each embedding is a grammatical unit that may be applied either as part of a continuous control function or as a member of a semantic data set.

The geometric representation discussed in Methodology below enables media resources of unlike types to be referenced according to attributes shared in common, including common semantic properties and common utilization of signal processing transformations. While many attributes of diverse media resources are not shared in common, a display grammar functions in a presentation system where resources of different types share common usage of DSP under interactive presentation architecture. Following is a review of attributes of semantic data and signal processing data, relevant to the presentation of a prototype geometric method that demonstrates the potential functional capacity of formalized display grammar.

22.3.3.1 *Characteristics of Semantic Structure and Order*   Semantic structures are discrete and organized in set membership representing relationships, such as similarity, subclass–superclass hierarchy, or context-based semantic association. Set membership is unordered. While interactive media requires ongoing scheduling of events in time sequence, relations, such as linear ordering are not easily expressed semantically, requiring relational predicates such as "nextThing" or "previousThing." A linear semantic scale may be valid within its defined context, but is cumbersome for semantic structure in general.

Semantic structure is relevant for MMIE as a *de facto* target for a recognition function. Display grammar can provide a coupling of semantic context with signal processing data to aid MMIE methods that tend toward optimization for narrow classes of targets.

22.3.3.2   Characteristics of Signal Processing Structure and Order   Signal processing functions are implemented as numerical expressions that constitute quantitative control state spaces, having numerical order. A DSP algorithm can have many control variables, and these can be represented as multidimensional systems with potentially many degrees of freedom and numerical order along each dimension. The availability of quantitative structure in the signal processing domain is a complement to the semantic domain; combining the two enables a dual expressivity where one can navigate by discrete semantic relationship or continuous control space. However, a meaningful coupling of signal processing states with semantic terms requires interpretation of signal processing state-spaces in a particular semantic context.

22.3.4   Example: Auditory Signatures for Spatial Cues

As an example of a semantically expressive coupling, an audio signal processing channel may be used to generate reverberation for audio signals. Reverberation attributes are determined by combinations of parameter control values. Select combinations of reverberation control values produce coherence of reverberation characteristics that are recognizable in terms of empirically observed environmental conditions. A recognizable coherence can be described using semantic references, such as "cathedral," "phone booth," or "concert hall"—terms that reflect the auditory signatures of simulated environmental conditions. These examples demonstrate the rationale of context and empirical observation for linking signal processing to semantic structure. Not every combination of DSP control parameters will result in a recognizable environmental coherence. There are parametric "sweet spots" that are relevant in terms of simulated environmental characteristics. These select control parameter states in a signal processing state space take on a semantic function based upon empirical observation and the relevant media use case.

22.3.5   Grammar in Context of an MMIE Application

The following demonstrates the role of a grammatical representation in the application of MMIE. Wold et al. (1996) presents an empirical rationale applied to the organization of MMIE contexts for media feature target definitions. With the Sound-Fisher application, a user specifies a target sound and initiates a search for acoustically similar sounds. The application performs a search analysis based upon spectral characteristics—purely signal processing with no semantic metadata. Chapter 23 provides an example of the results of a SoundFisher search, showing an array of sounds that are not from a common source, but are acoustically alike (Choi, Chapter 23, this volume). Pattern-based MMIE search results are often robust with respect to spectral similarities and differences, but may not be semantically consistent with structured vocabularies representing content. The SoundFisher analysis may be thought of as "machine listening," an automated form of empirical observation that is confirmed or rejected by the human observer. Iterative use of such a system can build up a semantic space representing audio signals in a robust relationship to signal processing characteristics. The process is useful both for audio production, as well as for analysis of audio signal content.

In the SoundFisher system, the relationship between semantic and DSP representations is purely case- based. There is no formal designation of a symbolic unit related to semantic or signal data. A user may assign keywords to classify individual sounds returned with respect to specific targets, and this target–tag relationship is suggestive of formalized semantic structure across multiple searches. A grammatical formalization could be applied by exposing the signal processing state space of the search engine and allowing semantic identifiers to be registered with respect to quantitative search terms. The signal analysis search state in a SoundFisher search occupies a potentially pivotal position between a signal processing representation of a sound and the semantic representation assigned by an observer who identifies similarity or difference in found sounds with respect to the search target sound. This pivotal role is informal but consistent with the distinction of grammatical symbol from semantic data and signal processing data.

Establishing a consistent symbolic pivot between signal and semantic representations provides an anchoring function for MMIE. In Section 22.4, a method for robust anchoring is proposed. The envisioned benefits are the coupling of semantic targets with quantitative properties of signals, extensible beyond limited searches tailored for specific media content types. The formalization of semantic-to-signal coupling is proposed to achieve explicit representation of the pivotal function and to apply grammar-based transformations to the coupling itself in a larger state space of potential couplings.

22.4 DISPLAY GRAMMAR METHODOLOGY

As presented above the control parameters of a DSP algorithm may be represented as an n-dimensional state space. For n parameters, each control parameter in the DSP algorithm may be represented as one dimension or one axis in the state space. For n dimensions, the domain of values along each axis maps into a range of control values for one DSP parameter. Each state in the n-dimensional state space constitutes a set of n DSP parameter control values. A state may be represented as a single point in the n-dimensional space; the parameter control values of this state may be thought of as an array of size n associated with the point.

For a DSP algorithm having many control states, a subset of these states represents perceptually distinct DSP outputs. Through empirical observation a selection of distinct states is identified for use in a media production. To create a display grammar, each selected state is assigned a unique symbolic identifier. A symbolic identifier is a discrete symbol, whereas the state it represents belongs to a continuous control space. Consistent with generative grammars, a DSP state may be assigned a terminal symbol or a nonterminal symbol. Points in the state space that are not selected remain functional as DSP parameter control states, but are not assigned a member of the set of symbols that make up the display grammar.

This approach provides a dual representation of DSP states for a display grammar: (1) a set of points in a geometric space that may be ordered according to linear distance; (2) a corresponding set of discrete symbols that may be ordered according to set operations such as union, intersection, or subset–superset hierarchy. With reference to this dual representation, a display grammar may be used to represent transformations from one state to another, and, in parallel, transformations from one symbol to another. Points in DSP state space may be ordered by quantitative value, and distances between two points may be represented as a vector. Moving from one point to another may be thought of as a linear transformation using operations such as vector addition. Sets of discrete symbols may be organized in topologies such as networks, and transformed with set operations. For a set of discrete symbols, a transformation is represented as the evaluation of a logical expression or as the traversal of a graph from one node to another, each node representing a symbol in the grammar.

This dual representation is critical to the functionality of a display grammar. Dual forms of organization and transformation create a functional relationship between the continuous control of DSP parameter values and the syntactic ordering of discrete symbols necessary for semantic associations. Syntax in a display grammar is a sequence of points in state space and in parallel, a sequence of symbols. One or more symbols may be grouped to represent a semantic unit, such as a particular combination of display processes. For example, a Doppler shift is a semantic concept referring to the simulation of a moving sound source, and could be represented by a display grammar syntax that combines audio signal processing of stereo panning, pitch shift, an amplitude envelope, and reverberation, to create the impression of an audio sound source accelerating toward and then away from the listener.

22.4.1 State Space Representations of Symbolic Differences

Dual representations of state space and grammatical symbols provide a unique method to measure differences among grammatical symbols according to vector distances in DSP state space. These distances may represent degrees of perceptual similarity, such as gradual changes in loudness representing physical distance or changes in reverberation representing the size of an acoustic space. In such cases, there is a linear relationship between state space distance and semantic difference: the closer in state space two symbols appear, the more similar the perceptual qualities of their processing outputs. In other cases, the distances in state space may represent semantic regions that are bounded by distinct thresholds rather than continuous transitions. For example, a filter controlled by a nonlinear process, such as a chaotic attractor, can exhibit adjacent regions having sharp transitions defined by the edge of a basin of attraction. In this case, the state space distances would define perceptual regions and boundaries rather than linear perceptual differences.

A different form of distance metric can be obtained by measuring the number of transformations applied to generate a grammatical string. For example, two control points may be relatively distant in terms of state space, but their corresponding semantic strings may be relatively close in terms of logical operations required to transform one symbol to another. Replacement rules applied in grammatical space may be interpreted as linear movement in control state space. A display grammar may be designed for the overdetermined space of semantic context and signal processing coherence, where transformation rules designate the precedence of discrete or continuous operations when evaluating a transformation expression.

These examples have in common a capacity to measure distances between symbols by measuring distances between associated points in DSP state space. Discrete symbolic systems having semantic relationships lack continuous metrics, and cannot represent values "in between" the relationship of two symbols. Semantic data is structured in terms of set membership, not linear difference. There is no continuum between nodes in a graph. By coupling semantic values to a continuous signal processing space, and pivoting from discrete to continuous systems, parameter control values can be determined "in between" defined semantic nodes. When combining discrete symbolic systems and continuous parametric systems, a pivotal function relating one system to the other provides expressive flexibility that is not available in either system alone. This flexibility can be expressed as the ability to select either quantitative operations or logical operations to apply transformations and to generate order among symbols and corresponding states. For example, given an L-system operation replacing a symbol with a string, one of two cases may apply: (1) the added members of the string may be semantic and represent a traversal from one node to another on a concept graph; (2) the added members of the string may represent a vector transformation in state space, resulting in a new semantic expression representing a new location in control state space.

In the practical application of a display grammar, it is beneficial to move between these two methodologies in order to select the priority for a relationship of display properties. In some cases, dynamic properties are more important, such as a cross-dissolve. In other cases, static properties are more important, such as the use of edge detection to create a visual emphasis of shapes or the use of filter bands to highlight or eliminate select frequency components in an audio signal.

22.5   DISPLAY GRAMMAR USE CASE

An example application of a display grammar combines multiple sound and image sources. Additional signal processing is applied to simulate space and distance cues in the audio representations, displayed using an immersive audio system. The display grammar processing is controlled from a graphical user interface representing display states. Moving a cursor on the GUI applies transformations to the display grammar and affects the visual and audio displays.

The GUI is coupled to a semantic query engine that can select visual and audio content from an existing database. The semantic queries are coupled to display grammar states such that transformations to the display grammar can also bring changes to the semantic content being displayed. This semantic display system is described in detail in Choi (2008a,b).

22.5.1   A Manifold Representation and Interface

To investigate shared representation of semantic structure and signal processing, we apply a manifold representation of a high dimensional control space (Choi 2000b). Interactive media require continuous application of signal processing, necessitating continuous control systems. A manifold representation was designed as a scalable multidimensional interface for continuous control. This tool and its underlying data representation provide a platform for demonstrating semantic coupling with signal processing control space, and examine properties of this coupling in terms of a representative functional display grammar.

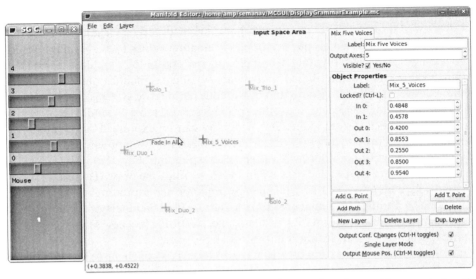

Figure 22.1. Generating points (GPs) on a manifold control surface, with a control path moving rightward from one GP to another. An *n*-dimensional array of parameter values is defined for each GP. In this example, *n* = 5; the fields on the right marked "Out" indicate the parameter values of the GP at screen center. Parameter values of the current cursor position are shown on the left.

Figure 22.1 shows a graphical user interface that represents in two dimensions a continuous and differentiable subspace of a phase space of three or more dimensions—five dimensions in this example. The manifold controller (MC) applies the 2D projection of a high dimensional subspace to a 2D graphical representation with a cursor that can be positioned continuously. The MC generates a high-dimensional array of values at each point on the control area. As the cursor moves through the 2D control area, the MC converts the cursor positions to positions in the high-dimensional state space. By this method, the MC generates a continuous and differentiable series of values for the high dimensional array at each 2D cursor position. These values are applied to real-time control of media signal processing, scheduling in this case sounds and acoustic models.

22.5.2 Configuring Manifold Control

Manifold control is configured in a graphical user interface by placing a set of generating points (GPs) on a bounded plane that represents a normalized 2D control area. A GP is an *n*-dimensional array of values associated to the *n*-dimensional phase space. The region of the 2D plane represents a subspace, or *manifold* of the full *n*-dimensional phase space. This subspace is defined by the array values of the GPs. GPs may be positioned arbitrarily on the 2D plane, and arranged in any spatial order preferred by the user. For any point in the 2D control region indicated by the cursor, the MC computes a value for each member of the *n*-dimensional array.

When a cursor is located at a GP, the MC returns the array of values defined for that GP. When the cursor is located between GPs, the MC determines values by weighting the distances of all GPs in the 2D control region relative to the position of the cursor. The GPs nearest the cursor will have the greatest influence on the values returned. Distances between GPs determine the degree of resolution of values in the spaces between points. Greater distance between two GPs creates finer resolution of values between them. Altering the positions of one or more GPs will modify the resulting n-dimensional values calculated between GPs.

The continuous dimensional representations of facial expressions presented in Chapter 6 (Stoiber et al. 2012) and emotional states of a speaker presented in Chapter 17 (Schuller 2012) both indicate a potential application of a manifold representation to a higher dimensional state space.

22.5.3   Symbolic Coupling to Signal Processing

In Figure 22.1, the control manifold ("Mix Five Voices") contains six GPs; each represents an array of five floating point values in the range (0.0, 1.0) assigned as scalars for the amplitudes of five audio sources. The value 0.0 scales an audio source to silence, and the value 1.0 scales a source to full amplitude. The audio source amplitudes are normalized such that the maximum loudness of each source is equivalent. Each dimension in the phase space is designated as an amplitude scalar for one audio source, such that the five-dimensional array at each GP represents a mix of the five audio sources. The GP "Mix_Trio_1" defines the values (0.65, 0.85, 0.0, 0.0, and 0.32) (not shown in Figure 22.1), resulting in the amplification of three sounds and complete attenuation of two others. The GP "Mix_5_voices" (shown in Figure 22.1) provides the values (0.42, 0.85, 0.25, 0.85, and 0.95), representing a mix of five voices. Moving the cursor to GUI positions between the GPs will produce a mix of continuously changing amplitude levels for all five sounds. The amplitude values at any point in the 2D control region will be weighted by the relative by the distance of the cursor to each GP.

The configuration in Figure 22.1 represents a rudimentary coupling of symbols to signal processing by indexing coordinates on the control surface to a designated sound source. The coupling assumes each sound source has semantic attributes. Each GP with its associated loudness control of five sound sources can be considered a nonterminal symbol of a display grammar. Terminals are related to dimensions in the control parameter state space. The display grammar includes the DSP loudness control function and the five-dimensional space of control values. Differences between terminal symbols in the grammar can be measured quantitatively by differences in array values at each GP and by geometric distances between the positions of the GPs. The symbolic differences of the GPs are semantically quantifiable according to the nature of the mix of five sources. For example, the name assigned to each GP, such as "Mix_Trio" or "Solo," represents the semantic value of that GP as a symbol in the display grammar.

22.5.4   Extending Display Grammar to Multiple Manifolds

In the above example, the amplitude processing of sounds provides a semantic function by generating mixes of sound sources; changes in the mix modify the semantic references provided by the sounds. However, this example configuration provides limited extensibility by relying upon direct coupling of sound sources and signal

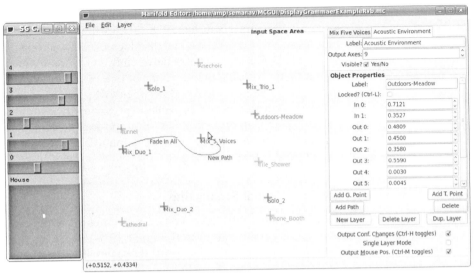

Figure 22.2. A second manifold is added with six new GPs representing parameterized spatial audio models. This "Acoustic Environment" manifold controls signal processing applied to the audio sound sources of the "Mix Five Voices" manifold. The control path of the "Mix Five Voices" manifold is continued from Figure 22.1; new parameter values of the path cursor position are shown on the left.

processing data to common GPs, and by assuming the semantic attributes of the sounds are appropriate for the semantics of each mix. Figure 22.2 represents an extension of semantic functions of signal processing. A second control manifold ("Acoustic Environment") is defined for a nine-dimensional space that provides parameter values for a different signal processing algorithm. Additional GPs that represent nine-dimensional arrays of parameter values (not shown) control a DSP algorithm applied to the mixtures of audio source signals. Each GP in the second manifold represents unique acoustic space properties; as stated in Section 22.3.2, the spatial models have audible semantic associations to acoustic properties of recognizable real-world spaces.

Note that in Figure 22.2, the "Mix Five Voices" manifold is still actively controlling the mix of sound sources. We use MC1, MC2, . . . , to refer to concurrent manifold layers. By navigating the coupled MC interfaces with a cursor, at each point, MC1 generates a mix of sound sources; in parallel, this mix is further processed by the acoustic model determined by the corresponding state of MC2. It is also possible to utilize two cursors and decouple the cursor positions of the two control regions, such that any simulated spatial quality of MC2 can be associated to any sound mix of MC1. The representation of a measurable grammatical unit can be extended to combine the arrays of parameter values from MC1 and MC2, and the relative geometric distances of multiple cursors in manifold state spaces. Quantitative differences between array values of multiple MC positions represent grammatical differences. When a cursor is moved, the resulting transformation of array values represents a transformation applied to symbols in the grammar.

22.5.5   Extending Display Grammar to Media of Multiple Types

The technique of coupling multiple manifolds to represent combined display process may be extended to MC control of visual media displays, such as images, video sources, and virtual camera positions, in a 3D graphical scene. Media types are presented using common or related signal processing, such as amplitude changes, compositing (mixing) of sources, spatial modeling, and simulated movements of media sources in scenes. Arrays of control manifolds can be defined and coupled to designate grammatical structures across multiple media types and related signal processing functions.

For example, a manifold representation is used to couple diverse media processing resources on a desktop platform, linking multiple MC layers (1) to graphics and audio subsystems represented in JavaFX™ or Adobe Flex™ that author for runtime engines, and (2) in parallel directly to a multimedia card with DSP capacity for acoustic modeling. MC1 associates sounds with graphics objects in a 2D or 3D scene; MC2 controls a 3D acoustic model applied to the sounds; MC3 couples virtual positions of camera and sound sources in the graphical scene to distance and directional parameters in the acoustic model. Doppler shift and similar physical phenomena may be modeled semantically in manifold layers. These coupled subsystems controls are often isolated in separate menus or control channels in an authoring interface. Display grammar provides a modeling space for media subsystems' semantic and signal processing relationships.

These examples present relatively simple semantic relationships between DSP applications in audio and visual media. They were selected to clarify the mechanics of the manifold control interface applied to display grammars. However, the proposed value of a display grammar is not limited to semantically unambiguous media display characteristics. The proposed value is in the creation of one or more n-dimensional display processing manifolds, and the coupling of these manifolds to create consistent and measurable relationships applied to transformations of DSP properties. The coupling of DSP transformations across multiple displays provides a methodology for establishing measured degrees of similarity or difference in the digital displays of media of multiple types. The deeper value of a display grammar methodology is the ability to create intervals of similarity and of difference from one display process to another, and to normalize these intervals across media of multiple types and across transformations applied to each media type.

22.6   FUTURE DIRECTIONS: APPLICATION OF DISPLAY GRAMMARS TO MMIE

Media production creates layers of signal processing that confound MMIE. For example, individual sounds are not only mixed in parallel audio tracks, they are processed with filters and spatial simulation. The cues that enable listeners to decode a complex layered signal include the harmonicity of spectral components and the common fate of spectral components in a sound. When a sound undergoes several layers of DSP processing, these cues become very difficult to identify computationally (Pardo 2006). If a media resource can be accompanied by data describing these layers in terms of algorithms and related control parameter values, the capacity to decode these layers and uncover the source content of the original sounds can become a regular preprocessing stage in MMIE.

MMIE data is relevant for optimized signal processing used in media production. Features in media content identified as MMIE search targets are not merely semantic objects. A recognizable feature in a media resource encodes a grammatical (symbolic and transformable) relationship between a media representation of semantic content and a media signal processing display function. MMIE techniques can support both semantic query and display synthesis representations in a display grammar. Semantic queries can be coupled to quantitative MMIE data representations of features as search targets. Semantic query results can be filtered according to MMIE data to select media resources that best fit a given display process, enabling MMIE-DSP criteria to contribute to the semantic selection.

Further in this vein, display processing engines may be tuned to leverage available MMIE data, for example, to help determine parameter settings for individual media resources. MMIE data that identifies patterns or features could help streamline the emphasis of those features when multiple resources are synthesized in a presentation. The measure of quantitative signal information across a range of resources could enhance consistency in perceptual space, such as color palette, contrast, tone, or dynamic range, by making adjustments as needed in individual resources to bring them into balance with the larger set.

At the front end of interactive media production, MMIE data may be related to content production through shared representation in a display grammar. With a normalized access to DSP data and algorithms, the process of authoring a media presentation could develop models of coherence across media using DSP attributes and transformations in addition to content-based semantic attributes. The desired result is the introduction of quantifiable ranges of sensory and semantic transformations applied in the signal processing domain.

ACKNOWLEDGMENTS

The term *display grammar* was introduced by Insook Choi, who provided critical insights. Sever Tipei, James Beauchamp, Donna Cox, and Katherine Syer made valuable manuscript suggestions.

CHAPTER 23

MEDIA AUTHORING WITH ONTOLOGICAL REASONING: USE CASE FOR MULTIMEDIA INFORMATION EXTRACTION

INSOOK CHOI

23.1 INTRODUCTION

During the twentieth century the majority of media content was generated in one of several well-defined systems—print, cinema, radio, and television—for transmission and reproduction largely within the same system. Today, media content is often created by mixing and "mashing up" diverse media types and deployed on diverse devices. Display systems, such as personal communications devices, can differ considerably from the production systems where media resources originate. And their roles can be reversed: personal devices can generate media in consumer formats that are repackaged and distributed by media syndication (Noguchi 2005). This is a relatively recent phenomenon that is extended by the capacity to exchange media through digital networks and pull technologies.

In an open, multiplatform media ecosystem where amateur-generated resources play side-by-side with those of professionals, the ability to classify, store, recognize, and retrieve media resources is of high value. Semiautomation of media applications through the practice of media authoring enhances the reusability of media resources in the creation of new content. Media applications can be created that combine preselected resources with ones automatically searched and pulled from diverse providers. RSS feeds, Twitter, and web-based streaming services provide industrial examples of this process, and indicate a promising future for application-specific and interactive content (Blekas et al. 2006; Hossain et al. 2008; O'Riordan and O'Mahoney 2008; Wagner et al. 2009). Multimedia information extraction (MMIE) tools could enhance this production process. However, diversity of media sources

Multimedia Information Extraction: Advances in Video, Audio, and Imagery Analysis for Search, Data Mining, Surveillance, and Authoring, First Edition. Edited by Mark T. Maybury.
© 2012 IEEE Computer Society. Published 2012 by John Wiley & Sons, Inc.

and end user situations increases challenges for structuring common and extensible descriptors.

23.1.1   Organization of This Chapter

This chapter demonstrates the use of ontology, a form of well-structured semantic data, as an organizing tool for media authoring. We hypothesize the application of ontology as a robust method for linking media authoring and MMIE. Interactive media is introduced as a context for media authoring, and the practice of authoring with media of multiple types is discussed to identify the relevance of semantic data. A working prototype of a semantic query-based authoring system is described, focusing on the design of ontological data and the use of reasoning to retrieve media resources. A GUI design for navigating semantic data enables queries to retrieve media resources of diverse types in real time. Analysis of the demonstration system is provided to introduce the relevant application of MMIE and the challenges of robust implementation. Prototype use cases are introduced combining authoring data with MMIE for non-speech audio.

23.2   INTERACTIVE MEDIA AND MEDIA AUTHORING: IMPLICATIONS FOR MMIE

Digital media technology both for consumers and media professionals provides increasing levels of support for interactive and procedural production. Characteristics of interactive media include multiple channels and multiple devices that introduce feedback and control from recipients into the production process. For example: (1) peer-to-peer transmissions of media resources may be captured as program content; (2) preproduced media may be designed as a template or frame for unspecified media resources added during interactive presentation; (3) media program assembly (editing, mixing) may be located at the point of delivery; and (4) transmission and display systems may be responsive to data about program content.

Interactive media formats enable the configuration of moment-by-moment content to be assembled with respect to users' actions: custom modifications to content are executed before it is transmitted and content configurations are determined at the point of delivery on a user's device. Broadcast-era formats are still dominant: preproduced programs are streamed or downloaded to a user's device. However, ISO standards, such as MPEG-4 (Koenen 2002), support the transmissions of programs that are not completely prepackaged, enabling users' preferences, interests, and actions to impact the final content.

23.2.1   Authoring

Authoring in the context of interactive media refers to the design of instruction sets integrating contents of multiple types, media devices, and users' actions. The instruction sets are multiplexed within media content or otherwise transmitted to recipients' devices. An authoring process configures initial conditions, combinations of media resources, and conditional procedures for generating program contents incorporating the recipients' actions. Authoring instructions not only display or modify content; they assemble content from multiple sources and generate content using purely procedural methods, such as graphics and sound synthesis (Delarue and Warusfel 2006).

23.2.2 Media Program Classification and MMIE

Interactivity creates a new media environment for MMIE, challenging traditional analysis workflow and creating opportunities for new applications, such as customized program production. Industrial MMIE applications have been established in response to assembly-line media manufacturing, addressing needs for offline archiving and postprocessing for information extraction. Broadcast media provide relatively stable context for MMIE by adhering to well-defined classes of contents that are targeted to well-developed markets. Content classes characterize invariants and meaningful variables in program content: weather forecasts, news broadcasts, sporting events, surveillance, and talk shows—each represent well-established patterns of media content presentation, including camera work, lighting, editing, segment duration, figure-ground pattern articulation, and separation of dialogue from music and sound effects. In some respects, these templates represent "vocabularies" that broadcast producers have developed to establish observers' expectations and then repeatedly satisfy those expectations.

Program templates provide essential baseline data for MMIE techniques. These techniques are reliable in relation to the uniformity within the class of media content. This uniformity is related to the broadcasting industry's model of establishing and maintaining audience expectations, akin to the marketing of commodities based on needs or interests many people have in common. As commodities, broadcast media programs have content variations, but their structural templates are relatively invariant. As markets diversify, these templates become less reliable at a large scale. With increased capacity for customized contents, the nature of media program templates becomes radically altered. Future applications of MMIE depend on the development of program classes for interactive media.

23.2.3 MMIE for Dynamic and Interactive Content

Authoring provides production context data relevant for MMIE. The usefulness of the data is determined by the implementation of procedural media processing, modes of user interaction, and quality of media resources. By definition, interactive media is dynamic, superseding the notion of a fixed version of program content. Interactive content is dynamically composed in a variety of sequences and layouts and imported from changing sources. Given a blog or YouTube video as a source for interactive content, the generated program content will reflect changes when the web source content changes (Han et al. 2008). Interactive media programs are rarely recorded and archived as definitive documents, only as versions or instances. The workflow for applying MMIE to an archived body of programs is less applicable in this environment due to the high degree of uncertainty regarding the anticipated content and its quality.

We look to authoring requirements to provide a new source of reliable templates for media producers creating interactive programs. In terms of computation and procedural media processing, templates are needed to generate coherent program content that meets users' expectations while incorporating users' actions and selections among content options. These templates will be realized in authoring data: computational instruction sets and scripts that encode the authoring decisions.

23.2.4 MMIE Use Case Overview

We anticipate that authoring data and MMIE data will be mutually supportive and can be shared. Section 23.5 presents use cases for these mutually supportive roles. To summarize the baseline use case: Media resources (sounds in this case) are indexed with a structured vocabulary—ontology concepts—then some of the concepts are used to author an interactive media sequence. The generated audio sequence is analyzed using an MMIE tool, with the objective of identifying the individual source sounds. Mixtures of sounds in the generated sequence partially confound the audio MMIE tool, such that search results include both correct and misidentified candidate source sounds. The search is refined by comparing authoring metadata with ontological data of the candidate source sounds; false positives are identified when candidate sounds' associated concepts do not match authoring concepts. Thus, a concept vocabulary identified with authoring may be used to constrain search space.

We hypothesize that MMIE techniques can be developed to utilize data extracted from patterns in authoring templates, as well as patterns in the resulting interactive media contents. Figure 23.1 shows the proposed scenario: context-rich authoring data provides context data for MMIE. Extracted information in turn can be incorporated as properties of ontological resources and referenced by authoring. This approach suggests a "tuning" cycle for alignment of semantic representations and pattern-based representations of features.

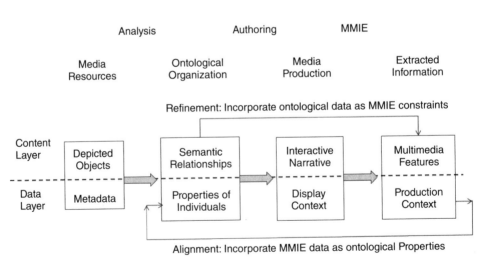

Figure 23.1. A data layer enables production context refinement for MMIE, and can incorporate MMIE data to align feature extraction with content production.

23.3 PROTOTYPE SYSTEM FOR MEDIA AUTHORING WITH ONTOLOGICAL REASONING

To study enhanced techniques for media authoring, a prototype system was developed to join semantic computation with user interaction. The prototype system tests a capacity for (1) *authoring interactive media*, with (2) an *interactive authoring process*. The first refers to the production of conditional procedures for processing media resources while responding to users' actions. The second refers to an authoring environment supported by real-time media processing to display results of procedural conditions. The objective is to support both capacities in close proximity with optimized system architecture and performance. Figure 23.2 represents the architecture of the prototype. Supported media resources include 2D graphic documents, such as photographs, diagrams, and architectural plans, prerecorded and procedurally generated sounds, videos, 3D graphical models, and camera movements in a 3D graphical scene. Semantic representations can be pivotal for linking MMIE across media of multiple types, as discussed in Chapter 10 (Tzoukermann et al. 2012).

For semantic organization and reasoning, we have adopted an ontological data design, discussed in Section 23.4. The authoring process is formalized as path planning through a semantic (ontological) data structure describing media resources of diverse types. Ontological structure defines a set of logical expressions interpreted as a directed graph of semantic nodes; edges represent concepts' relatedness. Structure is encoded in OWL file format using an open source editing tool (*Protégé* 2009;

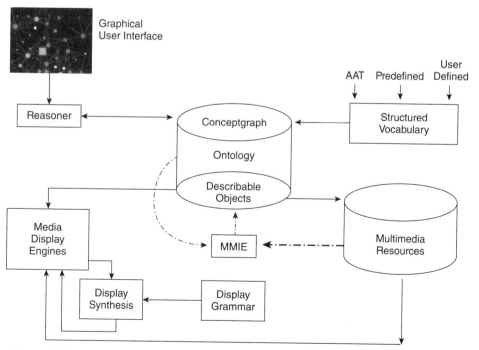

Figure 23.2. Architecture of the prototype authoring system with MMIE enhancement.

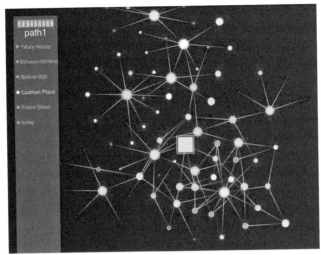

Figure 23.3. Graphical user interface of concepts as interactive nodes. In the original interface, color is used to visualize relationship. Size indicates number of links to a node.

W3C 2004). Paths are sequences of nodes that traverse the ontological data graph. A node can be queried and reasoning identifies semantically related media resources (Tskarov and Horrocks 2006).

23.3.1 Graphical User Interface for Navigating Relationships of Multiple Media Types

A graphical user interface (GUI) supports path-making, and a media scheduling engine displays the results of each query as a real-time mix of media resources. The GUI visualizes the ontological data graph as a 2D network of nodes and edges. The GUI snapshot in Figure 23.3 displays a limited region of a much larger ontology. Several levels of interaction are defined. Mouse over a node displays its concept name. Double-click on a node generates a resource query and modifies the display to reveal all nodes that are nearest neighbors. Nodes remain hidden until a nearest neighbor is selected. Nodes are displayed with animated ball-and-spring dynamics, aiding visual identification of relationships. The square node is anchored and can only be moved by direct mouse dragging; it represents a concept's membership in a *query path*, authored as a starting point for concept exploration. The "current location of the user" is defined as the most recently selected node generating the most recent query. Various criteria are applied to hide nodes that become remote from the current query location.

23.3.2 Path-Planning and Interactive Authoring

The idea of making paths through a digital document space can be traced to multiple sources, including the Memex proposed by Vannevar Bush in the mid-1940s (Bush 1945). These proposals focus on "trails of documents" using text processing for cross referencing and indexing to achieve more efficient storage and retrieval. Media asset management systems are beginning to adopt these approaches; however, computational path planning is not widely adopted for interactive media production.

Our prototype introduces path-planning techniques for interactive media production. Path-planning is computationally robust for combining interactive media and prestructured media. A path-planning model can accommodate user exploration and improvisation while maintaining linear structures as priorities. Our prototype differs from "trails of documents" proposals by implementing *paths of queries;* paths through concept space generating queries as acts of creative inquiry, creating real-time sequences of composite displays of resources, functioning both as dynamic media content and as semantic navigation feedback to the user. Queries generate sets of related resources; queries organized in paths may be designed to generate linear structures by making a series of selections from media resources that can function in multiple semantic contexts.

In Figure 23.3, the leftmost vertical array is a path of concept nodes. Path members can be traversed in any order. Each path member displays a square anchor node and a neighborhood expanded for exploration. Selecting a path member generates a query that returns a set of media resources and visualizes the concept neighborhood; exploration of neighboring nodes produces further queries returning related resources.

23.3.3 Interactive Media Use Case Example

A system is configured to respond to queries by scheduling the display of 2D images, sounds, and virtual camera movements in a 3D environment. Sounds and images have been entered as media resources in the ontological data set; also entered are virtual camera movements determined by positional data of 3D models. When a query returns one or more 2D images, sounds, or 3D objects, separate media display engines receive the addresses of these resources and schedule their display using a sound synthesis system and two image projections, one for compositions of 2D images and the other for 3D scenes.

To create a large-scale working prototype, we gathered or generated many media resources related to present-day and historical Brooklyn (Choi 2008a,b). The 2D and 3D images are displayed side-by-side in a tiled large-screen format. The GUI is part of a small kiosk. (1) In an example query path, the first node is the concept "FultonStreet2000toPresent." Selecting this concept returns photographs of storefronts, sounds of bus traffic, pedestrians, and street vendors recorded on Fulton Street from 2006 to 2008, and a 3D camera movement slowly "flying" (tracking) along virtual Fulton Street with contemporary photographs of real-world Fulton building exteriors applied as texture maps to the building models. (2) Selecting a second path node while these resources are displayed, "BoroHall2000toPresent" introduces new photos and sounds, with smooth visual and audio cross-fades effecting the transition. The 3D camera movement interpolates from Fulton Street to a new position hovering above the model of Borough Hall. Some images and sounds are returned by both queries; these persist in the display across the transition. (3) The third path node "FultonStreet1880to1920" returns the 3D camera to resume a flyover of Fulton Street; however, contemporary building texture maps are replaced by historically accurate storefront textures, also the 3D scene now includes an elevated train that ran above Fulton Street in the early twentieth century. Photographs of hip-hop shops and cell phone vendors are replaced by historical drawings, lithographs, and photographs—including images of the elevated train that provided references for modeling a 3D counterpart. Sounds recorded on Fulton Street are replaced by sounds from an SFX library: horses, carriages, a steam engine, and pedestrians on a boardwalk, synchronized by concept with the images and 3D scene.

Transitions in each media display are computed to dynamically compose image sequences, sound mixes, and combinations of virtual camera movements in the 3D scene. When a user generates a query at the GUI, transitions are effected immediately to provide feedback to the user. Scheduling constraints impose minimum duration between queries. We introduce *Display Grammar* for the configuration of display signal processing and scheduling of multiple resources. Chapter 22 discusses Display Grammar in detail (Bargar 2012).

23.4 ONTOLOGICAL DATA DESIGN FOR NAVIGATING MEDIA RESOURCES OF MULTIPLE TYPES

Authoring applied to media of multiple types requires structured access to diverse media resources; it is desirable to develop uniform and extensible authoring procedures rather than tailoring separate authoring for each media type. Ontological data can be designed to support uniform criteria for organizing media resources of multiple types. This task is akin to designing an MMIE meta-program to organize MMIE across multiple types of media. Ontologies are relationships of *concepts* that describe *individuals*; in this case, individuals are media resources. "Describe" refers to set membership: concepts describe sets, and resources are unordered members of one or more sets. Concept relatedness may be taxonomic subclass–superclass hierarchy or nontaxonomic and nonhierarchical. This flexibility is desirable for authoring both level-of-detail and syntactic relationships.

23.4.1 Dual Root Structure

Figure 23.4 summarizes the main components in the media ontology encoded in OWL: a dual root node structure of Concepts and Describable Objects. *Concepts* describe media resources of multiple types, *Describable Objects* include individual media resources and entities depicted by those resources—"Content Objects" in Figure 23.4. *Content Objects* distinguish specific nameable entities that can be depicted in more than one resource. Content Object types include unique objects detected across multiple resources discussed in Chapter 3 (Das et al. 2012), and named entities discussed in Chapter 11 (Natarajan et al. 2012). *Properties* denote metadata about media resources and content objects, including related objects and quantitative data.

Concepts and individuals may be associated by assertion and by inference. Assertion is a direct assignment of set membership to an individual resource. Inference is a computational evaluation that discovers relationships that may be emergent among the media resources. Ontological reasoning combines both types of discovery when a query is performed at a concept node.

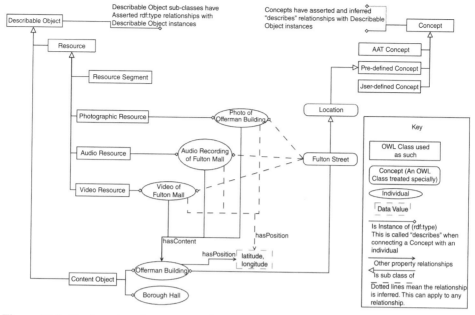

Figure 23.4. Dual root node structure. Concept and Describable Object are parallel root nodes.

23.4.2 Concepts

Concepts are semantic classes used in logical expressions to show relationships among objects, including other concepts and describable objects. Logical expressions use set membership to represent relationships, which may also be represented as graphs with concept nodes and predicate edges. An ontological data structure may exhibit one of several topologies, including trees (taxonomies), directed acyclic graphs, and cyclic graphs. In media authoring, most relationships are syntactic rather than taxonomic.

Concepts may have relationships asserted to specific media resources; however, many concepts have relationships only to other concepts. Edges between nodes in the concept graph may be asserted or eliminated without modifications to associated media resources. The dual root design enables concept relationships to be modified without affecting the representations of individual media resources. By minimizing direct dependencies between concepts and resources, changes can be applied to the concept graph without requiring modifications to resources already stored in the system, and resources may be added or removed without modifications to the concept graph.

23.4.3 Complementarity of Ontological Data and Metadata

Authoring can incorporate both semantic data and quantitative data of media resources. Ontological query can reason over both semantic and quantitative relationships, and across media resources of unlike types. Metadata queries cannot; they are limited to individual media types. For example, a metadata name-value pair from a photograph might indicate "focal length = 27 mm" and from a sound recording might indicate "reverb decay time = 150 ms." Taken together, these values represent complementary audio-visual data: a visual wide-field perspective and a highly reverberant acoustic ambience. This complement is relevant for representations of building interiors. However, neither the audio nor the visual metadata provides a structure to define relationships of lens settings to audio signal processing, even though both sound and image metadata may indicate building interiors as a subject. Image metadata can provide focal length information and audio metadata can provide reverb information, but searching on image metadata cannot return an associated sound, nor can sound metadata be queried to return an image.

To address this, we apply ontological data design, which can support evaluations of data of unlike types. In the above audiovisual example, the concept "Large Room" is common to both image and sound classifications, and a query can be structured over specific ranges of quantitative values in fields of both sound and image metadata.

23.4.3.1 *Ontological Reasoning Over Resource Metadata for MMIE*   Ontological data can encompass both a controlled vocabulary of concepts and metadata of individual media resources. Concepts are limited to semantic values and cannot express quantitative values. Metadata can be quantitative but is limited to individual resource types. Concept queries traverse the ontology to retrieve metadata values from individual resources. This indirect access to quantitative values enables comparisons of dates to determine membership in a historical concept, or GPS coordinates to determine geographical location. MMIE data may be stored for individual resources, for example, spectral coefficients or pattern recognition data from specific MMIE analyses. Including MMIE data properties in the ontology would enable concept reasoning over known features or patterns identified in media resources.

23.4.4 Properties and Metadata

Properties designate data or relationships between individual resources or content objects, illustrated in Figure 23.4. Media resource metadata is stored as Properties of individual resources, including tags, terms, and numerical data. For example, the property *hasPhotoSpecific* includes focal length metadata, and *has3DModelSpecific* includes polygon count metadata. Properties are either Object Properties or Data Properties. *Object Properties* are extensible and inferable: they are terms and may refer to other properties. *Data Properties* are terminal, not extensible, and may be asserted only, not inferred.

Concept queries may reason over terminal values of Properties, including evaluating quantitative data. Properties may be used to store metadata relevant for MMIE, such as date, time, or conditions of capture of individual resources. Whereas ontologies describe resources in unordered sets, resources may be ordered using metadata values stored as Properties. By accessing Data Properties, a semantic query can evaluate quantitative expressions using values stored in metadata, returning ordered information that cannot be represented directly by ontology.

23.4.5 Design of Structured Vocabulary

Large-scale organization of a concept structure is difficult to maintain for broad applications and tends to become taxonomic. To provide an initial semantic order for contemporary and historical resources depicting downtown Brooklyn, a controlled vocabulary was needed that would enable accurate classification of the built environment past and present, interior and exterior, land and water, urban and rural, and industrial and agrarian. The Art and Architectural Thesaurus (AAT) (Getty Trust 2005) was selected as a controlled vocabulary that provides both hierarchical and associative relationships among concepts. The AAT does not provide all concepts needed for structuring queries to support media authoring; dates independent of cultural and historical periods, for example, are not included. For the present prototype, the AAT provides a semantic anchor for technical accuracy across many types of describable objects, a baseline for building additional concepts needed for media authoring.

Predefined Concepts are created to meet the narrative needs of projects. Considerable design is required to minimize redundancy or contradictions with existing vocabulary to create a limited reusable non-AAT authoring vocabulary. Combinations of preexisting concepts may be grouped as *User Concepts*, created on-the-fly by selecting already available concepts and applying operations, such as unions, intersections, and filters, on metadata values. The intent is to enable queries to be captured, stored, and customized to generate results that meet unique needs. Examples of metadata filters in user-defined concepts include dates, GPS locations, polygon counts, and focal length settings.

23.5 EXAMPLE USE CASES: SOUND AUTHORING DATA WITH AUDIO MMIE

A set of use cases was developed to hand-test the relationship of authoring and MMIE. The tests were confined to sound resources, for simplicity of procedure, and because a small number of sounds when mixed together can generate a large range of complexity for pattern recognition. The MMIE was performed with SoundFisher (Blum et al. 1997), an application for non-speech audio, particularly effective with nonmusical natural sounds. SoundFisher receives a target soundfile and searches a collection of sounds, returning a list of soundfiles rated in order of similarity. The feature analysis includes distribution patterns and rate of change for loudness, pitch, and spectral brightness. The number of sounds returned varies; a threshold omits sounds with little or no similarity. The SoundFisher algorithm is ingenious and viable over a large range of sound qualities. Only audio signals are analyzed; semantic tags are disregarded. This is critical to SoundFisher's power and flexibility. The working concept of auditory similarity is unbounded by arbitrary and often misleading terminology that populates many professional sound libraries. The similarity function is unconstrained by classifications of sound sources, which typically dominate a listener's orientation to a sound. SoundFisher is able to identify similarities in sounds of widely diverse origins—sounds that are acoustically similar but generated from dissimilar sources. A listener's cognitive semantic space may be greatly enriched in the presence of this technological capacity. The SoundFisher classification methodology is complementary to ontological approaches, and provides an excellent enhancement of semantic structure with signal processing analyses. Non-speech audio is increasingly useful for contextual MMIE, as discussed in Chapters 14 and 18 (Hu et al. 2012; Guerini et al. 2012).

23.5.1 Baseline MMIE Use Case

The baseline use case applies MMIE to sound resources that are already members of an ontological data set. Given a stream of sounds generated by an interactive ontology, MMIE is used to identify the sound sources that occur in the stream, and authoring data is applied to refine the MMIE search results, as follows:

1. A query path is authored then traversed interactively, synthesizing a stream of mixed sounds. The sound stream is recorded as a sound file, referred to as the *generated sound*.
2. Temporal data from the path traversal is stored as metadata synchronized with the generated sound, marking the query time of each path node timed from the first query.
3. The generated sound is segmented into 3-second increments, and each segment is used as a SoundFisher search target. For each segment, a series of candidate source sound files is returned with similarity ranking. Due in part to sound mixtures in the generated sound, SoundFisher may return many candidate sounds, both correct sources and imposters.
4. To refine the search over the candidate sounds for a given target segment of the generated sound, each candidate is queried in the ontology to determine its related concepts. Sounds often belong to multiple concepts. Using the authoring metadata synchronized with the generated sound, the concept set for each candidate sound is compared with the authoring concept active for the current target segment. Authoring concepts that were queried up to 30 seconds prior to the current segment are included to account for sound file duration overlaps.
5. For each generated sound segment, the candidate sound files are discarded if none of their associated concepts match the corresponding query concept of the segment.
6. For candidate sounds not discarded, common sounds are identified across adjacent segments and compared with the concept authoring metadata to determine overlaps. Durations of the candidate sound files are compared to their contiguous adjacencies across segments. Poor fit of contiguous adjacency to sound file duration demotes a candidate sound.
7. Finally, SoundFisher similarity ranking is applied to resolve conflicts among remaining top candidates, promoting each highest ranked sound at its onset segment.

Figure 23.5 illustrates step 3 of this process for one segment of the generated sound, showing the candidate source sounds' similarity rankings and related concepts.

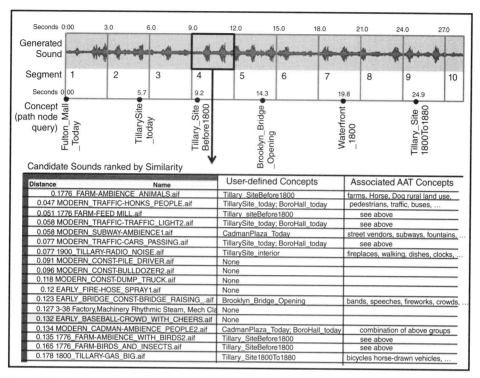

Figure 23.5. For one segment of a generated sound, MMIE candidate source sounds ranked by similarity. Concepts of each candidate sound are compared with the current path concept.

23.5.1.1 Expanded Search

23.5.1.1 Expanded Search   When no candidate sounds are returned for a generated sound segment, a "reverse concept search" technique is applied. (1) From the authoring metadata of the generated sound, the current concept for the segment is identified. (2) Given the current concept, the ontology is queried and all source sounds associated to the concept are returned. (3) One at a time, each concept-related source sound is used as a SoundFisher target with the generated sound segment as the sole sound compared with the target. Among the results of these 1:1 tests, the strongest similarities are identified as the most likely source sounds of the segment. These results are given a further confidence rating by comparison with results of adjacent segments.

Authoring data can also be used to constrain a search for a target sound within a generated sound. All concepts related to the target sound can be identified from the ontology. The authoring metadata of the generated sound is searched to identify possible locations of these concepts. Then SoundFisher is used to search for target sound similarities only in generated sound regions that correspond to concepts of the target sound.

23.5.2 MMIE Data Encoded in Ontologies

To complete the symmetry illustrated in Figure 23.1, we enable the alignment of MMIE data with ontological data to complement the refinement of MMIE using the authoring ontology. SoundFisher similarity results are entered as Data Properties of the individual sound resources returned by each search. We do not have access to the signal processing internal representation of the SoundFisher engine, so for test purposes, we adopt a cumbersome approach and enter the rank similarity ordering of each candidate sound with its target sound segment and related concept. The predicate "SoundsLike" was created to support these queries, with additional exposure of the relevant data property. This enables reasoning over the relative similarities of sounds, either with respect to a given concept or disregarding the concept and using only the ordered similarity data. Given that ontological inference cannot return ordered results at the conceptual level, the availability of quantitative and ordered search results is a useful extension for organizing media resources. We are presently experimenting with extended queries, such as unions and intersections of sounds, according to their similarity. We do not have conclusive results; however, we hypothesize that this may be a way to construct semantic representations of short-duration isolated sound components that can be composed through iterative inferences to sculpt more extended and complex sounds.

23.5.3 Extending Ontologies to New Media Resources

In cases where the original source sound library is not available for MMIE, the authoring data of the generated sound can be used to search surrogate sound libraries. The results of the search will give an indication of similarity to the original source sounds, and can be used to create an extended ontology. If the surrogate sounds are not already members of the ontology, the initial search can be conducted following the baseline use case, applying each segment of the generated sound as a target for a SoundFisher search. Ontological analysis can be performed on the resulting candidate sounds to classify them in the ontology. Results of the SoundFisher analysis can be entered into the data properties of each sound added to the ontology. Ontological inference can be applied to identify additional concept and MMIE data associations, supporting refined and extended MMIE. Given the eventuality of rich extended media resource ontologies, we can expect fruitful results using inference to identify new concept associations to MMIE candidate media resources. In this method, the ontological relationships and the media resource data sets are mutually enriched and increased in membership and semantic differentiation.

23.6 CLOSING STATEMENTS AND FUTURE DIRECTION

This chapter introduces multimedia authoring as a context for applications of MMIE. Two types of production data benefit MMIE: apparatus variables (device parameters) and production context (location, device, and performance conditions). Authoring with ontological reasoning encodes semantic information, includes useful data about production context, and bridges media resources of multiple types. Semantic structure applied to multimedia authoring can provide a formal structure for semantic analysis applied to MMIE.

Our future direction undertakes ontological data design to host a formalized methodology shared by the two practices, multimedia authoring and MMIE. Formalization of shared data protocols will facilitate the use of MMIE as a front-end media production tool. We envision a methodology in three stages.

23.6.1 Semantic Orientation

Media authoring can encode semantic information; MMIE optimization requires such information. Media concepts may be used to group MMIE-related data properties to represent well-defined production contexts such as standard media program templates. When MMIE is optimized for a type of media program, many assumptions are made about production context. These assumptions may be inaccurate if unsupported by production data. Ontology-based media authoring can host the supporting data while formalizing semantics of the MMIE process. Semantics describe the structures used to situate meaning, indicating potential situated features sought in MMIE. The identification of a semantic context ascertains a related production context, aiding the selection of MMIE techniques.

23.6.2 Semantic Detailing

Content Objects embody semantic details that differentiate the general contents of scenes. Semantic details may be coupled to key features—recognizable patterns in signals that are targets for MMIE. Features may be represented as named, recognizable entities, and Content Objects can track them across multiple resources. Content Objects can be grouped to represent combinations of features, stored as MMIE data properties of individual resources. These feature sets may be entities colocated in a single resource or distributed in adjacent resources, such as a sequence of shots in film or an album of images on a web page. Semantic detailing is extensible to *multimodal features*, such as the co-occurrence of a voice with a face, or a visual scene with a set of environmental sounds (Xiong et al. 2006). Detailing can use concepts to encode cross-media feature sets of MMIE data properties for 2D and 3D visual attributes, 3D model-based attributes, video segments, audio segments, and model-based spatiotemporal attributes, such as camera movements in 3D environments. Aspects of multi-modal features are elaborated in Chapters 8, 10, 11, 13, 14, and 18.

23.6.3 Feature Encoding

MMIE feature analysis data may be encoded as Properties of Describable Objects. Figure 23.1 refers to feature encoding as an alignment process; and refinement of concepts by grounding in MMIE data. Concepts could reference classes of MMIE data of known feature types, and could include cross-modal MMIE data extracted from multiple resources. A Content Object–Property relationship can index MMIE analysis data for features identified across multiple resources consistent with their semantic context. Once encoded, the MMIE properties will be accessible to reasoning performed by computational semantics in the authoring process.

We anticipate the extension of these techniques beyond the canonical examples of broadcast media, impacting the production and analysis of interactive media. Our goal is to enable the use of MMIE to support shared user-authored media in social networks. New canons and semantically rich techniques are anticipated in the production contexts created by media producers who are also end users.

ACKNOWLEDGMENTS

Thanks to Thom Blum and Audible Magic, Inc. for the use of the SoundFisher tool. Additional thanks go to Arthur Peters for software development, and to Robin Bargar for software design and project supervision. Tatiana Malyuta contributed insights on ontological reasoning. Robert Zagaroli and Robin Michals and their students contributed to media resources.

CHAPTER 24

ANNOTATING SIGNIFICANT RELATIONS ON MULTIMEDIA WEB DOCUMENTS

MATUSALA ADDISU, DANILO AVOLA, PAOLA BIANCHI, PAOLO BOTTONI, STEFANO LEVIALDI, and EMANUELE PANIZZI

24.1 INTRODUCTION

Annotation is a fundamental activity for information extraction. Annotation of large corpora provides a basis for building ontologies and thesauri (Braschler and Schauble 2000), while annotation of existing data helps adding semantics (Volz et al. 2004). The elements to be annotated range from simple text (Kahan and Koivunen 2001), to structured data (Geerts et al. 2006), images (Herve and Boujemaa 2007), and video (Del Bimbo and Bertini 2007), while the annotation content can be as simple as a tag (Zheng et al. 2008) or as complex as a whole new document (Bottoni et al. 2006), most commonly being text. While traditional annotation on paper alter the physical support of the document, digital annotations can be added at will on a digital document without modifying it, still maintaining their relationship to the original document through suitable metadata.

Automatic annotation of complex documents is still a hard problem for computational systems, hence any support to the manual work of the human annotators, for example, retrieval of existing information or versatility in managing different types of media is helpful. Moreover multimedia documents can be both the subject and the content of the annotation, making the combined management of documents and annotations a must. On the other hand, as we focus on in this chapter, annotation can prove useful not only for wide communities, but also for groups of interest or at the enterprise level, or even for individuals, allowing them to accumulate knowledge on specific topics by constructing a web of annotations.

In this sense, the annotation activity can be used to extract and retrieve two types of information. In the first type, which we may call "objective," well-known facts, for example, dates, places, or names, are extracted, which need to be related, structured, and documented, possibly according to known, domain-dependent conventions. In

Multimedia Information Extraction: Advances in Video, Audio, and Imagery Analysis for Search, Data Mining, Surveillance, and Authoring, First Edition. Edited by Mark T. Maybury.
© 2012 IEEE Computer Society. Published 2012 by John Wiley & Sons, Inc.

401

the second, "subjective," type, the information which is extracted is related to the user's goal in the context of a particular activity. Users may want to associate different, possibly unrelated parts of a document, such as salient features of an event or location, or of the psychological profile of a person, or information about a product or service, with a view to what is needed for a given task, for example, a presentation, a lecture, or the construction of a personal archive. Moreover, they want to do so in a nondisruptive way, while perusing the document.

The MADCOW system (for *M*ultimedia *A*nnotation of *D*igital *C*ontent *O*ver the *W*eb) (Bottoni et al. 2004, 2006), allows users to annotate web pages containing different types of media with *web notes* composed of text, images, video, and, in general, any type of digital document, which can then be retrieved from the originally annotated document (or directly through queries to an annotation server), and which can be made public. The MADCOW client is integrated as a bookmarklet on the toolbar of the most common browsers and allows readers to create or retrieve annotations on the current page without interfering with their normal behavior when accessing information on the Web.

We have recently enriched MADCOW with the ability to create notes pertaining not only to single blocks of text or to structures within pictures contained in the page, but also referring to any combination of these individual elements. As an example, writers involved in the cooperative construction of a web page, or a scholar reading a scientific document, could create a single note on two portions of text that appear as contradictory, or as a repetition. A detailed analysis of a picture might immediately refer to the text describing it. More sophisticated uses might uncover the logical relations between different parts of the document as described in the first scenario presented in the paper. These actions need not be done by the author of the document, but provide a dynamic construction of the interpretation of the document by its readers, in a sense materializing the notion of "open work" (Eco 1962). To our knowledge, no existing system for manual web annotation tackles the problem of linking a single annotation to different portions of the document.

In the following, we introduce our running example on two scenarios, concerning cooperative enrichment of available material between teacher and students, and extraction of structured information by a single user, illustrating the use of MADCOW to organize the two types of information discussed above. We present the notion of multistructure, allowing the creation of multinotes, which associate a single annotation with several elements of a Web document, and present the relevant data structures and the interaction by which they are created exploiting the MADCOW client. Finally, we show how multinotes can further be manipulated and reused by readers accessing them.

24.2 RELATED WORK

While annotation for multimedia and web content is a topic addressed by several groups,[1] and several systems share some of the MADCOW features, the MADCOW

---

[1] http://www.sharedcopy.com, http://www.reframeit.com, and http://www.diigo.com.

system offers some unique features and a unique combination of them. In fact, while most current systems offer annotation of text and some of them allow users to annotate areas in the page that include both text and images, MADCOW adopts different policies from those of most systems: (1) Annotations are linked to annotated documents instead of copying the document and modifying it with annotations as in Fleck or SharedCopy. (2) Javascript is used to modify the Document Object Model (DOM), thus being portable over different browsers, instead of being a plugin/toolbar for specific browsers, as in MyAnnotations or ReframeIt. (3) An annotation is considered as a new document itself, which can be annotated in turn; none of the other systems, including Diigo, the most similar to MADCOW under other aspects, define annotations as independent documents, or allow reannotation. MADCOW also deals with peculiar situations in the retrieval of notes on a given document. One of these is the case of duplicated documents, at different URLs, that are in fact the same document and to which the same set of annotations can be linked. Another important case is that of documents in which the position of some content has been moved, for which annotations must be retrieved with reference to its new position (Bottoni et al. 2007).

A current line of research aims at extracting semantic information from specific types of information. As an example, Carberry et al. (Chapter 15, this volume) extract information contained in particular types of graphical format for data presentation, while ontological information is used to support authoring with concept formation in Choi (Chapter 23, this volume).

Hierarchical annotation structures have been used for manual annotation of videos in BRAHMA (Dan et al. 1998), while ANVIL (Kipp, Chapter 21, this volume) allows synchronized annotation of several media. We are integrating video and audio portions of the document in a multistructure, while annotation of individual parts is already available in MADCOW.

24.3   TWO SCENARIOS

We present two scenarios, illustrating the concept of "objective" and "subjective" information discussed in the introduction. In the first, drawn from e-learning, a multistructure annotation allows a teacher and his students to highlight elements in a page relative to a well-known taxonomy. In the second, a researcher preparing a presentation exploits multistructures to organize information contained in several web pages on the same subject, so as to construct a quick reference data-base on that subject.

24.3.1   e-Learning Scenario (Extraction of Objective Information)

Annotation systems have a natural field of application in e-learning, supporting communication among students, and between them and their teachers, by annotating parts of the teaching material on which they require explanations, propose alternative interpretations, refer to other texts, or even relate to the exercises, testing their understanding. For example, a student of Fine Arts analyzing a particular work could annotate some detail on a picture of it, referring to pieces of text illustrating relevant facts about such a detail, creating notes which make up questions

Figure 24.1. Creation of a multistructure for Mammals.

or suggestions for the teacher or for other students. She might link other information to the work, such as sources relative to the period it was produced, the author, or accomplished restorations, if any.

We illustrate here a more complex scenario, in which a high school Biology teacher has created a course website, including pages from different sources, as well as newly created ones. The site also includes a page where examples of mammals are collected (see Figure 24.1).

Mammals are classified under three subclasses with respect to their reproductive behavior and the reproductive female apparatus: *monotremes* (laying eggs), *marsupials* (giving birth to tiny animals kept in a pouch by the mother), and *placentals* (with long pregnancies giving birth to completely formed individuals). To make this clear, the teacher wants to create an annotation where exemplars of marsupials are grouped and commented on both singularly and as a collection. The teacher also wants students to be able to perform simple information extraction activities and create similar annotations on the page in order to assess their understanding of the subject. He wants similar information to be collected for monotremes and placentals, also leaving the possibility open of associating a global content with mammals as a whole, encompassing other notes in a single *multistructure*.

Other annotation systems do not support such processes directly. Indeed, the teacher must be able to operate directly on the Web document while keeping his bearings in the intricacies of the multistructure. The interface must give the teacher immediate feedback as to what the annotations refer to and how they are grouped. Both individual annotated elements and groups of elements must be readily accessed, and the hierarchical structure of the annotation must be clear to the user. The interface elements allowing creation of and access to annotations must support the user during the whole annotation lifecycle, also allowing independent ways of accessing its content. In order to have this kind of experience, the teacher activates the MADCOW system by clicking on the MADCOW button on the browser toolbar. A new toolbar, visible on the upper-right part of Figure 24.1, is opened to float in the browser, through which the user accesses the buttons to interact with the MADCOW subsystem, allowing the manipulation of multistructures.

To create the multistructure for the class of mammals, the teacher clicks on the fully gray button in the toolbar and a new node is created, as shown in Figure 24.1. It is surrounded by a dotted line to indicate that it is currently selected, and constitutes the root of a tree growing with the composition of the annotated multistructure.

To create the multistructure for monotremes and make it a child of the Mammals node, the teacher clicks again on the fully gray button. He then constructs the roots for the other classes, always selecting the mammals node first. After these operations, the tree appears as in Figure 24.2.

The teacher then selects elements from the page and relates them to nodes in the hierarchy. He selects the two pictures of marsupials and the portion of text giving the definition of marsupials. Hence, the node in "Marsupials" has three children. By repeating the procedure for the other subclasses, the multistructure on the right of Figure 24.3 is obtained. The teacher saves the annotations to the MADCOW server of his school, which also manages access rights, to make them available to students and for future modifications. He maintains the property of the annotation, but makes it public for reading and interacting with it.

When a student accesses the annotated page through a browser on which the MADCOW client plug-in has been incorporated and enabled, annotated parts of the document appear highlighted. By clicking on one of them, the associated tree

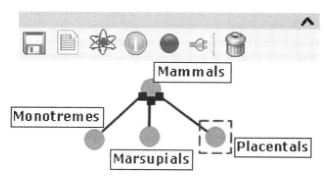

Figure 24.2. Extending the Mammal hierarchy.

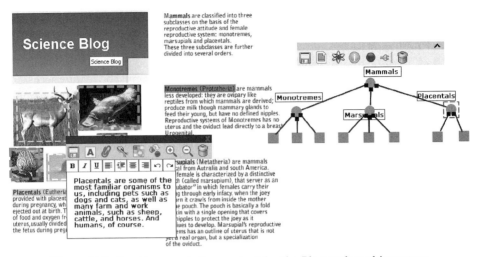

Figure 24.3. Creating annotation content for the Placentals multistructure.

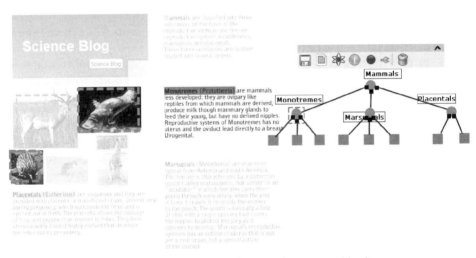

Figure 24.4. Highlighting selections on the page and in the tree.

is presented for her to access and explore the annotation content. The student can produce new annotations on the same page, or ask for the annotation to be loaded as an HTML page, packaged and delivered by the MADCOW server. New annotations can in turn be produced by any student on such a page (see Figure 24.3), thus opening a discussion channel with the teacher and with the other students. In order to give control to the user on the created annotations, those parts of the document related to a node in the multistructure are highlighted whenever their parent node is selected. Figure 24.4 shows the elements associated with the Monotremes node. Annotations, for example, concerning marsupials, can also be retrieved through direct MADCOW queries.

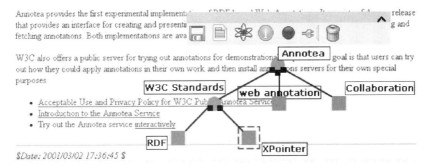

Annotea - Web Annotations as Metadata

Annotea is a W3C LEAD project that has two main goals. 1) to support W3C collaboration by developing experimental tools that support shared Web annotations, and 2) to demonstrate RDF based metadata infrastructure and other W3C standards, such as XPointer.

Annotations are external comments, remarks, deletions, bookmarks etc. that can be attached remotely to any Web document or a selected part of it. Annotations offer users a document based view for the current issues, which is often useful when developing documents for Web standards as a group effort.

Annotea provides the first experimental implement...release that provides an interface for creating and presentu..g and fetching annotations. Both implementations are ava...............................

W3C also offers a public server for trying out annotations for demonstration .... goal is that users can try out how they could apply annotations in their own work and then install an........ns servers for their own special purposes

- Acceptable Use and Privacy Policy for W3C Pub...Annotea Service
- Introduction to the Annotea Service
- Try out the Annotea service interactively

$Date: 2001/03/02 17:36:45 $

Figure 24.5. Constructing a multistructure to describe Annotea.

24.3.2 Research Scenario (Extraction of Subjective Information)

We consider a researcher preparing a presentation (or a teacher preparing a lesson) on the tools available for annotation of Web content. She is therefore searching the Web for such applications. As she visits the main page of each tool, she exploits MADCOW to construct structured descriptions, by annotating parts of the presentation and organizing them into multistructures whose nodes reflect the most important features of the tool.

As an example, on the Web page for Annotea, she extracts the fundamental concepts pertaining to it, such as *collaboration* or *annotation*, and makes a note on the use of standards (see Figure 24.5). To provide more focus, the user decides to consider in particular tools similar to MADCOW. For example, in Figure 24.6, she annotates a general description of DIIGO. Also, in this case, besides noting the tool main features, such as support for *tagging*, integration with *blogs* and *bookmarks* and *sticky notes*, the user exploits the tree organization of multistructures to provide a second level of specialization for the *search* topic of annotation. Finally, the user constructs an annotation for the A.nnotate tool, with reference to the actions provided to users to *organize* and *share* annotations (see Figure 24.7).

After completing this exploration and saving the multistructured annotations to the MADCOW server, the user exploits the retrieval features of MADCOW to organize the information thus extracted. To this end, she queries MADCOW to retrieve the produced notes. The answer comes as a new web page (see Figure 24.8),

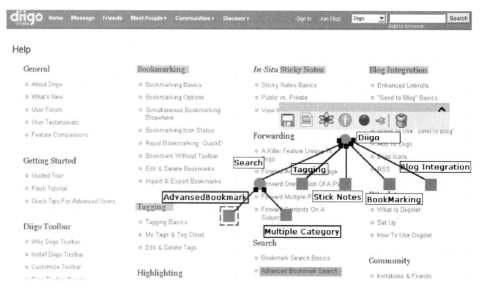

Figure 24.6. Structuring information concerning DIIGO.

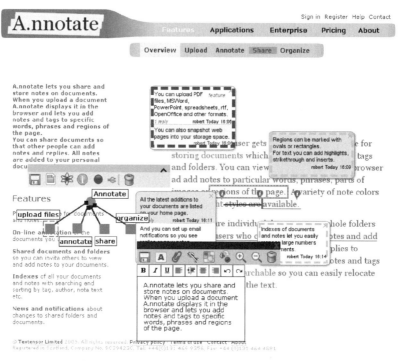

Figure 24.7. The multistructure for `A.nnotate`.

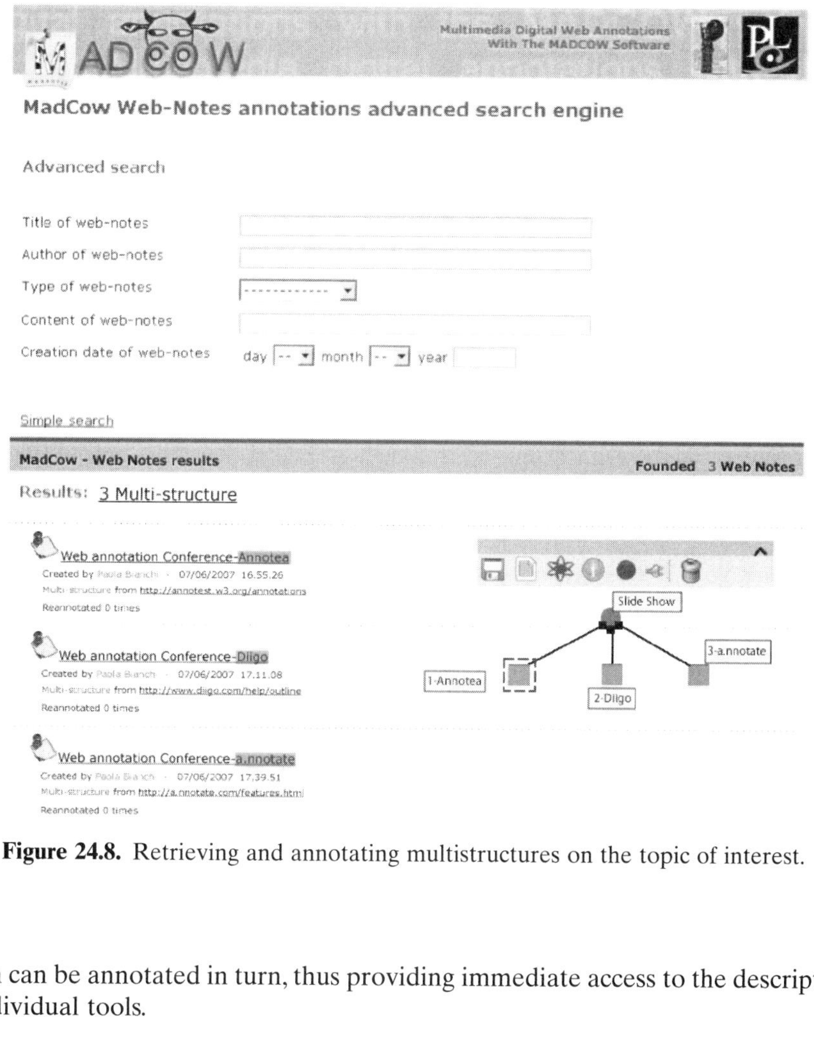

Figure 24.8. Retrieving and annotating multistructures on the topic of interest.

which can be annotated in turn, thus providing immediate access to the descriptions of individual tools.

24.4 MADCOW BASIC ARCHITECTURE

MADCOW is based on a client–server architecture that closely follows the Model–View–Controller (MVC) pattern requirements and is designed to be as platform-independent as possible. In particular, as shown in Figure 24.9, the *business logic* processes are carried out by both Model and Controller layers (in PHP 5.2.4), dealing respectively with data management (and related operations) within the database and user-interaction management, while the *presentation logic* processes are carried out by the View layer (in JavaScript 1.7). More specifically, the main features of the three layers can be summarized as follows:

Model Layer: Provides a set of information management functionalities (e.g., insert, validate, retrieve, and update), for single- and multistructured annotations contained in the database (DB). Moreover, this layer performs the

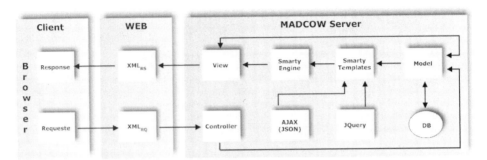

Figure 24.9. MADCOW basic architecture.

heaviest business logic operations, such as DOM processing, node indexing, XML parsing, and writing. Finally, the model layer notifies changes in its content or state to the view layer to update the presentation to the user.

View Layer: Manages the whole presentation logic processes, accessing data (as allowed by the model layer) according to the user requirements. It selects how and in which way both the different GUIs and the related information contents have to be presented to the user. Specifically, any single- or multistructured annotation is suitably shown to the user taking into account the types of element that compose it: texts, images, video, and/or audio streams, or other minor elements (icons, links, and so on). In the MADCOW server architecture, the view layer manages the basic tools for enriching a Web page to allow the user to post and/or visualize single or multistructured annotations: HTML, CSS, XML, JavaScript, JSON, and JQuery. In Figure 24.9, the roles of the JSON and JQuery modules have been highlighted to point out the main flow in client–server communication and the Web 2.0-style advanced MADCOW features. More specifically, the JSON module encapsulates client–server basic communication within an XML file, and JQuery allows high level interaction functionalities, such as *in place* editing of fields, outgrowing of areas, and so on. Finally, Smarty provides a template-based engine to build GUIs and related information contents. Every user requirement (e.g., retrieval of an annotation) is satisfied by transparently filling a suitable template and processing it with an interpretation engine.

Controller Layer: Defines the application behavior. It has to interpret the user actions and select a suitable presentation. Hence, the layer interprets user inputs and maps them into actions to be performed by the model. This layer also performs the business logic operations tied to the control process of the application. Finally, it selects the next view to display based on the user interactions and the outcome of the model functionalities and operations.

As shown in Figure 24.10, the physical communication process between client and server is performed via the XML_{RS} and XML_{RQ} files, whose content depends on the user action, that is, posting or retrieving of single or multistructured annotations on a Web page.

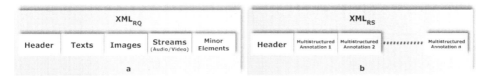

Figure 24.10. XML formats for single and sets of multistructured annotations.

The left of Figure 24.10 shows the XML structure built for posting a multistructured annotation. The header block contains all the "technical" information about the annotation, such as the URL of the annotated web page, author information, state of the annotation (public/private), and so on. The remaining blocks contain specific information about the annotation content on texts, images, streams, and minor elements, respectively. The annotation of every element of every remaining block is performed via the *Range Object* technology. On text elements, this allows the system to identify a range of content in a web page. It is also possible to obtain additional subranges. On elements of different types (images, streams, and minor elements), further information has a primary role, such as: shapes representing portion on images, time intervals to identify segments on streams, etc. Even a non-multistructured annotation (e.g., on a single text portion) can be represented in the XML_{RQ} format (with only one element in the text block and the other blocks empty).

The right of Figure 24.10 shows the XML structure downloaded to the client when a user needs to view annotations belonging to a Web page. In this case, the header block contains a summary of the related annotations, while the other blocks contain single or multistructured annotations for the current Web page. As each annotation (single or multistructured) presented to the user tends to modify the DOM structure of the Web page, it is necessary to identify the exact location of each element in the original page. In addition, each annotation presented to the user enriches the basic components of DOM (through the insertion of new tags), which complicates the task of the positioning algorithm (based on XPath). In order to overcome this problem, when a user posts an annotation, the DOM computation is performed taking into account the "original" DOM structure of the source Web Page. During the presentation process, the annotation elements are added to the DOM with a bottom-up, right-left strategy. Hence, every annotation will only need the original location on the DOM and will not interfere with the following ones; furthermore, no annotations can be added "below" an already presented one (or part of it, in case of multistructured annotation) where the DOM structure has been modified.

24.5 IMPLEMENTATION OF MULTISTRUCTURES

This section illustrates some implementation issues for management of multistructures and discusses some features facilitating their production and retrieval.

Application of Pattern Composite

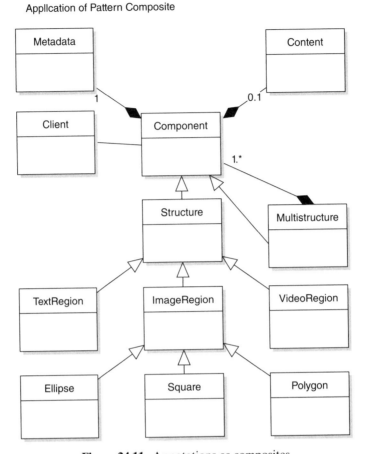

Figure 24.11. Annotations as composites.

24.5.1 Multistructures as Composites

For multistructures, the *Composite* pattern (Gamma et al. 1994) has been adopted, allowing uniform manipulation of individual objects and aggregates.

Figure 24.11 shows the conceptual model for annotating hierarchically organized multistructures, where a simple structure takes the role of Leaf and the multistructure plays the role of Composite. A common interface is provided for accessing and manipulating structure and multistructure objects through the Client (plugins on the browser). With each object of type Component, metadata are associated, describing information on the annotation's author, date, and so on, as well as its content, as text and multimedia attachments.

24.5.2 The MADCOW Database

The MADCOW entities to accommodating multistructures are organized as in Figure 24.12. In particular, they store: annotation *metadata*; the *content* associated with a selection, consisting of text and attachments; the *text interval* for a text selec-

Entity Relationship

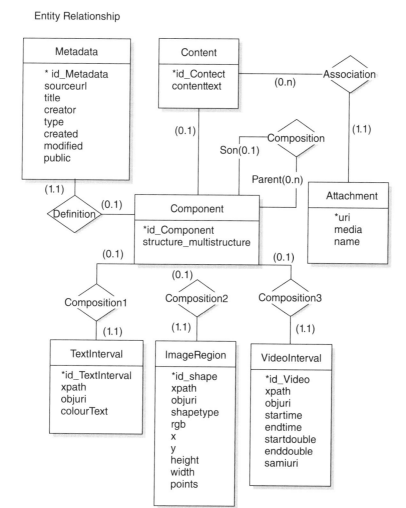

Figure 24.12. The conceptual model for the MADCOW database as ER diagram.

tion; the *video interval* for a video sequence range; the data related to a grouping of *image regions*; and those for *attachments*. *Component* stores information about structures and multistructures, where its Boolean attribute `structure_multi-structure` determines its role. In the physical organization, a table has been added to manage links from annotations to other documents.

Considering Figure 24.4, one sees a text selection (i.e., a *TextInterval* entity) and two rectangular boxes enclosing the exemplars of monotremes (i.e., two *ImageRegion* entities, containing information on the shape, and the RGB color). Information about the author, the created date, the title of the annotation is managed by the *Metadata* entity. Each selection will use the *xpath* attribute to describe the position in the page.

Figure 24.13 summarizes the relations between the conceptual model, the representation, and the storage of a multistructure. From a conceptual point of view, the

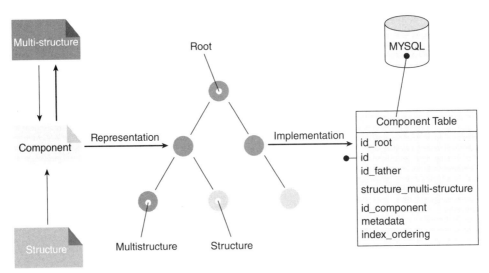

Figure 24.13. Representation and implementation of multistructures.

multistructure is a grouping of components that can themselves be multistructures or simple structures. From a representational standpoint, a multistructure has a tree representation, with a root that can be either a structure or a multistructure node. Multistructure nodes may appear both as leaves and as internal nodes. A multistructure node appearing as a leaf can at a later stage evolve further, as it can have children of type *multistructure* or *structure*, giving rise to a recursive hierarchical organization. On the contrary, a structure node may appear only as leaf and cannot subsequently evolve to a parent node. The fact that the multistructure is presented as a tree does not prevent the construction of complex relations between elements. Indeed, selected regions may be included in different multistructures, and different selections may overlap. In this way, new relations may be discovered among elements, which in turn can lead to the production of new nodes to represent these relations.

Structures and multistructures are stored in `Component`, where `id_father` refers to a node immediate parent, while `id_root` provides access to the root of the tree. For the root, `id_root` has its own identifier as value, while `id_father` has value −1. In Figure 24.3, all the tree nodes, except the root, will have `id_root` equal to the value of `id_component` for the *Mammals* node. The latter will also be the value of `id_father` for the *Monotremes*, *Marsupials*, and *Placentals* nodes. The leaves associated with text and image regions on the page will have as value for `id_father` the value of `id_component` for the *Marsupials* node.

24.5.3 Fast Retrieval of Elements

The information provided by `id_root` minimizes the number of queries to retrieve multistructures in the same tree. The DB exploits a linear ordering for children of the same node, expressed through an attribute `order_index`, thus making this information independent of the physical organization. To retrieve a multistructure tree from the `Component` table, one simply looks for all the records with a common value for `id_root`. This is the value of `id_root` for a selected node, or an external parameter of the query. Similarly, finding all the roots in the database requires selecting those records for which `id_father` = −1. In general, retrieving elements involves selections and projections on the attributes `id`, `id_father` and `order_index`. MADCOW supports several types of annotation retrieval. Besides exploiting links starting from the annotated content, a user can access the MADCOW main page on the server and perform queries exploiting metadata, for example, author, date, title its type, for example, *comment*, *question*, and *answer*, or on the annotation textual content, as shown in Figure 24.8.

24.6 INTERACTIVE CREATION AND USAGE OF ANNOTATIONS ON MULTISTRUCTURES

The annotation of multistructures is performed by interacting with two toolbars: for creation of the annotation proper (CLCS: content, link, color, shape) and for direct manipulation of the multistructure composition (MH: multistructure hierarchy).

24.6.1 The CLCS Interaction System

The CLCS subsystem provides facilities, shown in Table 24.1, for the user to create and edit the annotation text, and to select and attach the multimedia documents to

TABLE 24.1. Icons in the CLCS Toolbar

Button	Functionality
	Local save to a local XML file.
	Text insertion.
	Attachments.
	Association of a link to a URL or to an already annotated component.
	Choice of color for text or image region selection.
	Choice of shape for selection of an image region.
	Zoom In for the selected image region.
	Zoom Out for the selected image region.
	Deletion of the selected (multi-) structure.
X	Close toolbar.

Figure 24.14. Writing text, attaching documents, and selecting color.

TABLE 24.2. Icons in the MH Toolbar

Button	Functionality
	Save local XML files on the on-line DB.
	Show the toolbar of the CLCS system.
	Construct a node in the current multistructure.
	Enable/disable interaction with the working area of the mini-tree.
	Delete the selected structure or multistructure.
	Disable MADCOW.

be incorporated in the annotation content. Moreover, the annotator can configure the appearance of the links, color, and shape of the selections. Hence, it allows the production and personalization of the selections on the page: it is activated by selecting a structure in the document—in which case it opens near the selection—or by clicking on a node in the multistructure tree, enabling the user to define the annotation content or to modify the properties of the selection representation.

Figure 24.14 shows the appearance of the CLCS interface while the annotator is inserting text or attachments, or selecting colors, respectively. To facilitate interaction, the user is offered a working space directly under the toolbar, adapted to the task to be performed (e.g., with formatting commands for text insertion, or a browsing button for attachments). Manipulation of existing annotations is also possible by direct selection of nodes.

24.6.2 The MH Interaction System

The MH toolbar in Table 24.2 allows advanced management of multistructure trees. In particular, MH: (1) offers a view of the hierarchical composition of the multistructure at construction time; (2) allows interactive modification of the hierarchy structure, for example, moving subtrees between parents, or modifying the order in which siblings appear; (3) supports coherence between selection of nodes and focus on document parts; and (4) allows access to the CLCS subsystem to modify or examine existing annotations.

The toolbar can be opened at any time, to build a new multistructure or manipulate an existing one, and remains visible until the user explicitly closes it to commit the changes.

As MH offers direct manipulation of a hierarchy, care must be taken when specific semantics are attached to it, as can be the case for the mammal scenario, while in the scenario for tool reporting, subjective organizations can be constantly rearranged. As of now, no specific semantic control has been considered for operations on MH, but a simple solution could be of tagging parts of the hierarchy as unmodifiable.

24.7 CONCLUSIONS

Annotation is becoming an ubiquitous activity when interacting with Web and multimedia content, but many systems present several limitations: they only support proprietary formats, require separate environments, deal with different types of content separately (e.g., images and texts), allow only one annotation, or do not support incremental annotation.

The MADCOW system provides users with an annotation experience integrated within their normal navigation patterns on a browser: They can annotate different types of content on the same page, integrate several types of content within the annotation, and perform open-ended collaborations by making annotation public for other users to peruse and annotate upon.

In this chapter, we have presented a unique feature of MADCOW, namely the possibility of adding annotations not only to single portions of a document, but to multistructures formed by several portions, even of different nature, organizing them in a hierarchical structure, which may reveal new relations about them, while maintaining the same level of integration with the browsing experience provided by the traditional MADCOW tools. Moreover, we also added the possibility of exploring and manipulating both the annotation content and the hierarchical organization of a multistructure via different types of presentation.

The use of standard open technologies in MADCOW makes it available for incorporation in Web-based application besides usage through the browser. For example, organizations maintaining large collections of documents, such as digital libraries or press agencies, could integrate MADCOW facilities when serving their documents. The adoption of MADCOW can enhance the ability to extract, organize, and enrich the information on documents, and to support cooperative activities related to them. The MADCOW proposal extends the content and subject of annotations to fully exploit multimedia material, as well as making the whole Web a possible source of annotation content and content annotation alike.

ACKNOWLEDGMENTS

We gratefully acknowledge the work of Rosa Trinchese, Roberta Civica and Laura Orso on the first implementation of MADCOW.

ABBREVIATIONS AND ACRONYMS

AAAI	Association for the Advancement of Artificial Intelligence
AAM	Active appearance models
ACE	Automated content extraction
ACL	Association for Computational Linguistics
ACM	Association for Computing Machinery
ACT-R	Adaptive control of thought—rational
AHS	Audio hot spotting
ANVIL	Annotation of Video and Spoken Language
AP	Average precision
API	Application programming interface
ARR	Average reciprocal rank
ASR	Automatic speech recognition
AUC	Area under curve
BBN	Bolt, Beranek, and Newman
BLOB	Binary Large OBjects
BoF	Bag-of-feature representation
BONG	Bag of n-grams

Multimedia Information Extraction: Advances in Video, Audio, and Imagery Analysis for Search, Data Mining, Surveillance, and Authoring, First Edition. Edited by Mark T. Maybury.
© 2012 IEEE Computer Society. Published 2012 by John Wiley & Sons, Inc.

BOW	Bag of words
B-rep	Boundary representations
CAD	Computer aided design
CAIR	Cross-lingual audio information retrieval
CBCR	Content-based copy retrieval
CBMI	Content-based multimedia indexing
CBR	Content-based recommender
CBVIR	Content-based video indexing and retrieval
CC	Correlation coefficient
CER	Character error rate
CFS	Correlation-based feature selection
CGM	Consumer-generated media
CIVR	International Conference on Image and Video Retrieval
CLEAR	Classification of events, activities and relationships
CLEF	Cross-Language Evaluation Forum
CMU	Carnegie Mellon University
CORPS	CORpus of tagged Political Speeches
CUNY	City University of New York
DARPA	Defense Advanced Research Projects Agency
DB	Database
DER	Detection error rate
DL	Digital library
DOM	Document object model
DRM	Digital rights management
DUC	Document Understanding Conferences (duc.nist.gov)
EDC	Event detection and characterization
EDT	Entity detection and tracking
EER	Equal error rate
ELDA	Evaluations and Language Distribution Agency
EMNLP	Conference on Empirical Methods in Natural Language Processing
EVITAP	Enhanced video text and audio processing
EXIF	Exchangeable image format
FACS	Facial action coding system
FAQ	Frequently asked question
FBIS	Foreign Broadcast Information Service
FIRE	Flexible image retrieval engine
FPR	False positive rate
FRCS	Functional role coding scheme
GATE	General architecture for text engineering
GIFT	GNU Image Finding Tool
GML	Generative modeling language
GMM	Gaussian mixture model
GPE	Geopolitical entity
GUI	Graphical user interface
HLT	Human language technology
HMM	Hidden Markov model

HNR	Harmonics-to-noise-ratio
HTML	HyperText markup language
IAEA	International Atomic Energy Agency
IAPS	International Affective Picture System
IBM	International Business Machines
IDF	Inverse document frequency
IE	Information extraction
IEEE	Institute of Electrical and Electronics Engineers
IJCAI	International Joint Conference on Artificial Intelligence
IR	Information retrieval
ISMIR	International Conferences on Music Information Retrieval
ISODATA	Iterative self-organizing data
JSEG	J measure based SEGmentation
KB	Knowledge base
KL	Kullback–Leibler
LDC	Linguistic Data Consortium
LLDs	Low-level descriptors
LM	Language model
LNAI	Springer Lecture Notes in Artificial Intelligence
LNCS	Springer Lecture Notes in Computer Science
LNK	Entity linking
LPC	Linear predictive coding
LREC	International Conference on Language Resources and Evaluation
LSCOM	Large-Scale Concept Ontology for Multimedia
MADCOW	Multimedia Annotation of Digital Content over the Web
MAP	Mean average precision
MFCC	Mel-frequency cepstral coefficients
MHI	Motion history images
MIL	Multiple instance learning
MIR	ACM International Conference on Multimedia Information Retrieval
MIREX	Music Information Retrieval Evaluation eXchange
MLB	Major League Baseball
MLE	Mean linear error
MMIE	Multimedia information extraction
MPEG	Motion Pictures Expert Group
MPQA	Multiperspective Question Answering
MSC	Mission Survival Corpus
MT	Machine translation
MUC	Message Understanding Conference
NASA	National Aeronautics and Space Administration
NIST	National Institute of Standards and Technology
NLG	Natural language generation
NLP	Natural language processing
NSF	National Science Foundation
NURBS	Nonuniform rational B-splines

OCR	Optical character recognition
OWL	Ontology web language
PCA	Principal component analysis
PETS	Performance evaluation of tracking and surveillance
PLSA	Probabilistic latent semantic analysis
POS	Part of speech
QA	Question answering
QBIC	Query by image content
RANSAC	Random sample consensus
RDC	Relation detection and characterization
RDF	Resource Description Framework (http://www.w3.org/RDF)
RGB	Red, green, blue
RI	Relevance intervals
ROC	Receiver operating characteristic
RT	Rich transcription
SDR	Spoken document retrieval
SIFT	Scale invariant feature transform
SIGIR	ACM Special Interest Group in Information Retrieval
SIGMOD	ACM Special Interest Group on Management of Data
SMO	Sequential minimal optimization
SNE	Same news event
SNR	Signal-to-noise ratio
SQL	Standard query language
STT	Speech-to-text
SUSAD	Speech Under Simulated and Actual Stress Database
SVM	Support vector machine
SVR	Support vector regression
TAC	Text Analysis Conference
TDT	Topic detection and tracking
TF	Term frequency
TIDES	Translingual Information Detection Extraction and Summarization
TIMEBANK	Time bank of gold standard of temporally annotated documents
TimeML	Time markup language
TIPSTER	DARPA-funded text and information processing program (Not an acronym)
TREC	Text REtrieval Conference
TRECVID	TREC Video Evaluation
UAV	Unmanned aerial vehicle
UIMA	Unstructured information management architecture
UN	United Nations
URL	Uniform resource locators
USC	University of Southern California
VAM	*Vera am Mittag* corpus
VD	Virtual document
VEM	Visual extraction module
ViPER	Video Performance Evaluation Resource
VIVID	Video verification of identity

VOC	Visual object classes
VS	Visual surveillance
W3C	World Wide Web Consortium
WER	Word error rate
WWW	World Wide Web
XML	eXtensible markup language

REFERENCES

Abelson, R.P. and Carroll, J.D. 1965. Computer Simulation of Individual Belief Systems. *The American Behavioral Scientist* 8: 24–30.

ACE (Automatic Content Extraction). 2005.05.23. English Annotation Guidelines for Entities. *Linguistic Data Consortium*, Version 5.6.1. http://www.ldc.upenn.edu/Projects/ACE

Adomavicius, G. and Tuzhilin, A. 2005. Toward the Next Generation of Recommender Systems: A Survey of the State-of-the-Art and Possible Extensions. *IEEE Transactions on Knowledge and Data Engineering* 17(6): 734–749.

Ai, H., Litman, D.J., Forbes-Riley, K., Rotaru, M., Tetreault, J., and Purandare, A. 2006. Using System and User Performance Features to Improve Emotion Detection in Spoken Tutoring Dialogs. In *Proceedings of the Ninth International Conference on Spoken Language Processing* (INTERSPEECH), 797–800. Pittsburgh, PA, September 17–21, 2006. http://www.isca-speech.org/archive/interspeech_2006/i06_1682.html

AIM@SHAPE. 2006. A.I.M.A.T.S.H.A.P.E.—Advanced and Innovative Models And Tools for the Development of Semantic-Based Systems for Handling, Acquiring, and Processing Knowledge Embedded in Multidimensional Digital Objects'. http://www.aimatshape.net

Ajot, J., Fiscus, J., Garofolo, J., Michel, M., Over, P., Rose, T., Yilmaz, M., Simpson, H., and Strassel, S. 2008. Event Detection in Airport Surveillance: The TRECVid 2008 Evaluation. Presentation *at TRECVid*. http://www-nlpir.nist.gov/projects/tvpubs/tv8.slides/event-detection.pdf

Albrecht, I., Schröder, M., Haber, J., and Seidel, H. 2005. Mixed Feelings: Expression of Non-Basic Emotions in a Muscle-Based Talking Head. *Virtual Reality* 8(4): 201–212.

Allan, J. 2002. Knowledge Management and Speech Recognition. *IEEE Computer* 35(4): 60–61.

Allan, J., Papka, R., and Lavrenko, V. 1998. On-line New Event Detection and Tracking. In *Proceedings of the 21st Annual International ACM SIGIR Conference on Research and*

Development in Information Retrieval, 37–45. Melbourne, Australia, August 24–28, 1998. ACM, New York, NY.

Allwood, J., Loredana, C., Jokinen, K., Navarretta, C., and Paggio, P. 2005. The MUMIN Multimodal Coding Scheme, Technical Report. http://www.ling.gu.se/~shirley/jenspublications/bfiles/B70.pdf

Ambady, N. and Rosenthal, R. 1992. Thin Slices of Expressive Behaviors as Predictors of Interpersonal Consequences: A Meta-Analysis. *Psychological Bulletin* 111: 256–274.

Anderson, J.R., Matessa, M., and Lebiere, C. 1997. ACT-R: A Theory of Higher Level Cognition and its Relation to Visual Attention. *Human-Computer Interaction* 12(4): 439–462.

André, E., Klesen, M., Gebhard, P., Allen, S., and Rist, T. 1999. Integrating Models of Personality and Emotions into Lifelike Characters. In Paiva, A. and Martinho, C. (eds.), *Proceedings of the Workshop on Affect in Interactions—Towards a New Generation of Interfaces*, 136–149. In conjunction with the 3rd i3 Annual Conference, Siena, Italy, October, 21–22, 1999.

Andrews, S., Tsochantaridis, I., and Hofmann, T. 2003. Support Vector Machines for Multiple-Instance Learning. *Advances in Neural Information Processing Systems* 15: 577–584.

Ang, J., Dhillon, R., Krupski, A., Shriberg, E., and Stolcke, A. 2002. Prosody-based Automatic Detection of Annoyance and Frustration in Human-Computer Dialog. In *Proceedings of the 7th International Conference on Spoken Language Processing (ICSLP)*, 2037–2040. Denver, CO, September 16–20, 2002.

Arango, M. 2005. Vanishing Point. In Zhang, H., Chua, T.-S., Steinmetz, R., Kankanhalli, M.S. and Wilcox, L. (eds.), *Proceedings of the 13th Annual ACM International Conference on Multimedia*, 1067–1068. Hilton, Singapore, November 6–11, 2005. ACM, New York, NY.

Arikan, O., Forsyth, D.A., and O'Brien, J.F. 2003. Motion Synthesis from Annotations. *ACM Transactions on Graphics* 22(3): 402–408.

Arnold, D. 2006. Procedural Methods for 3D Reconstruction. *Recording, Modeling and Visualization of Cultural Heritage* 1: 355–359.

Arunachalam, S., Gould, D., Andersen, E., Byrd, D., and Narayanan, S. 2001. Politeness and Frustration Language in Child-Machine Interactions. In *Proceedings of Seventh European Conference on Speech Communication and Technology (Eurospeech)*, 2675–2678. Aalborg, Denmark, September 3–7, 2001.

Atkinson, J. 1984. Public Speaking and Audience Response: Some Techniques for Inviting Applause. In Atkinson, J.M. and Heritage, J. (eds.), *Structures of Social Action*, 370–409, Cambridge University Press, Cambridge, England.

Attias, H. 2000. A Variational Bayesian Framework for Graphical Models. *Advances in Neural Information Processing Systems* 12: 209–215.

Babaguchi, N., Kawai, Y., Ogura, T., and Kitahashi, T. 2004. Personalized Abstraction of Broadcasted American Football Video by Highlight Selection. *IEEE Transaction on Multimedia* 6(4): 575–586.

Bakeman, R. and Gottman, J.M. 1987. Applying Observational Methods: A Systematic View. In Osofsky, J.D. (ed.), *Handbook of Infant Development*, 818–854, Wiley, New York.

Bales R.F. 1970. *Personality and Interpersonal Behavior*. Holt, New York.

Barbic, J., Safonova, A., Pan, J., Faloutsos, C., Hodgins, J.K., and Pollard, N.S. 2004. Segmenting Motion Capture Data into Distinct Behaviors. In *Proceedings of the International Conference on Graphics Interface*, 185–194. London, ON, Canada, May 17–19, 2004.

Bargar, R. 2012. Toward Formalization of Display Grammar for Interactive Media Production with Multimedia Information Extraction, this volume.

Barnard, K., Duygulu, P., de Freitas, N., Forsyth, D., Blei, D., and Jordan, M. 2003. Matching Words and Pictures. *Journal of Machine Learning Research* 3: 1107–1135.

Barnard, K. and Forsyth, D. 2001. Learning the Semantics of Words and Pictures. In *Proceedings of the Eighth IEEE International Conference on Computer Vision* (ICCV), Vol. 2, 408–415. Vancouver, BC, Canada, July 7–14, 2001. IEEE Computer Society.

Bates, J. 1994. The role of Emotion in Believable Agents. *Communications of the ACM* 37(7): 122–125.

Batliner, A., Fischer, K., Huber, R., Spilker, J., and Nöth, E. 2003. How to Find Trouble in Communication. *Speech Communication* 40(1–2): 117–143.

Batliner, A., Schuller, B., Schaeffler, S., and Steidl, S. 2008. Mothers, Adults, Children, Pets— Towards the Acoustics of Intimacy. In *Proceedings of the International Conference on Acoustics, Speech, and Signal Processing (ICASSP)*, 4497–4500. Las Vegas, NV, March 30–April 4, 2008.

Batliner, A., Steidl, S., Schuller, B., Seppi, D., Laskowski, K., Vogt, T., Devillers, L., Vidrascu, L., Amir, N., Kessous, L., and Aharonson, V. 2006. Combining Efforts for Improving Automatic Classification of Emotional User States. In Erjavec, T. and Gros, J. (ed.), *Proceedings of Fifth Slovenian and First International Language Technologies Conference (IS-LTC)*, 240–245. Ljubljana, Slovenia, October 9–10, 2006.

Bay, H., Tuytelaars, T., and Van Gool, L. 2006. Surf: Speeded Up Robust Features. In *Proceedings of the 9th European Conference on Computer Vision (ECCV)*, 404–417. Graz, Austria, May 7–13, 2006.

Beacham, R., Denard, H., and Niccolucci, F. 2006. An Introduction to the London Charter. *The e-Volution of Information Communication Technology in Cultural Heritage: Where Hi-Tech Touches the Past* 1: 1–13.

Bechara, A., Damasio, H., and Damasio, A.R. 2000. Emotion, Decision Making and the Orbitofrontal Cortex. *Cerebral Cortex* 10(3): 295–307.

Beckman, R. and Cook, R. 1979. Testing for Two-Phase Regressions. *Technometrics* 21: 65–69.

Benkő, P., Kós, G., Várady, T., Andor, L., and Martin, R. 2002. Constrained Fitting in Reverse Engineering. *Computer Aided Geometric Design* 19(3): 173–205.

Benne, K. D. and Sheats, P. 1948. Functional Roles of Group Members. *Journal of Social Issues*, 4: 41–49.

Bernardini, F., Bajaj, C., Chen, J., and Schikore, D. 1999. Automatic Reconstruction of 3D CAD Models from Digital Scans. *International Journal on Computational Geometry and Applications* 9(4–5): 327–369.

Berndt, R., Fellner, D.W., and Havemann, S. 2005. Generative 3D Models: A Key to More Information within Less Bandwidth at Higher Quality. In *Proceedings of the 10th International Conference on 3D Web Technology*, Vol. 1, 111–121. Bangor, UK, March 29–April 1, 2005.

Bertoldi, N., Brugnara, F., Cettolo, M., Federico, M., and Giuliani, D. 2002. Cross-Task Portability of a Broadcast News Speech Recognition System. *Speech Communication* 38(3–4): 335–347.

Biasotti, S., Marini, S., Spagnuolo, M., and Falcidieno, B. 2006. Sub-Part Correspondence by Structural Descriptors of 3D Shapes. *Computer-Aided Design* 38(9): 1002–1019.

Biederman, I. 1987. Recognition-by-Components: A Theory of Human Image Understanding. *Psychological Review* 94(2): 115–147.

Bigbee, T., Loehr, D., and Harper, L. 2001. Emerging Requirements for Multi-Modal Annotation and Analysis Tools. In *Proceedings of the 7th European Conference on Speech*

Communication and Technology (Eurospeech), 1533–1536. Aalborg, Denmark, September 3–7, 2001.

Bikel, D., Schwartz, R., and Weischedel, R. 1999. An Algorithm that Learns What's in a Name. *Journal of Machine Learning* 34(1–3): 211–231.

BioCreative II. September, 2008. Critical Assessment for Information Extraction in Biology Challenge. *Special Issue of Genome Biology* 9(Suppl. 2).

Bird, S. and Liberman, M. 2001. A Formal Framework for Linguistic Annotation. *Speech Communication* 33(1–2): 23–60.

Bishop, C.M. 2007. *Pattern Recognition and Machine Learning*. Springer, New York.

Black, M.J. and Rangarajan, A. 2005. On the Unification of Line Processes, Outlier Rejection, and Robust Statistics with Applications in Early Vision. *International Journal of Computer Vision* 19(1): 57–91.

Blei, D.M., Ng, A.Y., and Jordan, M.I. 2003. Latent Dirichlet Allocation. *Journal of Machine Learning Research* 3(5): 993–1022.

Blekas, A., Garofalakis, J., and Stefanis, V. 2006. Use of RSS Feeds for Content Adaptation in Mobile Web Browsing. In *Proceedings of the 2006 international Cross-Disciplinary Workshop on Web Accessibility (W4A): Building the Mobile Web: Rediscovering Accessibility?* Vol. 134, 79–85. Edinburgh, UK, May 22–22, 2006. ACM, New York, NY.

Bligh, M.C., Kohles, J.C., and Meindl, J.R. 2004. Charisma Under Crisis: Presidential Leadership, Rhetoric, and Media Responses Before and After the September 11th Terrorist Attacks. *The Leadership Quarterly* 15(2): 211–239.

Blum, T., Keislaer, D., Wheaton, J., and Wold, E. 1997. Audio Databases with Content-Based Retrieval. In Maybury, M. (ed.), *Intelligent Multimedia Information Retrieval*, 113–135, AAAI/MIT Press, Menlo Park, CA.

Bobick, A.F. and Intille, S.S. 1999. Large Occlusion Stereo. *International Journal of Computer Vision* 33(3): 181–200.

Bocconi, S. 2006. Vox Populi: Generating Video Documentaries from Semantically Annotated Media Repositories. PhD thesis, Technical University of Eindhoven.

Bocconi, S. and Nack, F. 2004. Automatic Generation of Biased Video Sequences. In *Proceedings of the First ACM Workshop on Story Representation, Mechanism and Context (SRMC)*, 9–16. New York, NY, October 15–15, 2004. ACM, New York, NY.

Boer, J. 2003. *Game Audio Programming*. Charles River Media, Hingham, MA.

Boersma, P. and Weenink, D. 2005. Praat: Doing Phonetics by Computer (Version 4.3.14), [Computer Program] Retrieved from http://www.praat.org

Bookstein, F.L. 1989. Principal Warps: Thin-Plate Splines and the Decomposition of Deformations. *Transactions on Pattern Analysis and Machine Intelligence* 11(6): 567–585.

Bottoni, P., Civica, R., Levialdi, S., Orso, L., Panizzi, E., and Trinchese, R. 2004. MADCOW: A Multimedia Digital Annotation System. In *Proceedings of the Working Conference on Advanced Visual Interfaces (AVI)*, 55–62. Gallipoli, Italy, May 25–28, 2004. ACM, New York, NY.

Bottoni, P., Cuomo, M., Levialdi, S., Panizzi, E., Passavanti, M., and Trinchese, R. 2007. Differences and Identities in Document Retrieval in an Annotation Environment. In *Proceedings of 5th International Conference on Databases in Networked Information Systems*, 139–153. Aizu-Wakamatsu, Japan. October 17–19, 2007. Bhalla, S. (ed.) Lecture Notes on Computer Science 4777. Springer Verlag, Berlin/Heidelberg.

Bottoni, P., Levialdi, S., Pambuffetti, N., Panizzi, E., and Trinchese, R. 2006. Storing and Retrieving Multimedia Web Notes. *International Journal of Computational Science and Engineering (IJCSE)* 2(5/6): 341–358. dx.doi.org/10.1504/IJCSE.2006.014780.

Bouganis, A. and Shanahan, M. 2008. Flexible Object Recognition in Cluttered Scenes using Relative Point Distribution Models. In *Proceedings of the 19th International Conference on Pattern Recognition (ICPR)*, 1–53. Tampa, FL, December 8–11, 2008.

Bouthemy, P. and Lalande, P. 1993. Recovery of Moving Object Masks in an Image Sequence using Local Spatiotemporal Contextual Information. *SPIE Optical Engineering* 32(6): 1205–1212.

Boykov, Y., Veksler, O., and Zabith, R. 1998. A Variable Window Approach to Early Vision. *IEEE Transactions on Pattern Analysis and Machine Intelligence (PAMI)* 20(12): 1283–1294.

Bradley, D.C., Steil, G.M., and Bergman, R.N. 1995. OOPSEG: A Data Smoothing Program for Quantitation and Isolation of Random Measurement Error. *Computer Methods and Programs in Biomedicine* 46(1): 67–77.

Bradshaw, B. 2000. Semantic Based Image Retrieval: A Probabilistic Approach. In *Proceedings of the 8th ACM International Conference on Multimedia*, 167–176. Marina del Ray, CA, October 30–November 3, 2000. ACM, New York.

Braschler, M. and Schauble, P. 2000. Using Corpus-Based Approaches in a System for Multilingual Information Retrieval. *Journal of Information Retrieval* 3(3): 273–284.

Breck, E., Choi, Y., and Cardie, C. 2007. Identifying Expressions of Opinion in Context. In *Proceedings of the Twentieth International Joint Conference on Artificial Intelligence (IJCAI)*. Hyderabad, India, January 6–12, 2007.

Breese, J. and Ball, G. 1998. Modeling Emotional State and Personality for Conversational Agents. Technical Report MS-TR-98-41, Microsoft.

Browne, P. and Smeaton, A.F. 2004. Video Information Retrieval Using Objects and Ostensive Relevance Feedback. In *Proceedings of the ACM Symposium on Applied Computing*, 1084–1090. Nicosia, Cyprus, March 14–17, 2004. ACM.

Browne, P., Smeaton, A.F., Murphy, N., O'Connor, N., Marlow, S., and Berrut, C. 2000. Evaluating and Combining Digital Video Shot Boundary Detection Algorithms. In *Proceedings of Irish Machine Vision and Image Processing Conference (IMVIP)*, 93–100, Belfast, Northern Ireland.

Bull, P. and Noordhuizen, M. 2000. The Mistiming of Applause in Political Speeches. *Journal of Language and Social Psychology* 19: 275–294.

Bunt, H., Kipp, M., Maybury, M., and Wahlster, W. 2005. Fusion and Coordination for Multimodal Interactive Information Presentation. In Stock, O. and Zancanaro, M. (eds.), *Multimodal Intelligent Information Presentation*, 325–339, Springer, Amsterdam, The Netherlands.

Burke, R. 2002. Hybrid Recommender Systems: Survey and Experiments. *User Modeling and User-adapted Interaction* 12(4): 331–370.

Bush, V. 1945. As We May Think. *Atlantic Monthly* 176 (July): 101–108.

Bustos, B., Keim, D., Saupe, D., and Schreck, T. 2007. Content-Based 3D Object Retrieval. *IEEE Computer Graphics and Applications* 27(4): 22–27.

Calbris, G. 2008. From Left to Right: Coverbal Gestures and Their Symbolic Use of Space. In Cienki, A. and Müller, C. (eds.), *Metaphor and Gesture*, 27–53, John Benjamins, Amsterdam, The Netherlands.

Carberry, S., Elzer, S., Burns, R., Wu, P., Chester, D., and Demir, S. 2012. Information Graphics in Multimodal Documents, this volume.

Carberry, S., Elzer, S., and Demir, S. 2006. Information Graphics: An Untapped Resource of Digital Libraries. In *Proceedings of 9th International ACM SIGIR Conference*, 581–588. Seattle, Washington, August 6–11, 2006.

Carbonell, J.G. 1978. POLITICS: Automated Ideological Reasoning. *Cognitive Science* 2: 27–51.

Cardie, C., Wiebe, J., Wilson, T., and Litman, D. 2004. Low-level Annotations and Summary Representations for Multiperspective QA. In Maybury, M. (ed.), *New Directions in Question Answering*, 87–98, AAAI/MIT Press, Cambridge.

Cardillo, P., Clements, M., and Miller, M. 2002. Phonetic Searching vs. Large Vocabulary Continuous Speech Recognition. *International Journal of Speech Technology* 5: 9–22.

Carenini, G., Ng, R., and Zwart, E. 2005. Extracting Knowledge from Evaluative Text. In *Proceedings of the 3rd International Conference on Knowledge Capture (K-CAP)*, 11–18. Banff, Canada, October 2–5, 2005.

Carli, G. and Gretter, G. 1992. A Start-End Point Detection Algorithm for a Real-Time Acoustic Front-End based on DSP32C VME Board. In *Proceedings of the International Conference on Signal Processing Theory and Applications (ICSPAT)*, 1011–1017. Boston, MA, November 2–5, 1992.

CS 2008, Cassel, L., Clements, A., Davies, G., Guzdial, M., McCauley, R., McGettrick, A., Sloan, B., Snyder, L., Tymann, P., and Weide, B. 2008. Computer Science Curriculum 2008: An Interim Revision of CS 2001 Report from the Interim Review Task Force. December 2008. Association for Computing Machinery and IEEE Computer Society. See: http://computer.org/educate

Castelfranchi, C. and de Rosis, F. 1999. How can Personality Factors Contribute to Make Agents More "Believable." In *Proceedings of the Workshop on Behavior Planning for Lifelike Characters and Avatars*, 25–35. Sitges, Spain, March 9–10, 1999.

Castellano, G., Kessous, L., and Caridakis, G. 2008. Emotion Recognition through Multiple Modalities: Face, Body Gesture, Speech. In Peter, C. and Beale, R. (eds.), *Affect and Emotion in Human-Computer Interaction: From Theory to Applications, LNCS 4868*, 92–103, Springer-Verlag, Düsseldorf, Germany.

Castelluccio, M. 2006. The Music Genome Project. *Strategic Finance* 88(6): 57–58.

Černeková, Z., Nikou, C., and Pitas, I. 2002. Shot Detection in Video Sequences Using Entropy-based Metrics. In *Proceedings of the 2002 IEEE International Conference on Image Processing*. (ICIP), Vol. III, 421–424. Rochester, NY, September 22–25, 2002. IEEE.

Cha, M., Kwak, H., Rodriguez, P., Ahn, Y.-Y., and Moon, S. 2007. I Tube, You Tube, Everybody Tubes: Analyzing the World's Largest User Generated Content Video System. In *IMC '07: Proceedings of the 7th ACM SIGCOMM Conference on Internet Measurement*, 1–14. San Diego, CA, October 24–26, 2007. ACM, New York, NY.

Chang, Y., Hu, C., and Turk, M. 2004. Probabilistic Expression Analysis on Manifolds. *IEEE Computer Society Conference on Computer Vision and Pattern Recognition (CVPR)* 2: 520–527. Washington, DC, June 27–July 2, 2004.

Chang, Y., Hu, C., Feris, R., and Turk, M. 2006. Manifold Based Analysis of Facial Expression. *Image and Vision Computing* 24(6): 205–614.

Chen, D.-Y., Tian, X.-P., Shen, Y.-T., and Ouhyoung, M. 2003. On Visual Similarity Based 3D Model Retrieval. *Computer Graphics Forum* 22(3): 223–232.

Cheng, K., Wang, W., Qin, H., Wong, K., Yang, H., and Liu, Y. 2004. Fitting Subdivision Surfaces to Unorganized Point Data using SDM. In *Proceedings of 12th Pacific Conference on Computer Graphics and Applications*, Vol. 1, 16–24. October 6–8, 2004, Seoul, Korea.

Cheng, X., Dale, C., and Liu, J. 2007. Understanding the Characteristics of Internet Short Video Sharing: YouTube as a Case Study, Cornell University. Technical Report arXiv:0707.3670v1.

Chester, D. and Elzer, S. 2005. Getting Computers to See Information Graphics so Users Do Not Have To. In *Proceedings of the 15th International Symposium on Methodologies for Intelligent Systems*, 660–668. May 25–28, 2005. Lecture Notes in Artificial Intelligence 3488, Springer-Verlag, Saratoga Springs, NY.

Chippendale, P. 2006. Towards Automatic Body Language Annotation. In *Proceedings of the 7th International Conference on Automatic Face and Gesture Recognition—FG2006 (IEEE)*, 487–492. Southampton, UK, April 10–12 2006.

Choi, F.Y.Y. 2000. Advances in Domain Independent Linear Text Segmentation. In *Proceedings of the First Conference of the North American Chapter of the Association for Computational Linguistics (NAACL)*, 26–33. Seattle, WA, April 29–May 4, 2000.

Choi, I. 2000b. A Manifold Interface for Kinesthetic Notation in High-Dimensional Systems. In Battier, M. and Wanderley, M. (eds.), *Trends in Gestural Control of Music*. Paris: IRCAM (CD-ROM Publication).

Choi, I. 2008a. Ontologically and Graphically Assisted Media Authoring with Multiple Media Types. In Maybury, M. and Walter, S. (eds.), *Proceedings of AAAI Fall Symposium on Multimedia Information Extraction*, Arlington, Virginia, November 7–9, 2008. AAAI Technical Report FS-08-05. Association for the Advancement of Artificial Intelligence.

Choi, I. 2008b. idBrooklyn: An Interactive Documentary. Live Presentation, Music and the Moving Image Conference, New York University.

Choi, I. 2012. Media Authoring with Ontological Reasoning: Use Case for Multimedia Information Extraction, this volume.

Chomsky, N. 1965. *Aspects of the Theory of Syntax*. MIT Press, Cambridge, MA.

Choudhury, T. and Pentland, A. 2003. Sensing and Modeling Human Networks Using the Sociometer. In *Proceedings of the 7th International Symposium on Wearable Computers*, 216–222. Crowne Plaza Hotel, White Plains, NY, October 21–23, 2003.

Christel, M., Smith, M., Taylor, R., and Winkler, D. 1998. Evolving Video Skims into Useful Multimedia Abstractions. In *Proceedings of the SIGCHI Conference on Human Factors in Computing Systems*, 171–178. Los Angeles, CA, April 18–23, 1998. ACM Press/Addison-Wesley Publishing Co.

Chuah, M., Roth, S., and Kerpedjiev, S. 1997. Sketching, Searching, and Customizing Visualizations: A Content-Based Approach to Design Retrieval. In Maybury, M. (ed.), *Intelligent Multimedia Information Retrieval*, 83–111, AAAI/MIT Press, Cambridge.

Chuang, E.S., Deshpande, H., and Bregler, C. 2002. Facial Expression Space Learning. In *Proceedings of the 10th Pacific Conference on Computer Graphics and Applications*, 68–76. Tsinghua University, Beijing, October 9–11, 2002.

Chuang, Z.J. and Wu, C.H. 2004. Emotion Recognition Using Acoustic Features and Textual Content. In *Proceedings of IEEE International Conference on Multimedia and Expo (ICME)*, Vol. 1, 53–56. Taipei, Taiwan, June 27–30, 2004.

Cohen, J.A. 1960. A Coefficient of Agreement for Nominal Scales. *Educational and Psychological Measurement* 20: 37–46.

Collier, K. 2006. Writing for the Great Communicators: Speechwriting for Roosevelt and Reagan. Presented at *Southwest Political Science Association Meetings*, San Antonio, TX, March. http://www.kencollier.org/research/CollierSWPSA2006Full.pdf

Colthurst, T., Kimball, O., Richurdson, F., Han, S., Wooters, C., Iyer, R., and Gish, H. 2000. The 2000 BBN Byblos LVCSR System. In *Proceedings of the 6th International Conference of Spoken Language Processing (ICSLP)*, Vol. 2, 1011–1104. Beijing, China.

Computer Science Curricula 2008: An Interim Revision of CS 2001. Report from the Interim Review Task Force. December 2008. Association for Computing Machinery and IEEE Computer Society. www.acm.org/education/curricula/ComputerScience2008.pdf

Cootes, T.F., Edwards, G.J., and Taylor, C.J. 1998. Active Appearance Models. In *Proceedings of the European Conference on Computer Vision (ECCV)*, Vol. 2, 484–498. Freiburg, Germany, June 2–6, 1998, Lecture Notes in Computer Science 1407. Springer.

Cope, D. 2006. *Computer Models of Musical Creativity*. MIT Press, Cambridge, MA.

Cortes, C. and Vapnik, V. 1995. Support-Vector Networks. *Machine Learning* 20(3): 273–297.

Cousins, K. and Mcintosh, W. 2005. More than Typewriters, More than Adding Machines: Integrating Information Technology into Political Research. *Quality and Quantity* 39: 581–614.

Cowie, R., Douglas-Cowie, E., Apolloni, B., Taylor, J., Romano, A., and Fellenz, W. 1999. What a Neural Net Needs to Know about Emotion Words. In Mastorakis, N. (ed.), *Computational Intelligence and Applications*, 109–114, World Scientific & Engineering Society Press.

Cowie, R., Douglas-Cowie, E., Savvidou, S., McMahon, E., Sawey, M., and Schroder, M. 2000. FEELTRACE: An Instrument for Recording Perceived Emotion in Real Time. In *Proceedings of the ISCA Workshop on Speech and Emotion: A Conceptual Framework for Research*, 19–24. September 5–7, 2000. ISCA, Belfast, UK.

Cowie, R., Douglas-Cowie, E., Tsapatsoulis, N., Votsis, G., Kollias, S., Fellenz, W., and Taylor, J.G. 2001. Emotion Recognition in Human-Computer Interaction. *IEEE Signal Processing Magazine* 18(1): 32–80.

Crasborn, O., Sloetjes, H., Auer, E., and Wittenburg, P. 2006. Combining Video and Numeric Data in the Analysis of Sign Languages within the ELAN Annotation Software. In Vetoori, C. (ed.), *Proceedings of the Fifth International Conference on Language Resources and Evaluation (LREC) Workshop on Representation and Processing of Sign Languages*, 82–87. Genoa, Italy, May 28, 2006. ELRA.

Creswell, C., Beal, M., Chen, J., Cornell, T., Nilsson, L., and Srihari, R. 2006. Automatically Extracting Nominal Mentions of Events with a Bootstrapped Probabilistic Classifier. In *Proceedings of the COLING/ACL 2006 Main Conference Poster Sessions*, 168–175. Sydney, Australia, July 17–18, 2006. Association for Computational Linguistics: Morristown, NJ.

Cristani, M., Perina, A., Castellani, U., and Murino, V. 2008. Geo-located Image Analysis using Latent Representations. In *Proceedings of IEEE Computer Vision and Pattern Recognition (CVPR)*, 8 pages, June 2008. Anchorage, Alaska, June 23–28, 2008.

Crofts, N., Doerr, M., Gill, T., Stead, S., and Stiff, M. (eds.). 2003. CIDOC CRM Special Interest Group. Definition of the CIDOC Conceptual Reference Model, International Council of Museums (ICOM)/International Committee for Documentation (CIDOC) Documentation Standards Group.

Csurka, G., Bray, C., Dance, C., and Fan, L. 2004. Visual Categorization with Bags of Keypoints. In *8th European Conference on Computer Vision (ECCV), Proceedings of ECCV Workshop on Statistical Learning in Computer Vision*, 59–74. Prague, May 11–14, 2004.

Curhan, J. and Pentland, A. 2007. Thin Slices of Negotiation: Predicting Outcomes from Conversational Dynamics Within the First 5 Minutes. *Journal of Applied Psychology* 92(3): 802–811.

Curio, C., Breidt, M., Kleiner, M., Vuong, Q., Giese, M., and Bülthoff, H. 2006. Semantic 3D Motion Retargeting for Facial Animation. In Spencer, S.N. (ed.), *Proceedings of the 3rd Symposium on Applied Perception in Graphics and Visualization* (APGV06), 77–84. Boston, MA, July 28–29, 2006. ACM Press, New York, NY.

Dan, A., Sitaram, D., and Song, J. 1998. BRAHMA: Browsing and Retrieval Architecture for Hierarchical Multimedia Annotation. *Multimedia Tools and Applications* 7: 83–101.

Darwin, C. 1872. *The Expression of the Emotions in Man and Animals*. John Murray, London.

Das, M., Farmer, J., Gallagher, A., and Loui, A. 2008. Event-Based Location Matching for Consumer Image Collections. In *Proceedings of IEEE Conference on Image and Video Retrieval (CIVR)*, 339–349. Niagara Falls, Canada, July 7–9, 2008. ACM, New York, NY.

Das, M. and Loui, A. 2008. Matching of Complex Scenes Based on Constrained Clustering. In Maybury, M. and Walter, S. (eds.), *Proceedings of AAAI Fall Symposium on Multimedia Information Extraction*, AAAI Technical Report FS-08-05. November 7–9, 2008, Arlington, VA.

Das, M., Loui, A., and Blose, A. 2012. Visual Feature Localization for Detecting Unique Objects in Images, this volume.

Dasgupta, D. and Forrest, S. 1996. Novelty Detection in Time Series Data Using Ideas from Immunology. In Harris, F.C. (ed.), *Proceedings of the 5th International Conference on Intelligent Systems*, 82–87. Reno, NV, June 19–21, 1996. International Society for Computers and their Applications (ISCA).

Davenport, G., et al. 2000. Synergistic Storyscapes and Constructionist Cinematic Sharing. *IBM Systems Journal* 39(3–4): 456–469.

Davis, A., Rennert, P., Rubinoff, R., Sibley, T., and Tzoukemann, E. 2004. Retrieving What's Relevant in Audio and Video: Statistics and Linguistics in Combination. In *Proceedings of RIAO*, 850–873. Avignon, France, April 26–28, 2004.

de Kok, I. 2006. A Model for Valence Using a Color Component in Affective Video Content Analysis. In *Proceedings of the Fourth Twente Student Conference on IT*, Faculty of Electrical Engineering, Mathematics and Computer Science, University of Twente, The Netherlands, January 30, 2006.

de Rosis, F., Batliner, A., Novielli, N., and Steidl, S. 2007. You are Sooo Cool, Valentina! Recognizing Social Attitude in Speech-Based Dialogues with an ECA. In Paiva, A., Prada, R., and Picard, R.W. (eds.), *Affective Computing and Intelligent Interaction*, 179–190, Springer, Berlin/Heidelberg.

Delarue, O. and Warusfel, O. 2006. Mixage Mobile. In *Proceedings of the 18th International Conference of the Association Francophone d'Interaction Homme-Machine*, 75–82. Montreal, Canada, April 18–21, 2006.

Del Bimbo, A. 1999. *Visual Information Retrieval*. Morgan Kaufman Publishers, San Francisco, CA.

Del Bimbo, A. and Bertini, M. 2007. Multimedia Ontology Based Computational Framework for Video Annotation and Retrieval. In *Proceedings of Multimedia Content Analysis and Mining 2007*, 18–23. Lecture Notes on Computer Science 4577. Springer, Berlin/Heidelberg.

Deng, Y. and Manjunath, B.S. 2001. Unsupervised Segmentation of Color-texture Regions in Images and Video. *IEEE Transactions on Pattern Analysis and Machine Intelligence* 23(8): 800–810.

Deselaers, T., Keysers, D., and Ney, H. 2008. Features for Image Retrieval: An Experimental Comparison. *Information Retrieval* 11(2): 77–107.

Devillers, L., Lamel, L., and Vasilescu, I. 2003. Emotion Detection in Task-Oriented Spoken Dialogs. In *Proceedings of the IEEE International Conference on Multimedia and Expo (ICME)*, Vol. 3, 549–552. Baltimore, MD, July 6–9, 2003.

Dietz, R. and Lang, A. 1999. Affective Agents: Effects of Agent Affect on Arousal, Attention, Liking and Learning. In *Proceedings of the Third International Cognitive Technology Conference*, San Francisco, CA. http://rick.oacea.com/misc/polara/pubs/cogtech1999.html (visited July 9, 2009).

DiMicco, J.M., Hollenback, K.J., Pandolfo, A., and Bender, W. 2007. The Impact of Increased Awareness while Face-to-Face. *Special Issue on Awareness Systems Design Human-Computer Interaction* 22(1): 47–96.

DL. 2009. *Curriculum on Digital Libraries*. http://en.wikiversity.org/wiki/Curriculum_on_Digital_Libraries. See also http://curric.dlib.vt.edu

Douglas-Cowie, E., Campbell, N., Cowie, R., and Roach, R. 2003. Emotional Speech: Towards a New Generation of Databases. *Speech Communication* 40(1–2): 33–60.

Douglas-Cowie, E., Cowie, R., Sneddon, I., Cox, C., Lowry, O., Mcrorie, M., Martin, J.-C., Devillers, L., Abrilian, S., Batliner, A., Amir, N., and Karpouzis, K. 2007. The HUMANE

Database. In *Proceedings of the 2nd International Conference on Affective Computing and Intelligent Interaction (ACII)*, 488–500. Lisbon, Portugal, September 12–14, 2007.

Downie, J.S. 2008. The Music Information Retrieval Evaluation Exchange (2005–2007): A Window into Music Information Retrieval Research. *Acoustical Science and Technology* 29(4): 247–255.

Doyle, M. and Straus, D. 1993. *How to Make Meetings Work*. The Berkley Publishing Group, New York.

Du, Y., Bi, W., Wang, T., Zhang, Y., and Ai, H. 2007. Distributing Expressional Faces in 2D Emotional Space. In *Proceedings of the Conference on Image and Video Retrieval*, 395–400. Amsterdam, The Netherlands, July 9–11, 2007.

Du, Y. and Lin, X. 2002. Mapping Emotional Status to Facial Expressions. In *16th International Conference on Pattern Recognition (ICPR)*, Vol. 2, Mapping Emotional Status to Facial Expressions, 524–527. Quebec City, QC, Canada. August 11–15, 2002.

Dublin Core Metadata Initiative. 1995. Dublin Core Metadata Initiative. http://dublincore.org/

Duda, R.O., Hart, P.E., and Stork, D.G. 2001. *Pattern Classification*, 2nd ed., 526–528, Wiley, New York.

Dumais, S., Platt, J., Heckerman, D., and Sahami, M. 2006. Inductive Learning Algorithms and Representations for Text Categorization. In *Proceedings of 7th International Conference on Information and Knowledge Management*, 148–155. Bethesda, MD, November 2–7, 1998.

Dupuis, K. and Pichora-Fuller, K. 2007. Use of Lexical and Affective Prosodic Cues to Emotion by Younger and Older Adults. In *Proceedings of Interspeech*, 2237–2240. Antwerp, Belgium, August 27–31, 2007.

Duygulu, P., Barnard, K., de Freitas, J., and Forsyth, D. 2002. Object Recognition as Machine Translation: Learning a Lexicon for a Fixed Image Vocabulary. In *Proceedings of European Conference on Computer Vision*, Vol. IV, 97–112.

Eakins, J.P. 1996. Automatic Image Content Retrieval—Are We Getting Anywhere? In *Proceedings of the Third International Conference on Electronic Library and Visual Information Research*, 123–135. De Montfort University, Milton Keynes, UK: ASLIB.

Eco, U. 1962. Opera Aperta. Milano: Bompiani (English Edition: Eco, U. 1989. *The Open Work*. Harvard University).

Efron, E. 1972. *The News Twisters*. Manor Books, New York.

Efros, A.A., Berg, A., Mori, G., and Malik, J. 2003. Recognizing Action at a Distance. In *Proceedings of the Ninth IEEE International Conference on Computer Vision*, Vol. 2, 726–733. Nice, France, October 13–16, 2003.

Ekman, P. 1982. *Emotion in the Human Face*. Cambridge University Press, New York.

Ekman, P. 1999. Basic Emotions. In Dalgleish, T. and Power, M. (eds.) *Handbook of Cognition and Emotion*, 40–61, John Wiley and Sons, Inc., West Sussex, England.

Ekman, P. and Friesen, W.V. 1978. *The Facial Action Coding System: A Technique for the Measurement of Facial Movement*. Consulting Psychologists Press, Palo Alto, CA.

Ekman, P. and Friesen, W.V. 2003. *Unmasking the Face*. Malor Books, Cambridge, MA.

Ekman, P., Friesen, W.V., and Hager, J.C. 2002. *Facial Action Coding System The Manual*. Research Nexus Division of Network Information Research Corporation, Salt Lake City, UT.

Eleftheriadis, A. and Puri, A. 1998. MPEG-4 Systems, Text for ISO/IEC FCD 14496-1 Systems. *MPEG-4 SNHC*.

Elgammal, A., Duraiswami, R., Harwood, D., and Davis, L. 2002. Background and Foreground Modeling using Nonparametric Kernel Density Estimation for Visual Surveillance. *Proceedings of the IEEE* 90(7): 1151–1163.

Elliott, C. 1992. The Affective Reasoner: A Process Model of Emotions in a Multi-agent System. PhD thesis, Northwestern University.

Elzer, S., Carberry, S., Chester, D., Demir, S., Green, N., and Zukerman, I. 2005a. Exploring and Exploiting the Limited Utility of Captions in Recognizing Intention in Information Graphics. In *Proceedings of the Annual Meeting of the Association for Computational Linguistics*, 223–230. Ann Arbor, MI, June 25–30, 2005.

Elzer, S., Carberry, S., Zukerman, I., Chester, D., Green, N., and Demir, S. 2005b. A Probabilistic Framework for Recognizing Intention in Information Graphics. In *Proceedings of the International Joint Conference on Artificial Intelligence*, 1042–1047. Edinburgh, Scotland, UK, July 30–August 5, 2005.

Elzer, S., Green, N., Carberry, S., and Hoffman, J. 2006. A Model of Perceptual Task Effort for Bar Charts and its Role in Recognizing Intention. *User Modeling and User-adapted Interaction* 16(1): 1–30.

Enser, P. and Sandom, C. 2003. Towards a Comprehensive Survey of the Semantic Gap in Visual Image Retrieval. In *Proceedings of the 2nd International Conference on Image and Video Retrieval (CIVR'03)*, Erwin M. Bakker, Michael S. Lew, Thomas S. Huang, Nicu Sebe, and Xiang Zhou (eds.). Springer-Verlag, Berlin/Heidelberg, 291–299.

Essa, I.A. and Pentland, A.P. 1997. Coding, Analysis, Interpretation, and Recognition of Facial Expressions. *Transactions on Pattern Analysis and Machine Intelligence* 19(7): 757–763.

Esuli, A. and Sebastiani, F. 2006. SentiWordNet: A Publicly Available Lexical Resource for Opinion Mining. In *Proceedings of the 5th Conference on Language Resources and Evaluation*, 417–422. Genova, Italy, May 22–26, 2006.

Everingham, M., Van Gool, L., Williams, C.K.I., Winn, J., and Zisserman, A. 2009. The PASCAL Visual Object Classes Challenge 2009 (VOC2009) Part 1—Challenge & Detection Task. Kyoto, Japan in conjunction with ICCV 2009. October 3, 2009. Online proceedings: http://www.pascal-network.org/challenges/VOC/voc2009/workshop/index.html

Everingham, M., Van Gool, L., Williams, C.K.I., Winn, J., and Zisserman, A. 2010. The PASCAL Visual Object Classes (VOC) Challenge. *International Journal of Computer Vision* 88(2): 303–338.

Falaleeva, N.G. and Johnson, R.D. 2002. Influence of Individual Psychological Traits on Attribution toward Computing Technology. In *Proceedings of the Eighth Americas Conference on Information Systems*, 1028–1033. Dallas, TX, August 9–11, 2002.

Fan, J., Gao, Y., and Luo, H. 2004. Multi-level Annotation of Natural Scenes Using Dominant Image Components and Semantic Concepts. In *Proceedings of the 12th ACM International Conference Multimedia*, 540–547. New York, NY, October 10–16, 2004.

Farin, G. 2002. A History of Curve and Surfaces in CAGD. In Hoschek, J. and Kim, M.S. (eds.), *Handbook of Computer Aided Geometric Design*, Vol. 1, 1–22, Elsevier, Amersterdam, The Netherlands.

Farma, T. and Cortivonis, I. 2000. Un Questionario sul "Locus of Control": Suo Utilizzo nel Contesto Italiano (A Question on the "Locus of Control": Its Use in the Italian Context). *Ricerca in Psicoterapia* 2: 127–142.

Fei-Fei, L., Fergus, R., and Perona, P. 2004. Learning Generative Visual Models from Few Training Examples: An Incremental Bayesian Approach Tested on 101 Object Categories. In *Proceedings of IEEE Computer Vision and Pattern Recognition (CVPR) Workshop on Generative Model Based Vision*, Vol. 12, 178–186. Washington, DC, June 27–July 2, 2004.

Fellner, D.W. 2001. Graphics Content in Digital Libraries: Old Problem, Recent Solutions, Future Demands. *Journal of Universal Computer Science* 7: 400–409.

Fellner, D.W. and Havemann, S. 2005. Striving for an Adequate Vocabulary: Next Generation Metadata. In *Proceedings of the 29th Annual Conference of the German Classification Society*, Vol. 29, 13–20. Magdeburg, Germany, March 9–11, 2005. Springer, Heidelberg.

Fellner, D.W., Saupe, D., and Krottmaier, H. 2007. 3D Documents. *IEEE Computer Graphics and Applications* 27(4): 20–21.

Feng, Y. and Lapata, M. 2008. Automatic Image Annotation Using Auxiliary Text Information. In *Proceedings of 46th Annual Meeting of the Association for Computational Linguistics: Human Language Technologies*, 272–280. Columbus, OH, June 15–20, 2008.

Ferryman, J. and Shahrokni, A. 2009. An Overview of the PETS2009 Challenge. In *Proceedings 11th IEEE International Workshop on PETS*, 25–30. Miami, FL, June 25.

Ferryman, J. and Tweed, D. 2007. Overview of the PETS2007 Challenge. In *Proceedings 10th IEEE International Workshop on PETS*, 49–53. Rio de Janeiro, October 14, 2007.

Fikkert, W., van der Kooij, H., Ruttkay, Z., and van Welbergen, H. 2008. Measuring Behavior using Motion Capture Symposium. In *Proceedings of 6th International Conference on Methods and Techniques in Behavioral Research*, 13. Maastricht, The Netherlands, August 26–29, 2008.

Fischler, M.A. and Bolles, R.C. 1981. Random Sample Consensus: A Paradigm for Model Fitting with Applications to Image Analysis and Automated Cartography. *Communications of the ACM* 24(6): 381–395.

Fiscus, J., Ajot, J., and Garofolo, J. 2007. The Rich Transcription. In Stiefelhagen, R. (ed.), *2007 Meeting Recognition Evaluation*, Multimodal Technologies for Perception of Humans: International Evaluation Workshops CLEAR 2007 and RT 2007, Baltimore, MD, May 8–11, Revised Selected Papers, LNCS 4625, 373–389, Springer-Verlag, Berlin.

Fisher, R.B. 2002. Applying Knowledge to Reverse Engineering Problems. In *Proceedings of Geometric Modeling and Processing*, Vol. 1, 149–155.

Fleischman, M., Evans, H., and Roy, D. 2007. Unsupervised Content-based Indexing for Sports Video Retrieval. In *Proceedings of the 15th International Conference on Multimedia*, 473–474. Augsburg, Germany, September 25–29, 2007.

Fleiss, J. L. 1981. *Statistical Methods for Rates and Proportions, 2nd ed.* 38–46, John Wiley, Hoboken, NJ.

Flickner, M., Sawhney, H., Niblack, W., Ashley, J., Huang, Q., Dom, B., Gorkani, M., Hafner, J., Lee, D., Petkovic, D., Steele, D., and Yanker, P. 1997. Query by Image and Video Content: The QBIC System. In Maybury, M. *Intelligent Multimedia Information Retrieval*, 7–22, AAAI Press, MIT Press.

Flickner, M., Sawhney, H., Niblack, W., Ashley, J., Huang, Q., Dom, N., Gorkani, M., Hafner, J., Lee, D., Petkovic, D., Steele, D., and Yanker, P. 1995. Query by Image and Video Content: The QBIC System. *IEEE Computer* 28(9): 23–32.

Flickr. 2008. (November 3, 2008) Flickr . . . 3 billion photos. Retrieved February 22, 2010 from http://mashable.com/2008/11/03/flickr-3-billion-photos-uploaded

Foote, J. 1999. An Overview of Audio Information Retrieval. *ACM Multimedia Systems* 7(1): 42–51.

Franzosi, R. 2004. *From Words to Numbers: Narrative, Data, and Social Science*. Cambridge University Press, Cambridge.

Fruh, C. and Zakhor, A. 2003. Constructing 3D City Models by Merging Aerial and Ground Views. *IEEE Computer Graphics and Applications* 23(6): 52–61.

Futrelle, R.P. 1999. Summarization of Diagrams in Documents. In Mani, I. and Maybury, M. (eds.), *Advances in Automated Text Summarization*, 403–421, MIT Press, Cambridge, MA.

Futrelle, R.P. and Nikolakis, N. 1995. Efficient Analysis of Complex Diagrams Using Constraint-Based Parsing. In *Proceedings of the Third International Conference on Document Analysis and Recognition*, 782–790. Montreal, QC, Canada. August 14–16, 1995.

Gallant, S.I. 1990. Perception-Based Learning Algorithms. *IEEE Transactions on Neural Networks* 1(2): 179–191.

Gamma, E., Helm, R., Johnson, R., and Vlissides, J. 1994. *Design Patterns: Elements of Reusable Object-Oriented Software*. Addison Wesley, Reading, MA.

Garofolo, J., Auzanne, C., and Voorhees, E. 2000. The TREC Spoken Document Retrieval (SDR) Track: A Success Story. In *Proceedings of the 8th Text Retrieval Conference (TREC 8)*, 107–129.

Gatica-Perez, D. 2009. Automatic Nonverbal Analysis of Social Interaction in Small Groups: A Review. Image and Video Computing. *Special Issue on Human Naturalistic Behavior* 27(12): 1775–1787.

Geerts, F., Kementsietsidis, A., and Milano, D. 2006. MONDRIAN: Annotating and Querying Databases through Colors and Blocks. In *Proceedings of the 22nd International Conference on Data Engineering*, 82–91. Atlanta, GA, April 3–7, 2006. IEEE CS Press, Los Alamitos.

Gero, J.S. (ed.). 2006. *Design Computing and Cognition '06*. Springer, Amsterdam.

Gero, J.S. and Kumar, B. 1993. Expanding Design Spaces through New Design Variables. *Design Studies* 14(2): 210–221.

Getty Trust. 2005. *Art and Architecture Thesaurus (AAT)*. Getty Trust Publications, Los Angeles, CA.

Gibbon, D. and Liu, Z. 2008. *Introduction to Video Search Engines*. Springer, Berlin.

Goertzel, B., Silverman, K., Hartley, C., Bugaj, S., and Ross, M. 2000. The Baby Webmind Project. In *Proceedings of the Annual Conference of The Society for the Study of Artificial Intelligence and the Simulation of Behaviour (AISB)*. April 17–20, 2000, University of Birmingham, England, In *Proceedings of the AIS'00 Symposium on How to Design a Functioning Mind*.

Goleman, D. 2006. *Social Intelligence*. Hutchinson. Bantam Dell (A Division of Random House), New York, NY.

Gong, Y., Sin, L., Chuan, C., Zhang, H., and Sakauchi, M. 1995. Automatic Parsing of TV Soccer Programs. In *Proceedings of the International Conference on Multimedia Computing and Systems (ICMCS)*, 167–174. Washington, DC, May 15–18, 1995.

González, G., López, B., and Rosa, J.L. 2004. Managing Emotions in Smart User Models for Recommender Systems. In *Proceedings of 6th International Conference on Enterprise Information Systems ICEIS*, 187–194. INSTICC—Institute for Systems and Technologies of Information, Control and Communication, Universidade Portucalense, Porto, Portugal, April 14–17, 2004.

Goren-Bar, D., Graziola, I., Pianesi, F., and Zancanaro, M. 2006. Influence of Personality Factors on Visitors' Attitudes towards Adaptivity Dimensions for Mobile Museum Guides. *User Modeling and User-Adapted Interaction: The Journal of Personalization Research* 16(1): 31–62.

Gossweiler, R. and Limber, M. 2006. SketchUp: An Easy-to-Use 3D Design Tool that Integrates with Google Earth. In *Adjunct Proceedings of the 19th annual ACM Symposium on User Interface Software and Technology (UIST06)*, Vol. 19, 3. Montreux, Switzerland, October 15–18, 2006.

Green, N.L., Carenini, G., Kerpedjiev, S., Mattis, J., Moore, J., and Roth, S. 2004. Autobrief: An Experimental System for the Automatic Generation of Briefings in Integrated Text and Information Graphics. *International Journal of Human-Computer Studies* 61(1): 32–70.

Griffiths, T.L. and Steyvers, M. 2004. Finding Scientific Topics. In *Mapping Knowledge Domains, Proceedings of the National Academy of Sciences of the United States of America (PNAS)*, Vol. 101, 5228–5235. Irvine, CA, May 9–11, 2003.

Griffiths, T.L., Steyvers, M., Blei, D., and Tenenbaum, J. 2005. Integrating Topics and Syntax. In Saul, L.K., Weiss, Y., and Bottou, L. (eds.), *Advances in Neural Information Processing Systems*, Vol. 17, 537–544, MIT Press, Cambridge, MA.

Grimm, M. and Kroschel, K. 2005. Evaluation of Natural Emotions Using Self Assessment Manikins. In *Proceedings of the IEEE Automatic Speech Recognition and Understanding Workshop (ASRU)*, 381–385. November 27–December 1, 2005, San Juan, Puerto Rico.

Grimm, M., Kroschel, K., and Narayanan, S. 2007. Support Vector Regression for Automatic Recognition of Spontaneous Emotions in Speech. In *Proceedings of the IEEE ICASSP*, 1085–1088.

Grimm, M., Kroschel, K., and Narayanan, S. 2008. The "Vera am Mittag" German Audio-Visual Emotional Speech Database. In *Proceedings of IEEE International Conference on Multimedia and Expo (ICME)*, 865–868. Hannover, Germany, June 23–26, 2008.

Grosz, B. and Sidner, C. 1986. Attention, Intentions, and the Structure of Discourse. *Computational Linguistics* 12(3): 175–204.

Guerini, M., Stock, O., and Zancanaro, M. 2007. A Taxonomy of Strategies for Multimodal Persuasive Message Generation. *Applied Artificial Intelligence Journal* 21(2): 99–136.

Guerini, M., Stock, O., Zancanaro, M., O'Keefe, D.J., Mazzotta, I., de Rosis, F., Poggi, I., Lim, M.Y., and Aylett, R. 2011. Approaches to Verbal Persuasion in Intelligent User Interfaces. In Zancanaro, M. (ed.), *Persuasion and Communication*, [Volume 6 in: P. Petta, R. Cowie, & C. Pelachaud (eds.), *The HUMAINE Handbook on Emotion-Oriented Systems Technologies*]. 559–584, Springer, London.

Guerini, M., Strapparava, C., and Stock, O. 2008a. CORPS: A Corpus of Tagged Political Speeches for Persuasive Communication Processing. *Journal of Information Technology & Politics* 5(1): 19–32.

Guerini, M., Strapparava, C., and Stock, O. 2008b. Valentino: A Tool for Valence Shifting of Natural Language Texts. In *Proceedings of the 6th International Conference on Language Resources and Evaluation (LREC)*. Marrakech, Morocco, May 26–June 1, 2008, European Language Resources Association.

Guerini, M., Strapparava, C., and Stock, O. 2012. Audience Reactions for Information Extraction about Persuasive Language in Political Communication, this volume.

Haas, M., Lew, M.S., and Huijsmans, D.P. 1997. A New Method for Key Frame Based Video Content Representation. In Smeulders, A. and Jain, R. (eds.), *Image Databases and Multimedia Search*, 191–200, World Scientific, Singapore.

Hall, J.W. and Watson, W.H. 1970. The Effects of a Normative Intervention on Group Decision-Making Performance. *Human Relations* 23(4): 299–317.

Hall, M.A. 1999. Correlation-based Feature Selection for Machine Learning. PhD thesis, University of Waikato.

Han, Y., Ho Lee, S., Kim, J., and Kim, Y. 2008. A New Aggregation Policy for RSS Services. In *Proceedings of the 2008 International Workshop on Context Enabled Source and Service Selection, Integration and Adaptation (CSSSIA), 17th International World Wide Web Conference*, Article No. 2. Beijing, China, April 22, 2008.

Hang, B.K. 2003. Affective Content Detection Using HMMs. In *Proceedings of the Eleventh ACM International Conference on Multimedia*, Vol. 2003, 259–262. November 2–8, 2003. ACM, Berkeley, CA.

Hanjalić, A. 2006. Extracting Moods from Pictures and Sounds. *IEEE Signal Processing Magazine* 23(2): 90–100.

Hanjalić, A. and Xu, L. 2005. Affective Video Content Representation and Modeling. *IEEE Transactions on Multimedia* 7(1): 143–154.

Hansen, J.H.L. and Bou-Ghazale, S. 1997. Getting Started with SUSAS: A Speech Under Simulated and Actual Stress Database. In *Proc. EUROSPEECH-97: Inter. Conf. On Speech Communication and Technology*, Vol. 4, 1743–1746.

Hastie, T., Tibshirani, R., and Friedman, J.H. 2001. *The Elements of Statistical Learning*. Springer Series in Statistics, New York.

Hauptmann, A.G. 2005. Lessons for the Future from a Decade of Informedia Video Analysis Research. In *Proceedings of the 4th International Conference on Image and Video Retrieval*, Singapore, *(CIVR)*, 1–10, Springer.

Hauptmann, A., Christel, M., Concescu, R., Gao, J., Jin, Q., Lin, W., Pan, J.Y., Stevens, S., Yan, R., Yang, J., and Zhang, Y. 2005. CMU Informedia's TRECVID 2005 Skirmishes. In *Proceedings of the TREC Video Retrieval Conference (TRECVID'05)*. November 2005. NIST, Gaithersburg, MD.

Hauptmann, A., Rong, Y., and Lin, W. 2007a. How Many High-Level Concepts will Fill the Semantic Gap in News Video Retrieval? In *Proceedings of the International Conference on Image and Video Retrieval (CIVR)*, 627–634. University of Amsterdam, Amsterdam, The Netherlands, July 9–11, 2007.

Hauptmann, A. and Witbrock, M. 1997. Informedia: News-on-Demand Multimedia Information Acquisition and Retrieval. IMIR. In Maybury, M. (ed.), *Intelligent Multimedia Information Retrieval*, 213–239, MIT Press, Cambridge.

Hauptmann, A., Yan, R., Lin, W., Christel, M., and Wactlar, H. 2007b. Can High-Level Concepts Fill the Semantic Gap in Video Retrieval? A Case Study with Broadcast News. *IEEE Transactions on Multimedia Journal* 9(5): 958–966.

Hauptmann, A.G. and Christel, M.G. 2004. Successful Approaches in the TREC Video Retrieval Evaluations. In *Proceedings of the Twelfth ACM International Conference on Multimedia*, 668–675. New York, NY, October 10–16, 2004. ACM, New York, NY.

Hauptmann, A.G., Jin, R., and Ng, T.D. 2002. Multi-modal Information Retrieval from Broadcast Video Using OCR and Speech Recognition. In *Proceedings of the 2nd ACM/IEEE-CS Joint Conference on Digital Libraries*, 160–161.3. Portland, OR, July 14–18, 2002.

Havemann, S. 2005. Generative Mesh Modeling. PhD-Thesis, Technische Universitot, Braunschweig, Germany, Vol. 1, 1–303.

Havemann, S. and Fellner, D.W. 2004. Generative Parametric Design of Gothic Window Tracery. In *Proceedings of the 5th International Symposium on Virtual Reality, Archeology, and Cultural Heritage*, Vol. 1, 193–201. Oudenaarde, Belgium, December 7–10, 2004. Eurographics Association.

Havemann, S. and Fellner, D.W. 2007. Seven Research Challenges of Generalized 3D Documents, *IEEE Computer Graphics and Applications* 27(3): 70–76.

Haykin, S. 1991. *Adaptive Filter Theory*. Prentice Hall, Upper Saddle River, NJ.

Hays, J. and Efros, A.A. 2008. IM2GPS: Estimating Geographic Information from a Single Image. In *Proceedings of IEEE Computer Vision and Pattern Recognition (CVPR)*, 1–8. Anchorage, Alaska, June 24–26, 2008. IEEE Computer Society.

Heloir, A., Neff, M., and Kipp, M. 2010. Exploiting Motion Capture for Virtual Human Animation. In *Proceedings of the Workshop on Multimodal Corpora: Advances in Capturing, Coding and Analyzing Multimodality*. LREC-2010, ELDA, Paris, 59–62.

Heritage, J. and Greatbatch, D. 1986. Generating Applause: A Study of Rhetoric and Response at Party Political Conferences. *American Journal of Sociology* 92: 110–157.

Herlocker, J.L., Konstan, J., Terveen, L., and Riedl, J. 2004. Evaluating Collaborative Filtering Recommender Systems. *ACM Transactions on Information Systems* 22(1): 5–53.

Herve, N. and Boujemaa, N. 2007. Image Annotation: Which Approach for Realistic Databases? In *Proceedings of the 6th ACM international Conference on Image and Video*

Retrieval (CIVR), 170–177. Amsterdam, The Netherlands, July 9–11, 2007. ACM, New York.

Hilaga, M., Shinagawa, Y., Kohmura, T., and Tosiyasu, L. 2001. Topology Matching for Fully Automatic Similarity Estimation of 3D Shapes. In *Proceedings of the 28th Annual Conference on Computer Graphics and Interactive Techniques (SIGGRAPH)*, Vol. 28, 203–212. Los Angeles, CA, August 12–17, 2001.

Hirschberg, J., Whittaker, S., Hindle, D., Pereira, F., and Singhal, A. 1999. Finding Information in Audio: A New Paradigm For Audio Browsing/Retrieval. In *ESCA ETRW Workshop Accessing Information in Spoken Audio*, 117–122.

Hofmann, T. 1999. Probabilistic Latent Semantic Indexing. In *22nd Annual International ACM SIGIR Conference on Research and Development in Information Retrieval*, 50–57. Berkeley, CA, August 15–19, 1999.

Hofmann, T. 2001. Unsupervised Learning by Probabilistic Latent Semantic Analysis. *Machine Learning* 43: 177–196.

Hossain, M., Atrey, P., and El Saddik, A. 2008. Gain-Based Selection of Ambient Media Services in Pervasive Environments. *Mobile Networks and Applications* 13(6): 599–613.

Hu, C., Chang, Y., Feris, R., and Turk, M. 2004. Manifold Based Analysis of Facial Expression. In *Proceedings of the 2004 Conference on Computer Vision and Pattern Recognition (CVPR) Workshop*, 81. Washington, DC, June 27–July 2, 2004. IEEE Computer Society.

Hu, Q., Goodman, F., Boykin, S., Fish, R., and Greiff, W. 2003. Information Discovery by Automatic Detection, Indexing, and Retrieval of Multiple Attributes from Multimedia Data. In *3rd International Workshop on Multimedia Data and Document Engineering*, 65–70.

Hu, Q., Goodman, F., Boykin, S., Fish, R., and Greiff, W. 2004a. Audio Hot Spotting and Retrieval Using Multiple Audio Features and Multiple ASR Engines. In *Proceedings of ICASSP 2004 Rich Transcription 2004 Spring Meeting Recognition Workshop*.

Hu, Q., Goodman, F., Boykin, S., Fish, R., and Greiff, W. 2004b. Audio Hot Spotting and Retrieval Using Multiple Features. In *Proceedings of the HLT-NAACL 2004 Workshop on Interdisciplinary Approaches to Speech Indexing and Retrieval*, 13–17.

Hu, Q., Goodman, F., Boykin, S., Fish, R., and Greiff, W. 2009. System and Method for Audio Hot Spotting. United States Patent no. 7,617,188.

Hu, Q., Goodman, F., Boykin, S., Fish, R., Greiff, W., Jones, S., and Moore, S. 2012. Automatic Detection, Indexing and Retrieval of Multiple Attributes from Cross-Lingual Multimedia Data, this volume.

Hu, Q., Goodman, F., Boykin, S., and Peet, M. 2002a. Multimedia Indexing and Retrieval Technologies Using the Audio Track. In *IEEE 2002 Conference on Technologies for Homeland Security*.

Hu, Q., Goodman, F., Boykin, S., and Peet, M. 2002b. The MITRE Audio Hot Spotting Prototype—Using Multiple Speech and Natural Language Processing Technologies. In *International Conference on Text, Speech and Dialog (TSD 2002)*.

Huffman, S., Lehman, A., Stolboushkin, A., Wong-Toi, H., Yang, F., and Roehrig, H. 2007. Multiple-Signal Duplicate Detection for Search Evaluation. In *Proceedings of the 30th Annual International ACM SIGIR Conference on Research and Development in Information Retrieval*, 223–230. Amsterdam, The Netherlands, July 23–27, 2007. ACM.

Huiskes, M.J. and Lew, M.S. 2008. The MIR Flickr Retrieval Evaluation. In *ACM International Conference on Multimedia Information Retrieval (MIR)*, 39–43. Vancouver, BC, Canada, October 30–31, 2008.

Ireson, B. 2004. Minions. In *Proceedings of the 12th ACM International Conference on Multimedia*, 991–992. New York, NY, October 10–16, 2004.

IT. 2008. Curriculum Guidelines for Undergraduate Degree Programs in Information Technology. *Association for Computing Machinery and IEEE Computer Society*. November 2008.

Jain, A., Murty, M., and Flynn, P. 1999. Data Clustering: A Review. *ACM Computing Surveys* 31(3): 264–323.

Jeon, J., Lavrenko, V., and Manmatha, R. 2003. Automatic Image Annotation and Retrieval Using Cross-Media Relevance Models. In *Proceedings of the Annual International ACM SIGIR Conference on Research and Development in Information Retrieval*, 119–126. Toronto, July 28–August 01, 2003.

Jing, H. 1998. Usage of WordNet in Natural Language Generation. In Harabagiu, S. (ed.), *Proceedings Conference on the Use of WordNet in Natural Language Processing Systems*, 128–134. COLING-ACL '98 Workshop, August 16, 1998, Université de Montréal, Montréal/Canada. Association for Computational Linguistics, Somerset, NJ.

Joachims, T. 1998. Text Categorization with Support Vector Machines: Learning with Many Relevant Features. In Nedellec, C. and Rouveirol, C. (eds.), *Proceedings of the Tenth European Conference on Machine Learning (ECML), Lecture Notes in Computer Science 1398*, 137–142. Chemnitz, Germany, April 21–23, 1998. Springer Verlag, Heidelberg.

Joachims, T. 1999. Making Large-Scale Support Vector Machine Learning Practical. In Schoelkopf, B., Burges, C.J.C., and Smola, A.J. (eds.), *Advances in Kernal Methods: Support Vector Learning*, 169–184, MIT Press, Cambridge.

Jodoin, P.-M., Konrad, J., and Saligrama, V. 2008. Modeling Background Activity for Surveillance Applications. In *Proceedings of the IEEE International Conference on Distributed Smart Cameras*, 1–10. Stanford, CA, May 7–8, 2008.

John, J. 2006. Pandora and the Music Genome Project. *Scientific Computing* 23(10): 14, 40–41.

John, O.P. and Srivastava, S. 1999. The Big Five Trait Taxonomy: History, Measurement and Theoretical Perspectives. In Pervian, L.A. and John, O.P. (eds.), *Handbook of Personality Theory and Research*, 211–218, Guilford Press, New York.

Johnson, S.E., Jourlin, P., Jones, S.S., and Woodland, P.C. 2000. Spoken Document Retrieval for TREC-9 at Cambridge University. In *Proc. TREC-9*, 117–126.

Joly, A., Buisson, O., and Frelicot, C. 2007. Content-Based Copy Retrieval Using Distortion-Based Probabilistic Similarity Search Multimedia. *IEEE Transactions on Multimedia* 9(2): 293–306.

Jones, G.J.F. and Chan, C.H. 2012. Affect-Based Indexing for Multimedia Data, this volume.

Jones, K.S. 1993. What Might be in a Summary? *Information Retrieval 93: 9-26. Von der Modellierung zur Anwendung*. Universitatsverlag Konstanz.

Joshi, D. and Luo, J. 2008. Inferring Generic Activities and Events from Image Content and Bags of Geo-Tags. In *Proceedings of ACM International Conference on Image and Video Retrieval*, 37–46. Niagara Falls, Canada, July 7–9, 2008.

Jurafsky, D. and Martin, J.H. 2003. *Speech and Language Processing*. Prentice Hall, Upper Saddle River, NJ.

Kahan, J. and Koivunen, M. 2001. Annotea: An Open RDF Infrastructure for Shared Web Annotations. In *Proceedings of the 10th International Conference on World Wide Web*, 623–632. May 1–5 2001, Hong Kong. ACM, New York.

Kalnikaite, V. and Whittaker, S. 2008. Social Summarization: Does Social Feedback Improve Access to Speech Data? In *Proceedings of the ACM Conference on Computer supported Cooperative Work (CSCW)*, 9–12. San Diego, CA, November 8–12, 2008. ACM Press.

Karner, K., Bauer, J., Klaus, A., Leberl, F., and Grabner, M. 2001. Virtual Habitat: Models of the Urban Outdoors. In *3rd International Workshop on Automatic Extraction of*

Man-Made Objects from Aerial and Space Imaging, Vol. 3, 393–402. Centro Stefano Franscini, Monte Verità Ascona, Switzerland, June 10–15, 2001.

Kennedy, C. and Boguraev, B. 1996. Anaphora for Everyone: Pronominal Anaphora Resolution without a Parser. In *Proceedings of the 16th International Conference on Computational Linguistics*, 113–118. Center for Sprogteknologi, Copenhagen, Denmark, August 5–9, 1996.

Kennedy, L. and Hauptmann, A. 2006. LSCOM Lexicon Definitions and Annotations Version 1.0. In *DTO Challenge Workshop on Large Scale Concept Ontology for Multimedia*, 1–88. ADVENT Technical Report #217-2006-3, Columbia University, New York, March 2006.

Kenny, D.A. 1994. *Interpersonal Perception: A Social Relations Analysis*. Guilford Press, New York.

King, B.D., Wertheimer, M. (eds.). 2005. *Max Wertheimer and Gestalt Theory*. Transaction Publishers, Piscataway, New Jersey.

Kipp, M. 2001. Anvil—A Generic Annotation Tool for Multimodal Dialogue. In *Proceedings of the 7th European Conference on Speech Communication and Technology 2nd INTERSPEECH Event*, 1367–1370. Aalborg, Denmark, September 3–7, 2001.

Kipp, M. 2008. Spatiotemporal Coding in ANVIL. In *Proceedings of the 6th International Conference on Language Resources and Evaluation (LREC)*. Marrakech, Morocco, May 28–30, 2008.

Kipp, M. 2012. Multimedia Annotation, *Querying and Analysis in ANVIL*, this volume.

Kipp, M. and Martin, J.-C. 2009. Gesture and Emotion: Can Basic Gestural form Features Discriminate Emotions? In *Proceedings of the 3rd International Conference on Affective Computing and Intelligent Interaction (ACII-09)*, 1–8. September 10–12, 2009. IEEE Press, Amsterdam.

Kipp, M., Neff, M., Kipp, K., and Albrecht, I. 2007. Toward Natural Gesture Synthesis: Evaluating Gesture Units in a Data-Driven Approach. In Pelachaud, C., et al. (eds.), *Proceedings of the 7th International Conference on Intelligent Virtual Agents (IVA-07)*, 15–28. September 17–19, 2007, Paris. Springer.

Kita, S., van Gijn, I., and van der Hulst, H. 1998. Movement Phases in Signs and Co-speech Gestures, and Their Transcription by Human Coders. In Wachsmuth, I. and Frohlich, M. (eds.), *Gesture and Sign Language in Human-Computer Interaction*, 23–35, Springer, Berlin.

Koch, R., Pollefeys, M., and Van Gool, L. 2000. Realistic Surface Reconstruction of 3D Scenes from Uncalibrated Image Sequences. *Journal of Visualization and Computer Animation* 11(3): 115–127.

Koenen, R. (ed.). 2002. Overview of the MPEG-4 Standard. International Organisation for Standardisation (ISO) JTC1/SC29/WG11 Coding of Moving Pictures and Audio.

Kohavi, R. 1995. A Study of Cross-Validation and Bootstrap for Accuracy Estimation and Model Selection. In *14th International Joint Conference on Artificial Intelligence*, Vol. 14, 1137–1145. Montréal, QC, Canada, August 20–25 1995. Morgan Kaufmann.

Konrad, J. 2005. Motion Detection and Estimation. In Bovik, A. (ed.), *Handbook of Image and Video Processing*, Vol. 2, Chapter 3.10, 253–274, Academic Press.

Koskela, M., Smeaton, A.F., and Laaksonen, J. 2007. Measuring Concept Similarities in Multimedia Ontologies: Analysis and Evaluations. *IEEE Transaction on Multimedia* 9(5): 912–922.

Krallinger, M., Valencia, A., and Hirschman, L. 2008. Linking Genes to Literature: Text Mining, Information Extraction, and Retrieval Applications for Biology. *Genome Biology* 9(Suppl. 2): S8. Epub. September 1, 2008. http://genomebiology.com/2008/9/S2/S8

Kressel, U. 1999. Pairwise Classification and Support Vector Machines. In Scholkopf, B., Burges, C.J.C., and Smola, A.J. (eds.), *Advances in Kernel Methods: Support Vector Learning*, 255–268, MIT Press, Cambridge, MA.

Kubala, F. 1999. Broadcast News Is Good News. In *Proceedings of the DARPA Broadcast News Workshop*. Herndon, Virginia.

Kubala, F., Colbath, S., Liu, D., and Makhoul, J. 1999. Rough "n" Ready: A Meeting Recorder and Browser. *ACM Computing Surveys* 31(2es): 7.

Kubala, F., Colbath, S., Liu, D., Srivastava, A., and Makhoul, J. 2000. Integrated Technologies for Indexing Spoken Language. *Communications of the ACM* 43(2): 48–56.

Kullback, S. and Leibler, R.A. 1951. On Information and Sufficiency. *Annals of Mathematical Statistics* 22: 79–86.

Landis, J.R. and Koch, G.G. 1977. The Measurement of Observer Agreement for Categorical Data. *Biometrics* 33(1): 159–174.

Lang, P.J., Bradley, M.M., and Cuthbert, B.N. 2005. International Affective Picture System (IAPS): Affective Ratings of Pictures and Instruction Manual. Technical Report, A-6. The Center for Research in Psychophysiology, University of Florida, Gainesville, FL.

Laske, O. 1993. In Search of a Generative Grammar for Music. In Schwanauer, S. and Levitt, D. (eds.), *Machine Models of Music*, 215– 242, MIT Press, Cambridge, MA.

Laver, M., Benoit, K., and Garry, J. 2003. Extracting Policy Positions from Political Texts Using Words as Data. *American Political Science Review* 97(2): 311–331.

Law, E. and von Ahn, L. 2009. Input-Agreement: A New Mechanism for Collecting Data Using Human Computation Games. *CHI 2009, Proceedings of the 27th International Conference on Human Factors in Computing Systems*. April 4–9, 2009, Boston, MA. 1–10. ACM, New York. 1197–1206.

Leavitt, N. 2006. Recommendation Technology: Will It Boost E-Commerce? Computer May: 13–16. DOI: http://doi.ieeecomputersociety.org/10.1109/MC.2006.176

Lee, C.M., Narayanan, S., and Pieraccini, R. 2002. Combining Acoustic and Language Information for Emotion Recognition. In *Proceedings of Interspeech*, 873–376. September 16–20, 2002, Denver, CO.

Lehman, E.L. and Romano, J.P. 2005. *Testing Statistical Hypotheses*. Springer Science + Business, Inc., New York.

Lepri, B., Mana, N., Cappelletti, A., Pianesi, F., and Zancanaro, M. 2009. Modeling the Personality of Participants during Group Interaction. In *Proceedings of 17th International Conference on User Modeling, Adaptation, and Personalization (UMAP)*, 114–125. Trento, Italy, June 22–26, 2009. Springer LNCS 5535.

Lerdahl, F. and Jackendoff, R. 1983. *A Generative Theory of Tonal Music*. MIT Press, Cambridge.

Lew, M.S., Sebe, N., Djeraba, C., and Jain, R. 2006. Content-Based Multimedia Information Retrieval: State of the Art and Challenges. *ACM Transactions on Multimedia Computing* 2(1): 1–19.

Leyton, M. 2001. *A Generative Theory of Shape*. Springer-Verlag, New York.

Li, J. and Wang, J.Z. 2003. Automatic Linguistic Indexing of Pictures by a Statistical Modeling Approach. *IEEE Transactions on Pattern Analysis and Machine Intelligence* 25(9): 1–14.

Liberman, M. et al. 2002. Emotional Prosody Speech and Transcripts. Linguistic Data Consortium Catalog #LDC2002S28.

Lienhart, R. 2001. Reliable Transition Detection in Videos: A Survey and Practitioner's Guide. *International Journal of Image and Graphics (IJIG)* 1(3): 469–486.

Lin, J., Keogh, E., Patel, P., and Lonardi, S. 2002. Finding Motifs in Time Series. In *Proceedings of the 2nd Workshop on Temporal Data Mining at the 8th ACM SIGKDD International Conference on Knowledge Discovery and Data Mining*, 53–68. July 23–26, 2002, Edmonton, Alberta, Canada.

Lin, W.-H. 2008. Identifying Ideological Perspectives in Text and Video. Language Technologies Institute, School of Computer Science, CMU-LTI-08-008, Carnegie Mellon University, Pittsburgh.

Lin, W.-H. and Hauptmann, A. 2006. Are These Documents Written from Different Perspectives? A Test of Different Perspectives Based on Statistical Distribution Divergence. In *Proceedings of the 21st International Conference on Computational Linguistics and the 44th Annual Meeting of the ACL*. Sydney, Australia, July 17–18, 2006. Association for Computational Linguistics, Morristown, NJ.

Lin, W.-H. and Hauptmann, A. 2012. Automated Analysis of Ideological Bias in Video, this volume.

Lin, W.-H., Xing, E.P., and Hauptmann, A. 2008. A Joint Topic and Perspective Model for Ideological Discourse. In *Proceedings of the European Conference on Machine Learning and Principles and Practice of Knowledge Discovery in Databases (ECML PKDD 08)*, 17–32. Antwerp, Belgium, September 15–19, 2008, Proceedings, Part II.

Litman, D. and Forbes, K. 2003. Recognizing Emotions from Student Speech in Tutoring Dialogues. In *Proceedings of IEEE Workshop on Automatic Speech Recognition and Understanding (ASRU)*, 25–30. St. Thomas, Virgin Islands, November 30–December, 2003.

Liu, H., Liebermann, H., and Selker, T. 2003. A Model of Textual Affect Sensing using Real-World Knowledge. In *Proceedings of the 8th International Conference on Intelligent User Interfaces*, 125–132. Miami, FL, January 12–15, 2003.

Liu, L., Lai, W., Hua, X.-S., and Yang, S.-Q. 2007. Video Histogram: A Novel Video Signature for Efficient Web Video Duplicate Detection. In *Proceedings of the 13th International Conference on Multimedia Modeling—Volume Part II (MMM'07)*, Cham, T.-J. et al. (eds.), Springer-Verlag, Berlin/Heidelberg, II: 4352.

Loui, A.C. and Savakis, A.E. 2003. Automated Event Clustering and Quality Screening of Consumer Pictures for Digital Albuming. *IEEE Transactions on Multimedia* 5(3): 390–402.

Lovins, J.B. 1968. Development of a Stemming Algorithm. *Mechanical Translation and Computational Linguistics* 11: 22–31.

Lowe, D.G. 2004. Distinctive Image Features from Scale-Invariant Keypoints. *International Journal of Computer Vision (IJCV)* 60(2): 91–110.

Luo, J., Yu, J., Joshi, D., and Hao, W. 2008. Event Recognition: Viewing the World with a Third Eye. In *Proceedings of the 16th ACM International Conference Multimedia*, 1071–1080. Vancouver, BC, Canada, October 26–31, 2008.

Ma, S., Wang, W., Huang, Q., Jiang, S., and Gao, W. 2008. Effective Scene Matching with Local Feature Representatives. In *Proceedings of the 19th International Conference on Pattern Recognition (ICPR)*, 1–4. Tampa, FL, December 8–11, 2008.

Mairesse, F., Walker, M.A., Mehl, M.R., and Moore, R.K. 2007. Using Linguistic Cues for the Automatic Recognition of Personality in Conversation and Text. *Journal of Artificial Intelligence Research* 30: 457–500.

Mallory, P. and Miller, V. 1958. A Possible Basis for the Association of Voice Characteristics and Personality Traits. *Speech Monograph* 25: 255–260.

Mani, I. and Maybury, M. (eds.). 1999. *Advances in Automatic Text Summarization*. MIT Press, Cambridge, MA.

Manning, C.D., Raghavan, P., and Hinrich Schütze, H. 2008. *An Introduction to Information Retrieval*. Cambridge University Press, Cambridge.

Manohar, V., Boonstra, M., Korzhova, V., Soundararajan, P., Goldgof, D., Kasturi, R., Prasad, S., Raju, H., Bowers R., and Garofolo, J. 2006. PETS vs. VACE Evaluation Programs: A Comparative Study. In *Proceedings 9th IEEE International Workshop on PETS*, 1–6. New York, June 18, 2006.

Marini, S., Spagnuolo, M., and Falcidieno, B. 2007. Structural Shape Prototypes for Automatic Classification of 3D Objects. *IEEE Computer Graphics and Applications* 27(4): 28–37.

Martin, J.-C. and Kipp, M. 2002. Annotating and Measuring Multimodal Behaviour—Tycoon Metrics in the Anvil Tool. In *Proceedings of the Third International Conference on Language Resources and Evaluation (LREC)*, 31–35. Las Palmas, Canary Islands, Spain, May 29–31, 2002.

Martin, L.W. and Vanberg, G. 2007. A Robust Transformation Procedure for Interpreting Political Text. *Political Analyst* 16(1): 93–100.

Martínez, J.M. and Pereira, F. 2002. MPEG-7: The Generic Multimedia Content Description Standard. *IEEE Multimedia* 9(2): 78–87.

Mateas, M. and Stern, A. 2005. Procedural Authorship: A Case-Study of the Interactive Drama Façade. In *Proceedings of Digital Arts and Culture: Digital Experience: Design, Aesthetics, Practice (DAC 2005)*, Copenhagen, Denmark, December 1–4, 2005.

Mateas, M., Vanouse, P., and Domike, S. 2000. Generation of Ideologically-Biased Historical Documentaries. In *Proceedings of the Seventeenth National Conference on Artificial Intelligence and Twelfth Conference on on Innovative Applications of Artificial Intelligence*, 236–242. Austin, TX, July 30–August 3, 2000.

Maybury, M. 2009. Audio and Video Processing to Enhance Homeland Security. In *IEEE Homeland Security Conference (HST '09)*. Westin Hotel, Waltham, MA, May 11–12, 2009.

Maybury, M., Merlino, A., and Morey, D. 1997. Broadcast News Navigation using Story Segments. In *ACM International Multimedia Conference*, 381–391. Seattle, WA, November 8–14, 1997.

Maybury, M. and Walter, S. 2008. Working Notes from the AAAI Fall Symposium on Intelligent Multimedia Information Extraction. Arlington, VA, November 6–8, 2008. http://www.aaai.org/Symposia/Fall/fss08symposia.php#fs06

Maybury, M.T. (ed.). 1993. *Intelligent Multimedia Interfaces (1993)*. AAAI/MIT Press, Menlo Park, CA/Cambridge, MA.

Maybury, M.T. (ed.). 1997. *Intelligent Multimedia Information Retrieval*. AAAI/MIT Press, Cambridge, MA.

Maybury, M.T. (ed.). 2004. *New Directions in Question Answering*. AAAI/MIT Press, Palo Alto, CA.

Maybury, M.T. and Wahlster, W. (eds.). 1998. *Readings in Intelligent User Interfaces*. Morgan Kaufmann Press, Burlington, MA.

Mcintyre, G. and Gocke, R. 2008. The Composite Sensing of Affect. In Peter, C. and Beale, R. (ed.), *Affect and Emotion in Human-Computer Interaction LCNS 4868*, 104–115, Springer Verlag, Berlin.

Mehrabian, A. 1996. Pleasure-Arousal-Dominance: A General Framework for Describing and Measuring Individual Differences in Temperament. *Current Psychology* 14(4): 261–292.

Merlino, A., Morey, D., and Maybury, M. 1997. Broadcast News Navigation Using Story Segmentation. In *Proceedings of ACM Multimedia*, 381–391. Seattle.

Mikolajczyk, K. and Schmid, C. 2004. Scale and Affine Invariant Interest Point Detectors. *International Journal of Computer Vision (IJCV)* 60(1): 63–86.

Millen, D., Feinberg, J., and Kerr, B. 2006. Dogear: Social Bookmarking in the Enterprise. In *Proceedings of the SIGCHI Conference on Human Factors in Computing Systems*, 111–120. Montréal, Québec, Canada, April 22–27, 2006. ACM Press.

Mirghafori, N., Fosler, E., and Morgan, N.H. 1996. Towards Robustness to Fast Speech in ASR. In *Proc. ICASSP-96*, 335–338.

Mitra, N.J., Guibas, L.J., and Pauly, M. 2006. Partial and Approximate Symmetry Detection for 3D Geometry. *ACM Transactions on Graphics* 25: 560–568.

Mitra, N.J., Guibas, L.J., and Pauly, M. 2007. Symmetrization. In *International Conference on Computer Graphics and Interactive Techniques (SIGGRAPH 2007)*, Vol. 26, 1–8. San Diego, CA, August 7–9, 2007.

Morgan, N. and Fosler-Lussier, E. 1998. Combining Multiple Estimators of Speaking Rate. In *Proc. ICASSP-98*, 729–732.

Mori, Y., Takahashi, H., and Oka, R. 1999. Image-to-Word Transformation Based on Dividing and Vector Quantizing Images with Words. In *Proceedings of the First International Workshop on Multimedia Intelligent Storage and Retrieval Management (MISRM)*, 405–409. Orlando, FL, October 30, 1999.

MovieLens. 2009. MovieLens Data Sets web page, http://www.grouplens.org/node/73. Last accessed: September 2010.

Moxley, E., Kleban, J., Xu, J., and Manjunath, B.S. 2009. Not All Tags are Created Equal: Learning Flickr Tag Semantics for Global Annotation. In *Proceedings of IEEE International Conference on Multimedia and Expo (ICME)*, 452–458. Waldorf-Astoria Hotel, New York, NY, June 28–July 3, 2009.

Müller , H., Marchand-Maillet, S., and Pun, T. 2002. The Truth about Corel—Evaluation in Image Retrieval. In Lew, M.S., Sebe, N., and Eakins, J. (eds.), *Proceedings of the First International Conference on Image and Video Retrieval (CIVR)*, 38–49. London, UK, July 18–19, 2002. Lecture Notes in Computer Science, Vol 2383. Springer-Verlag, London.

Müller, M., Röder, T., and Clausen, M. 2005. Efficient Content-Based Retrieval of Motion Capture Data. *ACM Transactions on Graphics* 24(3): 677–685.

Müller, P., Wonka, P., Haegler, S., Ulmer, A., and Van Gool, L. 2006. Procedural Modeling of Buildings. In *Proceedings of the 33rd International Conference and Exhibition on Computer Graphics and Interactive Techniques (ACM SIGGRAPH 2006)*, Vol. 25(3), 614–623. Boston, MA, August 1–3, 2006.

Müller, P., Zeng, G., Wonka, P., and Van Gool, L. 2007. Image-Based Procedural Modeling of Facades. *ACM Transactions on Graphics* 26(3): 1–9.

Murray, I.R. and Arnott, J.L. 1993. Toward the Simulation of Emotion in Synthetic Speech: A Review of the Literature on Human Vocal Emotion. *Journal of Acoustical Society of America* 93(2): 1097–1108. ASA.

Musicovery. 2010. Musicovery: Interactive Web Radio. http://musicovery.com, last accessed: August 2010.

Naaman, M., Song, Y.J., Paepcke, A., and Garcia-Molina, H. 2004. Automatic Organization for Digital Photographs with Geographic Coordinates. In *Proceedings of the 4th ACM/IEEE-CS Joint Conference on Digital Libraries (JCDL)*, 53–62. Tuscon, AZ, June 7–11, 2004. ACM, New York, NY.

Nakatsu, R. 1998. Toward the Creation of a New Medium for the Multimedia Era. *Proceedings of the IEEE* 86(5): 825–826.

Naphade, M., Smith, J.R., Tesic, J., Chang, S.-F., Hsu, W., Kennedy, L., Hauptmann, A., and Curtis, J. 2006. Large-Scale Concept Ontology for Multimedia. *IEEE Transactions on Multimedia* 13(3): 86–91.

Naphade, M.R. and Huang, T.S. 2002. Extracting Semantics from Audio-Visual Content: The Final Frontier in Multimedia Retrieval. *IEEE Transactions on Neural Networks* 13(4): 793–810.

Naphade, M.R. and Smith, J.R. 2004. On the Detection of Semantic Concepts at TRECVID. In *Proceedings of the 12th Annual ACM International Conference on Multimedia, Special Session on Brave New Topics: The Effect of Benchmarking on Advances in Semantic Video Retrieval*, 660–667. October 10–16, 2004. ACM, New York, NY.

Naqvi, N., Shiv, B., and Bechara, A. 2006. The Role of Emotion in Decision Making: A Cognitive Neuroscience Perspective. *Current Directions in Psychological Science* 15(5): 260–264.

Natarajan, P., Emjeh, B., Schwartz, R., and Makhoul, J. 2001b. Videotext OCR using Hidden Markov Models. In *Proceedings of the 6th International Conference on Document Analysis and Recognition (ICDAR)*, 947–951. Seattle, WA, September 10–13, 2001.

Natarajan, P., Lu, Z., Schwartz, R., Bazzi, I., and Makhoul, J. 2001a. Multilingual Machine Printed OCR. *International Journal of Pattern Recognition and Artificial Intelligence* 15(1): 43–63.

Natarajan, P., MacRostie, E., Prasad, R., and Watson, J. 2012. Extraction of Human Language Content in Video, this volume.

National Institute of Standards and Technology (NIST). 1997. Speech Recognition Scoring Toolkit (SCTK). http://www.nist.gov/speech/tools/

Neff, M., Kipp, M., Albrecht, I., and Seidel, H.-P. 2008. Gesture Modeling and Animation Based on a Probabilistic Recreation of Speaker Style. *ACM Transactions on Graphics* 27(1): 1–24.

Neri, A., Colonnese, S., Russo, G., and Talone, P. 1998. Automatic Moving Object and Background Separation. *Signal Processing* 66(2): 219–232.

Netica. 2005. Norsys software corp. http://www.norsys.com/netica.html

Nguyen, L., Anastasakos, T., Kubala, F., LaPre, C., Makhoul, J., Schwartz, R., Yuan, N., Zavaliagkos, G., and Zhao, Y. 1995. The 1994 BN/BYBLOS Speech Recognition System. In *Proceedings ARPA Spoken Language Systems Technology Workshop*, 77–81. Austin, TX, January 1995. Morgan Kaufmann Publishers, San Mateo, CA.

Niblack, W. 1999. SlideFinder: A Tool for Browsing Presentation Graphics Using Content-Based Retrieval. In *Proceedings of the IEEE Workshop on Content-Based Access of Image and Video Libraries (CBAIVL)*, 114. June 22–22, 1999. IEEE Computer Society: Washington, DC.

Noguchi, Y. 2005. Camera Phones Lend Immediacy to Images of Disaster. *Washington Post*. Friday, July 8, 2005, p. A16.

Nowak, E., Jurie, F., and Triggs, B. 2006. Sampling Strategies for Bag-of-Features Image Classification. In *Proceedings of 9th European Conference on Computer Vision*, Vol. IV, 490–503. Graz, Austria, May 7–13, 2006.

Oberlander, J. and Nowson, S. 2006. Whose Thumb is It Anyway? Classifying Author Personality from Weblog Text. In *Proceedings of the 21st International Conference on Computational Linguistics and 44th Annual Meeting of the Association for Computational Linguistics*, 627–634. Sydney, Australia, July 17–21, 2006. Association for Computational Linguistics, Morristown, NJ.

O'Connor, E., Hayes, J., Smeaton, A.F., O'Connor, N., and Diamond, D. 2009. Environmental Monitoring of Galway Bay: Fusing Data from Remote and In-Situ Sources. In *Remote Sensing for Environmental Monitoring, GIS Applications, and Geology IX*, SPIE Europe Remote Sensing 2009, Berlin, Germany, August 31-September 3, 2009.

Ogale, A.S. and Aloimonos, Y. 2005. Shape and the Stereo Correspondence Problem. *International Journal of Computer Vision (IJCV)* 65(3): 147–162.

Olguin, D.O., Gloor, P.A., and Pentland, A. 2009. Capturing Individual and Group Behavior with Wearable Sensors. In *Proceedings of the AAAI Spring Symposium on Human Behavior Modeling*. Stanford University, CA, March 23–25, 2009.

Olston, C., Reed, B., Srivastava, U., Kumar, R., and Tomkins, A. 2008. Pig Latin: A Not-so-Foreign Language for Data Processing. In *Proceedings of the ACM SIGMOD International Conference on Management of Data*, 1099–1110. June 10–12, 2008. ACM Press, Vancouver, BC, Canada.

Oostveen, J., Kalker, T., and Haitsma, J. 2001. Visual Hashing of Digital Video: Applications and Techniques. In Tescher, A.G. (ed.), *Applications of Digital Image Processing XXIV, SPIE*, Vol. 4472(1), 121–131, SPIE.

O'Riordan, A. and O'Mahoney, M. 2008. InterSynd: A Web Syndication Intermediary that Makes Recommendations. In *Proceedings of the 10th International Conference on Information Integration and Web-based Applications & Services (iiWAS2008)*, 299–304. 24–26 November 2008, Linz, Austria.

Ortony, A., Clore, G.L., and Collins, A. 1988. *The Cognitive Structure of Emotions*. Cambridge University Press, Cambridge, UK.

Over, P. 2009. TRECVID 2008 –Goals, Tasks, Data, Evaluation Mechanisms and Metrics. In *Proceedings of TRECVID 2008, 2009*. NIST, Gaithersburg, MD, November 17–18, 2008. http://www-nlpir.nist.gov/projects/tvpubs/tv8.papers/tv8overview.pdf

Over, P., Ianeva, T., Kraaijz, W., and Smeaton, A. 2005. An Overview. In *Online Proceedings of the NIST TRECVID 2005 Video Retrieval Evaluation*. Gaithersburg, MD, November 14–15, 2005.

Over, Paul, Awad, George M., Fiscus, Jon, Michel, Martial and Smeaton, Alan F., and Kraaij, Wessel. 2010. TRECVID 2009–Goals, Tasks, Data, Evaluation Mechanisms and Metrics. In *TRECVID Workshop 2009*, Gaithersburg, MD, November 16–17.

Oviatt, S. 2008. Multimodal Interfaces. In Jacko, J. and Sears, A. (eds.), *The Human-Computer Interaction Handbook*, 413–432, Lawrence Erlbaum, Mahwah, NJ.

Ozkar, M. and Kotsopoulos, S. 2008. Introduction to Shape Grammars. In *Proceedings of the International Conference on Computer Graphics and Interactive Techniques ACM SIGGRAPH 2008* [Course Notes] Vol. 36, 1–175. Los Angeles, CA, August 11–15, 2008.

Page, L., Brin, S., Motwani, R., and Winograd, T. 1999. The PageRank Citation Ranking: Bringing Order to the Web. *Stanford Digital Library Technologies Project*, Technical Report. Stanford InfoLab http://dbpubs.stanford.edu/pub/1999-66

Palmer, D., Reichman, M., and White, N. 2012. Multimedia Information Extraction in a Live Multilingual News Monitoring System, this volume.

Palmer, F.R. 2001. *Mood and Modality*, 2nd ed., Cambridge University Press, Cambridge.

Pang, B., Lee, L., and Vaithyanathan, S. 2002. Thumbs Up? Sentiment Classification Using Machine Learning Techniques. In *Proceedings of the 2002 Conference on Empirical Methods in Natural Language Processing (EMNLP)*, 79–86. University of Pennsylvania, Philadelphia, PA, July 6–7, 2002.

Pantić, M. and Rothkrantz, L.J.M. 2000. Automatic Analysis of Facial Expressions: The State of the Art. *Transactions on Pattern Analysis and Machine Intelligence* 22(12): 1424–1445.

Paolillo, J.C. and Penumarthy, S. 2007. The Social Structure of Tagging Internet Video on del.icio.us. In *Proceedings of the 40th Annual Hawaii International Conference on System Sciences (HICSS'07)*, 85b. January 3–6, 2007, Hilton Waikoloa Village Resort Waikoloa, Big Island, HI.

Paoluzzi, A., Pascucci, V., and Vicentino, M. 1995. Geometric Programming: A Programming Approach to Geometric Design. *ACM Transactions on Graphics* 14: 266–306.

Paragios, N. and Deriche, R. 2000. Geodesic Active Contours and Level Sets for the Detection and Tracking of Moving Objects. *IEEE Transactions on Pattern Analysis and Machine Intelligence (PAMI)* 22: 266–280.

Pardo, B. 2006. Finding Structure in Audio for Music Information Retrieval. *IEEE Signal Processing Magazine* 23(3): 126–132.

Parikh, D. and Chen, T. 2007. Hierarchical Semantics of Objects (hSOs). In *Proceedings of the 11th IEEE International Conference on Computer Vision (ICCV)*, 1–8. Rio de Janeiro, Brazil, October 14–20, 2007.

Pauly, M., Mitra, N.J., Wallner, J., Pottmann, H., and Guibas, L. 2008. Discovering Structural Regularity in 3D Geometry. *ACM Transactions on Graphics* 27(43): 1–11.

Pazzani, M. and Billsus, D. 2007. Content-Based Recommendation Systems. In Brusilovsky, P., Kobsa, A., and Nejdl W. (eds.), *The Adaptive Web. Lecture Notes in Computer Science*, Vol. 4321, 325–341, Springer Verlag, Berlin.

Pelachaud, C., Badler, N.I., and Steedman, M. 1996. Generating Facial Expressions for Speech. *Cognitive Science* 20(1): 1–46.

Pentland, A. 2006. A Computational Model of Social Signaling. In *Proceedings of the 18th International Conference on Pattern Recognition (ICPR'06)*, 1080–1083. Hong Kong, August 20–24, 2006.

Pentland, A. 2008. *Honest Signals: How They Shape Our World*. MIT Press, Cambridge.

Perugini, M. and Di Blas, L. 2002. Analyzing Personality-Related Adjectives from an Eticemic Perspective: The Big Five Marker Scales (BFMS) and the Italian AB5C Taxonomy. In De Raad, B. and Perugini, M. (eds.), *Big Five Assessment*, 281–304, Hogrefe und Huber Publishers, Gottingen.

Peters, I. and Peters, W. 2000. The Treatment of Adjectives in SIMPLE: Theoretical Observations. In *Proceedings of the Second International Conference on Language Resources and Evaluation (LREC)*, Vol. III, 1385–1390. Athens, Greece, May 31–June 2, 2000. European Language Resources Association.

Pham, T.D. 2003. Unconstrained Logo Detection in Document Images. *Pattern Recognition*. 36(12): 3023–3025.

Phillips, J., Todd Scruggs, W., O'Toole, A., Flynn, P., Bowyer, K., Schott, C., and Sharpe, M. 2007. Face Recognition Vendor Test (FRVT) 2006 and ICE 2006 Large-Scale Results, 1–56. National Institute of Standards and Technology.

Pianesi, F., Lepri, B., Mana, N., Cappelletti, A., and Zancanaro, M. 2012. Extracting Information from Human Behavior, this volume.

Pianesi, F., Nadia, M., Cappelletti, A., Lepri, B., and Zancanaro, M. 2008a. Multimodal Recognition of Personality Traits in Social Interactions. In *Proceedings of the 10th International Conference on Multimodal interfaces (ICMI)*, 53–60. Chania, Crete, Greece, October 20–22, 2008.

Pianesi, F., Zancanaro, M., Bruno, L., and Cappelletti, A. 2008b. Multimodal Support to Group Dynamics. *Personal and Ubiquitous Computing* 12(3): 181–195.

Pianesi, F., Zancanaro, M., Lepri, B., and Cappelletti, A. 2007. Multimodal Annotated Corpora of Consensus Decision Making Meetings. *Journal of Language Resources and Evaluation* 41(3–4): 409–429.

Pianta, E. and Zanoli, R. 2007. Tagpro: A System for Italian POS Tagging Based on SVM. *Intelligenza Artificiale* Numero Speciale Strumenti di Elaborazione del Linguaggio Naturale per l'Italiano, 4(2): 8–9.

Picard, R.W. 1997. *Affective Computing*. MIT Press, Cambridge, MA.

Picard, R.W. and Cosier, G. 1997. Affective Intelligence—The Missing Link? *BT Technology Journal* 14(4): 150–161. British Telecom.

Picard, R.W. and Daily, S.B. 2005. Evaluating Affective Interactions: Alternatives to Asking What Users Feel. In *CHI Workshop on Evaluating Affective Interfaces: Innovative Approaches*, 2119–2122. Portland, OR, April 2–7, 2005. ACM, New York, NY.

Pinker, S. 1990. A Theory of Graph Comprehension. In Freedle, R. (ed.), *Artificial Intelligence and the Future of Testing*, 73–126, Psychology Press, East Sussex, UK.

Piwek, P. 2002. An Annotated Bibliography of Affective Natural Language Generation. Technical Report ITRI-02-02. University of Brighton.

Platt, J. 1999. Fast Training of Support Vector Machines Using Sequential Minimal Optimization. In Scholkopf, B., Burges, C.J.C., and Smola, A.J. (eds.), *Advances in Kernel Methods: Support Vector Learning*, 185–208, The MIT Press, Cambridge, MA.

Plutchik, R. 2001. The Nature of Emotions. *American Scientist* 89(4): 344.

Pogačnik, M. and Tasič, J. 2005. An Overview of User-Oriented Data Mining Approaches. *Elektrotehniski vestnik* 72(4): 177–182.

Pogačnik, M., Tasic, J., Marko, M., and Andrej, K. 2005. Personal Content Recommender Based on a Hierarchical User Model for the Selection of TV Programmes. *User Modeling and User Adapted Interaction* 15: 425–457.

Polzin, T.S. and Waibel, A. 2002. Emotion-Sensitive Human-Computer Interfaces. In *Proceedings of the ISCA Tutorial and Research Workshop (ITRW) on Speech and Emotion*, 201–206. Newcastle, Belfast, Northern Ireland, September 5–7, 2000.

Porter, M. 2008. Snowball Programming Language for Stemmers. http://snowball.tartarus.org

Posner, J., Russell, J.A., and Peterson, B. 2005. The Circumplex Model of Affect: An Integrative Approach to Affective Neuroscience, Cognitive Development, and Psychopathology. *Development and Psychopathology* 17(3): 715–734.

Povey, D. and Woodland, P.C. 2002. Minimum Phone Error and I-smoothing for Improved Discriminative Training. In *Proceedings of the IEEE International Conference on Acoustics, Speech and Signal Processing*, Vol. I, 105–109. Renaissance Orlando Resort, Orlando, FL, May 13–17, 2002.

Pratt, M.J. 2004. Extension of ISO 10303, The STEP Standard, for the Exchange of Procedural Shape Models. In *Proceedings of the International Conference on Shape Modeling and Applications*, 317–326. Genova, Italy, June 7–9, 2004.

Press, W.H., Teukolsky, S.A., Vetterling, W.T., and Flannery, B.P. 2007. *Numerical Recipes: The Art of Scientific Computing*, 3rd ed., Cambridge University Press, New York.

Protégé. 2009. Protégé Ontology Editor Knowledge Acquisition System. http://protégé.stanford.edu

Prusinkiewicz, P. 2000. Simulation Modeling of Plants and Plant Ecosystems. *Communications of the ACM* 43(7): 84–93.

Purpura, S. and Hillard, D. 2006. Automated Classification of Congressional Legislation. In *Proceedings of the Seventh International Conference on Digital Government Research*, 219–225. San Diego, CA, May 21–24, 2006.

Rabbani, T. and van den Heuvel, F. 2004. Methods for Fitting CSG Models to Point Clouds and their Comparison. In *Proceedings of Computer Graphics and Imaging (CGIM)*, Vol. 1, 1–6. Kauai, HI, August 17–19, 2004.

Ramamoorthi, R. and Arvo, J. 1999. Creating Generative Models from Range Images. In *Proceedings of ACM SIGGRAPH*, Vol. 1, 195–204. Los Angeles, CA, August 8–13, 1999.

Rao, K.R., Bojkovic, Z., and Milovanovic, D. 2006. *Introduction to Multimedia Communications*. Wiley and Sons, Hoboken, NJ.

Rasheed, Z., Sheikh, Y., and Shah, M. 2005. On the Use of Computable Features for Film Classification. *IEEE Transactions on Circuits and Systems for Video Technology* 15(1): 52–64. IEEE.

Reede, R. and Jose, J.M. 2005. Football Video Segmentation Based on Video Production Strategy. In Losada, D. and Fernandez-Luna, J. (eds.), *Advances in Information Retrieval: Proceedings of the 27th European Conference on Information Retrieval*, 433–446. Santiago de Compostela, Spain, March 21–23, 2005. *Lecture Notes in Computer Science 3408*, Springer.

Reiter, E. and Dale, R. 2000. *Building Natural Language Generation Systems.* Cambridge University Press, Cambridge, England.

Remondino, F. 2003. From Point Cloud to Surface: The Modeling and Visualization Problem. In *International Archives of Photogrammetry, Remote Sensing and Spatial Information Sciences (ISPRS)*, Vol. XXXIV-5/W10. *International Workshop on Visualization and Animation of Reality-based 3D Models*, Vol. 34, 228–238. Tarasp-Vulpera, Switzerland, February 24–28, 2003.

Rendals, S. and Abberley, D. 2000. The THISL SDR System at TREC-9. In *Proc. TREC-9*, 627–634.

Reynolds, D. 1995. Speaker Identification and Verification Using Gaussian Mixture Speaker Models. *Speech Communications* 17: 91–108.

Rienks R. and Heylen D. Dominance Detection in Meetings Using Easily Obtainable Features. In *Revised Selected Papers of the 2nd Joint Workshop on Multimodal Interaction and Related Machine Learning Algorithms*. Edinbourgh, Scotland, October 2006.

Rigoll, G., Muller, R., and Schuller, B. 2005. Speech Emotion Recognition Exploiting Acoustic and Linguistic Information Sources. In *Proceedings of the 10th International Conference on Speech and Computer (SPECOM)*, 61–67. University of Patras, Patras, Greece, October 17–19, 2005.

Rodden, K. 2001. Does Organisation by Similarity Assist Image Browsing? In *Proceedings of the SIGCHI Conference on Human Factors in Computing Systems*, 190–197. Seattle, WA, March31–April 5 2001.

Rodden, K, Basalaj, W., Sinclair, D., and Wood. K.R. 2001. Does Organisation by Similarity Assist Image Browsing? In *Proceedings of ACM CHI 2001*, 190–197.

Rodgers, J.L. and Nicewander, W.A. 1988. Thirteen Ways to Look at the Correlation Coefficient. *The American Statistician* 42(1): 59–66.

Roetenberg, D., Luinge, H., and Slycke, P. 2008. 6 DOF Motion Analysis Using Inertial Sensors. In *Proceedings of Measuring Behavior, 6th International Conference on Methods and Techniques in Behavioral Research*, 14–15. Maastricht, The Netherlands, August 26–29, 2008.

Rohlfing, K., Loehr, D., Duncan, S., Brown, A., Franklin, A., Kimbara, I., Milde, J., Parrill, F., Rose, T., Schmidt, T., Sloetjes, H., Thies, A., and Wellinghoff, S. 2006. Comparison of Multimodal Annotation Tools—Workshop Report. *Gesprachsforschung* 7: 99–123.

Rose, T., Quek, F., and Shi, Y. 2004. MacVissta: A System for Multimodal Analysis. In *Proceedings of the 6th International Conference on Multimodal Interfaces (ICMI)*, 259–264. New York, New York. July 2004. State College, Pennsylvania, USA, October 14–15, 2004.

Rosen-Zvi, M., Griffiths, T., Steyvers, M., and Smyth, P. 2004. The Author-Topic Model for Authors and Documents. In *Proceedings of the 20th Conference on Uncertainty in Artificial Intelligence*, 487–494. Banff, Canada, July 7–11, 2004.

Rothwell, S., Lehane, B., Chan, C., Smeaton, A., O'Connor, N., Jones, G., and Diamond, D. 2006. The CDVPlex Biometric Cinema: Sensing Physiological Responses to Emotional Stimuli in Film. In *Adjunct Proceedings of the Fourth International Conference on*

Pervasive Computing, 103–106. May 7–10, 2006, The Burlington Hotel, Dublin, Ireland. Austrian Computer Society (OCG).

Rotter, J.B. 1966. Generalized Expectancies for Internal versus External Control of Reinforcement. In Kimble, G.A. (ed.), *Psychological Monographs*, 80, American Psychological Association, Washington.

Rousseeuw, P.J. and Leroy, A.M. 1987. *Robust Regression and Outlier Detection*. Wiley Series in Probability and Statistics. John Wiley and Sons, Inc., New York.

Russell, J.A. and Mehrabian, A. 1977. Evidence for a Three-Factor Theory of Emotions. In *Journal of Research in Personality* 11(3): 273–294.

Sadlier, D. and O'Connor, N. 2005. Event Detection Based on Generic Characteristics of Field Sports. In *IEEE International Conference on Multimedia and Expo (ICME)*, 759–762. Amsterdam, The Netherlands, July 6–9, 2005.

Salazar, A. 1996. An Analysis of the Development and Evolution of Roles in the Small Group. *Small Group Research* 27(4): 475–503.

Salvucci, D.D. 2001. An Integrated Model of Eye Movements and Visual Encoding. *Cognitive Systems Research* 1(4): 201–220.

Salway, A. and Graham, M. 2003. Extracting Information about Emotions in Films. In *Proceedings of the Eleventh ACM International Conference on Multimedia*, 299–302. ACM, Berkeley, CA, November 2–8, 2003.

San Pedro, J., Denis, N., and Dominguez, S. 2005. Video Retrieval Using an EDL-Based Timeline. *Pattern Recognition and Image Analysis, Lecture Notes in Computer Science* 3522, 401–408. Springer-Verlag, Berlin.

San Pedro, J. and Dominguez, S. 2007a. Network-Aware Identification of Video Clip Fragments. In *Proceedings of the 6th ACM International Conference on Image and Video Retrieval (CIVR)*, 318–324. Amsterdam, The Netherlands, July 9–11, 2007.

San Pedro, J. and Dominguez Cabrerizo, S. 2007b. Synchronized Digital Video Subsampling to Achieve Temporal Resolution Independence. In *Proceedings of the 5th IEEE International Symposium on Industrial Electronics (ISIE)*, 1785–1790. Vigo, Spain, June 4–7, 2007.

Scharstein, D. and Szeliski, R. 1998. Stereo Matching with Nonlinear Diffusion. *International Journal of Computer Vision* 28(2): 155–174.

Scharstein, D. and Szeliski, R. 2002. A Taxonomy and Evaluation of Dense Two-Frame Stereo Correspondence Algorithms. *International Journal of Computer Vision* 47(1–3): 7–42.

Scherer, K.R. 1979. Personality Markers in Speech. In Scherer, K.R. and Giles, H. (eds.), *Social Markers in Speech*, 147–209, Cambridge University Press, Cambridge, UK.

Schindler, G., Brown, M., and Szeliski, R. 2007. City-Scale Location Recognition. In *Proceedings of IEEE Conference on Computer Vision and Pattern Recognition (CVPR)*, 1–7. Minneapolis, MN, June 18–23, 2007. IEEE Computer Society.

Schlosberg, H. 1952. The Description of Facial Expressions in Terms of Two Dimensions. *Journal of Experimental Psychology* 44(4): 229–237.

Schmidt, T. 2004. Transcribing and Annotating Spoken Language with Exmaralda. In *Proceedings of the LREC-Workshop on XML based Richly Annotated Corpora*. Centro Cultural de Belem, Lisbon, Portugal. May 24–25, 2004.

Schmidt, T., Ehmer, O., Hoyt, J., Kipp, M., Loehr, D., Rose, T., Sloetjes, H., Duncan, S., and Magnusson, M. 2009. An Exchange Format for Multimodal Annotations. In *Multimodal Corpora: From Models of Natural Interaction to Systems and Applications, Lecture Notes on Artificial Intelligence (LNAI) 5509*, 359–365. Springer.

Schnabel, R., Wahl, R., and Lein, R. 2007a. Efficient RANSAC for Point-Cloud Shape Detection. *Computer Graphics Forum* 26(2): 214–226.

Schnabel, R., Wahl, R., Wessell, R., and Klein, R. 2007b. Shape Recognition in 3D Point Clouds. *Technical Report* 1: 1–9.

Schröder, M. 2009. Emotion Markup Language (EmotionML) 1.0. W3C Working Draft, October 29, 2009. http://www.w3.org/TR/emotionml

Schröder, M. (ed.), Baggia, P., Burkhardt, F., Martin, J., Pelachaud, C., Peter, C., Schuller, B., Wilson, I. and Zovato, E. 2008. Elements of an EmotionML 1.0. W3C Final Incubator Group Report, World Wide Web Consortium, November 2008. http://www.w3.org/2005/Incubator/emotion/XGR-emotionml

Schuller, B. 2006. Automatic Recognition of Emotion from Speech and Manual Interaction. PhD thesis, Technische Universitat Munchen, Munich, Germany.

Schuller, B., Ablaßmeier, M., Müller, R., Reifinger, S., Poitschke, T., and Rigoll, G. 2006a. Speech Communication and Multimodal Interfaces. In Kraiss, K. (ed.), *Advanced Man Machine Interaction*, 141–190, Springer Verlag, Berlin/Heidelberg.

Schuller, B., Batliner, A., Seppi, D., Steidl, S., Vogt, T., Wagner, J., Devillers, L., Vidrascu, L., Amir, N., Kessous, L., and Aharonson, V. 2007a. The Relevance of Feature Type for the Automatic Classification of Emotional User States: Low Level Descriptors and Functionals. In *Proceedings of INTERSPEECH 2007, ISCA*, 2253–2256. Antwerp, Belgium, August 27–31, 2007.

Schuller, B., Batliner, A., Steidl, S., and Seppi, D. 2009. Emotion Recognition from Speech: Putting ASR in the Loop. In *Proceedings of the International Conference on Acoustics, Speech, and Signal Processing (ICASSP)*, 4585–4588. IEEE, Taipei, Taiwan, April 19–24, 2009.

Schuller, B., Köhler, N., Müller, R., and Rigoll, G. 2006b. Recognition of Interest in Human Conversational Speech. In *Proceedings of the Ninth International Conference on Spoken Language Processing (ICSLP)—INTERSPEECH 2006*, 793–796. Pittsburgh, PA, September 17–21, 2006. International Speech Communication Association.

Schuller, B., Müller, R., Hörnler, B., Höthker, A., Konosu, H., and Rigoll, G. 2007b. Audiovisual Recognition of Spontaneous Interest within Conversations, invited talk. In *Proceedings of the ACM 9th International Conference on Multimodal Interfaces (ICMI), Special Session on Multimodal Analysis of Human Spontaneous Behavior*, 30–37. Nagoya, Japan. November 12–15, 2007.

Schuller, B., Müller, R., Lang, M., and Rigoll, G. 2005. Speaker Independent Emotion Recognition by Early Fusion of Acoustic and Linguistic Features within Ensembles. In *Proceedings of INTERSPEECH 2005, Special Session: Emotional Speech Analysis and Synthesis: Towards a Multimodal Approach*, 805–809. Lisbon, Portugal, September 4–8, 2005.

Schuller, B., Rigoll, G., and Lang, M. 2004. Speech Emotion Recognition Combining Acoustic Features and Linguistic Information in a Hybrid Support Vector Machine-belief Network Architecture. In *Proceedings of the 28th IEEE International Conference on Acoustics, Speech, and Signal Processing (ICASSP)*, Vol. 1, 577–580. IEEE Computer Society. Montreal, QC, Canada, May 17–24, 2004.

Schuller, B., Wöllmer, M., Eyben, F., and Rigoll, G. 2012. Retrieval of Paralinguistic Information in Broadcasts, this volume.

Schwartz, R., Nguyen, L., and Makhoul, J. 1996. Multiple-pass Search Strategies. In Lee, C.-H., Soong, F.K., and Paliwal, K.K. (eds.), *Automatic Speech and Speaker Recognition: Advanced Topics*, 429–456, Kluwer Academic Publishers, Norwell, MA.

Settgast, V., Ullrich, T., and Fellner, D.W. July–August 2007. Information Technology for Cultural Heritage. *IEEE Potentials* 26(4): 38–43.

Shan, C., Gong, S., and McOwan, P.W. 2005. Appearance Manifold of Facial Expressions. In Sebe, N., Lew, M.S., and Huang, T.S. (eds.), *Computer Vision in Human-Computer Interaction*, 221–230, *Lecture Notes in Computer Science 3723*. Springer, Berlin.

Shapiro, L.G. and Stockman, G.C. 2001. *Computer Vision*. Prentice Hall, Upper Saddle River, NJ.106–107.

Shapiro, V. 2002. Solid Modeling. In Farin, G., Hoschek, J., and Kim, M.-S. (eds.), *Handbook of Computer Aided Geometric Design*, Vol. 20, 473–518, Elsevier Science B.V., Amsterdam, The Netherlands.

Shriberg, E. 2005. Spontaneous Speech: How People Really Talk and Why Engineers Should Care. In *Proceedings of Interspeech*, 1781–1784. Lisbon, Portugal, September 4–8 2005.

SIGCHI. 1996. ACM SIGCHI Curricula for Human-Computer Interaction See: http://old.sigchi.org/cdg

Singhal, A., Buckley, C., and Mitra, M. 1996. Pivoted Document Length Normalization. In *Proceedings of the 19th Annual International ACM SIGIR Conference on Research and Development in Information Retrieval*, 21–29. Zurich, Switzerland, August 18–22, 1996.

Slaney, M. and McRoberts, G. 2003. BabyEars: A Recognition System for Affective Vocalizations. *Speech Communication* 39(3–4): 367–384.

Smeaton, A., Over, P., and Kraaij, W. 2006. Evaluation Campaigns and TRECVid. In *Proceedings of the 8th ACM International Workshop on Multimedia Information Retrieval (MIR)*, 321–330. Santa Barbara, CA, October 26–27. ACM, New York, NY.

Smeaton, A., Over, P., and Kraaij, W. 2009. High-Level Feature Detection from Video in TRECVid: A 5-Year Retrospective of Achievements. In Divakaran, A. (ed.), *Multimedia Content Analysis, Theory and Applications*, 151–174, Springer Verlag, Berlin.

Smeulders, A.W., Worring, M., Santini, S., Gupta, A., and Ramesh, J. 2000. Content-Based Image Retrieval at the End of the Early Years. *IEEE Transactions on Pattern Analysis and Machine Intelligence* 22(12): 1349–1380.

Smola, A.J. and Schoelkopf, B. 1998. A Tutorial on Support Vector Regression. NeuroCOLT2 Technical Report NC2-TR-1998-030.

Snavely, N., Seitz, S., and Szeliski, R. 2006a. Photo Tourism: Exploring Photo Collections in 3D. *ACM Transactions on Graphics (SIGGRAPH)* 25(3): 835–846.

Snavely, N., Seitz, S., and Szeliski, R. 2006b. Modeling the World from Internet Photo Collections. *International Journal of Computer Vision (IJCV)* 80(2): 189–210.

Snoek, C.G., Worring, M., and Hauptmann, A.G. 2006. Learning Rich Semantics from News Video Archives by Style Analysis. *ACM Transactions on Multimedia Computing, Communications and Applications* 2(2): 91–108.

Snyder, J.M. and Kajiya, J.T. 1992. Generative Modeling: A Symbolic System for Geometric Modeling. In *Proceedings of the 19th Annual ACM Conference on Computer Graphics and Interactive Techniques (SIGGRAPH)*, Vol. 1, 369–378. Chicago, IL, July 27–21, 1991.

Srihari, R.K. and Burhans, D.T. 1994. Visual Semantics: Extracting Visual Information from Text Accompanying Pictures. In *Proceedings of AAAI-94*, 793–779. Seattle, WA, July 31–August 4, 1994.

Srihari, R.K., Li, W., Niu, C., and Cornell, T. 2008. InfoXtract: A Customizable Intermediate Level Information Extraction Engine. *Journal of Natural Language Engineering* 14(1): 33–69.

Stauffer, C. and Grimson, E. 2000. Learning Patterns of Activity Using Real-time Tracking. *IEEE Pattern Analysis and Machine Intelligence (PAMI)* 22(8): 747–757.

Steidl, S., Ruff, C., Batliner, A., Nöth, E., and Haas, J. 2004. Looking at the Last Two Turns, I'd Say This Dialogue is Doomed—Measuring Dialogue Success. In Sojka, P., Kopecek, I., and Pala, K. (eds.), *Proceedings of the 7th International Conference Text, Speech and Dialogue (TSD)*, 629–636. September 8–11, 2004. Springer, Berlin/Heidelberg.

Stein, A. and Hebert, M. 2005. Incorporating Background Invariance into Feature-Based Object Recognition. In *Proceedings of Workshop on Applications of Computer Vision (WACV)*, 37–44. Breckenridge, CO, January 5–7, 2005.

Stevens, K.N. and Hanson, H.M. 1995. Classification of Glottal Vibration from Acoustic Measurements. In Fujimura, O. and Hirano, H. (eds.), 147–170, *Vocal Fold Physiology: Voice Quality Control*, Singular Publishing Group, San Diego, CA.

Stevenson, D.J. 2004. Laughter and Leadership. Paper presented at *The International Center for Studies in Creativity*. Buffalo State College, June 2004.

Stiefelhagen, R. 2007. The CLEAR 2007 Evaluation. In Stiefelhagen, R. (eds.), *Multimodal Technologies for Perception of Humans: International Evaluation Workshops CLEAR 2007 and RT 2007*, Baltimore, MD, May 8–11, 2007, Revised Selected Papers, *Lecture Notes on Computer Science 4625*, 3–34. Springer-Verlag, Berlin.

Stiny, G. and Gips, J. 1972. Shape Grammars and the Generative Specification of Painting and Sculpture. In Freiman, C.V. (ed.), *Information Processing 71*, 1460–1465, North-Holland, Amsterdam. Republished in Petrocelli, O. R. (ed.) 1972. *The Best Computer Papers of 1971*, 125–135. Auerbach, Philadelphia.

Stiny, G. and Gips, J. 1978. *Algorithmic Aesthetics: Computer Models for Criticism and Design in the Arts*. University of California Press, Berkeley and Los Angeles.

Stoiber, N., Breton, G., and Seguier, R. 2012. A Data-Driven Meaningful Representation of Emotional Facial Expressions, this volume.

Stoiber, N., Seguier, R., and Breton, G. 2009. Automatic Design of a Control Interface for a Synthetic Face. In *Proceedings of the ACM International Conference on Intelligent User Interfaces (IUI)*, 207–216. Sanibel Island, FL, February 8–11, 2009.

Stolcke, A., Shriberg, E., Bates, R., Ostendorf, M., Hakkani, D., Plauchu, M., Tur, G., and Lu, Y. 1998. Automatic Detection of Sentence Boundaries and Disfluencies Based on Recognized Words. In *Proc. ICSLP'98*, 2247–2250.

Stolcke, A., Shriberg, E., Hakkani-Tur, D., Tur, G., Rivlin, Z., and Sonmez, K. 1999. Combining Words and Speech Prosody for Automatic Topic Segmentation. In *Proc. DARPA Broadcast News Workshop*, 61–64.

Sturm, J., Houben-Van Herwijnen, O., Eyck, A., and Terken, J. 2007. Influencing Social Dynamics in Meetings through a Peripheral Display. In *Proceedings of ACM 9th International Conference on Multimodal Interfaces (ICMI)*. Nagoya, Aichi, Japan, November 12–15, 2007.

Suga, A., Fukuda, K., Takiguchi, T., and Ariki, Y. 2008. Object Recognition and Segmentation using SIFT and Graph Cuts. In *Proceedings of International Conference on Pattern Recognition (ICPR)*, 1–4. Tampa, FL, December 8–11, 2008.

Sugihara, T., Diltz, M., Averbeck, B., and Romanski, L.M. 2006. Integration of Auditory and Visual Communication Information in the Primate Ventrolateral Prefrontal Cortex. *The Journal of Neuroscience* 26(43): 11138–11147.

Sun, A. and Datta, A. 2009. On Stability, Clarity, and Co-occurrence of Self-Tagging. In *Proceedings of the Second ACM International Conference on Web Search and Data Mining (WSDM)*, Barcelona, Spain, February 9–12, 2009. http://www.wsdm2009.org/sun_2009_self_tagging.pdf

Tian, Y.-L., Kanade, T., and Cohn, J. 2001. Recognizing Action Units for Facial Expression Analysis. *Transactions on Pattern Analysis and Machine Intelligence* 23(2): 97–115.

Tkalčič, M., Tasič, J., and Košir, A. 2012. The Need for Affective Metadata in Content-Based Recommender Systems for Images, this volume.

Toshniwal, D. and Joshi, R. 2005. Finding Similarity in Time Series Data by Method of Time Weighted Moments. In *Proceedings of the 16th Australasian Database Conference*, 155–164. Newcastle, Australia.

Toyama, K., Krumm, J., Brumitt, B., and Meyers, B. 1999. Wallflower: Principles and Practice of Background Maintenance. In *Proceedings of the Seventh IEEE International Conference on Computer Vision (ICCV)*, 255–261. Kerkyra, Greece, September 20–27, 1999.

Toyama, K., Logan, R., and Roseway, A. 2003. Geographic Location Tags on Digital Images. In *Proceedings of the Eleventh ACM International Conference Multimedia*, 156–166. Berkeley, CA, November 2–8, 2003.

Tsapatsoulis, N., Raouzaiou, A., Kollias, S., Cowie, R., and Douglas-Cowie, E. 2002. Emotion Recognition and Synthesis Based on MPEG-4 FAPs. In *MPEG-4 Facial Animation*, Igor Pandzic, R. Forchheimer (eds.), John Wiley & Sons, UK.

Tskarov, D. and Horrocks, I. 2006. FaCT++ Description Logic Reasoner: System Description.

Tzanetakis, G., Essl, G., and Cook, P.R. 2001. Automatic Musical Genre Classification of Audio Signals. In *Proceedings of the International Symposium on Music Information Retrieval (ISMIR)*, 205–210. Bloomington, IN, October 15–17, 2001.

Tzoukermann, E., Ambwani, G., Bagga, A., Chipman, L., Davis, T., Farrell, R., Houghton, D., Jojic, O., Neumann, J., Rubino, R., Shevade, B., and Zhou, H. 2012. Semantic Multimedia Extraction using Audio and Video, this volume.

Tzoukermann, E., Davis, A., Houghton, D., and Rennert, P. 2005. Knowledge Discovery via Content Indexing of Multimedia and Text. In *International Conference on Intelligence Analysis*. McLean, VA, May 2–6, 2005. http://analysis.mitre.org//proceedings/Final_Papers_Files/211_Camera_Ready_Paper.pdf

Ullrich, T. and Fellner, D.W. 2007. Robust Shape Fitting and Semantic Enrichment. In *Proceedings of the 2007 International Symposium of the International Committee for Architectural Photogrammetry (CIPA)*, Vol. 21, 727–732. Athens, Greece, October 1–6, 2007.

Ullrich, T., Settgast, V., and Fellner, D.W. 2008. Semantic Fitting and Reconstruction. *Journal on Computing and Cultural Heritage* 1(2): 1201–1220.

Ulusoy, I. and Bishop, C.W. 2005. Generative versus Discriminative Methods for Object Recognition. In *Proceedings of the IEEE Computer Society Conference on Computer Vision and Pattern Recognition*, Vol. 2, 258–265. San Diego, CA, June 20–26, 2005.

Valdez, P. and Mehrabian, A. 1994. Effects of Color on Emotions. *Journal of Experimental Psychology: General* 123(4): 394–409. APA.

Van De Sande, K.E.A., Gevers, T., and Snoek, C.G.M. 2008. Evaluation of Color Descriptors for Object and Scene Recognition. In *Proceedings of IEEE Conference on Computer Vision and Pattern Recognition (CVPR)*, 1–8. Anchorage, AK, June 24–26, 2008.

Van Thong, J., Goddeau, D., Litvinova, A., Logan, B., Moreno, P., and Swain, M. 2000. Speech-Bot: A Speech Recognition Based Audio Indexing System for the Web. In *Proceedings of International Conference on Computer-Assisted Information Retrieval, Recherche d'Informations Assistee par Ordinateur* (RIAO2000), 106–115. Paris.

Veksler, O. 2002. Stereo Correspondence with Compact Windows via Minimum Ratio Cycle. *IEEE Pattern Analysis and Machine Intelligence (PAMI)* 24(12): 1654–1660.

Ververidis, D. and Kotropoulos, C. 2003. A State of the Art Review on Emotional Speech Databases. In *Proceedings of the First Richmedia Conference*, 109–119. Lausanne, Switzerland, October 9–10, 2003.

Vinciarelli, A., Pantic, M., and Herve, B. 2009. Social Signal Processing: Survey of an Emerging Domain. *Journal of Image and Vision Computing* 27(12): 1743–1759.

Vlahos, J. 2008. Surveillance Society: New High-tech Cameras Are Watching You. In *Popular Mechanics*, 64–72, Hearst Communications, Inc., New York. http://www.popularmechanics.com/technology/military/4236865.

Vlasenko, B., Schuller, B., Wendemuth, A., and Rigoll, G. 2008. On the Influence of Phonetic Content Variation for Acoustic Emotion Recognition. In *Perception in Multimodal Dialogue Systems, Proceedings 4th IEEE Tutorial and Research Workshop on Perception and Interactive Technologies for Speech-Based Systems, Lecture Notes in Computer Science 5078*, 217–220. Kloster Irsee, Germany, June 16–18, 2008. Springer, Berlin/Heidelberg.

Vogt, T., Andre, E., and Wagner, J. 2008. Automatic Recognition of Emotions from Speech: A Review of the Literature and Recommendations for Practical Realization. In Peter, C. and Beale, R. (eds.), *Affect and Emotion in Human-Computer Interaction. Lecture Notes in Computer Science*, Vol. 4868, 75–91, Springer Verlag, Berlin/Heidelberg.

Volz, R., Handschuh, S., Staab, S., Stojanovic, L., and Stojanovic, N. 2004. Unveiling the Hidden Bride: Deep Annotation for Mapping and Migrating Legacy Data to the Semantic Web. *Journal of Web Semantics: Science, Services and Agents on the World Wide Web* 1(2): 187–206.

von Luxborg, U. 2006. A Tutorial on Special Clustering. Max Planck Institute for Biological Cybernetics Technical Report TR-149.

Vradi, T., Martin, R.R., and Cox, J. 1997. Reverse Engineering of Geometric Models—An Introduction. *Computer-Aided Design* 29(4): 255–268.

W3C. 2004. OWL Web Ontology Language Overview. http://www.w3.org/TR/owl-features

Wactlar, H., Hauptmann, A., Gong, Y., and Christel, M. 1999. Lessons Learned from the Creation and Deployment of a Terabyte Digital Video Library. *IEEE Computer* 32(2): 66–73.

Wagner, E., Liu, J., Birnbaum, L., and Forbus, K. 2009. Rich Interfaces for Reading News on the Web. In *Proceedings of the 13th ACM International Conference on Intelligent User Interfaces (IUI)*, 27–36. Sanibel Island, FL, February 8–11.

Wahl, R., Guthe, M., and Klein, R. 2005. Identifying Planes in Point-Clouds for Efficient Hybrid Rendering. In *Proceedings of the 13th Pacific Conference on Computer Graphics and Applications*, Vol. 1, 1–8. Macao, China, October 12–14, 2005.

Wang, Y., Jiang, H., Drew, M., Li, Z., and Mori, G. 2006. Unsupervised Discovery of Action Classes. In *Proceedings of the IEEE Computer Society Conference on Computer Vision and Pattern Recognition—(CVPR)*, Vol. 2, 1654–1661. New York, NY, June 17–22, 2006.

Watson, B. and Wonka, P. 2008. Procedural Methods for Urban Modeling. *IEEE Computer Graphics and Applications* 28(3): 16–17.

Weintraub, W. 1986. Personality Profiles of American Presidents as Revealed in Their Public Statements: The Presidential News Conferences of Jimmy Carter and Ronald Reagan. *Political Psychology* 7(2): 285–295.

Whissell, C.M. 1989. The Dictionary of Affect in Language. In Plutchik, R. and Kellerman, H. (eds.), *Emotion: Theory, Research and Experience (Chapter 5)*, 113–131, Academic Press, New York.

Wilson, T., Wiebe, J., and Hwa, R. 2004. Just How Mad are You? Finding Strong and Weak Opinion Clauses. In *Proceedings of AAAI*, 761–769. San Jose, CA, July 25–29.

Wimmer, M., Schuller, B., Arsic, D., Radig, B., and Rigoll, G. 2008. Low-Level Fusion of Audio and Video Feature for Multi-modal Emotion Recognition. In Ranchordas, A. and Araújo, H. (eds.), *Proceedings of the Third International Conference on Computer Vision Theory and Applications (VISAPP 2008)*, Vol. 2, 145–151. Funchal, Portugal, January 22–25, 2008.

Witten, I.H. and Frank, E. 2005. *Data Mining—Practical Machine Learning Tools and Techniques*, 2nd ed., Morgan Kaufmann, San Francisco.

Wittenburg, P., Brugman, H., Russel, A., Klassmann, A., and Sloetjes, H. 2006. ELAN: A Professional Framework for Multimodality Research. In *Proceedings of the Fifth International Conference on Language Resources and Evaluation (LREC)*, 1556–1559. Genoa, Italy, 22–28 May.

Wittgenstein, L. 1974. *Philosophical Grammar*. Basil Blackwell, Kenny, A. (trans). Oxford.

Wold, E., Blum, T., Keislar, D., and Wheaten, J. 1996. Content-Based Classification, Search, and Retrieval of Audio. *IEEE Multimedia* 3(3): 27–36.

Wollmer, M., Eyben, F., Reiter, S., Schuller, B., Cox, C., Douglas-Cowie, E., and Cowie, R. 2008. Abandoning Emotion Classes—Towards Continuous Emotion Recognition with Modelling of Long-Range Dependencies. In *Proceedings of the 9th Annual Conference of the International Speech Communication Association (INTERSPEECH2008)*, 597–600. Brisbane, Australia, September 22–26, 2008.

Wu, J. and Rehg, J.M. 2008. Where am I: Place Instance and Category Recognition Using Spatial PACT. In *Proceedings of the IEEE Conference on Computer Vision and Pattern Recognition (CVPR)*, 1–8. Anchorage, AK, June 24–26, 2008.

Wu, L., Hua, X., Yu, N., Ma, W., and Li, S. 2008. Flickr Distance. In *Proceedings of the 16th ACM International Conference Multimedia*, 31–40. Vancouver, BC, Canada, October 26–31, 2008.

Wu, T., Khan, F., Fisher, T., Shuler, L., and Pottenger, W. 2005. Posting Act Tagging Using Transformation-Based Learning. In Lin, T.Y., Ohsuga, S., Liau, C.J., and Tsumoto, S. (eds.), *Data Mining: Foundations, Methods, and Applications*, 319–331, Springer, Berlin/Heidelberg.

Wu, X., Hauptmann, A., and Ngo, C.-W. 2007. Practical Elimination of Near-Duplicates from Web Video Search. In *MULTIMEDIA '07: Proceedings of the 15th International Conference on Multimedia*, 218–227. Augsburg, Bavaria, Germany, Sept. 25–29, 2007. ACM, New York, NY.

Wu, X., Ngo, C., and Hauptmann, A. 2008. Multi-modal News Story Clustering with Pairwise Visual Near-Duplicate Constraint. *IEEE Transactions on Multimedia* 10(2): 188–199.

Wu, X., Ngo, C.-W., Hauptmann, A.G., and Tan, H.K. 2009. Real Time Near-Duplicate Elimination from Web Video Search with Content and Context. *IEEE Transactions on Multimedia* 11(2): 196–207.

Xiong, Z., Regunathan, R., Divakaran, A., Rui, Y., and Huang, T. 2006. *A Unified Framework for Video Summarization, Browsing and Retrieval*. Elsevier Academic Press, Burlington, MA.

Xu, C., Wang, J., Wan, K., Li, Y., and Duan, L. 2006. Live Sports Event Detection Based on Broadcast Video and Web-Casting Text. In *Proceedings of the 14th Annual ACM International Conference on Multimedia. MULTIMEDIA '06*, 221–230. Santa Barbara, CA, October 23–27, 2006. ACM, New York, NY.

Xu, D., Cham, T., Yan, S., and Chang, S.-F. 2008. Near Duplicate Image Identification with Spatially Aligned Pyramid Matching. In *Proceedings of IEEE Conf. on Computer Vision and Pattern Recognition (CVPR)*, 1–7. Anchorage, AK, June 23–28, 2008.

Yacoob, Y. and Davis, L.S. 1996. Recognizing Human Facial Expressions from Long Image Sequences Using Optical Flow. *Transactions on Pattern Analysis and Machine Intelligence* 18(6): 636–642.

Yaegashi, K. and Yanai, K. 2009. Can Geotags Help Image Recognition? In *Proceedings of the 3rd Pacific-Rim Symposium on Image and Video Technology (PSIVT2009)*, 361–373. Tokyo, Japan, January 13–16.

Yan, W.-Q., Wang, J., and Kankanhalli, M.S. 2005. Automatic Video Logo Detection and Removal. *Multimedia Systems* 10(5): 379–391.

Yanai, K. 2003. Generic Image Classification Using Visual Knowledge on the Web. In *Proceedings of the Eleventh ACM International Conference on Multimedia*, 167–176. Berkeley, CA, November 2–8, 2003.

Yanai, K. and Barnard, K. 2005. Image Region Entropy: A Measure of "Visualness" of Web Images Associated with One Concept. In *Proceedings of the 13th Annual ACM International Conference on Multimedia*, 419–422. Hilton, Singapore, November 06–11, 2005.

Yanai, K., Kawakubo, H., and Qiu, B. 2009. A Visual Analysis of the Relationship between Word Concepts and Geographical Locations. In *Proceedings of the 8th ACM International Conference on Image and Video Retrieval (CIVR)*, 1–8. Santorini Island, Greece, July 8–10, 2009.

Yang, J. and Hauptmann, A. 2008. (Un)Reliability of Video Concept Detection. In *Proceedings of the 7th ACM International Conference on Content-based Image and Video Retrieval (CIVR)*, 85–94. Niagara Falls, Canada, July 7–9, 2008.

Yang, J. and Hauptmann, A.G. 2004. Naming Every Individual in News Video Monologues. In *Proceedings of the 12th Annual ACM International Conference on Multimedia*, 580–587. New York, NY, October 10–16, 2004.

Yu, J., Hunter, J., Reiter, E., and Sripada, S. 2002. Recognising Visual Patterns to Communicate Gas Turbine Time-Series Data. In *Proceedings of The Twenty-Second SGAI International Conference on Knowledge Based Systems and Applied Artificial Intelligence*, 105–108. Peterhouse College, Cambridge, UK, December 10–12, 2002.

Yu, J. and Luo, J. 2008. Leveraging Probabilistic Season and Location Context Models for Scene Understanding. In *Proceedings of the International Conference on Content-Based Image and Video Retrieval (CIVR'08)*, 169–178. Niagara Falls, Canada, July 7–9, 2008.

Yu, J., Reiter, E., Hunter, J., and Mellish, C. 2007. Choosing the Content of Textual Summaries of Large Time-Series Data Sets. *Natural Language Engineering* 13(1): 25–49.

Yu, T. and Zhang, Y. 2001. Retrieval of Video Clips using Global Motion Information. *IEEE Electronics Letters* 37(14): 893–895.

Yuan, J., Luo, J., Kautz, H., and Wu, Y. 2008. Mining GPS Traces and Visual Words for Event Classification. In *Proceedings of ACM SIGMM International Workshop on Multimedia Information Retrieval*, 2–9. Vancouver, British Columbia, Canada, October 30–31, 2008.

Zancanaro, M., Lepri, B., and Pianesi, F., 2007. Automatic Detection of Group Functional Roles in Face to Face Interactions. In *Proceedings of ACM-ICMI '07*. Nagoya, Japan.

Zancanaro, M., Lepri, B., and Pianesi, F. 2006. Automatic Detection of Group Functional Roles in Face to Face Interactions. In *Proceedings of the 8th International Conference on Multimodal Interfaces (ICMI'06)*, 28–34. Banff, Alberta, Canada, November 2–4, 2006.

Zebedin, L., Klaus, A., Gruber-Geymayer, B., and Konrad, K. 2006. Towards 3D Map Generation from Digital Aerial Images. *International Society for Photogrammetry and Remote Sensing (ISPRS) Journal of Photogrammetry and Remote Sensing* 60: 413–427.

Zeng, Z., Pantić, M., Roisman, G.I., and Huang, T.S. 2009. A Survey of Affect Recognition Methods: Audio, Visual, and Spontaneous Expressions. *IEEE Transactions on Pattern Analysis and Machine Intelligence* 31(1): 39–58.

Zhai, Y. and Shah, M. 2005. Tracking News Stories Across Different Sources. In *Proceedings of the 13th ACM International Conference on Multimedia*, 2–10. Singapore, November 6–11 2005. ACM.

Zhai, Y., Shah, M., and Rasheed, Z. 2004. A Framework for Semantic Classification of Scenes Using Finite State Machines. In *Proceedings of the Third International Conference Image and Video Retrieval (CIVR)*, 279–288. Dublin, Ireland, July 21–23, 2004. Springer.

Zhang, B., Li, H., Liu, Y., Ji, L., Xi, W., Fan, W., Chen, Z., and Ma, W. 2005. Improving Web Search Results Using Affinity Graph. In *Proceedings of the 28th Annual International ACM SIGIR Conference on Research and Development in Information Retrieval (SIGIR)*, 505–511. Salvador, Brazil, 25–19 August 2005. ACM.

Zhang, D. and Lu, G. 2001. Segmentation of Moving Objects in Image Sequence: A Review. *Circuit Systems Signal Processing (CSSP)* 20(2): 143–183. Springerlink 2001.

Zhang, S., Wu, Z., Meng, H., and Cai, L. 2007. Facial Expression Synthesis Using PAD Emotional Parameters for a Chinese Expressive Avatar. In Paiva, A. et al. (ed.), *Proceedings of the Second International Conference on Affective Computing and Intelligent Interaction (ACII)*, Lisbon, Portugal, September 12–14, 2007. Springer, Berlin. *Lecture Notes in Computer Science 4738*, 24–35.

Zhang, T. and Jay Kuo, C.-C. 2001. *Content-Based Audio Classification and Retrieval for Audiovisual Data Parsing*. Kluwer Academic Publisher, Boston, MA.

Zhang, Y., Callan, J., and Minka, T. 2002. Novelty and Redundancy Detection in Adaptive Filtering. In *Proceedings of the 25th International ACM SIGIR Conference on Research and Development in Information Retrieval*, 81–88. Tampere, Finland, August 11–15, ACM.

Zhang, Z. 1997. Parameter Estimation Techniques: A Tutorial with Application to Conic Fitting. *Image and Vision Computing Journal* 15(1): 59–76.

Zhao, Q., Zhang, D., and Lu, H. 2005. Supervised LLE in ICA Space for Facial Expression Recognition. In *Proceedings of the International Conference on Neural Networks and Brain*, 1970–1975. Beijing, China, October 13–15, 2005. IEEE.

Zhao, W.L., Ngo, C.W., Tan, H.K., and Wu, X. 2007. Near-Duplicate Keyframe Identification with Interest Point Matching and Pattern Learning. *IEEE Transactions on Multimedia* 9(5): 1037–1048.

Zhe, X. and Boucouvalas, A.C. 2002. A Text-to-Emotion Engine for Real-Time Internet Communication. In *Proceedings of the International Symposium on Communication Systems, Networks, and DSPs*, 164–168. Staffordshire University, UK.

Zheng, H., Wu, X., and Yu, Y. 2008. Enriching WordNet with Folksonomies. In *Proceedings of the 12th Pacific-Asia Conference on Advances in Knowledge Discovery and Data Mining*, 1075–1080. Osaka, Japan. Lecture Notes in Computer Science 5012. Springer, Berlin/Heidelberg.

Zheng, J., Franco, H., Weng, F., Sankar, A., and Bratt, H. 2000. Word-Level Rate-of-Speech Modeling Using Rate-Specific Phones and Pronunciations. In *Proc. ICASSP-2000*, Vol. 3, 1775–1778.

Zhou, X. and Conati, C. 2003. Inferring User Goals from Personality and Behavior in a Causal Model of User Affect. In *Proceedings of the 8th International Conference on Intelligent User Interfaces (IUI)*, 211–218. Miami, FL, January 12–15, 2003.

Zhu, G. and Doermann, D. 2007. Automatic Document Logo Detection. In *Proceedings of the 9th International Conference on Document Analysis and Recognition (ICDAR)*, Vol. 2, 864–868. Curitiba, Parana, Brazil, September 23–26.

Zhu, G., Huang, Q., Xu, C., Rui, Y., Jiang, S., Gao, W., and Yao, H. 2007. Trajectory Based Event Tactics Analysis in Broadcast Sports Video. In *Proceedings of the 15th International Conference on Multimedia*, 58–67. Augsburg, Germany, September 23–29, 2007.

Zhu, J., Hoi, S., Lu, M., and Yan, S. 2008. Near-duplicate Keyframe Retrieval by Nonrigid Image Matching. In *Proceedings of the 16th International Conference on Multimedia*, 41–50. Vancouver, BC, Canada, October 26–31.

INDEX

AAAI Fall Symposium on Multimedia Information Extraction, xiii, 38

AAM, 101–105, 110

AAT, *see* Art and Architectural Thesaurus (AAT)

ABC, 115, 180–181, 236

ACE, 16, 17, 115, 180

ACM SIGCHI, 10, 11, 13

Acoustic features, 8, 20, 219, 255–256, 264–267, 274–275, 279–286

Active appearance models (AAM), 101–105, 110

Activity matching, 210

Activity of speech, 255–256

ACT-R, 245–247

Addisu, Matusala, 348, 401

Affect, xi, 5, 9, 11, 35, 46, 100, 186, 245, 270–271, 273–276, 280–288, 290, 305–319, 322–339, 341–345. *See also* Recognition of emotion

Affect extraction, 8, 11, 35, 269, 271, 324

Affective computing
  metadata, 112, 270–271, 305–307, 310–316
  Picard, Rosalind, 35, 274, 305, 307, 310, 313, 323–324, 328
  states, 273–274, 276

Age, 255, 269, 270, 273, 275, 278, 282, 285–287, 340

Age recognition, 285

Agreeableness, 262, 270, 305

Ahmadinejad, 151

AHS, *see* Audio hot spotting

Alerting, 151, 175

Algorithms
  active appearance models (AAM), 101–105, 110
  arousal modeling, 329, 333, 343
  association analysis, 347, 352, 364, 366
  audio analysis, 115–116, 329, 348, 355
  automatic speech recognition, 17, 145
  bag of words, 24, 71, 120, 269, 275, 281, 283
  Bayesian, 7, 149, 236, 240, 242, 246–248, 250–252, 274
  Bayesian networks, 250, 274
  caption processing, 240, 242–243, 251
  content based recommender (CBR), 270, 305–319
  content-based copy retrieval (CBCR), 186–192
  correlation based Feature Selection (CFS), 278–280, 284–286
  digital signal processing, 347, 370

Multimedia Information Extraction: Advances in Video, Audio, and Imagery Analysis for Search, Data Mining, Surveillance, and Authoring, First Edition. Edited by Mark T. Maybury.
© 2012 IEEE Computer Society. Published 2012 by John Wiley & Sons, Inc.